THE THEOLOGY OF
Thomas Aquinas

Bologna, Museo Civico, Corale 545 (formerly 36), fol. 75r. The folio shows the office for the feast of St. Thomas Aquinas and probably dates to the years just after his canonization in 1323. The unusual inclusion of Dominican nuns as eager students of the saint, and the roundel depicting the Apparition of Christ to the Maries, suggest that this choirbook was made for the women's convent of St. Agnes in Bologna. In the folio Thomas is represented as a teacher to all members of the Church, both clerical and lay. The illumination has been attributed to a Bolognese artist known as the Second Master of San Domenico, who participated in the decoration of several manuscripts produced for Dominicans.

THE THEOLOGY OF
Thomas Aquinas

edited by

RIK VAN NIEUWENHOVE
and
JOSEPH WAWRYKOW

University of Notre Dame Press
Notre Dame, Indiana

Manufactured in the United States of America

Library of Congress Cataloging-in-Publication Data
The theology of Thomas Aquinas / edited by Rik Van Nieuwenhove and
Joseph Wawrykow.
    p.   cm.
    Includes bibliographical references and index.
    ISBN 0-268-04363-9 (cloth : alk. paper)
    1. Thomas, Aquinas, Saint, 1225?–1274—Theology.
    I. Van Nieuwenhove, Rik, 1967–   II. Wawrykow, Joseph Peter.
    B765.T54T35   2005
    230'.2'092—dc22
                                                                2004027610

To Rose and Dianne

Contents

Acknowledgments

The essay by David B. Burrell, "Analogy, Creation, and Theological Language," has appeared in slightly different form in *American Catholic Philosophical Association Proceedings*, vol. 74 (2001): 35–52, and is printed here with the permission of the editor.

The essay by Gilles Emery, "Trinity and Creation," was translated from the French by Patrick I. Martin.

The essay by Thomas Prügl, "Thomas Aquinas as Interpreter of Scripture," was translated from the German by Albert K. Wimmer.

Publication of a full-color dust jacket was made possible by a grant from the Institute for Scholarship in the Liberal Arts, College of Arts and Letters, University of Notre Dame.

The editors have benefitted from their dealings with the capable staff of the University of Notre Dame Press. Two people in particular are deserving of our profound thanks: Jeff Gainey, former Associate Director of the Press, for his interest and enthusiasm from the outset of the project; and Rebecca DeBoer, for her diligent, patient, and unfailingly intelligent copyediting.

Finally, the book is dedicated to our wives, Rose Cunningham and Dianne Phillips; their encouragement and commitment are a constant source of strength.

Contributors

David B. Burrell, C.S.C., Department of Theology, University of Notre Dame

Gilles Emery, O.P., Faculty of Theology, University of Fribourg, Switzerland

Paul Gondreau, Department of Theology, Providence College

Harm Goris, Department of Systematic Theology and Thomas Instituut, Katholieke Theologische Universiteit te Utrecht

Carlo Leget, Department of Ethics, Philosophy and History of Medicine, University Medical Centre Nijmegen

Bruce D. Marshall, Perkins School of Theology, Southern Methodist University

D. Juvenal Merriell, C.O., St. Philip's Seminary, Toronto

Paul O'Grady, Department of Philosophy, Trinity College Dublin

Thomas F. O'Meara, O.P., St. Thomas Aquinas Priory, River Forest, Illinois

Jean Porter, Department of Theology, University of Notre Dame

Thomas Prügl, Department of Theology, University of Notre Dame

Herwi Rikhof, Department of Systematic Theology and Thomas Instituut, Katholieke Theologische Universiteit te Utrecht

Eugene F. Rogers, Jr., Department of Religious Studies, The University of Virginia

Rudi A. te Velde, Department of Theology, University of Tilburg, The Netherlands

Rik Van Nieuwenhove, Department of Theology and Religious Studies, Mary Immaculate College, University of Limerick, Ireland

Liam G. Walsh, O.P., Professor Emeritus, Faculty of Theology, University of Fribourg

Joseph Wawrykow, Department of Theology, University of Notre Dame

Abbreviations

Bibliographical Abbreviations

AHDLMA *Archives d'histoire doctrinale et littéraire du moyen âge.* Paris: J. Vrin, 1926 –.

Albert the Great, Cologne Edition Albertus Magnus. *Opera omnia ad fidem codicum manuscriptorum edenda, apparatu critico, notis, prolegomenis, indicibus instruenda curavit Institutum Alberti Magni Coloniense, Bernhardo Geyer praeside.* In progress. Münster i. W.: Aschendorff, 1951 –.

BGPTMA *Beiträge der Philosophie und Theologie des Mittelalters.* Münster i. W., 1895 –, 43 vols. Neue Folge, 1970 –.

Bonaventure, Quaracchi Edition *Doctoris seraphici S. Bonaventurae s.r.e. episcopi cardinalis Opera omnia.* Edited by the Fathers of the College of St. Bonaventure. 10 vols. Quaracchi: Collegium S. Bonaventurae, 1882 – 1902.

Borgnet *B. Alberti Magni Ratisbonensis episcopi, Ordinis praedicotorum. Opera omnia, ex editione lugdunensi religiose castigata, et pro auctoritatibus ad fidem vulgate versionis accuratiorumque patrologiae textuum revocatur.* Edited by Auguste Borgnet. 38 vols. Paris: Vives, 1890 – 99.

CCSL *Corpus Christianorum Series Latina.* Turnhout: Brepols, 1954 –.

CSEL *Corpus Scriptorum Ecclesiasticorum Latinorum.* Vienna: Geroldi, 1866 –.

DS *Enchiridion Symbolorum Definitionum et Declarationum de rebus Fidei et Morum.* Quod primum edidit Henricus Denzinger et quod funditus retractavit auxit notulis ornavit Adolfus Schönmetzer. Editio XXXII. Rome: Herder, 1963.

PL   *Patrologiae cursus completus: Series Latina.* Edited by J.-P. Migne. 221 vols. Paris, 1844–64.

Peter Lombard,   *Magistri Petri Lombardi Parisiensis episcopi Sententiae in IV libris*
Sent.   *distinctae* (Spicilegium Bonaventurianum 4–5). Edited by the Fathers of the College of St. Bonaventure (Quaracchi). 2 vols., vol. 1 in 2 parts. 3rd ed. Grottaferrata: Editiones Collegii S. Bonaventurae ad Claras Aquas, 1971–.

RTAM   *Recherches de Théologie ancienne et médiévale.* Louvain: Abbaye du Mont César, 1929–96.

SC   *Sources Chrétiennes.* Paris: Les Éditions du Cerf.

Summa Halensis,   *Summa theologica.* Edited by the Fathers of the College of St. Bona-
Quaracchi   venture. 4 vols. Quaracchi: Collegium S. Bonaventurae, 1924–48.
Edition

Writings of Thomas Aquinas

Leonine Edition   *Sancti Thomae Aquinatis doctoris angelici Opera omnia iussu impensaque/ Leonis XIII P.M. edita.* (Some volumes have the general title: *Opera omnia iussu edita Leonis XIII P.M.*) Edited by the members of the Leonine Commission. Rome: Sta. Sabina, 1882–.

Theological syntheses:

ScG   *S. Thomae Aquinatis Doctoris Angelici Liber de veritate Catholicae fidei contra errores infidelium, qui dicitur Summa contra gentiles.* Edited by P. Marc with the help of C. Pera and P. Caramello. 3 vols. Turin: Marietti, 1961.

English translation by A. C. Pegis (Bk. I), J. F. Anderson (Bk. II), V. J. Bourke (Bk. III), C. J. O'Neill (Bk. IV), published by the University of Notre Dame Press, 1975.

Citations of *ScG* give Book, chapter, and the paragraph number according to the English translation. Thus, *ScG* IV.27.1 = Book IV, chapter 27, paragraph 1.

Sent.   *Scriptum super libros sententiarum magistri Petri Lombardi Episcopi*
             Parisiensis. 4 vols. Vols. 1–2 edited by P. Mandonnet, vols. 3–4 edited
             by M. F. Moos. Paris: P. Lethielleux, 1929–47.

             Citations of *Sent.* are prefaced by the Book and followed by the dis-
             tinction, question, article, and part of article. Thus, III *Sent.* d.1 q.2
             art.5 ad 4 = *Scriptum* on Book III, 5, response to fourth objection.

ST   *Summa Theologiae*

             Citations of *ST* give Part, question, article, part of article. Thus, *ST*
             I.1.10 ad 1 = *ST* Part One, question 1, article 10, the response to the
             first objection.

             English translations:

             Summa Theologica. Complete English Edition in 5 vols. Translated by
             the Fathers of the English Dominican Province. Westminster, Md.:
             Christian Classics, 1981.

             Summa Theologiae. Latin text and English translation, Introductions,
             Notes, Appendices, and Glossaries. London: Blackfriars in conjunc-
             tion with Eyre and Spottiswoode; New York: McGraw-Hill, 1964–.
             60 vols. Various translators.

Disputed questions:

De Car.   *Quaestio disputata de caritate*

De Malo   *Quaestiones disputatae de malo*

             English translation by Jean T. Oesterle, *Saint Thomas Aquinas, On*
             Evil. Notre Dame, Ind.: University of Notre Dame Press, 1995.

De Pot.   *Quaestiones disputatae de potentia*

             English translation, *Saint Thomas. On the Power of God,* by the En-
             glish Dominican Fathers [L. Shapcote], 3 vols. Westminster, Md.:
             Newman Press, 1952.

De Spe   *Quaestio disputata de spe*

De Spir. Creat.   *Quaestio disputata de spiritualibus creaturis*

De Ver.	*Quaestiones disputatae de veritate*

English translation, *Saint Thomas, On Truth,* by R.W. Mulligan (vol. 1), J.V. McGlynn (vol. 2), R. W. Schmidt (vol. 3). Chicago: Henry Regnery, 1952–54.

De Virt.	*Quaestiones disputatae de virtutibus in communi*

Quodl.	*Quaestiones de quodlibet I–XII*

Commentaries on the Bible:

In Is.	*Expositio super Isaiam ad litteram*

In Ier.	*Postilla super Ieremiam*

In Iob	*Expositio super Iob ad litteram*

Cat. in Ioh.	*Catena aurea in Ioannem*

In Matt.   *Lectura super evangelium S. Matthei. S. Thomae Aquinatis Doctoris Angelici evangelium S. Matthaei lectura.* Edited by Raphael Cai, O.P. Turin-Rome: Marietti, 1951.

Citations of this commentary give biblical chapter and verse, and the paragraph in this edition. Thus, *In Matt.* 2:1, no.161 = on chapter 2, verse 1, paragraph 161.

In Ioh.   *S. Thomae Aquinatis Doctoris Angelici Super evangelium S. Iohannis lectura.* Edited by Raphael Cai, O.P. Turin-Rome: Marietti, 1952.

In Ioh. 6:1, no.839 = on chapter 6, verse 1, paragraph 839.

In Psalmos	*Postilla super Psalmos*

Ad Rom.   *Expositio super Epistolam ad Romanos.* In *S. Thomae Aquinatis Doctoris Angelici Super Epistolas S. Pauli lectura.* Edited by Raphael Cai, O.P. 2 vols. Turin-Rome: Marietti, 1953.

Citations of the commentaries on the Pauline Epistles give biblical chapter and verse, and paragraph in this edition. Thus, *Ad Rom.* 8:1, no.595 = on chapter 8, verse 1, paragraph 595.

In I Cor.	*Super I ad Corinthios*
In II Cor.	*Super II ad Corinthios*
In Gal.	*Super ad Galatas*
In Eph.	*Super ad Ephesios*
In Phil.	*Super ad Philippenses*
In Col.	*Super ad Colossenses*
In I Thess.	*Super I ad Thessalonicenses*
In II Thess.	*Super II ad Thessalonicenses*
In I Tim.	*Super I ad Timotheum*
In II Tim.	*Super II ad Timotheum*
In Tit.	*Super ad Titum*
In Heb.	*Super ad Hebraeos*

Commentaries on Aristotle:

De An.	*Sententia libri De anima*
De Caelo	*Sententia De Caelo et mundo*
De Sensu	*Sententia De sensu et sensato*
Ethica	*Sententia libri Ethicorum*
Meta.	*Sententia super Metaphysicam*
Periherm.	*Sententia super Peri hermenias*
Phys.	*Sententia super Physicam*
Post. Anal.	*Sententia super Posteriora Analytica*

Other commentaries:

De Causis	*Expositio super librum De Causis*
De Div. Nom.	*Super librum Dionysii De divinis nominibus*
De Trin.	*Expositio super librum Boethii de Trinitate*

Polemical writings:

De Aet. Mundi	*De aeternitate mundi*
De Uni. Int.	*De unitate intellectus contra Averroistas*

Treatises:

Comp. Theol.	*Compendium Theologiae*
De Ente	*De ente et essentia*
De Rat. Fid.	*De rationibus fidei*
De Sub. Sep.	*De substantiis separatis*

Editorial Abbreviations

a., aa.	articulus, articuli
ad (cum numero)	responsio ad obiectionem (argumentum)
arg.	argumentum
art.	articulus
c.	corpus (= body of article)
ch., chs.	chapter, chapters
d., dd.	distinctio, distinctiones
lect., lects.	lectio, lectiones
lin.	linea, lineae
n., nn.	note, notes
N. F.	Neue Folge
no., nos.	numero, numeros
n.s.	new series
ob., obj.	obiectio
q., qq.	quaestio, quaestiones
qc.	quaestiuncula
resp.	responsio
sol.	solutio
tr.	tractatus

Editors' Preface

This volume offers an introduction to the theology of the great thirteenth-century Scholastic, Thomas Aquinas, covering the major areas of theological investigation. After an initial essay on the nature of theology according to Aquinas (Marshall), there are contributions on his trinitarian thought (Rikhof, Emery) and his teaching about speaking the Christian God (Burrell); on God's providential rule (Goris); on theological anthropology, the moral life, and the movement of the human person to God as end (Merriell, te Velde, Porter, Wawrykow); on Christ (Wawrykow, Gondreau), his saving work (Van Nieuwenhove), and its communication (O'Meara, Walsh); and on the end things (Leget). The volume concludes with essays on Aquinas' scriptural exegesis as part of his theological project (Prügl); on Aquinas' concern for "philosophy" and possible openness to more recent philosophical trends (O'Grady); and on the rapprochement between Aquinas and Protestant theology (Rogers). The intended audience of this volume is broad. By engaging Aquinas' texts on their own terms and presenting his ideas in a style that is meant to be straightforward as well as theologically sophisticated, the volume should be of considerable service both to newcomers to Aquinas and to those who are already conversant with his thought.

In commissioning these essays, the editors were direct in their instructions. Each essay was to be on an important aspect of Aquinas' theology or its reception. The approach was to be historically sound, sensitive to Aquinas' strategies as a theologian, and attentive to his ways of proceeding in addressing significant topics in theology. Each essay was also to be alert to the overall form of Aquinas' theology, relating the topic of the essay to Aquinas' most basic theological convictions. And, finally, the contributors were asked to ponder, where possible, the contributions that Aquinas might make to contemporary theological discourse. The result is a volume that will be of interest to a wide range of readers—to those who crave to know more about this great Scholastic theologian and about his theological work in its historical setting; to those who in their own attempts to resolve the issues that are of abiding concern to working theologians want to consider, at least, Aquinas' point of view.

The cast of contributors to this volume is international in scope. No fewer than eight nations (Canada, Flanders, the United States, Ireland, Germany, England, the Netherlands, and Switzerland) are represented in this volume. Major locales for the study of Aquinas find representation in the volume: Fribourg, Utrecht, and Notre Dame, Indiana. The essays are by a judicious mix of younger and more established scholars. Each takes historical theology very seriously, as both interrogation of the past and retrieval of the basic, most vital insights of classical theologians. As a rule, the essays are shaped by close reading of the pertinent texts of Aquinas himself. The reader should come away with a good grasp of Aquinas' major theological claims, as well as guidance in how best to read Saint Thomas.

While the contributors are united by their appreciation of Aquinas' theological genius and their use of a historical-theological approach to his writings, there are occasional disagreements in the essays that follow on particular points of interpretation. Marshall, O'Grady, and Rogers differ on the status of the "philosophical" in the theology of Aquinas. Wawrykow (in his chapter on grace) offers an assessment of the importance of efficient causality in providence that departs from that offered by Van Nieuwenhove. Sufficent textual information is provided in each case to allow the reader to decide the adequacy of each interpretation. Nonetheless, the overall picture of Aquinas that emerges from this volume is quite consistent—not surprising, given the commitment of all of our authors to close reading of texts as well as their refusal to bend Aquinas to the demands of some modern or postmodern scholarly agenda, whether theological or philosophical.

Appended to the volume is a bibliographical orientation, that is, a set of instructions on how to learn about editions and translations of Aquinas' writings, as well as about the scholarly research over the past century.

Quod Scit Una Uetula

Aquinas on the Nature of Theology

BRUCE D. MARSHALL

During the season of Lent, perhaps as late as 1273, Thomas Aquinas gave a series of instructional sermons on the Apostles' Creed in his Neapolitan vernacular.[1] We have them only in later Latin summaries by his secretary, Reginald of Piperno, but the simplicity and directness of Aquinas' address to the faithful gathered for Lenten Vespers still comes through. He begins by observing the radical difference Christian faith makes in human life, including human knowing. Even the humblest believer in Christ knows more about God and how to lead a good life than the most profound philosopher was able to know without faith in Christ.

> Despite all of their effort, none of the philosophers before the coming of Christ was able to know as much about God, and about what is necessary for life, as one old woman [*uetula*] knows by faith after Christ's coming. Hence it is said: "The earth is full of the knowledge of God" [Isaiah 11:9].[2]

Not only soteriologically and morally, but epistemically, Christ's advent is the decisive event in human history. The faith it calls forth makes unlettered Neapolitan crones wiser in the ways of God than Plato and Aristotle.

This may seem remarkable, since we do not "see" what we believe, but simply cling to it by faith on the authority of God, who instructs us in Christ about what we ought to hold true. Aquinas firmly insists, however, that believing what we cannot see would only be a mistake if we could see everything—if we "could know perfectly all things visible and invisible." But of course we cannot. In fact, in its present state "our knowledge is so weak that no philosopher has been able completely to investigate the nature of a single fly." Therefore the genuinely foolish course is the philosopher's unwillingness, rare in a *uetula*, "to believe anything about God save what a human being is able to know by his own resources [*per se*]." God subdues this epistemic pride, as Job teaches: "God is great, and conquers our knowledge" (Job 36:26).[3]

Indeed, even in the most ordinary worldly matters we cannot get along without holding countless beliefs on the authority of others. This may happen because we want to learn some science or art, and have to assume that the person teaching it to us knows more about it than we do. But the weakness of our intellect goes deeper than this. Even on a seemingly obvious matter like who our own father is, we have no choice but to believe the testimony of others. On this important issue, as with so many others, we have no way to transform our believing into seeing. Aquinas finds nothing wrong in this. We could not survive unless we were willing to accept the weakness of our intellect and act accordingly. "If a human being were willing to believe only what she knew with certainty, she could not live in this world. How can one person live without believing another?" When it comes to God, where the weakness of our intellect is most telling and our need for instruction most profound, the epistemic lesson is unmistakable: "No one ought to doubt concerning the faith, but ought to believe what belongs to faith more certainly than she believes what she sees, because human vision can be deceived, but God's knowledge is never mistaken."[4]

Thomists past and present would probably be puzzled at the inclusion of Aquinas' praise of the *uetula* in an account of his idea of theology. Every faithful Catholic, including the old woman chattering to her crucifix (in Newman's phrase, kindly meant), of course has some important items of knowledge which, in the nature of the case, are unavailable to human beings who knew nothing of Christ's advent: that the one God is three distinct persons, that Jesus Christ is God, incarnate for the world's salvation, and so forth. But for many interpreters of Aquinas this has little to do with his conception of theology. For Aquinas theology, after all, is a science, of which the *uetula* knows nothing. Theology is knowledge of a quite particular kind, for which the model is provided, in Aquinas' view, by just those Greek philosophers who lacked the items of Christian knowledge that the old woman has.

More than that: about even the most mundane matters, to say nothing of God, the *uetula* does not have a single cognition that approaches the epistemic rigor regularly attained by the ancient philosophers, even about God—despite their lack of Christian faith. As Aquinas does not fail to note in the *Collationes Credo in Deum*, however much we human beings need faith in this life, it is not to be confused with knowledge, in the properly demanding sense of the term. "It is necessary that one human being believe another *concerning those things which she is not able to know perfectly by her own resources.*"[5] To many Thomists it has seemed that the science of theology must take these rationally accessible certainties as given, and build on them as far as it can. Christian faith no doubt includes truths beyond reason's grasp. As Aquinas famously observes, however, "grace does not destroy nature, but perfects it"—a phrase often taken to sum up his understanding of theology.[6] It seems that Aquinas attributes to the elderly illiterates in his Naples congregation only a modest epistemic advantage, which must retreat into insignificance when we come to consider the nature and tasks of theology.

One way to approach Aquinas' conception of theology is to see whether his apparent celebration of the *uetula's* epistemic advantage genuinely conflicts with his ideas about theology as a science, and about the superiority of "scientific" knowledge. In order to do this, we will need to look in some detail at the way Thomas handles three questions:

1. Why do we need theology in the first place?
2. In what sense is theology a science?
3. How is the wisdom of theology connected to that knowledge which we human beings can attain by our own resources?

Salvation and *sacra doctrina*

Aquinas opens his *Summa Theologiae* with a question, comprising ten articles, on "holy teaching" (*sacra doctrina*).[7] He thinks it important to clarify, at the outset of the enterprise, "what sort [of teaching] this is, and how far it extends."[8] This is not surprising, since from beginning to end the *Summa* is an exercise in *sacra doctrina*.[9] For Aquinas the first thing to consider is why we have to have this sort of teaching at all.

Aquinas often gives multiple reasons in support of the positions he takes, but here he relies on only one. We need *sacra doctrina* because our salvation depends on it. The goal of life for which God has made us—the enjoyment of God himself, seen face to face—is wholly beyond our power to attain. In particular, life's aim exceeds the grasp of our reason. Left to our own cognitive devices, we would never be able to know what the aim of life is, let alone be able to attain it. Sin makes this problem much worse, but since we are creatures, finite and contingent, yet made for an end beyond all creation, we would have this problem even without the burden of sin—it just goes with being the sort of creatures we are. "The human being is ordered by God to an end which exceeds the comprehension of reason, as Isaiah 64[:4] says: 'Without you, O God, the eye has not seen what you have prepared for those who love you.'"[10]

Unless we can rely on God to tell us what we can never find out on our own, there will be no salvation for us. In order to attain any goal we first of all have to know what the goal is, so that we can direct our intentions and actions to it. For just this reason—*unde,* as Aquinas tersely says—"it was necessary for human salvation that certain matters which exceed human reason be known to [us] by divine revelation," and, correlatively, "received through faith."[11] Precisely these saving matters, into which reason has no business seeking to pry, are the province of *sacra doctrina.*[12] This saving doctrine includes, in fact, "that which is known to [God] alone concerning himself, and is shared with others through revelation."[13] Knowledge of the glory which God has prepared for those who love him "is not received from sensible things, but from divine revelation"; as such it cannot "ascend" into our minds from our interaction with the world, but must, like every perfect gift, "descend from the Father of lights (James 1:17)."[14]

The whole weight of *sacra doctrina,* and with that the whole work of the *Summa Theologiae,* turns on Aquinas' cryptic *"unde."* We need a teaching "beyond the philosophical disciplines, which reason investigates," because we need to know the aim of life, and we need to know the aim of life in order to attain it—to be saved.[15] If the aim of life could be known (*praecognitum*) without this "holy teaching," then there would be no need for such teaching. Our need for it indicates that reason's shortcoming goes beyond an inability to demonstrate or know with certainty what life's final goal is. By itself, reason appears unable even to give us an adequate *idea* of life's true aim—adequate, that is, to orient our intentions and actions toward this goal.

Reason can, to be sure, "investigate" at least some truths about God on its own, by attending to what creatures tell it of their source. Even with regard to matters where God may be known *per creaturas,* however, divine revelation is required if this knowledge is to have any saving effect. This is partly because of the weakness of even the best human intellect. Any truths about God which we might attain by reason would be grasped only "by a few, after a long time, and with the admixture of many errors."[16] But Aquinas evidently also thinks that the kinds of truths accessible to reason are, by themselves, unable to provide us with the needed knowledge of life's ultimate aim. For that we need access to what God alone can tell us about himself. "The deep things of God," Aquinas observes in comment on 1 Corinthians 2:10, "are those which lie hidden in him, and not those which can be known about him *per creaturas;* these latter seem to reach only as far as the surface."[17] Without knowledge of these depths, we cannot recognize God as our last end. The surface truths available to reason cannot tell us this.[18] We thus need God's instruction not only in order to reach life's aim, but even to know what it is.[19]

Since salvation "is accomplished by the incarnate Son and by the gift of the Holy Spirit," the truth beyond reason which we most need to know concerns the distinction of the Son and the Holy Spirit from the Father. The doctrine of the Trinity—or more precisely, "the knowledge of the divine persons"—is a *saving* truth for Aquinas. The chief reason we need to know it is "in order to think rightly concerning the salvation of the human race."[20] Or as Aquinas elsewhere maintains, "The Christian faith," which clings to that body of saving doctrine we receive from God, "consists above all [*principaliter*] in the confession of the Holy Trinity, and it glories especially in the cross of our Lord Jesus Christ."[21] The knowledge of Jesus Christ is, indeed, "the consummation of the whole enterprise of theology."[22] On account of being one of the holy Trinity, Jesus Christ is himself the goal of human life, and on account of being that divine person incarnate, crucified, and risen, he is at the same time "our way of reaching God" (*via . . . nobis tendendi in Deum*).[23]

Thus *sacra doctrina* always has a soteriological purpose. Even at its most recondite—and "holy teaching" in Aquinas' hands can become a highly intricate affair—theology always serves the practical aim of helping human beings attain their ultimate destiny. No merely speculative knowledge belongs to *sacra doctrina,* no knowledge, that is, acquired as an end in itself, apart from any consideration of the wider human purposes it may serve. To put it differently: no talk of God can belong to genuine knowledge of him which cannot aid in the attainment of God as life's final aim. Aquinas does, of course, argue that *sacra doctrina* is a contemplative (*speculativa*) as well as a practical science, indeed that it is primarily contemplative. By this he does not mean, however, that this teaching may ever be divorced from the purpose which alone justifies its existence, which is human salvation. Instead, Aquinas' point is that the saving aim of *sacra doctrina,* God seen and contemplated by human beings, gives the whole of this teaching its basic character. Since the final aim is not made by us, the product of our own act, but is God himself, who makes human beings and makes them blessed, *sacra doctrina* should be thought of as more contemplative than practical in character.[24] At the same time, the end of life *is,* in a sense, a human act, but an act of seeing—*speculatio*, as Aquinas sometimes calls it—rather than of making. As a result, the teaching by which this end is reached is, once again, primarily "speculative" in nature.[25]

After Aquinas the view that theology is, on the contrary, primarily practical rather than speculative or contemplative became quite common outside his own Dominican order. This need not amount to a significant substantive difference from Aquinas. Thus Duns Scotus, for example, argues that theology is practical rather than speculative just because there is nothing in it which is incapable of increasing our love for God and the practices which enact that love. His reason for calling theology practical is pretty much the same as Aquinas' reason for calling it speculative: everything in it is at least capable of directing us to the attainment of life's ultimate aim.[26]

Evidently Aquinas' *sacra doctrina* embraces considerably more than we now customarily mean by "theology." The Bible itself—the text, and not simply its interpretation—belongs to holy teaching, and indeed scripture forms the basis for the whole of *sacra doctrina.* Holy teaching can use concepts and arguments drawn from any quarter, not least from the ancient philosophers, even though they knew nothing of Christ. But no such use of "philosophical authorities" establishes the truth of a claim in *sacra doctrina.* Only the use of canonical scripture can do that, since by it God teaches us those truths about the depths of his own life which alone can lead us to him. Even the teaching of the fathers and doctors of the church, while closer to the heart of *sacra doctrina* than that of the philosophers, can serve only as probable, rather than conclusive, support for a teaching.[27] It is thus unsurprising that Aquinas sometimes uses "holy teaching" and "holy scripture" interchangeably.[28]

To be sure, on occasion Aquinas also treats theology as co-extensive with *sacra doctrina.* Literally, "theology" just means talk about God (*sermo de Deo*), and in that broad sense all of Christian holy teaching is theology.[29] But not all theology is *sacra doctrina.* Philosophers certainly talk about God, but since their enterprise lacks by definition that apprehension of, and reliance upon, God's teaching about himself which is constitutive of Christian *sacra doctrina,* their theology "differs in kind" (*secundum genus*) from "the theology which belongs to holy teaching," and is not to be confused with it.[30] Aquinas' thoroughly scriptural notion of *sacra doctrina,* and thereby of theology, conforms to his own vocation. His professional title, as we would call it, was not "theologian," but *magister in sacra pagina*—master of the sacred page—and his daily work was teaching the Bible.[31]

So far, Aquinas' conception of theology—of holy teaching—apparently accords to the *uetula* a considerable epistemic advantage over even the most intellectually accomplished non-Christian. She does not simply possess some cognitive items additional to those which human reason can arrive at on its own. She knows the final aim of human life, and she knows the way to reach it. She has this knowledge because she believes what God teaches about himself in Christ. The *uetula* gets her knowledge by relying on God's attestation of himself in scripture, as interpreted under God's guidance in the community of faith to which she belongs. There is no other way for human beings to know life's final aim. So while human reason can know much of which the *uetula* has not the slightest inkling, she has knowledge of the highest things, of that which it is best to know. This is worth far more than even the greatest knowledge of lesser things, since it enables the old woman to do what even the most accomplished philosopher, absent Christian faith, cannot: orient her whole life, including the life of her mind, modest though it may be, to her final end.[32] Her advantage is therefore great, and genuinely epistemic. With her knowledge of life's end goes the capacity to accomplish the chief purpose for which she has a mind in the first place—to see God.

Theology as a Science

1. Aristotle and the Logic of Holy Teaching

Having established that only God can teach us the true aim of our life and how that aim—God himself—may be reached, Aquinas spends much of the remaining space in the *Summa Theologiae*'s opening question trying to specify how the saving doctrine which God imparts can be thought of as a science. His idea of a "science" comes not from the modern experimental and mathematically rigorous study of nature, of course, but from Aristotle's *Posterior Analytics*. Aquinas knew this treatise well (it was one of only two parts of Aristotle's *Organon* upon which he wrote a commentary), although the idea that Christian theology verifies Aristotle's notion of a science was not original with him.[33]

On the Aristotelian view which Aquinas takes up, a science is a system of thought at once deductive and empirical. It aims to explain states of affairs which we observe or otherwise accept (for example, that the planets, unlike the stars, do not twinkle) by tracing them back with syllogistic necessity to principles which provide a causal account of these states of affairs (for example, that planets are near, and what is near does not twinkle).[34] When we reach principles which cannot be syllogistically resolved into further and yet more basic premises, we have arrived at the first and most essential truths of a particular science, and so of the part of nature which it treats. These truths cannot themselves be demonstrated, but are known in a direct and non-inferential way. They are what Aquinas often calls "*principia per se nota*," principles known "through themselves," rather than through some other and more basic premises, and thus principles which are in some way self-evident.[35]

Aquinas' effort to think of *sacra doctrina* as more or less an Aristotelian science runs into several problems. Of these perhaps the most obvious is that the "principles" of Christian holy teaching fail to meet the chief requirement for premises of scientific knowledge. *Sacra doctrina* takes for its principles truths about God and God's saving works which God himself makes known, and which form the articles of the church's faith.[36] But these Christian teachings are not "known through themselves." They do not elicit unhesitating assent from anyone who understands the terms in which they are put. On the contrary, they may reasonably be doubted, and many people in fact hold them false. So it seems that Christian holy teaching cannot count as a science.

We may be puzzled as to why Aquinas cares that it should. Having established that sacred doctrine relies on saving truths beyond reason's reach, what is to be gained by trying to show that this teaching conforms to an ideal of knowledge suited to what lies within reason's grasp? Aquinas' chief motives on this score perhaps come to light when he considers whether having a reason for what you believe reduces the merit (the fitness for salvation, we might say) of Christian faith. Not, he argues, if the urge for rational clarity stems from faith's willing embrace of the truths God reveals. In that case "a person loves the truth which he believes, turns it over in his mind, and eagerly considers whether any reasons can be found for it."[37] Love for the saving truth by which God leads us to himself elicits in the believer a longing to understand what he believes, to turn his mind as best he can from the surface to the depths of the self-revealing God.[38] In beings who think discursively—who cannot, like God, apprehend everything at once but must move from thought to thought—the believing mind's yearning to share in the inherent luminosity of divine truth naturally takes the form of a desire to see the rational connections among the truths of faith, and indeed among all the beliefs we hold true. This being the case, we cannot be indifferent to whether our best idea of a rationally connected body of knowledge describes *sacra doctrina*. And if it does not, then it seems we will have to grant that, as far as we can tell, Christian teaching itself will forever frustrate the believer's desire for reasoned understanding.[39]

Aquinas bids to save theology as a science while granting the evidently unscientific character of theology's first principles, by adapting a further notion from Aristotle. According to the *Posterior Analytics* a hierarchical relation obtains among the sciences, in which some sciences are subordinated to others.[40]

This can happen in several ways, but when it comes to theology the one which interests Aquinas occurs when a "subalternate" science (*sub altero*—under another) relies on principles delivered to it by another science. The higher science (say, physics) demonstrates conclusions which the lower science (say, engineering) accepts as its own axioms, trusting that these principles have been established as items of genuine knowledge in the higher science.[41] Thus the practitioners of a "subalternate" science like engineering credit the practitioners of physics with a kind of grasp upon the basic premises of *engineering* which they do not themselves possess, but upon which the scientific character of their own enterprise depends. So it is with *sacra doctrina*. It "proceeds from principles known by the light of a higher science, namely that of God and the blessed. Hence, just as music credits principles taught (*tradita*) to it by arithmetic, so holy teaching credits principles revealed by God."[42]

This argument for the scientific character of theology has evident limitations. In the case of the sciences whose principles are available to human reason, it is always possible to ascend from the epistemic position of the lower science to that of the higher—for the engineer to become a physicist. But the principles of *sacra doctrina* can never, at least in this life, become *per se nota* for us. We must content ourselves with an epistemic situation in which certainty about the principles which lead to life's consummation depends on trusting our teacher about life's end—God in Christ—and not on resolving these convictions into premises which are rationally unavoidable (whose opposite, as Aquinas suggests, is unthinkable).[43] Nor are the principles of our earthbound holy teaching the conclusions of a science practiced by the blessed in heaven (still less by God), as the engineer's premises are conclusions of the physicist's arguments. Rather, we believe the very same things that God and the blessed, each knowing in a quite different and radically more direct way than we, see to be true.

Still, theology shares certain features with those sciences which are humanly attainable. Though the engineer might become a physicist, she normally does not. Instead she, like the theologian, takes on trust premises of which she presumes others have a more rigorous knowledge. But no one thereby doubts the scientific character of engineering. And just as the engineer might attain the more rigorous level of knowledge upon which her science finally depends, so the person who holds true the articles of faith rightly hopes to know better what she now believes, "when we shall be like him, for we shall see him as he is" (1 John 3:2).[44]

For all the difference in the way they are known, the principles of *sacra doctrina* also display a certain similarity with *principia per se nota*. The articles of faith cannot be demonstrated to those who deny them, but neither can the *principia per se nota* upon which other sciences eventually depend. Yet we can show the difficulties into which a person falls who denies these naturally knowable *principia*. Similarly, we can defend the articles of faith against those who deny them, showing that "what the faith proclaims is not impossible."[45]

Finally, in theology, as in the other sciences, we can infer conclusions from principles. These conclusions may expand our stock of true beliefs, or they may be convictions we already hold, but in either case our field of knowledge is increased, since we now have a reason why our conviction is true. In this way theology genuinely addresses the mind's yearning for *scientia* (which faith "does not destroy, but perfects"). It gives a grasp of the rational connections among Christian beliefs, and so displays something of the intelligibility, the radiant divine luminosity, of the Christian faith.[46] These shared features are enough, in Aquinas' view, for *sacra doctrina* to verify the Aristotelian idea of a science, though it conforms to this notion of knowledge only in part—the articles of faith are "*like* principles in this science" (*quasi principia*), and inferences we draw from them are "like conclusions" (*quasi conclusiones*) in a science.[47]

Aquinas' commentators have sometimes been concerned to classify in detail the different types of inferences which may be drawn from the articles of faith, and have argued over the doctrinal and theological status of the conclusions thus deduced.[48] Aquinas himself is less systematic, and less syllogistic. His stock example for an argument based on an article of faith is 1 Corinthians 15:12 ff., where Paul takes Christ's resurrection as the basis of an argument for the general resurrection of the dead (itself, of course, an article of faith).[49] In his own detailed analysis of this passage, Aquinas does not take Paul's argument to be a syllogism (and thus a bit of science, by the standards of the *Posterior Analytics*), but simply a case of *modus ponens*, where the conditional premise is "If Christ has risen, then the dead will rise."[50] As Aquinas reads him, Paul develops multiple arguments both for the truth of the conditional itself and for the truth of its antecedent ("Christ has risen"), and Aquinas offers further arguments of his own, mostly in the form of replies to objections. The supporting arguments for both the conditional and its antecedent draw freely on truths of faith. In both cases, moreover, Aquinas is clear that even then the arguments establish only the *inconvenientia* (the unsuitability) of denying that Christ is risen, not the logical necessity of affirming it.[51]

This means that the tightest rational connection we can draw between the creedal truths concerning Christ's resurrection and the general resurrection is suitability (*convenientia*). Even granted the Christian conviction that Christ is risen, we cannot *demonstrate* the general resurrection—show it to be logically necessary. That Aquinas calls this argument *ex convenientia* a "proof of the coming resurrection of the dead" should not mislead.[52] It simply means that he takes showing the *inconvenientia* of denying something to be a kind of proof. In fact, Thomas often relies on argument *ex convenientia*—"*ratio persuasoria*" rather than syllogistic demonstration—to exhibit the rational connections among Christian beliefs.[53] He does so not only with regard to beliefs about contingent states of affairs, such as divine actions in time, but also with regard to beliefs about matters which cannot be otherwise, such as the triunity of God. Thus he appeals to the pseudo-Dionysian principle that God's goodness is self-diffusive to argue *ex convenientia* for God's incarnation, and allows the same principle to be used to argue *ex convenientia* for the Trinity.[54]

2. Knowing the First Truth

It may seem as though sacred doctrine has now left the *uetula* far behind, and moved into a realm of inference and argument in which she has no part. I will suggest at the end that Aquinas does not see it exactly this way. But in any case his account of theology as a science points up a problem which the most learned Parisian master shares with the untutored old woman who cleans up his room. How can we be certain that the teaching of scripture and creed about God and his works is true, and so directs us toward the real aim of life, and not toward a goal of our own imagining? The master is aware that articles of Christian faith cannot be the basis of a science unless we can be certain that they are true. The *uetula* knows nothing of the master's science, but she is a Christian, and so, like him, needs certainty about the truth of Christian teaching regardless of its scientific utility.

Aquinas' answer, as we have seen, is that we can be certain of what scripture and creed teach because this teaching is revealed by God through his witnesses, even though it is for us neither self-evident nor reducible to principles which are. But apparently this just relocates the problem. How can we be certain that these particular teachings have actually been revealed by God? When it comes to the articles of Christian faith, it seems that we need a way to ensure that we are better off than Aristotle's physicians, who justifiably took the word of their physicists regarding the number and nature of the elements, but were thereby misled.[55]

Yet in this question Aquinas shows remarkably little interest. It is his modern commentators who have been preoccupied with it, as far back as the seventeenth century. Sharing (perhaps to some extent originating) modernity's enchantment with the epistemological, they have sought ways of showing that even though the *contents* of Christian faith cannot be demonstrated, their *status* as divine revelation can become intellectually evident to us.

This apologetic project has been pursued since early modern times mainly by arguing that the miracles of Christ and the apostles, the holiness and self-sacrifice of the saints, and other visible signs are evidence of the divine presence sufficient to show that what Christ, the apostles, and the church teach must come from God. It was often held that this evidence is available to natural reason, without the aid of divine grace. As such it is enough to compel any reasonable and attentive person to conclude that what the church teaches must be true—indeed cannot reasonably be doubted. Our assent to the articles of faith is thereby rational, even though the contents of the articles cannot, by themselves, be demonstrated or known *per se*.

Many of Aquinas' modern interpreters have held this to be not only his teaching, but an effective antidote to the rationalist and subjectivist excesses of modernity alike.[56] Other Thomists have taken a rather different tack, arguing that while the credibility of Christianity does depend on the availability of public signs of its divine origin, the significance of these signs as evidence of revelation cannot be appreciated except by a mind lit up by the grace of God—a mind infused, as Aquinas puts it, with the "light of faith." They too seek support for their views in Aquinas, and the issue has generated much inner-Thomistic controversy.[57]

However executed, as an interpretation of Aquinas this apologetic strategy runs into considerable difficulty. Aquinas apparently just rejects any attempt to root certainty about the contents of Christian faith in certainty about their status. We cannot *infer* that the articles of faith must be true because miracles or other naturally available signs establish their revealed status. On Aquinas' account, this would be to base what is more certain on what is less certain. The faith which assents to the teaching of scripture and creed deliberately clings to the God who makes himself known through them as the source and measure of all truth—the first truth (*prima veritas*), in Aquinas' phrase.[58] To hold this teaching true in the distinctive manner of Christian faith is thus to regard it as that body of statements than which there can be none more certain: "A human being is much more certain about what he hears from God, who cannot be deceived, than about what he sees by his own reason, because his reason can be deceived."[59] So even if we could demonstrate by unaided reason that Christian teaching is revealed by God, we could not use this conclusion about the status of faith's articles to warrant the belief that they must be true. Far from giving faith adequate rational grounds, this would eliminate faith's own certainty, since it seeks to establish that which cannot be false on the basis of that which might be.

For this reason Aquinas holds that miracles are in fact epistemically dispensable for Christian faith. We would have to believe what Christ teaches even if it were accompanied by no visible signs. As the Father's Word become our flesh, the human being Jesus Christ is in his own distinctive way the *prima veritas*. As such we have to believe his teaching simply because it is his, and not because of any evidence we might have for its divine status (or, as we would now suppose, any arguments to support the claim that he actually said it).[60]

These considerations may make more attractive the suggestion that the light of faith gives an immediate or intuitive certainty that the first premises of Christian teaching stem from the *prima veritas*. In fact Aquinas himself held a strong version of this claim early on, arguing that the light of faith makes the articles themselves *per se nota* for us.[61] But he soon changed his mind about this, and by the time of his *quaestiones* on Boethius' *De Trinitate* had reached the position which he firmly maintains in the *Summa Theologiae:* we can neither know the articles of faith *per se,* nor resolve them into principles known in this way.[62] The thought that God imparts to us a cognitive power which renders it self-evident that the articles of faith are his own self-testimony (or revelation) as *prima veritas* seems to require either that the truth of the articles themselves becomes self-evident, or that it follows necessarily from our grasp of their status. Either way, we apparently fall afoul of Aquinas' insistence on our inability in this life to "see" that the articles are true.

If we are blocked from any telling appeal to the revealed status of Christian doctrines, how *can* we gain surety about their truth? The will, Aquinas argues, elicits the mind's assent to the teaching of scripture and creed. Even though the mind can "see" neither that the content of this teaching must be true, nor that its status compels assent, the will clings to the good which is held out in this teaching, and induces the intellect to hold it true. "Faith . . . is an enigmatic cognition, but . . . the will makes good use of this cognition, assenting to what it does not see, for God's sake."[63] Lit by grace, the heart (as we might now say) finds in the triune God of whom this teaching speaks its true desire, and so cleaves to this teaching not only as true, but as the first truth, "which is the goal of all our desires and actions."[64] Thus faith's distinctive certainty. It reposes in the church's teaching as our only way of apprehending in this life, where we must think discursively and in words, the first truth in whom our ultimate good—our salvation—consists.[65] But the first truth is not grasped at all—is not grasped as *first*—unless it is believed for its own sake, and not on account of any other belief, which must be less than the first truth.[66] So faith holds to the articles as the most certain statements there could be, even though they seem less obvious to us than many other beliefs.[67]

This may not seem especially helpful, since we normally give little epistemic credit to a person who believes what she wants, regardless of whether there is any evidence for it. Aquinas argues, though, that the believer's assent to the articles of faith springs not from a mere wish for what one would like there to be, but from a prior intimacy with the God who makes himself available to us in the articles as our last end. This grace-wrought intimacy with God—or "connaturality," as Aquinas sometimes puts it—spontaneously recognizes in the creedal articles the God of whose goodness and love it already enjoys a taste. Arraigned before Pilate, Christ does not, Aquinas notes, say "Everyone who hears my voice is of the truth"—everyone who believes my teaching becomes truth's intimate—but rather, "Everyone who is of the truth hears my voice" (John 18:37). We do not draw close to the saving truth of which Christ speaks because we believe his words or those of his witnesses; rather, "we believe because we are 'of the truth,' in that we have received the gift of God by which we believe and love the truth."[68]

The truth we believe and love is of course Jesus Christ himself (cf. John 14:6). But the incarnate *prima veritas* does not simply call upon us from afar to believe in him; he dwells within us and gives us the gift of his own Spirit, whose very being is to kindle love. This indwelling by grace of the one who is the truth itself, inseparable from the donation of the Spirit who is love itself, brings our intellect to the highest perfection it can enjoy in this life. The indwelling Christ gives us "a kind of instruction by which the intellect bursts out in love's affection," a taste of himself which is "a certain experiential knowledge," so that we might hold fast to what he says, to a truth we do not see.[69] The name for this sort of knowledge is "wisdom, a kind of knowledge by taste"—a wisdom which comes not first from learning, but from "suffering divine things" (*patiens divina*).[70] In the end, it seems, we believe the teaching of scripture and creed not because reason gives us compelling grounds to do so, still less because we merely wish that it were true, but because we have already suffered the things of which it speaks. For this reason, faith's assent to what God teaches amounts to a "certain participation in . . . and assimilation to God's own knowledge, in that by the faith infused in us we cling to the first truth for its own sake."[71] And so "*sacra doctrina* is like an impression of God's own *scientia*" in us.[72]

The Wisdom of God and the Wisdom of the World

The Parisian master knows the basic premises of Christian teaching in the same way as the illiterate *uetula:* by a connatural apprehension of the first truth attested in the language of scripture and creed. For the master this holy teaching takes the form of an articulated science, a body of warranted beliefs connected by various sorts of argument. This naturally leads one to wonder about broader epistemic connections. What does the holy teaching of the Christian master have to do with the rest of the knowledge human beings have, or think they have? We especially need to know what links there are between sacred doctrine and the rest of the sciences, those bodies of warranted belief which depend on human reason and not on the self-testimony of the first truth. Curiosity on this score naturally gravitates in particular toward beliefs about *God*—to the connection between the knowledge of God which belongs to Christian teaching and that *theologia,* different in kind, which belongs to philosophy.[73]

Aquinas handles the main epistemic question by arguing that *sacra doctrina* is not only science, but wisdom. To have *scientia* is to understand effects in light of their causes, but wisdom (*sapientia*) goes further. It grasps ultimate causes, in an entire area of nature or human practice. Thus the distinctive mark of wisdom is the capacity, as Aquinas puts it, "to order and judge." The wise person understands how everything in her area of knowledge fits together under the highest causes, and can assess the correctness of all beliefs and practices pertinent to that domain. Thus the engineer has an intricate science regarding certain sorts of material things, but the physicist is genuinely wise in the ways of matter and motion, grasping first principles. She can therefore correct the engineer, but the engineer cannot correct her.[74]

Christian teaching, however, knows God as the highest cause of everything, not just of one or another sort of thing. It knows the supreme cause, moreover, in the highest possible way available to human beings in this life, since its creedal premises are those "deep things" which only God would know about himself, had he not freely willed to share them with us in Christ.[75] Therefore, "among all the wisdom available to human beings this teaching is the greatest, not just in one area, but without qualification."[76] As highest wisdom, it belongs to sacred doctrine to judge the truth of beliefs and the correctness of practices not simply in one area or another, but across the board.[77] In just this way sacred doctrine is a participated likeness of God's own knowledge. It not only receives from God an apprehension of the ultimate divine cause of all things—of the persons of the Trinity, without the knowledge of whom we can understand neither the coming forth of creatures from God nor their return to him, neither creation nor salvation.[78] Sacred doctrine is an *impressio* of God's *scientia* just because it can understand and judge all things in light of their causes in God, and so emulate in human knowledge God's own ordering of things.[79]

From this conception of Christian teaching as the highest wisdom follow two epistemic consequences, which Aquinas clearly specifies. It is not the business of sacred doctrine, he argues, to prove the principles of the other sciences, but only to judge them. For any-thing found in any other science which is opposed to the truth of this science is false, and must be totally rejected. For this reason it is said in II Cor. 10:5, "We destroy arguments, and bring down all arrogance which exalts itself against the knowledge of God."[80]

Christian wisdom is connected to the rest of our beliefs in two basic ways: (1) it does not prove the beliefs which are held or proposed in any other realm of human knowledge and practice; (2) it does judge the truth of beliefs which are held or proposed in all other realms of human knowledge and practice. It will be clearest to take these in reverse order.

1. "Only to Judge"

Since no statement can be true which conflicts with the contents of sacred doc-trine, the scriptural and creedal principles of Christian teaching are the primary criteria for deciding which beliefs are true. The epistemic primacy of sacred doc-trine is of a negative or limiting kind (*sacra doctrina* does not prove, but judges). No true statement can be inconsistent with the contents of Christian teaching. This stricture applies on the widest possible scale. No statement whatever—including any we may regard as observationally, historically, scientifically, or philo-sophically justified—can definitively be established as true without being tested for its agreement with the contents of Christian teaching. For Aquinas the stan-dard against which all other beliefs are to be tested is, at least in the passage just cited, quite broad. The measure is simply "this science"—the whole of *sacra doc-trina*. Since within this science the articles of faith are the first principles, pri-macy in decisions about truth belongs ultimately to them. This should not sur-prise. Assenting to the articles, Christian faith cleaves for his own sake to the triune God as first truth, and so is in a position to judge every claim to truth in light of the source and measure of all truth.

This means that Aquinas' epistemology is, at bottom, a kind of theological coherentism. Proposals for belief may come with all manner of imposing war-rants attached. They may be *per se nota*, evident to the senses, agreed on by every-body, and so forth. They may be conclusions of a rigorous science. The articles of Christian faith lack all these epistemic desiderata. They are not self-evident, beyond rational doubt, or widely agreed on. Yet we cannot tell for sure whether any statement is true, no matter what its epistemic qualifications, save by seeing whether it agrees—coheres—with the articles of Christian faith. Of course there are many kinds of coherentism. The sort of coherence Aquinas regards as epistemically telling is not symmetrical. He does not hold that a large and generally coherent body of beliefs must for the most part be true. Rather, we may recognize as true no statement which is logically inconsistent with the articles of faith, and we may not regard the articles of faith as false on account of their inconsistency with any other statement. The giving of reasons thus has certainties in which it can come to an end, though we may be assured of their truth only by faith. Aquinas is thus immune to the charge of circularity sometimes thought to be telling against coherentist views of epistemic justification.[81]

A tension in Aquinas' epistemology comes to the surface at this point. He thinks of human knowing, and certainly the knowledge generated by the sciences, as depending on beliefs which are self-evidently true, on principles known "through themselves." At the same time he holds that no belief can be true unless it is at least consistent with the articles of Christian faith. This means that even a seemingly self-evident statement like "the whole is greater than the part" cannot be conclusively established as true until it has been checked for compatibility with the creedal articles. Such statements would *not* then be principles known through themselves, but would be known through other beliefs.

Aquinas seems to be aware of the problem, and indeed to take a firm position on it. Human reason is feeble, and can be mistaken; God's knowing cannot. Therefore the faith which relies connaturally on God's own knowledge imparted through scripture and creed is, despite its lack of self-evidence, more certain than any science which relies on reason's grasp of *principia per se nota*.[82] This confirms the epistemic primacy of faith's articles over even the most obvious of reason's certainties: "The believer assents more firmly to those things which belong to faith than even to the first principles of reason."[83] But while the weakness of reason accounts for the need to test even seemingly self-evident beliefs against the articles of faith, it fails to explain how such beliefs, thus tested, could still be regarded as known "through themselves." One might handle this problem by utilizing Aquinas' distinction between statements which are *per se nota* in themselves, and those which are grasped as such by us.[84] The point would then be that as some statements are known *per se* by the wise, and not by the rest of us, so in the final vision of God we will have *per se* knowledge of all those matters of which we can now be certain only by testing them against the articles of faith. But since our knowledge in the final vision will not be propositional anyway—indeed we will grasp all things we know simultaneously through the vision of God's essence, and not piecemeal "through themselves"—it would seem that this recourse fails to solve the problem.[85]

So far, *sacra doctrina*'s office of epistemic judgment involves, for Aquinas, a quite basic but modest claim. Consistency with the teaching of scripture and creed is a necessary condition for any belief to be true. However, at times Aquinas also makes a much bolder claim about the epistemic significance of the articles of faith. At least when it comes to beliefs about *God,* consistency with the articles of faith is not enough to secure their truth, even when these beliefs are warranted by self-evident premises. For claims about God to be true, the person who makes them actually has to believe the articles of faith. For example, someone who makes an argument for the existence of God not only has to reach a warranted conclusion which is consistent with the articles of faith; he has to believe the whole package of articles himself. Otherwise sacred doctrine judges his belief to be false.

Aquinas makes this claim in several passages. Considering whether the belief that God exists belongs to the distinctively Christian act of faith (since non-Christians also often hold that God exists), he argues that it does. Even though non-Christians (*infideles*—"unbelievers") may believe that there is a God, they do not assent to the full range of creedal teachings by which God makes himself known, and to which Christians assent by the grace of faith. As a result the assent of non-Christians to the statement that God exists differs in kind from that of Christians. Lacking faith in Christ and the Trinity, "they do not really believe that God exists." Their epistemic location outside the scriptural and creedal faith of the Christian community engenders a cognitive defect so great that they "totally fail to attain" the object of their belief, namely, God; as held by them, the belief that God exists is simply false.[86] Elsewhere Aquinas explicitly applies this argument to the ancient philosophers who demonstrated God's existence, with, if anything, an even more stringent result: "even if they erred in the smallest way regarding the knowledge of God, they are said to be completely ignorant of him."[87] This is a bold sort of coherentism. When it comes to God, the web of belief is so tightly woven that for any one statement to be true, it has to be believed together with many other statements, above all the articles of Christian faith.[88]

Because the bold coherentism for which Aquinas argues here effectively rules out natural theology (unless, of course, it is practiced by Christians), Thomists may find it difficult to believe that Aquinas means what he plainly says.[89] Since the mid-nineteenth century, many Thomists have seen a consummate natural theology as Aquinas' greatest achievement. He put belief in God's existence and nature on a firm rational foundation, whence it could be defended against the assaults of modern skepticism, and serve as a basis for the acceptance of revealed truths about God beyond reason's grasp.[90] But had Aquinas simply meant that the Christian believer and the non-Christian natural theologian hold the same true belief that God exists, if by different means (the believer by faith, the natural theologian by demonstrative argument), he would have said that even though the natural theologian lacks Christian faith, she nonetheless really believes that God exists, and her belief, like the Christian's, "attains" God.[91] Instead he denies these claims. Had Aquinas thought that the natural theologian's cognitive handicap is simply one instance of the imperfection of all human knowledge of God in this life, including that of Christians, he would not have said the natural theologian's belief that God exists is false—totally fails to attain God—while the Christian's is true. He apparently thinks that some epistemic defects have considerably more drastic consequences than others.

Most puzzling, of course, is how to square this rejection of natural theology apart from Christian faith with Aquinas' repeated insistence that the existence and at least some of the attributes of God can be rationally demonstrated from God's created effects. But while this may seem almost hopelessly paradoxical to us, after generations of Thomist natural theology, Aquinas himself seems not to think the matter especially mysterious. Scripture (from which alone holy teaching may argue *ex necessitate*) assures us that the invisible things of God may be known from the things that are made (Romans 1:19 – 20). So it must be possible to demonstrate God's existence and attributes from creatures. But scripture equally instructs us that human beings have failed to honor and worship the God whom they knew in this way, with the result that their minds have become lost in vanity, their foolish hearts darkened (Romans 1:21): God has "deprived them of the light of wisdom, by which a human being knows God truly" (*vere Deum cognoscit*).[92] So absent the restoration of this cognitive light—the *lumen fidei* and the Spirit's gift of wisdom—the human mind cannot attain God from creatures.

That there can be no knowledge of God without faith in Christ and the Trinity is an ancient and deep-laid Christian conviction.[93] The difficulty lies in how to understand it. In the passages we have just been looking at, Aquinas utilizes Aristotle's theory of simple or incomposite entities in order to account for this Christian conviction. On this view simple entities are such that we have to know all their properties at once; we either know all of them or none of them. God is supremely simple, so unless we know what he has told us about himself, we do not know him at all.

Objections against this notion and its theological application are numerous. But without entering into the disputed metaphysics of simples, it is not difficult to get a sense of what Aquinas is driving at. Well before the visual discovery of the planet Pluto, astronomers had solid mathematical arguments for the belief that there must be another planet beyond Neptune, whose gravity would account for eccentricities in Neptune's orbit. But this is not exactly to say that they had knowledge of Pluto itself, and some doubted the existence of a ninth planet. People who have a valid argument for God's existence but lack knowledge of the Trinity and the incarnation, Aquinas seems to argue, are in a similar position.

Still, in neither case does it seem quite right to say that people with sound arguments, but also a serious cognitive defect, have *no* true beliefs about God or Pluto. Pluto, for example, is a planet whose gravity causes eccentricities in Neptune's orbit, and even before its discovery there were astronomers who believed that there is a planet whose gravity causes eccentricities in Neptune's orbit. So they had a true belief about Pluto, but were not yet aware that they did. Thus it seems more plausible to say that they did not have true beliefs sufficient to *identify* Pluto than to say that they had no true beliefs about Pluto at all. On this line of argument, it is not clear why the same would not apply to the natural theologian's beliefs about God. (This would, to be sure, limit the natural theologian to a far more modest knowledge of God than most modern Thomists have thought to find in Aquinas.) In fact, Aquinas himself says as much at an early stage, when he touches on the epistemic bearing of God's simplicity in his commentary on Boethius' *De Trinitate.*[94] But, as we have seen, he clearly changed his mind later on, perhaps as a result of writing his commentary on Aristotle's *Metaphysics,* where the knowledge of simples comes in for detailed treatment.[95]

The matter might be approached differently, by way of linguistic meaning. The beliefs of the non-Christian and the Christian are different enough that they do not mean the same thing by "God" when they each assert that God exists. If the Christian's belief is true, then the non-Christian will have failed to form a belief about God in the first place, and so will obviously have failed to form a true belief.[96] Aquinas suggests such an approach when he argues that the *infidelis* who asserts that God exists does not "really believe" what the Christian believes, indeed does not actually succeed in having an opinion about God at all.[97] Here too problems arise. If a non-Christian cannot mean the same thing by "God" as a Christian, then she might be completely ignorant of God, but it is hard to see how she could actually disbelieve what Christians say about God. She would be disbelieving in some other god, and so would not really be an *infidelis* at all (unless she could somehow mean the same thing when she denied that God is the Trinity, but—perhaps because of this denial—something different when she asserted that God exists). Aquinas' bolder coherentism thus faces some serious challenges. But this is clearly the position he holds, at least in his later writings.

2. "Not to Prove"

Aquinas' second claim about the epistemic status of Christian teaching complements his theological coherentism, in both its modest and bold forms. It does not belong to this holy teaching to prove the principles of any other science. That is, consistency with the articles of faith is a necessary condition for the truth of all other beliefs, but it is not enough to establish the truth of those beliefs. In order to decide what to believe in doubtful cases, or to give an account of why we believe what we do, we need reasons or explanations beyond the principles and contents of sacred doctrine. For Aquinas this can come from many places, including the evidence of the senses, principles which look self-evident to us, and inferences from other beliefs of whose truth we are convinced, but also from the testimony of other people whom we believe are reliable. When our beliefs about a particular subject matter take the form of a science, this will be a body of knowledge with its own principles and its own procedures for testing beliefs about that subject matter. Theology provides neither these principles nor these procedures for warranting beliefs.

In science, as in ordinary life, sacred doctrine should thus see its epistemic role as indispensable but limited. It rightly rejects as false any belief, in any area, which is contrary to Christian teaching. But save in matters which have a logically close tie to the articles of Christian faith, it cannot provide reasons for beliefs or enable us to decide between competing alternatives. *Sacra doctrina* thus has only a limited stake in the arguments of the philosophers. Where philosophers (or scientists) hold competing positions among which, as is very often the case, theology has no way to decide, it is best for theologians simply not to become entangled with such disputes. It only encourages them to think that the Christian faith itself has some vital interest in the outcome of these disputes, and so to take as a binding matter of Christian conviction what is only a philosophical opinion.

Thus Aquinas replied with a hint of impatience when John of Vercelli, the master of the Dominican order, interrupted his Holy Week devotions in April of 1271 to ask a number of questions about disputed philosophical matters, particularly pertaining to Aristotle's cosmological writings. Aquinas felt bound in obedience to reply right away, but he protests at the outset that

> many of these questions belong not to the doctrine of the faith, but to the dogmas of the philosophers. It does a great deal of harm, however, either to assert or deny claims which make no contribution to the teaching of piety, as though they pertained to sacred doctrine.

Taking his cues from Augustine, Aquinas summarizes his view about the safest course for Christian theology to follow in handling those claims which are widely made by the philosophers, as long as "they are not contrary to our faith." They should not be asserted as teachings of the faith, although from time to time they can be introduced into theology under the name of the philosophers who hold them. Nor should they be rejected as though they were contrary to the faith, since this might give the wisdom of the world needless occasion to hold the doctrine of the faith in contempt.[98] Aquinas goes on dutifully to answer the master's questions, "even though many of them are outside the limits of theology," that is, are not matters which theology can or need decide one way or the other.[99] A question about the interpretation of a knotty passage of Aristotle on animal generation does, however, prompt an observation about the usefulness, for a *magister in sacra pagina,* of being concerned about matters beyond these limits: "I do not see what the interpretation of the words of Aristotle has to do with the doctrine of the faith."[100]

That theology has only a limited stake in the arguments of the philosophers does not mean that theology can do without philosophy, still less that it can be basically hostile to philosophy (including, once again, much that now belongs to the natural and social sciences). Theology uses philosophy, to be sure, not out of any inherent need (the way engineering uses physics), but as a pragmatic means to its own pedagogical ends.[101] Of these Aquinas characteristically lists three.[102] When philosophers argue for conclusions which are against the faith, sacred doctrine uses the resources of philosophy itself to show that these arguments are not compelling. Since what the faith teaches cannot be false, no argument against the faith can have genuinely demonstrative force.[103] Where it can, Christian teaching uses philosophy to develop demonstrative arguments for those aspects of the faith which can be supported in this way (the so-called "preambles" to the articles)—though in its bold form Aquinas' coherentism limits, as we have observed, the circumstances under which these arguments actually yield true beliefs.[104] And sacred doctrine uses philosophical concepts and arguments to clarify and explain what the faith teaches, not because the content of the faith is inherently obscure, but because in the current feeble state of our intellect what lies within the scope of philosophy is more obvious to us than what is epistemically primary and most certain. Thus *sacra doctrina* "does not accept anything from other sciences as from its superiors, but uses them as inferiors and handmaids."[105]

In practice all this works out in complex and not always predictable ways. The eternity of the world, for example, was much debated while Aquinas was teaching at the University of Paris. That the universe had no beginning in time is against the faith, and so must be rejected as false.[106] Sacred doctrine thus prescribes a teaching in another science, against Aristotle's conclusion (in book VIII of his *Physics*) that the world is eternal. On this Aquinas agrees with the rest of the theologians at Paris. That the teaching of classical physics on the eternity of the world is false means that the arguments for it cannot be genuinely demonstrative, even if Aristotle thought they were.[107] But this is not to say that the arguments are shoddy, or the conclusion unreasonable or absurd. On the contrary—and here Aquinas disagrees with most of the Parisian theologians—there is no contradiction in the idea of an eternal world. Indeed it derogates from God's power as free creator *ex nihilo* to deny that he could make a world whose duration had no onset. Therefore it cannot be demonstrated that the world has a temporal beginning, any more than it can be demonstrated that it lacks one.[108] On the basis partly of considerations in logic and physics, and partly in the Christian doctrine of creation, Aquinas seems content to let physics reach its own conclusions in its own ways, even though theology may not always be able to accept them. Yet this issue, at least, is close enough in logical space to the heart of Christian doctrine that theology does not simply veto the conclusion of classical physics, but provides its own reason why it must be false: to posit an eternal world would be to put a creature where only the uncreated *Verbum* can be, in the beginning with God (John 1:2).[109]

Aquinas' basic teaching on the universal epistemic primacy of sacred doctrine seems clear enough. Theology does not attempt to settle the competing claims of worldly wisdom, so long as they are compatible with Christian teaching. But the wisdom we have from God judges all our claims to be wise, rejecting whatever contradicts the wisdom from above. Yet this teaching has been widely ignored, and often implicitly repudiated, in modern Thomism. Philosophy, Thomists regularly insist, has to be autonomous. It has to be purely philosophical, free to certify its own conclusions in its own ways, and so needs to proceed in a theologically antiseptic fashion. At the same time, these Thomists assume that philosophy's autonomously established results have to be capable of inclusion in a harmonious Christian view of the world.

According to Aquinas, though, we can only be sure that philosophy's results will fit into a Christian view of the world if Christian teaching has the epistemic right to judge, and if need be to reject, even the most thoroughly certified philosophical claim. For Aquinas philosophy is evidently not autonomous, but is always subject to correction from another quarter. It has, more precisely, about the same autonomy with respect to theology as stonecutting has with respect to architecture (in Aquinas' terms, philosophy is autonomous not *simpliciter*, but *secundum quid*). Stonecutting has its own goals and methods, which the architect is normally willing to leave to the mason. But if the architect's well-designed edifice crumbles because the stones would not bear the load, he rightly judges that the mason, whatever his protests that the stones were flawless, needs to produce a different result. The architect may, indeed, help him figure out how. In the relationship between faith and reason, grace, modern Thomists often observe, does not destroy nature but perfects it. As Aquinas immediately goes on to say, however, this does not justify the unfettered autonomy of philosophy, but rather eliminates it: "therefore it is necessary that natural reason be subservient to faith."[110]

Modern Thomism has various motives for its preoccupation with philosophical questions. Vatican I's teaching of a *"duplex ordo cognitionis"* has sometimes been taken as a compelling endorsement of philosophy's autonomy.[111] The urge to make Thomism convincing in the face of many apparently opposed currents in modern philosophy has no doubt played a considerable role. But over the last century or so the dominance of Thomism by philosophy has produced some odd results.

It has long been fashionable to bash the tradition of handbook or "manual" Thomism from, say, Franzelin's treatises in the 1860s to the *Sacrae Theologiae Summa* of the Spanish Jesuits in the early 1950s. Distorted by the exigencies of Vatican I and blind to the dynamic development of Aquinas' thought, this tradition produced, so it is charged, strained, over-systematized, and ahistorical interpretations of Aquinas. Whatever their deficiencies, though, the manualists at least read Aquinas as a theologian, composing long treatises *secundum mentem Thomae* (as they understood it) on the Trinity, the incarnation, grace, and the sacraments. To that extent they were interested in the same things as is Aquinas, not least because Aquinas is so evidently concerned about them (which is not to say that these Thomists always upheld the properly ancillary character of philosophy). More recent Thomism prides itself on its greater fidelity to the mind of Aquinas, but one is struck by the amount of interest this Thomism has taken in a matter like the proofs for the existence of God (on which the *Summa Theologiae* includes only one article), and how little it has taken in, say, Christology (to which Aquinas devotes the bulk of the *Tertia Pars*).

The Thomism of recent generations has, to be sure, not simply set store by a robust and autonomous philosophy. It has sought to explain and defend *Aquinas'* philosophy in particular. But from the point of view of *sacra doctrina* as Aquinas understands and practices it, this passion to vindicate his own philosophy is also somewhat curious. It has resulted, among other things, in a long-standing and often deliberate isolation of much Thomistic philosophy from the analytic tradition which has come to dominate philosophy in most parts of the world. The barriers between the two are now being widely breached, from both sides. How much of Aquinas' metaphysics and philosophy of mind will stand the test of a sustained engagement with analytic philosophy, and how much will go the way of his physics and biology, only attention to individual cases will tell.[112] It may be that relatively little will survive. Thomists need not, however, be especially alarmed by this prospect, at least if they think of Thomism as a way of practicing *sacra doctrina*. "To the extent that sacred doctrine uses philosophical texts for its own purposes, it does not receive them on account of the authority of those who wrote them, but on account of the reasons they give for what they say. What is well said it accepts, the rest it discards."[113] The same surely goes for whatever philosophy is to be found in the pages of Thomas Aquinas.

What the Old Woman Knows

In considering sacred doctrine's right to judge the truth claims of other sciences, it might seem once again as though we have left the *uetula* behind. But here too, as with the capacity for knowing the articles of faith upon which theological science is based, Aquinas thinks otherwise. In fact the opposite is the case. The holy teaching of the Parisian master is a partial and incomplete attempt to catch up, by the laborious path of learning and argument acquired by study, to the wisdom the unlettered charwoman already possesses as a free gift from God. Like every faithful Christian, the *uetula* receives through baptism and the sacramental life the Holy Spirit's own gift of wisdom. That she has divine wisdom is not in doubt; the question, as Aquinas sees it, is whether the science of theology can also aspire to the title of wisdom by the standard she sets.[114]

Theology can count as wisdom, Aquinas argues, because right judgment can be learned. One way to be wise is "by taking thought" (*per modum cognitionis*), having acquired by long study, trial, and accumulation of argument the skill of fine discrimination in one's area of knowledge. In this way, Aquinas argues, a person learned in the discipline of ethics can become genuinely wise about where virtue lies in human action, even though he may not be virtuous himself. Similarly a person can with effort learn to be a skilled judge of what truth claims Christians ought to accept or reject, and what actions they ought to regard as right and wrong, based on the articles of faith which God has revealed. *Sacra doctrina* is painfully acquired wisdom, as Aquinas sees it, of just this sort.[115]

There is, however, a less arduous and more reliable way of being wise in the ways of God. The *uetula* knows nothing of the complex apparatus of textual tradition, technical concept, and rigorous argument by which the theological master judges rightly about what "is in agreement with Christ," what accords with Christian teaching, and what must be rejected as false.[116] But she has no need to. She has already suffered divine things, and she is already wise. The connatural affection by which she clings to the self-revealing first truth enables her to judge what is with this truth and what is against it, what she should believe and what she should reject. An intimate of the triune God through the Spirit's gifts, she judges rightly not by taking thought, but by a spontaneous inclination (*per modum inclinationis*), not like someone who knows about virtue, but like someone who has it. She is "the spiritual person, who judges all things" (1 Corinthians 2:15), the person who has been taught not by study, but "by suffering divine things."[117]

Of course there is much that the *uetula* has not been given to understand. But she knows the aim of life. With her connatural grasp of life's end goes the capacity to judge rightly about everything necessary for the attainment of that end. The *uetula* is thus able to realize, as far as human beings may in this present life, the one purpose for which God has taught us concerning himself, which otherwise only he would know. The theological master simply strives to make explicit, to recapture *in modo cognitionis*, what the faithful heart of any old woman already knows.

Notes

1. *Collationes Credo in Deum;* Nicholas Ayo gives the provisional Leonine text and an English translation in *The Sermon-Conferences of St. Thomas Aquinas on the Apostles' Creed* (Notre Dame, Ind.: University of Notre Dame Press, 1988). Here, as usual with Aquinas' works, fixing a date and location is difficult and uncertain. Ayo follows the established view that the sermons were preached in Naples in 1273; Jean-Pierre Torrell questions this late date. For this and more on these *Collationes,* see Ayo's introduction to *The Sermon-Conferences,* 1–14, and Torrell, *Saint Thomas Aquinas,* vol. 1, *The Person and His Work,* trans. Robert Royal (Washington, D.C.: Catholic University of America Press, 1996), 69–74, 357–58.

2. *Collationes Credo in Deum* I (ed. Ayo, 20). All translations are my own.

3. All from *Collationes Credo in Deum* I (ed. Ayo, 20–22).

4. *Collationes Credo in Deum* I (ed. Ayo, 22–24).

5. Ibid. (ed. Ayo, 22), my emphasis.

6. *ST* I.1.8 ad 2.

7. As a quick glance at the *Summa* shows, each of Aquinas' "articles" actually answers a question, and his "questions" are collections of such articles. Other medieval theologians sometimes reverse the terminology (such as Bonaventure in his commentary on the Lombard's *Sentences*).

8. *ST* I.1, proem.

9. Aquinas concludes his brief preface to the entire work with a statement of its task: "Confident of divine help, we will attempt to present briefly and clearly those things which belong to holy teaching, to the extent that the matter allows" (*ST* I, prol.).

10. *ST* I.1.1c. Jean-Pierre Torrell emphasizes that for Aquinas *sacra doctrina* is, first of all, teaching which saves. Cf. "Le savoir théologique chez saint Thomas," in Torrell, *Recherches thomasiennes* (Paris: J. Vrin, 2000), 132, 143.

11. *ST* I.1.1c; and ad 1. Faith, Aquinas later stresses, has to do precisely with that in which the aim of life consists. *ST* II-II.1.8c: "Those matters of which we will enjoy the vision in eternal life inherently [*per se*] belong to faith, as do those by which we are led into eternal life." Cf. II-II.1.6 ad 1; 2.5c.

12. *ST* I.1.1 ad 1: "Those matters which are above human thought are not to be sought after by human beings through reason, but they are nevertheless revealed by God. . . . And in these matters holy teaching consists."

13. *ST* I.1.6c.

14. *In I Cor.* 2:9, no.98. Cf. *ST* II-II.2.3c: "The ultimate blessedness of a human being consists in a vision of God which exceeds our natural reach [*in quadam supernaturali Dei visione*]. A human being cannot attain this vision except by learning from God, his teacher. As John 6[:45] says: 'Everyone who hears from the Father and learns, comes to me.'" Such passages indicate that whatever we make of Aquinas' famous claim that "all our knowledge has its beginning from sense" (*ST* I.1.9c), this dictum cannot be taken to mean that our contact with sensible objects is by itself sufficient to yield every item of knowledge we actually have. Aquinas regularly cites Ecclesiasticus 3:25 in this connection: "Much has been shown to you which is above human sense" (cf. *ST* I.1.1 ad 1; II-II.2.3 ad 3; *ScG* I.5.6).

15. The quoted phrase is from *ST* I.1.1c. For Aquinas, as for Aristotle, the "philosophical disciplines" embrace physics, astronomy, biology, psychology, and politics—that is, much of what we now regard as belonging to the natural and social sciences, and not only those matters (logic, metaphysics, and ethics) which remain the province mainly of philosophers.

16. *ST* I.1.1c. Cf. II-II.2.4c: "When it comes to things divine human reason is greatly deficient. An indication of this is that the philosophers, even when they looked into things human by their natural powers of investigation, made many mistakes and contradicted themselves."

17. *In I Cor.* 2:10, no.102.

18. Aquinas is quite explicit about this. *ST* I-II.113.4 ad 2: "By natural knowledge a human being is not turned toward God insofar as he is the object of blessedness and the cause of justification"; *ST* II-II.4.7c: "Natural knowledge cannot aim at God [*attingere ad Deum*] as the object of blessedness, which is the way in which [Christian] hope and love tend toward him"; *ScG* I.5.2: because God calls us to a higher good than we can experience in this life, "it is necessary that the mind be called forth into something [good] in a higher way than our reason is capable of attaining in the present life, in order that the mind may in this way learn to desire, and by zeal to tend toward, that which surpasses the whole state of the present life."

19. Therefore when Aquinas argues that God helps us by revelation even regarding those truths about him which can be known by reason, "in order that salvation might come about for human beings more suitably [*convenientius*—or perhaps, *communius*, 'more widely'; cf., in this sense, *ST* II-II.2.4c] and certainly" (I.1.1c), he does not mean that our salvation would come about less suitably, widely, and certainly without revelation. It would not come about at all, since we would lack knowledge sufficient to locate the end in which it consists. The point, rather, is that God's generosity provides us not only with that knowledge of him we would otherwise lack, but also with that knowledge of him we might otherwise attain, and so gives us all we need for salvation.

20. All from *ST* I.32.1 ad 3. As Aquinas here observes, we also need to know about the Trinity "in order to think rightly about creation." This adds a particular and delicate problem to the concept of knowing God from creatures, since we cannot know about the Trinity *per creaturas*.

21. *De Rat. Fid.*, ch. 1 (Leonine Edition 40 B [1967], 57, lin.15–17). See also *ST* II-II.174.6c: "The whole faith of the church is founded on the revelation made to the apostles concerning faith in the unity and trinity [of God]."

22. *ST* III, prol.: "Consummationem totius theologici negotii."

23. *ST* I.2, proem. In the commentary on John (*In Ioh.* 14:6, nos.1868, 1871), Aquinas writes: "Because this 'way' is not distant from the goal, but joined to it, [Jesus] adds, 'the truth and the life.' Thus he is at once the way, and the goal. . . . The Lord is for us the way by which we go to him, and through him to the Father."

24. *ST* I.1.4c: *sacra doctrina* "is more speculative than practical, since it treats mainly of God [*de rebus divinis*] rather than mainly of human acts. It deals with the latter insofar as by them a human being is ordered to the perfect knowledge of God, in which eternal blessedness consists."

25. Cf. Aquinas' own title for *ST* I-II.3.8: "Whether blessedness consists only in that vision [*speculatione*] by which God is seen through his own essence" (*ST* I-II.3, proem.), to which the answer is, of course, affirmative. On the vision of God as itself a human act (*operatio*), though one with no product outside the agent, cf. I-II.3.2.

26. See Richard Cross, *Duns Scotus* (Oxford: Oxford University Press, 1999), 8–10.

27. *ST* I.1.8 ad 2: "The use of philosophical authorities is, as it were, extrinsic to holy teaching, and yields only probable conclusions, while the use of canonical scripture's authorities belongs to the very nature of the enterprise, and yields necessary conclusions." The authority "of the other teachers of the church" (besides the authors of scripture) lies midway between these two. *Sacra doctrina* uses them naturally (*quasi arguendo ex propriis*), rather than "extrinsically," but the results remain probable rather than necessary.

28. E.g., *ST* I.1.8c ("Unde sacra Scriptura . . . disputat"); cf. Torrell, "Le savoir théologique," 132.

29. Thus *ST* I.1.7, sed contra: "this science . . . is called theology, a kind of talk about God."

30. *ST* I.1.1 ad 2. On this see the last section of this chapter.

31. Cf. Torrell, *Saint Thomas Aquinas*, 1:55: "'To read' Scripture was the first task for the master in theology, and therefore also for Thomas. . . . Though long overlooked in favor of the *Sentences* or the *Summa*, this kind of biblical teaching was nevertheless Thomas's ordinary labor."

32. *ST* I.1.5 ad 1: "The least knowledge we can have of the highest things is more desirable than the most certain knowledge of lesser things," applying a dictum of Aristotle in a way in which, on Aquinas' account, Aristotle himself never could.

33. On this the classic work remains M.-D. Chenu, *La théologie comme science au XIIIe siècle*, 3rd ed. (Paris: J. Vrin, 1969).

34. For this example, see *Posterior Analytics* I, 23 (78a39–b3), and Aquinas' commentary, *Post. Anal.* I, 23 (Leonine Edition 1*/2 [Editio altera retractata, 1989], 85, lin.73 ff.).

35. The notion of being known "*per se*" actually collects a considerable number of ideas for Aquinas. For a representative list, cf. *ST* I.2.1: that is known *per se* "of which the knowledge is naturally present in us" (obj.1); "which is known as soon as the terms are known," such as "every whole is greater than its part" (obj.2); "of which no one can think the opposite" (sed contra); of which "no one is ignorant" (corpus; cf. *De Trin.* q.2 a.2 obj.5: "which everyone approves who hears them"); and of which "the predicate is included in the meaning of the subject, such as 'a human being is an animal'" (corpus). This last is the dominant note in Aquinas' discussions of *principia per se nota*, but the connection of these ideas with one another, and the role they play in the formation of a single and coherent concept, is not always clear.

36. *ST* I.1.7c: "The principles of this science . . . are the articles of faith, which has to do with God." For Aquinas' enumeration of fourteen articles of faith on the basis of the Apostles' Creed, see II-II.1.8. The Creed is itself based on scripture, and adds nothing to it; cf. II-II.1.9 ad 1.

37. *ST* II-II.2.10c.

38. "The aim of faith for us is that we reach an understanding of what we believe" (*De Trin.* q.2 a.2 ad 7). The teacher of theology therefore aims "to instruct his hearers in order that they may be lead to an understanding of the truth which they hold. It is necessary that such teaching rely upon reasons which search out the root of this truth, and make it known how what is said, is true." Otherwise the hearers "will acquire no knowledge or understanding, and will go away empty" (*Quodl.* IV, 9, 3c).

39. Aquinas has other motives for defending theology's claim to be a science, not least the view of some among the faculty of arts at the University of Paris—soon to be hit by the condemnation of 1277—that theology (unlike philosophy as practiced in the arts faculty) cannot be a science, since its principles are not *per se nota*. On this see Torrell, "Le savoir théologique," 47–48, with references to the considerable literature on this subject.

40. *Posterior Analytics* I, 25 (78b34–79a16); Aquinas, *Post. Anal.* I, 25 (Leonine Edition 1*/2, 89–91).

41. Aquinas' own examples of course come from the arts and sciences of his day. Thus optics is subalternate to geometry and music to arithmetic. Cf. *ST* I.1.2c.

42. *ST* I.1.2c.

43. On this see Aquinas' discussion of the distinction between faith and vision as epistemic situations in *ST* II-II.1.4c, also above, n. 35. It is not entirely clear, in fact, that Aquinas thinks the articles of faith can ever be converted into principles "known through themselves," even by the saints in heaven. He does say that the articles, as the principles of sacred doctrine, are "known by the light of a higher science" (I.1.2c), but he also insists that the knowledge of the blessed (to say nothing of the knowledge God enjoys) is nondiscursive; they have altogether left behind our current cognitive need for propositions (cf. II-II.1.2 ad 3). So while the blessed surely know that the articles of faith which we wayfarers believe are true, the articles are in no sense cognitive principles for the blessed themselves.

44. "Even in the sciences which are taught by human beings there are in some cases principles which are not known by all, but must be accepted from higher sciences [*oportet ea supponere a superioribus scientiis*] . . . and are known *per se* only to those possessing the higher science. The articles of faith, which are the principles of this science, are related to God's knowledge in this way. Those things which are known *per se* in the science which God has concerning himself are accepted in our science, and we believe the God who makes these things known to us through his witnesses, just as a physician believes the physicist when he teaches that there are four elements" (*De Trin.* q.2 a.2 ad 5). On 1 John 3:2 as a scriptural locus for the teaching that the mind's vision of God is the final aim of human life, cf. *ST* I.12.1, sed contra; 12.5c; II-II.1.2 ad 3; *De Ver.* q.8 a.1 ad 1. This vision converts what we now believe about God into knowledge *per se,* indeed knowledge through the divine essence itself (which is not exactly to say, as we have observed, that the propositions we currently hold true become *per se nota*). But it cannot normally take place within the bounds of this life (cf. I.12.11), though scripturally attested exceptions to this rule—Moses and Paul—help to structure Aquinas' overall account of the *visio* (cf. I.12.11 ad 2; II-II.175.3). For the rest of us, the hope of seeing what we now believe, and so of attaining blessedness, is constitutive of the faith by which we assent to the contents of scripture and creed (cf. II-II.4.1c; *In Heb.* 11:1, no.557).

45. *ST* I.32.1c. Cf. I.1.8c: "If an adversary believes none of the articles which are divinely revealed, no way is left to prove articles of faith to him by reason, but only to dismantle the arguments (if any) which he brings against the faith." See this same passage on the parallel between the principles of "metaphysics" and "sacred scripture," as well as *De Trin.* q.2 a.2 ad 4: "The articles of faith are not like conclusions in this science, but like principles, which are both defended against those who contest them (as Aristotle argues against those who deny first principles in *Metaphysics* IV) and clarified by various comparisons (just as principles naturally known are manifested inductively, and not proven by a demonstrative reason)." Aquinas is quite clear that the premises of *sacra doctrina* are ultimately lodged in scripture. "If there is someone who . . . totally contradicts the holy scriptures, he is utterly removed from our wisdom. For it is not the business of the theologian to prove the things of faith to a person who does not receive the scriptures, since faith is above reason. . . . It is necessary that we who receive the manifestation of God from holy scripture guard those things which have been placed in holy scripture, since they are the best possible rule of truth" (*De Div. Nom.* 2, 1, nos.124–25).

46. *ST* I.1.8 ad 2: "Sacred doctrine uses human reason," including its inferential procedures, "not in order to prove the faith . . . but to clarify [*ad manifestandum*] various matters which are treated in this teaching." Cf. II-II.10.7 ad 3.

47. *De Trin.* q.2 a.2c (my emphasis); cf. ad 4 (above, n. 45).

48. For a brief sample of the possibilities, see Reginald Garrigou-Lagrange, *Reality: A Synthesis of Thomistic Thought,* trans. (from the French *La synthèse thomiste*) Patrick Cummins (St. Louis: Herder, 1950), 65–68.

49. Cf. *ST* I.1.8c.

50. *In I Cor.* 15:12, no.911.

51. Cf. *In I Cor.* 15:14, nos.918–25; 15:21, no.931.

52. *In I Cor.* 15:12, no.911; cf. *ST* I.1.8c: "ad resurrectionem communem probandum."

53. *De Trin.* q.2 a.1 ad 5; cf. *ST* II-II.5 ad 2.

54. *ST* I.32.1 ad 2: "It is introduced in order to illuminate the Trinity [*ad manifestationem Trinitatis*]"; on the *convenientia* of the incarnation, cf. III.1.1.

55. Cf. *De Trin.* q.2 a.2 ad 5; above, n. 44.

56. For an argument in defense of the claim that "the mysteries of faith . . . are fit to be believed because the most certain signs present them to our reason as revealed by God," and deeply engaged with the modern Thomistic discussion, see Reginald Garrigou-Lagrange, *De Revelatione per Ecclesiam Catholicam Proposita,* 5th ed. (Rome: F. Ferrari, 1950), 1:487. There are surely texts of Aquinas which seem to point in this direction. Considered "under the general notion of that which may be believed," the articles of faith "are seen by the person who believes. For he would not believe [them] unless he saw that they were to be believed, either on account of the evidence of signs or something else of this kind" (*ST* II-II.1.4 ad 2; cf. 2.1 ad 1; 2.9 ad 3; 8.4 ad 2).

57. On the *lumen fidei* in this sense, cf. *ST* II-II.1.4 ad 3: "It is the light of faith which causes one to see those things which are believed. . . . By the habit of faith the human mind is inclined to assent to those things which belong to the correct faith and not to others" (cf. also 1.5 ad 1). The classic work on these modern apologetic disputes is Roger Aubert, *Le problème de l'acte de foi,* 3rd ed. (Louvain: E. Warny, 1958); for a useful summary see Avery Dulles, *The Assurance of Things Hoped For: A Theology of Christian Faith* (New York: Oxford University Press, 1994), especially 208–14.

In much Roman Catholic (to say nothing of Protestant) theology, including Aquinas interpretation, these arguments have come to seem old-fashioned and largely pointless since appeals to transcendental theories of knowledge became commonplace (though in theological hands these theories often rely on notions quite like that of an interior light of faith). Philosophers of religion have been more interested in these issues of late, and have tried to cast them in a contemporary philosophical idiom. For a recent interpretation of Aquinas along these lines, which seeks to reclaim the *lumen fidei* as the key to certainty about the revealed status, and thus the truth, of the articles of faith, see John I. Jenkins, *Knowledge and Faith in Thomas Aquinas* (Cambridge: Cambridge University Press, 1997).

58. On faith as assent to the *prima veritas,* cf. *ST* II-II.1.1; 1.3. The first truth is the triune God (and not a remote divine essence), but Aquinas consistently refuses to play off faith's apprehension of the self-revealing God against its assent to particular statements, as though holding sentences true were adventitious to having faith. The "formal object" of faith is "the first truth proposed to us in scripture, rightly interpreted according to the teaching of the church" (II-II.5.3 ad 2; cf. 1.2). On this see Bruce D. Marshall, "Faith and Reason Reconsidered: Aquinas and Luther on Deciding What Is True," *The Thomist* 63 (1999): 8–9.

59. *ST* II-II.4.8 ad 2. Aquinas discusses several other ways of assenting to what the creedal articles say besides Christian faith, though to his mind these are radically defective.

60. *Quodl.* II, 4, 1, sed contra [3]: "Human beings are obligated to believe the first truth more than to believe visible signs. But while Christ might have done no miracles, nevertheless he, being true God, was the *prima veritas.* Therefore even if he had done no miracles, he would still have to be believed." Cf. *ST* III.43.1 ad 3. On the human being Jesus as the *prima veritas,* cf. also *In Ioh.* 1:14, no.188; 1:17, no.207. In his comment on this argument (*Quodl.* II, 4, 1, ad 3) Aquinas simply grants the point, and observes that Christ, as the first truth, can make himself known to human beings in other ways: "he illuminates and teaches a person inwardly."

61. Christian teaching "has for its first principles the articles of faith, which the person who has faith knows *per se* by the infused light of faith, just as principles naturally implanted in us are known by the light of the agent intellect" (I *Sent.* q.1 art.3 qc.2 ad 2).

62. Cf. *De Trin.* q.2 a.2 ad 5 (above, n. 44); *ST* I.1.2 obj.1; II-II.1.4c; 5.2c. For some suggestions about the development of Aquinas' thought on this score, cf. Michel Corbin, *Le chemin de la théologie chez Thomas d'Aquin* (Paris: Beauchesne, 1974), 713–27.

63. *De Malo* q.1 a.3 ad 11. "'To believe' is an act of the intellect, assenting to divine truth at the will's command" (*ST* II-II.2.9c; cf. 1.4c; 4.2; 5.2). Thomist apologetics of both the naturalist and illuminationist sort has sensed its own difficulty in maintaining the genuinely voluntary (and thereby meritorious) character of faith, and has tried to cope with this problem in various ways. Cf., e.g., Garrigou-Lagrange, *De Revelatione,* 1:510–11.

64. *ST* II-II.4.2 ad 3. On the vision of God, "three and one," as the goal to which faith leads, cf. *In Heb.* 11:1, no.557. At just this point, miracles and other "external signs" can be "an inducement sufficient to believe" what the faith teaches (*ST* II-II.2.9 ad 3)—not as the basis of a proof of the faith's divine status, but as an incentive which attracts the will to the God whom the faith proclaims. Still, Aquinas argues, the scriptural example of doubting Thomas shows that it is better to believe without the inducement (John 20:29). Thomas "saw the wounds, and believed that it was God. But a more perfect faith does not require this sort of help in order to believe" (III.55.5 ad 3).

65. *ST* II-II.4.1c: "The first beginning of 'things hoped for' is in us by faith's assent, which contains in a virtual way everything we hope to attain."

66. *De Trin.* q.2 a.2c: "By the faith infused in us we cling to the first truth for its own sake [*propter se ipsam*]." Cf. *In Ioh.* 4:42, no.662: "When . . . a person has been led to believe, she can

say that she does not believe on account of any of these things: not on account of natural reason, nor the testimony of the law, nor the preaching of others. Rather she believes only on account of the truth itself [*propter ipsam veritatem tantum*]." This may help explain why Aquinas does not come to the aid of naturalist apologetics by appealing, as one might expect, to the distinction between what is more certain in itself and what is more certain to us (cf. *ST* I.1.5 ad 1). If you treat the articles of faith as in some way warrantable on the basis of other convictions, however obvious they may be, you are not taking the articles to be the first truth (or his testimony) at all.

67. Cf. *ST* II-II.4.8c; *De Ver.* q.14 a.1 ad 7. The faith which grasps the first truth, and so enjoys infallible certainty, is surely a kind of light, lit in us by grace: "Faith has certainty from a light divinely infused" (*In Ioh.* 4:42, no.662). But this light yields voluntary assent rather than intellectual vision. "The light of faith, which is like an impress of the first truth in the mind, cannot be mistaken, just as God can neither be deceived nor lie. Thus it suffices for [right] judgment. However this habit does not move us by way of the intellect, but rather by way of the will. Hence it does not make us see what is believed or compel assent, but works assent voluntarily" (*De Trin.* q.3 a.1 ad 4). This suggests how we might best interpret Aquinas' comments, even in his later writings, about the *lumen fidei* enabling us to "see" what we believe (or to see that the articles are to be believed). Faith's "vision" depends upon, or perhaps just is, the will's confident inclination to assent to Christian teaching and not to its denial (cf. II-II.1.4 ad 3, above, n. 57). As Aquinas already observes in the *Scriptum* on the *Sentences*, "The certainty of faith comes from outside the realm [*genus*] of knowledge, existing in the realm of affection" (III *Sent.* d.23 q.2 art.3 qc.1 ad 2; cited in Aubert, *Le problème de l'acte de foi*, 54).

68. *In Ioh.* 18:37, no.2363.

69. *ST* I.43.5 ad 2; on *cognitio experimentalis* cf. II-II.97.2 ad 2; I *Sent.* d.14 q.2 art.2 ad 3; d.15 q.2 art.1 ad 5. That our assent to Christian teaching has to stem from love for the God of whom it speaks is apparently not, for Aquinas, simply an exigency of our present epistemic situation. It follows from who the triune God is—from the particular dynamics of the trinitarian processions and their associated missions. Since knowledge of the Trinity is beyond our natural capacity, it requires a definite action of the triune God himself, in particular the *instinctus interior* by which the Son moves us to know him (cf. *Quodl.* II, 4, 1, ad 3; *In Ioh.* 15:24, no.2055). The Father's eternal Son, however, "is not just any sort of Word, but one who brings forth Love [*spirans Amorem*]," that is, the Holy Spirit (*ST* I.43.5 ad 2). So this Son cannot dwell in us without breathing out this Love in us, and this Love cannot be in us without issue—without our own love for the one who gives Love to us. It seems, therefore, that the Trinity cannot be known save by being in some way loved.

70. *ST* I.43.5 ad 2. On "suffering divine things" cf. II-II.45.2c: "To have right judgment concerning divine things by way of a certain connaturality to them belongs to that wisdom which is a gift of the Holy Spirit, just as Dionysius says: a certain Hierotheus was perfected when it comes to matters divine, 'not only learning, but suffering, divine things.' This suffering with, or connaturality to, divine things happens through love [*caritatem*], which unites us to God." Cf. also II-II.97.2 ad 2; I.1.6 ad 3 (on which more at the end of this essay); and *De Div. Nom.* 2, 4 (nos.191–92). I owe my attention to this idea in part to Reinhard Hütter, *Suffering Divine Things: Theology as Church Practice*, trans. Douglas W. Stott (Grand Rapids: Eerdmans, 1999).

The thought that our assent to the articles of faith springs from a connatural affection for the God of whom they speak poses, no doubt, a delicate conceptual problem. We cannot love, Aquinas assumes, what we do not know—what we do not believe to be, and to be worthy of desire. This means that the love which initially prompts our assent cannot be that divinely given *caritas* by which we cling to the articles with certainty (the love by which faith, as Aquinas puts it, "is infallibly ordered to the final end, for whose sake the will assents to what is true" [*ST* II-II.4.5c]). *Caritas,* on the contrary, presupposes faith (II-II.4.7c; and ad 5). The will's initial assent to the truths of faith must therefore stem not from the full connaturality of charity, but from something less: "a certain desire for the promised good" (*De Ver.* q.14 a.2 ad 10).

71. *De Trin.* q.2 a.2c (cf. above, n. 66).

72. *ST* I.1.3 ad 2.

73. Cf. *ST* I.1.1, ad 2.

74. *ST* I.1.6c. Aquinas' own example is more suggestive, since between physics and engineering we probably do not presume the sort of thoroughly hierarchical relationship he has in mind: the stonecutter and the bricklayer have genuine arts of which they are the master, but in the domain of knowledge which pertains to building the architect is the wise one, who can correct the judgment of the stonecutter, while he cannot correct hers.

75. Christian wisdom "is not only about the highest things, but from them" (*De Trin.* q.2 a.2 ad 1). Cf. *ST* I.1.6c; *In I Cor.* 2:7, no.85.

76. *ST* I.1.6c.

77. The wisdom which goes with Christian faith "can judge and order everything [*omnia*] according to divine rules." *ST* II-II.45.1c.

78. Cf. *ST* I.32.1 ad 3 (see also n. 20); I *Sent.* d.10 q.1.

79. Cf. *ST* I.1.6 ad 1.

80. *ST* I.1.6 ad 2. More colorfully, echoing Rev. 3:16: "Whatever is not in agreement with Christ is to be spewed out" (*In Col.* 2:9, no.96).

81. On the articles of faith as "epistemic trump" in Aquinas, and on the coherentist character of his epistemology, cf. my "Faith and Reason Reconsidered," 5–21, also my articles "Thomas, Thomisms, and Truth," *The Thomist* 56 (1992): 499–524, and "Aquinas as Postliberal Theologian," *The Thomist* 53 (1989): 353–402. Coherence in Aquinas pertains to the justification of beliefs, not to their truth, which Aquinas thinks of as the correspondence or *adaequatio* of the mind to reality.

82. "Just as science is certain, so also faith—indeed much more so, because science relies for its certainty on human reason, which can be deceived, while faith relies for its certainty on divine reason, which cannot be contradicted" (*In Ioh.* 4:42, no.662). Cf. *De Trin.* q.3 a.1 ad 4; *ST* I.1.5c; II-II.4.8 ad 2 (above, n. 59); *Collationes Credo in Deum* I (ed. Ayo, 22–24; above, n. 4). On the possibility of error even concerning "principles naturally known," see *ScG* IV.95.2.

83. I *Sent.* q.1 art.3 sol.3.

84. Cf. *De Ver.* q.10 a.12c; *ST* I.2.1c; I-II.94.2c.

85. Cf. *ST* I.12.9–10. This puzzle about Aquinas' view touches on issues much discussed in recent philosophy, especially concerning epistemological holism and the intelligibility of the analytic/synthetic distinction. As we have observed, Aquinas considerably revises Aristotle's understanding of knowledge in order to make it useful in a theological account of faith's supreme certainty. It seems that his account of the relationship between the knowledge we have by faith and the rest of what we know might have gone more smoothly if he had revised yet further, and dropped Aristotle's version of the idea of analytic truths.

86. *ST* II-II.2.2 ad 3.

87. *In Ioh.* 17:25, no.2265. Aquinas reaches much the same conclusion—that your assent to any of the creedal articles does not yield a true belief unless you assent to all of them—when he reflects on the vice of infidelity. The person who rejects one of the articles, even if he accepts

all the others, is *infidelis* (he declines to believe what God himself teaches). And "infidelity puts the human being at the maximum distance from God. . . . It cannot be that a person knows God in part who holds a false opinion about him, because that about which he opines is not God" (*ST* II-II.10.3c).

88. For analysis of these texts and replies to objections about how they should be read, see the articles cited in n. 81. These essays would have been clearer if they had distinguished explicitly between the modest and bold claims of Aquinas' coherentism.

89. For a case in point, see Paul O'Grady's essay in this volume.

90. Perhaps the most influential, though by no means the only, version of this Thomistic outlook is Étienne Gilson, *The Christian Philosophy of St. Thomas Aquinas*, trans. L. K. Shook (New York: Random House, 1956).

91. In his technical idiom for different aspects of the act of faith (*ST* II-II.2.2), he would have said that would-be natural theologians "non credunt Deo, sed tamen vere Deum credunt," whereas what he actually says is "nec vere Deum credunt" (ad 3).

92. *Ad Rom.* 1:21, no.130; cf. Marshall, "Faith and Reason Reconsidered," 13–15. *Ad Rom.* 1, lects.6–7 offer a detailed account of the epistemic consequences of sin; see especially nos.126–30.

93. For an analysis of various traditional views on this point, including those of Aquinas, see Bruce D. Marshall, "Do Christians Worship the God of Israel?" in *Knowing the Triune God*, ed. James J. Buckley and David S. Yeago (Grand Rapids: Eerdmans, 2001), 231–64.

94. God is entirely simple, "but those things which are one in God are multiple in our intellect. For this reason our intellect can apprehend one of them without apprehending another" (*De Trin.* q.1 a.4 ad 10).

95. Cf. *Meta.* 9, 11 (nos.1901–16).

96. On this cf. my "Faith and Reason Reconsidered," 11–13.

97. *ST* II-II.2.2 ad 3; 10.3c (above, n. 87).

98. *Responsio ad magistrum Ioannem de Vercellis de 43 articulis*, proem. (Leonine Edition 42 [1979], 327).

99. *Responsio de 43 articulis*, 43 (ed. cit., 335, lin.616–17).

100. *Responsio de 43 articulis*, 34 (ed. cit., 333, lin.481–83). Cf. the discussion of this passage in Otto Hermann Pesch, *Thomas von Aquin: Grenze und Größe mittelalterlicher Theologie*, 2nd ed. (Mainz: Matthias-Grünewald-Verlag, 1989), 79–81.

101. Sacred doctrine "can accept something from the philosophical disciplines, though not as if it had need of them by necessity" (*ST* I.1.5 ad 2); cf. I.1.8 ad 2 (above, n. 27).

102. Cf. *De Trin.* q.2 a.3c.

103. Cf. *ST* I.1.8c (and above, n. 45).

104. The "preamble" to which Aquinas devotes the most attention is the existence of God. The extensive modern discussion of the preambles has generated confusion about Aquinas' epistemic priorities. By the seventeenth century a number of Thomists took the preambles to be a kind of epistemic basis for holding the articles of faith to be true. On this view one cannot rationally assent to those Christian beliefs which are beyond demonstration, like the Trinity and the incarnation, unless one has demonstrated that God exists, or at least implicitly assented to such a demonstration. This fits with the naturalist apologetics we have already looked at: we know by demonstration that a God with certain attributes exists, and we assent to certain suprarational teachings as the revelation of this God on the evidence of miraculous signs. This treatment of the preambles fails, however, to fit with Aquinas' insistence that we judge the truth even of what we take to be demonstrated by its compatibility with the indemonstrable articles, or with

his insistence that one can quite well believe, and normally does believe, in the existence of God without any demonstration (cf. *ST* I.2.2 ad 1). Aquinas' own consistent position is that the preambles are not an epistemic warrant for believing the articles, but logical presuppositions of the articles, statements which must be true since the articles are true. They are distinguished from other such presuppositions by also belonging to what God himself reveals, and from the articles of faith in the narrower sense by being knowable *per creaturas*. For a detailed account see Guy de Broglie, "La vraie notion thomiste des 'praeambula fidei,'" *Gregorianum* 34 (1953): 341–89.

    105. *ST* I.1.5 ad 2; cf. above, n. 46.

    106. Cf. *De Aet. Mundi* (Leonine Edition 43 [1976], 85).

    107. Cf. *ST* I.46.1c.

    108. This is the aim of the arguments in *De Aet. Mundi;* cf. also *ST* I.46.2.

    109. "Aristotle . . . said that the world was co-eternal with God. This is contrary to what the Evangelist says: 'This one'—that is, the Word alone—'was in the beginning with God.' John's 'this one' excludes another nature co-eternal with God, though not another person" (*In Ioh.* 1:2, no.65). This passage suggests that in the end Aquinas does not think an eternal world is a real possibility. While neither self-contradictory nor incompatible with the conviction that God creates freely out of nothing, the eternity of the world is, Aquinas seems to suppose, incompatible with God's triunity.

    110. *ST* I.1.8 ad 2.

    111. See *DS* 3015.

    112. I am surprised to see myself numbered by Paul O'Grady, in his contribution to this volume, among those who seek to insulate Aquinas from the rigors of analytic philosophy. On theology, Aquinas, and analytic philosophy, see Bruce D. Marshall, *Trinity and Truth* (Cambridge: Cambridge University Press, 2000); "Theology after Cana," *Modern Theology* 16 (2000): 517–27; "In Search of an Analytic Aquinas: Grammar and the Trinity," in *Grammar and Grace* (Festschrift in honor of Victor Preller), ed. Robert McSwain and Jeffrey Stout (London: SCM, forthcoming).

    113. *De Trin.* q.2 a.3 ad 8.

    114. Thus the objection Aquinas seeks to answer: "Wisdom . . . is numbered among the gifts of the Holy Spirit . . . therefore this [sacred] doctrine is not wisdom" (*ST* I.1.6 obj.3).

    115. *ST* I.1.6 ad 3.

    116. Cf. above, n. 80.

    117. *ST* I.1.6 ad 3.

Two

Trinity

HERWI RIKHOF

One of the striking features of contemporary systematic theology is the remarkable renaissance of the theology of the Trinity. Both Catholic and Protestant theologians have contributed to the retrieval of what is commonly confessed to be the heart of the Christian faith but is often rather a dead weight within theology and spirituality alike. Most of the time, traditional or classical theology of the Trinity is blamed for this irrelevancy of the Trinity.

Classical theology is blamed, first, for turning its attention from the role of Father, Son, and Spirit in the history of salvation, the so-called economic Trinity, to the inner life of the Trinity, the so-called immanent Trinity. A second criticism is that this predominant attention to the immanent Trinity is couched in an abstract language. And to make matters worse, concepts used for the immanent Trinity (such as "person") have undergone in modern times a development different from the original (theological) meaning. That increasingly creates more questions and problems than insight and understanding.

A somewhat different point of criticism concerns the place of the theology of the Trinity. Due to developments in modern philosophy, the oneness of God has become central in discussions about the proofs for the existence of God or about the problem of evil. But this "theistic" approach, using a general conception of God and not a trinitarian one, and its atheistic reaction are also based on or furthered by internal theological developments. In the standard Catholic theology manuals of the nineteenth and twentieth centuries, the oneness of God (*de Deo Uno*) is treated before and dissociated from the Trinity (*de Deo Trino*), turning the Trinity into an optional appendix. An additional point of criticism is that classical theology appeals to the rule that in God's dealing with creation, salvation, and fulfillment, the three persons act as one. This appeal means that a mockery is made of distinct roles of Father, Son, and Spirit in the history of salvation.

When this tragic development into irrelevancy is mentioned, Thomas Aquinas figures prominently. He is portrayed as an example of this classical theology and denounced as a crucial influence on its development. Given these circumstances, a presentation and a discussion of Aquinas' theology of the Trinity cannot consist in an easy and obvious exposition—certainly not if one wants to consider him, as I do, as a theologian who does not merely have some historical or antiquarian importance, but who can, and as doctor of the Church should, contribute to the continuing reflection on the mystery of our God. A complex presentation and discussion is called for, containing both an assessment of that common criticism and a presentation of Aquinas' views, as determined by the positive insights and the genuine concerns that characterize the current debate on the Trinity. But a complete discussion would be too lengthy for this volume. In this essay I shall concentrate on the contribution Aquinas can make to the current renaissance of the theology of the Trinity.[1]

Can Aquinas provide us with insights that will help us in our further reflections on the mystery of our God? It seems to me that on at least three points, he can. The first two are concerned with content and the third with style. The first point is related to the Trinity acting in our history, and the second to an important aspect of that activity: the inhabitation of the Spirit in us. The way Aquinas deals with these topics shows his style of doing theology, and I will make a few comments about this more technical aspect in my conclusion.

The Current Debate

In the current debate on the theology of the Trinity, theologians, supposedly in reaction to classical theology, stress the importance of the economic Trinity over and against the immanent Trinity. An implication of this reversal of interest is that the distinct roles of Father, Son, and Spirit within the history of salvation receive (or should receive) attention. The terms "immanent" and "economic" are somewhat confusing, since they might suggest two Trinities. It is better to use the distinction *theologia-oikonomia,* indicating that two different perspectives are used to talk about the same reality.

The consensus among contemporary theologians—that the theology of the Trinity should in the first place be about the Father, the Son, and the Spirit acting "for us and for our salvation"—seems to me a crucial insight. Some theologians not only accept the priority of the *oikonomia*, they also argue that the *theologia* is superfluous and a misguided enterprise. All we know about the Trinity we know from revelation in history. To go beyond that is to indulge in mere speculation. The development of the *theologia* and the concentration on God *in se* has, so they argue, facilitated the wrong kind of curiosity. It is undoubtedly correct to warn against a kind of trinitarian speculation that seems to know too much about God, especially if that speculation, and not the biblical revelation, is used as a starting-point in theology. But there is also a "theological" curiosity that is helpful and appropriate to the *oikonomia* and that is, moreover, required for the interpretation and protection of the *oikonomia*. A short reflection on the creed of the councils of Nicaea and Constantinople can clarify this point.

In the creed, the passage about Jesus' life, death, and resurrection is preceded by a passage that focuses on the person. Or, to put it differently, the passage about what Jesus did and suffered "for us and for our salvation" is introduced by the passage concentrating on his identity ("God from God, light from light," and so forth): thus, first *theologia*, then *oikonomia*. In those two passages one finds not only two different perspectives but two different kinds of language. In the passage on the identity of Christ, one encounters an argumentative, conceptual, analytical language; in the passage on the meaning of Jesus' life, death, and resurrection, a narrative and biblical language. Perspective and language are connected, as becomes clear when one realizes that the order in the creed is not the historical order. At the council of Nicaea, an argumentative section was added to a narrative creed that originally belonged to the context of baptism and catechism. The council of Constantinople followed this pattern. The addition could be made because the point at stake was neither what was narrated, nor the relevancy of the life, death, and resurrection of Christ for us, but rather their precise meaning. The answer to the question about the precise meaning of what Christ did and suffered required not only a focus on the one who acted and suffered, but also a language that could interpret and determine this narrative as clearly as possible. Thus, problems raised with regard to the history of salvation, the *oikonomia*, required a reflection on the level of God-self, the *theologia*. In the creeds of Nicaea and of Constantinople, one can discern a certain reluctance to discuss the identity of Christ in terms other than those used in Scripture. But one can also discern the discovery of the need to use these other terms, since the available biblical terms allow for a variety of interpretations, including deficient ones. In the Niceno-Constantinopolitan creed, the term *homoousion* is the final term in a series of concepts with diminishing biblical connotations, which determine more and more precisely the identity of Jesus Christ.

When one takes the *oikonomia* as starting-point for the theology of the Trinity, the next question becomes: which part of the *oikonomia?* Most contemporary theologians take the Paschal mystery as the main and even exclusive focus of their attention. The passion story becomes the foundation for the doctrine of the Trinity. However important this focus may be, it tends to overlook the role of the Spirit in the economy of salvation. The role of the Holy Spirit can receive more attention if the focus is not merely on the suffering, death, and resurrection of Jesus Christ, but also on his life, baptism, actions, and preaching. The recent rediscovery of Spirit-Christology shows how fruitful this approach is, and reveals the importance of Jesus' baptism. More than the passion story, the account of Jesus' baptism calls for a trinitarian understanding.[2] However, even this broadening of perspective does not do full justice to the "breadth and length and height and depth" (Ephesians 3:18) of the mystery of our God. The doctrine of the Trinity should not only explain who Jesus Christ is (and his Father and the Spirit), it should also explain who we, as Christians, are. This focus on ourselves is the logical consequence of accepting the history of salvation as the starting-point for the theology of the Trinity and as the criterion for what that theology should contain and how the themes should be treated. But this focus on ourselves also asks for a sustained attention to the role of the Spirit. In the classical theology of the Trinity, the concept *missio* is used to describe and systematize the activity of the triune God in our history. Or, to be more precise, the concept is the plural, *missiones.* For there are two missions, one of the Son and one of the Spirit, and together they structure the history of salvation.

The importance of paying attention to the role of the Spirit is borne out by reading Aquinas' discussion of the *missiones* in his *Summa Theologiae.* Aquinas also makes clear what this attention entails, and how it can determine and shape our understanding of God and of ourselves, in a beautiful text from the *Summa contra Gentiles,* in which he deals with the work of the Spirit.[3] Both passages make important contributions to the current debate. I will discuss them not in chronological order, but rather in such a way that the text from the *Summa contra Gentiles* reveals the implications of the text from the *Summa Theologiae.* In both cases I follow the text rather closely, for only then will Aquinas' insights become clear.

I start with some comments about the place each text occupies in the *Summa Theologiae* and the *Summa contra Gentiles,* respectively. I thereby place the texts in a broader context and show that those texts as presented here reveal important insights of Aquinas on the theology of the Trinity. I also want to counter the suggestion that this selection is merely inspired by contemporary, or even idiosyncratic, interests.

Aquinas on the *missiones:* A Reading of *ST* I.43

1. The *quaestiones* on the *distinctio personarum:* Structure and Method

In 1265 Aquinas was given the task of establishing a new *studium* in Rome and teaching the young brethren theology. While regent master in Rome (1265–67), he apparently started to revise his commentary on Peter Lombard's *Sentences* but then decided to write something quite different, the *Summa Theologiae.*[4] In the introduction he indicates that he was dissatisfied with the available textbooks for students in theology. He wants to provide them with a clear and concise account of sacred doctrine. He also wants to treat the topics according to an *ordo disciplinae,* an educational method. That remark is an important key to understanding the structure on the level of the *quaestiones.*

Aquinas has composed and ordered the *quaestiones* that form his discussion of the "Trinity of persons in God," the *distinctio personarum,* with pedagogic principles in mind. One principle is that the student should first acquire the conceptual tools necessary for understanding the way the Trinity of persons is talked about, namely, Father, Son (Word, Image), and Spirit (Love, Gift). So, before discussing the meaning of those (biblical) terms, Aquinas pays attention to concepts like "procession," "relation," "person," "unity," and "plurality."[5] He repeats the same pattern when he discusses the way the Trinity of persons is acting in our history. Before he discusses the *missiones* of Son and Spirit, he pays attention to properties and characteristics of the persons.[6]

Within a *quaestio,* the order of the *articuli* may be patterned in the same way. In *ST* I.43, the question about the *missiones,* Aquinas dedicates the first two articles to the clarification and determination of the concept *missio,* before proceeding with the inquiry into the content of the missions of Son and Spirit, and the inhabitation of the Trinity in the believer.[7]

If one is not aware of Aquinas' procedure, one might think that his primary interest is in the more technical and conceptual issues, since he starts with those. If one does not take his way of ordering into account, one might easily misconstrue Aquinas' theology of the Trinity as an abstract and theoretical game. If, however, one keeps in mind his pedagogic principle, then those discussions are the introductions to the real issues, to the meaning of the terms used in Scripture and to the meaning of the missions. From this perspective, Aquinas' theology of the Trinity is profoundly scriptural and geared toward the history of salvation. The final question about the *distinctio personarum* is therefore not an afterthought, but rather the culmination of all the preceding questions on the Trinity. The stage is set. Names and titles have already introduced the three persons that play the central role in the history of salvation. Conceptual questions have been discussed at length so that, if necessary, a short remark is sufficient. It is therefore appropriate to concentrate on the *missiones* in Aquinas' theology of the Trinity.

Another pedagogic principle of Aquinas is that the student should be aware of the kind of knowledge involved and, consequently, of the kind of arguments that can be given. In his discussion *de Deo* (the *Prima Pars*), Aquinas inserts in his discussion of both the *essentia Dei* (qq.2–26) and the *distinctio personarum* (qq.27–43) reflections on knowledge: q.2 (aa.1,2), q.12, and q.32. These three discussions form a sequel. In q.2 Aquinas discusses the type of knowledge (self-evident or by effects), and in q.12 he explores knowledge by effects. In the final article of that question, he introduces another type of knowledge: knowledge through grace. That type of knowledge, concerned with the divine persons, is the topic of q.32. Aquinas qualifies this knowledge as necessary for us because it gives us the right understanding of salvation, that is, it helps us understand that our salvation is realized by the Son, who became incarnate, and by the Spirit, who is given.[8] The sequel formed by these discussions shows a gradual concentration on what could be called an "economic" knowledge of God, culminating in knowing the three Persons.

Precisely because knowledge of the Trinity is knowledge through grace, based on revelation and taken from Scripture, there is a given, a "God-given," to start with.[9] That means that the form of the theological discourse will depend on the acceptance of revelation and of the authority of Scripture. If one accepts revelation and Scripture, then the truth of faith can be proven or rather can be manifested. Given the belief in the Trinity (*Trinitate posita*), one can proceed, and explore and clarify the content of faith.[10] If one does not accept the authority of Scripture, however, then the only way open is to show that what is held in faith is "not impossible."[11]

Earlier in the *Summa Theologiae*, in a discussion about the status of theology (q.1), Aquinas makes similar remarks. Instead of the twofold division (belief-unbelief) he uses in q.32, he envisions in *ST* I.1.8 three different kinds of discourse. Theology is argumentative, not in the sense that it argues to prove its principles, but in the sense that given the principles—the articles of faith—it proceeds to show something. In the case of heretics, the discussion will be about the articles of faith, for they accept the truth of faith but not all of the articles. The way to proceed, then, is to argue on the basis of the articles they accept in favor of the articles they reject. In the case of those who do not accept the articles of faith, only the arguments they put forward against these articles can be answered.[12]

The middle position Aquinas indicates here, namely, the discussion with the heretics, is interesting, for it makes clear that it is a discussion among believers. From a historical point of view it might appear that those discussions are passé, since they have led to the conclusion that certain positions are not to be considered as faithful or orthodox and consequently that those who held them do not belong to the community of the faithful. The qualification "heretical" signals the end of a discussion and even suggests that it is not necessary to inquire further. But if those who held those positions are considered to hold the faith, be it only partially, the discussion is, from a systematic point of view, still interesting and possibly relevant for the ongoing debates. Why did those believers hold these views, and why did others think these views were insufficient?

In the *Summa contra Gentiles* the heretical positions receive separate and extensive attention (discussed later in this essay), but in the *Summa Theologiae* they are merely mentioned in the course of the discussion, as part of an overall argument. When Aquinas presents these views, he deals with them as he indicated in *ST* I.1.8. For instance, in the article with which he opens the whole discussion about the *distinctio personarum* (q.27 a.1), Aquinas refers to the views of Arius and Sabellius with regard to *processio*. Both views amount to denying the Trinity. Arius argues that Son and Spirit proceed from the Father as creatures. Sabellius argues that the Father is called Son and Spirit because of some likeness or action. To counter Arius' arguments, Aquinas quotes 1 John 5:20 and 1 Corinthians 6:19 and introduces these quotations with "this is contrary to what is said" (in Scripture). And, "the words of the Lord" refute the views of Sabellius, while "many other passages" in Scripture show that Father and Son are different persons.[13]

But disputes with heretics are not the main concern in the *Summa Theologiae*. In his final work Aquinas is more interested, so to speak, in the next step, namely, understanding the faith of the Church. His main interlocutors are therefore Augustine, Hilary, and other fathers. He quotes and discusses their views in order to reach a better understanding of the data of faith. That means that even when Aquinas turns to the *oikonomia*, he is not so much concerned with telling the story of salvation as with understanding it. He presupposes that story, and he presupposes that his readers are familiar with it. Aquinas does not start q.43 about the *missiones* with the question whether there are missions of Son and Spirit in our history, but with another type of question: is *missio* an appropriate term? That is to say, given the fact of the missions, is the term *missio* an adequate term?

The rest of the question is determined by the issue of visibility-invisibility of the missions. Aquinas introduces this issue for two reasons: first, because of problems in relation to the visible mission of the Spirit; second, and more importantly, because he is especially interested in understanding the invisible *missiones*, as we will see. That is, Aquinas is not so much interested in the nonrecurrent visible *missiones* that occurred at specific moments in history, as in the salvific, invisible *missiones* that continue throughout the ages and that constitute God's presence by grace in the faithful.

This interest makes I.43 not only the culmination of the preceding *quaestiones*, but also the bridge to what follows: first, the subsequent *quaestiones* that deal with the *processio* of the creatures from God (qq.44ff.), and second, the other parts of the *Summa*. Moreover, it contains in barest outline and in very general and abstract terms Aquinas' view of the pattern of God's dealing with humanity. *ST* I.43 contains therefore the key to understanding those *quaestiones* in which Aquinas develops the various aspects of the *oikonomia* more fully. The reference to grace and sacraments in one of the articles is an indication of this function. That Aquinas refers to grace and sacraments in a rather matter-of-fact way shows how self-evident that link is for him.[14]

2. *Quaestio* 43

Having sketched the wider context of *ST* I.43, I shall now take a closer look at the text itself. The first two articles contain, as already indicated, introductory discussions. Via the question of appropriateness, Aquinas is able to specify the precise meaning of *missio*. At first sight, that term cannot be used in the theology of the Trinity. *Missio* connotes movement and subordination—associations that do not fit God.[15] Moreover, it contradicts the co-equality of the persons that is at the heart of the theology of the Trinity.[16] But a closer look at how we use *missio* in ordinary language shows that we use it also without those associations.[17]

Aquinas introduces in this analysis a distinction that will play a crucial part in the further discussion, namely, the distinction between being sent to a place where one was not before (this does not apply to God) and being present in a new capacity (this does apply to God). Aquinas does not give an example of this second type, but one could think of someone who is asked to act as a diplomatic consul or, perhaps even better, of a colleague with whom one falls in love. Why this second example is better will become clear when Aquinas uses this "new capacity" later in his discussion.

Although the term *missio* is found in Scripture, the concepts "visible-invisible" are not. The use of these concepts in relation to the missions is not strange, however, since Scripture mentions, on the one hand, the coming of the Son (incarnation) and the Spirit (baptism of Jesus, Pentecost), which are visible, and on the other hand, the inhabitations of the Trinity and especially of the Spirit, which are invisible. It is remarkable that Aquinas is mainly interested in the invisible missions. That is already obvious from the way he formulates the various questions to be discussed at the beginning of the *quaestio*. Three times he mentions *invisibilis* (a.3, a.5, and a.6), while *visibilis* is mentioned only once (a.7). If one compares these formulations with the questions formulated in the various articles, one can see that this interest is even more pronounced. Article 7 is about the appropriateness (*conveniens*) of the visible mission of the Spirit. However, as the objections show, the discussion also focuses on the relationship between the missions of Son and Spirit, stressing the difference between them, and emphasizing the visible character of the mission of the Son (obj.1, 2, and 4). In his response Aquinas argues not only for the appropriateness of the visible mission of the Spirit, but also for the appropriateness (*conveniens*) of the visible as pointer to the invisible. The discussion in a.5 shows a similar attention to the invisible mission of the Spirit. Article 5 is about the appropriateness of the invisible mission of the Son. But the objections show that Aquinas' interest is more specific. The objections refer to the gifts of grace, which are normally attributed to the Spirit. So, the question is about the mission of the Spirit as well as about the relationship between the missions of Son and Spirit. This attention to the invisible missions in q.43 is significant, for it shows that Aquinas is primarily interested in the grace-giving role of the Spirit, with whom the invisible mission is especially associated. The discussions in articles 5 and 7 do not contradict this observation, but specify and augment it. How important the Spirit is and, consequently, how concerned Aquinas is about "our side" is shown by the third article in a subtle way.

The third article deals with what is at stake (*secundum quid*) in the missions. The way Aquinas formulates the problem suggests that the issue is somewhat contentious, for he starts with the thesis that sanctifying grace (*gratia gratum faciens*) is not the only effect of the mission. There appear to be two other possible effects: the gift of grace that one receives for others (*gratia gratis data*) (obj.3) and the divine person himself (obj.1 and 2). Thus, the discussion is in fact one about the depth or the impact of the *missio*. Does the *missio* mean that the creature on the receiving end becomes someone who is an instrument of grace, edifying and helping others? Does the *missio* mean that the creature on the receiving end becomes a grace-filled and holy person? Does the *missio* mean that the divine person is given? Apparently, there is a tendency to select just one of these. The way Aquinas formulates the question shows something else as well. In three of the four objections and in the *sed contra*, the Spirit, and only the Spirit, is mentioned explicitly. And the quotation from Scripture (in obj.2) is Romans 5:5, Aquinas' favorite quotation about the Spirit.[18] The discussion about the depth or the impact of the *missio* is especially about the depth or impact of the *missio* of the Spirit.

Aquinas' response amounts in fact to the view that the *missio* entails all three effects, even though in the corpus of the article he is mainly concerned with sanctifying grace and the divine person. The way he formulates his answer and the way he argues for it show two things: first, the primary importance of the coming and indwelling of the divine person, and second, Aquinas' attention to the Spirit.

Aquinas opens his answer with a thesis about the divine person: it is appropriate that a divine person (*divinae personae convenit*) is "sent" and "given"—two verbs that have rich biblical connotations—insofar as "to send" is understood as beginning to exist in a new capacity, and "to be given" implies possession, in the human person. In other words, the existence of a divine person in a new capacity and the possession of a divine person have a consequence: the sanctification of the human person.[19]

In order to argue for this thesis, Aquinas provides two analyses, one of "to send" and one of "to give." Both analyses are condensed and merit unpacking. For his analysis of "to send" Aquinas concentrates on the result, the presence, the new capacity. He starts with a distinction between two types of God's presence: on the one hand, the presence of God in all things, i.e., the presence of the Creator in creation; on the other hand, the presence of God in a human person, in rational beings. He qualifies these two types as "common" versus "special," and he indicates the relationship of this special presence as "over and above" (*super*) the common one and as a new way (*novo modo*), using the clarification he has introduced earlier in a.1 of this question. This second type of presence is the one relevant for the discussion.

Aquinas' next step is to point to two features that characterize the rational capacity of the human person: knowing and willing (or loving). The fact that two features are mentioned, the theoretical and the practical, or, the intellectual and the affective, suggests already that the mission is not partial in the sense that just one aspect of human existence is concerned, but rather that the whole human being is involved. The special presence fits that capacity. At this stage of his analysis Aquinas does not explicitly mention Son and Spirit; he only says that according to this special presence, "God is said to be as the known in the knower and as the loved in the lover." His attention in this article is primarily directed to the human person, to the receiving end of the *missio*. The other aspect of the *missio*—who is being sent—will concern him in the following articles. So, in his analysis of the *oikonomia* he is not only discussing the *missiones*, God's activity in our history, but he also starts with "our side."

Aquinas' third step is to specify this new way, this special presence, by concentrating on its intensity. He does that by drawing out the implication of the formulation "as the known in the knower and as the loved in the lover." In those acts of knowing and loving, the human person reaches the object. And so, the human person "touches God-self" (*attingit at ipsum Deum*). This is what Scripture refers to as "inhabitation." In this perspective, the human person is not just a rational creature in which God is present as in other creatures, but is God's temple, a phrase with biblical connotations. Given this intensive presence, the human person must be sanctified. The new way turns out to be a change on our side, an intense relationship with God-self.

This analysis of "to send" is sufficient for his answer to the question. But Aquinas adds another analysis, namely, of "to give." Given his intention to be economic with his arguments, so clearly expressed in the introduction to the *Summa Theologiae*, he must have had some reasons. They can be found in Scripture. The term "to give" is a term used to refer to the *missio* of Son and Spirit, and mostly to the *missio* of the Spirit (cf. Romans 5:5 and 8:15, 23; 1 Corinthians 2:12 and 6:19; 2 Corinthians 1:22 and 5:5; Galatians 3:2, 14; Ephesians 1:17; and 1 Thessalonians 4:8). Aquinas reflects this biblical usage in his second analysis.

As in his analysis of "to send," he concentrates on the result of "to give," namely, to have, or having. This was already indicated right at the beginning, where he used the passive *dari* (cf. also *mitti*). Aquinas' second analysis, like the first, is dense, and some careful reading is called for if one wants to discover its richness. Aquinas starts with appealing to the distinction between "to use" and "to enjoy" (*uti-frui*). "We are said to possess something when we can freely enjoy or use it." But Aquinas neither develops that distinction nor explains the way the distinction is understood in theology. He presupposes that knowledge and moves quickly to the conclusion: "to have the power to enjoy a divine person is only according to sanctifying grace." Earlier in the *Summa Theologiae*, when discussing the name "gift" for the Spirit (q.38), Aquinas had examined the distinction in some greater detail.

As in q.43 a.3, Aquinas determines in q.38 a.1 the meaning of "to possess" as "to be able to use or enjoy something freely." He then takes three steps. He first expresses the fundamental difference between rational creatures and the rest of creation. Only rational creatures can enjoy a divine person when conjoined to God; others cannot. He then remarks that this enjoyment "sometimes" happens. This somewhat cautious remark emphasizes that this type of relationship should be seen not in terms of creation, but in terms of the history of salvation. In terms of creation, all creatures, by being creatures, are de facto related to the Creator.[20] But in history, this special relationship is not de facto present.

The realm of history implies volatility and the realm of grace implies the divine initiative, as Aquinas remarks a little later, and a positive or negative reaction on the human side. Enjoyment happens when a rational creature becomes "a participant to the divine Word and the Love proceeding [from Father and Son], so that he can truly know and rightly love God."[21] This important formulation reveals that, for Aquinas, there is an intimate relationship between the missions of Son and Spirit, on the one hand, and the human acts of knowing and loving God, on the other. Aquinas concludes with a reminder. The rational creature cannot become a participant by his own power: that has to be given from above. That is why "given" is being used: we have received something from elsewhere.

When stating the difference between the rational and other creatures, Aquinas does not merely say that rational creatures can enjoy a divine person. The rational creature can also use (*uti*) the effects of the divine person. The difference between person and effect is crucial. This explains why in q.43 a.3 Aquinas only mentions the enjoyment, since he talks about the divine person. But it does not explain the distinction itself or the specification. And although his three steps do show the importance of *frui-uti* for the history of salvation and for the relationship to God, they do not reveal the richness implied in that distinction. In order to uncover that, we have to go back to Augustine, who introduced it into theology. Peter Lombard extensively quotes Augustine in the very first distinction of his *Sentences,* and in his *Scriptum* Aquinas comments upon these views.

Augustine in *De doctrina christiana* presents the pair *uti-frui* as two forms of appreciation, liking, and loving (*deligere*). To enjoy something is to love something for its own sake; to use something is to love something for the sake of something else. Moreover, enjoyment is related to things that make us happy, use to things that help us to reach happiness.[22] Augustine does not merely employ this distinction to describe the difference between purpose and means, he also uses it as a prescription: "There are realities one has to enjoy, others one has to use." If something that should be used is enjoyed, it will cause damage to our pursuit of happiness, for one is in fact focused on a means as if it were a purpose; one is satisfied too quickly, one is misguided.[23]

This analysis becomes theologically relevant when Augustine argues that there is only one reality we should enjoy: "Father, Son, and Spirit, who form the Trinity." Only the triune God is our ultimate purpose, only God can make us happy, the rest we should use.[24] Consequently, a just and holy person is someone who judges these matters correctly: "His love is in order; he does not love what he should not, he does not forget to love what he should; he does not love more what he should love less and vice versa or love equally what he should love less and vice versa."[25]

With this in mind, we can return to Aquinas' analysis of "to be given" in q.43 a.3. As mentioned earlier, Aquinas introduces the distinction *uti-frui*, but only develops the concept of *frui*. It is now clear why. *Frui* is the term that is used (or should be used) exclusively in connection with God. It refers to the quality our relationship with God can have or should have. One can enjoy a divine person only if one's love is "in order" or, in other words, if one is filled with grace, sanctified. Aquinas finishes his short analysis and conclusion with a reminder (*sed tamen*), a *nota bene*. In that gift of grace, "the Spirit is possessed and dwells in the person. The Spirit himself is given and sent." This point deserves to be stressed, since there is a tendency not to think sufficiently profoundly about the mission of the Spirit.

Aquinas' attention to the profundity and intensity of the missions, especially the mission of the Spirit, seems to me to touch on one of the central points of the belief in God Father-Son-Spirit and therefore on a crucial element for every theology of the Trinity. The incarnation of the Son and the inhabitation of the Spirit in the believers are the amazing center of our faith. Aquinas' insistence on this profundity seems to be relevant as well. There has always been a reluctance to believe and accept the extraordinary ordinariness of God as revealed in incarnation and inhabitation. The discussions in the early Church about Christ and the Spirit, resulting in the creed of the councils, bear witness to that, precisely because those discussions occurred among believers. Arius' views, in which Christ was given a high and exclusive position within creation, were inspired by a great esteem for God's excellence and otherness. The distinction of creator from creature was an insurmountable division, the ultimate great divide. This kind of view and this incredulity among believers are a continuation of the discussions in the New Testament. Again and again one encounters in the gospel amazement and rejection. Is what Jesus says and does "from God"? Can one so familiar and so ordinary be the Son of God? ("Is this not the carpenter . . . ?" Mark 6:3; "Can anything good come out of Nazareth?" John 1:46.) Can someone who dwelt among us be the exegesis of the unseen God (John 1:14, 18)? In Paul's letters, Paul does not merely refer to the Spirit; he also puts a distinct emphasis on the effects of the Spirit's coming and presence resulting in a new and different life. The presence of the Spirit is constitutive for being a Christian believer and a Christian community. The dignity and responsibility Christians have is based upon their being temples of the Holy Spirit. The intimacy they have with "Abba, Father" is due to the presence of the Spirit in their hearts. The discussion about the Spirit in the early Church is also a discussion about this newness, dignity, responsibility, and intimacy.[26] Some complicated theories or abstract terminology may contribute to the problems people have with the doctrine of the Trinity, but this amazing center probably causes the real resistance. For, if one is to take seriously the incarnation of the Son and the inhabitation of the Spirit, one cannot continue to live with God at a distance. Aquinas' attention to the *missiones* and his insistence on the profundity of their impact make clear that to believe in God Father-Son-Spirit is intimately connected with a "different" life. I shall return to this when I discuss Aquinas' views on the role of the Spirit in the *Summa contra Gentiles*.

Although Aquinas concentrates in the third article of q.43 on the presence of the divine persons and the consequences their presence has for us, in the following articles he considers God's side. The responses to the objections of a.5 are especially interesting since they contain a further specification of the invisible missions of Son and Spirit and their mutual relationship.

On the one hand, Aquinas stresses the deep connection between the two missions: with respect to grace, they have a common root (*radix*). On the other hand, he points to a difference. There is a difference in effect: an enlightenment (*illuminatio*) of the intellect and an enkindling (*inflammatio*) of the affect.[27] And, Aquinas adds, one effect cannot be without the other. This is not just to say that both the intellectual and the practical side of the human person are involved in the grace-filled relationship to the triune God. Aquinas wants to say more. The Son, the Word, is "not just any word, but the Word breathing Love." The Son is, therefore, not sent "to whatever perfection of the intellect, but to such an instruction of the intellect that it bursts forth into love." The ultimate purpose of the coming of the Son and the Spirit is to draw the human person into a new relationship of love. To believe in the triune God is to live a new life, a different life, a life of love. That is why Aquinas introduced right at the beginning "the new way" as a central element in his determination of *missio*. That is why I suggested that the example of falling in love might be a good example of this new way. Without this new way, the amazing center of our faith would go unnoticed. In the *Summa contra Gentiles* Aquinas gives a beautiful text about this different, and new, life.

Aquinas on the Work of the Spirit: A Reading of *ScG* IV.20–22

1. The Theology of the Trinity in the *Summa contra Gentiles:* Place and Method

According to an old tradition, Aquinas wrote the *Summa contra Gentiles* as a manual to help missionaries, especially in their discussion with the Muslims. But this apologetic purpose is now generally questioned.[28] It seems more reasonable to consider this *summa* as the work of a theologian who wants to contemplate and to clarify his faith and even to consider it as Aquinas' most personal work.[29] Aquinas' work lacks the explicit personal and existential references that are so obvious in Augustine. But in the introduction to the *Summa contra Gentiles* one can find a rare exception, be it in the form of a quotation: "that I may use the words of Hilary: I am aware that I owe this to God as the chief task of my life: that all my words and thoughts speak of him."[30] Aquinas views the contemplation and clarification of faith as a twofold task: to show the truth and to refute the errors. Although these errors are often connected with the names of historical figures, Aquinas' interest is geared not so much to the historical aspects, but to the systematic and conceptual problems that gave rise to these errors.

The *Summa contra Gentiles* consists of four books, and the discussion of the Trinity is the opening of the final book, followed by a discussion of incarnation, sacraments, and the eternal life. The discussion of these themes in Book IV is based upon Aquinas' view that the truth of God has to be manifested in two ways, not because there is a double truth in God, but because of our capacity. Human reason can reach some truths, but others are beyond that reach.[31] Books I–III deal with topics that lie within that reach, Book IV with topics that are beyond.

In the introduction to Book IV Aquinas qualifies his discussion about the Trinity as *de ipso Deo*. This phrase suggests to the modern reader that Aquinas starts with or even concentrates on the immanent Trinity, without much attention to the economic Trinity. But when one begins to read, that suggestion is quickly proven incorrect. Aquinas starts with the *oikonomia* and then moves to the *theologia*. He does so for the same reason that the *theologia* and the type of language connected with it were introduced in the early Church: to clarify the story of our salvation. An indication is already to be found in the structure of his chapters on the Trinity. These can be divided in two groups: chapters on the Son and chapters on the Spirit. That structure is revealing: it suggests that the point of the theology of the Trinity is not so much the Father as the Son and the Spirit. Aquinas does pay some attention to the Father in chapter 2, but in relation to the Son and from the perspective of the Son.[32] The attention to Son and Spirit reveals that our knowledge of the Trinity is from Son and Spirit.

An important consequence of the distinction Aquinas makes between the truth of God that is within our reach and truth that is beyond our reach is that his method in Books I–III differs from the one he uses in Book IV.[33] In chapter 9 of his introduction to Book I, Aquinas writes that in the first three books he wants to establish the truth and convince adversaries. To that purpose he can use both demonstrative and probable arguments borrowed from philosophers and the fathers. In Book IV, though, his intention is necessarily more humble.

He wants to dissolve the arguments against faith and to show the truth of Scripture by merely probable arguments and by authorities. In I.9 he also mentions "likely" arguments (*rationes verisimiles*) that can support and comfort the faithful. The term *rationes verisimiles* does not recur in the introduction to Book IV, where Aquinas again discusses the question of method. He does, however, outline three steps that will prove relevant when one examines the series of chapters on Son and Spirit. First, he will start with the data of Scripture, then he will discuss and interpret these data, and finally, he will reflect upon them.

In the first two chapters on Jesus Christ, Aquinas presents some basic data from Scripture. He concentrates on three elements: the term "Son" (and "Father"), the implication of that term, namely, *generatio*, and the Son being God (*deus*). The next six chapters contain Aquinas' presentation and discussion of three heretical positions. His summary at the beginning of chapter 3 shows that he presents them as three different positions that, taken together, cover all the possible alternatives to "what we are taught by Scripture, that the Son of God, begotten of God, is God."[34] Photinus (and others, like Paul of Samosata) held that the Son of God took his beginning from Mary; Sabellius held that the Father began to be the Son by taking the flesh; and Arius held that although the Son existed before the world was created, he was not eternal and not of the same nature as the Father. For each position, Aquinas gives the passages from Scripture that its proponents used to support their views. He then counters these positions (*improbatio*) by giving other passages from Scripture that contradict their conclusions. Sometimes he introduces this *improbatio* with the remark that if one reads Scripture carefully, one cannot but reject the position they held.[35] Finally, Aquinas argues that the passages they have quoted in favor of their position do not prove what they taught (*solutio*). At this stage he uses the heresies, that is, the interpretations of Scripture that were rejected by the Church in the course of history, to assist us in uncovering the right interpretation of Scripture.[36] In the introduction, Aquinas comments that this whole procedure will make what is dark and unclear in Scripture somewhat clearer.[37] After a long discussion about the correct understanding of the data or the testimonies of Scripture, Aquinas reflects upon these data. He concentrates on *generatio*. How can one understand that concept (chapters 10 and 11)? How is it related to what is said in Scripture about Wisdom (chapter 12) and about Word (chapter 13)?

In the chapters on the Spirit, the same pattern can be seen, but the structure shows something else as well: the interaction between *oikonomia* and *theologia*. Aquinas starts with a short chapter (15) that consists mainly of passages from Scripture. Those passages indicate, on the one hand, that *in divinis* not only Father and Son are mentioned but also the Holy Spirit, and, on the other hand, that some kind of *processio* is alluded to. These two issues recur in the chapters that follow.

The next four chapters are concerned with the status of the Holy Spirit. Some scriptural passages suggest that the Spirit is a creature, and these passages, Aquinas points out, were used in the discussion in the early Church about the Spirit (chapter 16). But there are also passages clearly indicating that the Spirit is divine (chapter 17). In the next chapter Aquinas moves, at first sight, to another level of discourse: the question is whether the Spirit is a subsisting person, or merely the divinity of Father and Son, or even some accidental perfection we receive from God. But a closer look shows that Aquinas continues the discussion of Scripture, and that a main point is to establish the profundity of the inhabitation Scripture talks about.[38] The last chapter on the identity of the Spirit (19) consists of a number of reflections aiming at elucidating that the Spirit is "true God, subsistent and personally distinct from Father and Son." Aquinas' interest in these chapters is "theological." He reads Scripture from the perspective of *theologia*. The issue of the *processio* returns in the two final chapters (24–25). They contain Aquinas' discussion of the *filioque*. Although the problem originally arises out of the *oikonomia*—how is the *missio* of the Spirit related to the *missio* of the Son?—the problem calls for a discussion on the level of the *theologia*.

Right in the middle of these "theological" chapters, Aquinas inserts three chapters (20–22) in which he presents the working of the Spirit according to Scripture, a topic belonging to the *oikonomia*. The structure *theologia-oikonomia-theologia* is further underlined by chapter 23, in which he returns to the passages from Scripture used to argue that the Spirit is a creature, in order to refute them. Therefore, chapters that call attention to *who* is working surround the three chapters dealing with the working of the Spirit. These three chapters contain a remarkable and profound insight into the working of the Spirit.

2. Chapters 20–22

The three chapters on the working of the Spirit form the heart of Aquinas' analyses and arguments. Of these three, Aquinas dedicates one to the working of the Spirit regarding all creatures and two to the working of the Spirit regarding human beings. The first chapter, which contains some major themes of the theology of creation, including the insight that "creation" refers first of all to God's continuing care and to his keeping all things in existence, is also a good example of the importance of the theology of the Trinity for understanding creation. In the *Summa Theologiae* Aquinas will reiterate that one of the reasons why knowledge of the Trinity is necessary for us is that it provides us with the correct understanding of creation: a free act of God out of love.[39] The other two chapters move to the level of the history of salvation. The reason why Aquinas divides his material between two chapters lies in the two aspects or the two movements he discerns in that history: things done by God in us through the Holy Spirit and our movement toward God through the Holy Spirit (*a Deo* and *in Deum*). But beneath that division lies a profound insight unifying both movements.

In order to appreciate fully what Aquinas does in these two chapters (the same is true for the chapter on creation), one must realize that here he is not arguing for or against certain interpretations of passages from Scripture, as he did in the chapters dealing with "theological" issues. In chapters 21 and 22 he is concerned with showing the deep structure of what Scripture reveals to us about the Spirit, that is, with showing how well Scripture speaks and how fitting is what we read. The linguistic markers *unde dicitur* and *convenienter attribuitur* that occur again and again are signals of this part of his task as theologian. Aquinas is concerned not so much with establishing the truth as with contemplating the truth.

What he discovers in contemplating the various texts about the Spirit from the Gospels (mainly John) and the Epistles (mainly Paul) is that they can be best understood as texts about friendship. To put it differently, Aquinas proposes friendship as the model that makes sense of the biblical data about the Spirit. In both chapters he introduces elements that constitute friendship, that are "proper" to friendship, in order to show why in Scripture the working of the Spirit is presented as it is.

Of course, Aquinas does not invent that model, in the sense that he introduces something completely new. He builds upon Scripture. The first quotation in chapter 21 is Romans 5:5, where Paul speaks about the *caritas Dei* "that has been poured into our hearts through the Holy Spirit which has been given to us." Aquinas, in his commentary on that passage, remarks that *caritas Dei* can be understood in two ways: either the love with which God loves us, or the love with which we love God.[40] The double meaning corresponds to the mutual relationship that is characteristic of friendship.[41] Aquinas also quotes John 15:15, where the Lord says to his disciples that he no longer calls them servants but friends. In his commentary on that text Aquinas again remarks that "friend" has a double meaning: the one that loves and the one that is loved.[42] In chapter 21 he adds that we are God's friends through the Holy Spirit.

In his analysis of friendship and of what is proper to friendship, Aquinas is clearly inspired by Aristotle. He mentions the following characteristics. It is proper to friendship to be of one heart, to be of one affect, to reveal one's secrets.

That is why it is so appropriate for Scripture to say that the Spirit reveals to us God's mysteries (1 Corinthians 2:9–10; cf. 14:2), that under certain circumstances the Spirit will speak through us (Matthew 10:20), and that men moved by the Spirit spoke of God (2 Peter 1:21; cf. the words of the creed, "who has spoken through the prophets"). It is proper to friendship that a friend is an alter ego, and so friends share what they have, want the best for each other, do the best for each other. That is why it is so appropriate to say that all God's gifts are given to us through the Spirit (1 Corinthians 12:8), that we, by the zeal of the Spirit, are configured to God (2 Corinthians 1:21–22; Ephesians 1:13–14), and that we, through the Spirit, become adoptive children of God (Romans 8:15). It is proper to friendship that offences are removed, for offences and friendship are contrary. And since we are friends of God through the Spirit, it is appropriate to say that through the Spirit our sins are forgiven (John 20:22), that those who blaspheme against the Spirit do not receive forgiveness (Matthew 12:31), and that the Spirit renews and cleans (Psalm 103:30; Ephesians 4:23; James 4:4). It is very proper to friends to converse with each other. Our conversation with God is by contemplating him. We contemplate God through the Spirit. That is why the Apostle says that we behold the glory of God by the Spirit (2 Corinthians 3:18). It is proper to friendship to enjoy a friend's company and in anxiety to seek a friend's support and comfort. That is why Scripture says that we, through the Spirit, enjoy God (Romans 14:17; cf. Acts 9:31), and why the Spirit is called the Paraclete, that is, Comforter (John 14:26). It is proper to friendship to consent to a friend's will. To consent to God's will is to fulfill his precepts, and we do that through the Spirit. Hence Paul says that whoever acts by the Spirit is a child of God (Romans 8:14). Aquinas adds a reminder: this acting by the Spirit does not entail force and violence, but is done in such a way that we freely become children of God. That is why Paul says that we have not received a spirit of slavery but of sonship (Romans 8:15).

By explaining the texts about the Spirit on the model of friendship, Aquinas indicates that the proper way of dealing with God and of thinking about God should be characterized by surplus and surprise, by luxury and abundance, and not by demands and needs, or by rights and rewards. To give in order to get (*do ut des*) might be a natural pattern of expectation in society, and it might also be the "natural" way of dealing with God and thinking about God, but it does not fit friendship and certainly not the divine friendship which is at the heart of our belief in the Trinity. To believe in God Father-Son-Spirit is not just to believe in a god ("there must be something"), or even to believe in a creator, but rather to believe in a God who loves us. The relationship with God Father-Son-Spirit breathes the atmosphere of personal warmth, open-heartedness, and generosity.

Conclusion

Aquinas' theology of the Trinity, both in the *Summa contra Gentiles* and in the *Summa Theologiae*, differs at least in one crucial respect from contemporary theology of the Trinity. Aquinas presupposes knowledge of Scripture, familiarity with Scripture, and, to a degree, a certain self-evidence of the faith in the Trinity. He acknowledges that he does not know the fundamental critical questions about faith from his own experience.[43] Our situation is different. Because of the development in theology, a general or generic theistic understanding of God has become predominant. Because of the development in biblical studies, the historical critical method profoundly influences our scholarly reading of the Bible and, consequently, our theological reflection. The Christian faith has become one among others in a multi-religious society. Faith has lost its self-evident and public place, at least in Western (European) society. Because of these developments, theologians at present not only experience those fundamental critical questions at first hand, but also feel the need to ask those questions first. The attention to the *oikonomia* therefore entails a way of telling the story of salvation so that it becomes clear once again that this is a story about God Father-Son-Spirit acting in and through our history, in and through us.

If we keep in mind this difference and what it entails (e.g., we might not want to keep Aquinas' pedagogic order of the *Summa Theologiae*), Aquinas' method in doing theology contains valuable insights. It is not enough to present some biblical data, nor is it enough to present the data of faith as such. The task of a theologian is to reflect upon them and to go backward and forward between the *oikonomia* and the *theologia*. Only then will the richness and the profundity of these data become clear and, most of all, the amazing philanthropy (cf. Titus 3:4) of our God, as shown in what Aquinas says about the missions of Son and Spirit.

Notes

1. For a critical assessment of some critics, see H. Rikhof, "Aquinas' Authority in the Contemporary Theology of the Trinity," in *Aquinas as Authority*, ed. P. van Geest, H. Goris, and C. Leget (Louvain: Peeters, 2002), 213–34.

2. P. Schoonenberg, *De Geest, Het Woord en de Zoon: Theologische overdenkingen over Geest-christologie, Logos-christologie en drieëenheidsleer* (Averbode: Kampen, 1991); R. Del Colle, *Christ and the Spirit: Spirit Christology in Trinitarian Perspective* (New York: Oxford University Press, 1994).

3. I first encountered this text while reading Matthias Scheeben, a nineteenth-century theologian. In his *Mysterien des Christentums* (1865) he adds to his chapter on the mystery of the Trinity the complete text of chapters 20–22 of Book IV of the *Summa contra Gentiles*.

4. Cf. J. Weisheipl, *Friar Thomas d'Aquino: His Life, Thought and Works,* rev. ed. (Washington, D.C.: Catholic University of America Press, 1983), 216–19; J.-P. Torrell, *Initiation à saint Thomas d'Aquin: Sa personne et son oeuvre* (Paris: Cerf, 1993), 210–11.

5. *ST* I.27–31.

6. *ST* I.39–42.

7. *ST* I.43.1 and 2.

8. *ST* I.32.1 ad 3; Cf. also *ST* I.1, where Aquinas argues that a revealed doctrine is necessary for human salvation.

9. Cf. *ST* I.32.1 ad 3.

10. *ST* I.32.1 ad 2.

11. *ST* I.32.1.

12. *ST* I.1.8.

13. Cf. *ST* I.31.2, where Aquinas discusses Arius and Sabellius in a systematic way.

14. *ST* I.43.6 ad 2 and ad 4.

15. Cf. *ST* I.9.

16. Cf. *ST* I.42.

17. For a more extended analysis, see H. Rikhof, "Trinity in Thomas: Reading the *Summa Theologiae* against the Background of Modern Problems," in *Jaarboek* 1999 (Utrecht: Thomas Instituut Utrecht, 2000), 81–100.

18. Even the single objection referring to the Son is also about the *missio* of the Spirit, as Aquinas reveals in his response to it: he alludes to the discussion in article 5, where he discusses the invisible mission of the Son and shows that this is tied up with the invisible mission of the Spirit (a.5 ad 1, ad 2, ad 3).

19. *ST* I.43.3: "Dicendum quod divinae personae convenit mitti secundum quod novo modo existit in aliquo; dari autem secundum quod habetur ab aliquo. Neutrum autem horum est nisi secundum gratiam gratum facientem."

20. Aquinas uses the term *relatio realis* to express that all creatures, by being creatures, are *de facto* related to the Creator. A *relatio realis* indicates that the relationship is constitutive for the *res*. The term "father" or "mother" implies necessarily a relationship to "child." Cf. *ST* I.13.7 and 45.3 ad 1.

21. *ST* I.38.1: "Ad quod quandoque pertingit rationalis creatura, ut puta cum sic fit particeps divini Verbi et procedentis Amoris ut possit libere Deum vere cognoscere et recte amare."

22. Augustine, *De doctrina Christiana libri quattuor,* ed. G. M. Green, CSEL 80 (Vienna, 1963), Book 1, 3.

23. Ibid.

24. Ibid., Book 1, 5.

25. Ibid., Book 1, 27.

26. See, e.g., Basile Le Grand, *Sur L'Esprit Saint,* ed. B. Pruche, SC 17 (Paris: Cerf, 1947), esp. chaps. 10–16.

27. *ST* I.43.5 ad 3: "Si autem quantum ad effectum gratiae, sic communicant duae missiones in radice gratiae, sed distinguuntur in effectibus gratiae, qui sunt illuminatio intellectus et inflammatio affectus."

28. Cf. Torrell, *Initiation,* 153–56, for a survey of the discussion.

29. Aquinas probably would not recognize the phrase "his faith" as an adequate description of his attitude; "the faith of the Church" would be more correct.

30. Aquinas refers to Hilary, but in *De Trinitate* I, 37, Hilary addresses God: "Ego quidem hoc vel praecipuum vitae meae officium debere tibi Pater omnipotens Deus, conscius sum ut te omnis sermo meus et sensus loquatur."

31. *ScG* I.3 and 9.

32. Cf. *ST* I.34 proem.: "sed ratio Filii ex ratione Patris consideratur."

33. For an extended and illuminating discussion of the introduction to the *ScG* as a whole and of chapter 1 of Book IV, see M. Corbin, *Le chemin de la théologie chez Thomas d'Aquin* (Paris: Beauchesne, 1974), 475–680.

34. *ScG* IV.3.3.

35. "Diligenter autem verba sacrae Scripturae considerantibus apparet . . ." (c.5); "Hanc autem positionem divinae Scripturae repugnare manifeste potest percipere, si quis sacrarum Scripturarum dicta diligenter considerat" (c.7).

36. Cf. also his remark later in c.55: "qui tamen errores exercuerunt fidelium ingenia ad diligentius divinorum veritatem exquirendam et intelligendam."

37. Aquinas stresses (*ScG* IV.1) that the understanding will not be complete: "ea quae in sermonibus praedictis occulte nobis traduntur studeamus utcumque mente capere a laceratione infidelium defendendo, ut tamen praesumptio perfecte cognoscendi non adsit."

38. Cf. the discussion of *ST* I.43.3 earlier in this essay.

39. *ST* I.32.1 ad 3. Cf. also the discussion in the first part of the second main section ("Aquinas on the *missiones:* A reading of *ST* I.43") of this essay.

40. *Ad Rom.* 5:5, nos.392–93.

41. Cf. his analysis of friendship in *ST* II-II.23.1: "requiritur quaedam mutua amatio, quia amicus est amico amicus."

42. *In Ioh.* 15:13, no.2011.

43. *ScG* I.2.

Three

Trinity and Creation

GILLES EMERY, O.P.

In contemporary theological research, we see renewed interest in a trinitarian doctrine of creation. In the field of trinitarian theology, reflection strives to overcome the "isolation" that threatens the doctrine of the Trinity, according to the account put forward some time ago by Karl Rahner.[1] Christian thought has been careful ever since to insist on the relationship between trinitarian faith and the whole of the divine economy, of which creation is the first work: since God is Trinity, his action must be understood in a trinitarian manner.[2] One finds a comparable concern expressed within the field of the theology of creation: a Christian doctrine of creation cannot be limited to an approach of philosophical theology, however legitimate this approach may be. Rather, it must ground creative work in the trinitarian mystery of God, in order to emphasize its distinctively Christian characteristics.

Many scholars today express dissatisfaction with the thought of Saint Thomas Aquinas in this domain: according to a widely held view, Thomist trinitarian theology consists in a logical and metaphysical reflection detached from the Bible and separated from those actions in which God manifests himself as Trinity.[3] In a related and no less prevalent view, the Trinity does not play a constitutive role in the Thomist treatment of creation: Saint Thomas has a monistic conception of divine creative activity, "at the expense of mediation through the Son and the Spirit."[4] Such judgments, examples of which abound in recent theological literature, indicate perhaps the shortcomings of certain currents in Thomistic neo-scholasticism during the first half of the twentieth century. But they fail to do justice to the authentic thought of Saint Thomas, and cannot withstand an attentive reading of his works. In fact, contrary to these all-too-often widespread misrepresentations, Saint Thomas developed a profoundly trinitarian conception of creation. He systematically set forth the trinitarian principles of creative action and their repercussions for the understanding of the created world in a coherent synthesis that intimately unites faith in God the Trinity, creation, and the economy of salvation. Without attempting to present an exhaustively detailed account of the Thomist position, I will describe the trinitarian structure of the Thomist theology of creation and of divine action in the world.

The *ordo creationis:* The Causality of the Trinitarian Processions

As early as his first theological synthesis, the *Scriptum super libros Sententiarum,* Saint Thomas formulates the central thesis of his trinitarian doctrine of creation: "The eternal processions of the persons are the cause and the reason [*causa et ratio*] of the production of creatures."[5] The words "cause" and "reason" are completed by other terms to make precise the trinitarian foundation of creation: Saint Thomas explains that the procession of the persons is the origin (*origo*) of the procession of creatures,[6] or the principle (*principium*) of creatures;[7] the procession of creatures has as its exemplar (*exemplatur, exemplata*) the procession of the divine persons.[8] This affirmation is presented as a theological exegesis of the biblical texts that deal with the creative action of the Son and of the Holy Spirit. It occurs nearly twenty times in the works of Saint Thomas, in the same terms[9] or in related expressions: "the temporal going-forth of creatures is derived [*derivatur*] from the eternal going-forth of the persons,"[10] "the going-out [*exitus*] of the persons in the unity of essence is the cause of the going-out of creatures in the diversity of essence."[11] Saint Thomas discovered this theological thesis in the works of his master, Saint Albert the Great, who twice expressed it in his commentary on the *Sentences*.[12] He also clearly relied on Saint Bonaventure, who, without expressly formulating that thesis, also taught that the procession of the Son and of the Holy Spirit possessed a causality and an exemplarity with respect to creation: the "extrinsic diffusion" of the good (creation) has as its reason the "intrinsic diffusion" of the sovereign Good in the divine persons, in the way in which that which is first (*primum*) is the cause of all secondary realities that are derived from it. And yet neither Saint Albert nor

Saint Bonaventure systematically developed the creative causality of the trinitarian processions; the use of that thesis appears to be a trait particular to and characteristic of Saint Thomas' theology.[13]

The causality of the trinitarian processions constitutes that which Saint Thomas calls the "order of creation" (*ordo creationis*).[14] The *order* consists in the relation of a thing with its principle. It is comprised of three elements,[15] which, in the case of creation, are as follows: (1) the fundamental distinction of God and of the world (the exclusion of pantheism); (2) the fact that God is absolutely first (*primum, prius*), while the created world is second, existing through participation in the divine perfection (participation through creation, analogy);[16] (3) the threefold causality—efficient, exemplar, and final—that characterizes God as *principle* with regard to the world.[17] When Saint Thomas explains that the trinitarian processions are the cause and the reason of the procession of creatures, all the elements of that "order of creation" are present. Special significance is attached here to exemplar causality. Saint Thomas in fact applies to the trinitarian processions the famous Aristotelian adage of the "causality of the highest instance": that which is first and that possesses a perfection to the highest degree is the cause and the reason of that which comes afterwards and possesses that perfection in a limited manner.[18] This principle, which constitutes the soul of the *quarta via* establishing the existence of God in the *Summa Theologiae*,[19] indicates that here we are at the heart of the Thomistic metaphysic of participation. When it is applied to the Trinity, this metaphysical principle signifies that the trinitarian processions are the cause (exemplar, efficient, and final) of the procession of creatures, the "motive" of God's creative action, and the principle of creatures both in the ontological order and in the intelligible order. The full and precise understanding of creation therefore requires the knowledge of the procession of the divine persons.

Saint Thomas does not attribute creation in a proper and exclusive way to one divine person in particular. God is creator by virtue of his divine essence, which is common to the three persons: the three persons are a single creator.[20] Creative causality is properly attributed not to one divine person, but rather to the trinitarian processions (*processiones, processus, exitus*). The word "procession" signifies the origin, the coming forth of a reality from its principle (*eductio principiati a suo principio*).[21] By considering the Trinity and creation in an analogous way, under the aspect of *procession* (the Son and the Spirit *proceed* eternally, and creatures also *proceed* from God in another order), Saint Thomas uses a concept that makes it possible to conceptualize analogically the communication of being.

In God, procession signifies the essential communication of the fullness of divinity: the Father eternally communicates the fullness of divinity to the Son, and together with the Son, he communicates it to the Holy Spirit. Our mind conceives of the processions as the foundation of the relations that maintain the divine persons, but procession designates in fact the same reality (*res*) as relation. It is the manner of signifying that reality (*modus significandi*) which differs: procession refers to the relationship of the divine persons in the manner of an *act* (to beget, to breathe forth, to be begotten, to be breathed forth), whereas relation signifies this same reality in the manner of a form or of a property (paternity of the Father, filiation of the Son, spiration or procession of the Spirit).[22] When speaking of "procession," therefore, Saint Thomas considers the persons under the dynamic aspect of the eternal communication of the divinity. In an analogous way, he considers creation under the dynamic aspect of the participation of creatures in being and in the divine perfections. It is on this level of the *communication of being*, implying the doctrine of analogy, that trinitarian causality is situated. The communication of the entire divine essence in the Trinity is the cause and reason of the communication to creatures, in a radically different order, of a participation in the divine essence: "the going-out of the persons in the unity of essence [*exitus personarum in unitate essentiae*] is the cause of the going-out of creatures in the diversity of essence [*exitus creaturarum in essentiae diversitate*]."[23]

Creation thus finds its foundation in the trinitarian mystery of *personal communication or communication of being*. God's activity in the world is rooted in the intra-divine activity of the processions. Saint Thomas applies here, in theology, an elementary Aristotelian distinction. With Aristotle, Saint Thomas in fact considers two principal types of action: (1) immanent action, which remains in the subject who acts (*quae in ipso operante manet*), as do the actions of knowing, wishing, feeling, loving, rejoicing, and so on; (2) transitive action, which is exercised on an exterior reality or matter (*quae in exteriorem rem transit*), as are those actions by which something is done (to make, to heat, to eat, etc.).[24] The distinction of these two sorts of action constitutes the point of departure for trinitarian theology. Since the Son and the Holy Spirit are truly God, their procession cannot be a transitive activity of the Father, for then the Son and the Holy Spirit would be exterior (*extra*) to the intimate being of God; this, according to Saint Thomas, is the error common to both Arianism and Sabellianism. When God accomplishes a transitive activity (*ad aliquid extra*), that activity results in a reality that is of an essence other than God: the creature. Only immanent activities, which remain in God, make it possible to account for the procession of persons who are God. Which are those immanent activities of God that have divine persons as their term? Only two among them make it possible to assert the procession of truly distinct persons: the intellectual activity of the utterance of the Word and the voluntary activity of the spiration of Love.

The trinitarian theology of the mature works of Saint Thomas is built on these two modes of procession.[25] It is, for Saint Thomas, the only way in which understanding guided by faith can coherently represent the *real distinction* of persons who are truly *God*. Saint Thomas is so convinced of this position that, in his *Quaestio disputata de potentia*, he explains, "If the procession of the Word and of Love are not sufficient to introduce the personal distinction, no personal distinction in God will be possible."[26]

In order to understand the creative causality of the trinitarian processions, one must take into account the relationship between immanent and transitive activity: "The first of the operations [the immanent operation] is the reason [*ratio*] of the second [the transitive operation] and precedes it by nature, as the cause is the reason of its effect, which it precedes."[27] The usual example given by Saint Thomas is that of the artisan or architect; the conception of the house in the mind of the architect, and the will to carry out its design (immanent actions), are the cause of the construction of the house (transitive action). In an analogous way, in God, the immanent activities of understanding and of will are the reason of creation. Now, as we have seen, these fruitful immanent actions are the procession of the Word and of the Holy Spirit. In order to appreciate the creative causality of the Trinity, therefore, it is not enough to consider the trinitarian processions in an indiscriminate manner. Rather, one must further examine the proper mode of the personal procession of the Son and of the Holy Spirit.

The Father Creates All Things through His Word and through His Spirit

The trinitarian theology of Saint Thomas includes two major stages that must be treated separately. In his earliest writings, Saint Thomas considers the generation of the Son principally as a communication of the *nature*. The proper characteristic of the procession of the Son, which is distinguished from the procession of the Spirit—for these two persons are distinct—is to proceed by mode of nature (*per modum naturae*). Correlatively, Saint Thomas teaches that the proper characteristic of the procession of the Spirit is to proceed by mode of will or by mode of love (*per modum voluntatis, per modum amoris*); in the synthesis of his earliest writings, Saint Thomas therefore conceives of the Holy Spirit as a subsisting Act of Love.[28] It is therefore by means of the procession *by mode of nature* and *by mode of will* that Saint Thomas explains theologically the biblical texts that deal with the creative role of the Son and of the Holy Spirit. The act by which the Son eternally receives from the Father the fullness of the divine *na-*

ture is the origin and exemplar cause of the action by which creatures receive a participation in the divine nature in creation.[29] Saint Thomas considers the procession of the Son by mode of nature as the reason and eternal model of the procession of creatures who receive a likeness of the divine nature. This thesis applies to the Son, in particular, the causality of the trinitarian processions that we have previously examined. It is not a matter of an appropriation, but rather of a trait *proper* to the procession of the Son: only the Son, in God, proceeds by mode of nature, in such a way that he is properly the only divine person whose procession is truly the exemplar reason of the procession of creatures by way of the communication of nature. The Son appears here as the causal archetype of all reception of being.

In the development of this theological explanation, Saint Thomas therefore conceives of the procession of the Spirit as the reason and exemplar cause of all the gifts that the will of God makes to creatures, and first among them, the gift of being through creation.[30] The eternal procession of the Holy Spirit by mode of will and of love is here considered as the causal archetype of all the gifts that God makes outside of himself through his free generosity. As with the procession of the Son, it is not a matter of an appropriation but rather of a trait proper to the procession of the Spirit: the Spirit is the only person, in God, that proceeds by mode of will and of love, in such a way that his procession is the principle of every other gift proceeding from the will of God. Saint Thomas here applies to the Holy Spirit, according to the proper mode of his procession, the causality of the trinitarian processions: on the basis of faith in the Trinity, which one cannot prove but which one receives by Revelation, "it is necessary that the procession of the persons, which is perfect, be the reason and cause of the procession of creatures."[31] Saint Thomas further explains: "That which is first in a genus is the cause of all that is in that genus, as Aristotle teaches in the *Metaphysics*. But the Holy Spirit has the formal aspect of the first Gift [*habet rationem primi doni*], inasmuch as the Spirit is the love of the Father and of the Son. It appears therefore that it is through this Gift that all is given [*per hoc Donum omnia dentur*]."[32] The Holy Spirit is therefore the exemplar cause of every gift, as much in the order of nature as in the order of grace. In this way, since God accomplishes all things by virtue of his nature and his free will, creation and all the effects of the activity of God in the world have as their foundation the procession of the Son and that of the Spirit who are their principle, their exemplar, their cause and reason. All things find their source of being and their explanatory principle in the trinitarian going-forth of the persons.

In these explanations, Saint Thomas exercises particular care in making the distinction between the essential going-forth of the persons (processions in the unity of the divine essence), and the going-forth of creatures (procession in the diversity of essence), in order to avoid all pantheistic confusion of God and of the world. Creatures are realities produced (*principiata*) by God, by his essence, by his understanding and will, which are their principle (*principium*). For its part, the eternal procession of the Son and of the Spirit is the reason of the production of creatures (*ratio principiandi*). Between the creatures produced (*principiata*) and the divine persons who are the reason of the production of creatures (*ratio principiandi*), there remains the chasm that separates the created from the uncreated.[33] Saint Thomas sums up this causal relationship and this radical distinction in the following manner: "The creature proceeds from the divine will as a thing made [*res operata*] by that will; but the Holy Spirit proceeds as the reason [*ratio*] of every work accomplished by the divine will; in the same way, the Son proceeds as the Art of all things that are made by the divine intellect."[34] These explanations from the commentary on the *Sentences* are not marginal in character; they are at the very heart of the doctrine of generation and of pneumatology, and they furnish an instrument of preeminent importance for elaborating trinitarian theology. With them, Saint Thomas conceives of the divine processions in their transcendence but also in the relationship that they freely maintain with creation and the economy of redemption.

In his mature works, beginning with the *Summa contra Gentiles*, Saint Thomas constructs his trinitarian theology on a more precise doctrine of the procession of the Word by mode of intellect and of the Holy Spirit by mode of Love. This evolution leads him to a more refined explanation of the causality of the trinitarian processions. Without going into detail, let us recall that Saint Thomas thereafter has a clearer conception of what constitutes a word: the word (*verbum*) is not the intellect, nor the act of knowing, nor the *species* that actualizes the intelligence causing it to know, but rather the product of the intelligence, that is the concept (*conceptio intellecta, conceptus*) that the intellect conceives or forms. In God, the name *Verbum* is therefore a proper name of the Son, because it includes in its signification a relation of origin with respect to the Father who "speaks" it: the name *Word* properly designates the Son of God in his personal property, distinct from the Father and from the Spirit. Henceforth Thomas considers the generation of the Word *per modum intellectus* as the best way of accounting for the generation of the Son.[35]

Thanks to this progress, Saint Thomas can treat the entire creative work of the Son by means of the doctrine of the Word. Since the Word perfectly expresses the Father who speaks it, it expresses everything that is in the Father: the Word represents everything that the Father knows, it expresses all the creatures that preexist in the understanding of the Father. For this reason the Word is not only the "Word of the Father," but also the "Word of all things" (*Verbum omnium rerum*): since God does not act by a necessity of nature but by his wisdom, the Father accomplishes all things by his Word. By begetting his Word, the Father engendered the One by whom he produces creatures in being.[36] In fact, divine knowledge of creatures is not only cognitive but also actualizing (transitive action), the efficient cause of creatures: "So, the Word of God is purely expressive of what is in God the Father, but he is both expressive and causative of the creatures [*creaturarum vero est expressivum et operativum*]."[37] The Word is thus the reason of creatures from a double point of view, that of exemplar causality (the expression, the conception of creatures) and that of efficient causality (the accomplishment of results, the production of creatures in being). In this way, the name *Verbum* signifies first of all the divine person of the Son in his relation to the Father, but, in a secondary sense, this name equally includes an expressive and causal relationship with regard to creatures. It is by virtue of his property as *Word*, in all its extension, that the Son is the creative Art of the Father and the *ratio* of the production of creatures.

It is again by means of the doctrine of the Word that Saint Thomas explains the expression "the Father works all things through his Son." The preposition "through" (*per*) does not make of the Son the formal or efficient cause of the action of the Father, nor an instrument inferior to the Father. The Son acts by the same principle of action (the divine essence) as the Father, but the Son eternally receives his creative power from the Father, insofar as he is the Word proceeding from the Father. Creative power is eternally communicated to the Son in his generation: the Son receives it and possesses it in the mode of his personal property. In other words, the Son expresses and causes creatures inasmuch as he is the Word. In this way, Saint Thomas explains, "when we say that the Father does all things 'though his Son' this statement is not mere appropriation but proper to the Word [*non est appropriatum Verbo sed proprium eius*], because the fact that he is a cause of creatures is had from someone else, namely the Father, from whom he has being."[38] These explanations drawn from the commentary on Saint John, one of the last works of Saint Thomas, reveal the continuity of his thought concerning the creative causality of the divine persons. The concept of appropriation, despite its value, does not represent Aquinas' last word on the action of the Trinity. By taking into account the processions and the order of the persons within the Trinity, Saint Thomas teaches a trinitarian structure of creative action in which the persons participate according to their property.

In the development of this insight, the theological understanding of the procession of the Holy Spirit is based on the presence of "God loved" in "God who loves himself." As in the case of *verbum*, Thomas comes here to a deeper understanding of love, which he henceforth conceives of as an "affection to-ward" (*affici ad aliquid*), an impulsion (*impulsio, impulsus*), an attraction (*attrac-tio*), an impression (*impressio*) of the reality loved, an ardent movement toward the thing loved, and no longer as a kind of informing of the will by the good (which was the more "static" perspective of the *Sentences*).[39] In the will of the one who is engaged in the act of loving, he discerns therefore a dynamic pres-ence of the object loved: the being that I love is present to my will, bending me, as it were, in his direction. It is this affection, impression, or impulsion of love that constitutes henceforth the preferred approach to understanding the person of the Holy Spirit. The procession of the Holy Spirit is the spiration, in God, of that impression or impulsion of love by which God loved is present in God who loves himself. It is thus that the Spirit is Love as person (personal Love). The Spirit proceeds precisely in the mode of the love by which God loves his own goodness. The creative and redemptive action of God has as its reason (*ratio*) the will by which God loves his own goodness. Saint Thomas attributes ever after to the Holy Spirit all the divine works which result from the loving will of God: "the Holy Spirit is therefore the principle of the creation of things; that is the meaning expressed in the *Psalm* (103:30): 'Send forth your Spirit and all will be created.'"[40]

The Thomist doctrine of creative love is eminently dynamic. Saint Thomas attributes creation to the Holy Spirit, because Love encompasses a force of im-pulsion, a motive power (*vis quaedam impulsiva et motiva*).[41] For this reason, not only creation but the entire divine economy is placed under the dynamic action of the Spirit. In his *Summa contra Gentiles,* Saint Thomas thus connects the en-tire economy of salvation to the Holy Spirit: providence, the divine government of the world, life, charity which causes human beings to resemble God by giv-ing them divine friendship, revelation, prophecy, the keeping of the command-ments, the road toward eternal beatitude, the forgiveness of sins and the renewal of hearts, contemplation, consolation, the spiritual freedom of the children of God, and so forth.[42] In this vast fresco of the works of the Spirit, the speculative doctrine of Love makes it possible to show why the Holy Spirit is the principle that animates the entire divine economy. This teaching is summarized in the fol-lowing explanations:

> Even as the Father utters himself and every creature by the Word he begets, inasmuch as the Word begotten completely expresses the Father and every creature, so also he loves himself and every creature by the Holy Spirit, inas-much as the Holy Spirit proceeds as Love for the primal goodness by whom the Father loves himself and every creature.[43]

In this way Saint Thomas reunites in the study of the Holy Spirit all that concerns the love of God, the love by which God loves himself, and the love by which he loves his creatures. There is only one personal Love, who is the Holy Spirit, and by whom God accomplishes all things.

The Trinitarian Structure of the Divine Economy

The procession of the Word and that of the Spirit are not only the source of creation; they extend their influence to the entire divine economy. For Saint Thomas, the causality of the trinitarian processions constitutes more than a particular theme of theological reflection. It offers a structure of doctrinal synthesis that makes it possible to conceive of all divine work in a trinitarian manner:

> Just as the procession of persons is the reason of the production of creatures by the first principle [*processio personarum est ratio productionis creaturarum a primo principio*], so too this same procession is the reason for the return of creatures to their end [*est eadem processio ratio redeundi in finem*]; since, just as we have been created by the Son and the Holy Spirit, so too it is by them that we are united to our ultimate end.[44]

The trinitarian processions provide the doctrinal foundation of the *exitus-reditus* structure of the world and of history. If everything comes from God (*exitus*) and if humans receive the grace to return to God and participate in his beatitude (*reditus*), it is by virtue of the influence of the trinitarian processions who are the cause and the reason both of the *exitus* and of the *reditus*. Saint Thomas observes here a certain "circular movement" of creatures (*circulatio, regiratio*), of which the trinitarian processions are the dynamic pivot; the *exitus* and the *reditus* are accomplished by the same trinitarian processions (*per eadem*), who exercise their influence in a varied way.[45] In more Aristotelian terms, the *Summa Theologiae* talks about God as the "beginning and end," but it is the same structure of going-out and return that governs the thought of Saint Thomas.[46] The trinitarian processions thus exert a double transcendent "mediation."

How must one understand the causality of the trinitarian processions in the *reditus* of creatures to God? It is no longer a question of the creation that establishes creatures in their natural being, but a question of the gifts of sanctifying grace and of glory which bring about union with God in the theologal order. The processions that are the cause of the *reditus* are the missions of the Son and of the Holy Spirit. Let us recall that the mission (*missio*) of the divine person consists in his eternal procession to which a created effect is joined, namely, sanc-tifying grace.[47] The structure of the divine missions is the following: the proper effect of the mission of the Spirit is to conduct us to the Son, and the proper ef-fect of the mission of the Son is to conduct us to the Father.[48]

In the mission or temporal procession, explains Saint Thomas, the divine person who is sent forth impresses on the soul of the saints a likeness of his eter-nal property. This likeness impressed as a kind of seal on the soul makes it pos-sible for humans to participate in the personal relationship of the Son and of the Spirit. Saint Thomas is speaking here of a "sealing" (*sigillatio*) of the divine per-sons: the theologal gift of love, which is a shared likeness of the personal property of the Spirit, offers us the possibility of entering into relationship with the Son in a mode comparable to that of the Spirit, by imitating the Spirit (Love which proceeds from the Son). The theologal gift of wisdom, which is a shared likeness of the personal property of the Son, offers us the possibility of entering into re-lationship with the Father in a mode comparable to that of Word, that is, by imi-tating the Word (Word of the Father). Rational creatures can enter into theolo-gal relation with the Father because charity lets them participate in the personal relation that the Holy Spirit maintains with the Father, and because faith (wis-dom) lets them participate in the personal relation that the Son maintains with the Father. The reality of contact with God in the *reditus* comes from the fact that the eternal properties of the Word and of the Spirit are the *origin* and *exem-plar* of the created gifts of wisdom and charity.[49]

This "sealing," which imprints in us the likeness of the eternal processions, constitutes the ontological foundation of the intentional union with God in the theologal acts of faith and charity: through the missions of the Son and of the Spirit, those in the state of grace participate in the trinitarian *activity*. In its full-ness, the image of the Trinity in the soul of the saints consists in an assimilation to the divine Persons, through a created representation, in an active way (*secun-dum actus*), of the trinitarian processions.[50] In the mission of the Son and of the Spirit, the human person attains by his operation God himself, and God lives then in the saints "as that which is known is in the person who knows and that which is loved is in the person who loves."[51]

In the *reditus* of humanity to God, the divine persons live in the saints in a dynamic mode, as we have just seen: the likeness imprinted in the soul of the saints represents the *relation* through which the Spirit and the Son are in rela-tion with the Father. The Son and the Spirit, by imprinting a likeness of their respective personal property, inscribe in us the *dynamic ardor for returning to our end*. In the gifts of grace, the persons are possessed "insofar as they lead to this end" or "insofar as they unite us to this end."[52] As for the Father, explains Saint

Thomas, he is the "ultimate end" to which the missions of the Son and of the Spirit lead: *ultimum ad quod recurrimus.*[53] The missions of the Son and of the Spirit lead us to the Principle without principle who is the Father (*principium ad quod recurrimus*), and it is thus that the procession of the divine persons is the reason for the return to our end (*ratio redeundi in finem*).[54] In Christological terms, Saint Thomas can therefore explain that, in the mystery of the incarnation of the Son, the entire redeemed universe returns to its principle.[55] In this way, the causality of the trinitarian processions provides the fundamental structure of the real, of the world and of history. It also offers the theologian the organizing principle of theology: through the procession of the Son and of the Spirit who are the reason of creation and of the return to God, everything comes from the Father and returns to the Father.

Two Complementary Rules

When he treats creation and the works of God *ad extra,* Saint Thomas always applies the fundamental rule of the unity of operation of the three divine persons: since the principle of divine action is the essence common to the three persons, creation and the effects of divine action are not the proper or exclusive work of one person, rather they are brought about by the three persons by virtue of their inseparable divinity. However, the rule of the common efficacy of the Trinity is not sufficient to explain all the richness of the action of the three persons. By insisting too exclusively on the unity of operation of the Trinity, the neo-Thomist tradition has undoubtedly impoverished the thought of Saint Thomas. Aquinas in fact explains: "the procession of the divine persons is, in a certain way, the origin of the procession of creatures [*processio divinarum personarum est et quaedam origo processionis creaturarum*], since everything that is first in its genus is the cause of that which comes after it; but efficacy with regard to the creatures is attributed to the common essence."[56] The creative action of the Trinity includes therefore *two complementary aspects,* which must neither be separated nor isolated but rather must be taken together: (1) the causality of the Trinitarian processions; (2) the common efficacy of the three persons by virtue of their unique essence. Saint Thomas explains these two complementary aspects by reconsidering the elements that we have already encountered here above: the unique essence of the three persons accounts for the common efficacy of the Trinity (*efficientia totius Trinitatis*), whereas the personal procession provides the reason of the efficacy (*ratio efficientiae*). That is why the proper name of a person (*Word, Love*) can include a relationship to creatures. It is also the reason for which we say, in the proper sense of the terms, that "the Father speaks all things through his Word" and that "the Father loves us through the Holy Spirit."[57]

In his commentary on the *Sentences,* when he sets forth these two aspects, Saint Thomas applies the principle of the "causality of the first" and explains that the divine persons proceed as the principle of creatures: the divine persons who proceed (the Son and the Spirit) are the *ratio principiandi;* the creatures, for their part, are designated as the *principiata.*[58] In the *Summa Theologiae,* the explication is more succinct: "The comings forth of the divine Persons are the reasons of the production of creatures [*processiones personarum sunt rationes productionis creaturarum*], inasmuch as they include the essential attributes of knowing and willing."[59] In the two cases, the thought of Saint Thomas remains the same, and the *Scriptum super libros Sententiarum* allows us to understand better the teaching of the *Summa Theologiae.* The Son and the Holy Spirit proceed eternally as the term of an immanent operation in God; these immanent operations are the intellectual activity (the speaking of the Word which is the natural begetting of the Son) and the voluntary loving activity (the spiration of personal Love which is the Holy Spirit). In this way, the personal processions really include in themselves the essential operative attributes that are the knowledge and will of God. Thus, the processions of the persons include in their very *ratio* the attributes of God the creator: the Son proceeds as the reason of that which God accomplishes by his creative knowledge; the Holy Spirit proceeds as the reason of that which God accomplishes by his creative love. Creation is not attributed in an exclusive manner to the Son, nor to the Holy Spirit, and yet the theologian discerns in the Son and in the Spirit the personal reason of God's creative action. This personalist view provides the foundation for the realism of the appropriations. Thus, according to Saint Thomas, faith in the Trinity is *necessary* in order to understand the depth of God's creative action:

> To know the divine persons was necessary for us for two reasons. One in order to have a right view of the creation of things. For by maintaining that God made everything through his Word we avoid the error of those who held that God's nature compelled him to create things. By affirming that there is in him the procession of Love we show that he made creatures, not because he needed them nor because of any reason outside himself, but from love of his own goodness. . . . The other and more important reason is so that we may have the right view of the salvation of mankind, accomplished by the Son who became flesh and by the gift of the Holy Ghost.[60]

For Saint Thomas, the affirmation of creation by the Word shows the wisdom of God's creative activity, by excluding the thesis of a necessary emanatism; the affirmation of creation by the Holy Spirit guarantees for its part the free generosity of divine activity, by pure grace. These explanations clearly show the personal mode of creative action: it is by reason of his personal Word and of his personal Love that the Father creates. This "personalism" of the doctrine of creation is necessary to understand clearly the reality of redemption: we are saved by the persons who have created us, and we are conducted to the Father (*reditus*) by the persons who are also the reason of creation (*exitus*). The trinitarian order of salvation thus presupposes the trinitarian order of creation that provides its foundation.

To these explanations, one must still add the proper mode of action of each person. The divine person, according to Saint Thomas, is constituted by a relational property (paternity, filiation, procession); the person, in God, *is* that subsisting relation.[61] Saint Thomas also designates the divine person as a "mode of existence" (*modus existendi*).[62] That personal mode of existence is a *relational* mode of being: the proper mode of existence of the Word is to exist as the Word in relation to the Father who speaks it; the proper mode of existence of the Spirit is to exist hypostatically as Love in relation to the Father and to the Son; the proper mode of the Father is to exist as the Source in relation to the Son that he begets and to the Spirit that he breathes forth. Just as the *mode of existence* of the person is relational, the *mode of action* of the person is relational, in conformity with the mode of existence. For this reason, creative and redemptive action is common to the entire Trinity (shared efficacy), but in this common action each person is involved according to his personal mode, that is, according to his *proper relational mode*.

This is why Saint Thomas can affirm that, in the expression "the Father works all things through his Son," the working *through the Son* is not only appropriate to the Word, but *proper* to the Word.[63] It is not efficacy with regard to creatures that is proper to the Word; that efficacy is common to the entire Trinity. That which is proper to the Word is to act in the mode of his personal property, in conformity with his personal mode of being, which is to be in relation to the Father who speaks him. The Holy Spirit acts in conformity with his personal mode of being, which is to be Love in relation to the Father and to the Son who breathe him forth. The Father acts in conformity with his personal mode of being, which is to be the Source, the Principle without principle from which proceed the Son and the Holy Spirit; that which is proper to the Father is to act "through his Son and through his Spirit." Trinitarian action is accomplished in conformity with the *order* in the Trinity.[64] In this way, Saint Thomas maintains a strict monotheism (a single action of the entire Trinity), while taking into account the personal *mode* of action of each hypostasis and while emphasizing the *order* of the persons. This teaching reveals a profound personalism in the treatment of trinitarian action. Without weakening the truth of the unity of operation of the three persons, one must hold together two complementary rules: the common efficacy of the Trinity, and the causality of the trinitarian processions.

The Meaning of Plurality in the World

When he explains the plurality and multiplicity of creatures, Saint Thomas most often has recourse to the theme of the representation of divine perfection. The argument is as follows: God has created the world by reason of his goodness, which he communicates to creatures; a single creature, because of its finitude, would be incapable of representing sufficiently divine goodness; God has therefore created a universe (*universum*), that is, a multiplicity of creatures in a well-ordered plurality, capable of better representing his goodness.[65] This thesis of Neoplatonic origin is not, however, the only explanation of Saint Thomas. Here again he introduces the causality of the trinitarian processions:

> In its dignity and causality, the distinction [of the divine persons] surpasses all distinctions. And, in the same way, the relation that is the principle of that distinction surpasses in its dignity all principles of distinction in creatures, not by the fact that it is a relation, but by the fact that it is a divine relation. That relation surpasses them also in its causality, since every procession and multiplication of creatures is caused by the procession of the distinct divine persons [*excellit etiam causalitate, quia ex processione personarum divinarum distinctarum causatur omnis creaturarum processio et multiplicatio*].[66]

In the context of the study of relation, Saint Thomas explains that the *distinction* of the divine persons, if one looks at it under the aspect of quantity, is the smallest of all real distinctions, since it does not divide the unity of being of the three hypostases in God. Following Averroës, Saint Thomas therefore considers *relation* as the reality having the least degree of being (*ens minimum*), since relation does not constitute a determination which would intrinsically modify the subject; relation, unlike the other categories of being, consists in the pure relationship to something else (*ad aliud*). But if one considers them under the aspect of dignity and causality, distinction and relation in the Trinity surpass all other distinctions and all other relations. Personal relation does not claim this prerogative by the fact that it is a relation, but by the fact that it is a *divine* relation: relation, in God, is really identified with the person and with the divine essence. For this reason, divine relation possesses the universal causality of the divine essence. Saint Thomas considers divine relation not only in its efficacy, but also in its exemplar causality; divine relation and the distinction of which this relation is the principle, are the cause of the procession and the multiplication of creatures.

Thus, creation finds its source in the trinitarian *distinction* and *relations*. The first distinction, that of the divine persons, is the cause of that other distinction which is creation (creation is the production of a world really distinct from God, and in this sense creation is a distinction). In the same way, writes Saint Thomas, the personal plurality of which relation is the principle is the cause of the multiplication (*multiplicatio*) of creatures: the plurality of genera and species in creatures, the multiplicity of individuals within the species, and the multiplicity of events that constitute history, have the trinitarian relations as their source. One cannot emphasize more forcefully the positive value of the multiplicity of creatures; Saint Thomas does not conceive of plurality as a decline from unity, but to the contrary, as a participation in the fullness of the trinitarian life of God. This theological audacity expresses the consequences of the revolutionary idea of a "transcendental multitude" that Saint Thomas recognizes in the Trinity.[67] This teaching casts a very illuminating light on the meaning of plurality and differences in our world. As the principle of distinction in the intratrinitarian going-forth, personal relation appears as the ultimate source of creation and all plurality in our world.

Conclusion

The doctrine of the creative Trinity, in Saint Thomas, does not constitute an isolated chapter in theology. It provides a key to the interpretation of all of reality. In his commentary on the *Sentences*, Saint Thomas finds in the causality of the trinitarian processions the structural principle of theology: the processions of the persons are the cause and reason of the *exitus* and of the *reditus* of creatures to God. The *Summa Theologiae* does not explicitly place this trinitarian principle in the foreground, but the linking of the trinitarian processions and the divine attributes makes it possible to recognize the permanence of the same theological thesis: the processions of the persons, inasmuch as they include the essential attributes which account for the activity of God *ad extra*, are the cause of creation. The study of God's action, for Saint Thomas, is not only governed by the rule of the unity of operation of the Trinity; it also implies a complementary rule, that of the causality of the trinitarian processions. That leads to emphasizing the *mode of action* of each person, in conformity with his personal property, as well as the *order* of the Trinity in its creative and redemptive action. In the final analysis, plurality in the created world has as its efficient and exemplar cause the plurality of the divine persons in their relations and in their distinction; relation occupies a central place in the theology of Saint Thomas, and this primacy of the trinitarian relation is reflected in the doctrine of creation.

Three consequences must be drawn from this summary. First, the trinitarian doctrine of creation constitutes for Saint Thomas the *foundation* of the trinitarian doctrine of salvation. The world is saved by the missions of the divine persons (incarnation of the Son and gift of the Spirit), but it is above all created and established in its natural principles by the action of the Trinity; the procession of the divine persons is the cause of creation and of the return to God, the *exitus* and the *reditus* are brought about *per eadem*. Second, the doctrine of trinitarian action reveals the personalism of Saint Thomas' theology. Aquinas rejects the false opposition of divine essence and divine persons; he attributes creation to the persons, in virtue of their common essence and in virtue of the trinitarian processions. It is in the doctrine of the *person* that the synthesis of the double aspect of trinitarian action (essence and relation/property)[68] is accomplished. Third, speculative reflection on what we call today the "immanent Trinity" constitutes the foundation of a theology of the trinitarian economy (the "economic Trinity"). The economic doctrine of the Trinity is not prior to speculative reflection on the being of the Trinity; on the contrary, speculative reflection on the being of the Trinity, on the properties of the persons, and on their procession makes possible a true theological doctrine of the trinitarian economy. Because it is properly speculative, the theology of Saint Thomas can provide a trinitarian understanding of the economy of creation and redemption.

Notes

1. Karl Rahner, "Bemerkungen zum dogmatischen Traktat 'De Trinitate,'" in *Schriften zur Theologie*, vol. 4 (Einsiedeln: Benzinger, 1964), 103–33.

2. See Gerald Collins, "The Holy Trinity: The State of the Question," in *The Trinity: An Interdisciplinary Symposium on the Trinity*, ed. S. T. Davis, D. Kendall, and G. O'Collins (Oxford: Oxford University Press, 1999), 1–25.

3. For these critiques, see, for example, Anne Hunt, *The Trinity and the Paschal Mystery: A Development in Recent Catholic Theology* (Collegeville, Minn.: Liturgical Press, 1997), 120–21; *What Are They Saying about the Trinity?* (Mahwah, N.J.: Paulist Press, 1998), 2–4, 75–76.

4. Colin E. Gunton, *The Triune Creator: A Historical and Systematic Study* (Edinburgh: Edinburgh University Press, 1998), 99–102.

5. Aquinas, I *Sent.* d.14 q.1 art.1: "Processiones personarum aeternae sunt causa et ratio productionis creaturarum."

6. I *Sent.* d.32 q.1 art.3.

7. I *Sent.* d.35, *divisio textus.*

8. I *Sent.* d.29 q.1 art.2 qc.2; *De Pot.* q.10 a.2 sed contra 2.

9. I *Sent.* d.10 q.1 art.1; I *Sent.* d.14 q.2 art.2; I *Sent.* d.26 q.2 art.2 ad 2; I *Sent.* d.27 q.2 art.3 ad 6; *De Pot.* q.10 a.2 arg. 19 et ad 19; *ST* I.45.6c and ad 1 (*processiones divinarum personarum sunt causa creationis*); 45.7 ad 3.

10. General *Prologue* of the *Scriptum super libros Sententiarum: Super Boetium de Trinitate, Prologus:* "De Trinitate personarum, ex quarum processione omnis alia nativitas vel processio derivatur."

11. I *Sent.* d.2, *divisio textus.*

12. St. Albert, I *Sent.* d.20 a.3 sed contra: "processio personarum est causa processionis creaturarum"; I *Sent.* d.29 a.2 sed contra 2.

13. For the sources of Saint Thomas in Saint Bonaventure and Saint Albert, and for the comparison of their thought, see Gilles Emery, *La Trinité créatrice* (Paris: Vrin, 1995); more briefly, "Trinité et création: Le principe trinitaire de la création dans les commentaires d'Albert le Grand, de Bonaventure et de Thomas d'Aquin sur les *Sentences,*" *Revue des Sciences Philosophiques et Théologiques* 79 (1995): 405–30.

14. St. Thomas, General *Prologue* of the *Scriptum super libros Sententiarum.*

15. I *Sent.* d.20 q.1 art.3 qc.1; cf. *ST* I.42.3.

16. I *Sent.* prol., q.un. art.2 ad 2; cf. II *Sent.* d.3 q.3 art.3 ad 2.

17. *ST* I.44.

18. General *Prologue* of the *Scriptum super libros Sententiarum:* "Semper enim illud quod est primum est causa eorum quae sunt post"; I *Sent.* d.18 q.1 art.3 contra 2; I *Sent.* d.32 q.1 art. 3. Cf. Aristotle, *Metaphysics* II (a), 993b24–30; Emery, *La Trinité créatrice,* 276–85.

19. *ST* I.2.3.

20. *ST* I.45.6.

21. I *Sent.* d.13 q.1 art.1.

22. *ST* I.40.1–4.

23. I *Sent.* d.2, *divisio textus.*

24. *ScG* II.1.2 (Edition Marietti, no.853).

25. *ST* I.27; *ScG* IV.11 and 19.

26. *De Pot.* q.9 a.9 ad 7.

27. *ScG* II.1.3 (Ed. Marietti, no.854).

28. I *Sent.* d.4 q.1 art.1; d.10 q.1 art.1; d.32 q.1 art.1–3.

29. I *Sent.* d.10 art.1: "Processionem creaturarum naturae divinae perfectionem imperfecte repraesentantium reducimus in perfectam imaginem, divinam perfectionem plenissime continentem, scilicet Filium, tanquam in principium et quasi naturalis processionis creaturarum a Deo, secundum scilicet imitationem naturae, exemplar et rationem"; cf. the general *Prologue.*

30. I *Sent.* d.10 art.1: "Ita oportet quod, inquantum processio creaturarum est ex liberalitate divinae voluntatis, reducatur in unum principium, quod sit quasi ratio totius liberalis collationis. Haec autem est amor, sub cujus ratione omnia a volontate conferuntur; et ideo oportet aliquam personam esse in divinis procedentem per modum amoris, et haec est Spiritus Sanctus."

31. Ibid.

32. I *Sent.* d.18 q.1 art.3 contra 2.

33. I *Sent.* d.6 q.1 art.2.

34. I *Sent.* d.10 q.1 art.1 ad 3.

35. *ScG* I.53; IV.11; *ST* I.34. See Gilles Emery, "Le traité de saint Thomas sur la Trinité dans la *Somme contre les Gentils*," *Revue Thomiste* 96 (1996): 5–40; Yves Floucat, "L'intellection et son verbe selon saint Thomas d'Aquin," *Revue Thomiste* 97 (1997): 443–84 and 640–93.

36. *ScG* IV.13.7 (Ed. Marietti, no.3491): "Verbum produxit, per quod res in esse produxit, sicut per earum rationem perfectam."

37. *ST* I.34.3c.

38. *In Ioh.* 1:3, no.76; cf. I *Sent.* d.12 q.1 art.3; II *Sent.* d.13 q.1 art.5.

39. *ScG* IV.19; *Comp. Theol.* I, ch. 46; *ST* I.37.1.

40. *ScG* IV.20.2 (Ed. Marietti, no.3570).

41. *ScG* IV.20.3 (Ed. Marietti, no.3571).

42. *ScG* IV.20–22.

43. *ST* I.37.2 ad 3.

44. I *Sent.* d.14 q.2 art.2; cf. I *Sent.* d.14 q.1 art.1.

45. I *Sent.* d.14 q.2 art.2: "Et ideo oportet ut per eadem quibus est exitus a principio, et reditus in finem attendatur."

46. See Jean-Pierre Torrell, *Saint Thomas Aquinas*, vol. 1, *The Person and His Work*, trans. Robert Royal (Washington, D.C.: Catholic University of America Press, 1996), 150–56.

47. *ST* I.43.1–3.

48. *In Ioh.* 14:26, no.1958.

49. I *Sent.* d.15 q.4 art.1: "In reductione rationalis creaturae in Deum intelligitur processio divinae personae, quae et missio dicitur, inquantum propria relatio ipsius personae divinae repraesentatur in anima per similitudinem aliquam receptam, quae est exemplata et originata ab ipsa proprietate relationis aeternae."

50. *ST* I.93.7–8.

51. *ST* I.43.3.

52. I *Sent.* d.15 q.4 art.1: "Unde in receptione hujusmodi donorum habentur personae divinae novo modo quasi ductrices in finem vel conjungentes."

53. Ibid.

54. I *Sent.* d.14 q.2 art.2.

55. III *Sent.*, prol.

56. I *Sent.* d.32 q.1 art.3.

57. Ibid.

58. I *Sent.* d.6 q.1 art.2; I *Sent.* d.32 q.1 art.3.

59. *ST* I.45.6c.

60. *ST* I.32.1 ad 3.

61. *ST* I.29.4.

62. *ST* I.30.4 ad 2; *De Pot.* q.2 a.5 ad 4, ad 5; *De Pot.* q.9 a.5 ad 23.

63. *In Ioh.* 1:3, no.76. See also *ST* I.39.8.

64. *ST* I.45.6 ad 2.

65. See, for example, *ST* I.47.1.

66. I *Sent.* d.26 q.2 art.2 ad 2.

67. *ST* I.30.3c: "multitudo secundum quod est transcendens"; cf. *De Pot.* q.9 a.7.

68. See Gilles Emery, "Essentialism or Personalism in the Treatise on God in Saint Thomas Aquinas?" *The Thomist* 64 (2000): 521–63.

Four

Analogy, Creation, and Theological Language

DAVID B. BURRELL, C.S.C.

What singles Thomas Aquinas out from an array of medieval thinkers, and sets him off decisively from many who followed him, is the way in which he was able to transform the philosophical frameworks given him, yet do so in a way that respected their logical and semantic integrity.[1] Part of that transformation, certainly, was to exploit the analogical reaches of language to which Aristotle had alluded, and which he himself had employed to call attention to the fact that "'being' is said in many ways."[2] In Aquinas' case, however, his encounter with Dionysius the Areopagite, with his typology of discourse *in divinis*, led him to a more constructive strategy regarding predicating "perfection terms" of creator as well as of creatures. Taking the perfection terms in question, Aquinas found a far more potent metaphysical use for the altogether ordinary semantic distinction of *res significata* and *modus significandi*— "thing signified" and "manner of signifying," customarily used to show how a shift in syllogistic terms from a nominal to an adjectival "manner of signifying" need not alter the argument. His argument in the *Summa Theologiae* is that perfection terms

> do say that God is; they are predicated of him in the category of substance, but fail to represent adequately what he is. The reason for this is that we speak of God as we know him, and since we

know him from creatures we can only speak of him as they represent him. [Yet] any creature, in so far as it possesses a perfection, represents God and is like him, for he, being simply and universally perfect, has pre-existing in himself the perfections of all his creatures. . . . But a creature is not like to God as it is like to another member of its species or genus, [so] words like 'good' and 'wise' when used of God do signify something that God really is but they signify it imperfectly because creatures represent God imperfectly.[3]

Both Aristotle and Dionysius help frame this response, with Aristotle reminding us how our knowledge is derived from sensible objects—"we know God from creatures"; and Dionysius insisting that whatever we find of perfection in our universe "represents God and is like him," yet is more unlike than like, "since a creature is not like to God as it is to another member of the species or genus."[4]

The crucial element being factored in at this point is what Robert Sokolowski calls "the distinction" of creator from creatures: a pre-philosophical stance which marks the thought and practice of all Abrahamic faiths, though each in a distinctive way, and becomes especially acute in Christian life and practice.[5] Injecting the creator/creature relation directly into the argument at this point displays what Josef Pieper has so astutely noted: that creation is the "hidden element" in the philosophy, or here, the epistemology, of Aquinas.[6] By calling attention to the fact that the items which serve as the proper objects of our cognition are also creatures, Aquinas can argue that certain terms—evaluative rather than descriptive ones, of course—can properly be predicated of both creator and creature, though we cannot know how to use them properly of God, since as we use them they "signify [what God really is] imperfectly." In the previous article of the *Summa* he had called attention to the fact that we can help correct our inevitable misuse by reminding ourselves how, in their concrete (or adjectival) form, terms like "just" or "wise" are predicated of subsistent things; saying "God is just" will remind us of that fact, whereas the abstract (or nominal) form of such terms articulates an identity rather than a predication, thereby indicating a simple form: "God is justice." Yet since "God is both simple, like the form, and subsistent, like the concrete thing," we need to use both forms of expression for him, for "neither way of speaking measures up to his way of being."[7] In this way, we remind ourselves that language as we use it "will fail to represent adequately what God is." Yet since any warrant we have for using human language at all—even perfection terms—turns on the grounding fact of creation, such terms cannot be univocal, since they must be able to span "the distinction" of creatures from creator without collapsing it. For creation, with the all-important "distinction" it introduces, at once assures that our human language will possess such terms and demands that we rely on them if we would speak coherently of God, still recognizing ourselves to be creatures with a creaturely mode of knowing. Any attempt—on semantic or other grounds—to deny human language that capacity must also deny that we can say anything whatsoever about God.[8] And that is indeed what Moses Maimonides had to insist, for his keen understanding of the import of God's revelation to Israel would not allow him to forsake "the distinction"; in contrast, a current consensus among "philosophers of religion" is to elide "the distinction" in the service of a semantics that makes sense to them.[9]

So how did Aquinas manage to walk the tightrope he did? And why has it proven to be so difficult to assimilate or to present his teaching properly? I suggest that the answer to both questions is latent in his lapidary argument to "imperfect signification," which put an already sophisticated semantics in the service of "the distinction" by honing it to a yet finer point. But what permitted him the freedom to put philosophy to such a strategic use? The answer lies in his explicit conviction that revelation gives direction to reason itself, inviting reason to give expression to its internal orientation to its source and goal. So even if argument as such demands univocity, "the distinction" flowing from a revealed free creation will demand that certain terms be able to outstrip their use among creatures to indicate their source in the creator, while that insight will direct how we use the arguments that we can construct. For the way we use arguments is always subject to goals quite beyond the rules for constructing arguments themselves, and revelation introduces a new context for the genre of reasoning. Aquinas articulates this in addressing the query whether "besides the knowledge we have of God by natural reason there is in this life a deeper knowledge that we have through grace." He responds:

By grace we have a more perfect knowledge of God than we have by natural reason. The latter depends on two things: images derived from the sensible world and the natural intellectual light by which we make abstract intelligible concepts from these images. In both respects human knowledge is helped by the revelation of grace. The light of grace strengthens the intellectual light and at the same time prophetic visions provide us with God-given images that are better suited to express divine things than those we receive naturally from the sensible world. Moreover God has given us sensible signs and spoken words to show us something of the divine, as at the baptism of Christ when the Holy Spirit appeared in the form of a dove and the voice of the Father was heard saying "this is my beloved Son."[10]

Starting with a succinct encapsulation of the epistemology he has derived from Aristotle, Aquinas shows how this can be enhanced without being undermined or circumvented. Moreover, the use of "image" to include the complex literary images offered by scripture also indicates how developed his ear had become by the extensive reflection carried out in the twelfth century into the multiple senses of scripture.[11]

It is illuminating to contrast the positive valence which Aquinas gives to the *image* with the opposition that Averroës (Ibn Rushd) consistently represents between the deliverances of reason and those of the imagination. In a fashion all too characteristic of philosophers, this earnest disciple of "the Philosopher" could not but oppose the idiom proper to philosophy to the images which fill the Qur'an. Without ever denying that the Qur'an is the revealed Word of God, Averroës nonetheless deemed its idiom better adapted to common folk than to those trained in reason, and thus was constrained to test its utterances against the bar of reason.[12] Aquinas seems led to a more positive evaluation of the "God-given images [provided by] prophetic visions," by contrasting them not with reason as such but with the material human reason is given to work with: "those we receive naturally from the sensible world." In this respect, Aquinas seems more faithful to Aristotle than even Averroës. As an example of the way in which these "God-given images are better suited to express divine things," he states that "God has given us sensible signs and spoken words to show us something of the divine, as at the baptism of Christ when the Holy Spirit appeared in the form of a dove and the voice of the Father was heard saying 'this is my beloved Son.'" The example is chosen appositely: asserting the triunity of God, for Aquinas, must surpass the power of human reason, since philosophical wisdom reaches its apex in the idea of divine unity.[13] Indeed, any observer of the history of Christianity should be startled to find that it took four centuries for that cultural system to delineate its central teaching: who and what is Jesus.[14] Yet the reason is obvious: affirmation of God as "Father, Son, and Holy Spirit" could never be so articulated as to contradict the insistence which immediately follows those names in terminating each liturgical prayer: "one God." Hence, asserting the divinity of Jesus had to be accomplished in a way which ensured that God would "have no associate" (as the Qur'an insists), as well as that God was *One* in the fashion insisted upon by the rabbis: not just one numerically, but the One from Whom the universe comes and to Whom all things return.[15]

If images are to be valorized, however, they must be able to direct us beyond any image at all, to a God who is so utterly one that nothing can properly be attributed to that One—not even *unity*. This demand of Moses Maimonides was shared by Aquinas, as shown in the passage cited above, where Aquinas first distances himself from "Rabbi Moses" only to affirm in the end his Jewish mentor's overriding concerns.[16] We cannot expect these "God-given images" to offer us concepts tailored to philosophical argument, of course, yet we can employ them to direct that argument properly. For just as the images of scripture, in the case Aquinas offers, gesture beyond themselves toward a triune God, so the elaborated doctrine of the Trinity can serve to keep reason from egregious error when it ventures beyond its proper limits—say, in trying to articulate the origins of the universe. Aquinas offers a paradigmatic instance of philosophical inquiry being shaped by premises from faith in a telling text imbedded in a question regarding God's triunity, where he asks whether the Trinity of the divine persons can be known by natural reason. Aquinas captures the opportunity offered by a sophistical objection—that knowledge of the Trinity must be accessible to reason since it would be superfluous to teach what cannot be known by natural reason, yet it would hardly be becoming to say that the divine tradition of the Trinity was superfluous—to offer "two reasons why the knowledge of the divine persons was necessary for us." The first envisages "the right idea of creation: the fact of saying that God made all things by His Word excludes the error of those who say that God produced things by necessity; [while] when we say that in Him there is a procession of love, we show that God produced creatures not because He needed them, nor because of any other extrinsic reason, but on account of the love of His own goodness."[17] If creation will prove to be the underlying warrant for employing language analogously, as the passage cited above already suggests, and if the revelation of a triune God is indispensable lest we be misled into substituting a necessary emanation scheme for a free creator, then the proper exercise of reason in these domains will require our assent to revelation.

This straightforward conclusion suggests a quite radical reprise of an entire tradition of reading Aquinas. Simply put, we must infer that Aquinas was not a Thomist! Recent scholarship, notably by Edward Booth and Wayne Hankey, has already shown how misleading it is to identify Aquinas as an Aristotelian. For it was specifically the works of Dionysius the Areopagite that facilitated the breakthrough to *esse*, which allowed Aquinas (in Booth's terms) to overcome the *aporia* bequeathed by Aristotle to philosophy, and especially to subsequent commentators on his work.[18] This *aporia*, evident to anyone trying to teach Aristotle's metaphysics, is revealed in the way Aristotle sets himself to recover (from Plato, as he sees it) the inherent worth of *substance* as an individual existing thing, only to find himself (in the culminating treatment in the *Metaphysics*) identifying *substance* with *form* (9.8 [1050b]). Some have called it Plato's revenge. Central to the *aporia* is Aristotle's inability to identify anything other than their form that makes substances exist. Even though he had shown how our quest for understanding the world elicits two questions—"is it?" and "what is it?"—he focused on the second, leaving the first entirely implicit.[19] Yet how can *form* convey existence to individual existing things, if form is what makes each of them be the kind of thing they are? This lacuna would seem linked to Aristotle's insouciance about the origin of things, which are simply presumed always to have been, even though individuals are generated and die. It would take, it seems, the revelation of a free creator to alert readers of Aristotle's *Metaphysics* to its unsatisfactory conclusion, and notably to Aristotle's failure to ask why there might be anything at all. The first thinker to question this effectively was Ibn Sina (Avicenna), who read the *Metaphysics* many times, yet by his own admission failed to grasp it, until he availed himself of the guidance of his compatriot, al-Farabi.[20] His questioning led Avicenna to formulate a key distinction between *essence* (*mahiyya*) and *existence* (*wujud*)—a distinction faithful to Aristotle's celebrated two questions, yet clearly motivated by Avicenna's desire to distinguish beings from their source. He formulated that difference as one between *possible* and *necessary being*, but the *necessity* in question differed radically from Aristotle's "necessary beings" in that it is explicitly identified with the source of all-that-is. So we must conclude that Avicenna's distinction was motivated more by the Qur'an than by anything internal to Aristotle, since previous commentators had not made this crucial move.[21]

Yet for Aquinas, as we have seen, as well as for Ibn Sina's co-religionist al-Ghazali, Avicenna's distinction did not go far enough. For the resulting "necessary emanation" failed to capture the insistence of the Qur'an (or the Bible) that creation was free. Even if that requirement is primarily religious—to properly acknowledge "the distinction" of creator from creatures—its philosophical ramifications nonetheless prove immense. For what is at stake is an adequate way of conceiving what revelation led reason to assert: a cause of being. As Harm Goris has shown, Aquinas takes Avicenna's account of God as "necessary being" and shifts the focus to God as "cause of being," removing any hint of "ontotheology," since the cause of being cannot itself *be* in the manner of anything which it causes. As "the source and goal of all things,"[22] God cannot be one of those things, so we are less tempted to think of being as a generic term including creator and creature—the germ of any "onto-theology."[23] Thus the key to the metaphysics which Aquinas had to develop lies in "the distinction," while its challenge is to find a proper expression for a cause of being, since Aristotle had never used his crucial technical terms in so radical a fashion: to refer to a cause whose activity presupposes nothing at all. Indeed, as medieval philosophy sought to retrieve a Hellenic tradition, it was also impelled to build upon it in undreamt ways, and Aquinas seemed destined to be its principal architect.[24] It proved to be the concept of a creator, and indeed a free creator—thus resolving the ambiguities attending the emanation scheme introduced by Plotinus and adopted by Islamic *falâsifâ*—which pushed Aquinas to exploit Aristotle's hints about language and to find in Aristotle's broad category of *equivocal* terms a proper subset whose ambiguity would be systematic: analogous expressions. Aquinas displayed the inner differentiation of such terms by the way he used them, notably, in his grand attempt to show that "Christian teaching" (*doctrina Christiana*) could qualify as a mode of knowing, a *scientia* (*epistēmē*), in Aristotle's terms.[25] Yet since knowledge, properly speaking, proceeds by demonstration—a point which Averroës repeatedly emphasized—Aquinas had to square the syllogistic requirement of univocity with the demand internal to a "knowledge of God" (*theologia*) that human discourse about the One (who must be both transcendent and immanent) can only be analogous.

In spite of these clear concerns, however, the sole systematic account of analogous usage in Aquinas is the passage entitled "on divine names,"[26] which Herbert McCabe translates "theological language" (in the Blackfriars edition of the *Summa*), as if to remind us to look here to find a discussion of these thorny semantic issues regarding analogous language and *scientia*. Aquinas' treatment turns, as we have seen, on the use to which he puts a standard semantic distinction between *res significata* and *modus significandi*, "thing signified" and "manner of signifying": inherently analogous terms like "just" do indeed signify the transcendent source of justice (as the *res significata* toward which they must point to be used properly), but as we use these terms, they cannot but signify it "imperfectly" since our manner of signifying will be tied to our experience. (If modern readers find anticipations of Kant in this treatment, they will be correct, but they should note that Aquinas also finds a way through the ceiling which Kant puts on transcendent use: one which—to my mind—turns on Aquinas' explicit avowal of a creator.) He makes other remarks about analogous usage throughout his works, to be sure, but numerous efforts to collate them into a systematic account show that it cannot be done.[27] In fact, the most enlightening of these invoke the Platonic notion of *participation*, which again reminds us of creation as the logical and metaphysical presupposition for attending properly to analogical usage. So it could be that Aquinas eschewed a systematic account, rather than omitting one, realizing that semantics alone can only show the *potential* for analogical use inherent to a certain class of expressions; something else must activate that use.[28] Gilson's observation that analogy for Aquinas was a matter of judgment and not of concepts was directed at the time against Cajetan's attempt to develop a systematic treatment of the issue in what Bernard Lonergan calls "conceptualist" terms, yet Gilson's perception continues to guide these reflections.[29]

The *judgment* to which Gilson alludes is that required to *discriminate thing signified* from *manner of signifying*, since we use terms which we might tend to treat as univocal descriptions of the matter at hand—analogous terms do not always show their inherent potential for inner differentiation on their face. According to Yves Simon, this judgment will discern which prime analogate is functioning in our usage, and so direct us beyond the mode of signifying endemic to our ordinary discourse.[30] There is more at stake here than the usual concern of philosophical theologians to avoid anthropomorphic language about the One, a concern epitomized in Maimonides; by insisting on the centrality of *judgment* in Aquinas' use of analogy, Gilson is rendering judgment on later Scholastics, notably Duns Scotus, who epitomized that penchant for univocity prominent in philosophers trained in syllogistic reasoning.[31] As Gilson notes, any attempt to show how "sacred doctrine" can become an Aristotelian mode of knowing (*theologia*) can easily be diverted from attending to the inherently analogous form of language which must characterize human discourse *in divinis*, precisely by the demands of the mode of knowing identified as *scientia*. Gilson was in fact gesturing toward the late medieval roots of "onto-theology."[32] That was, of course, the direction taken by Thomists in celebrating the "analogy of being," which undergirded the entire edifice of baroque theology that Karl Barth found it necessary to reject with his famous "nein." McInerny"s corrective— namely, that analogy as Aquinas used it was primarily a semantic rather than an ontological instrument—provided the impetus for a fresh approach to the issues, especially within the context of the "linguistic turn" in philosophy.[33] Yet the further considerations rendered possible by this fresh approach have alerted us to the ways in which Aquinas' concerns to establish "sacred doctrine" as *theologia*, that is, as a *scientia*, may have obscured the quality of judgment which his readers need to activate the inherently analogous character of the language he employs. In short, it is Aquinas' preoccupations with *scientia* that his texts tend to display most prominently, in their lapidary construction and the "systematic" (though never deductive) ordering of the topics. As a result, his peculiar transformations of standard philosophical terms or distinctions (like that of *res significata/ modus significandi*) are often left implicit, and contemporary analytic philosophers can display egregious misunderstandings when they simply try to read Aquinas' texts, for they have few overt clues to the presuppositions latent in his use of language.[34]

How, then, can we identify those presuppositions, and especially the ones latent in his use? I have so far focused on creation and "the distinction," but it turns out that every philosophical theologian will avow some form of each of these, although that avowal may have little effect on their mode of reflection, given that the philosophical resources available to contemporary thinkers make it difficult, if not impossible, to formulate a "cause of being."[35] What is at issue is the relation between creator and creation, already expressed in faith and practice as "the distinction," yet demanding a proper philosophical articulation. What seems to be required is a particular quality of *imagination,* to which Aquinas alludes in remarking that the images of the scriptures can direct our reason beyond its inherent limits to grasp something of its inherent orientation to its very source and goal. If we combine these orienting remarks of Aquinas with Gilson's observations about the discerning judgment needed to be alert to the analogical resources of language as well as to use them properly, we shall find ourselves on the track of his operative presuppositions. If all this sounds utterly bizarre, given Aquinas' own apparent inattention to the *imaginaire,* operative in his own use of language, we need only recall how concerned he was to validate "sacred doctrine" as a *scientia,* and so to establish *theologia,* properly speaking. Yet the fact remains, as many have shown, that a strong inner gyroscope kept him from falling into the inertial tendency of philosophers to univocal language. It is that inner gyroscope which I am attempting to identify and delineate. My suggestion is that we might do so by examining the directions in which two manifest successors took his work—Meister Eckhart and John of the Cross. Neither of them were preoccupied with establishing "sacred doctrine" as a form of knowledge, for Aquinas had already accomplished that. Meister Eckhart, I shall propose, extended Aquinas' philosophical theology in a less "systematic" fashion, which allowed him to underscore the unique quality of the relation between creator and creatures; while John of the Cross astutely extended Aquinas' transformations of Aristotle's epistemology to explore the peculiarities of faith as a mode of knowing, by focusing on its inner dynamics of presence and absence.

Meister Eckhart: Distinction as Nonduality

My contention here is quite straightforward: the apparently radical statements of Meister Eckhart regarding the relation between creator and creatures are simple workings out of Aquinas' transformation of Aristotelian *substance* in the face of a free creator. For if the creator must be identified philosophically as the "cause of being" of each thing which is—that is, of every substance—and if such a cause cannot be identified with any of Aristotle's four causes (which together purport to explain the being of each substance), then what Aristotle presumed to exist "in itself"—substance—must be said to exist "from another." Or, as Aquinas puts it, the very *esse* (existence, to-be) of a creature is *esse-ad* (existence toward, to be toward) its creator, so that what Aristotle presumed existed "in itself" actually exists in-relation-to its creator.[36] This will put incredible strains on Aristotle and our ordinary way of thinking about things, as the tradition testifies, yet the opening was already present in the maverick category of *relation*. Each of the rest of the nine categories besides *substance* can be identified with an accident of substance: what is said to be both "in and of" substance (*Categories* 2a–b). Yet relations are more properly "between" things, requiring (as Russell and Whitehead pointed out) a two-place predicate rather than the single predicate that articulates accidents, properly speaking: "Joan is a fast runner" versus "Joan won the race." The strains emerge whenever we overlook the difference between relations and accidents and are tempted to reduce relations to accidents. For then the radical dependency of substances on their creator, in such a way that being related to the creator is part of their very being, could be construed as making the entire universe an *accident* of divinity. That way of thinking leads, of course, to some form of pantheism. On the other hand, to try to resist that move by reasserting Aristotle's dictum that substances are what exist "in themselves" (and *not* in relation to anything else) is to render the creator just as separate from creatures as creatures are from themselves, and so to deny the pervasive dependency which creation entails.

There is a way through this impasse, however, which discerning readers should perceive immediately: namely, to recognize just how unique (and analogous) this category of *relation* can be, and to forbear assimilating it to an accidental predicate. Indeed, *relation* is a category so malleable that it offered a way for Christian theologians to formulate the "persons" in a triune God without prejudice to the ontological simpleness of divinity. As Aquinas summarized the achievement of the Cappadocians: Father, Son, and Holy Spirit cannot subsist separately, as Tom, Dick, and Harry do; their distinctness lies precisely in the way in which they relate one to another (the Father is not generated; the Son is), so they can be denoted "subsistent relations."[37] Kierkegaard picks up this thread in his celebrated definition of the self: "the self is spirit; but what is spirit? Spirit is a . . . relating [and] a relating completed when, relating itself to itself, it is grounded transparently in the power which constitutes it."[38] Thus the transcendence of the self is realized when its constituting link to the creator becomes transparent. Moreover, for Aquinas, "the coming forth of all of being from the universal cause, which is God,"[39] or alternatively, "the production of existence entire by the universal cause of all beings, which is God,"[40] is itself modeled on the intratrinitarian processions, since "the comings forth of the divine persons can be seen as types for the comings forth of creatures."[41] Hence, the relation relating creatures and creator will be *sui generis,* much like the relations within divinity, though that of creation will be free while those within God belong to divinity itself.

In a prescient example of the fruitfulness of comparative inquiry, Sara Grant has articulated this relation in terms reminiscent of Sankara's concept of *nonduality:* namely, as a nonreciprocal relation of dependence.[42] For as the cause of being, the creator cannot be an extrinsic cause of creatures, since their very to-be is to-be-in-relation to the creator. That is why Aquinas can say that to-be (*esse*) is "more intimately and profoundly interior to things than anything else,"[43] and that precisely this *esse* accounts for whatever similarity can be had between creator and creature. Indeed, created *esse* brings them so close that the nonreciprocal relation of dependence, which is participated being, can be likened to Sankara's notion of *nonduality:* the distinction cannot amount to a separation, for separated from their source, creatures would perish. Nor can God be pictured as one more being over against the universe, for as creator, God is the very source of being of all that is, and so cannot be assimilated to a being within (or over against) the universe. As the "beginning and end of all things," God is not one of those things, and hence not (in any ordinary sense) a *thing*. As Aquinas puts it, "God is not contained within the category of *substance*."[44] The metaphor which Aquinas used to articulate this *sui generis* relation was a Neoplatonic one: *participation*.[45] So Meister Eckhart's insistence that God alone exists, and that creatures have borrowed existence, can be read as parsing that metaphor. Moreover, Eckhart's contention that the existence whereby creatures exist must itself be "something divine" reflects the gnomic assertion of Aquinas that "while the measure of becoming is time, the measure of existence is eternity."[46] The present moment denotes the connection between temporal and eternal existence in that whatever is, is now; hence, the perspective of a creator as the cause of all-that-is existing and being what it is, allows the present moment to fulfill Plato's description of time as the "moving image of eternity."[47] Yet Aquinas' language remains so wedded to the paradigm of *scientia* borrowed from Aristotle that it takes the more evocative prose of a Meister Eckhart (or in our time, a Sara Grant) to underscore the uniqueness of this very relation by which all things have their being, and which relates each thing to its creator from within its very being-toward that One.

It has been claimed, however, that Eckhart's mode of expression presumes a univocal notion of *being* (or *esse*) and that this assumption makes him insist that creatures, in existing, have "something divine."[48] I respond rather that Eckhart realizes that no notion whatsoever can capture the reality of *esse* as it emanates from the One; thus the oppositions he represents between the nothingness of creatures and the plenitude of the creator can also be read as alerting us to the dialectical drama inherent in the use of all analogical expressions.[49]

A language born of "the distinction" must be able to evoke difference within similarity, for no other form of *similarity* can possibly attend creator and creature, as Maimonides rightly insisted. Rather than proposing something new, Eckhart, in my view, is reminding readers of Aquinas just what is at stake in accepting Aquinas' thoroughgoing analogical view of language. Or, considered another way, Eckhart is unpacking the crucial metaphor of *participation* to offer us a glimpse of its import. For he intends to follow Aquinas' insistence that the "proper effect of the first and most universal cause, which is God, is existence itself [*ipsum esse*]."[50] When we remind ourselves, however, that Aquinas' celebrated formula for God is *ipsum esse subsistens* (subsisting existence itself), and that the sole *similarity* linking creator with creatures attends creatures' very existing,[51] then we can be no more surprised to find Meister Eckhart insisting that this *esse* is "something divine" than we are that philosophers inattentive to the metaphysical centrality of creation or to analogical discourse find the entire notion baffling.[52] Yet it is equally true that those who avow *esse* and give it the pride of place in metaphysics are at a loss to identify it.[53] So one can hardly contend that there is a "Thomistic notion of *esse* which Eckhart contravenes" indeed, it would be more accurate to remind ourselves that the substance of this notion eludes even those who aver its centrality.[54] So it appears that Eckhart's language has underscored an element of Aquinas' own thought to which trusted commentators like Josef Pieper have taken pains to alert us: the "negative" or inherently mysterious dimension of some of his key notions—in this case, *esse*.[55] And, Pieper insists, such a perspective will attend any attempt to parse "the distinction," or to identify the creator-creature relation which Aquinas deems to constitute substance.

Since the *distinction* in question proves to be unlike any other, so does the *relation*. The best language we have for characterizing both, as I have suggested, turns out to be that of an Indian philosopher, Sankara: the language of *advaita* or "nonduality." My authority here is Sara Grant, whose Teape lectures succeed in unveiling this dimension of Aquinas by reading him after extended absorption in the thought of Sankara. Bradley Malkovsky defines *advaita* for western readers as follows: "non-duality always refers to the unity of all being in the One. The world in all its multiplicity is never 'outside' or external to its infinite simple Source nor can the two be added up as if they were entities in a series. The world exists by participation in the supremely Real, so that it may be said that while the two—the world and its Source—are distinct they are not realities set apart."[56] In Aquinas' terms, if the *to-be* (*esse*) of each creature is in fact an *esse-ad* (*creatorem*), since creation is *in* each creature not as a feature but as a *relation*,[57] then Aristotle's characterization of *substance* as "what subsists in itself" is radically relativized. Whatever *subsists* (other than the source of being, God) does so as gifted with existing (*esse*, to-be). Hence, no creature "exists of itself"—or, as Eckhart loved to put it, "whatever is, in itself is *nothing.*"

There is no gainsaying this implication once one has yoked biblical or Qur'anic revelation to Hellenic philosophy to arrive at a "cause of being"—something toward which Plato gestured, but which found no place in Aristotle, nor would such a cause fit in Aristotle's taxonomy of causes. Yet most varieties of "Christian philosophy," and most notably "Thomism," have succeeded in avoiding this implication for centuries, spooked as they were by the specter of "pantheism" or "monism." Perhaps it is the lot of our generation, chastened by the horrors of two centuries intoxicated by "autonomy," to be reminded of the need to find a way to give constructive articulation to this elusive yet constitutive *distinction* of all-that-is from its transcendent source. And when we try to do so, to explicate not merely what it is to be something of a kind (Aristotle), but what it is for things of such a kind to *be*, as creatures, we find that nothing can be unless it is internally related to what causes it to be. Yet that relation cannot be a feature of the thing, since without it there would be no such thing; rather, the being of each thing is such that it reflects its source, from which it cannot be separated under pain of annihilation.[58] So in itself it is nothing! "Nonduality" is the paradoxical term invented to articulate this constituting relation whereby each thing's *to-be* (*esse*) is a *to-be-toward* (*esse ad*). But to keep on saying this is a lot like going around in circles, as dervishes do, so astute composers like Meister Eckhart and John of the Cross have recourse to figures of speech: Eckhart to a preacher's paranetic use of contrasting images, John to a poetic allusion. As Robert Sokolowski states, "in [this] distinction God is understood as 'being' God entirely apart from any relation of otherness to the world or to the whole. . . . No distinction made within the horizon of the world is like this, and therefore the act of creation cannot be understood in terms of any action or any relationship that exists in the world."[59]

John of the Cross: Faith as a Journey to Union

John of the Cross, in comparison to Meister Eckhart, employs a more poetic idiom to describe and analyze the intentional journey of a person of faith to this One who is the source of anyone's existence. John is disarmingly forthright in identifying the goal of that journey—"the union and transformation of the [person] in God" (*Ascent to Mount Carmel* 2.5.3)—as well as the means: "faith alone, which is the only proximate and proportionate means to union with God" (2.9.1).[60] He is at pains to distinguish this intentional union from the "union between God and creatures [which] always exists [by which] God sustains every soul and dwells in it substantially. . . . By it He conserves their being so that if the union would end they would immediately be annihilated and cease to exist" (2.5.3). So John assumes the unique metaphysical relation of all creatures to their source that Meister Eckhart elaborates from Aquinas' "distinction," and does not hesitate to call it a *union*—indeed, an "essential or substantial union." This grounding fact attends all creatures, hence it is *natural* and found in everything (though it is displayed differently in animate and inanimate beings, and among animate beings it differs from animals to humans; yet among humans it can still be found in "the greatest sinner in the world"). In contrast, the intentional union is *supernatural* and can only be found "where there is a likeness of love [such that] God's will and the [person's] are in conformity" (2.5.3). As we shall see, what eliminates any prospect of "heteronomy" between those two wills is precisely this "nonreciprocal relation of dependence," which attends all creatures.

Consider first the internal connection between *faith* and *union* that John confidently asserts. What makes this sound so startling is our propensity to confine such talk to "mystics," while reducing faith to belief, that is, holding certain propositions to be true. This is a long and complex debate in Christian theology, which often cuts oddly across denominational lines. The best we can do here is to remind ourselves that John of the Cross could well have been responding, from the Iberian peninsula, to the religious upheavals of sixteenth-century northern Europe. He does so by elaborating some key assertions of Aquinas in order to cut through the debates that polarized intellect and will in the act of faith. First, according to Aquinas: "Faith is a sort of knowledge [*cognitio quaedam*] in that it makes the mind assent to something. The assent is not due to what is seen by the believer but to what is seen by him who is believed."[61] The one who is believed is, of course, the Word of God incarnate, Jesus, as mediated through the scriptures, so this peculiar "sort of knowledge" is rooted in an interpersonal relation of the believer with Jesus. That relation, at the root of faith, is what John of the Cross sets out to explore, quite aware that what results from it will "fall short of the mode of knowing [*cognitio*] which is properly called 'knowledge' [*scientia*], for such knowledge causes the mind to assent through what is seen and through an understanding of first principles."[62]

More positively, Aquinas characterizes faith as an "act of mental assent commanded by the will, [so] to believe perfectly our mind must tend unfailingly towards the perfection of truth, in unfailing service of that ultimate goal for the sake of which our will is commanding our mind's assent."[63] Unlike ordinary belief, then, faith must be an act of the whole person, involving a personal and critical quest for a truth which outreaches our proper expression. John focuses critically on our concepts: "nothing which could possibly be imagined or comprehended in this life can be a proximate means of union with God" (2.8.4), since "nothing created or imagined can serve the intellect as a proper means for union with God; [indeed], all that can be grasped by the intellect would serve as an obstacle rather than a means, if a person were to become attached to it" (2.8.1). So, following Aquinas, we must be able to let our concepts "lead us on by the hand" (*manuductio*), as John does, to a goal which transcends them. That goal, we recall, is "union and transformation of the [person] in God," and it is already intimated in the sort of *faith* of which Aquinas and John are speaking. As Augustine had already worked out, Christian faith differs from ordinary belief in being a response to an utterly gratuitous invitation, which could never be initiated by persons themselves. This treatment of faith and union anticipates the critiques of both Freud and Marx, while leaving room for both. For if Freud would reduce religious faith to projections, Aquinas would insist that "faith that does not rely on divine truth can fail and believe falsehood."[64] Yet if we regard John of the Cross as developing Aquinas' lapidary exposition of faith, then authentic faith always involves a journey of responding rather than initiating, with intermediate projections being submitted to a searing critique. And John's forthright insistence on *union* responds to Marx's characterization of Christian faith as alienating human beings from their authentic life and work by offering a distracting "heavenly reward," since the union of which John speaks begins now. Yet Marx's account may well address a Christian ethos quite innocent of the tradition, which John articulates, of an internal critique that John's account of faith demands. Indeed, the demands of the journey of faith that John outlines are utterly rigorous: "we shall explain how in order to journey to God the intellect must be perfected in the darkness of faith, the memory in the emptiness of hope, and the will in the nakedness and absence of every affection [unrelated to the goal of union]" (2.6.1).

A poetic characterization of that intentional union is offered in the first stanza of John's "Living Flame of Love":

O living flame of love
That tenderly wounds my soul
In its deepest center! Since
Now You are not oppressive,
Now Consummate! If it be your will:
Tear through the veil of this sweet encounter!

John's commentary begins:

The soul now feels that it is all inflamed in the divine union, . . . and that in the most intimate part of its substance it is flooded with no less than rivers of glory, abounding in delights, and that from its bosom flow rivers of living waters [John 7:38], which the Son of God declared will rise up in such souls. Accordingly it seems, because it is so vigorously transformed in God, so sublimely possessed by Him, and arrayed with such rich gifts and virtues, that it is singularly close to beatitude—so close that only a thin veil separates it (579). . . . This flame of love is the Spirit of the Bridegroom, which is the Holy Spirit. . . . Such is the activity of the Holy Spirit in the soul transformed in love: the interior acts He produces shoot up flames for they are acts of inflamed love, in which the will of the soul united with that flame, made one with it, loves most sublimely. . . . Thus in this state the soul cannot make acts because the Holy Spirit makes them all and moves it towards them. As a result all the acts of the soul are divine, since the movement toward these acts and their execution stems from God. Hence it seems to a person that every time this flame shoots up, making him love with delight and divine quality, it is giving him eternal life, since it raises him up to the activity of God in God. (580–81)

There is no hint of "heteronomy" here, I suggest, because John assumes the unique metaphysical relation of person ("soul") to its source that Meister Eckhart develops from Aquinas.

Epilogue

Do these developments of Meister Eckhart and of John of the Cross represent monism? Or pantheism? Or do they represent valiant efforts to articulate the crucial distinction of creator/creature, one that is *sui generis* because the creator cannot be another item in the universe, but is its ever-present source and goal? Once a creator has been introduced into the Hellenic philosophical schemes, we will have great difficulty using inherited categories, tailored (we now realize) to creatures, to articulate this founding relation to a creator. So what can we do? We cannot simply adopt Wittgenstein's famous *caveat* at the end of the *Tractatus*— "that whereof one cannot speak one must remain silent." We must rather follow his example and look carefully at the bizarre forms of language which this *distinction* elicits. Negatively, that will mean a constant endeavor to correct "crude and false pictures" of the relation. Positively, one might offer a poetic path—like John of the Cross or Dante, if one had the talent. For those of us who do not, however, and who can only admire from afar as (at best) critics rather than poets, we can at least allow ourselves to be carried on by the power of language whose analogical potential has been unleashed to unveil that toward which it points. The veil is an image as dear to Sufi thinkers as to John of the Cross—indeed, his axial use of this image offers one more indication of Islamic influence. What do we veil, for such thinkers, and why do we veil it? We veil what entices us, and do so precisely that it may entice us the more; the secret of gender relations in Islamic society! Where the West sees oppression, the East sees its opposite as exploitation—who is right? What is at issue, of course, is *eros:* truth or reality (*al-haqq*) in its appealing aspect as "the good," together with the stubborn fact that human beings can only approach this reality as at once present and absent. That is what the analogous reaches of language open us up to, and why not? For once we have been introduced to a free creator, should not *poiēsis* (with its ac-companying practical reason) outstrip speculative reason as the highest way in which creatures can emulate the creator? The traditional hierarchy, articulated by "philosophers" or those adept at conceptual inquiry, regards poetry and its at-tendant imagination as an inferior stepping-stone to knowledge. But should not the centrality of creation transform what we mean by knowledge into a creativity imitative of the creator's agency, hoping thereby to unveil something of that con-stituting relation of nonduality? Conceptual play remains, of course, as the image of unveiling reminds us of the inevitable place of *presence* and *absence* on the path of coming-to-know what surpasses our capacity for proper expression. Indeed, that is how the play goes on.

Should one infer, however, that granting such valence to creative language and to imagination rules out philosophical discourse, one would be misled by the force of my language in trying to dislodge a particular hierarchical view of discourse. What these reflections should remind us, however, is just how crucial is an ear for analogical discourse: especially in matters divine, of course, but also in assessing human goals and attainments. Yet univocity seems to emerge as the default position for philosophy and philosophers. This penchant for the univocal on the part of philosophers should hardly be surprising, of course, since philo-sophical inquiry intends to proceed by *argument,* and arguments demand univo-cal terms if they are to proceed. There is nothing novel here; that has been a clear requirement from the time of Plato and Aristotle, and it was underscored by the medievals.[65] Yet a closer look at the way philosophers actually proceed finds them employing modes of argumentation that defy any simple classification: "argu-ment" itself turns out to be analogous. If that be the case, then one is tempted to indict philosophers who scorn analogy with lack of imagination for alternative ways of proceeding—an indictment they would surely share with all too many academics in any settled discipline. In a more constructive spirit, however, we should eschew indictments of any sort, while keeping *imagination* in mind. For

I have been counting on a sensitivity to diverse uses of language which normally presupposes the kind of training in imagination that can be found in liturgical forms of worship or cognate "spiritual exercises."[66] Moreover, as Hans Frei reminds us, it will not do simply to read the scriptures, outside such liturgical contexts, if we are otherwise infected with an empiricist mindset that must keep the past *past*, so making us unable to appreciate the way Passover or Holy Week liturgies can portray scripture as "realistic narrative," precisely by "making it present."[67]

Alongside these requisite practices, however, appreciation of the analogous richness of language turns out to require some metaphysical commitments as well, though these need not precede the practices. In fact, they are often concomitant, as we can appreciate in a paradigmatic medieval thinker like Thomas Aquinas, and find emerging as a moment of revelation for our contemporaries who have been introduced to metaphysics devoid of any practices except a straightened form of "argument." So the direction of these reflections begins to emerge: metaphysics proceeds at its own peril without attention to analogous uses of language, yet philosophers have a predilection for univocity unless suitably shaken from their default mode. Who or what can do that? Nothing so much as the prospect of a free creator, as tradition testifies. But acknowledging a free creator cannot be a mere conclusion of metaphysics. Something more is required: something akin to practices of a faith community. Moreover, when examined more closely, these practices body forth language so as to display its "inner differentiation," that is, ways in which terms come to reveal their inherently transcendent reach. The practices, then, at once presuppose as well as prepare us to acknowledge a "metaphysics of participation," according to which the universe in which we quite naturally live becomes de-centered in such a way as to become a created world. In this way, "spiritual exercises" become part of metaphysics, just as this metaphysics of participation authenticates those exercises. Thus, language use and metaphysics interpenetrate, as philosophers from Aristotle to Wittgenstein have insisted and as nearly every philosopher endorses, though often unwittingly. And the intentional link between them will be reflected in a "form of life" embodying a characteristic set of practices, which serve to make the thinkers themselves aware of that connection.

The form of argument which can be most revelatory of the cogency of the "positions" we claim to hold will not be apodeictic in nature but rather will be one that shows inconsistencies between our characteristic practice and what we assert to be the case.[68] For standard forms of argumentation that we credit as apodeictic will perforce adopt the presuppositions of the framework in which we are accustomed to operate, whereas laying bare the connections of those frameworks with practices can display them as a domain into which we may or may not wish to enter. Discussions of *justice,* for example, which presuppose the parameters of a liberal society, can either be taken as setting the terms for philosophical debate on matters of justice, or used to remind people that there are other ways to frame the questions involved. Such reminders will only emerge, however, as one traces the way in which the arguments presuppose characteristic practices, and then goes on to expose how those practices themselves may offend against justice.[69] Such critiques can reveal how terms like "justice" must be analogous in order to function properly in moral argument, thus expanding the very notion of *argument* itself. For a purely conceptual form of argumentation would have to ask how we could recognize such practices to be unjust, and would only be able to answer that question in terms of prior conceptions, inviting one to ask where those conceptions came from; whereas arguments designed to reveal the inner connection between practices and conceptions can show us how those conceptions are internally linked to practices, and so introduce one to specifically ethical argumentation. Perceptive readers will detect an indebtedness to Alasdair MacIntyre here.[70] By this exploration into the internal connections among creation, analogy, and theological language, I hope to have carried the argument a step further, to show how the discourse proper to metaphysics presupposes practices as well, signaling my indebtedness throughout to Pierre Hadot.[71]

It should be superfluous to add that the examples—Meister Eckhart and John of the Cross—chosen to illustrate an "underground" legacy of Aquinas have been just that—exemplary. Others could well be chosen, including examples from later centuries. Kierkegaard and Blondel would be useful candidates. What such thinkers illustrate is a style of argumentation which is self-involving and which directs inquirers into inevitably analogous uses of language to express their conclusions.

Notes

1. For a recent example, see John Jenkins, *Knowledge and Faith in Thomas Aquinas* (Cambridge: Cambridge University Press, 1997).

2. *Metaphysics* 4.2; Aquinas, *In Duodecim Libros Metaphysicorum Aristotelis* (Rome: Marietti, 1950), Liber IV, lectio iv [534–39].

3. *ST* I.13.2c.

4. Wayne Hankey's masterful study, *God in Himself* (Oxford: Oxford University Press, 1987), details the contribution of Dionysius to Aquinas' doctrine of God.

5. Robert Sokolowski, *God of Faith and Reason* (Notre Dame, Ind.: University of Notre Dame Press, 1982; Washington, D.C.: Catholic University of America Press, 1995).

6. Josef Pieper, "The Negative Element in the Philosophy of St. Thomas," in *Silence of Saint Thomas* (New York: Pantheon, 1957), 47–67.

7. *ST* I.13.1 ad 2.

8. This is how I read Maimonides' celebrated "agnosticism"; unable to identify and exploit the analogical reaches of human language, he could only insist that "God's essential attributes . . . must not be like the attributes of other things and must not be comprised in the same definition." *The Guide of the Perplexed*, trans. Schlomo Pines (Chicago: University of Chicago Press, 1963), 1.56. Much of Aquinas' discussion has been shaped in response to Maimonides; see Avital Wohlman, *Thomas d'Aquin et Maimonide: Un dialogue exemplaire* (Paris: Cerf, 1988).

9. For a biased survey of such writing, see my "Creation, Metaphysics, and Ethics," *Faith and Philosophy* 18 (2001): 204–21.

10. *ST* I.12.13c.

11. Marie-Domenique Chenu, "Grammaire et théologie," in *La théologie au douzième siècle* (Paris: Vrin, 1957).

12. See Dominique Urvoy, *Ibn Rushd, Averroës*, trans. Olivia Stewart (New York: Routledge, 1991), 76–79, as well as the nuanced treatment of Roger Arnaldez in *Encyclopedia of Islam* (Leiden: Brill, 1999–), 3:912–14 [Ibn Rushd].

13. *ST* I.11.

14. For an account of this development which reads almost like a detective story, see Thomas Weinandy's *Does God Change? The Word's Becoming in the Incarnation* (Still River, Mass.: St. Bede's Publications, 1985).

15. See my *Knowing the Unknowable God* (Notre Dame, Ind.: University of Notre Dame Press, 1986).

16. See Alexander Broadie, "Maimonides and Aquinas on the Names of God," *Religious Studies* 23 (1987): 157–70.

17. *ST* I.32.1 ad 3.

18. Hankey, *God in Himself*; Edward Booth, *Aristotelian Aporetic Ontology in Islamic and Christian Thinkers* (Cambridge: Cambridge University Press, 1983). See my review of Booth in MIDEO [=*Mélanges Institut Dominicain d'Etudes Orientales*] (Cairo) 17 (1986): 235–38.

19. *Posterior Analytics* 2.1 89b23–25; Aquinas, *In Aristotelis Libros Posteriorum Analyticorum Expositio* (Rome: Marietti, 1955), Liber II, lectio 1 [408–10].

20. See my "Essence and Existence: Avicenna and Greek Philosophy," MIDEO (Cairo) 17 (1986): 53–66.

21. See Booth, *Aristotelian Aporetic Ontology*, for a detailed perusal of commentators.

22. *ST* I.2, prol.

23. For a careful treatment of these issues, see Harm Goris, *Free Creatures of an Eternal God* (Leuven: Peeters, 1996). For an attack on "onto-theology," see Jean-Luc Marion, *God without Being* (Chicago: University of Chicago Press, 1991), complemented by his "Saint Thomas d'Aquin et l'onto-théo-logie," *Revue Thomiste* 95 (1995): 31–66.

24. On Aquinas' unique placement in this regard, see Booth, *Aristotelian Aporetic Ontology*, and Hankey, *God in Himself*, as well as my *Knowing the Unknowable God*.

25. See Jenkins, *Knowledge and Faith in Thomas Aquinas*.

26. *ST* I.13.

27. See James Ross, *Portraying Analogy* (Cambridge: Cambridge University Press, 1981), and my review in *New Scholasticism* 59 (1985): 347–57.

28. I am indebted here to John Milbank, whose treatment of these issues in "Intensities," *Modern Theology* 15 (1999): 445–97, suggests ways in which my earlier theses about the semantics of analogy needed to be bolstered, esp. n. 104.

29. Étienne Gilson, *History of Christian Philosophy in the Middle Ages* (New York: Scribners, 1955), 105–7, and *Jean Duns Scot* (Paris: J. Vrin, 1952), 101. Bernard Lonergan's battle against "conceptualism" is legendary: see his *Insight* (New York: Philosophical Library, 1958), passim.

30. Yves Simon, "On Order in Analogical Sets," *New Scholasticism* 34 (1960): 1–42; reprinted in *Philosopher at Work*, ed. Anthony Simon (Lanham, Md.: Rowan and Littlefield, 1999), 135–71.

31. See Gilson, *Jean Duns Scot*, and also Eric Alliez, *Capital Times*, trans. G. van den Abbeele (Minneapolis: University of Minnesota Press, 1996).

32. See John Milbank's provocative essay, "Only Theology Overcomes Metaphysics," in his *The Word Made Strange* (Oxford: Blackwell, 1997), 36–52.

33. Ralph McInerny's initial study, *The Logic of Analogy* (The Hague: Martinus Nijhoff, 1961), has now been crowned with his latest reflections: *Aquinas and Analogy* (Washington, D.C.: Catholic University of America Press, 1997). See my attempt at a formulation in *Analogy and Philosophical Language* (New Haven, Conn.: Yale University Press, 1973). Nicholas Lash develops this line of reflection admirably in his "Ideology, Metaphor and Analogy," in *The Philosophical Frontiers of Christian Theology: Essays Presented to D. M. McKinnon*, ed. Brian Hebblethwaite and Stewart Sutherland (Cambridge: Cambridge University Press, 1982), 68–94.

34. A notable example is Christopher Hughes, *On a Complex Theory of a Simple God: An Investigation in Aquinas' Philosophical Theology* (Ithaca, N.Y.: Cornell University Press, 1989).

35. See my "Creation, Metaphysics, and Ethics."

36. *ST* I.45.3.

37. *ST* I.30.2.

38. Søren Kierkegaard, *Sickness unto Death*, trans. Alastair Hannay (New York: Penguin, 1989), 43.

39. *ST* I.45.1c.

40. *ST* I.45.3c.

41. *ST* I.45.6c.

42. Sara Grant, R. S. C. J., *Towards an Alternative Theology: Confessions of a Nondualist Christian* (Bangalore: Asian Trading Corp., 1991).

43. *ST* I.8.1c.

44. *ST* I.3.5 ad 1.

45. For a sterling treatment of this topic, see Rudi te Velde, *Participation and Substantiality in Thomas Aquinas* (Leiden: Brill, 1995); see my review in *International Philosophical Quarterly* 37 (1997): 101–4.

46. *ST* I.10.4c.

47. *Timaeus* 37d.

48. See Vladimir Lossky, *Théologie négative et connaissance de Dieu chez Maître Eckhart* (Paris: J. Vrin, 1973), 25, 297–98.

49. See *ibid.*, 73–75; Bernard McGinn, ed., *Meister Eckhart: Teacher and Preacher* (New York: Paulist, 1986), introduction, esp. 26.

50. *ST* I.45.5c.

51. *ST* I.13.5c.

52. Peter Van Inwagen, "Meta-Ontology," *Erkenntnis* 48 (1998): 233–50.

53. See the seminal study of Joseph de Finance, *Être et agir dans la philosophie de Saint Thomas* (Rome: Gregorian University Press, 1960).

54. Herein lies the sole weakness of Lossky's magisterial rendering of Eckhart's thought in relation to Aquinas. He assumes something called "Thomism," which faithfully transmits

Aquinas to us, and contrasts Eckhart's developments with those of that "tradition," whereas I can just as easily (and I believe more fruitfully) use his work to show the opposite: that Eckhart's very paradoxical formulations often better extend and interpret the thought of Aquinas than the "tradition" which has adopted his name and claimed his legacy.

55. Pieper, *Silence of Saint Thomas.*

56. Introduction by Bradley Malkovsky, in Sara Grant, R. S. C. J., *Toward an Alternative Theology: Confessions of a Non-dualist Christian* (Notre Dame, Ind.: University of Notre Dame Press, 2002), xvi.

57. *ST* I.45.3c.

58. When Aquinas asks, under the rubric of God's perfection, whether "creatures can be said to resemble God," just after demonstrating that the God whom Jews, Christians, and Muslims worship must be ontologically simple and so utterly unlike anything else (*ST* I.3), he responds by invoking the axiom that effects resemble their agent; yet he recalls that this agent— "the all-embracing cause of existence entire" (*causa universalis totius esse*) (*ST* I.45.2c)—cannot share a form with its effect, yet "will present the sort of analogy that holds between all things because they have existence [*esse*] in common. So this is how things receiving existence from God resemble God; for precisely as things possessing existence they resemble the primary and universal source of all existence" (*ST* I.4.3c).

59. Sokolowski, *God of Faith and Reason,* 32–33.

60. *The Collected Works of John of the Cross,* trans. Kieran Kavanaugh, O. C. D., and Otilio Rodriquez, O. C. D. (Washington, D.C.: Institute of Carmelite Studies, 1970). References to each work will be by part, section, and paragraph, e.g., 2.4.6.

61. *ST* I.12.13 ad 3.

62. Ibid.

63. *ST* II-II.4.5c.

64. Ibid.

65. See I. M. Bochenski, "On Analogy," *The Thomist* 11 (1948): 424–47; reprinted and corrected in *Logico-Philosophical Studies,* ed. A. Menne (Dordrecht: D. Reidel Publishing Co., 1962).

66. See Catherine Pickstock, *After Writing: On the Liturgical Consummation of Philosophy* (Oxford: Blackwell, 1998), and Pierre Hadot, *Exercices spirituelles et philosophie antique* (Paris: Institut d'Études Augustiniennes, 1993), whose essays are translated by Arnold Davidson, *Philosophy as a Way of Life* (Oxford: Blackwell, 1995).

67. Hans Frei, *The Eclipse of Biblical Narrative* (New Haven, Conn.: Yale University Press, 1975).

68. See my "Convictions and Operative Warrant," in Stanley Hauerwas, Nancey Murphy, and Mark Nation, eds., *Theology without Foundations* (Nashville, Tenn.: Abingdon Press, 1994), 43–48.

69. This has consistently been the thesis of my longtime colleague and friend, Stanley Hauerwas, whose favorite target has been John Rawls' way of approaching questions of justice, and the manner in which that has set the tone for subsequent discussion, precisely by obscuring the operative presuppositions.

70. Alasdair MacIntyre, *Three Rival Versions of Moral Enquiry* (Notre Dame, Ind.: University of Notre Dame Press, 1990).

71. See Hadot, *Exercices spirituelles et philosophie antique,* and his summary, *Qu'est-ce que la philosophie?* (Paris: Gallimard, 1995).

Five

Divine Foreknowledge, Providence, Predestination, and Human Freedom

HARM GORIS

Aquinas maintains that divine foreknowledge, providence, and predestination are compatible with creaturely contingency and freedom. He does so throughout his career and in many of his texts, from the early commentary on Peter Lombard's *Sentences*, written in the mid-1250s, to his letter to the abbot of Monte Cassino, written around mid-February 1274, about three weeks before he died.[1] It is, however, less clear how exactly Aquinas argues for that compatibility, and whether his arguments are cogent.

The first question, how to interpret Aquinas' texts, was one of the points over which a fierce debate arose among Catholic theologians around the end of the sixteenth century, known as the *De Auxiliis* controversy. The theological issue at stake was the coherence of God's foreknowledge, predestination, the efficacy of grace, and human freedom. In this debate, each of the two rival parties claimed that its position was supported by Aquinas, who had been proclaimed Doctor of the Church by Pope Pius V in 1567. But both parties also assumed that Aquinas had not fully explicated his view, and they sought to supplement the Thomistic doctrine. The Dominican party, led by Domingo Báñez, introduced the notion of "physical premotion" (*praemotio physica*). According to the Dominican theory, God has predetermined the eternal decrees of his will to concur in an irresistibly efficacious way with the activities of creatures in time, even when they act freely. Their major adversaries were the Jesuits Luis de Molina and Francesco Suárez, who saw in "physical premotion" a denial of human freedom. As an alternative, they developed the theory of the *scientia media,* the contingent knowledge God has of what a possible creature would actually choose, given any possible set of circumstances. The controversy came officially to an end in 1607, when the pope intervened. Both parties were directed not to charge each other with heresy—either Calvinism or (semi-) Pelagianism—and to submit all writings on the subject to the Inquisition prior to publication. The Holy See would promulgate its decision in the matter at an opportune moment—which, apparently, is still pending.[2] Although officially the dispute was left undecided, the Dominican Bañezians emerged victorious, in the sense that their theory became generally recognized as the Thomistic doctrine.

From the 1960s on, analytical philosophers of religion have regained interest in the classical question of whether and how God's foreknowledge and providence are compatible with human freedom. While the Molinist theory of the *scientia media,* or middle knowledge, features prominently in this present-day debate, Aquinas' views have received relatively little attention.[3] It seems that the predominance of the Bañezian interpretation, with its deterministic implications in particular, is the major reason for this neglect.

Only in recent times have some begun to question the identification of the Bañezian theory with Aquinas' own view. Apart from the systematic problem of determinism, it has been pointed out that the expression *praemotio* (or *praedeterminatio*) *physica* does not appear in Aquinas' texts at all. Moreover, if God's will and causality suffice to account for the certainty of God's foreknowledge, then the argument that Aquinas usually offers, namely, that God foreknows because all of time is present to his eternity, becomes superfluous.[4] Finally, it has been argued that Bañez's theory does not do justice to God's transcendence because it suggests that God is merely the first element of a physical chain of movement.[5]

In order to get a better grasp of Aquinas' own views, I first present some elements from his discussions on theological language. An analysis of the terms "foreknowledge," "providence," and "predestination" make it clear that Aquinas distinguishes two different problems when it comes to the compatibility of divine agency with contingency in the world. One problem has to do with the diachronic relation of foreknowledge and future contingents, and the other with the synchronic relation of a necessary cause and its effect.

Divine Names

Aquinas does not aim at constructing a watertight, logically deducible theological system from scratch. He analyzes and reflects on what has been given to him:

the Catholic faith and its religious language, as it is used and handed down by Scripture and the Church. As a theology professor, he wants to gain, and pass on, insight into the mysteries of faith, show the noncontradictory coherence of the *nexus mysteriorum*, and explore the limits and possibilities of our understanding *in divinis*. In this life, we cannot understand what God is (*quid Deus sit*), and hence, all the words we use for God ("divine names") are radically imperfect. No one concept or name captures and represents adequately the mystery of God. In Aquinas' view, all divine names refer to the one, simple divine reality, but this does not mean that they are synonymous. For the conceptual content that each name expresses differs, giving us only a partial, limited, and opaque inkling of the mystery of divine perfection. Each name leaves God's being, or wisdom, or knowledge as "not comprehended and exceeding the signification of the name."[6] This basic insight permeates the whole of Aquinas' theological enterprise. He is always very aware of the limits and radical imperfection of our language and understanding *in divinis*, but he also insists that this does not prevent us from speaking both properly and truly of God.[7]

In analyzing the semantics of divine names, Aquinas uses several methods of classification. One is the distinction between (relative) names that signify immanent acts and those that signify transitive acts. Logically, immanent acts do not require at the same time the real existence of the objects; a person may be said to know or will things that exist only intentionally. On the other hand, the grammar of transitive acts like "causing," "creating," or "justifying" does imply the real existence of the external effect. When used *in divinis*, this distinction coincides with divine names that are predicated of God "from eternity" (*ab aeterno*) and those that apply to him in time (*ex tempore*).[8] "Creating" and "causing" belong to the latter. Furthermore, Aquinas points out that we should not think of God's causation as the setting in motion of a chronologically successive series of events that, after some time, results in a final effect. We should speak of God's causation as instantaneous: at the very moment God causes something, it is.[9] This explains why we can say that God knows from eternity what will happen tomorrow, but not that he creates from eternity tomorrow's events. Aquinas would consider "eternal causation" to be a misnomer. Again, this does not imply any real distinction or change in God. God's acts of knowing and willing do not differ in reality from his act of being, nor does he create or govern by any supervenient act(s).[10] The distinctions are merely conceptual. They come from the inability of our language and understanding to capture fully God's perfect being and activity. Saying that God "knows" or "wills" does not yet express the fact that God communicates being to the object known or willed, so that it exists in its own right. For that, we need other verbs, like "to create" or "to cause."

Strictly speaking, "willing" belongs to the names that signify immanent acts and that are said of God from eternity. But Aquinas acknowledges that, in practice, theological language is not that rigid. He states that, unlike the term "knowing," the term "willing" also has the connotation of causality.[11] For it expresses the fact that God's acting *ad extra* is free, is directed to the good, and does not imply any real change in God. Therefore, it can be used for signifying God's efficient causation of creatures in time.[12] In a discussion on God's will, Aquinas distinguishes between the intentional and the external object of the will:

> The will has a twofold relation to what is willed. First, insofar as it is willed; secondly, insofar as it is to be actually produced by the will. And the latter presupposes the first relation. For we understand first that the will wills something; next, from the fact that it wills it, we understand that it produces the thing in reality, if the will is efficacious.[13]

Aquinas further points out that, when considered as (intentionally) willed, the object of God's will is not necessary. For God is free to choose. But when God's will is regarded as the cause of the object, then the object exists necessarily, for nothing can thwart divine causation:

> For the first relation of divine will to what is willed is not necessary in an absolute sense, because of the lack of proportion of what is willed to its end. . . . But the second relation is necessary because of the efficacy of divine will; and therefore it follows necessarily, if God wills something by the will of pleasure, that it happens.[14]

It is the second relation that is relevant to the question of determinism: God's will as cause *ad extra* of created reality, and, hence, signified as a transitive act in time.

The terms "providence" and "predestination" express God's plan to lead creatures to their end. In the case of "providence," it is the ordering of all beings to their end in general. "Predestination," on the other hand, is a particular part of providence. It concerns specifically the ordering of rational creatures to a supernatural end, which they cannot reach by their own, natural powers: the beatific vision of God himself. Because "providence" and "predestination" signify intellectual planning and intention, they belong to both God's knowledge and his will.[15] Usually Aquinas classifies "providence" and "predestination" as immanent acts from eternity, and distinguishes them from their transitive counterparts in time. "Governance" (*gubernatio*) signifies the execution of providence, while "justification by grace" and "glorification" signify the effects of predestination in time.[16]

But, as we shall see below, when it comes to the problem of determinism, Aquinas also takes into account the determinism that seems to follow from the causal aspect of God's will, that is, from "providence" and "predestination" taken as transitive acts and as causes of what happens in time.

Another important element in mapping out the logic of the divine names "foreknowledge," "providence," and "predestination" concerns the prefix "*prae*." Augustine, Boethius, and Anselm had argued that because God is timeless, he does not really have foreknowledge or foresight (*praevidentia*). Aquinas agrees that God is outside of time, but in his view this does not render the use of "*prae*" false or improper. For it is we temporal beings who speak about God, and the things that we say God foreknows or predetermines are future for us.[17] That is why the terms "foreknowledge," "providence," and "predestination" can be used properly, and only with regard to the future.[18]

In discussing the question of how foreknowledge, providence, and predestination can have contingent things or events as their objects, Aquinas distinguishes two problems. One has to do with the relation of knowledge to future contingencies, and the other with the relation of a necessary cause to contingent effects. When Aquinas discusses the problem of foreknowledge for the first time in the commentary on the *Sentences*, he writes:

> For contingencies seem to elude divine knowledge for two reasons: Firstly, because of the order of cause to what is caused. For the effect of a necessary and immutable cause seems to be necessary; therefore, as God's knowledge is the cause of things and as it is immutable, it does not seem that it can be of contingencies. Secondly, because of the order of knowledge to what is known; for, as knowledge is certain cognition, it requires from the notion of certainty, even if causality is excluded, certainty and determination in what is known, and contingency excludes this; that knowledge, because of its certainty, requires a determination in what is known, is clear in our knowledge, which is not the cause of things, and in God's knowledge with regard to evil things.[19]

The reference at the end of this quotation to human knowledge and to God's noncausal knowledge of evil specifies again that the concept of "knowledge" by itself does not include causality. According to Aquinas, it poses its own kind of problem. This is why he usually separates the discussions of the two problems. The problem of causality is dealt with under the heading of God's will, and the problem of knowledge is discussed within the context of divine knowledge. Since the notions of "providence" and "predestination" imply both God's knowledge and causal will, they combine the two problems.[20]

What exactly are the two problems? The text from the commentary on the *Sentences,* quoted above, states that the notions of "knowledge" (or "certain, non-conjectural cognition") and of "necessary cause" each require a determination or certainty of their objects which is excluded by the notion of "contingency." In another text, while discussing the certainty of predestination, Aquinas distinguishes the two kinds of determination as follows:

> There is a twofold certainty: one of cognition, and the other of order. There is certainty of cognition when cognition does not deviate in any way from what is found in reality, but judges in such a way about reality as it is. Because a certain judgement is held about things especially through their cause, the noun "certainty" has been transferred to the order of a cause to its effect. Consequently, the order of the cause to its effect is said to be certain when the cause produces the effect infallibly.[21]

Elsewhere Aquinas explains that it is not the contingent as such, but the contingent insofar as it is future and not present or past, that lacks the determination or certainty which knowledge requires.[22]

An example may clarify the distinction between the two problems. Let us take "I shall have waffles for breakfast tomorrow" as a neutral phrase that can be the object of different acts. First, consider it as an object of knowledge. What I am having for breakfast in general is contingent; it depends on my choice. But when it comes to particular events, there is a difference between, on the one hand, past and present and, on the other, the future. My choice for yesterday's breakfast was contingent, but precisely because it is now past, it is determinate and is expressed by the true statement "I had waffles for breakfast yesterday." Therefore, it is possible for someone to know that I had waffles for breakfast yesterday. This is not the case with my choice for waffles tomorrow. That event is not determinate. I may be inclined now to take a cheese omelette tomorrow, but between now and tomorrow morning I may change my mind (or I may even die). What (or even, if) I shall choose tomorrow is not determinate. Consequently, the statement "I shall have waffles for breakfast tomorrow" cannot be said to be either true or false. Therefore, it cannot be the object of knowledge, for knowledge is, by definition, of what is true.

Next, consider the same phrase as an object of will. In this case it need not be determinate and true. If, however, it is stipulated that the will is an infallibly efficacious and instantaneous cause, and if "I shall have waffles for breakfast tomorrow" is considered not as an intentional object, but as a real, external event, then my having waffles tomorrow will be caused tomorrow in such a way that it will not depend upon my choice anymore and I shall not be able to refrain from it.

"Necessity" is an ambiguous term. We speak, for example, of logical, hypothetical, moral, natural, metaphysical, and causal necessity. It is important to note that the two problems at stake involve two different kinds of necessity. Divine causation seems to imply causal necessity, but the problem of foreknowledge concerns temporal or factual necessity. This is a kind of necessity that has to do with the nature and passage of time. Intuitively, we think that past and present as such have a kind of necessity and determinateness that the future lacks.[23] This is what in present-day philosophy of time is spelled out in the so-called "tensed" or "dynamic" or "A-series" view of time as having an "open" future. In general, a tensed view considers the monadic and changing notions of "future," "present," and "past" as the basic, metaphysical characteristics of temporal events themselves: an event that was future, is now present, and will be past. It should be noted, however, that on a specific version of the tensed theory, a future event cannot be identified as an individual, particular event in the same way as present and past events can be. One may only refer to types of future events. We can imagine this version of the tensed theory as the tip of a pen— representing the present—which constantly moves on and draws the line of the past behind it. In front of the tip there is nothing: it is blank, the future is open.[24] The rival theory, called the "tenseless" or "static" or "B-series" view, reduces the dynamic, monadic categories of "future," "present," and "past" to the unchanging relations of "later than," "simultaneous with," and "earlier than." For example, instead of "Caesar was murdered in the past," the tenseless view holds that "Caesar is murdered forty-four years earlier than Christ is born," where the two finite verbs "is" are logically understood as tenseless, though grammatically they have a present tense.[25] The tenseless theory considers time as a fourth dimension and states that what is earlier or later relative to this moment is in itself as determinate and factual as what happens now. It pictures time as a static, straight line that includes all that is future relative to this moment.[26] On such a theory, one may admit that not all events, whether past, present, or future relative to this moment, are either causally or logically necessary, and that some of them could have been counterfactually otherwise.[27] But on the tensed view with an open future, it does not make sense to talk about the future "that could counterfactually have been otherwise." For on this view there are no future facts, and hence, no future counter-facts: the future lacks the factual or temporal necessity and determinateness of the past and present.

By carefully mapping out the semantics of divine names, Aquinas concludes that there are two distinct problems regarding the compatibility of foreknowledge, providence, and predestination with creaturely contingency and freedom. The first one concerns the diachronic relation between foreknowledge and a future contingent object, and the other one the synchronic relation between a necessary, instantaneous cause and its contingent effect. For reasons of clarity and convenience, I label them "temporal fatalism" and "causal determinism." How does Aquinas deal with each problem, and are his arguments convincing?

Temporal Fatalism

At first sight, Aquinas' answer to the question how God can know future contingents looks quite simple. He adopts Boethius' well-known solution of God's "eternal vision" and the presence of all things to eternity. God, Boethius argues, is eternal, outside of time, and thus the whole stretch of time—past, present, and future—is equally present to him and lies open to his gaze. Boethius illustrates this with a spatial metaphor: God is like someone who observes from on high a procession that moves along down on the plain below. A person who is part of the procession can only see those that have preceded him, but not the ones that will come after him. But from his elevated position, the observer sees in one glance the entire procession.[28]

Three important objections have been raised against this solution: it is logically incoherent, it presupposes metaphysically a tenseless view of time, and it makes God's knowledge observational and dependent, which is theologically unacceptable.

Anthony Kenny is famous for the logical reduction to absurdity of Boethius' solution. "Present to" or "simultaneous with," he points out, is a transitive notion: if A is present to B, and B is present to C, then A is also present to C. Consequently, if all of time is present to God, then every temporal event must also be present to every other temporal event.[29] In short, the whole of temporal extension would collapse into one singularity.

Eleonore Stump and Norman Kretzmann have tried to overcome Kenny's objection by introducing the notion of E(ternity)-T(ime)-simultaneity, in a pivotal article published in 1981.[30] It provoked a lively debate, in the course of which the notion was refined and redefined.[31] It is beyond the scope of this essay to give a detailed analysis of the whole debate, but the gist of ET-simultaneity is as follows. Kenny's argument is based on ordinary language, in which we talk about "simultaneous with" and "present to" as relations that hold between temporal events. Stump and Kretzmann draw attention to the fact that in Boethius' solution one of the *relata* is not temporal but eternal. Therefore, we have to take into account two distinct and irreducible reference frames or modes of existence, that is, time and eternity. According to Stump and Kretzmann, an event in time is ET-simultaneous with the eternal God, without becoming eternal itself (E-simultaneous) or simultaneous with another temporal event (T-simultaneous). In other words, because it presupposes two different reference frames, ET-simultaneity is not transitive: if temporal event x is ET-simultaneous with the eternal God and if temporal event y is also ET-simultaneous with the eternal God, it does not follow that x and y, both of which are in one and the same reference frame, are ET-simultaneous (or T-simultaneous) with each other. Just as Boethius' metaphor of the observer who watches from on high does not exclude the spatial extension and succession of the procession in the plain, in the same way, ET-simultaneity allows for temporal extension and succession. How this works will become clearer if we take into account the metaphysical presupposition of ET-simultaneity.

Although Stump and Kretzmann claimed that their theory is compatible with a tensed theory of time, Craig has argued convincingly that it is not.[32] It presupposes a tenseless view on which all events, whether they are (tenselessly) earlier than, simultaneous with, or later than this moment, are (tenselessly) in themselves ontologically on a par and equally real. This does not mean that they are temporally on a par and equally present in themselves. If that were the case, Kenny's absurdity would follow. On the tenseless view, each event has its own temporal location and extension within the tenselessly existing time-space matrix of the "block-universe." Moreover, on the tenseless theory of time, it does not make sense at all to speak of an event being "present in itself": an event is present to, or better, simultaneous with another event, but not present in itself. So it seems that the only way to save the Boethian solution is to adopt a tenseless view of time. God, then, is conceived as being outside of, and encompassing, the whole time-space matrix, in the same way that the present moment encompasses all of space.[33] In order to prevent the misunderstanding that leads to Kenny's absurdity, one might better rephrase Boethius' statement that all events in time are "equally present to God" as "all events are (tenselessly) equally real to God." This might also be the reason why Aquinas sometimes qualifies the presence of temporal beings and events to God by inserting terms such as "as if" (*quasi*) and "in a certain way" (*quodammodo*).[34]

Apart from the fact that it seems the only way to account for God's foreknowledge, there is another reason why a tenseless theory of time is attractive to theologians: it can account for God's knowledge of what is future to us without suggesting that he derives it from observation. If the whole time-space continuum exists tenselessly, it also makes sense to say that it is caused tenselessly. Moreover, the tenseless view seems to offer an easy way of defending divine immutability. If temporal becoming is illusory, we can imagine the whole of reality having come forth "at once" from an immutable cause. In accordance with

Christian doctrine and most present-day scientific cosmologies, its temporal extension can very well be limited, having a begin- and an end-term, but it would exist as tenselessly and immutably as its temporally non-extended cause.

In recent years, a number of scholars have claimed that in fact Boethius and Aquinas adopted a tenseless theory of time, though they were not aware of it.[35] If this were true, there would be a serious flaw in the way they proceed. For both raise the problem of foreknowledge by presupposing a tensed theory with an open, indeterminate future, but allegedly solve the problem by adopting a tenseless theory, in which whatever is later than this moment is in itself as determinate and real as what is earlier than this moment. In the end, they would have accepted what they intended to refute, namely, temporal fatalism.

A tenseless theory, moreover, is not consistent with Boethius' and Aquinas' views on statements (propositions) about future contingents. In commenting on the famous ninth chapter of Aristotle's *De interpretatione*, Aquinas adopts the same interpretation as Boethius. Statements about future events that are already fully causally determined by present-day tendencies and laws of nature are "determinately true" (*determinate verum*), but statements about future contingents are not. There has been much discussion on how to read the expression "determinately true." The major reason for the confusion among present-day commentators seems to be that Aristotle and the Scholastics base their views on so-called indexical and temporally indefinite statements, whose truth value depends on when, where, and by whom the statement is uttered. Most modern logicians convert such statements (e.g., "I was here yesterday") into non-indexical, temporally definite ones (e.g., "Harm Goris is in Utrecht on July 24, 2001"). It can be argued, however, that Aquinas and other Scholastics do take temporal definiteness into account, while, at the same time, considering indexical tenses essential to statements.[36] "Not determinately true," then, means that statements about future contingents do not have a truth value: they are not true, but they are not false either.[37] The lack of a truth value is not because of our ignorance, as Boethius explicitly points out, but stems from the "variable and indeterminate outcome of the things themselves."[38] This metaphysical indeterminateness of the future is precisely what the tenseless theory of time denies.

Despite the apparent systematic advantages of a tenseless view on time, I think that it is possible to give a coherent interpretation of Aquinas' texts that (1) confirms God's foreknowledge, (2) accepts a tensed theory of time with an open future and hence denies temporal fatalism, (3) does not make God's knowledge dependent on observation, and (4) coheres with Aquinas' basic theological insight that in this life we cannot conceptualize God.

As we saw earlier, Aquinas sometimes says that all of time is "quasi present" to God. This may be understood as meaning "tenselessly real" to God. But it is possible to give a different interpretation, one that is based not on a tense-less mode of being of creatures, but on the unknowable mode of God's being: eternity.

Eternity

Aquinas discusses eternity in the context of his "negative theology": it indicates how and what God is not.[39] Aquinas does adopt Boethius' definition of eternity as the "complete possession all at once of illimitable life," but he reinterprets it in a negative way. Eternity means that God's being has no beginning, no end, and no succession.[40] From Boethius, Aquinas also borrows the Neoplatonic image of eternity as the "standing now" (*nunc stans*).

Stump and Kretzmann have criticized the idea of eternity as a *nunc stans*. Eternity, they argue, is not "a frozen, isolated and static instant," but should be conceived as "atemporal duration."[41] Like their suggestion of ET-simultaneity, this notion of "atemporal duration" has also led to much discussion, the main point of criticism being that it is not coherent: duration, that is, extension without any distinguishable parts (because atemporal), is no extension at all.[42]

Aquinas is somewhat ambiguous about predicating "duration" of God. On the one hand, he says that it implies extension (*distensio*) and therefore should not be said of God. On the other hand, he states that eternity does signify duration because of God's actuality.[43] Instead of concluding that Aquinas contradicts himself, I prefer to read his words analogously within the context of a negative theology.

In commenting on a text from the Neoplatonic *Book on Causes* (*Liber de causis*) stating that "there are two kinds [*species*] of durability, one eternal and the other temporal," Aquinas distinguishes the two as follows:

> These perpetual durations differ in three ways. Firstly, eternal perpetuity is fixed, standing immobile, while temporal perpetuity is flowing and mobile. . . . Secondly, eternal perpetuity is all at once, as it were gathered in one, but temporal perpetuity has successive extension according to earlier and later, which belong to the notion of time. Thirdly, eternal perpetuity is simple, existing as complete by itself, while the whole or completeness of the temporal is by different parts, each succeeding the other.[44]

Aquinas gives here an interpretation of eternal duration that is very similar to, if not identical with, Stump and Kretzmann's concept of atemporal duration. But he makes such strong distinctions between temporal and eternal duration that "duration" in fact can no longer be seen as a univocal term, nor can temporal and eternal duration be seen as two species of a generic duration. "Duration" becomes an analogical term. In reaction to some criticisms, Stump and Kretzmann also acknowledged the analogical character of "duration" in atemporal duration.[45] But if this is so, why not admit the same about "now" in the classical expression "standing now"? Then the standing now is no longer a static, frozen, isolated instant, just as atemporal duration is neither a tenseless extension nor a tensed succession. In other words, if understood analogously, "standing now" and "atemporal duration" are two sides of the same coin. God endures, we may say, but not by temporal extension or succession, and he is present, but his presence is not limited by past and future. The words "standing" in "standing now" and "duration" in "atemporal duration" remind us not to think of God's existence as a static, frozen, isolated instant, or as an evanescent instant which elapses as soon as it occurs, or as the atemporality of abstract entities like numbers or universals. On the other hand, the words "now" and "atemporal" in the two formulas tell us not to conceptualize God's existence as tenseless extension or as tensed succession.

This negative/analogous interpretation of eternity is mirrored in our talking about the presence of temporal beings to God. The relative expression "being present to" has an analogous meaning when God fills in the blank. We can understand that a temporal being is present to another temporal being or event, or that it is past or future to it. But we do not know exactly what it means when a temporal being is said to be present to the eternal God. For if we did, we would also understand what God's own mode of being, eternity, is. And this, Aquinas repeats over and again, we do not know, at least not in this life. It does not follow that "being present to God" is just idle and nugatory talk. We may truly say that a temporal event is now present to God, but not that it ever was future to God or past to God. As Aquinas says, "nothing can coexist by way of presence with the eternal, unless with the whole of it; for the eternal does not have successive duration."[46] It is not the case that "something future" only means that it is (tenselessly) later relative to this moment; whatever it will turn out to be, it is now future and indeterminate in itself. But we cannot say that it is also now future to God. Related to God, it is present and determinate, not because of its own, alleged tenseless existence, but because of God's transcendent, eternal mode of being.

Even if divine foreknowledge is compatible with an open, indeterminate future on the basis of God's eternity, the question remains whether this does not imply that God's knowledge is causally dependent on the presence of temporal beings and events. Is it the case that the presence of such beings to God's eternity is a necessary condition for his observation of them, as Boethius' visual metaphor suggests? Although he does not address this question in particular, Aquinas would reject any suggestion of God's knowledge being dependent. Some have argued that what Aquinas means by "the presence of all of time to God" is not the real (sometimes called "existential" or "physical") presence of temporal beings themselves, but their intentional ("epistemological" or "objective") presence through the divine Ideas, insofar as these are determined by the divine will. Bonaventure and other Franciscans read Boethius in this way, but most commentators agree that Aquinas means the real presence of all temporal beings to God and that this presence justifies the epistemological claim that God's knowledge is related to its objects as present objects.[47]

For Aquinas, God's knowledge of temporal beings is indeed practical and creative, but this causality is not expressed by the notion of "knowledge" as such. "Knowledge" is signified as an eternal, immanent act, while "causation" is signified by a transitive act in time. The point is that one must distinguish between the question of what is the source of God's knowledge of temporal reality, and the question of what conditions that reality must meet in order to qualify as object of God's knowledge. Future contingents as such lack the determinate being that is required for knowledge. God cannot know them as such, that is, as future, not because of a deficiency on his side, but because of a deficiency on their side.[48] But, since God exists eternally, whatever is future both in itself and to us is not future but present (in an analogical sense) to him. Consequently, God can know future contingents, but, as Aquinas puts it, "not under the concept of future" (*non sub ratione futuri*). This does not mean that he does not know that they are future. For then his knowledge would be either false or incomplete. The expression "not under the concept of future" concerns the mode of knowing, not the mode of being of the external objects. The human intellect is subject to time, and that is why we know temporal things in a temporal mode, namely, under the notions of past, present, and future; our intellect knows by forming tensed propositions. But according to Aquinas, the isomorphism between the mode of being of the external objects and the mode of knowing is not necessary. Objects, he often states, are known according to the mode of the knower, not according to the mode of their being.[49] The human intellect, for example, knows material, concrete things in an immaterial, universal way. Likewise, Aquinas states, the divine intellect knows temporal beings in his own, atemporal, eternal way, which we cannot understand or express.[50] Therefore, if we say "God knows that future contingent *x* will be," we signify God's knowledge inevitably in a human way, by using the tensed proposition "*x* will be."[51] It does not follow, however, that *x* exists tenselessly and determinately or that the proposition by itself is true. Such consequences are drawn only if we are not sufficiently aware of the irremediable imperfection of our understanding and speaking of God, and if we forget our inability to conceptualize and express his transcendent, eternal mode of being and knowing.

Causal Determinism

If God's will is the all-encompassing cause, which brings about everything and cannot be hindered, is all that is or happens necessary, in the sense of causally determined? As we saw earlier, this problem arises when the divine will is considered as the efficient cause of what happens in time. One might also focus on God's will as free, with the apparent consequence that everything is contingent. Occasionally, Aquinas addresses this problem:

> Although everything depends on God's will as on the first cause, which is not necessitated in its operation unless on the supposition of its intention, still absolute necessity is not excluded from things because of this, so that we would have to acknowledge that all things are contingent—what someone might think from the fact that things have not come forth from their cause by absolute necessity.[52]

But more often Aquinas directs his attention to the irresistible efficacy of God's will, and to its compatibility with created contingent causes in particular. Following Aristotle, Aquinas distinguishes two kinds of created contingent causes: voluntary causes, and natural causes that occasionally do not produce the effect they are determined to by nature. The latter may occur for different reasons: another cause intervenes, the agent cause has some defect, or the matter upon which the cause acts is not suitably disposed.[53] Both kinds of contingent causation have their own specific problems, with which Aquinas deals in separate discussions. He speaks about human will in his anthropological texts, moral treatises, and the doctrine of grace and justification. Coincidence in nature is treated in Aquinas' works on natural philosophy and on the theory of science. But in discussing explicitly the question how God's causation can go together with contingent causation by creatures, he always lumps both kinds of contingent causation together, and aims at offering a general, overall framework for refuting the apparent incompatibility and for indicating the transcendence of the divine cause.

It seems that Aquinas only gradually developed his view on the transcendence of divine causation.[54] In the commentary on the *Sentences,* he uses Aristotle's model of ordered causes: the first, remote cause may be necessary, in the sense that it always operates in the same way, but if it produces its effect by mediation of a secondary, proximate cause that is contingent, then the effect will also be contingent, for an effect always takes the condition of its proximate cause. Aquinas takes as an example the necessary movement of the sun, which causes a tree to bloom. Yet, he says, the blooming of the tree is a contingent event, for its proximate cause is the vegetative force of the tree, which is a contingent cause and may fail. But Aquinas realizes that the comparison with divine causality breaks down: though the movement of the sun cannot be hindered, it can go together with a defect of the secondary, proximate cause, so that the effect does not take place. This, Aquinas admits, cannot be the case with God's causation. The unsatisfactory solution Aquinas comes up with is that the ultimate effect is still certain, not because of God's causation, but only because of his eternal knowledge, to which all is present.[55]

The next stage in Aquinas' development is that he attributes a kind of statistic certainty to God's causality. This is found in the discussion on the certainty of predestination in De veritate, question 6. Aquinas says that if God's causal influence is mediated through a created, necessary cause, then the ultimate effect will follow in each particular instance. But when the created, proximate cause is a contingent one that occasionally fails, the ultimate effect only comes about by and large (in universali). This explanation, Aquinas says, will do to secure the general causal certainty (certitudo ordinis) of divine providence, but it is insufficient in the case of predestination. He ignores the objection that the proximate, created cause in the realization of predestination is not a natural but a voluntary cause, namely, free will, which, by its nature, is not a contingent cause inclined to one alternative (contingens ut in pluribus) and failing only occasionally, but one that is completely indifferent (ad utrumlibet). Instead, he focuses on the doctrinal point that predestination does not regard humanity in general, but rather concerns the final end of each individual person.[56] Furthermore, in contrast with the discussion in the commentary on the Sentences, Aquinas acknowledges that it is theologically unacceptable to state that the certainty of predestination depends only on the certainty of God's knowledge.[57] His answer to the problem is that at a particular instance human free will may fail and turn away from God and his final destination, but that God offers so many opportunities that, in the end, he is successful (so to speak), and the person reaches the predestined goal.[58]

Aquinas' mature view consists in pointing out the transcendence of God's causality: God causes being as such, including its modal differences. Aquinas restricts the validity of the Aristotelian rule that an effect has the modal status not of its remote, first cause, but of its proximate, secondary cause, to ordered created causes, and he no longer thinks that this rule is sufficient to explain the relation between divine and created causation. For the rule suggests that divine causation is a kind of mediated, indirect emanation which happens by blind necessity of nature and not intentionally. But this, Aquinas says, is not in accordance with Christian faith. God is not a first, necessary cause in the way the sun is. First, God's causal activity itself is not necessitated by his nature, but is voluntary. Second, the efficacy of his causal activity exceeds that of any created cause: it not only causes the effect to be, but also causes the mode in which the effect exists, namely, contingently or necessarily.[59] It does not destroy creaturely causality, but sustains it. God causes necessary created causes to bring forth necessary effects and contingent causes to produce contingent effects. Elsewhere, Aquinas states that God's will is beyond the order of contingency and necessity, for it is the very cause of being as such and, hence, of the modal order.[60] We may use different models, derived from our created reality, to illustrate the relation between divine and created causation: the Aristotelian models of first and secondary causes, remote and proximate causes, and principal and instrumental causes, or the Platonic idea of participation.[61] But none of them captures adequately or expresses univocally the transcendence of the divine cause.[62]

What does Aquinas mean when he says that God causes being, and how does that relate to created causes?[63] Being, Aquinas states, is the common effect of every cause.[64] Created causes, however, are limited in their essence and, hence, in their power. Their causal agency always presupposes something upon which to act, and is confined to the categorical determinations of being: substantial and accidental being.[65] Only God, who is subsistent being itself, causes being as such (*ens inquantum ens*), and to him belongs exclusively that causal act that does not presuppose anything, namely, creation out of nothing. Within the existent created order, creatures do have their proper causal role: they cause something to be this, or to be such. But this created causation is not independent from God. While creatures cause something to be this or such, they do not cause something to be this or such. This is what Aquinas means when he says that every created agent causes or gives being, not by its own power, but "in virtue of the divine power" (*in virtute divina*).[66] One should not understand by this that God gives a kind of generic being, while created causes subsequently determine and particularize it.[67] For Aquinas, "to be" is not a univocal, generic notion, but "the actuality of each thing," "more intimate and deeper than anything else."[68] As each cause operates at a different level, the divine one on the transcendental level of being itself, and the created one on the level of its categorical determinations, there is no competition between the two, nor is there mutual exclusion: "by keeping reality in being . . . God immediately operates within every agent, without excluding the operation of the will and of nature."[69]

Conclusion

At the beginning of this essay, I asked how Thomas Aquinas argues for the compatibility of God's foreknowledge, providence, and predestination with human freedom, and whether his arguments are cogent. With regard to the first question, I have tried to show that Aquinas distinguishes between two problems. The first one has to do with the infallibility of God's foreknowledge of the future, and the second one with the irresistible efficacy of God's will as the First Cause. Providence, when understood not only as God's eternal plan to bring creatures to their destination, but also as the execution of that plan in time, presupposes conceptually both God's foreknowledge and divine causation. The same goes for predestination, which Aquinas calls "a part of divine providence," and which concerns the supernatural end of rational creatures. It is important to note that this distinction does not reflect any real distinction in God, but stems from the special semantics of the divine names, which differ only conceptually.

The cogency of the arguments with which Aquinas solves both problems must be assessed within the framework of his negative theology. God's incomprehensible, eternal mode of being allows us to say that events which are future and contingent, and hence indeterminate in themselves and in relation to us, are present and determinate in relation to God. Likewise, God's incomprehensible act of giving being as such, including its modal qualifications, allows us to say that the Creator sustains the causal action of creatures and gives being to their effects in accordance with the necessity or contingency of the secondary causes. "Presence" and "causation" are said analogously of the Eternal One and of the Creator, and signify modes of presence and of causation that elude our grasp.

In his discussions on the compatibility of God's foreknowledge, providence, and predestination with human freedom, Aquinas develops only the general conceptual and linguistic framework within which the theologian has to think and speak. For a more concrete and detailed analysis of human freedom, we must turn both to Aquinas' anthropology, where he deals with the human will as distinguished from natural contingent causes, and to his theology of sin and grace, where he discusses our deliverance from evil and our new life in community with the triune God.

Notes

1. A selection of the most important texts is I *Sent.* d.38 q.1 art.5; d.40 q.3; *De Ver.* q.2 a.12; q.6 a.3; q.23 a.5; *ScG* I.67; II.30; III.72 – 75; *ST* I.14.13; 19.8; 22.4; *Meta.* VI, 3; *Periherm.* I, 13 – 14. I have discussed these texts in more detail in my *Free Creatures of an Eternal God: Thomas Aquinas on God's Infallible Foreknowledge and Irresistible Will* (Louvain: Peeters, 1996).

2. Cf. H. Denzinger, *Enchiridion symbolorum, definitionum et declarationum de rebus fidei et morum,* bilingual edition Latin-German, ed. P. Hünermann (Freiburg im Breisgau: Herder, 1991), no.1997 and 1997a (1610 – 11).

3. Interest in Molinism revived in the mid-1970s due to the work of Alvin Plantinga. Some recent studies are Eef Dekker, *Middle Knowledge* (Louvain: Peeters, 2000), and Thomas P. Flint, *Divine Providence: The Molinist Account* (Ithaca, N.Y.: Cornell University Press, 1998).

4. Cf. Bañez, *Scholastica Commentaria in Primam Partem Summae Theologiae S. Thomae Aquinatis* (Madrid: F. E. D. A., 1934), 350 – 51: "si Deus per impossibile cognosceret tantum futura contingentia, prout habent esse in suis causis, et non prout sunt praesentia in aeternitate, ejus cognitio esset certa et infallibilis [350]. . . . Deus cognoscit futura contingentia in suis causis particularibus, quatenus ipsae causae particulares subjiciuntur determinationi et dispositioni divinae scientiae et voluntatis, quae est prima Causa."

5. Already in 1910, the Dominican Thomist A.-D. Sertillanges objected to Bañezianism as a distortion of Aquinas' own position. See his *S. Thomas d'Aquin* (Paris: Alcan, 1925), vol. 1, 265 – 67. But prominent neo-Thomists like G. Manser and, in particular, R. Garrigou-Lagrange defended vigorously the *praemotio physica.* More recent criticisms of Bañezianism are Kathryn Tanner, *God and Creation in Christian Theology: Tyranny or Empowerment?* (Oxford: Blackwell, 1988), 141 – 52, and Brian J. Shanley, "Divine Causation and Human Freedom in Aquinas," *American Catholic Philosophical Quarterly* 72 (1998): 99 – 122.

6. *ST* I.13.5.

7. I *Sent.* d.22 q.1 art.2 ad 4: "sed hoc quod in modo significandi importetur aliqua imperfectio, quae Deo non competit, non facit praedicationem esse falsam vel impropriam, sed imperfectam." See also the contribution of David Burrell in this volume.

8. I *Sent.* d.37 q.2 art.2: "Omnis autem relatio quae fundatur super aliquam operationem in creaturas procedentem, non dicitur de Deo nisi ex tempore, sicut dominus et creator et huiusmodi; quia huiusmodi relationes actuales sunt, et exigunt actu esse utrumque extremorum." Cf. also, e.g., *ST* I.13.7 ad 3 and 14.15 ad 1.

9. *ST* I.46.2 ad 1: "causa efficiens quae agit per motum, de necessitate praecedit tempore suum effectum. . . . Sed si actio sit instantanea et non successiva, non est necessarium faciens esse prius facto duratione." See also *ST* I.45.2 ad 3 and 104.1 ad 4. Aquinas' usual example of instantaneous causation is illumination. He did not know yet that light travels at a limited speed.

10. Cf. *ST* I.45.3 ad 1: "creatio active significata significat actionem divinam, quae est eius essentia, cum relatione ad creaturam."

11. I *Sent.* d.38 q.1 art.1: "scientia secundum rationem scientiae non dicit aliquam causalitatem, alias omnis scientia causa esset," and *De Ver.* q.2 a.14: "scientia inquantum scientia, non dicit causam activam . . . a scientia nunquam procedit effectus nisi mediante voluntate, quae de sui ratione importat influxum quemdam ad volita."

12. *De Ver.* q.23 a.4 ad 13: "Cum vero dicitur Deum velle aliquid, non significatur illud aliquid inesse Deo, sed tantum modo importatur ordo ipsius Dei ad illius constitutionem in pro-

pria natura," and ibid., ad 6: "illa quae important comparationem Dei ad exitum creaturarum in esse, sicut velle, creare, et huiusmodi. . . ."

13. *De Ver.* q.23 a.4 ad 15: "voluntas ad volitum habet duplicem respectum: primum quidem habet ad ipsum in quantum est volitum; secundum vero habet ad idem, in quantum est producendum in actu per voluntatem; et hic quidem respectus praesupponit primum. Primo enim intelligimus voluntatem velle aliquid; deinde ex hoc ipso quod vult illud, intelligimus quod producat ipsum in rerum natura, si voluntas sit efficax."

14. *De Ver.* q.23 a.4 ad 15: "Primus ergo respectus divinae voluntatis ad volitum non est necessarius absolute, propter improportionem voliti ad finem. . . . Sed secundus respectus est necessarius propter efficaciam divinae voluntatis; et exinde est quod de necessitate sequitur, si Deus vult aliquid voluntate beneplaciti, quod illud fiat." The "will of pleasure" (*voluntas beneplaciti*) is a technical Scholastic term. It signifies God's will in the proper sense of the word. It is contrasted with the "will of the sign" (*voluntas signi*), which is metaphorically called "will" and signifies God's commandments; cf. *De Ver.* q.23 a.3.

15. Cf. especially *De Ver.* q.5 a.1 and q.6 a.1.

16. Cf. I *Sent.* d.40 q.1 art.1; *ST* I.22.1 ad 2 and 23.2.

17. I *Sent.* d.40 q.3 art.1 ad 5: "Unde cum dicitur Deus praescit hoc, non intelligitur quod sit futurum respectu divinae scientiae, sed respectu huius temporis in quo profertur." Cf. also *De Ver.* q.2 a.12 (*in fine*); *ScG* I.67.9.

18. I *Sent.* d.41 q.1 art.5 ad 1: "[C]um dicimus, Deus praescivit Christum moriturum, designatur respectus ad futurum; unde quando desinit esse futurum, Deus iam non praescit illud. . . ." Cf. also I *Sent.* d.35, exp. txt.; *De Ver.* q.6 a.1 ad 6.

19. I *Sent.* d.38 q.1 art.5: "Contingentia enim videtur duplici ratione effugere divinam cognitionem. Primo propter ordinem causae ad causatum. Quia causae necessariae et immutabilis videtur esse effectus necessarius; unde cum scientia Dei sit causa rerum, et sit immutabilis, non videtur quod possit esse contingentium. Secundo propter ordinem scientiae ad scitum; quia cum scientia sit certa cognitio, ex ipsa ratione certitudinis etiam exclusa causalitate, requirit certitudinem et determinationem in scito, quam contingentia excludit; et quod scientia ex ratione certitudinis suae requirat determinationem in scito, patet in scientia nostra, quae non est causa rerum, et in scientia Dei respectu malorum."

20. Cf. I *Sent.* d.40 q.3 art.1; *ST* I.23.6; *De Ver.* q.6 a.3; *Periherm.* I, 14, 192; *De Malo* q.16 a.7 ad 15; *ScG* III.95.9 and 16; *Comp. Theol.* I, 140; *Quodl.* 12, 3.

21. *De Ver.* q.6 a.3: "duplex est certitudo: scilicet cognitionis et ordinis. Cognitionis quidem certitudo est, quando cognitio non declinat in aliquo ab eo quod in re invenitur, sed hoc modo extimat de re sicut est; et quia certa extimatio de re praecipue habetur per causam rei, ideo tractum est nomen certitudinis ad ordinem causae ad effectum, ut dicatur ordo causae ad effectum esse certus, quando causa infallibiliter effectum producit."

22. *ScG* I.67.2: "Contingens enim certitudini cognitionis non repugnat nisi secundum quod futurum est, non autem secundum quod praesens est. Contingens enim, cum futurum est, potest non esse. . . . Ex quo autem praesens est, pro illo tempore non potest non esse."

23. What I call "temporal necessity" is Aquinas' *"quaedam necessitas"* in *ST* II-II.49.6: "Praeterita autem in necessitatem quandam transeunt: quia impossibile est non esse quod factum est. Similiter etiam praesentia, inquantum huiusmodi, necessitatem quandam habent: necesse est enim Socratem sedere dum sedet." Cf. I *Sent.* d.42 q.2 art.2 and d.44 q.1 art.4; *ScG* II.25.15; III.86.6; *Eth.* VI, 2, 1138; *Resp. de art.* 108, 82, 1; *De Caelo* I, 29, 10. The Scholastics also called it *"necessitas per accidens"* or *"necessitas ut nunc."*

24. The metaphor of the moving tip of the pen also illustrates the difficulties in imagining and conceptualizing time: the metaphor itself includes what it is supposed to clarify, namely, time.

25. The so-called "old" tenseless theory held that the tensed and the tenseless phrase have exactly the same meaning. According to the "new" tenseless theory, semantic equivalence is not necessary; it suffices that the tenseless phrase expresses effectively the extensional truth conditions or facts.

26. A clear introduction to contemporary philosophy of time is Quentin Smith and L. Nathan Oaklander, *Time, Change and Freedom: An Introduction to Metaphysics* (London: Routledge, 1995).

27. A solution to the problem of foreknowledge along these lines has been labeled the "Ockhamist" solution. It hinges upon the notion of counterfactuality: God's foreknowledge would have been different, if I would have made a different choice than I actually shall make. It considers knowledge to be a "future-infected soft fact," depending semantically on what will actually happen. This line of reasoning is followed, among others, by William L. Craig. See, for instance, his *Divine Foreknowledge and Human Freedom. The Coherence of Theism: Omniscience* (Leiden: Brill, 1991). In this study Craig defends the compatibility of the Ockhamist solution with a tensed theory of time. Later he advocated the tenseless view in "The Tensed vs. Tenseless Theory of Time: A Watershed for the Conception of Divine Eternity," in *Questions of Time and Tense,* ed. R. Le Poidevin (Oxford: Clarendon, 1998), 221–50, esp. 246–48. Aquinas disagrees with the counterfactuality solution: I *Sent.* d.38 q.1 art.5 ad 4; *De Ver.* q.2 a.12 ad 7; *ST* I.14.13 ad 2.

28. Boethius, *De Consolatione Philosophiae* V, 6, Loeb Classical Library (London: William Heinemann, 1973), 422–35. Like Boethius, Aquinas also uses the Neoplatonic metaphor of the center of a circle, to which the whole circumference is equally present.

29. A. Kenny, "Divine Foreknowledge and Human Freedom," in *Aquinas: A Collection of Critical Essays,* ed. A. Kenny (London: McMillan, 1969), 255–70. Kenny concludes (264): "But on St. Thomas' view, my typing of this paper is simultaneous with the whole of eternity. Again, on his view, the great fire of Rome is simultaneous with the whole of eternity. Therefore, while I type these very words, Nero fiddles heartlessly on." The same objection had already been raised by the late-thirteenth-century Dominican William Peter of Godin: cf. Maarten Hoenen, *Marsilius of Inghen: Divine Knowledge in Late Medieval Thought* (Leiden: Brill, 1993), 169–70.

30. Eleonore Stump and Norman Kretzmann, "Eternity," *Journal of Philosophy* 78 (1981): 429–58.

31. For a survey of the debate and a critical evaluation, see Craig, "Tensed vs. Tenseless Theory," 232–40.

32. Craig, "Tensed vs. Tenseless Theory," 235, 239.

33. The analogy with the present moment of time encompassing all of space is used by Anselm in *De Concordia praescientiae et praedestinationis et gratia Dei cum libero arbitrio* I, 5.

34. Cf. *ScG* I.66.8; *ST* II-II.95.1. In *De Rat. Fid.* 10 Thomas uses the metaphor of the circle: "in circulo, cuius centrum . . . aequaliter respicit omnes circumferentiae partes, et omnes sibi sunt quodammodo praesentes, quamvis una earum alteri non sit praesens. . . . Deus omnia quae nobis sunt vel praeterita vel praesentia vel futura, quasi praesentia inspiciens, infallibiliter et certitudinaliter cognoscit. . . . Deus autem de excelso suae aeternitatis per certitudinem videt quasi praesentia omnia quae per totum temporis decursum aguntur." Also Boethius uses *quasi* once: "omnia quasi iam gerantur in sua simplici cognitione considerat" (*De Cons. Phil.* V, 6, 65–66 [p. 426]).

35. Among others, William L. Craig, "Was Thomas Aquinas a B-Theorist of Time?" *New Scholasticism* 59 (1985): 475–83; Delmas Lewis, "Eternity, Time and Tenselessness," *Faith and Phi-*

losophy 5 (1988): 72–86. John Yates stresses that God's knowledge is not dependent on observation in his *The Timelessness of God* (Lanham, Md.: University Press of America, 1990), esp. 221–32. Craig has argued that Scotus criticized Aquinas for endorsing a tenseless view in his *The Problem of Divine Foreknowledge and Future Contingents from Aristotle to Suarez* (Leiden: Brill, 1988), 129–33.

36. Cf. my *Free Creatures*, 101–36, 220–35. A more detailed survey of thirteenth-century tense logic can be found in my "Tense Logic in 13th-Century Theology," *Vivarium* 39 (2001): 161–84.

37. For Boethius and Aquinas, statements about future contingents have the disjunctive property of being either-true-or-false, but this property is not truth-functional and the truth values are not distributed. Cf. the detailed study by Richard Gaskin, *The Sea Battle and the Master Argument: Aristotle and Diodorus Cronus on the Metaphysics of the Future* (Berlin: De Gruyter, 1995).

38. Boethius attributes the epistemic reduction to the Stoics. Cf. his second commentary on *De Interpretatione* III, 9, 192, 194, 245 (New York: Garland, 1987; reprint of the Leipzig edition of C. Meiser, 1887–90).

39. For example, *ST* I.10 (cf. the prologue in *ST* I.3) and *ScG* I.30.4.

40. Boethius, *De Consolatione Philosophiae* V, 6: "Aeternitas est interminabilis vitae tota simul et perfecta possessio" (422). Aquinas' apophatic reading of the Boethian definition is pointed out, among others, by Yates, *Timelessness,* 39–40, and Brian Shanley, "Eternity and Duration in Aquinas," *The Thomist* 61 (1997): 525–48.

41. Stump and Kretzmann, "Eternity."

42. For a survey of the discussion, see William L. Craig, "The Eternal Present and Stump-Kretzmann Eternity," *American Catholic Philosophical Quarterly* 73 (1999): 521–36.

43. Cf. I *Sent.* d.8 q.2 art.1 ad 6, in commenting on Boethius' definition: "[D]uratio dicit quamdam distensionem ex ratione nominis: et quia in divino esse non debet intelligi aliqua talis distensio, ideo Boetius non posuit durationem, sed possessionem." Cf. also *De Caelo* I, 21, 9. On the other hand, in I *Sent.* d.19 q.2 art.1 (cf. II *Sent.* d.2 q.1 art.1): "[T]ria praedicta nomina [*aeternitas, aevum, tempus*] significant durationem quamdam. Duratio autem omnis attenditur secundum quod aliquid est in actu." Eternity is also called *duratio Dei* in *ScG* II.35.6 and II *Sent.* d.1 q.1 art.5 ad 7.

44. *De Causis* 30 (no.450 in the Marietti edition of 1972): "Et differunt hae perpetuae durationes tripliciter: primo quidem quia perpetuitas aeternalis est fixa, stans immobilis; perpetuitas autem temporalis est fluens et mobilis. . . . Secundo, quia perpetuitas aeternalis est tota simul quasi in uno collecta; perpetuitas autem temporalis habet successivam extensionem secundum prius et posterius quae sunt de ratione temporis. Tertio, quia perpetuitas aeternalis est simplex, tota secundum seipsam existens, sed universalitas sive totalitas perpetuitatis temporalis est secundum diversas partes sibi succedentes."

45. Eleonore Stump and Norman Kretzmann, "Eternity, Awareness and Action," *Faith and Philosophy* 9 (1992): 463–82, esp. 464–65 and 468–69.

46. *ScG* I.66.8: "Aeterno autem non potest aliquid praesentialiter coexistere nisi toti: quia successionis durationem non habet."

47. Cf. Albert Michel, "Science de Dieu," *Dictionnaire de théologie catholique* 14.2 (Paris: Letouzey, 1941): 1598–1620; and the references in Lewis, "Eternity," 85 n. 21. In *ST* I.14.13 Aquinas says that all of time is present to God "non solum ea ratione qua habet rationes rerum apud se praesentes, ut quidam dicunt. . . ." The reference is probably to Bonaventure. See also I *Sent.* d.38 q.1 art.5 (*in fine*).

48. *ST* I.89.7 ad 3: "futura, quae distant secundum tempus, non sunt entia in actu. Unde in seipsis non sunt cognoscibilia, quia sicut deficit aliquid ab entitate, ita deficit a cognoscibilitate." Cf. also *De Malo* q.16 a.7. In other texts, Aquinas states that sometimes we cannot know certain things due to a deficiency of our cognitive powers, as in the case of the mystery of the Trinity, while other things cannot be known (by any cognitive faculty) because of a deficiency from their side, like future contingents: *ST* II-II.171.3; *De Ver.* q.12 a.2; and *Ad Rom.* 12:7, no.978.

49. Cf. John F. Wippel, "Thomas Aquinas and the Axiom 'What Is Received Is Received According to the Mode of the Receiver,'" in *A Straight Path: Studies in Medieval Philosophy and Culture, Essays in Honor of Arthur Hyman,* ed. R. Link-Salinger et al. (Washington, D.C.: Catholic University of America Press, 1988), 279–89.

50. Cf. I *Sent.* d.38 q.1 art.3 ad 3: "temporalia intemporaliter cognoscit," and *Periherm.* I, 14, 195: "omnino eternaliter sic videt unumquodque eorum que sunt in quocunque tempore." Nor does God know by forming tenseless propositions. Such propositions imply a tenseless view on time.

51. Cf. *De Ver.* q.2 a.12: "Difficultas autem in hoc accidit eo quod divinam cognitionem significare non possumus nisi per modum nostrae cognitionis consignificando temporum differentias." In the answer to the seventh objection, Aquinas states: "et ideo magis esset dicendum 'si Deus scit aliquid, hoc est' quam 'hoc erit'." Aquinas' counterfactual phrase already indicates that 'hoc est' is also imperfect, for the future contingent does not exist now. Cf. also *Epistola ad Bernardum abbatem Casinensem* (Leonine Edition, vol. 42): "Eo ergo modo ab eterno prescivit hunc tali tempore moriturum si modo nostro loquimur, cum tamen eius modo dicendum esset, videt eum mori. . . ."

52. *ScG* II.30.1: "Licet autem omnia ex Dei voluntate dependeant sicut ex prima causa, quae in operando necessitatem non habet nisi ex sui propositi suppositione, non tamen propter hoc absoluta necessitas a rebus excluditur, ut sit necessarium nos fateri omnia contingentia esse; quod posset alicui videri, ex hoc quod a causa sua non de necessitate absoluta fluxerunt."

53. Cf. *Meta.* VI, 3, 1210. Aquinas' views on coincidence in natural causation receive little attention, partly because they are interwoven with outdated scientific (cosmological) theories, partly because "coincidence" is also a problematic notion in modern science. Still, Aquinas' texts contain valuable discussions on the concept of cause and on the compatibility of natural coincidence with divine providence: cf. my *Free Creatures,* 281–89.

54. The development is sketched by Bernard McGinn in his "The Development of the Thought of Thomas Aquinas on the Reconciliation of Divine Providence and Contingent Action," *The Thomist* 39 (1975): 741–52.

55. I *Sent.* d.38 q.1 art.5: "Sed adhuc manet dubitatio maior . . . quia causa prima necessaria potest simul esse cum defectu causae secundae, sicut motus solis cum sterilitate arboris; sed scientia Dei non potest simul stare cum defectu causae secundae. Non enim potest esse quod Deus sciat simul hunc cursurum, et iste deficiat a cursu; et hoc est propter certitudinem scientiae et non propter causalitatem eius." As we saw earlier (cf. n. 19 above), Aquinas discusses divine knowledge both as cause and as knowledge in this text. Cf. also II *Sent.* d.35 q.1 art.5, exp. txt., where Aquinas says that what happens rarely in nature is fortuitous or casual compared to its proximate cause, but not "in ordine ad causam primam, cuius praesentiam nihil praeterfugit."

56. *De Ver.* q.6 a.3: "Et sic nihil potest deficere a generali fine providentiae, quamvis quandoque deficiat ab aliquo particulari fine. Sed ordo praedestinationis est certus non solum respectu universalis finis, sed etiam respectu particularis et determinati. . . . Nec tamen hoc modo est certus ordo praedestinationis respectu particularis finis, sicut erat ordo providentiae: quia in providentia ordo non erat certus respectu particularis finis, nisi quando causa proxima necessario

producebat effectum suum; in praedestinatione autem invenitur certitudo respectu singularis finis; et tamen causa proxima, scilicet liberum arbitrium, non producit effectum illum nisi contingenter." On the expression "certitudo ordinis," see n. 21 above.

57. *De Ver.* q.6 a.3: "Non enim potest dici quod praedestinatio supra certitudinem providentiae nihil aliud addat nisi certitudinem praescientiae. . . . Sic enim non diceretur praedestinatus differre a non praedestinato ex parte ordinis, sed tantum ex parte praescientiae eventus. Et sic praescientia esset causa praedestinationis, nec praedestinatio esset per electionem praedestinantis; quod est contra auctoritatem Scripturae et dicta sanctorum."

58. *De Ver.* q.6 a.3: "Tamen in eo quem Deus praedestinat, tot alia adminicula praeparat, quod vel non cadat, vel si cadit, quod resurgat, sicut exhortationes, suffragia orationum, gratiae donum, et omnia huiusmodi. . . ."

59. *De Ver.* q.23 a.5 is one of the first texts that represents Aquinas' mature view. He begins by quoting the Aristotelian rule, adduced by *"quidam"* (including the young Aquinas himself!). After having given the objections, he concludes: "Et ideo oportet aliam principalem rationem assignare contingentiae in rebus, cui causa praeassignata [Aristotle's rule] subserviat. . . . Voluntas autem divina est agens fortissimum, unde oportet eius effectum ei omnibus modis assimilari, ut non solum fiat id quod Deus vult fieri . . . sed ut fiat eo modo quo Deus vult illud fieri, ut necessario vel contingenter. . . . Et sic non dicimus quod aliqui divinorum effectuum sint contingentes solummodo propter contingentiam causarum secundarum, sed magis propter dispositionem divinae voluntatis, quae talem ordinem rebus providit." Cf. also *Quodl.* II, 3, written around Easter 1259, in the same period as *De Ver.* q.23.

60. Cf. *Periherm.* I, 14, 197: "Nam voluntas divina est intelligenda ut extra ordinem entium existens, velut causa quedam profundens totum ens et omnes eius differencias; sunt autem differencie entis possibile et necessarium, et ideo ex ipsa voluntate divina originatur necessitas et contingencia in rebus, et distinctio utriusque secundum rationem proximarum causarum." All effects of created causes depend on God's will, the "prima causa que transcendit ordinem necessitatis et contingencie" (ibid.). Discussing the efficacy of divine providence in *Meta.* VI, 3, 1222, Aquinas says: "Sed necessarium est effectus esse contingenter, vel de necessitate. Quod quidem singulare est in hac causa, scilicet in divina providentia. Reliquae enim causae non constituunt legem necessitatis vel contingentiae, sed constituta a superiori causa utuntur." Cf. also *ST* I.19.8; *De Malo* q.16 a.7 ad 15; *ScG* III.94.10; *Quodl.* 12, 3, ad 1.

61. Cf. for example *De Pot.* q.3 a.7, where Aquinas uses all of these models.

62. On the apophatic character of Aquinas' account of divine causation, see Shanley, "Divine Causation."

63. For a more detailed account of this question, see Rudi te Velde, *Participation and Substantiality in Thomas Aquinas* (Leiden: Brill, 1995), 160–83; John F. Wippel, "Thomas Aquinas on Creatures as Causes of Esse," *International Philosophical Quarterly* 40 (2000): 197–213.

64. *ScG* III.66.3: "esse sit communis effectus omnium agentium, nam omme agens facit esse actu"; *De Pot.* q.7 a.2: "Omnes autem causae creatae communicant in uno effectu qui est esse. . . . Conveniunt ergo in hoc quod causant esse." Cf. also *Meta.* V, 1, 751; *ScG* III.67.1; *Phys.* II, 10, 15.

65. Cf. *ScG* II.21.4: "Alia vero agentia non sunt causa essendi simpliciter, sed causa essendi hoc, ut hominem vel album"; *De Pot.* q.3, a.1: "nulla earum est activa entis secundum quod est ens, sed eius entis secundum quod est hoc ens, determinatum in hac vel illa specie."

66. Cf. *ScG* III.66.1: "omnia inferiora agentia non dant esse nisi inquantum agunt in virtute divina"; *De Pot.* q.3 a.1: "nulla res dat esse, nisi inquantum est in ea participatio divinae virtutis."

67. Sometimes Aquinas' wordings might suggest this. Cf. *De Pot.* q.3 a.1: "Causalitas vero aliorum quae ad esse superadduntur, vel quibus esse specificatur, pertinet ad causas secundas," and *ScG* III.66.6: "Secunda autem agentia, quae sunt quasi particulantes et determinantes actionem primi agentis, agunt sicut proprios effectus alias perfectiones, quae determinant esse."

68. Cf., e.g., *ST* I.4.1 ad 3: "ipsum esse est actualitas omnium rerum," and 8.1: "Esse autem est illud quod est magis intimum cuilibet, et quod profundius omnibus inest."

69. *De Pot.* q.3 a.7: "tenens rem in esse . . . ipse in quolibet operante immediate operetur, non exclusa operatione voluntatis vel natura."

Six

Trinitarian Anthropology

D. JUVENAL MERRIELL, C.O.

At the beginning of his *Summa Theologiae* St. Thomas explains that the proper study of the theologian is God as He exists in Himself and also as the beginning and end of all things, especially the rational creature.[1] In fact, the main subject of the long exposition of *sacra doctrina* that follows is man, because the holy teaching that comes primarily from God is concerned mainly with the relation of man to God. The theologian does not study man as man is in himself—that is the subject of philosophy and its subordinate sciences. In the *Summa* Aquinas teaches about man *sub ratione Dei:* man as ordered to God as his beginning and end.[2] Man is the work of God's hands, and God has made man for Himself. Man comes from God and returns to God in the end. In the *Prima Pars* Aquinas covers the *exitus* of creatures, especially man, from God. In the *Secunda Pars* he begins with the consideration of God as the ultimate end that draws man to His perfection, and then he treats the acts and habits that direct man to this end. Finally, in the *Tertia Pars,* Christ and his sacraments are the way and the means to salvation in God. The theologian looks at man in terms of this dynamic of movement from and to God, and not simply in terms of the constant, unchanging nature of man.

From the early days of the Church, theologians have been fascinated with the biblical notion of the creation of man in the image of God because of the key it provides for understanding the relation of man to God. Aquinas was heir to the patristic tradition of reflection on the text of Genesis 1:26, which bears a more dynamic sense in the Vulgate: *Faciamus hominem ad imaginem et similitudinem nostram* (Let us make man *to* our image and likeness). Scholars of the twentieth century, in particular Ghislain Lafont, have noted that the theme of the *imago Dei* is a key concept in Aquinas' theological anthropology and in the structure of the *Summa Theologiae*.[3] It is not that Aquinas harps continually on the idea, but rather that he refers to it at key points in the *Summa*. He places his extended study of man as image of God (I.93) in the section on the creation of man (I.90 – 102): here man is related to God as to his first cause or beginning (*principium*). Then, after the final section of the *Prima Pars* (on God's governance of the world), Aquinas recurs to the idea of the image of God at the very beginning of the *Secunda Pars*, in which man is now seen as directed to God as his end (*finis*). In the prologue he introduces the study of human activity toward an end by relating the human act to God's creative action as an image is related to its exemplar. We have considered the exemplar, God, as the free and autonomous creator in the *Prima Pars*. Now we turn to study God's image, man, as a free and autonomous agent.[4] Yet because man is created for God, his activity is necessarily directed toward the achievement of his final end, which is the beatific vision of God.[5] J.-P. Torrell explains the significance of Aquinas' reference to the image of God in this prologue:

> If the human being has God for end, it is because he has been made by Him "to His image and likeness" (Gen. 1:26), and so there results an irresistible attraction inscribed in his very nature to become like Him as an image is like the model to which it has been made. The human person finds his completion in striving to imitate Him more and more. This is why Thomas dwells on the theme of the image of God when he speaks of the creation of man and his nature in the *prima pars* (q.93), and he spontaneously returns to it when he comes to discuss his action. Thus the theme of the image of God provides an organic connection between the *prima* and the *secunda pars*.[6]

Man's fundamental orientation toward God, his capacity for God, is tied to his creation to the image of God. In explaining why there is a certain aptitude in human nature for the Incarnation of the Son of God, Aquinas says: "the likeness of image is found in human nature inasmuch as it is able to receive God [*capax Dei*], that is, by attaining to Him by its own operation of knowledge and love."[7] Whatever he may say about the fulfillment of this capacity for God in the beatific vision, Aquinas insists that the capacity is rooted in human nature. God has created man with this capacity, and in the *Summa* Aquinas connects this capacity to the image of God in man. Aquinas discusses the image of God in man on purpose in the section on God's production of man. After covering the creation of the human soul and the production of Adam and Eve, Aquinas considers the end or terminus of this production of the human being: "Next we must consider the end or terminus of the production of man, inasmuch as he is said to be made to the image and likeness of God."[8] The end or terminus of the production of a thing is not the final cause for which the thing is made. It is not the *finis operantis* but the *finis operationis*. The end for which a craftsman makes a thing (the *finis operantis*) is the purpose it is meant to serve. The end of the production of a thing (*finis operationis*) is simply the form of the thing at which the process of production terminates.[9] When a thing acquires its substantial form, the process of generation has reached its terminus. God gives to man as his form a soul that bears the express likeness of its creator, because the rationality of man's soul gives man a "likeness according to species" that makes man truly, although imperfectly, an image of God.[10] The defining characteristic of the image of God is simply the intellectual nature that God and man both possess in their own ways.[11] In Augustinian parlance, it is according to his mind (*mens*) that the rational creature is made to the image of God.[12] Thus, the image of God is implanted in the nature of man from the moment of his creation, because man's mind, his rational soul, is in itself an image of the all-knowing God.

Aquinas places the treatment of the image of God in the context of the creation of man after he has considered the nature of the human soul and its intellectual capacity (I.75–89). This arrangement reflects a development in his thinking about the image of God. In his earlier systematic exposition of Christian doctrine the discussion of the image of God is differently located. In the *Scriptum super Sententiis* Aquinas had to follow the order of Peter Lombard's compilation, in which there is a distinction near the beginning (Book 1, d.3) of the long section on the Trinity that deals with the image of the Trinity in man. A shorter discussion of the image of God is found in the section on the creation of man (Book 2, d.16). This division impeded Aquinas from giving a unified treatment of the image. Following in the medieval Augustinian tradition, it tended to make the image of God in man primarily an analogical guide to understanding the divine Trinity.

For the medieval theologian of Latin Christendom, the great authoritative source for thinking about the image of God was Augustine's *De trinitate*, the most brilliant and sustained investigation of the dogma of the Trinity from the patristic period. Study of the twelfth- and thirteenth-century Scholastics seems to indicate that before Aquinas there was limited understanding of Augustine's work, its character as an investigation (*inquisitio*), and its real teaching.[13] Perhaps few Scholastics actually tackled Augustine's daunting work, but after his first teaching of the *Sentences* (1252–56), it seems that Aquinas read and perhaps re-read the *De trinitate*. This is reflected in the comprehension of Augustine's teaching that appears in *De veritate*, question 10 (1257), where Aquinas discusses some of the chief points about the image of God in man in the context of a theological treatment of human cognition. Further development in Aquinas' assimilation of Augustine's thought is indicated in the short texts on the image of the Trinity in *Summa contra Gentiles* IV.26 (1263–64) and *De potentia* q.9 a.9 (1266), as well as in the rough articles that belong to the *reportatio* of Aquinas' lectures on Book 1 of the *Sentences* at the Dominican studium at Rome (1265–66).[14] Only when he came to write the *Summa Theologiae* did he have the opportunity to put his knowledge of Augustine's *De trinitate* to full use, both in his treatment of the Trinity and in a unified exposition of man as image of the triune God.

The Dynamic Image

God is pure act, according to Aquinas.[15] God is not an inert lump of substance. God is active, He is *per se* the pure act of being, and this divine act of being is also one eternal act of knowing and loving.[16] Furthermore, God has revealed that the fecundity of His being eternally gives rise to two divine Persons, the Son and the Holy Spirit, who proceed from the Father in the unique acts of the divine intellect and will.[17] In the beginning was the Word, who proceeds eternally in the simple act by which God knows Himself and all things. Coeternally there proceeds the Holy Spirit in the simple act of God's will that follows naturally upon the act of intellect. In this act by which God loves Himself and all things and by which the Father and the Son love each other, the Spirit proceeds as subsistent Love, a third Person in God, distinct from the Father and the Son.

In his concise and masterful presentation of the two trinitarian processions, Aquinas reveals his grasp of the psychological analogy of the Trinity that Augustine had worked out in his *De trinitate*, especially in its final Book 15. Here is one of the key texts in which Aquinas deploys the analogy, which is dependent on the exemplar relationship between the image of God in man and the divine Trinity:

> [Immanent] action in an intellectual nature is found in the act of the intellect and the act of the will. But the procession of word is found in connection with the intellect's act. With regard to the operation of the will there is found in us another sort of procession, namely, the procession of love, inas-

much as the loved object is in the lover, just as through the conception of a word the thing spoken or understood is in the one who understands. Hence in addition to the procession of word we posit also another procession in God, which is the procession of love.[18]

Combining Augustine's psychological analogy with the more Aristotelian identification of intellect and will as the only faculties of the mind, Aquinas was able to give a clearer and more explicit answer to the chief question Augustine wrestled with in *De trinitate:* "Why is the Holy Spirit not also to be either believed or understood to be begotten by God the Father, so that He also may be called a Son?"[19] Whereas Augustine saw the distinction of the procession of love from the procession of word in terms of the difference between love's unitive function and the generative function of the intellect in producing the interior word, Aquinas contrasts the will and the intellect in terms of the circle between the mind and its object.[20] For Aquinas the act of intellect entails the action of the object upon the mind that produces a likeness of the object in the mind, that is, the interior word or concept of the object. In contrast, the act of the will moves in the opposite direction, starting from the concept in the mind and being drawn outward to the object itself. This outward-directed impulse is what Aquinas identifies as the love that proceeds in the act of will—a thing that is very different from the inner word that is a likeness of the object reproduced within the mind.[21] Thus, in God, as in man, there are two distinct interior processions belonging to the acts of intellect and will and resulting in two entities: word and love.

Man is the image of the divine Trinity. This truth was largely unchallenged among the medieval schoolmen. To have done so would have meant contradicting St. Augustine, although in general the Greek fathers had not dwelt much on man as the image of the entire Trinity.[22] Aquinas says that if a thing is the image of God inasmuch as it imitates the divine nature, it will also necessarily be the image of the Trinity, "for in God Himself one nature exists in three Persons."[23] The image, like the exemplar, will also be trinitarian.

In the development of Aquinas' thought from the *Scriptum super Sententiis* to the *Summa Theologiae,* his improved understanding of Augustine's *De trinitate* produces similar results both in the teaching on the Trinity and in the treatment of the image of the Trinity in man. Aquinas moves from a view of the image of the Trinity as a static reality consisting of the three faculties of memory, intellect, and will in the human mind, to an acceptance of Augustine's developed notion of the image as the *acts* of remembering, understanding, and willing. In his mature teaching, Aquinas sees the image as a dynamic imitation of God's eternal acts of knowing and willing according to which there are two processions in God, the processions of the Son as Word and of the Holy Spirit as Love. The human mind reflects and imitates the divine Trinity in its own human processions of word and love. The capacity to participate in the dynamic life of the Trinity is rooted in man's nature, but it is only when the mind is actively engaged in knowing and willing that the two processions actually occur in man's mind.

In his commentary on the *Sentences* Aquinas considers the two triads Augustine discerned in man's soul as images of the Trinity: mind, knowledge, love (*mens, notitia, amor,* Book 9); and memory, understanding, will (*memoria, intelligentia, voluntas,* Books 10 and 14). Peter Lombard presented Augustine's second triad first, and Aquinas interpreted this order in the *Sentences* as a judgment on the relative value of the two triads as offering an adequate analogy for the Trinity. Aquinas devotes only one article to examining Augustine's earlier triadic analogue: he analyzes *mens, notitia, amor* as the essence of the mind and two consubstantial habits of knowledge and love.[24] For Aquinas this triad lacks the equality between its members that would make it a satisfactory image of the three equal Persons in God, for a habit is not equal ontologically to the essence of the mind in which it is located.

In the *Scriptum* Aquinas prefers to devote most of his discussion of the image of the Trinity to the second triad (*memoria, intelligentia, voluntas*), which, he realized, Augustine preferred. Peter Lombard had described these three as "natural properties or powers [*vires*] of the mind."[25] As Beaurecueil has judged in his study of Aquinas' evolving view about the image of God, Lombard's ontological description of the triad as properties or powers of the mind is not an accurate reading of Augustine.[26] However, it became and remained the common interpretation of Augustine's triad, even after Aquinas had corrected it. In the *Scriptum* Aquinas by and large accepted this common view and designated the three powers as *potentiae,* or faculties of the soul in the Aristotelian sense.[27] A major problem arose for this interpretation of the triad as faculties of the mind: Aristotelian psychology recognizes only two powers at the intellective level of the soul, namely, intellect and will. Memory belongs at the level of sensation as a function of the faculty of imagination. Is there some sort of higher memory that can be called a faculty of the mind? Aquinas asserts that the mind has its own special ability to retain the intelligible species of things it has come to know.[28] However, this higher memory is not a faculty in the proper sense, because it has no act of its own toward which it is oriented. Instead, it is a capacity of the faculty of intellect to retain the forms or intelligible species of things to which the intellect can recur in order to reactivate its knowledge of those things. Memory in the mind is a faculty (*potentia*) only in the sense of a natural property of the soul: "any property that follows upon the essence of the soul according to its nature is here called a faculty [*potentia*] of the soul, whether it is directed toward operation or not."[29]

Aquinas evaluates the triad of memory, intellect, and will as an "express representation" of the Trinity by showing that the three faculties possess characteristics that make them like the Trinity.[30] The three faculties are distinct from one another and yet consubstantial, as are the three divine Persons. There is also a similar order and equality between the three faculties when they are directed toward the higher objects, namely, one's own soul and God.[31] The mind thus exhibits a sort of parallel or mirror image of the Trinity. Aquinas adds a more dynamic dimension to his view of the image by studying a fifth characteristic, which he calls *actualis imitatio*. Having defined the word "image" in terms of "imitation," Aquinas here explains that the mind *imitates* the Trinity in an active way, that is, by means of its acts. The mind actively intends God as object of its intellect and will, and so becomes an "image that expressly leads to God."[32] A question Aquinas then faces is whether the mind is always actively intending God (either directly or through considering itself as image of God). The *Summa fratris Alexandri* tied actual imitation to the state of grace.[33] But if the mind is only truly an image of God when it actively knows and loves God, how can the image of God be permanent in man? Aquinas' uncomfortable answer in the *Scriptum* is that there is a sort of preconceptual activity of memory, intellect, and will that continues unbrokenly in the human mind with regard to God and itself.[34] There is a simple act of intuition (*simplex intuitus*) by which certain intelligible objects are simply present to the intellect and known in some sort of way.[35] Students of Aquinas have been embarrassed by this early opinion, since later, in *De veritate*, question 10, he only allows this simple cognition to be habitual, not active.[36] However, it seems more likely that Aquinas already had some idea that Augustine tied the image of the Trinity in the human mind to a state of activity. If the image is a permanent reality of the mind, then somehow the mind must always be actively directed to the higher objects, that is, God, and secondarily, one's own soul—so Aquinas seems to have reasoned in the *Scriptum*.

When Aquinas returned to the question of the image of the Trinity in the course of his *Quaestio disputata de veritate* (probably in the fall of 1257 for question 10), his new, more mature approach shows a greater comprehension of Augustine's thought. Aquinas is no longer constrained to identify Augustine's triad of *memoria, intelligentia, voluntas* as faculties of the mind. Instead, faithful to Book 14 of *De trinitate*, he considers memory in the mind to be simply the habitual state of knowledge in the intellect. He calls it a *vis* (power) but not a *potentia*, an Aristotelian faculty of the soul.[37] In fact, the mind's memory is simply a function of the faculty of intellect. Thus, the triad at the level of mere potency is reduced to two faculties, intellect and will, although there is a sufficient distinction in function between memory and understanding to speak of the triad at the level of faculties.[38]

Aquinas is much more interested in the active level of the triad, by which the mind *perfectly* imitates the Trinity.

> The soul, in fact, perfectly imitates the Trinity in this, that it remembers, actually understands, and actually wills. This is so because in the uncreated Trinity the middle Person in the Trinity is the Word. However, there can be no word without actual thinking. Hence, according to this way of perfect imitation, Augustine assigns the image in these three things—memory, understanding, and will—inasmuch as memory refers to habitual knowledge, understanding to actual thought that proceeds from that knowledge, and will to the actual movement of the will that proceeds from thought.[39]

Aquinas goes on to quote from Book 14 of *De trinitate,* showing a perfect understanding of why Augustine stressed that *acts* of intellect and will are required for the proper realization of the image of the Trinity.[40] The key to the image of the Trinity is the imitation of the processions of the Word and Love in God. These processions only occur when the intellectual nature is engaged actively in knowing and willing. Although we can say that the image of the Trinity exists in an imperfect way when the human mind has only a habitual knowledge and love of its object and even when the faculties of intellect and will are in a state of bare potentiality, nevertheless, the image only exists in a complete and fulfilled way when the mind actively knows and wills and consequently gives rise to an inner word and love that reflect the processions in the divine Trinity.

Ten years later St. Thomas gave his mature treatment of the image of the Trinity in the *Prima Pars* of his *Summa Theologiae,* question 93. He had taught on this subject when lecturing on the *Sentences* at the Dominican studium in Rome in the year 1265–66. Some idea of his teaching can be found in his second *lectura* on Book 1 of the *Sentences* and in the *Quaestio disputata de potentia* (q.9 a.9), both from this same year. These works witness to a development in Aquinas' thought that finds fuller and more systematic treatment in the *Summa.* Aquinas now focuses primarily on the two processions of word and love that represent the two trinitarian processions. Just as he begins his treatment of the Trinity with the processions of the Word and Love in God, so, as early as his discussion of creative causality in question 45, he notes that God imprints the trinitarian image upon rational creatures inasmuch as they give rise to an inner word and love:

Now the processions of the divine Persons are found according to the acts of intellect and will, as it was said above. For the Son proceeds as the Word of the intellect, and the Holy Spirit as Love in the will. Therefore, in rational creatures, in which there are intellect and will, there is found a representation of the Trinity by way of image, inasmuch as there is found in them a word that has been conceived and love that proceeds.[41]

In question 93, after affirming in article 5 the existence of the image of the Trinity in man, Aquinas describes in article 6 where the image is located in man and in what exactly it consists:

Because the uncreated Trinity is differentiated according to the procession of the Word from the One who speaks, and of Love from both, as it has been held above, we can speak of an image of the uncreated Trinity on account of certain representation of species in the rational creature, in which there is found a procession of word according to the intellect and a procession of love according to the will.[42]

From these two verbally similar texts we can see that Aquinas considered the two processions to be central, both to the exemplar causality of the divine Trinity at work in creation and to the created image of the Trinity in the human soul.

In article 7 of question 93 Aquinas once again tackles the problem of whether the image of the Trinity is found in the mind only in a state of activity or also at the level of habits and faculties. As in *De veritate,* he quotes Augustine to the effect that the procession of an inner word depends upon the act of thinking in the intellect. Therefore, the image exists principally according to the *acts* of the intellect and will, inasmuch as "from the knowledge that we have we form an inner word by thinking, and from this we burst forth into love."[43] Aquinas makes no mention of memory in the corpus of this article, although he deals with Augustine's two triads in the replies to the objections. Memory is simply the "habitual retention of knowledge and love."[44] Man is made to the image of the Trinity according to his *acts* of understanding and loving. Aquinas allows that these acts have some existence in their principles, that is, in their corresponding habits and faculties, but in effect he bypasses the discussion of Augustine's triads in terms of acts, habits, and faculties by simply stressing the two processions of word and love. In doing so he is following the lead of Augustine himself, who in the last book of the *De trinitate* focuses more on the two processions than on his triad of memory, understanding, and will. The human mind always has a potentiality for these two processions and therefore always possesses the image of the Trinity *in germine.* Nevertheless, the image exists primarily in the state of activity according to which the word proceeds in the act of knowing and love proceeds in the act of willing.

Assimilation to the Trinity

Aquinas had said in the *Scriptum super Sententiis* that the mind actively imitates the Trinity only when the mind has as its object either God or itself. The mind is assimilated to God and conformed to its exemplar when its faculties are directed to God Himself, either directly when God is the object or indirectly when the mind regards itself as the image of God. Aquinas even allowed that the mind is the image of the Trinity *quodammodo* when it has other things as its objects.[45] With a better knowledge of Augustine, he changed his opinion in the *De veritate.* The image of the Trinity depends upon the existence of an express likeness to the Trinity either according to analogy or according to conformation.[46] When the mind knows and loves itself, we have the highest case of analogy to the Trinity. The parts of the human analogue and their interrelations are a mirror image of the divine Persons and their relations. In this case the mind and its object are consubstantial because they are identical, as God is when He knows and loves Himself. Such is not the case when the mind considers temporal objects, which are not consubstantial with the mind. As Aquinas puts it, when the mind knows and loves itself, it offers the best analogy of the eternal unfolding of the Trinity:

> But in the likeness by which our mind knows itself there is a representation of the uncreated Trinity according to analogy, inasmuch as, in this case, the mind in knowing itself begets a word expressing itself, and love proceeds from both of these, just as the Father, uttering Himself, has begotten His Word from eternity, and the Holy Spirit proceeds from both.[47]

Here we have the highest analogy of proportionality between God and creature—A is to B as a is to b.

Yet Aquinas goes on to say that there is a more express likeness than likeness according to analogy, and that is likeness according to conformation, in which the image is assimilated or conformed to the exemplar by a sort of union. In the case of the image of the Trinity, when man turns his mind to God, the intentional presence of God conforms the mind more closely to God than when the mind is considering itself as object. Aquinas says, "there is a greater likeness through conformation, as of sight to color, than through analogy, as of sight to intellect, which is related in a similar way to its objects."[48] An object acting on a faculty makes the faculty like itself with a likeness that is closer than an analogical likeness between two faculties and their respective objects. As Beaurecueil has observed, "the one is communion, the other remains at the extrinsic level of 'parallelism.'"[49] There is a better image of the Trinity in man's mind when he knows and loves God, because God as objectively present makes man more like Himself. As Aquinas puts it, "in that cognition by which the mind knows God Himself, the mind itself is conformed to God, just as every knower, as such, is assimilated to that which is known."[50]

In the *Summa Theologiae* Aquinas in effect shows that the image of the Trinity properly involves elements both of analogy and conformation. In answering the question about which objects the mind must intend in order to be the image of the Trinity, he develops a fundamentally different argument from the one he used in the *De veritate*. Throughout the question on the image of God in the *Summa*, the key term in the definition of image is "representation of species." If we can speak of the "species" of the Trinity, we must say that what distinguishes the divine Persons is the double procession of Word and Love. And what specifies the processions is the object that specifies God's acts of knowing and loving. That object is, of course, God Himself. If the human mind is to represent the specificity of the Trinity, it also must have God as its object. Aquinas reasons:

> It is clear that a diversity of objects diversifies the species of the word and love. For in man's heart the word conceived from a stone is not the same in species as that conceived from a horse, nor is the love the same in species. Therefore, the divine image is noted in man according to the word conceived from the knowledge about God and the love derived from thence.[51]

According to Aquinas, not just any inner procession of word and love suffices for the mind to be the image of the Trinity. It has to be the inner word that expresses the mind's knowledge of God, the inner love that impels the mind toward God. God must be the object of the intellect and will; and reflexive acts of self-knowledge and self-love will suffice only if they in fact lead the mind to God.

At the principal and proper level of the image of the Trinity there is both a likeness of analogy and a likeness of conformation. The mind is conformed to God because it has God as its object. God assimilates the mind to Himself by His objective presence in the intellect and the will. Yet Aquinas also sees the analogical aspect involved in this assimilation. For there remains an analogy between the procession of the Word in God and the intellectual procession of the inner "word conceived from the knowledge about God" in man's mind. In effect, when the mind knows and loves the same object as God does, that is, God Himself as object, we have the case of the analogy *unius ad alterum*, according to which the human acts are a participation in the divine acts. Aquinas gives a suggestion of what this means when he says that in the human act of knowing God, "the Word of God proceeds from knowledge about God."[52] The human mind somehow participates in the procession of the eternal Word so that the Word of God can be said to proceed in the human mind through the assimilation caused by the objective presence of God to the human intellect.

We must now ask Aquinas how the human mind can know and love God in such a way that it participates in the divine life of the Trinity. Is grace required? Does this assimilation depend on the light of glory by which the blessed see God face to face? Aquinas always affirmed that every man bears the image of the Trinity from the first moment of his existence, although it may be only at an incipient stage. Aquinas tends to associate the image at the active level with the gifts of grace and glory. In the *Summa* he designates three levels of the image:

> in one way, according as man has a natural aptitude for understanding and loving God, and this aptitude consists in the very nature of the mind, which is common to all men; in another way, according as man knows and loves God actually or habitually, but imperfectly, and this is the image through the conformation of grace; in a third way, according as man actually knows and loves God perfectly, and in this way the image is noted according to the likeness of glory.[53]

In this life, grace with its virtues of faith, hope, and charity enables the mind to know and love God as He has revealed Himself, even if much of the time this knowledge and love are only at the habitual level.

However, Aquinas does allow that man can know and love God in the state of nature unaided by grace. Thomas always held that there can be a merely natural knowledge of God. In his treatment of the image of God in the *Summa* he replies to an argument that we need grace in order to know and love God by saying that "there is some natural knowledge and love of God," and furthermore, that the mind has a natural ability to know God by using its reason.[54] The image of the Trinity can exist at the active level even in the state of nature. Nevertheless, it would seem that grace is usually required to conform and assimilate the mind to God so that the mind can participate in the divine processions of the Word and Love. Man has an innate ability to know God by his natural faculty of reason, but in fact he often fails to know God when he is not aided by grace. Therefore, de facto, the image of the Trinity is usually elevated to the active level only by means of the gift of grace.

The Indwelling of the Trinity

Whatever man might be able to attain by the natural powers God has given him, God has willed to elevate man by supernatural grace to a more intimate share in His divine life. Aquinas connects the capacity or obediential potency for sharing God's beatitude with the image of God. "Rational creatures," he says in the *Tertia Pars*, "inasmuch as they are made to the image of God, are capable of divine beatitude [*capaces beatitudinis divinae*], which consists in the enjoyment of God."[55] The enjoyment or fruition of God in which beatitude consists involves the possessing of God as the object of one's knowledge and love. The capacity for God which God implants in man in making him to His image is realized by knowing and loving God. "The likeness of the image is found in human nature according as it has a capacity for God [*est capax Dei*], that is, by attaining to Him through its proper operation of knowledge and love."[56] The rational creature has an innate capacity to contact the eternal Word Himself in some way by its acts of knowing and loving.[57] Through the grace of Christ, Aquinas states, the image of God fulfills its capacity for the beatific knowledge of God,[58] a capacity that God has planted in the rational nature.

Although Aquinas does not make the connection explicit, it seems likely that he saw the graced indwelling of the Trinity as the fulfillment of the image of the Trinity in this life on earth. It is obvious that Aquinas applied his developed teaching on the Trinity in the *Prima Pars* (qq.27–43) to the analysis of the image of the Trinity in man (q.93). In both places there is the same consistent use of Augustine's psychological analogy with its final emphasis on the two processions of Word and Love.[59] At the end of the treatment of the Trinity, Aquinas discusses the sending, or mission, of the divine Persons into the world—a subject that really involves the whole of salvation history with its center in the visible sending of the Son to be born as man. In question 43 of the *Prima Pars*, Aquinas mainly deals with the invisible missions of the Son and the Spirit by which the entire Trinity is said to come and dwell in the souls of the just. This indwelling of the Trinity entails a new presence of God in man above the basic presence of God in all creatures (God's physical presence, or presence of immensity). Following the New Testament references to the new presence of God in the soul, Aquinas asserts that sanctifying grace is required for this presence.[60]

There was great controversy in the mid-twentieth century about Aquinas' teaching on the graced presence of God in the soul, and particularly about whether it involved a second physical presence of God in addition to the basic physical presence of God.[61] The texts of Aquinas on the indwelling of the Trinity support the view that the new divine presence in the soul is not a new physical presence but an objective presence: through grace, God makes Himself present in a new and higher way as the object of the mind's knowledge and love. Aquinas describes it in this way:

> There is one special way [above God's common presence] that pertains to the rational creature, in which God is said to exist as the thing known in the knower and the thing loved in the lover. Because the rational creature by knowing and loving attains to God Himself by its operation, God, according to this special way, is said not only to be in the rational creature, but also to dwell in it as in His temple. However, no effect other than sanctifying grace can thus be the reason that the divine Person should exist in a new way in the rational creature.[62]

Through grace man is enabled to know and love God in such a way that God can be said to come and dwell in the soul as in a temple in which He is worshipped and also, Aquinas adds, to be possessed and freely enjoyed by man. The Son and the Holy Spirit are not only sent to the redeemed soul, but also *given* to the soul. The soul in the state of grace possesses the Father, the Son, and the Holy Spirit within itself, a wonderful reality that contemplatives like St. Catherine of Siena and St. John of the Cross have spoken about from their own experience.

The indwelling of the Trinity assimilates the soul to the Trinity. Aquinas writes that the sending of the divine Person to a soul entails "assimilation to the divine Person through some gift of grace."[63] The soul is assimilated to the Holy Spirit who is Love through the gift of charity. It is assimilated to the Word through the gift of wisdom, the *sapida scientia* that gives a sort of experiential taste of a thing that results in a movement of love toward the thing. "Therefore, the Son is not sent according to any perfection of the intellect, but according to a conditioning, or informing, of the intellect such that by means of it the intellect bursts forth into the affection of love [*prorumpat in affectum amoris*]."[64] It is interesting that the only other text in which Aquinas uses the expression *prorumpere in amorem* is the description of the active level of the image of the Trinity in question 93: "we form an inner word by thinking, and from this we break forth into love [*in amorem prorumpimus*]."[65] The use of the same unusual phrase suggests that Aquinas saw the similarity between the graced *indwelling* of the Trinity and the active level of the *image* of the Trinity.[66] Nevertheless, he did not explicitly mention the connection, possibly because the focus in question 43 is on the sending of the divine Persons, not on the effect of their mission on the mind made to the image of the Trinity at the beginning of the world.

One other text from Aquinas' treatment of the Trinity sheds some light on the assimilation of the soul to the Trinity. In question 93 Aquinas teaches that God must be the object of the intellect and will if man is to be properly the image of the Trinity. He suggests there that the eternal Word of God somehow proceeds in the mind that knows God. In question 38, on the Holy Spirit as gift, Aquinas asks what it means to say that a divine Person is *given* to the soul— how can we have and possess a divine Person? Aquinas explains:

> We are said to have that which we can freely use or enjoy as we will. And in this way a divine Person can only be had by a rational creature that is conjoined to God. Other creatures can indeed be moved by a divine Person, but nevertheless it is not in their power to enjoy a divine Person and use His effect. Sometimes the rational creature attains to this when, that is, it is made a partaker of the divine Word and the Love which proceeds in such a way that it can freely know God in truth and love Him rightly.[67]

Aquinas says further that a divine Person cannot be possessed in this way unless He is given to the soul by God, because it is beyond the creature's own power. In fact, Aquinas ties the *giving* of the Persons to the *sending* of the Son and the Spirit in his treatment of the divine missions.

Thus, the indwelling of the Trinity is basically the graced presence of God to the mind's faculties of intellect and will in a way that makes the intellect participate in the divine procession of the Word and the will participate in the divine procession of Love. God brings this about by the gift of grace with the consequent habits of wisdom and charity, the appropriated effects of the Word and Love, which the soul uses at the same time as it enjoys those divine Persons in the acts of knowing and loving God as He shows Himself to man. This description of what takes place in the indwelling of the Trinity is basically equivalent to what transpires in the active level of the image of the Trinity, in which "the Word of God proceeds from knowledge about God."[68] It is properly by the graced missions of the Spirit and the Son that the soul truly comes to participate in their divine processions so that the soul knows and loves God by the very acts of God in which the Son and the Spirit proceed. It is as if the divine Word were proceeding in the mind of man, and from thence the Person of Love were proceeding in the human act of loving God. The missions of the Son and the Holy Spirit are temporal extensions of the eternal processions. "The mission," Aquinas says, "includes the eternal procession and adds something, namely, the temporal effect"[69]—which is the indwelling of the Persons in the soul. The Trinity draws its created image into the processional life of divine knowing and loving. The life of the Trinity unfolds in man through man's graced participation in the divine nature.

For Aquinas the proper study of the theologian is God, and especially God as the beginning and end of man. God is a Trinity of Persons, and man bears the imprint of the creative Trinity. In his fundamental being, man is oriented to God and capable of sharing the trinitarian life of God. The very structure of man's being as an intellectual creature is an image and imitation of God's interpersonal life of knowing and loving. Whether man is able in some limited way to actualize the trinitarian potentiality of his being at the natural level, God offers His grace to man to elevate him to a closer and higher sharing in the divine life of the Trinity. God sends His Word and His Love into the hearts of the just to make them participate in the processions of the divine Word and Love, by which they are enabled through grace to know God and love God better than mere nature allows. In this way the image of the Trinity is actualized in the soul that is turned to God by grace and led toward the supreme assimilation to God in the glory of heaven. Aquinas' doctrines of the image of the Trinity and the indwelling of the Trinity express his penetrating insight into the fundamental relationship between man and the God who is the source and the completion of human existence.

Notes

1. *ST* I.2, prol.

2. *ST* I.1.7c.

3. Ghislain Lafont, *Structures et méthode dans le Somme théologique de saint Thomas d'Aquin* (Paris: Desclée de Brouwer, 1961), 265–66: "La notion la plus capable de rassembler de manière simple l'anthropologie thomiste semble être celle de l'Image de Dieu; c'est aussi la notion classique en Tradition chrétienne. Elle n'est pas, chez saint Thomas, un instrument technique d'élaboration: c'est cette notion que les développements techniques ont mission d'éclairer." See also Louis B. Geiger, "L'homme, image de Dieu: A propos de *Summa Theologiae*, Ia, 93, 4," *Rivista di Filosofia Neo-Scolastica* 66 (1974): 511–32, for the importance of the notion *imago Dei* in the anthropological section of the *Prima Pars*. For a recent reconsideration of this subject, see Jean-Pierre Torrell, *Saint Thomas d'Aquin, Maître spirituel: Initiation 2* (Fribourg: Éditions Universitaires and Paris: Cerf, 1996), 105–9.

4. *ST* I-II, prol.: "Quia, sicut Damascenus dicit, homo factus ad imaginem Dei dicitur, secundum quod per imaginem significatur intellectuale et arbitrio liberum et per se potestativum; postquam praedictum est de exemplari, scilicet de Deo, et de his quae processerunt ex divina potestate secundum eius voluntatem; restat ut consideremus de eius imagine, idest de homine, secundum quod et ipse et suorum operum principium, quasi liberum arbitrium habens et suorum operum potestatem."

5. *ST* I-II.1, prol.: "Et quia ultimus finis humanae vitae ponitur esse beatitudo, oportet primum considerare de ultimo fine in communi; deinde de beatitudine."

6. Torrell, *Saint Thomas d'Aquin, Maître spirituel*, 108.

7. *ST* III.4.1 ad 2. See also *ST* III.6.2c. For the importance of this expression *capax Dei*, see C. O'Neill, "L'homme ouvert à Dieu (*Capax Dei*)," in *L'anthropologie de saint Thomas*, ed. N. A. Luyten (Fribourg: Éditions Universitaires, 1974), 54–74.

8. *ST* I.93, prol.

9. For this Aristotelian distinction, see *ST* II-II.141.6 ad 1; *De Pot.* q.3 a.16 resp.; and *Meta.* 8, lect.4, Marietti ed., no.1737: "Finis enim generationis hominis est anima."

10. *ST* I.93.2.

11. *ST* I.93.3c: "id in quo primo consideratur ratio imaginis, quod est intellectualis natura." See also *ST* I.93.4c: "cum homo secundum intellectualem naturam ad imaginem Dei esse dicitur."

12. *ST* I.93.6.

13. See the judgment of Michael Schmaus in "Die trinitarische Gottesebenbildlichkeit nach dem Sentenzenkommentar Alberts des Grossen," in *Virtus politica: Festgabe zum 75. Geburtstag von Alfons Hufnagel*, ed. Joseph Möller and Helmut Kohlenberger (Stuttgart–Bad Canstatt: Frommann-Holzboog, 1974), 295–98.

14. On the authenticity of this second *lectura* on the *Sentences*, Book I, see Leonard E. Boyle, "Alia lectura fratris Thome," *Mediaeval Studies* 45 (1983): 418–29. It is noteworthy that the manuscript (Lincoln College, Oxford, MS. Lat. 95), which is mostly a copy of Book I of Aquinas' Parisian *Scriptum super Sententiis*, did not have enough room in the margins of the *Scriptum* text to add the new articles that deal with the image of God. Instead, we find four articles on the image at the end of the manuscript, along with several other articles. This indicates significant development in Aquinas' thinking about the image between his two sets of lectures on the *Sentences*.

15. *ST* I.3.2c: "Deus est purus actus, non habens aliquid de potentialitate."

16. *ST* I.14.4c: "ipsum [Dei] intelligere sit eius essentia et eius esse." *ST* I.19.1c: "Et sicut suum intelligere est suum esse, ita suum velle."

17. Thomas neatly expounds Augustine's doctrine of the two processions of the divine Word and Love in *ST* I.27.

18. *ST* I.27.3c.

19. *De trinitate* 9.12.17; CCSL 50:308. Few scholars have noted the centrality of this question in the development of the *De trinitate*. It is one of two main questions Augustine addresses, beginning in Book 1: "Movet etiam quomodo spiritus sanctus in trinitate sit, quem nec pater nec filius nec ambo genuerint, cum sit spiritus patris et filii" (1.5.8; CCSL 50:36–37). The Spirit is not begotten, so how are we to understand His procession? Agostino Trapé noted how Augustine focused on this question and how at the very end of *De trinitate* he gives an answer that Aquinas read and developed in *ST* I.27.4. See Trapé, "Nota sulla processione dello Spirito Santo nello teologia trinitaria di S. Agostino e di S. Tommaso," in *Studi Tomistici*, vol. 1: *San Tommaso, Fonti e riflessi del suo pensiero* (Rome: Pontificia Accademia Romana di S. Tommaso d'Aquino, 1974), 119–25.

20. In places, Aquinas explicitly compares the double movement of intellect and will to a circle. See *ScG* IV.26; *De Pot.* q.9 a.9 resp.: "Est ergo in nobis quam in Deo circulatio quaedam in operibus intellectus et voluntatis; nam voluntas redit in id a quo fuit principium intelligendi: sed in nobis concluditur circulus ad id quod est extra . . . ; sed in Deo iste circulus clauditur in se ipso."

21. *ST* I.27.4c: "Processio igitur quae attenditur secundum rationem intellectus, est secundum rationem similitudinis; et intantum potest habere rationem generationis, quia omne generans generat sibi simile. Processio autem quae attenditur secundum rationem voluntatis, non consideratur secundum rationem similitudinis, sed magis secundum rationem impellentis et moventis in aliquid. Et ideo quod procedit in divinis per modum amoris, non procedit ut genitum vel ut filius, sed magis procedit ut spiritus; quo nomine quaedam vitalis motio et impulsio designatur, prout aliquis ex amore dicitur moveri vel impelli ad aliquid faciendum."

22. See Jean Kirchmeyer, "Grecque (Église)," *Dictionnaire de spiritualité* [1967], 6:812–22; H. Merki, "Ebenbildlichkeit," *Reallexikon für Antike und Christentum*, vol. 4 (1958), cols. 459–79; and Aimé Solignac, "L'image et ressemblance, II: Pères de l'Église," *Dictionnaire de spiritualité* [1967], 7:1406–25.

23. *ST* I.93.5c.

24. I *Sent.* d.3 q.5 a.1 sol.

25. I *Sent.* d.3, text.

26. Marie-Joseph Serge de Laugier de Beaurecueil, "L'homme image de Dieu selon saint Thomas d'Aquin," *Études et Recherches* 8 (1952): 62: "Notons seulement le gauchissement vers une interprétation ontologique, lorsqu'on nous parle de *naturales proprietates seu vires ipsius mentis*. Ces expressions conviendraient mal au plan de la conscience où se plaçait le docteur d'Hippone."

27. Thomas locates the image of God "*in potentiis mentis*" (I *Sent.* d.3 q.3 a.1 ad 1). In this, he was following in the steps of earlier theologians of the thirteenth century, including his immediate Franciscan and Dominican predecessors.

28. I *Sent.* d.3 q.4 a.1 sol.

29. Ibid.

30. I *Sent.* d.3 q.4 a.4 sol.

31. Ibid.

32. Ibid. The distinction between actual and habitual vs. potential imitation is found in Alexander of Hales, I *Sent.* d.3, no.34 (ed. Fathers of the College of St. Bonaventure [Quaracchi, 1951], 54–55); and *Qu. Disp. 'antequam esset frater,'* q.26, disp.1, membrum 5, no.23 (ed. Fathers of the College of St. Bonaventure [Quaracchi, 1960], 475); *Summa Halensis.* lib.1, no.50, sol.; and Albert, *Summa de creaturis*, p.2, tr.1, q.73, a.2, particula 1, qc.2, sed contra.2 (Borgnet [1896], 35:608) and particula 2, quaesitum 2, ad qc.1 and qc.2 (Borgnet [1896], 35:616). Albert speaks of *imitatio actualis, imitatio secundum actum,* and *actus imitandi exemplar.*

33. *Summa Halensis,* lib.1, no.50, sol.

34. I *Sent.* d.3 q.4 a.5 sol.

35. Ibid.

36. See A. Gardeil, "La perception expérimentale de l'âme par elle-même d'après S. Thomas," in *Mélanges Thomistes* (Paris: Vrin, 1923), 225. He contends that Thomas really means a habitual state of cognition.

37. *De Ver.* q.10 a.2 resp.

38. *De Ver.* q.10 a.3 resp.: "Nihilominus tamen, etsi memoria non est potentia distincta ab intelligentia prout intelligentia sumitur pro potentia, tamen invenitur trinitas in anima etiam considerando ipsas potentias secundum quod una potentia, quae est intellectus, habet habi-

tudinem ad diversa, scilicet ad tenendum notitiam alicuius habitualiter et ad considerandum illud actualiter."

39. *De Ver.* q.10 a.3 resp.

40. Walter H. Principe rightly pointed out that Augustine tends to use the verbal forms (*meminisse, intellegere, velle*), thus indicating that the image of the Trinity at its highest level is found when the mind is in a state of activity. See his "The Dynamism of Augustine's Terms for Describing the Highest Trinitarian Image in the Human Person," in *Studia Patristica*, vol. 18, ed. Elizabeth A. Livingstone (Oxford and New York: Pergamon Press, 1982), 1291–99.

41. *ST* I.45.7c.

42. *ST* I.93.6c.

43. *ST* I.93.7c.

44. *ST* I.93.7 ad 3.

45. I *Sent.* d.3 q.4 a.4 ad 2.

46. *De Ver.* q.10 a.7 resp.

47. Ibid.

48. Ibid.

49. Beaurecueil, "L'homme image," 46.

50. *De Ver.* q.10 a.7 resp.

51. *ST* I.93.8c.

52. *ST* I.93.8 ad 1: "Verbum Dei procedit a notitia de Deo." Does "Verbum Dei" here mean *the* Word of God, or simply "a word about God"? Torrell translates it: "il faut trouver un verbe au sujet de Dieu procédant d'une connaissance sur Dieu" (*Saint Thomas d'Aquin, Maître spirituel,* 130). But I prefer the interpretation of Beaurecueil ("L'homme image," 48): "il faut qu'il y ait communion à l'activité divine elle-même, selon laquelle le Verbe de Dieu procède d'une connaissance ayant Dieu pour objet." Cf. Lafont, *Structures et méthode,* 270: "C'est Dieu lui-même qui procède de Dieu au travers des actes humains."

53. *ST* I.93.4c.

54. *ST* I.93.8 ad 3.

55. *ST* III.23.1c.

56. *ST* III.4.1 ad 2.

57. *ST* III.4.1c: "nata est contingere aliqualiter ipsum Verbum."

58. *ST* III.8.2c.

59. See *ST* I.32.1 obj.2 for his open admission: "Augustine proceeds to manifest the Trinity of Persons from the procession of word and love in our mind. We have followed this way above."

60. *ST* I.43.3c.

61. See Lucien Chambat, *Présence et union: Les missions des personnes de la Sainte Trinité selon Saint Thomas d'Aquin* (Abbaye Saint-Wandrille: Fontenelle, 1945), for the proposal of the indwelling as a second physical presence of God. This interpretation is sufficiently refuted by Francis L. B. Cunningham, *The Indwelling of the Trinity: A Historico-Doctrinal Study of the Theory of St. Thomas Aquinas* (Dubuque, Iowa: Priory Press, 1955).

62. *ST* I.43.3c.

63. *ST* I.43.5 ad 2.

64. Ibid.

65. *ST* I.93.7c.

66. J.-P. Torrell has noted (*Saint Thomas d'Aquin, Maître spirituel,* 120–21) that the connection between image and indwelling in the *Summa* is allusive, not explicit, but that "the doctrine of

the indwelling of the Trinity is the crowning of the doctrine of the image of God." He criticizes my hesitation about affirming this connection in my book *To the Image of the Trinity: A Study of the Development of Aquinas' Teaching* (Toronto: Pontifical Institute of Mediaeval Studies, 1990), 230–34. However, it remains the fact that Aquinas does not mention the image in his treatment of the indwelling, and vice versa. I think it is fair to ask why his systematic mind did not explicitly indicate the connection. I do not deny that there is a close relation between image and indwelling and between Aquinas' treatments of the two themes.

67. *ST* I.38.1c.
68. *ST* I.93.8c.
69. *ST* I.43.2 ad 3.

Seven

Evil, Sin, and Death

Thomas Aquinas on Original Sin

RUDI A. TE VELDE

Although the idea of original sin is not one of the most popular topics of Christian teaching, it is still considered to be an essential part.
According to this doctrine, the first sin of Adam has been passed on to
the whole of mankind by way of origin, that is, transmitted through
sexual reproduction from generation to generation. That the sin of
Adam, acting as head of the human race, is the cause and source of
original sin is strongly suggested by the famous statement of St. Paul
in the Letter to the Romans (5:12): "By one man sin entered into this
world, and by sin death." Human nature was created at first faultless
and without sin; but as the result of the sin of Adam, that nature has
contracted a culpable defect. The first sin has led to the fall of all of humanity in this world.

The first Christian thinker to attempt a coherent explanation of this
seemingly mythical notion of original sin was Augustine of Hippo.[1] His
emphasis on the sexual act of procreation as the locus of transmission
of original sin from one generation to another may impress us as highly
paradoxical. All human beings are said to be somehow "infected" by sin,
simply by reason of their being born from human parents. The paradox
consists in the strange combination of the moral category of sin and
guilt with the biological notion of infectious transmission. From the
perspective of modern moral theory, based on human autonomy and

individual responsibility, the idea of original sin is likely to be rejected as some sort of relic from a "dark" religious past, which lacked a genuine moral conception of sin and guilt. For many people it is difficult to accept that newborn children—the paradigm of pure innocence in our still romantic age—are already tainted with guilt contracted from their parents, in consequence of which they should be ritually cleansed by baptism. But it is not only modern enlightened thought, with its emphasis on the autonomous individual, that finds this concept problematic. Aristotle also would probably have had difficulties with the notion that people are born with a moral defect. In his *Nicomachean Ethics* he observes, as a matter of moral fact, that no one would reproach a person blind from birth, but rather one would pity him.[2] The doctrine of original sin seems to be in flat contradiction with this common moral intuition.

For Thomas Aquinas the doctrine of original sin is neither a relic of a religious past nor, as I will argue, some sort of rational theory that pretends to explain the moral shortcomings of mankind in history in terms of a hereditary defect of human nature. For Aquinas, original sin is in the first place an integral part of the Catholic doctrine of faith. It is one of the elements in which the inexhaustible meaning of faith has been articulated throughout the theological tradition. Perhaps one should start by saying that the idea of original sin, as a culpable failure which bears on the whole of mankind in its relationship to God, has arisen from the faithful experience of the redemptive suffering of Jesus Christ, who is said to have died on the cross for "our sins."

Aquinas' treatment of the doctrine of original sin has its place in the *Prima Secundae* (I-II.81–83) of his *Summa Theologiae*, where it is part of a wider treatment of the moral categories of *peccatum* and *vitium*. The second part of the *Summa* is devoted to what is usually called moral theology. Its general subject matter is characterized by Aquinas as "the movement of the rational creature towards God."[3] It is about the ultimate end of human life and about the free human acts by means of which man strives to attain his end, which consists in the blessed union with God himself (*visio beatifica*). Within the systematic framework of the moral consideration of human acts, the moral category of sin is defined as an evil human act, that is, a voluntary act that fails to conform to the measure for attaining the human end. And original sin, one might say, denotes a more structural failure on the part of humanity to live and act in a free responsiveness to God's will.

Original sin is placed by Aquinas in the category of moral evil, which in its turn is a specification of evil in general. I therefore begin my exposition of Aquinas' account of original sin with a short discussion of evil in general, especially the issue of how evil can happen in a good creation. I also pay some attention to Aquinas' discussion of the traditional theological topic of the "Fall of the Angel," which functions as a contrasting background for the human moral condition. I then focus on the doctrine of original sin as expounded in the *Prima Secundae*. It is not my intention to give a complete doctrinal exposition of Aquinas' view on this matter. In particular, I explore and clarify the issue of the causality of original sin—its mode of transmission. Finally, I discuss some of the anthropological and theological notions that underlie Aquinas' view of the relationship between original sin and human death.

The Possibility of Evil within a Good Creation

The topic of evil is addressed by Aquinas for the first time in the middle of the *Prima Pars* (I.48), in the systematic context of the treatment of God's creative action. Evil is discussed here from the perspective of the distinctions which are proper to created reality. Two specific distinctions found in creatures merit attention from a theological point of view, to wit, the distinction between good and evil, and the distinction between spiritual and material creatures.[4] The distinction between good and evil is something that belongs properly to creatures, for evil can only occur within a reality which is distinguished from, and related to, the reality of God as the source of the good. In God there can be no evil. God is not only good, he is the essence of the good and therefore the measure both of created goodness and of its opposite. The ultimate criterion of good and evil in created reality lies in the creator, particularly in God as the providential law (*lex aeterna*) of all things.

The central question is how to understand the existence of evil within a reality which, as creation, is the expression of God's goodness. How should one conceive the possibility of evil in a good creation? The issue does not yet concern moral evil, which has its origin in the (human or angelic) will. The category of "*malum*" here applies to all kinds of bad things which happen in the physical world, phenomena such as corruption, decay, damage, disintegration, loss of natural goodness, and so forth—physical evil in contrast to moral evil.

Aquinas' general thesis is that evil cannot have the ontological status of a nature.[5] Evil is not an essence, nor is it part of the essential structure of a thing. One cannot speak of things as being in themselves and essentially evil. Even the devil does not have an "evil" nature. As a being and as a nature he, too, is good. Evil is the corruption of a nature, not a nature itself. The ontological status of evil must therefore be explained in terms of privation: it signifies the absence of the goodness a thing should have. Evil must be understood as not-good, and thus in terms of a deviation, a falling short of, as missing, or lacking in, and so on.

But the question still remains: how must the existence of evil and corruption in a divinely created reality be understood? Can a world in which "bad things" happen be understood as the work of a good and perfect creator? Aquinas' answer to this question, which draws on the basic principles of his metaphysics of creation, can be summarized as follows.[6] God intends to produce a creation which is as perfect as possible. The perfection of the created universe, however, requires that there should be a multitude of unequal things, so that every degree of goodness may be realized. To create means for God to induce a likeness (*similitudo*) of himself in something else. It is impossible that one creature alone bears the perfect likeness of God, so as to constitute another God. The likeness of each created effect falls short of the infinite perfection in God himself. Because of this, Aquinas argues, plurality and inequality in things are intended by God, so that each creature may mirror God's perfection in its own way and thus contribute to the multiplied way the universe as a whole expresses the goodness of its creator. The only way, so to speak, for God to recognize himself in his work of creation is to articulate and differentiate his simple and unified perfection into an ordered multitude of unequal creatures.[7]

Because of this inequality, the universe cannot consist only of spiritual creatures, whose nature is incorruptible and who are in an enduring possession of their goodness. Besides the superior degree of spiritual creatures, another degree of good things is required, namely, corporeal creatures, which can fail in goodness and may lose their being. But even corruptible things contribute to the perfection of the universe as a whole, and their existence is therefore required by that perfection. Without the existence of corruptible and corporeal things, the created universe would not be complete. Now, if the perfection of the universe requires that there should be things which can fail in goodness, it follows that sometimes (*interdum*) they do fail. And it is in this that evil consists, namely, in the fact that a thing fails in goodness.[8] The existence of corruptible things as such is not evil; rather, evil is their actual corruption, the fact that they sometimes, sooner or later, lose their goodness and perish.

It is therefore a good thing that God's creation contains corporeal and thus fragile and vulnerable creatures, which are liable to perish, to be damaged, or to be destroyed. Their corruption is not as such intended by God or by nature, but still, it is likely to happen sooner or later. The significant use of the term *interdum* points, in my view, to the factual, nonnecessary way that evil happens. One may compare this with the fragility of a beautiful vase. It is not necessary that the vase will break and fall to pieces. But it is something one can expect to happen "sooner or later." The loss of oneself, in which the evil of corruption consists, cannot be understood as the actualization of some potency, which is part of a thing's essential structure. But neither is the actual corruption purely contingent. The possibility of corruption and evil follows from the mode of being of corruptible things. Hence a bodily creature needs special protection and care in order to be preserved from the destruction and evil (sickness, corruption, death) to which it is susceptible.

Human beings are bodily creatures. They also are susceptible to evil in the sense of corruption and loss of natural goodness. Being corporeal creatures, they are vulnerable and can be deprived of what they need in order to live and to live well as human beings. These forms of evil are not yet moral, since they are independent from the will. In this connection, however, one should note that, according to the classical doctrine, physical evil which affects human life has some relationship to the will, insofar as it is opposed to the will. Seen from this perspective, as something which runs contrary to the human will and its free realization of the good, the evil that befalls a man has a penal character (*malum poenae*).[9] Aquinas is not saying that every evil which may happen to a human being is intended by someone (God) as a punishment. His main point seems to be that evil in the sense of corruption and damage has a special character in the case of creatures who are in possession of a will. More concretely, only human beings, who are both corporeal and spiritual, are capable of experiencing the bad things which may happen to them as something bad, as contrary to their will, and therefore as something they suffer from.

The Fall of the Angel

The second place in the *Prima Pars* where the issue of evil is addressed is in the question dealing with the malicious angels. Aquinas devotes two separate questions to the topic of moral evil in the angelic realm. First, he discusses the evil that angels willingly commit and of which they are guilty (I.63: *de angelorum malitia quoad culpam*); second, he examines the evil which the bad angels undergo as punishment (I.64: *de poena daemonum*).

It is a remarkable fact that angels—incorruptible and spiritual creatures—are thought to have the possibility of committing sin. How is it possible that something goes wrong in the spiritual life of the angel, who is created in the nearness of God? The possibility of moral evil (*malitia*) lies in the free exercise of a will which is not its own measure. In Aquinas' view, the angels are endowed with free will, a will, however, which is not from the outset firmly and finally attached to the divine good in the full enjoyment of beatitude. Although the angels are immediately perfect with respect to their nature, in the order of grace they are open to an additional perfection with respect to their ultimate end. One might say that even in the angel there is room for something like "spiritual growth," although not in a temporal sense. The angel is somehow reaching out for its end, which is achieved as a result of its free conversion to God. The ultimate end of any intellectual creature, angels as well as human beings, consists in the beatifying vision of God himself. An essential tenet of Aquinas is that the ultimate vision of God cannot be part of created nature, because it is the perfection of created nature as such, which necessarily surpasses its natural capacities. The ultimate beatitude is therefore not a perfection which is included in the angel's natural endowment. The angel acquires its final beatitude as reward (*meritum*) for its free conversion to God, which is made possible through divine grace. Through grace, God opens the created will of the angel to himself and enables a free and affirmative response.

The angel is created, according to Aquinas, in a state of grace. At the very moment of its creation, the angel can freely choose either to turn itself to God and to adhere firmly to his goodness, or to turn away from God in order to reach out for its happiness by its own power. The angel has but one single moment of free choice. After the choice is made, the good angels cannot sin any longer, and the bad angels cannot correct their fault. Once they have made their wrong choice, the will of the fallen angels remains fixed; their will is "obstinate in evil" (*obstinata in malo*), while the will of the good angels, who adhered to justice, is "confirmed in good" (*confirmata in bono*).[10]

Considering the "obstinacy" of their will, the bad angels are beyond redemption. Their sins are without remission, because the angelic will has been fixed forever and cannot retract or repent its choice. The angelic will *is* its once-made choice and does not have the possibility of disengaging itself from that choice. It is bound to it forever. And therefore the bad angel has cut itself off from God forever. Aquinas cites Damascene: "Death is to men, what the fall is to the angels."[11] The angelic fall is like death, that is, the definitive closure of freedom.

In contrast to the angelic state, the sins of human beings, grave or less grave, are still pardonable before death.[12] For humans there still is time in life, that is, time for contrition, repentance, penance, and reconciliation. As long as life endures, there remains the possibility of a new beginning. Thus, for human beings, who exist in time, a history of salvation is possible. The way of human freedom through history remains open and undecided with respect to "eternal punishment" or "everlasting life." But for angels there is no history of salvation, unless it is that single moment of their choice. Their wills adhere fixedly and immovably to their once-made choice.[13]

The fall of the angel will be considered by many as a piece of mythical imagining without any real theological significance. However, Aquinas' exposition of the moral state of the angel functions as an illuminating contrast to the human condition of freedom in time, a freedom which makes a history of salvation possible. In fact, one of the functions of angelology in Aquinas' theology is that of providing a contrasting background for his theologically-inspired anthropology of rational freedom. By means of the difference in nature between angel and man, Aquinas is able to clarify the typical structure of human rational freedom, which is open to history.

The "obstinacy" of the will of the fallen angel is said to be rooted in the condition of the angelic nature, which is purely intellectual. Whereas the angelic nature is completely intellectual and therefore immovable in its intuitive apprehension of the truth and its choice of the good, the intellectual part of human nature is merely the starting-point of a rational-discursive process by means of which humans freely realize their intellectual openness for the truth and the good. The rational nature of humans results in a typical flexibility of voluntary acts. Free will does not consist of a single act fixed once and for all, but remains flexible, even after a choice.[14] The consequence is that in the case of human life, wrong choices and sins are pardonable (*remissibile*). Because of rationality, humans have the moral capacity of disengaging themselves from their evil acts, of feeling remorse, and of trying to better their lives. The freedom of the angel consists in its single choice for or against God; the freedom of man, on the contrary, is a freedom in history, in which he is offered the divine chance of redemption and restoration.

What God created is good. For Aquinas it is unthinkable that evil has its origin in God himself, since evil is that which, in one way or another, is opposed to God and deviates from God's good order. Now, God created a corporeal nature and a spiritual nature. The evil in the realm of the corporeal nature is rooted in what may be termed an ontological "weakness," that is, the susceptibility of corporeal things to a deficiency in goodness. The spiritual nature is endowed with free will. Moral evil (*malitia*), which has its root in free will, is not so much a sign of impotence as a sign of perversion, since it consists in the voluntary deviation from God's law, which is nothing else than a perversion of created freedom. Humans share in both the spiritual and the corporeal nature.[15] In the human sphere of existence, therefore, evil is present in both senses: in the sense of suffering and death, and in the sense of moral sin and perversion of rational freedom. In Aquinas' theological account of human life and history, both manifestations of evil, the evil of suffering and the evil of sin, are closely related to one another. Theologically, the physical evil (suffering, sickness, death) to which man as a bodily creature is susceptible is seen from the perspective of sin. According to classical theology, the susceptibility to suffering from evil characterizes man after the Fall. In his primitive state (*in statu innocentiae*) man was exempt from suffering and death, since "God made man upright" and had granted him a favor which preserved him from bodily defects and death. From this one can draw the conclusion that human evil—in the twofold form of the evil man commits (*malum culpae*) and the evil he suffers from (*malum poenae*)—is in some respects similar to the evil in the angelic realm (fall and damnation), and in other respects similar to the evil in the corporeal realm. Man is neither an angel, in whom moral evil is purely a matter of perversion, nor a corporeal creature without a will, to which corruption and loss of itself happen without the specific human associations of suffering and death.

Moral Theory and the Facticity of (Original) Sin

Considering the fact that the human intellect has "being" as its object, which is convertible with the true, it appears that evil, properly speaking, resists understanding. Evil, in its twofold form of corruption and sin, is not wholly intelligible. Although it is true that evil exists in reality, it does not have in itself being or truth. So the question why evil happens remains in the last resort unanswered. There is no cause by which evil can be explained. From this it follows that the Christian claim of original sin has a certain factual character. It is not an intelligible truth about human nature as such, but a factual truth about human nature in its historical reality. Like any other sin, original sin results from human freedom in a way that remains ultimately inexplicable to us.

The issue I want to explore here is how Aquinas accounts for this facticity of original sin from the systematic perspective of his moral theory of sin. The idea of original sin, which entails the assertion of the factual sinfulness of the whole of humanity, does not seem to fit easily in a moral theory about human acts, especially when one considers that it cannot be a conclusion of a theory.

The three questions devoted to the topic of original sin in the *Prima Secundae* (qq.81–83) are part of a wider treatment of the notion of *peccatum* (qq.71–89), which falls under the moral consideration of the human act. The discussion of the different aspects of *peccatum* is organized according to a sixfold division: first, the examination of the vices and sins in themselves, then their distinction, their comparison with one another, the subject or the part of the person in which they occur, their causality, and finally, their effects. Aquinas' analysis by means of these divisions results in a refined and articulate moral understanding of the complex reality of human sin. Not every sin is the same; there are different species of sin according to the diversity of virtuous acts which are their positive counterparts. The differentiated account of sin in all its relevant aspects draws upon the intelligibility of the "good order" of human acts.

The treatment of original sin appears to be included under the heading of the causality of sin. This seems quite appropriate, since original sin derives its name from the way it is caused in human beings: *per modum originis*, by way of origin. The crucial question is whether this mode of causation can be reconciled with the character of *peccatum* as essentially a voluntary human act. According to Aquinas, *peccatum* is an evil human act that fails to conform to the measure for attaining the human end. The cause of a sinful human act primarily resides in the immediate principles of a human act, namely, reason and will. The notion of original sin, however, does not seem to fit in this moral understanding of *peccatum* as a voluntary act, because, in the first place, it is not an act at all, and in the second place, it is not voluntary by reason of one's own will. According to Aquinas, one should distinguish between an actual sin (*peccatum actuale*), which is a disordered human act, and original sin, which is a disordered disposition of human nature (*peccatum naturae*). Original sin does not consist in a voluntary act of a person, but is on the contrary a disposition of his nature, which precedes the free exercise of his will.

The distinction between two modalities of sin, actual and dispositional, leads to another observation. Aquinas' general analysis of *peccatum* as an evil human act is to be regarded as a form of categorial analysis that aims to describe the relevant structures and aspects of the complex reality of human sin. It deals with matters such as definition, species, causes, effects, and so forth. As such, it is part of moral theory (*scientia moralis*). Now, it is not at all clear how the notion of original sin, which characterizes the factual condition of mankind in history, coheres with the categorial analysis of human acts, since a categorial analysis necessarily abstracts from factual life. The theoretical analysis is restricted to describing and analyzing several types of sin, which may occur in human life. But the moral theory of sin does not express itself on the factual sinfulness of human beings in concrete (historical) life. It does not contend that this or that person has actually sinned or that all human beings are sinners. It merely clarifies the categorial structure of human acts that somehow fail to conform to their appropriate measure. And in doing this, it also considers possible external causes which may induce a human person to sin. Aquinas discusses two "external causes" which may exercise a "bad influence" on human moral conduct, namely, the devil and other people. Both may cause a man to sin by way of "suggesting" (*suggerendo*) or by persuasion.[16] But in taking into account these external causes of sin, one should never lose sight of the moral principle that it is one's own voluntary consent that makes one's act an act of sin. No external agent can necessarily move one's will to sin. However strong the pressure (seduction, persuasion, and the like) may be, it remains in one's own power to sin or not to sin (*remaneat in nobis peccare et non peccare*).[17]

The Christian doctrine of original sin claims that the whole of mankind has actually sinned in the person of Adam. It implies a factual claim about the moral condition of historical mankind, and it even contends that no one, by reason of original sin, is able to refrain from sinning. In contrast to Pelagianism, Catholic faith teaches that it is no longer in our power not to sin. After the fall of the first man, Aquinas says, no one is able to remain completely without sin, even if his reason has been cured by God's grace.[18] With respect to this claim of the factual sinfulness of mankind, the categorial analysis of moral theory appears to be inadequate. At the categorial level of moral consideration, one must say that it remains in one's own power to sin or not to sin, since the will is the perfecting principle of the act of sin. But the doctrine of original sin confronts one with a sort of "external cause of sin," which affects the moral condition of the whole of mankind in an inevitable way. As children of Adam, we find ourselves in a state of sinfulness. Inasmuch as moral theory does not express itself about the factual sinfulness of concrete human beings, it seems it cannot explain original sin, either. Even if original sin is treated under the heading of the causality of sin, which is one of the six items of the categorial consideration of acts of sin, it cannot be fully integrated with the moral theory, because it lies outside the scope of the categorial analysis of human acts.

It should be noted, however, that in the *Summa,* original sin is never presented as a conclusion of moral theory. On the contrary, it is a conclusion of faith. At the beginning of his treatment of original sin, Aquinas reminds us that original sin, insofar as it implies an existential claim, is part of the doctrine of Catholic faith.[19] Original sin characterizes the factual condition of humanity seen in the light of faith. The moral analysis of sin may be helpful to elucidate the Christian talk of original sin and to develop some sort of understanding which is appropriate to its factual character. But in extending its consideration to the facticity of the first sin and its prolongation in the subsequent generations of mankind, moral theory must be supplied, so to speak, with a theological hermeneutics of the Christian experience of factual human life, which is marked by an original guilt vis-à-vis God.

The shift in methodological perspective—from theory to hermeneutics—which occurs when Aquinas starts to deal with the Christian notion of original sin has some important consequences for how one should interpret his account. In the first place, Aquinas does not intend to provide a theoretical explanation of the moral imperfection of humanity. And in the second place, his talk about the "first parent" should not be taken literally as referring to a real biological ancestor of the human race, whose sin is transmitted to all members of humanity as some sort of hereditary defect. What Aquinas is in fact doing can be described in the following way. Granted that the first sin of the first man and woman is somehow "transmitted" to all human beings by way of origin, as it is claimed by the Catholic faith, how, then, should one understand this "transmission" and talk about it in a meaningful way without contradicting some essential truths of moral teaching about sin, for instance, that the notion of guilt always implies a voluntary element? The task is not so much to construct a pseudo-biological mechanics of the "transmission" of sin from parents to children, as to explore the question whether and in which sense the "we" of historical humanity can be understood to have a moral status.

The Meaning of "By Way of Origin"

According to Aquinas, all humans are linked together in a chain of innumerable generations, going back to the imaginary first parents, called Adam and Eve in the biblical narrative.[20] Human beings in their historical reality are not isolated individuals, independent from each other, but form a collective entity of "we humans" by reason of their common origin. One may compare this to a family, which has a collective unity constituted by common ancestors. This common origin has a symbolic value insofar as it enables humans to express their collective unity and solidarity throughout history. The chain of generations is somehow the foundation of this collective unity of humanity.

Human beings thus are connected to each other by the fact that each individual is the child of his or her parents. One may, therefore, feel tempted to explain the "transmission of sin" by means of the biological continuity of the human race. According to traditional accounts, new human life was generated by means of semen; through the semen human nature was passed on to the newborn individual, who could be affected in some way by the condition of his or her parents. From the biological perspective of human generation, the metaphor of an infectious disease may force itself upon us, suggesting that the original sin is passed on from generation to generation through the sexual act. The traditional interpretations of original sin in the wake of Augustine are all more or less indebted to the biological metaphor of infection through the life-giving act of propagation. In particular, the sexual act was thought to be the very locus of the transmission of sin, constituting, as it were, the reenactment of the first sin by reason of the concupiscence aroused by it. Thus, every human being is conceived in a sinful act, reminding us of the first disobedience.

The vocabulary of biology and sexuality is not absent in Aquinas. For him, too, original sin was transmitted from Adam to his posterity by means of the semen, which is like the instrumental cause of original sin.[21] But the interesting fact is that Aquinas decisively rejects certain traditional accounts that interpret the link between Adam and his posterity in a highly external and biological manner. Since having some defect by way of origin seems to exclude the character of guilt, which is essentially something voluntary,[22] the transmission of sin cannot be simply a matter of passing on a defect from parents to children. For Aquinas this is a very strong and important statement. It is not appropriate to speak about original sin in terms of a defect that is passed on biologically from parents to children, because this would cancel the moral character of sin.

Before elaborating his own positive account of the transmission of original sin, Aquinas discusses two traditional accounts, which are both judged to be inadequate. The first starts from the assumption that only the rational soul of a person can be the subject of sin, since sin is a moral quality, residing in the rational part of a human. In order to explain the "infection" of the rational soul, the soul of the newborn child is said to be transmitted with the semen from the parents, so that an infected soul would seem to produce another infected soul. In this way the rational souls of all human beings are derived from the rational soul of Adam, which incurred a defect as the result of the first sin.[23] The second view discussed by Aquinas rejects the first, traducianist theory of the soul's origin. Instead of an immediate transmission of sin from soul to soul, it argues that the soul becomes soiled as it enters the body, which has been born from the parents with a defect. The idea is that the sinful defect in the parent's soul somehow affects his body and is passed on by means of the corrupted seed to the body of the child; the bodily defects, in turn, exercise an influence on the child's soul, where it becomes a culpable defect.[24]

It is not difficult to see that both explanations are inadequate, since they do not succeed in accounting for the moral character of original sin. Original sin is conceived as a sort of defect which is passed on, like an infectious disease, directly from soul to soul or mediated through the generated body. Both accounts are "naturalizing" explanations of the transmission in terms of being "infected" by the sin of the parent through sexual propagation, which leaves the moral character of sin unexplained. As long as the transmitted defect of the child's soul is not in its will, it will not have the character of a guilty defect that deserves punishment, as Aquinas observes. He even cites the passage—mentioned before—from Aristotle's *Nicomachean Ethics:* "no one reproaches a man born blind; one rather takes pity on him."

It may seem surprising that Aquinas apparently approves of the important ethical distinction between natural defects, with which one is born and which therefore are not one's fault, and moral (voluntary) defects, of which one is guilty. In one form or another, this distinction has always been at the basis of the main objection against the Christian doctrine of original sin: how can a defect contracted by way of origin, namely, by the fact that one is born, constitute a moral defect of which one is guilty? But even when Aquinas accepts the Aristotelian principle in criticizing the naturalizing accounts of original sin, this does not mean that he is inclined to restrict moral fault to the individual person, independent from that person's belonging to the body of humanity. Although there is no guilt in the proper sense of the word outside the dimension of the voluntary, Aquinas nevertheless avoids a moralistic account of original sin, in which the essential distinction between actual and original sin is somehow obscured.

The matter must therefore be explained otherwise than in terms of a transmission from parents to their children. It is noteworthy that the focus of Aquinas' critique particularly concerns the attempt to explain the causality of original sin in the manner of an infectious disease. This attempt seems to result from overlooking the metaphorical character of the comparison with an infection. Although the way in which the sin of one person may induce others to sin can be metaphorically described in terms of an infectious disease, the biological connection, which is at the basis of any hereditary disease, cannot explain the transmission of moral guilt. Behind the traditional interpretation one can detect the following analogical reasoning: just as the body of the parent may cause some physical defect in the body of the child, similarly, the soul of the parent may cause some moral defect in the soul of the child, directly or indirectly through the body. In this way the metaphor is transformed into an explanation.

Aquinas' own account is based on the thesis that all humans born of Adam may be considered as "one man."[25] All humans share in one common nature, which they receive from their first ancestor. Instead of arguing from the continuity between human beings through the line of the body or the soul, Aquinas approaches the matter from the point of view of the common human nature, in which all individuals participate. All individuals may be considered as one, not unlike the way in which the members of a social community (e.g., church, army, or any professional community) are considered one. It is customary to speak of a social body, composed of its individual members and acting as one collective entity. The whole of humanity, Aquinas is suggesting, may be considered as a social body, consisting of the multitude of persons who are born from Adam. One should observe that even this notion of a collective entity is in some sense a metaphor, a way of looking at historical mankind as constituting a community, to which each member belongs by reason of being born from human parents.

As a metaphor, it cannot provide a rational explanation for the transmission of original sin. But in my view, this is not what Aquinas intends to do. His account does not pretend to be a rational theory that explains how each individual human being is infected by original sin, due to receiving a human nature by birth. It is more a matter of suggesting a way of speaking about humanity in its historical reality as constituting some sort of collective "self," to which each individual belongs by reason of being born into this "family of man." Considering all humans born of Adam as one, as constituting a concrete "we" of historical mankind in this world, might provide an intelligible model by means of which one can account for the moral dimension of the causality of original sin.

The model of a morally relevant causality, which explains the transmission of a moral fault within a collective entity, is elaborated by Aquinas in the following way. Consider the action of one member of the body, of the hand, for instance. The action of the hand is voluntary, not by its own will, but by the will of the soul, which is the first mover of the members. If, for instance, the hand commits a murder, it would not be held responsible for the murder, considered in itself, separate from the body, but only insofar as it belongs to a human being and is moved by that being's first moving principle, that is, its rational will. The point of this example is that the action of the hand only receives a moral quality when it is considered as part of the human being who acts voluntarily through its hand. The hand is, so to speak, part of the moral self, insofar as it is moved by the human will which is present in it. "In this way, then, the disorder which is in this man born of Adam, is voluntary, not by his will, but by the will of his first parent, who, by the movement of generation, moves all who originate from him, even as the soul's will moves all the members to their actions."[26] This is the crucial formula by which Aquinas proposes his solution to the problem of how a defect transmitted by propagation can still be voluntary. The whole of the human race is to be regarded as an extended moral self, of which Adam's will is the primary principle. Thus, the disorder found in the individual members of humanity by reason of their being born of Adam can be understood as voluntary and hence culpable in relation to the will of Adam. The sinful will of Adam prolongs itself, as it were, through the ongoing process of generation; the first sin resonates through the succession of human generations, insofar as the movement of generation, by which each new individual receives from its parents the human nature, has its origin in Adam's will.

It is important to note that Aquinas does not view the "body" of humanity primarily as the biological entity of the human species. The core of his interpretation seems to me to consist in suggesting a way in which one may consider oneself as part of humanity, not simply as a biological species, but more as a "historical self," to which one belongs by reason of being born from human parents, and from whose history of disorder and moral failure one cannot exempt oneself. Original sin is not a matter of personal sin, committed by my own free will; rather, it is a sin I find myself guilty of inasmuch as I am part of humanity, having been born into the factual history of mankind, which is from the start a history of damaged freedom (*status naturae corruptae*). Therefore, Aquinas says, original sin is called "the sin of nature," not the sin of the human person. "Nature" here does not mean either biological nature or the essential nature of the human being ("nature" in the categorial sense). It stands for human nature (including the dimension of reason and freedom) in its factual, historical condition.

The State of Original Justice

As we have seen, original sin must be distinguished from actual sin, that is, a sinful act of an individual human being. It is not a "human sin" in the ordinary sense of the word, but a "sin of (human) nature" (*peccatum naturae*). It does not, therefore, consist in a voluntary act of a human person, although original sin expresses itself at first in the human will, which is the first principle of human actions.[27] Consequently, one must say that it is not the individual as such who has committed original sin, but the human collectivity: "we all have sinned in Adam."[28] With respect to original sin, all human beings are considered as one. The principal mover of the "collective self" of humanity is symbolized by Adam, who in sinning has caused the disorder of human nature we received from him.

The essence of original sin is defined as a certain "disorder of human nature." Original sin consists in a disordered disposition of nature arising from the loss of harmony that was characteristic of the original rectitude of man.[29] This notion of "disorder" and the "original order" which is presupposed by it deserves further attention.

"Disorder" means lack of order. It implies a loss of an (original) order between the different parts of human nature, which is required in order that man may exercise his life in a right way. In the Christian tradition the original, well-ordered disposition of human nature is called "the state of original justice" (*status iustitiae originalis*). It is a counterfactual notion, in contrast to which the inherent "disorder" in the present life can be expressed meaningfully. Original justice characterized the Paradisian state of man, in which he lived in harmony with God, with himself, and with his body. Paradise does not lie in a historical past, but "precedes" the historical existence of humanity. It is in reference to this original state of man, as described by the mythical narrative in the book of

Genesis, that the morally deplorable situation in which humanity finds itself receives its theological expression.

For Aquinas, the historical existence of humanity began after the Fall. This
means that historical life ("the present life") is characterized theologically as
"the state of corrupted nature" (*status naturae corruptae*). When original sin is
defined as an inordinate disposition of nature, arising from the loss of harmony
in which original justice consisted, one should interpret this definition as expressing the Christian self-understanding of the historical existence of humanity
in the light of faith. Aquinas is not explaining anything in terms of a mythical
incident; he is theologically clarifying the symbolic narrative by means of which
the Christian religion expresses this understanding. It is, as it were, the human experience of moral failure, which expresses itself in the "we have sinned," in the
confession of the solidarity of all humans in committing evil.

The notion of "original justice" is construed on the basis of a passage in
Ecclesiastes 7:30, where it is said that "God made man upright." According to
traditional Augustinian interpretation, this means that man in his original
state was endowed by God with the grace of rectitude and integrity. This rectitude consisted primarily in the subjection of human reason to God, and consequently in the subjection of the lower powers to reason, and of the body to
the soul. As long as man's reason was subject to God, the lower powers of his
soul remained subject to his rational mind, and his body remained subject to
his soul.[30]

The gift of original justice enabled the first man to exercise his life in a free
and harmonious manner, controlled by reason and wholly responsive to God, in
which the measure of human freedom consists. In his original state there was
no conflict in man, either between his reason and the passions or between soul
and body, because there was no conflict between man and God. One might say
that the first man was able to experience his factual and bodily life as an adequate expression of his rational self, and thus found himself in perfect harmony
with how he wanted himself to be.

The original justice was a gift of grace. The subjection of the body to the
soul and of the lower powers to reason was not from nature. Man's rectitude in
his original state was not something that belonged to his essential nature, since
otherwise the loss of it would have meant the very end of human nature. After
the fall Adam remained a human being, but what he had lost was the ability, by
God's grace, to preserve in the actual exercise of his life the right order between
the different parts of human nature. After his own disobedience to God, he felt
"the impulse of disobedience in the flesh, as though it were a punishment."[31]
The life of the passions was no longer the obedient expression of man's self and

of his rational freedom; instead, the passions seemed to act like another self. The same applied to the body, of which man became aware, no longer as a harmonious part of the human self, but as a loathsome burden which causes trouble and pain and is subject to sickness and death.

It is this loss of original justice, and consequently the inability to preserve the right order between the parts of human nature in the actual exercise of life, that is transmitted together with human nature from generation to generation. It is not a defect of nature itself, but a disordered disposition of nature, a self-indebted lack of harmony in the complex human self, which underlies the actual exercise of human life in history.

Man is guilty of this "disorder," this inability to realize his freedom according to the moral order of justice and love, by reason of the will of Adam. The will of Adam, as the head of humanity, is the principal will of the collective human "self," the will which extends itself somehow in the "we" of historical mankind, that is to say, "we humans," who constantly stumble over our own impotence to do the good and to live according to God's law. Only by situating that impotence ("not to be able not to sin") in the heart of human freedom itself can one come to see the meaning of the redemptive act of Jesus Christ in the right perspective. If man were merely a victim of a tragic loss of his original moral perfection, or if it were only a matter of the "human condition," his freedom could only be restored to its original responsiveness to God from the outside, by a kind of divine magic. But since man is victim by his own fault, so to speak, the human self must be involved in its redemption and liberation, namely, in the person of Christ, who, as man, lived in perfect obedience to his Father and who has shown us in himself the way to God.

The Evil of Death

The famous statement of St. Paul, "By one man sin entered into this world, and by sin death," is often quoted by Aquinas when he comes to the consequences of the first sin.[32] As a consequence of Adam's sin, the human body, fragile and corruptible from nature, lost its special favor of divine protection and thus became susceptible to sickness and death. The Pauline view that human death is the punishment for sin has always been part of Christian doctrine. To the modern secularist mind, however, it is not easy to accept that human death, which seems so essential a part of what it means to be human, is a punishment that confronts man with the consequences of his sinfulness vis-à-vis God. For many, the traditional religious meaning attached to death, as something by which man is cut off from God as the source of life and happiness, seems to reveal an inability to accept human finitude.

In my view, the Christian vision of death as related to sin is based on an intuition that death is somehow connected with an original failure of human freedom in its historical reality to respond to a divine appeal, to which it nevertheless remains sensitive. Man is not created in order to die and perish forever. From a religious point of view, death means the final confirmation of the human inability to respond to this appeal and to come to share in the divine life to which man is called. Christians see in death, as the end of their factual lives in this world, a sign, which reminds them of the fact that human life—the project of human freedom in history—comes to a dead end.

Invited by the statement of St. Paul, Aquinas attempts to explain how sin affects the meaning which is attached by the Christian tradition to the experience of human death. His view about death is interesting because it combines a naturalistic approach to life and death with a Christian religious understanding of human life as destined to share in the eternal life of God. On the one hand, one must say, according to Aquinas, that death is something natural for humans; on the other hand, the God of biblical revelation shows himself to be a God who does not want to abandon us to death. The God of Christian faith is a God of life. To see how Aquinas succeeds in combining these different approaches to death, I shall first discuss certain aspects of his view of human nature, and then explain in what sense man was immortal in his primitive state of innocence and how, as a consequence of sin, he lost the divine protection against death.

As mentioned earlier, according to Aquinas, the human being shares in spiritual nature as well as in corporeal nature. The point of departure of Aquinas' theological anthropology is the principle that man is, by his nature, established midway between corruptible and incorruptible creatures.[33] The soul (*anima intellectiva*) is naturally incorruptible, while the body is naturally corruptible. Human nature appears to consist of a paradoxical unity of incorruptibility and corruptibility: it includes an incorruptible and spiritual soul, and a corruptible body, which is an essential part of human nature. One may wonder how such a complex being can exist at all.

The ontologically complex nature of man must be understood, Aquinas says, from the perspective of the spiritual soul, which is the formal element of human nature. The body exists for the sake of the soul, not the soul for the sake of the body. Following the principles of Aristotelian philosophy, Aquinas states that the spiritual soul of man stands in need of sensory perception—something which requires an organic body—in order to be able to realize itself according to its faculties of intellect and will. The human intellect cannot come to knowledge of its object unless it turns to the phantasma, the sensory representation of the object (*conversio ad phantasmata*). The reason is that the human intellect is in potency with respect to knowledge and must actualize itself in a rational-discursive manner on the basis of the sensory presence of its object. Its non-material operation requires sense perception and, therefore, a sensitive body. Thus, Aquinas understands the ontological genesis of sense perception and of the body as bearer of the sensory faculties as a requirement of the actualization of the human intellect. The spiritual soul of man is *anima in se subsistens*, subsisting by itself, but at the same time the soul is *forma corporis*, the form of the body, which serves the realization of the proper end of man, that is, the ultimate perfection of his spiritual nature. The body is therefore subordinate to the soul; ontologically speaking, the body exists for the sake of the soul inasmuch as it enables the realization of man's spiritual being.

Being naturally incorruptible, the human soul is proportionate to its end, that is, everlasting happiness.[34] The body, in turn, is proportionate to the soul, inasmuch as the body is the organically differentiated matter which is apt to receive the soul as its form, and in which the soul can exercise itself. The soul may be incorruptible in itself, but it cannot exist as a complete substance without the body. The body is part of the essential nature of man. Separated from the body, the soul (*anima separata*) is no longer a complete human being.

In another respect, however, the body is not proportionate to the soul. The body has a certain organic structure, which is required by sensory perception. But this same organic structure makes the body vulnerable and corruptible. A sensitive body is necessarily a corruptible body.[35] And this makes man naturally a mortal being. Aquinas calls death something "natural," insofar as the liability for death follows from the corporeal nature of man. Considered in his corporeal (= corruptible) nature, man is naturally mortal. At the same time, one must keep in mind that the spiritual soul of man is incorruptible; in virtue of its intellectual nature, the soul transcends the whole of corporeal reality. So the awkward conclusion seems to be that human life necessarily results in a failure, considering the paradoxical constitution of human nature. The corruptibility of the body prevents the soul from fulfilling its *telos*, namely, everlasting happiness. Man is naturally a mortal being, but as endowed with a spiritual soul he should not die. How does one solve this paradox?

One cannot help but say that the constitution of human nature has a certain defect, due to its material condition. One may compare this state of affairs, Aquinas says, with a saw made from iron. A saw needs to be made from iron, as iron suits its form and action. Its hardness makes the saw fit for cutting.

Unfortunately, iron is liable to rust, which is a necessary condition of such matter and not the craftsman's choice.[36] In the same way, the form of man requires a body which is suitable for sensory perception. But such a body is necessarily corruptible, since it is composed of contraries. What Aquinas is saying here is that the categorial constitution of human nature shows a defect, which, although not intended by the divine author of nature, nevertheless seems to make it impossible for man to fulfil the *telos* of his spiritual soul. One might be tempted to conclude that, when left to its natural state, human life would necessarily result in failure.

An essential feature of Aquinas' theological view of human life, however, is that in fact one cannot speak properly about a "natural state." Man is not simply created by God and consequently left to himself with a "defective" nature. When God first created man, he supplied the deficient human nature with an additional gift of original justice, which preserves man from death.[37] Man was created not in "the state of nature" but in grace, as endowed with a special divine favor which preserves man from corruption and death. This gift of grace was intended to enable man to realize himself according to the finality of his spiritual nature within the context of his bodily and earthly existence. As long as man is subject to God and lives according to God's rule, the body will remain subject to the soul and wholly pervaded by its life-giving power without any disturbance or defect. The natural liability of the body for corruption is prevented from showing itself. In this original state, human life enjoys an integrity and harmony that are lost as a result of sin. As a consequence of the loss of original justice and of the harmony which results from this justice, man became confronted in his life with his natural susceptibility to sickness, death, and other bodily defects.

It has become clear by now how Aquinas is able to say that death is both "natural" and "penal": natural, because of the condition of the matter, and penal (*poenalis*), because death entered into the life of man as consequence of the guilty loss of the favor preserving man from death.[38] Death is a *malum*, but a *malum* that, in the case of human life, cannot be understood sufficiently in terms of the natural corruptibility of a corporeal being. So death is not just a biological fact of human nature; it is something that reminds us of the original failure of human freedom to exercise itself in an obedient responsiveness to God and his rule of life. Death is a *malum incidens ex culpa humana,* an evil which happens through human fault.

Aquinas' reflections about human death are interesting and valuable because of the way he combines the categorial perspective of human nature, considered abstractly in itself, with the existential perspective of human nature as created by God in a certain state. From the categorial perspective, human nature is conceived as an essential unity of spirit and matter, a spiritual soul which is united with the body as its substantial form. This complex unity of soul and body, of incorruptibility and corruptibility, seems to make man in his "natural" existence an impossible being, at least, when the body is regarded as belonging essentially to the life of the human person. But, according to Aquinas, there is in fact no natural state of human existence. The state in which man exercises his (created) nature is determined by the presence or absence of the right order between the different parts of human nature. And this order cannot be part of the essential constitution of human nature. It is a gift of grace, a divine favor, which enables man to exercise his life in accordance with the end for which he is created by God. Man is said to be made "to the image of God," that is, he is brought into being with an orientation toward God himself.[39] God made man "to his image," in order that man may come to share in the divine life itself. In view of this end, man is made right, so that he would be able to orientate his life to God and thus become worthy of the eternal happiness in God, without being cut off from this fullness of life by natural death.

Conclusion

The theological challenge of the paradoxical notion of original sin consists in finding a morally adequate and religiously meaningful way of speaking about a nonpersonal sinfulness of all human beings in such a way that the link with human freedom and with the moral self can be maintained. Aquinas' interpretation of the doctrine of original sin stands out, in my opinion, by the balanced and subtle way he attempts to account for the moral character of original sin, notwithstanding the fact that it is not an actual sin committed by one's own will. What makes his interpretation especially interesting and valuable is his proposal to consider individuals as members of a human collective in a concrete and historical sense. Against traditional interpretations, he emphasizes the crucial point that the culpable character of original sin cannot be accounted for as long as human individuals are considered purely in themselves, isolated from the fact of belonging, through being born of human parents, to the collectivity of historical mankind. In other words, the idea of original sin presupposes a concept of a "we" in a morally relevant sense, prior to the individual moral agent. "All men born of Adam may be considered as one man." As human beings we have something in common, a common nature, and in coming to share this nature by means of generation we are moved by a will, by an impulse of freedom which causes the lack of moral order, and which we cannot but recognize in our historical existence and in ourselves, since we are all humans.

From the perspective of modern thought, in which human freedom and nature are often conceived in opposition to each other (compare the Kantian dualism of freedom and nature), the very notion of a "sin of nature" becomes incomprehensible and unacceptable. Even if it is thinkable that members of a later generation may assume responsibility for the moral faults of their forebears, insofar as they regard their particular history and descent as part of their moral identity, it seems quite absurd to hold the view that the moral fault has been transmitted to the later generation by a natural process. As we have seen, Aquinas is sensitive to this objection that moral fault or guilt cannot be passed along via a natural process, even if the solidarity of historical mankind in evil is not without the natural process of generation. After all, the process of generation is more than purely biological; it is through generation that one receives human nature from one's parents, and thus becomes a human individual. Everyone who is born of human parents counts as a human being. But still—if I may conclude with one critical remark—it seems to me that the aspect of recognition, by which a human individual assumes and freely acknowledges his belonging to the community of humans, is not given its full due in Aquinas' interpretation of original sin. If the whole of mankind, in its historical sequence of generations, is to have a moral status, as constituting the "we" of the announcement "we have all sinned in Adam," then this "we" should be understood in terms of the performative act by which we declare ourselves to be part of history, being all children of Adam.

Notes

1. For Augustine's view on original sin, see William E. Mann, "Augustine on Evil and Original Sin," in *The Cambridge Companion to Augustine*, ed. Eleonore Stump and Norman Kretzmann (Cambridge: Cambridge University Press, 2001), 40–48.

2. *Ethica Nicomacheia* III, 5.

3. See *ST* I.2, prol.: "de motu rationalis creaturae in Deum."

4. Cf. *ST* I.48, prol.

5. Cf. *ST* I.48.1: "utrum malum sit natura quaedam."

6. For an extensive treatment of Aquinas' doctrine of creation, see my *Participation and Substantiality in Thomas Aquinas* (Leiden: Brill, 1995).

7. Cf. *ST* I.47.1c: "distinctio rerum et multitudo est ex intentione primi agentis, quod est Deus. Produxit enim res in esse propter suam bonitatem communicandam creaturis, et per eas repraesentandam. Et quia per unam creaturam sufficienter repraesentari non potest, produxit multas creaturas et diversas, ut quod deest uni ad repraesentandam divinam bonitatem, suppleatur ex alia."

8. *ST* I.48.2c: "ita perfectio universi requirit ut sint quaedam quae a bonitate deficere possint; ad quod sequitur ea interdum deficere. In hoc autem consistit ratio mali, ut scilicet aliquid deficiat a bono."

9. Cf. *ST* I.48.5c [utrum malum sufficienter dividatur per poenam et culpam]: "Malum igitur quod est per substractionem formae vel integritatis rei, habet rationem poenae; . . . de ratione enim poenae est, quod sit contraria voluntati."

10. *ST* I.64.2c.

11. Ibid.: "Hoc enim est hominibus mors, quod angelis casus, ut Damascenus dicit."

12. Ibid.: "Manifestum est autem quod omnia mortalia peccata hominum, sive sint magna sive sint parva, ante mortem sunt remissibilia; post mortem vero, irremissibilia, et perpetuo manentia."

13. Ibid.: "postquam iam adhaesit, immobiliter adhaeret."

14. Ibid.: "liberum arbitrium hominis flexibile est ad oppositum et ante electionem, et post."

15. Cf. *ST* I.75, prol.

16. *ST* I-II.80.1c.

17. *ST* I-II.75.3 ad 1: "quod remaneat in nobis peccare et non peccare."

18. Cf. *ST* I-II.109.8: "utrum homo sine gratia possit non peccare."

19. *ST* I-II.81.1c: "secundum fidem catholicam est tenendum quod primum peccatum primi hominis originaliter transit in posteros."

20. Aquinas would, of course, never call Adam an "imaginary" first parent. But the role Adam plays in his treatment of original sin allows one to conclude that, for Aquinas, Adam symbolizes the idea of the common origin, in reference to which the collective identity of mankind in its historical reality can be expressed (cf. the meaning of statements such as "we all are children of Adam").

21. Cf. *ST* I-II.83.1.

22. *ST* I-II.81.1c: "tamen hoc ipsum quod est ex origine aliquem defectum habere, videtur excludere rationem culpae, de cuius ratione est quod sit voluntaria."

23. Ibid.: "Quidam enim, considerantes quod peccati subiectum est anima rationalis, posuerunt quod cum semine rationalis anima traducatur, ut sic ex infecta anima animae infectae derivari videantur."

24. Ibid.: "Alii vero, hoc repudiantes tanquam erroneum, conati sunt ostendere quomodo culpa animae parentis traducitur in prolem, etiam si anima non traducatur, per hoc quod corporis defectus traducuntur a parente in prolem."

25. Ibid.: "Et ideo alia via procedendum est, dicendo quod omnes homines qui nascuntur ex Adam, possunt considerari ut unus homo, inquantum conveniunt in natura, quam a primo parente accipiunt."

26. Ibid.: "Sic igitur inordinatio quae est in isto homine, ex Adam generato, non est voluntaria voluntate ipsius sed voluntate primi parentis, qui movet motione generationis omnes qui ex eius origine derivantur, sicut voluntas animae movet omnia membra ad actum."

27. *ST* I-II.83.3c: "peccatum originale per prius respicit voluntatem."

28. Cf. Romans 5:12: "In whom [= Adam] all have sinned."

29. *ST* I-II.82.1c: "quaedam inordinata dispositio proveniens ex dissolutione illius harmoniae in qua consistebat ratio originalis iustitiae."

30. *ST* I.95.1c: "ipsa rectitudo primi status, in qua Deus hominem fecit, secundum illud Eccl. 7,30: Deus fecit hominem rectum. Erat enim haec rectitudo secundum hoc, quod ratio subdebatur Deo, rationi vero inferiores vires, et animae corpus. Prima autem subiectio erat causa

et secundae et tertiae: quandiu enim ratio manebat Deo subiecta, inferiora ei subdebantur, ut Augustinus dicit." The reference is to Augustine's *De civitate Dei* 13, c.13.

31. Ibid., taken from a citation from Augustine, *De civitate Dei* 13, c.13.

32. *ST* I.97.1; I-II.85.5, 6; II-II.164.1.

33. *ST* I.98.1c: "Est ergo considerandum quod homo, secundum suam naturam, est constitutus quasi medium quoddam inter creaturas corruptibiles et incorruptibiles: nam anima eius est naturaliter incorruptibilis, corpus vero naturaliter corruptibile."

34. *ST* I-II.85.6c: "quod forma hominis, quae est anima rationalis, secundum suam incorruptibilitatem proportionata est suo fini, qui est beatitudo perpetua."

35. Ibid. "Similiter corpus humanum est materia electa a natura quantum ad hoc, quod est temperatae complexionis, ut possit esse convenientissimum organum tactus et aliarum virtutum sensitivarum et motivarum. Sed quod sit corruptibile, hoc est ex conditione materiae. . . ."

36. Ibid.: "Sicut faber ad faciendum cultellum eligit materiam duram et ductilem, quae subtiliari possit ut sit apta incisioni, et secundum hanc conditionem ferrum est materia proportionata cultello: sed hoc quod ferrum sit frangibile et rubiginem contrahens, consequitur ex naturali dispositione ferri, nec hoc eligit artifex in ferro, sed magis repudiaret si posset."

37. Ibid.: "Sed Deus, cui subiacet omnia natura, in ipsa institutione hominis supplevit defectum naturae, et dono iustitiae originalis dedit corpori incorruptibilitatem quandam."

38. *ST* II-II.164.1 ad 1: "Et sic mors et est naturalis, propter conditionem materiae: et est poenalis, propter amissionem divini beneficii praeservantis a morte."

39. See *ST* I.93.

Eight

Right Reason and the Love of God

The Parameters of Aquinas' Moral Theology

JEAN PORTER

We are currently in the midst of a revival of interest in Aquinas' moral theology. This revival is only the latest in a series of efforts over the past century to retrieve Aquinas' moral theology as a resource for contemporary moral thought. Even before the Second Vatican Council, the moral theologians Bernard Häring and Gerard Gilleman turned to Aquinas' doctrine of charity to provide a basis for a renewed, theologically richer account of the Christian moral life.[1] Somewhat later, the Catholic philosopher Ralph McInerny offered an interpretation of Aquinas' moral thought, emphasizing its philosophical and especially Aristotelian dimensions, which is still widely influential.[2] Still more recently, a wide variety of theologians and some religiously oriented philosophers, Protestants as well as Catholics, have attempted to retrieve aspects of Aquinas' moral thought for contemporary Christian ethics.

Whatever we may think of their work, these scholars cannot be accused of giving too much attention to a marginal aspect of Aquinas' thought. There can be little doubt that moral questions play a central role in Aquinas' theological writings. The second part of Aquinas' final and most extensive work, the *Summa Theologiae*, comprising 303 questions, is taken up with what we would describe as moral theology, including both general principles of the moral life (in the *Prima Secundae*) and specific normative content (in the *Secunda Secundae*). Yet this discussion, extensive as it is, hardly exhausts Aquinas' reflections on moral questions. Within the *Summa contra Gentiles*, forty-one chapters are devoted to a discussion of the divine law, virtue, sin, and related issues, and a number of Aquinas' public disputations are likewise focused on moral issues.[3] In addition, moral questions are prominent in a number of his commentaries, including most of his scriptural commentaries as well as his commentary on Aristotle's *Nicomachean Ethics*. Indeed, it is difficult to identify any of Aquinas' longer writings that does not offer some extended discussion of these issues.

It would take us well beyond the scope of this essay to examine either the contemporary appropriations of Aquinas' moral theology or the development of that theology over the course of his own work. My aim is more modest. In what follows, I offer an overview of Aquinas' mature moral theology as developed in the *Summa Theologiae*, which will highlight the overall plan of his moral theology and indicate how the central motifs of that theology—beatitude, virtue, law—are related to one another. I consult Aquinas' other writings to illuminate the key themes of the *Summa Theologiae*, but I do not attempt a comprehensive survey of all his writings on morality. Nor do I engage the work of contemporary exponents of Aquinas' ethic in any systematic way. Finally, I do not attempt any extended discussion of the anthropological presuppositions of Aquinas' moral thought, that is to say, his analyses of the intellect, passions, and will. By the same token, I offer only the briefest overview of his doctrine of grace, discussed elsewhere in this volume, with the aim of indicating how it completes his overall moral theology.

Even this modest aim is ambitious enough. The richness of Aquinas' reflections on morality makes it difficult to offer an overview of his theology of the moral life within the compass of a brief article. At the same time, while Aquinas renders the interpreter's task challenging by the sheer extent and richness of his writings on morality, he renders it at least manageable by his clarity and his capacity to organize complex ideas around a few guiding principles. I will organize my presentation of his moral thought around a principle which Aquinas takes from the fifth-century theologian known today as Pseudo-Dionysius, and to which he returns throughout all his writings, namely, that "the good of the human soul is to exist in accordance with reason."[4]

This remark might seem to suggest a philosophical rather than a theological approach to Aquinas' moral thought. Some interpreters have taken this line, arguing that Aquinas' emphasis on practical reason implies that for him, the theory of morality does not depend on theological claims, or indeed on broad metaphysical claims.[5] This line of interpretation presupposes that Aquinas brings the same assumptions to his interpretation of Pseudo-Dionysius' dictum as many contemporary philosophers would bring. In particular, it presupposes a view according to which practical reason is autonomous, in the sense of generating moral norms through the dynamics of its proper functioning, without any necessary relation to a more comprehensive context of purposes.

But this is not Aquinas' view of practical reason. Aquinas consistently interprets the Pseudo-Dionysian dictum in terms of a teleological interpretation of reason: "This pertains to right reason, that one should make use of those things which lead to an end in accordance with the measure which is appropriate to the end."[6] This implies that practical reason does not generate moral norms through its own dynamics alone, apart from any consideration of the relative value of the goods of human life and their proper relations to one another. Correlatively, the first principles of practical reason can only be applied in an appropriate way to specific acts by someone who has developed a capacity for judging particular acts in accordance with their appropriateness with respect to the end, which capacity is developed through the moral virtues, properly so called.[7]

Aquinas' teleological understanding of practical reason is particularly important from our perspective, because it allows him to integrate both pre-rational and super-rational aspects of human existence within his theory of morality. As he explains in some detail in *De virtutibus in communi,* all of the moral virtues can be understood in terms of the diverse ways in which they bring the order of reason to those operations that are in some way directed to the end of human life.[8] In addition, there are also virtues which pertain directly to our orientation toward our final end and serve to place us in right relation to that end; these are the theological virtues of faith, hope, and charity.[9] We might say that reason opens both downward and upward for Aquinas—downward, drawing on the inclinations and passions which we share with the other animals, and indeed to some extent with all creatures, and upward, toward union with God through the dynamisms of grace and the theological virtues. For this reason, Pseudo-Dionysius' dictum allows Aquinas to integrate the different aspects of his moral system within a unified theological system of morality. That, at least, is what I hope to show.

Sources and Interlocutors

One tendency among some interpreters of Aquinas is to treat him as if he were a solitary genius, whose location in an extended tradition and community of discussion is irrelevant to our understanding and appreciation of his accomplishments. It is doubtful that Aquinas himself would have been flattered by this kind of praise. At any rate, even a cursory examination of his writings indicates how deeply he is indebted to a wide range of Christian and classical authors. His indebtedness to his own recent predecessors and contemporaries, including Jewish and Islamic as well as Christian thinkers, is less evident, but it becomes apparent once we place him within the context of twelfth- and thirteenth-century thought.[10]

A second tendency among Aquinas scholars, almost as misleading and far more prevalent, is to read Aquinas as if he not only baptized Aristotle, but is himself little more than Aristotle baptized. On this view, there is little in Aquinas' ethical thought that does not come from the *Nicomachean Ethics*, together with whatever modifications are suggested by Aquinas' Christian context. This assumption has even led scholars to attempt to find Aristotelian roots for aspects of Aquinas' thought that can be traced to other sources. Certainly, Aquinas is deeply indebted to Aristotle's ethics, especially in his analysis of the virtues. But it is impossible to understand his thought in purely Aristotelian terms, even in his analysis of the virtues, and much less in his treatment of other topics.

What are these other sources? They include, first and most fundamentally, Scripture itself, which Aquinas, together with every other Scholastic theologian, considers to be the final authority on all questions. Aquinas wrote extended commentaries on scriptural texts, especially but not only New Testament writings, and these commentaries contain much that is directly relevant to his moral theology as developed in the *Summa*. Second, Aquinas shares with his contemporaries a reverence for, and indebtedness to, the fathers of the church. He is distinctive, although not unique among thirteenth-century Scholastics, for his attention to the Greek fathers, whom he had to read in translation, and both Pseudo-Dionysius and John of Damascus contribute central motifs to his moral thought. At the same time, Aquinas is profoundly indebted to Augustine, not so much for the articulation of specific theses as for the overall theological framework of his moral thought. Among classical authors, Cicero is nearly as important as Aristotle; indeed, a case could be made that he is more important, when his indirect influence on Aquinas through the latter's own interlocutors is taken into account.

This brings us to a further point. It would be misleading, at best, to interpret Aquinas' thought in the context of his sources alone, as if his writings developed out of an unmediated encounter with classical and Christian authorities. On the contrary, Aquinas' moral theology (like his theology generally) developed in the context of Scholastic debates over key questions, such as the nature of sin, the relation between natural or political virtues and theological virtues, and the origins and binding force of the natural law. His reception of his sources is mediated through these debates, and his own distinctive positions are best understood within this context. It is impossible to set out this context in any detail here, but I will attempt to indicate the main lines of central debates as they are relevant.

Beatitude: The Moral Description of Actions

Let us begin our examination of Aquinas' moral theology, then, as Aquinas himself begins it, by placing it within the wider context of the organizing principles of his theology. In his introduction to the *Summa*, Aquinas explains that his intention is to present a unified compendium of theology, in which the material is arranged logically, rather than following the vagaries of academic debates or the outlines of a given text. As he explains further on,[11] the structure for the *Summa* will be provided by the schema of emanation and return (a framework which can be traced back to pre-Christian Platonic philosophy, but which had long been a resource for Christian theology). Hence, Aquinas says, we will first consider God, from Whom all finite being proceeds; next, we will consider the return of the human person to God by means of the actions which comprise an individual life; and finally, we will consider Christ, who is the means through which we are able to return to God. Moral theology is located in the second part of this three-part schema; that is, morality, broadly construed to include all aspects of human action, is placed under the rubric of the human person's return to God.

In the *Secunda Pars*, Aquinas explains in more detail what he understands morality to be. The actions through which the human person returns to God can be considered from two perspectives.[12] In the first place, we can analyze human actions in terms of general principles. These are further divided into the internal principles from which human actions spring, and the external principles prompting us to act badly or well. Under the heading of internal principles, Aquinas includes the will, passions, and virtues, and the gifts of the Holy Spirit that perfect the operations of the virtues. Under this heading, he also includes a discussion of vices and sins, which are seen as corruptions of the powers and acts of the agent. The external principles include both Satan, who tempts us to evil, and God, who "both instructs us through law, and aids us through grace."[13] This leads Aquinas to a discussion of law, grace, and merit, each of which represents an aspect of the way in which God directs the human person toward his or her final end. This brings us to the end of the *Prima Secundae*.

So much for general principles. We can also analyze human actions with respect to the specific rules or ideals which govern them, and this is the kind of analysis that Aquinas offers in the *Secunda Secundae*. These specific norms are divided into norms which apply to everyone, and norms which apply only to those in a particular vocation. Aquinas organizes this part of his analysis around a schema of the theological and cardinal virtues, together with the concepts and ideals which are relevant to particular callings.

However, Aquinas does not begin his moral theology with an analysis of concepts of virtue or of other familiar concepts, such as law, obligation, and the like. He begins in the first question of the *Prima Secundae* by asking a more fundamental question: Is it proper to the human person to act for an end?[14] This question may seem strange to us, but it is Aquinas' way of raising a further question that provided the agenda for moral reflection throughout classical antiquity:[15] What is the end—that is to say, the purpose, the goal—of human life?[16] In order to pose this question, Aquinas must first establish that it makes sense to speak of the purpose of human life as something which informs human action and gives unity and structure to an individual life.

Hence, when we read further in the first question of the *Prima Secundae*, we find Aquinas arguing that it is indeed proper to the human person to act for a purpose.[17] Somewhat surprisingly, Aquinas denies that only rational agents act for a purpose; on the contrary, he says, every creature acts for a purpose, in the sense of moving toward its specific form of perfection through natural processes of development.[18] However, the rational agent may be said to act for a purpose in a distinctive way, that is, out of a reflective understanding of the purposes for which she acts. Of course Aquinas realizes that we sometimes act without deliberation, without thinking, as we might say—he gives the examples of someone waving his hand or foot or idly scratching his beard.[19] But these actions, while they are acts *of* a human person, are not distinctively human actions, in the sense of being the kinds of actions that are characteristic of human beings. Not only is it characteristic of the human person to act for an end, but, Aquinas argues, every human person necessarily acts for some single end, which provides the overarching motivation in terms of which all her actions can ultimately be explained.[20] Subjectively, this end varies—some people aim at riches, others aim at pleasure or something else.[21] Yet another sense, all persons do share in the same last end, because we are all seeking happiness, understood as the ultimate and complete fulfillment of all that we are seeking in our lives. Furthermore, there is objectively only one thing which can provide us with this happiness, and that is God Himself.[22]

It will be evident by now that Aquinas' remarks on the last end of human life, his equation of this end with God, and his claim that all creatures are similarly directed toward God as last end, raise many questions that cannot be pursued here. For our purposes, the point to be underscored is that Aquinas here sets forth the parameters for his interpretation of reason as it operates in moral contexts. First of all, human reason is one expression of a more general phenomenon, namely, the intelligible and goal-directed processes which characterize all created existence. Correlatively, practical reason for Aquinas is always oriented toward some goal, and this aspect of rational actions provides the touchstone for their evaluation.[23] Not only are actions goal-oriented—taken by itself, this would allow us to evaluate actions in terms of efficiency, but not in terms of morality—but there are better and worse human goals, better and worse relative to an ultimate end, which Aquinas identifies as *the* end of human life. At the same time, the continuities between human rationality and the natural processes of nonrational creatures are also important, because they imply that human morality is grounded in pre-rational tendencies and inclinations which we share with other creatures, and which human reason harmonizes and completes without destroying them. And finally, just as human reason is grounded in pre-rational dynamisms, it is also open to a super-rational, that is to say, a supernatural completion through union with God. This aspect of human reason makes it possible for God to transform the moral life through grace—as we will see further on.

Aquinas continues exploring the principles of human action in the *Prima Secundae,* moving from a further consideration of the end of human life to extensive discussions of the will, the criteria for evaluating human actions, and the passions. Since his analysis of the criteria for evaluating human actions is foundational for much of what follows, a brief examination of those criteria is in order.

As noted earlier, every agent acts for an end, which is at least apparently good, and which is furthermore related in some way to the overall end toward which all the agent's actions are directed. This implies that all the agent's acts are voluntary, that is to say, they stem from the will, which is nothing other than an appetite for the good as discerned through reason. Correlatively, no one incurs merit or guilt except through voluntary acts. Hence, Aquinas moves from his discussion of the end of human action to an analysis of the concept of voluntariness,[24] and from there to an analysis of the will and its basic operations.[25] These remarks prepare the way for his analysis of the criteria for judging human actions.

Aquinas identifies three criteria in terms of which a human act is to be evaluated, namely, by reference to its object, its circumstances, and the agent's aim in acting.[26] In order for an act to be morally justifiable, it must be good in every respect. That is, its object must be good or at least neutral, considered in itself; it must be appropriate to its circumstances; and the agent's aim in acting should be praiseworthy or at least permissible.[27] Hence, an action which is bad with respect to its object cannot be justified by a good aim, and by the same token, an act which is generically good will be corrupted by a bad aim or by inappropriateness in the given circumstances.

The object of an act, as Aquinas understands it, is expressed in terms of that description which indicates its moral species, that is to say, which correctly identifies the kind of action that it is, considered from a moral point of view.[28] For example, we may say that a given act is an act of murder, or theft, or adultery, or alternatively, an act of capital punishment, or making use of what is one's own, or marital intercourse. It is important to note that neither the agent's end in acting nor the circumstances of the act can be collapsed into the object. Thus, to take Aquinas' example, someone who steals in order to commit adultery is guilty of a twofold transgression in a single act; the object of the act of theft cannot be elided into the agent's aim, namely, to have the means to commit adultery.[29] Similarly, the circumstances in which the agent acts do not change its object, unless they have some intrinsic relation to the object.[30]

It is sometimes assumed that these criteria provide a straightforward procedure for evaluating actions: we determine the object of the act, we take note of the agent's aim and the circumstances, and we then arrive at a moral evaluation through applying the formula, "Any single defect causes evil; good, however, is brought about through a complete and intact cause."[31] But Aquinas does not present this analysis as a methodology for evaluating specific actions, much less as a procedure for moral decision-making. For his analysis to function as a moral methodology in the relevant way, we would need to be able to determine which of his three components of an action is which, *prior to* forming a moral evaluation of the action. However, the object of an action is not given simply and perspicuously in the description of an act. It certainly cannot be equated with "what is done," described in a simple, nonmoral way. For one thing, any action allows for indefinitely many possible true descriptions of "what is done." More to the point, the determination of the object of an act presupposes that we have described the act correctly, from a moral point of view, and that process requires normative judgments about the significance of different aspects of the action. In other words, the determination of the object of an act is the *outcome* of a process of moral evaluation, not its presupposition. Description is not prior to evaluation; on the contrary, to describe an action from the moral point of view *is* to form a moral evaluation of the action.

This becomes apparent when we turn to Aquinas' analysis of the relation of circumstances to object in determining the moral species of an action.[32] He observes that "the process of reason is not determined to any one thing, but when anything is given, it can proceed further. And therefore, that which is considered in one act as a circumstance added on to the object, which determines the species of the act, can be considered a second time by ordaining reason as a principal condition of the object that determines the species of the act." For example, it is not generally relevant to a description of a particular act of taking what is another's that the object is taken from a museum, or a private house, or from the street; in all these instances, the act is still an act of theft, and qualifications of place are circumstantial to that act. But for Aquinas, at least, it is not just a circumstantial detail that something is stolen from a church; that fact qualifies our essential understanding of the act itself, in such a way as to change its moral description from an act of simple theft to an act of sacrilege.

How, then, are we to determine the object of the act? Aquinas' response brings us back to the overarching principle of his moral thought. We are told that the object of an action is determined by reason, which determines whether what is done is appropriate (as, for example, to use what is one's own) or inappropriate (to take what is another's).[33] There can be no formula for answering this question, but neither are we left to answer it through intuitive judgments unsupported by any systematic reflection. Aquinas' subsequent discussions of virtue and law provide us with two vantage points from which to reflect on the meaning of reasonableness in action.

The Internal Principles of the Moral Life: The Virtues

Thanks to the work of the historian Odon Lottin, we are aware of the extensive twelfth- and thirteenth-century debates over the origin and nature of the virtues that formed the context for Aquinas' discussions of these topics. This work, together with more recent efforts to analyze Aquinas' virtue ethics, should caution us against assuming that Aquinas does not add anything of significance to Aristotle's analysis.[34] It is particularly noteworthy that Aquinas' preferred definition of a virtue, around which he structures his own systematic analysis, is the definition that the twelfth-century theologian Peter Lombard drew from the writings of Augustine: "Virtue is a good quality of the mind, by which we live righteously, of which no one can make bad use, which God brings about in us, without us."[35] Aquinas qualifies this definition by noting that the last clause applies only to the infused virtues, which God bestows on us without action on our part, in contrast to the acquired virtues, which, as the name suggests, can be attained through human effort without grace.

At the same time, Aquinas does draw on Aristotle at key points in his analysis of the concept of a virtue. Most fundamentally, he follows Aristotle in the view that a virtue is a *habitus*. It is important not to be misled at this point by the connotations of the English term "habit," which is generally applied to repetitive, unthinking behavior. For Aquinas, a *habitus* is simply a stable disposition, which, in the case of a habit of the intellect, will, or passions, inclines the person to act in one way rather than another.[36] Such dispositions are necessary if we are to be capable of action at all; for example, the child's innate capacities for speech must be developed through the *habitus* of a particular language before the child can actually talk.[37] So understood, the virtues include intellectual capabilities such as knowledge. These are of course morally neutral, although they are good in the sense of perfecting the agent in some respect.[38] However, those virtues that shape the passions and the will, and the intellect insofar as it is oriented to action, are necessarily morally significant.[39]

Because the faculties of the intellect, the will, and the desiring and irascible passions are all distinct, each has its proper virtue, identified with one of the four traditional cardinal virtues. Prudence or practical wisdom, strictly speaking an intellectual virtue, enables the agent to choose in accordance with a correct understanding of the human good, as applied to particular situations; justice orients the will toward the good of others or the common good, as discerned by reason; and temperance and fortitude shape the passions in such a way that the agent desires what is truly in accordance with reason, and is prepared to resist obstacles to attaining it.[40]

I observed earlier that for Aquinas, reason reaches downward as well as upward, drawing on those aspects of our nature which we share with the other animals as well as orienting us toward a final end that supersedes reason itself. Here we see a first example of the way in which reason draws on and perfects pre-rational components of our nature. The passions, which are regulated through temperance, fortitude, and the related virtues, are not distinctively human; we share them with the animals.[41] Yet in the human person they are not completely devoid of reason, either. Rather, Aquinas says, they have something of reason in them, and by the same token they can be shaped by reason in such a way as to aim toward the overall good of the person.[42] It is important to realize that for Aquinas, the passions are shaped and directed, but not suppressed, by reason—otherwise, the virtues of the sensitive part of the soul would render their subject otiose, rather than perfecting it.[43] Similarly, the will, which is intrinsically rational and therefore distinctively human, is shaped by the virtues of justice and ultimately charity to move beyond natural self-love to wider loves, toward the community, one's neighbors, and ultimately toward God Himself.[44]

We should also observe that Aquinas' overall teleological approach to reason informs his analysis of the virtues. Virtues by their nature are perfections of the powers that they inform, and this means that they are intrinsically oriented toward some good.[45] Nor can the goods toward which individual virtues are oriented be understood in isolation from wider contexts of overall human and social well-being. I have already cited Aquinas' view that it pertains to right reason to make an appropriate use of those things which are oriented toward an end.[46] As he explains in the same article of the *Summa,* this implies that exterior goods are ordered to the well-being of the body; that bodily goods are oriented toward the well-being of the soul; and that the goods proper to the active life are ordered to the goods of the contemplative life.

Aquinas' statement about right reason is not an isolated comment, but an expression of a fundamental principle. Each of the cardinal virtues is defined in relation to the overall good of the agent or the common good. But how is this orientation toward the good translated into specific ideals of virtue? Aquinas answers this through an appropriation of Aristotle's doctrine of the mean, according to which the virtues are stable dispositions leading to passions and actions in accordance with a mean that is determined by practical reason. The rational criterion, that is to say, the mean of the virtues of the passions (temperance and fortitude), is determined by the overall good of the organism, which places sensual goods in their correct relation to that overall good; hence, these virtues are said to observe a rational mean only.[47] The mean of justice, in contrast, is determined by the good of the neighbor or the community as a whole (depending on which form of justice is in question), and for this reason justice orients the will toward an aim that goes beyond the good of the individual; because it is determined by objective criteria of fairness, the mean of justice is said to be a real, as well as a rational, mean.[48] In either case, however, the mean is determined by reference to some good: to the agent's own overall good, in the case of temperance and fortitude, and to the good of others or the common good, in the case of justice.[49]

At the same time, Aquinas' references to the good of the agent call for further explication, as he himself notes, because the good of the agent, or happiness, can be understood in a twofold way. There is a kind of happiness, proportioned to the capacities of the rational creature, to which the virtues that we could acquire by our own efforts are oriented. Indeed, Aquinas frequently identifies this kind of happiness with the practice of the cardinal virtues.[50] But in fact, we have been called to a higher form of happiness, namely, direct union with God in the beatific vision. This form of fulfillment completely exceeds the natural capabilities not only of the human intellect, but of any created intellect, and for this reason we must be transformed in such a way as to receive new principles of action in order to attain such an end.[51] Correlatively, these new principles of action can only come to us through God's immediate action, transforming the soul and bestowing on it principles of action which it could not have attained by itself.[52] This transformation is brought about by grace, and the operative dispositions through which grace is rendered active are the infused virtues, including infused versions of the cardinal virtues as well as the theological virtues of faith, hope, and charity, and the gifts of the Holy Spirit.[53] We have already seen how reason operating through the virtues looks downward, drawing on and transforming the passions; now we see reason looking upward through the transforming effect of grace operating through the infused virtues and the gifts.

The infused cardinal virtues are specifically different from their acquired counterparts because they are directed toward a different end.[54] As such, they observe a different mean than do the acquired virtues; they are directed toward a different goal, and therefore they respect different standards of appropriateness. Acquired temperance takes its standards from the overall well-being and health of the body, and leads to an appropriate moderation in food and drink. Infused temperance, in contrast, takes its ultimate criterion from the person's desire for salvation, and incorporates forms of restraint and discipline, such as fasting, that will promote the individual's spiritual as well as physical health. Note, however, that I say *as well as,* rather than *instead of*—Aquinas claims that ascetical exercises which damage one's bodily well-being are vicious rather than virtuous.[55] The goal of acquired temperance, namely, physical health, is taken up and transformed by the infused virtue, rather than being ignored or undermined by it; grace perfects rather than destroys nature, as Aquinas repeatedly reminds us.

At this point, we see one of the most interesting and original aspects of Aquinas' analysis of the virtues, an aspect which is not apparent unless we place that analysis in the context of the discussions of the virtues among Aquinas' contemporaries. Aquinas' distinction between the acquired and infused virtues presupposes an older and more general distinction between the cardinal virtues and the theological virtues of faith, hope, and charity. Similarly, the distinction between acquired and infused virtues, while not so old, was well established by the time Aquinas wrote. What is distinctive about Aquinas' approach is the fact that he combines these two schema and develops them into an overarching framework for moral analysis.

To appreciate the originality of Aquinas' approach, it is helpful to compare it with the analysis of one of his predecessors. William of Auxerre (ca. 1150–1231), a secular theologian whose *Summa aurea* influenced Aquinas' own work, similarly devotes considerable space in his overall work to moral questions.[56] Moreover, like Aquinas, William organizes his discussion of specific questions through a schema of the virtues. However, when we turn to the specifics of William's analysis, we see a marked contrast with Aquinas. For William, the theological virtues of faith, hope, and charity are directly contrasted with the political virtues, which are necessary to social life and which stem from the natural law.[57] This may not seem to be much of a contrast, since William identifies the political virtues with the cardinal virtues. The point is, however, that for William the distinction between the theological and political virtues remains more or less fixed. The political virtues serve as a preparation for the theological virtues, and they provide a medium through which the theological virtues can be expressed in external acts.[58] Nonetheless, the theological and the political virtues remain in an external relation, with the former directing the latter. There is no place in William's schema for infused political or cardinal virtues.

The distinction between Christian, or theological, and civic or political virtues is almost universal among Scholastics up to Aquinas, and he is clearly familiar with it.[59] However, by the time he develops his mature theory of the virtues, he has replaced this distinction with a more complex set of divisions between the theological and the cardinal virtues, on the one hand, and between infused and acquired virtues, on the other. At first glance, these revisions to a well-established line of analysis would seem to introduce unnecessary complications. Why would he have made this move?

Part of the answer to this question lies in the specifics of Aquinas' concept of grace and its relation to the virtues. As we have already noted, grace is nothing other than a created transformation of the human soul, through which we are enabled to carry out actions that lead to salvation. The infused virtues are the operative principles through which this transformation is effectively translated into specific actions.[60] Correlatively, in order for an action to be meritorious, it must stem from grace in some way.[61] This implies that the standard Scholastic model, according to which the theological virtues direct the political or cardinal virtues, is inadequate. In order for grace to be fully efficacious in every dimension of human life, it must transform all the faculties of the human soul involved in the processes of deliberation and action.[62] And this means that on Aquinas' terms, it is not enough that the theological virtues should command the acts of the other virtues; rather, grace must be expressed directly through virtues appropriate to every faculty of the soul, namely, through infused versions of all the cardinal virtues.

This still does not explain why Aquinas prefers to speak of the cardinal rather than the (infused) political virtues. The reason for this shift only becomes apparent when we turn to the detailed moral analyses of the *Secunda Secundae.* Here we find that the division between virtues oriented toward beatitude and those oriented toward social life is too simple for Aquinas' purposes. Only one of the cardinal virtues, justice, has a direct and defining relation to the good of the community as a whole; indeed, strictly speaking, this is the case only for legal justice.[63] Both fortitude and temperance are primarily oriented toward maintaining the individual's equilibrium between her passions and her reasonable judgments about the overall good, and in that sense, they both have the good of the individual as their primary focus. Similarly, particular justice, which is further divided into commutative and distributive justice, is concerned with right relations toward individuals.[64] Prudence ranges over both sets of considerations and integrates them, and for that very reason Aquinas distinguishes between individual and political prudence.[65]

In recent years, several scholars have attempted to appropriate Aquinas' account of the virtues as a basis for a contemporary virtue ethic, which would provide an alternative to a more legalistic ethic based on concepts of law or rules.[66] It should be noted, however, that Aquinas consistently holds the ideas of virtue and law together in his moral thought. In his general analysis of habits, Aquinas argues that habits receive their species from their objects, which are further distinguished in accordance with a distinction between good and bad.[67] This language, reminiscent of Aquinas' general analysis of human actions, implies that the virtues are conceptually linked to the kinds of actions that instantiate them.[68] At the same time, these concepts of kinds of actions, which comprise what Aquinas calls the object or the moral species of particular actions, are also correlated with moral rules. This, in turn, implies that the virtues can be correlated with precepts of the natural or divine law, and when we turn to the *Secunda Secundae,* we find that each of the seven major virtues that Aquinas discusses is indeed correlated with one or more precepts.[69] By the same token, Aquinas argues in the *De malo* that every sin represents a deviation from the mean, thus expanding a concept proper to virtue theory into a general analysis of moral norms.[70]

None of this should be taken to imply that virtues are merely dispositions to act in particular ways. Aquinas recognizes that the virtues are also attitudinal dispositions, and as such, they must be understood in terms of the desires, feelings, and perceptions characteristic of them, as well as in terms of the kinds of actions that typify them.[71] I simply want to underscore the fact that for Aquinas, the virtues are correlated with norms for conduct; for this reason, they can only be fully understood in connection with the external positive principle of good action, which Aquinas identifies with God, but which takes the concrete forms of law and grace.

An External Principle of Action: Natural and Eternal Law

Aquinas' treatment of law and grace, including a discussion of merit as the immediate correlate of grace, comprises the last twenty-four questions of the *Prima Secundae.* I focus on his remarks on the natural law as a framework for moral action.

Aquinas' initial remarks about the natural law imply once again that morality is grounded in reason: "The natural law is something constituted through reason, just as a proposition is a certain work of reason."[72] As such, the natural law is grounded in the first principles of practical reason, which function in practical matters in much the same way that the first principles of speculative reason (for example, the law of noncontradiction) function in speculative thought. Indeed, the natural law understood in its primary sense is identified with these first principles, although the more specific precepts stemming from these principles are also associated with the natural law.[73]

Of course, Aquinas is neither the first nor the last moral theorist to claim that moral principles are in some way derived from reason. To appreciate the distinctiveness of Aquinas' position, we must press further and ask just how the precepts of the natural law are derived from reason. Two articles in the *Summa* are critical to understanding Aquinas' views on this point. The first is a very widely discussed passage, *ST* I-II.94.2, in which Aquinas begins by posing the rather odd question, "Whether the natural law contains many precepts, or one only?" In order to answer this question, he first observes that the diverse precepts of the natural law can all be understood as expressions of one fundamental precept: "Good is to be done and pursued and evil is to be avoided." This first principle, in turn, is given meaning and content through the various inclinations toward goodness which are innate to the human person as a creature, a sentient creature, and finally as a rational creature. The first of these, which we share with all other creatures, is the inclination to maintain our own existence; the second, which we share with other animals, includes tendencies to reproduce and to nurture our offspring; and the third includes all those tendencies which are distinctive to us as rational creatures, including the tendencies to live in a civil society, to inquire about truth through speculation, and to worship God.

Hence, the specific precepts of the natural law can be understood as expressions of a complex but well-ordered human inclination toward goodness. That is why the diverse precepts associated with the natural law can be understood as comprising one, rationally unified natural law: "All these precepts of the natural law, insofar as they are referred to one first precept, have the rational character of one natural law."[74] This does not mean that we could derive specific precepts of the natural law from these inclinations, taken by themselves. Of course we do experience these inclinations, but in order to understand their significance, they must be interpreted in light of a more comprehensive account of the ways in which all creatures are oriented toward the good through inclinations proper to their specific natures: "The natural inclination in those things devoid of reason indicates the natural inclination belonging to the will of an intellectual nature."[75]

Aquinas' point is that once we have a more or less correct understanding of the exigencies and the proper shape of human life, we will see that diverse moral principles are in fact all expressions of the first principle of practical reason. At the same time, the distinctively human good does not consist in fulfilling the inclinations, but rather consists in fulfilling them in a certain way, which is consonant with a rational discernment of the human good.[76] We are reminded once again of the link between virtue and law: "The virtues perfect us to follow natural inclinations in an appropriate way, which inclinations pertain to the law of nature. And therefore to the determination of each natural inclination there is ordered a particular virtue."[77]

We turn now to a second question, in which Aquinas develops his conception of the natural law. In common with most of his immediate predecessors and contemporaries, Aquinas explicitly identifies the precepts of the natural law with those of justice by identifying both with the precepts of the Decalogue.[78] He explains this identification by appealing to another traditional definition of the natural law, that is, the double commandment of love of God and neighbor. The link between the two great commandments and the Decalogue lies in the fact that both are presented in Scripture as summaries of morality. This raises the question, how are they related to one another?

Aquinas explains that the injunctions to love God and neighbor are not included in the Decalogue because they are immediately evident to everyone, "either through nature or through grace." The precepts of the Decalogue, in turn, are derived from these two commandments with only a modicum of reflection, and as such, they too are known to all persons.[79] That is why they are portrayed as being given to the people directly from God; not only the Israelites, but every person receives these precepts directly from God through the operation of natural human reason. The more detailed applications of these precepts are not included in the Decalogue, on the other hand, because these need to be worked out by "the wise" and so do not come to the people directly from God.[80] More specifically, the precepts of the Decalogue draw out the meaning of the love commandments by specifying what it means to love God and neighbor.[81] With respect to the neighbor, Aquinas adds, the command to love may be interpreted as a command to fulfill one's special obligations, represented by the primal obligation to one's parents, and to avoid harming anyone, represented by injunctions against basic forms of harm such as murder, theft, adultery, lying, and the like.[82]

We can hardly miss the point that for Aquinas, the fundamental precepts of the natural law, as summarized in the Decalogue, are derived from first principles which are also the basic precepts of the virtue of charity, namely, the injunctions to love God above all things and to love one's neighbor as oneself.[83]

Does this mean that the natural law is grounded in charity, or that it can only be known to those who have grace? Some interpreters have argued for such a reading of Aquinas, but in my view this is incorrect.[84] It is important to realize that for Aquinas, every creature naturally loves God.[85] But of course, the love of God means different things in different contexts. For irrational creatures, as we have seen, the love of God is equivalent to the creature's inclinations toward its own specific form of perfection and its proper place in the universe. There is a kind of love of God proper to the rational creature, correlated with the knowledge of God as the first principle of existence which can be attained through philosophical speculation. Given the realities of original and historical sinfulness, this kind of knowledge and love of God can be attained only in fragmentary forms, and for most people it cannot be attained at all. Yet our rational capacities for knowing and loving God provide the basis for the transforming effects of grace, working through charity and the other infused virtues to direct us toward a personal relationship with God that we could otherwise never have envisioned.[86] And even without grace, these rational capacities retain sufficient integrity to provide the basis for some knowledge of specific precepts of the natural law, albeit a distorted and incomplete knowledge.[87]

This brings us once again to the idea that for Aquinas, reason looks downward and opens upward; it draws on the intelligibilities inherent in pre-rational nature, and it is also open to the transforming effects of grace. How do both aspects of reason operate in the context of the natural law?

First, human reason stems out of the intelligibilities inherent in our nature as creatures and as animals, and while it goes beyond these, it also respects their essential structure. Among Aquinas' contemporaries, this idea was frequently summarized in the phrase "nature as reason," by which they understood the intelligibilities expressed in nonhuman nature and in the pre-rational aspects of our own nature. Aquinas does not use this phrase in his later writings (we find it in *De veritate* 16), but he clearly endorses the general idea that nature, considered as a pre-rational ground for human action, does have moral significance, a claim which he makes explicit in the context of his analysis of sexual sins: "the principles of reason are those which are according to nature, for reason, presupposing what is determined by nature, disposes other matters in accordance with what is appropriate to these."[88] As he says in the same article, this is why the sin against nature is the worst kind of sexual sin; in this kind of action, the human person "violates, against nature, that which is determined by nature concerning the use of the sexual act." This is particularly serious, because "just as the order of right reason is from the human person, so the order of nature is from God himself."[89] Earlier in this question, we read that the natural end of the sexual act which is thus violated is specifically its orientation to procreation.[90] Elsewhere, Aquinas explicitly says that this kind of action is said to be contrary to that nature which we share with all other animals, in contrast to those sins which are contrary to our nature as rational creatures.[91]

Aquinas' sexual ethics is of course one of the most controversial aspects of his moral thought. For this very reason, it is important to realize that he also affirms the moral significance of the pre-rational dimensions of human nature in a variety of other contexts. In the *Prima Pars,* in the course of analyzing the relationship between the natural love of God and charity in the angels, Aquinas observes that because reason imitates nature, it is natural for rational creatures to love both the good of the universe and the divine goodness of God more than themselves as individuals.[92] Otherwise, he adds, charity would be a perversion, rather than a perfection of nature.[93] Further on, he condemns suicide because it violates the natural inclination of all living creatures to stay alive.[94] By the same token, he defends killing in self-defense on the grounds that such an act is a legitimate expression of the inclination toward self-preservation.[95] Vengeance, understood as the infliction of penal suffering for some good cause, is an expression of the natural inclination to resist evil.[96] The obligations of obedience are grounded in a more general analysis of the ways in which secondary causes are hierarchically arranged; at the same time, these obligations are limited by the natural tendencies and needs of the body, since with respect to such matters we are all equal.[97] The virtue of temperance takes its norms from the natural necessities of human life;[98] hence, as we have already noted, fasting is an act of virtue when done for appropriate reasons, but it becomes vicious when taken to the extreme of actual harm.[99]

At the same time, reason also opens upward, as it were, by its participation in the divine wisdom through which each individual creature, and the universe as a whole, comes forth and moves toward its final fulfillment. This aspect of moral reason becomes apparent when we examine Aquinas' discussion of the eternal law, which, as the name suggests, is nothing other than God's providential wisdom, in which all true laws of whatever kind participate in some way.

Aquinas was not the first theologian to speak of an eternal law; the idea can be traced back to Augustine, and in the generation prior to Aquinas' own time, it was developed by Franciscan theologians as a way of providing a theological context for speaking about the natural law. As Lottin points out, Aquinas' account of the eternal law in the *Summa Theologiae* adopts the topics and the structure of the Franciscan account, almost point for point.[100] At the same time, however, Aquinas' account emphasizes God's providential reason more than do the Franciscans, and the idea of authority is less prominent: "eternal law is nothing other than the reason of divine wisdom, insofar as it directs all acts and motions."[101] By the same token, Aquinas holds that temporal laws are derived from the eternal law insofar as they are reasonable and directed to genuinely good ends.[102] In other words, human authority depends on conformity to God's wisdom, rather than being derived in a juridical fashion from God's authority.

When we view Aquinas' account of the eternal law in the wider context of his work, it becomes apparent that for him it functions as a way of placing the different kinds of law within an overarching theological framework. Lottin observes that just as Aquinas interprets the divine ideas as God's knowledge of the specific forms of creatures, seen as forms of participation in the divine essence, similarly, he understands the eternal law as God's knowledge of creatures seen in relation to God and to the good of the universe as a whole.[103] In other words, for Aquinas the eternal law is God's providential wisdom, directing all things toward their proper fulfillment in union with God, in the way appropriate to each kind of creature. He thus emphasizes Augustine's idea of the eternal law as the supreme ordering principle of the universe, while deemphasizing Augustine's remarks on the authority of the divine law.

At the same time, Aquinas understands the natural law as an expression of the intrinsic principles of operation through which each creature expresses its specific form and arrives at its appropriate form of union with divine goodness. Aquinas believes that, strictly speaking, only the human person can be said to follow a natural law.[104] Nonetheless, he also holds that the natural law represents the distinctively rational form of more general processes by which all creatures participate in God's providential wisdom, that is, God's eternal law: "Hence, since all things which are subject to divine providence are governed and given measure by the eternal law . . . it is clear that all things participate in some way in the eternal law, insofar as they receive from it inclinations toward their own acts and ends. . . . in the rational creature there is also a participation in eternal reason, through which he has a natural inclination toward a due act and end. And this participation of the eternal law in the rational creature is called the natural law."[105]

Through the motif of the eternal law, Aquinas develops a theological framework for understanding the universal principles of human morality, and interpreting them in the light of still more general principles of action as these are manifested throughout creation. We have already observed that this approach to the natural law does not imply that the natural law, or, by implication, moral knowledge and virtuous action, are impossible without grace. What Aquinas does establish, however, is the fundamental congruity between human morality and the operations of grace, considered as two expressions of God's wisdom: "the stance [*affectus*] of charity, which is the inclination of grace, is not less ordered than the natural appetite, which is the inclination of nature, because each of these inclinations comes forth from the divine wisdom."[106]

Conclusion

We have now come full circle. As noted earlier, Aquinas begins the *Prima Secundae* by examining the different ways in which human beings and all other creatures may be said to act for an end, that is, a final goal or purpose, which, correctly understood, is to be identified with God. This, I have suggested, is the key to understanding Aquinas' account of reason as it functions in moral contexts. Practical reason is always teleological in its operations, and this implies a twofold orientation: downward, toward the intelligible dynamisms of pre-rational nature, which it incorporates into its own operations, and upward, toward the divine wisdom from which it stems. At the most fundamental level, practical reason is grounded in the individual's overarching conception of happiness, that in which his or her ultimate perfection and well-being consists, a conception that Aquinas claims is at the basis of all the person's rational judgments and actions.

When we turn to Aquinas' analysis of virtue, we find the twofold character of reason at work through Aquinas' analysis of the relationship of the virtues to the passions and the will. The virtues harmonize and direct the passions, which are themselves pre-rational yet not completely devoid of elements of reason; and they reorient the will, which is naturally directed toward the individual's own private good, but which is transformed through justice and charity to love the common good and the supreme good that is God. These two aspects of reason's operation are expressed through Aquinas' appropriation of the Aristotelian idea of the mean of the virtues. Similarly, the natural law is a rational norm, in fact, a construction of reason, as Aquinas says. Yet it too is informed by pre-rational intelligibilities, which it appropriates and harmonizes, and at the same time it points beyond itself to the eternal law, in which it participates.

These dynamisms of the moral life are integrated through their relation to the end of human life, which, as we have observed, Aquinas identifies with God Himself. This aim (which, it should be remembered, we share in common with every other creature) can be attained in diverse ways.[107] Subrational creatures obtain God through attaining their specific form of perfection and their proper place in the universe, considered as an ordered cosmos. This mode of attaining God is also possible, at least abstractly possible, for the rational or intellectual creature, which also has a specific form of created perfection. For human beings, this consists of the practice of the virtues, which Aquinas identifies as the connatural happiness of human life, toward which the moral life apart from grace is oriented.

However, we are as a matter of fact oriented toward a higher and in that sense a supernatural aim, namely, the enjoyment of God in the beatific vision. This Aquinas understands to be the direct apprehension of God as He is in Himself, in contrast to a knowledge of God which apprehends Him as the First Cause through a consideration of created things. Yet—as Aquinas has already explained in the *Prima Pars,* and as he repeatedly reminds us in the *Prima Secundae*—this apprehension exceeds the capacities of the human intellect. Indeed, it exceeds the natural capacities of any creature, however exalted. For this reason, if we are to attain it, we must receive a new principle of action, bestowed on us directly by God. This principle is grace, and the transformation which it brings about in the human person is expressed through the infused virtues and the gifts of the Holy Spirit.

It would take us too far afield to examine Aquinas' doctrine of grace in detail. It is worth noting, however, that Aquinas sets forth the main lines of this doctrine by delineating the effects of grace, seen in comparison to the natural capacities of the rational creature. When we examine the relevant question, we find that the fundamental effects of grace have their parallels in our natural capacities; we are naturally capable of seeking the truth, doing the good, and loving God more than ourselves.[108] Grace restores these capabilities, which have been damaged by sin, and in addition it transforms them; we are able to love God above ourselves directly for Himself.

Once again, Aquinas' fundamental approach is that grace perfects rather than destroys nature, and this includes those aspects of nature which we share with the rest of creation. By the same token, the operations of grace are intelligible, at least up to a point, in terms of their relation to our natural capabilities and inclinations. Yet because grace renders us capable of attaining a direct union with God, and even brings about the first stages of that union in this life, it also goes beyond reason. In this life, our love for God through charity outstrips the knowledge of God that is possible through faith, and even in the life to come, our knowledge of God will eternally fall short of the full reality of God's inner life.[109]

The moral life is not an end in itself for Aquinas; it is oriented toward final union with God, and it will find its completion in that union. For that reason, Aquinas' moral theology can only be understood within the wider context of his metaphysics and theology.

Notes

An earlier version of this essay was presented at St. Mary's College, Notre Dame, Indiana, on April 1, 2001, and I am grateful to those present for their helpful comments.

1. Bernard Häring, C.S.S.R., *Das Gesetz Christi* (Frieburg im Breisgau: Erich Wewel Verlag, 1959); subsequently published in English as *The Law of Christ: Moral Theology for Priests and Laity*, 2 vols., trans. Edwin G. Kaiser, C.P.P.S. (Westminster, Md.: Newman Press, 1961–65); Gérard Gilleman, S.J., *Le Primat de la charité en théologie morale: Essai méthodologique* (Louvain: E. Nauwelaerts, 1952); the second edition was subsequently translated into English as *The Primacy of Charity in Moral Theology*, trans. William F. Ryan, S.J., and Andre Vachon, S.J., (Westminster, Md.: Newman Press, 1959).

2. Ralph McInerny, *Ethica Thomistica: The Moral Philosophy of Thomas Aquinas* (Washington, D.C.: Catholic University of America Press, 1982; rev. ed., 1997).

3. The most noteworthy of these are the *De malo, De virtutibus in communi, De virtutibus cardinalibus,* and *De caritate.*

4. *ST* II-II.47.6c. All translations of Aquinas are my own.

5. In particular, see Martin Rhonheimer, *Natural Law and Practical Reason: A Thomist View of Moral Autonomy,* trans. Gerald Malsbary (New York: Fordham University Press, 2000), and John Finnis, *Aquinas: Moral, Political, and Legal Theory* (Oxford: Oxford University Press, 1998).

6. *ST* II-II.152.2c.

7. That is why, as Aquinas explains at *ST* I-II.58.5c, prudence requires the moral virtues; cf. *ST* I-II.65.1c, II-II.47.6c.

8. *De Virt.* q. un., a.12; cf. *ScG* III.34.

9. *De Virt.* q. un., a.12.

10. Although it is now somewhat dated, M.-D. Chenu's *Toward Understanding St. Thomas,* trans. A. M. Landry and D. Hughes (Chicago: Henry Regnery Company, 1964), still provides a helpful introduction to the sources and the intellectual and social context of Aquinas' writings. For a more recent and very thorough discussion, see Jean-Pierre Torrell, *Initiation à saint Thomas d'Aquin: Sa personne et son oeuvre* (Fribourg: Éditions Universitaires, and Paris: Éditions du Cerf, 1993). For further detail on the social and intellectual contexts of Scholasticism, see John Marenbon, *Later Medieval Philosophy (1150–1350)* (London: Routledge, 1991), and (with special emphasis on the social context) R. W. Southern, *Scholastic Humanism and the Unification of Europe,* vol. 1, *Foundations* (Oxford: Blackwell, 1995).

11. *ST* I.2, prol.

12. See the introductions to *ST* I-II.6 and 49.

13. *ST* I-II.90, prol.

14. *ST* I-II.1.2.

15. As Julia Annas shows in *The Morality of Happiness* (New York: Oxford University Press, 1993), 27–46.

16. *ST* I-II.1.4.

17. *ST* I-II.1.1 and 2.

18. *ST* I-II.1.2c; *ScG* III.2 and 3.

19. *ST* I-II.1.1 ad 3.

20. *ST* I-II.1.5 and 6.

21. *ST* I-II.1.7c.

22. Ibid.

23. Cf. *ST* I-II.1.3.

24. *ST* I-II.6.

25. *ST* I-II.8–17.

26. *ST* I-II.18.2–4, respectively.

27. *ST* I-II.18.4 ad 3.

28. *ST* I-II.18.2c.

29. *ST* I-II.18.7c.

30. *ST* I-II.18.10 and 11.

31. *ST* I-II.18.4 ad 3.

32. *ST* I-II.18.10.

33. *ST* I-II.18.5c; cf. I-II.18.10.

34. The relevant papers are collected in *Psychologie et morale aux XIIe et XIIIe siècles,* vols. 2 and 3 of 6 (Louvain: Abbaye du Mont Cesar, 1948, 1949). For a more recent effort to show that Aquinas' virtue ethic is not fundamentally Aristotelian in its structure, see Mark Jordan, *The Alleged Aristotelianism of Thomas Aquinas,* Etienne Gilson Series 15 (Toronto: Pontifical Institute of Mediaeval Studies, 1990).

35. *ST* I-II.55.4 obj.1 and 4c, quoting Peter Lombard, *Sent.* Bk. II, d.27, c.1.

36. *ST* I-II.55.1c.

37. *ST* I-II.49.4c.

38. *ST* I-II.56.3c; I-II.57.1c; I-II.58.3c.

39. *ST* I-II.58.1c.

40. *ST* I-II.59.2c; I-II.60.3–5; cf. *De Virt.* q. un., a.12, which sets forth the relation of the virtues to the different faculties of the soul in more detail.

41. *ST* I-II.6 intro.

42. *ST* I-II.58.2c.

43. *ST* I-II.59.5c.

44. *ST* I-II.56.6c; I-II.60.2c; II-II.24.1c; II-II.58.4c.

45. *ST* I-II.55.1 and 3.

46. *ST* II-II.152.2c.

47. *ST* I-II.64.2c; note, however, that the infused cardinal virtues observe a different mean than do their acquired counterparts, as Aquinas explains at I-II.63.4c.

48. *ST* I-II.56.6c; II-II.58.10c.

49. *ST* I-II.63.2c; I-II.64.1c.

50. *ST* I-II.4.7c; I-II.5.5c; cf. *De virtutibus cardinalibus,* q. un., a.1.

51. *ST* I-II.62.1c; I-II.110.3c.

52. *ST* I-II.62.1c.

53. *ST* I-II.110.3c; with reference to the gifts in particular, I-II.68.1 and 2.

54. *ST* I-II.63.3 and 4.

55. *ST* II-II.147.1 ad 2.

56. *Summa aurea Magistri Guillelmi Altissiodorensis,* ed. J. Riballier (Paris: Éditions du Centre National de la recherche scièntique, 1980–).

57. *Summa aurea* III, tractatus 18, c.1.

58. *Summa aurea* III, tractatus 19, intro.

59. *De Virt.* q. un., a.9; *ST* I-II.61.5c.

60. *ST* I-II.110.3c.

61. *ST* I-II.114.2c.

62. *ST* I-II.63.3, especially ad 2.

63. *ST* II-II.58.7 and 8.

64. Ibid.; *ST* II-II.61.1c.

65. *ST* II-II.47.11c.

66. This is by no means a new approach; see, for example, Vernon J. Bourke, "Is Thomas Aquinas a Natural Law Ethicist?" *The Monist* 58 (1974): 52–66. For a more recent and highly influential example, see Daniel Mark Nelson, *The Priority of Prudence: Virtue and Natural Law in Thomas Aquinas and the Implications for Modern Ethics* (University Park: Pennsylvania State University Press, 1992).

67. *ST* I-II.54.2 and 3.

68. See, for example, *ST* II-II.27.1.

69. The relevant texts are *ST* II-II.16; 22; 44; 56; 122; 140; and 170.

70. *De Malo* q.2 a.1; sins are said specifically to be opposed to one or more virtues at 2.6.

71. Otherwise, there would be no basis for his distinction between the continent person, who does the right thing in the teeth of contrary desires, and the temperate individual, whose desires and actions are both harmoniously in accord with the demands of morality; see *ST* II-II 155.

72. *ST* I-II.94.1c.

73. *ST* I-II.90.1 ad 2; I-II.94.2c; note that these are also said to be the first principles of the virtues at *ST* II-II.47.6.

74. *ST* I-II.94.2 ad 1.

75. *ST* I.60.5c.

76. *ST* I-II.94.4 ad 3.

77. *ST* II-II.108.2c.

78. *ST* I-II.100.3 ad 3; II-II.122.1c.

79. *ST* I-II.100.1 and 3; II-II.122.1c.

80. *ST* I-II.100.3c.

81. *ST* I-II.100.3 ad 3.

82. *ST* I-II.100.5c.

83. *ST* II-II.27 and 44.

84. In particular, see Eugene F. Rogers, Jr., "The Narrative of Natural Law in Aquinas's Commentary on Romans 1," *Theological Studies* 59 (1998): 254–76.

85. *ST* I.6.1c.

86. *ST* I-II.109.1 and 3.

87. *ST* I-II.94.4–6; I-II.109.4c.

88. *ST* II-II.154.12c.

89. *ST* II-II.154.12 ad 1.

90. *ST* II-II.154.11c.

91. *In Rom.* 1:26, no.149; see also *ScG* III.122; *De Malo* q.15 a.3.

92. *ST* I.60.5c.

93. *ST* I.60.5c.

94. *ST* II-II.64.5c.

95. *ST* II-II.64.7c.

96. *ST* II-II.108.1 and 2.

97. *ST* II-II.104.1 and 5.

98. *ST* II-II.141.6c.

99. *ST* II-II.147.1 ad 2.

100. See Odon Lottin, "La Loi eternelle chez saint Thomas d'Aquin et ses predecesseurs," in *Psychologie et Morale,* 2:51–67.

101. *ST* I-II.93.1c.

102. *ST* I-II.93.3c.

103. Lottin, "La loi eternelle."

104. *ST* I-II.91.2 ad 3.

105. *ST* I-II.91.2c.

106. *ST* II-II.26.6c.

107. I owe this way of expressing the relation between our natural and our supernatural end to Kevin Staley; see "Happiness: The Natural End of Man?" *The Thomist* 53 (1989): 215–34.

108. *ST* I-II.109.1–3; cf. I.12.13.

109. *ST* I.12.7c.

Nine

Grace

JOSEPH WAWRYKOW

In this chapter, I will provide an introduction to Aquinas' doctrine of grace, as this is found, in particular, in ST I-II.109-114.[1] The treatise on grace does not, however, stand in isolation. It not only completes the *Prima Secundae*, bringing to a term Aquinas' reflections there on the movement of the human person to God as end;[2] it also continues and completes the depiction of predestination initiated in the *Prima Pars* of the *Summa* (I.23). Grace figures anew in the *Tertia Pars*, in the consideration of what might be termed a test or limit case: the unique situation of Jesus Christ, who is both God and human. Accordingly, I will devote most of my attention to I-II.109-114, and then end with brief reflections on I.23 and a group of the relevant questions from the treatise on Christ.

The actual starting-point of the *ex professo* analysis of grace in the *Prima Secundae* is in fact a matter of some scholarly dispute. Others might insist that Aquinas begins the discussion of grace proper with q.106, in the questions that handle the New Law.[3] That I-II.106-108 are important and provide the link between what comes before—on law in its various manifestations, including the Old Law—and what comes after—grace—is beyond question. Nonetheless, those questions add little to the presentation of grace itself; and their main insight— the interiority of the New Law, as the inward prompting of the Holy Spirit—is adequately advanced by Aquinas in the course of his detailed teaching on grace. Thus, we can safely begin with ST I-II.109.

ST I-II.109-114: Grace

In the six questions of the treatise on grace, Aquinas examines a healthy range of issues. In identifying these issues as worthy of inclusion, Aquinas is undoubtedly conditioned by his historical circumstances; he reflects on topics that other Scholastics also have found pertinent to a treatise on grace, although of course the full teaching is his own, distinctive and proper to himself.[4] The questions on grace are divided by Aquinas into three groups.[5] The first group reviews the need for grace (q.109), the essence of grace (q.110), and its division (q.111). In q.112, Aquinas looks at the cause of grace. And, in the remaining group of two questions of the treatise, he examines the effects of grace: justification (q.113) and merit (q.114).

Running throughout the first question on the need for grace, and informing most of the others, are three main distinctions. The first is the difference between what may be called the natural order, and the supernatural order. For Aquinas, what is natural lies within a being's powers. Thus, it is natural for a human to think discursively and to will, for the human is endowed with the capacity for such thinking and willing. And as embodied intellect, a human can come to know whatever presents itself to the senses; the intellect forms concepts and judgments on the basis of that evidence. In contrast, the squirrel lacks the capacity to think and will (the example is my own); it simply senses and acts on instinct. If, then, one were to ask the squirrel to follow, perhaps even contribute to, an argument, that would be to ask of the squirrel what lies beyond its natural capacity (which makes the squirrel capable of merely squirrel sorts of things). We are here provided with what can be termed a first introduction to the "supernatural" as Aquinas takes it. Something is considered "supernatural" when it lies beyond or above the natural capacities of a being. Aquinas is of course concerned, in drawing our attention to the difference between the natural and the supernatural, with humans in relation to God and especially to God as their end. Is the act in question something that is natural to the person, or is it natural to God, and so beyond the natural capacity of the human? In q.109, Aquinas asks the question about the need for grace in each of the articles, and so in effect asks the question of need ten times. Is grace needed for this or for that—for example, to know the truth of the things encountered in this world, or, to will God, akin to God's willing of Godself? In the early articles of the question, the answer is fairly easy and straightforward. If the act is natural to the human, then grace will not be needed, for intrinsic human capacity should suffice. If the act is supernatural or directed to God as by God, then grace is needed. As will be pointed out very shortly, by the end of the question the analysis has become more complicated.

The next distinction is between two kinds of grace. For Aquinas, acting presupposes a potential or capacity for that acting. Thus, to render possible acting on the supernatural level, God provides humans with a grace that enhances the person's capacity, granting the wherewithal for supernatural acting. This is habitual grace, a grace that sanctifies the person before God.[6] In referring to habitual grace, Aquinas is hardly innovative. His contemporaries tended to construe grace as principally, even exclusively, habitual; and in fact, in his earliest teaching on grace (in the *Scriptum* on the *Sentences* of Peter Lombard), Aquinas himself viewed grace as only habitual. A habit is a potency, a steady disposition to act in a certain way. Habitual grace thus is a power added to the soul which makes the person capable of, and inclined to, supernatural action. The medievals debated the connection between habitual grace and the theological virtues (faith, hope, and charity). For Aquinas, there is a difference, inasmuch as habitual grace is infused in the soul and is rooted in its essence. The theological virtues flow out of habitual grace and perfect the powers of the soul.[7]

The other grace is *auxilium*. In first introducing this grace in *ST* I-II.109,[8] Aquinas is content with a metaphysical observation. What is in potency to act does not reduce itself to act. The potency is reduced only by what is already in act. In terms of the person who has habitual grace, the mere potency of habitual grace is insufficient to account for graced action. For that action, the potency has to be reduced to act; and that occurs by *auxilium*, by God moving people to actions in accord with habitual grace.

As the question proceeds, however, *auxilium* is cast in an additional light, while continuing to be affirmed on metaphysical grounds. The moral need for grace comes into greater prominence as Aquinas proceeds with his inquiry into the necessity of grace. Here, a third distinction comes to the fore: the difference between the pre-Fall and the post-Fall state. Aquinas' point is that sin brings tremendous disruption—to the human self, inasmuch as the lower self because of sin is at war with the higher self, with the reason; to the human self before God, inasmuch as the person refuses and rebels against the will of God. Because of sin, then, even with regard to the good that is natural to the human person, the person will need grace. In terms of habitual grace, habitual grace will not only elevate the person to the supernatural level; habitual grace will be needed to heal the soul, to make it pleasing before God and to render the lower self prone to the promptings of the higher self, and to make the whole person ready to obey the will of God. Yet the healing brought by habitual grace is not complete in this life; full healing and full restoration awaits the next life, when the person is in the immediate presence of God. Hence, for as long as the person is in this world, the person will need more grace, to reduce the person endowed with habitual grace to correct moral and supernatural action. This further grace is *auxilium,* God's direct contribution to the moral and supernatural behavior required of the person to attain to God as end. To the metaphysical necessity of *auxilium* (as in *ST* I-II.109.1), then, Aquinas adds the moral contribution of this grace.[9]

All three of these distinctions appear already in the corpus of the second article of *ST* I-II.109, in which Aquinas asks whether grace is needed to will and to do good. That question receives a twofold qualification. In the first place, there are two "goods" that can be considered. If we are talking about supernatural good, then humans always needed habitual grace. If we are talking about natural good, then humans did not always need habitual grace. In related fashion, Aquinas mentions the difference between humans before and after sin. Before sin, humans did not need habitual grace for the good natural to them; their natural capacities sufficed. But after sin, they do need habitual grace, because of the disruption brought by sin. The question in this article also requires that one take account of both kinds of grace, not simply habitual grace. And with regard to *auxilium,* for Aquinas humans always need *auxilium,* whether their nature is considered as apart from or under sin. Prior to the Fall, *auxilium* is needed to reduce the person endowed with habitual grace to the supernatural action that God seeks from those who will reach God as end. After the Fall, *auxilium* is needed for that reason, but also to provide correct action, to overcome the sin that has disrupted the self in its internal relations, in its relations to others, and in relation, especially, to God.

In the treatise on grace, Aquinas makes use of another analytical tool to organize his presentation: a view of the life of the individual as a "journey." The end of the journey comes only in the next life, when the person is ushered into the immediate presence of God. God is the end of the journey. As ultimate Truth, God alone can fully fulfill the human's desire to know; as ultimate Good, God alone is the proper and fullest object of the human will. Life with God in heaven is, radically, a gift. There is nothing in the human person that can necessitate God setting God as the end of the person. Rather, God has freely established God as the end of the journey, inviting humans to come to share in God's own life of self-contemplation and love.

For Aquinas, as for other medievals who employ the model of life as journey, life in this world is divided into two states. Attaining the end of eternal life presupposes ending one's life in this world in the state of grace. In applying this model, medieval theologians take for granted that people will at some point in their lives lack grace and so will need to acquire it. The move from the state of non-grace to the state of grace involves conversion, a moving toward God as the end of human existence.

Different obstacles can hinder the successful journey. Some medieval theologians would speak of the great ontological gap that distinguishes the creature from God. If eternal life is the end of the journey, and eternal life is proper and natural to God, then the creature must be raised above her natural capacities in order to come to God as end. While eternal life is not incompatible with human capacity, it certainly lies beyond it; people thus need an aid to raise them to God's level, namely, God's grace.[10] When the ontological gap is the major problem that must be solved, grace is seen in primarily elevating terms: the function of grace will be to bridge the gap between the creature and God and so render possible the attainment of God as end. Other theologians could speak of another problem that makes difficult the attainment of God as end: the moral gap caused by sin. For these theologians, grace's principal function will be to heal, to overcome sin, and thus make the attainment of God possible.

As should already be clear, Aquinas in the *ST* speaks of both obstacles to the journey, the ontological and the moral; and therefore grace will have a twofold function, of healing and elevating. Neither seems for Aquinas to take precedence; he views both with equal seriousness.

In the treatise on grace, Aquinas can devote given articles to one or another of the states of the wayfarer in this life; as one reads through the treatise on grace, it is important to be aware of which part of the journey is in play. Thus, Aquinas can discuss the conversion of the person from non-grace to grace in such articles as I-II.109.6; 112.2 – 3; 113 (entire); and 114.5 – 6. Other articles in the treatise are given over to a consideration of the person who has moved into the state of grace. Once the person has moved into the state of grace, certain acts are expected of the person to complete the journey to God; in this regard, Aquinas can speak of merit in the state of grace. And, given the incompleteness of the healing brought by the habitual grace that is infused in the process of conversion, Aquinas can also talk about the grace—the *auxilium*—that works perseverance in grace, by enabling the graced person to overcome temptation and continue on the path to God as end.[11]

Each of Aquinas's two kinds of grace—habitual and *auxilium*—performs both functions of grace. Habitual grace as given at the term of the process of conversion heals the self (at least in principle) of the effects of sin, restoring right order within the self and before God, and so making the person pleasing to God. Habitual grace also elevates the person to the supernatural level, orienting the person and the person's acts to God as end. *Auxilium* too both heals and elevates. In the treatise on grace, Aquinas is clear that an *auxilium* in fact inaugurates the process of conversion. God moves the person who lacks grace into the state of grace, that is, to the reception of habitual grace. As in *ST* I-II.112.2, Aquinas can talk about conversion in terms of form and matter. Matter must be disposed for a formal perfection. In conversion, *auxilium* works the preparation for the form; once that disposition is achieved, the formal perfection of habitual grace is infused.

Each of his two graces can be further distinguished into "operative" and "cooperative." The classic text in the *Summa* for this way of talking about grace is I-II.111.2c. When used of habitual grace, "operative" refers to being: by operative habitual grace the being of the person, both morally and supernaturally, is enhanced, and the person is rendered pleasing to God. "Cooperative" habitual grace has to do with disposition; by cooperative habitual grace, one is inclined to the meritorious actions that complete the journey to God.

The discussion of operative and cooperative *auxilium* in this article is somewhat more complicated, giving rise to certain interpretive disputes. When used of *auxilium*, "operative" means that God moves the person and the person is simply moved. Here, Aquinas states that the "especial" example of operative *auxilium* is conversion. That is, when the person moves from the state of non-grace into the possession of habitual grace, God works the conversion: God moves the person away from sin and toward God as end; by operative *auxilium* God disposes the person for the infusion of habitual grace. The person is merely passive in this process. Some interpreters of Aquinas have seen conversion as the *only* example of operative *auxilium*, but this is wrong. Not only would that be a strained interpretation of his point that conversion is the special example of such grace (that is, "special" does not mean "only"). It ignores the fact that by this point in the treatise, Aquinas has already provided sufficient indication of where another operative *auxilium* would be found: in the perseverance in habitual grace of those who have already converted to God. As in the final articles of *ST* I-II.109, perseverance is not an act of the person, but is worked in the person by God, in accordance with God's will for the person to reach eternal life.

For its part, cooperative *auxilium* has to do with God moving the person, but here the moving is such that the person also moves him/herself. In distinction from operative *auxilium*, with cooperative *auxilium* the person is not merely passive; the person is also active, as this *auxilium* cooperates with the person in doing what God requires of those who will reach God as end.

In the discussion of operative and cooperative *auxilia*, Aquinas makes some effort to relate these graces to human acting. His language in this article, however, poses some difficulty for those who have read, much earlier in the *Prima Secundae*, about the human act. In the present article, Aquinas speaks of inward and external action, and links the former with operative *auxilium,* the latter with cooperative *auxilium.* The problem is that earlier in the *Prima Secundae,* Aquinas has divided the complete human act into three main parts or segments.[12] First is the willing of the end, or intention. Next is the choice of the means; this involves considering various strategies that might be deployed to reach the intended end, deliberating about them, and finally opting for or choosing one of these means. And finally, there is the performance of the act, implementing the chosen strategy to reach the intended end. To return to *ST* I-II.III.2c, it is relatively easy to match operative *auxilium* with the intention of the end that stands at the head of every complete human act. It is also easy to match cooperative *auxilium* with the third part of the complete human act, actual performance. The difficulty is in accounting for the middle part, choice of the means. Here, in effect, the question is about the extent of merit, about what people do to contribute to the working out of their own salvation. As Aquinas states at the head of *ST* I-II.114, merit is the effect of cooperative grace. Is external performance what alone accounts for merit? It is more likely that cooperative *auxilium* is responsible for choice of the means as well. Thus, when the person wills correctly, that is due to operative *auxilium,* by which the person is moved to correct intention. This is not, in itself, meritorious. When the person chooses the correct means to that end and actually does the act to attain that end, that is due to cooperative *auxilium.* God is contributing throughout the act. At the head of the act, God simply moves; in the second and third parts of the act, God moves, but does so in such a way that the person also moves him/herself. And thus, in this latter respect, there is room for merit, the voluntary action by which people deserve a reward from God.

There is considerable progress from *ST* I-II.109 to III.2c. On the basis of q.109, one can chart the following sequence of graces in the depiction of the journey to God: *auxilium* works conversion by preparing the person for habitual grace (a.6); at the term of that preparation, habitual grace is infused; once the person is in the state of grace/has habitual grace, further *auxilia* are required, to provide for perseverance in habitual grace and to keep the person moving to God as end (aa.9–10). On the basis of q.III.2c, the same sequence can be put as follows: operative *auxilium* works conversion. Habitual grace is infused at the term of the conversion. As operative, habitual grace enhances the being of the person, making the person both morally and supernaturally pleasing to God. As cooperative, habitual grace disposes its possessor to actions that are pleasing to God and conducive to bringing that person to the end that is God. In addition, in the state of grace additional *auxilia* are provided to the person by God. As operative, these *auxilia* keep the person on the path to God and make possible perseverance in grace; they do so by overcoming temptation and by providing correct intention to the person in the willing of the end of all of the acts that person will go on to do when in the state of grace. As cooperative, these *auxilia* also contribute to the merit of the person, allowing that person to contribute in a meaningful way to the achievement of eternal life. There will be as many *auxilia* as there are complete, good human acts of the person who is in the state of habitual grace.

ST I.23: Predestination

In Aquinas' analysis, grace does not stand on its own. The treatise on grace in the *Prima Secundae* presupposes the discussion of predestination in the *Prima Pars*, building on and completing that earlier teaching. In presenting his ideas about grace in the *Prima Secundae*, Aquinas is assuming that the reader is familiar with that earlier account. The grace that promotes the successful journey to God as end is given in accordance with God's predestining will for that individual.

Predestination is a matter of divine intellect and divine will.[13] By the time Aquinas gets to predestination (I.23), he has discussed in turn the divine knowledge (qq.14 ff.) and the divine will (qq.19 ff.) and so can turn to what pertains to them jointly. The discussion of predestination draws on what he has said about love in *ST* I.20, as part of the consideration of the divine will. For Aquinas, love in general has to do with willing good with respect to another. There is, however, a crucial difference between human loving and divine loving. Human loving presupposes a good, whether real or only apparent; human loving is elicited by a good that already exists or seems to exist. Divine loving, on the other hand, is causal of good. God loves, and therefore there is good.[14] It is not all that difficult to imagine how this account of God as loving will figure into an account of creation; and in fact *ST* I.20 anticipates the later, more complete discussion of creating (in *ST* I.44 ff.) Nothing other than God need exist. That things other than God do exist is due to the divine will: God wills things into existence, communicating good to what is not God. There is a hierarchy of beings, and different beings have different natures, which endow them with the capacity for different acts. In the course of his analysis of God's love, Aquinas asks whether God loves better things—that is, things that have greater capacity, and so more good—more than other things.[15] Aquinas uses that question to remind the reader of the proper sequence when it comes to God's love. Yes, God does love the better thing more. But, the reason is not because there is already, or apart from God's loving, more good in that thing, which would elicit a greater love from God. Rather, the better thing is better—possessed of more good—as a result of God's love. God wills more good to the better thing. And thus, to take the example of a human and of a squirrel, God loves both, and thus both exist. The human has greater capacity (can do such things as think discursively and will, which the squirrel cannot) because God has made this being a human rather than a squirrel; God has willed to that being the greater good of being human. God has loved the human more.

When he discusses providence (*ST* I.22) and predestination (*ST* I.23), Aquinas extends this account of God's love to include the ends of creatures and the reaching of these ends. God not only establishes beings with their proper natures; God also orders them to their ends, to their fulfillment as beings of that sort. Again, the ordering of beings to their respective ends is a matter of God's loving; the higher the end, the greater God's love for that being.

For Aquinas, providence is the plan that God has for all creatures. There are in fact two aspects of, or "notes" to, providence.[16] Primarily, providence is the ordering by God of every creature to their ends: it is the plan that God has for their fulfillment. Secondarily, however, providence also involves the implementation of this plan that extends to all creatures. God orders; God implements the ordering, bringing every creature to the end set for it by God. This implementing is called by Aquinas "government"; he returns to a fuller explication of government toward the end of the *Prima Pars* (in qq.103 ff.).

Predestination is that part of providence that deals with those rational creatures called to the special end of life with God in heaven. Although some readers of Aquinas would prefer that he teach the salvation of all, or at least the equal opportunity for the salvation of every human *qua* human, in the *ST,* at least, Aquinas is clear that predestination has to do with only some rational creatures.[17] As a matter of love, predestination means that God has so loved some rational creatures that God has willed for them the good of God's own life. By virtue of God's special love for them, they will reach God in heaven and come to participate in God's eternal self-love and contemplation. This is God's special gift to them, grounded in God's love.[18]

As with providence, there are two aspects of, or notes to, predestination. Primarily, it is the ordering by God of these rational creatures to eternal life. Secondarily, predestination is a matter of implementation; and this implementation occurs through grace.[19] It is by grace that God brings these rational creatures to the special end set for them, freely and in love, by God. Hence the need to relate the treatise on grace to the question on predestination; hence the need to continue reading into the treatise on grace, to complete the analysis of predestination.

Predestination is, of course, a tricky matter, and it certainly has elicited a variety of concerns. Three will be taken here as representative, as a way of indicating in fuller detail what Aquinas both does and does not want to do with this teaching. First, Aquinas does not advocate what later (as in Calvin) came to be called "double predestination." In such a teaching, God will have decided in eternity what will become of every human, such that when that person comes into existence and lives out her life, that person will come to the end set for the person by God. There is no escape; and predestination as double has to do with both salvation and damnation. The basic logic would seem to be that if God is not for you, God must be against you. And so, in eternity God has decided, prior to anyone's existence, what will become of that person. Those whom God loves, God will send to eternal life at the term of their earthly life; those whom, in eternity, God hates, God will send to eternal damnation. In such an account there is a basic symmetry. The elect make it to eternal life because of God's eternal decree; the reprobate go to hell, again in accordance with God's decree. What happens to humans follows on what God has decided for them.

In his own account of predestination, however, Aquinas in effect denies any such symmetry, and he refuses to implicate God in this manner in the sending of people to hell. He agrees, of course, that reaching heaven is the sign of God's special love for that human. God's will will be implemented, and what God wants in the case of the elect will occur. The salvation of the elect is due to the decision of God for them. But Aquinas denies a similar involvement of God in the damnation of others. Rather, he makes the damned themselves responsible for their going to hell. Hell is the just punishment for sin. By their sin, performed through their misuse of their own will, sinners become qualified for hell. To the extent that God enters into the account of damnation, it is to bring good out of the evil of sinners. By sending them to hell, God is giving sinners what they deserve for their bad acts.[20] Thus, human sinning provides the opportunity for God to show the good of God's justice: God is rendering to them what is owed to them for their sin. The dissymmetry, then, is plain. In terms of the elect, personal holiness will follow on and be due to God's loving decision in their case. In terms of the reprobate, first they sin—of their own accord—and then God responds, by punishing them with hell and so showing the good of justice.

To complete the point, Aquinas can parse what scripture would mean by talking about God's "hatred." This is not akin to a decision made by God in eternity and prior to the existence and mis-activity of the person who will go to hell, as if personal wickedness followed on God's eternal decree against that person. Rather, employing the rhetoric of God's loving, this has to do with God not loving such a person to the same extent as God loves the elect.[21] In terms of both the elect and the reprobate, God loves both. This love is shown, in both, by the very fact that they exist; and that they exist as humans, with the proper capacities of the human. In terms of the elect, however, God has loved them more, willing to them the greatest good, attaining the end of life with God in heaven whereby they partake of God's own existence. God has not willed that end to the reprobate, and so has not loved them to the same extent. Hence, they are left to their sin, by which they earn the end to which they come.

Even as a teaching about single predestination, however, Aquinas' account can elicit other concerns, having to do with the place of the human in a view of salvation in which divine initiative and sovereignty receive such great emphasis. In the questions on providence and predestination, Aquinas contemplates human freedom and the human contribution in a couple of venues. First, he asks about the compatibility of divine and human causing. Hence, in *ST* I.22.4 he asks whether God's providence imposes necessity on all things. He returns to the question, but this time explicitly with regard to predestination, in *ST* I.23.6. In both articles, he trades on the distinction between primary and secondary causality. As the primary efficient cause, God brings about all effects. Because God's will cannot be in vain, what God wants to cause does come about, just as God wills it. However, God employs secondary causes in achieving God's will. There are two kinds of secondary cause, necessary and contingent. A secondary necessary cause is one that, once posited, always brings about its effect and always brings about the same effect. A secondary contingent cause, on the other hand, does not always cause, and does not always bring about the same effect when it does cause. Thus, when God causes an effect through a secondary cause that is necessary, the effect is certain and infallible—because caused by God, whose will is certain and infallible—and necessary, because caused through a secondary cause that is necessary. When God causes an effect through a secondary cause that is contingent, the effect is, again, certain and infallible, because caused by God, and contingent, because caused by God through a secondary cause that is contingent.[22] That is where Aquinas leaves the matter, with the claim that some effects are certain, infallible, and yet contingent. In other words, he simply asserts that it is possible to ascribe real causing to the human will, while at the same time affirming the infallibility of divine willing. For modern readers, the simple assertion is jarring and perhaps puzzling. In all likelihood, Aquinas feels that he can make the claim without further explanation because he takes seriously divine transcendence. In terms of efficient causes within the world, those that are utterly successful would seem to be so at the expense of those through whom they work, achieving their ends by limiting or restricting the proper causality of these others. But God is not to be reduced to a cause in the world, even to the most successful cause; and so it should be possible to assert that God can be infallibly successful as cause through—not despite—the secondary causes whose source God is. Elsewhere in this volume (see the essay by Goris), the issue receives a fuller treatment. It suffices to note here that Aquinas continues the discussion of *ST* I.23.6 in I-II.111.2c, where he distinguishes between operative and cooperative *auxilium*. In particular, the insistence there that God can move the will so that it moves itself (cooperative *auxilium*) reflects anew Aquinas' keen sense of God as transcendent cause.

Aquinas also asks about the human contribution to salvation in *ST* I.23 by raising the issue of merit. "Merit" means a voluntary human act that deserves a reward from God. Can the person merit salvation? Aquinas subjects this issue to close scrutiny in *ST* I.23.5c. The actual putting of the question in this article is, at least initially, not altogether promising. Is God's "fore-knowledge" of merit the cause of predestination? That is, does God look into the future of a human, see that that human will do morally good acts, and therefore decide on the basis of that person's prospective works to give that person heaven? By this point in the discussion of providence and predestination, the reader will be well aware that neither providence nor predestination is a matter of simple "knowing"; they involve God's causing as well. And, by this point the reader knows well that the article's posing of the question has botched the sequence. It is not that first a person is good and then God decides that that person will end up in heaven. Rather, a person's holiness follows on God's predestining will. A person is good because God has willed the end of eternal life for that person and provided that person with the grace that will bring the person to that special end.

Having dispensed with a mistaken view of a possible compatibility of predestination and human merit, Aquinas completes the corpus of article 5 by explaining how and why merit does fit into his account of salvation. We meet, in fact, in this article one of the earliest mentions in the *Summa* of the model of human existence that will figure so prominently in the treatise on grace: life as journey. Here, Aquinas says that it is prudent to distinguish between the overall effect of predestination and particular effects. What he means is that the fact that a person reaches eternal life is due to God's will, God's special love, for that person. Eternal life is utter gift. And the presupposition of reaching eternal life is grace. Thus, in intending a human to eternal life, God also wills for that person the grace that will bring that person to this end. There is nothing in the person that could "earn" either this end or this grace; God, after all, loves the elect specially even before they are born. And yet, Aquinas continues, there is a place to speak of "meriting." For God has ordained a particular effect to another as meritorious of it, such that the other is rendered to the person as reward. That is, God has ordered good acts done in the state of grace to eternal life as meritorious of eternal life. For this reason, then, eternal life is susceptible to a double characterization. It is first and foremost a gift of God, reflecting the good of God's love and mercy. But because of this ordination, eternal life is also, secondarily, a reward rendered to the elect by God for their graced good acts. To return to the earlier comments about the lack of symmetry between election and reprobation, in damnation only the good of God's justice is shown: God renders to sinners what is owed them for their sin. In salvation, both the good of God's love (primarily) and the good of God's justice are shown. God renders to the elect the eternal life to which they are freely and lovingly destined as a reward for the good acts that they do under God's grace.

ST I.23 and *ST* I-II.109–114: Predestination and Grace

The question on predestination offers a sound introduction to major features of Aquinas' analysis of salvation. It too conceives human existence in terms of a journey, and it distinguishes two states in that journey (the state of non-grace and the state of grace). It portrays the movement from the first to the second state in terms of a conversion that is the gift of God. And while insisting that the entire salvific process, including its end in God, is the gift of God and the mark of God's special love, it also allows room for merit. The elect, by God's grace, earn through their good acts done in the state of grace the end of eternal life. Yet the human story of responding to grace and working under grace is only correctly told when viewed against the account of God's willing: in the fullest expression of God's love, God wills to some rational creatures enjoyment of the life proper to God, by willing to them in this light the grace needed for them to attain God.

The treatise on grace repeats this analysis, while nuancing it and adding considerable detail. Without aiming at being exhaustive, it seems to mark an advance in the account of human salvation in the following ways. First, the question on predestination is basically content to speak simply of "grace"; the articulation of the two kinds of grace—habitual and *auxilium*—must await the treatise on grace. The distribution of each of these graces into "operative" and "cooperative" is likewise absent in the account of predestination. Hence, Aquinas simply gestures at the interplay between grace and human freedom (as in *ST* I.23.6), without the specificity of *ST* I-II.111.2c. Next, the treatise on grace pays much more attention to the question of sin. In the question on predestination, Aquinas brings in sin to explain reprobation: through the misuse of their free will, people sin and so earn the penalty of hell. As for election, on the other hand, the stress is on the transcendent end of the elect, and so on the need for a grace that will elevate the human person beyond herself and to God's level. Fourth, in the question on predestination, Aquinas is content with a relatively basic account of the journey: he mentions conversion, and he asserts merit in the state of grace. In the treatise on grace, on the other hand, the account of the person in the state of grace is considerably deepened. Aquinas plays up the need for a grace that will work perseverance in grace. Such a grace is not earned—it is not merited. As is the case with the grace that works conversion, the grace of perseverance is given by God to the elect to ensure that they reach the end lovingly set for them by God, namely, eternal life. This additional claim about perseverance is not surprising, in light of the greater care that the treatise on grace gives to the problem of sin and the attendant claim that the healing wrought by habitual grace is never complete in this life. Thus, those moved into the state of grace must rely on God's continued contribution to their progress, through the operative *auxilium* that works perseverance.

Aquinas also ends up saying more about the role of prayer in the journey to God. In *ST* I.23.8 he explains in a basic way how prayer fits into the journey, by invoking the distinction between primary and secondary causes. One's prayer for oneself or for the salvation of another may be fruitful, provided that God has ordained to use such prayer to further one's own or another's salvation. In the final articles of *ST* I-II.109, on the other hand, prayer is linked to the request for perseverance. Those who are in the state of grace will ask God to keep them in this state; in this connection, Aquinas refers to the Lord's Prayer,[23] which in his telling is especially concerned with the perseverance of the elect.

Finally, the treatise on grace offers a much more sophisticated account of merit, of the value of human, graced acts in the salvific process. The final question of the treatise, *ST* I-II.114, masterfully reviews the extent and limits of merit before God. Its ten articles fall into two main parts. The first article itself constitutes the first part of the question, insisting that merit is possible precisely because of a divine ordination: God orders good acts to their reward from God in order to proclaim the goodness of God outside of God.[24] The echoes of *ST* I.23.5c are obvious, and intentionally so; the two articles are meant to be read in tandem. Articles 2 through 10 of *ST* I-II.114 look at various possible objects or rewards for merit: Can one merit eternal life (aa.2–4)? Can one merit conversion, whether for oneself or for another (aa.5–7)? Can those in grace merit more grace (aa.8–9) or temporal rewards (a.10)? Through these articles, the list of possible rewards is extended. In addition to the eternal life that is the reward of merit in *ST* I.23.5c, Aquinas adds here that while one cannot merit the first grace (the grace of conversion) for oneself, if it is God's will, one can merit it for another. Similarly, for those who are in grace, there is a secondary reward for the good acts that merit heaven: growth in and firmer possession of the habitual grace given to the elect in their conversion. Aquinas' insistence here on what *cannot* be merited is just as striking as the extended list of what can be merited. Thus, one cannot merit eternal life *unless* one is in grace (a.2);[25] one cannot merit the first grace for oneself (a.5), nor can one in grace merit restoration to the state of grace in case of a subsequent fall from grace (a.7); and one cannot merit perseverance in grace (a.9), repeating the lesson of the final articles of *ST* I-II.109. The effect is to insinuate the place of merit in the Christian life, without either making too much of merit or putting in question the divine preeminence and sovereignty in the salvific process.

Some Comparative Comments

Aquinas thoroughly reworked his teaching on grace over the course of his career, and the account of human salvation offered in the earliest major work, his *Scriptum* on the *Sentences* of Peter Lombard, looks rather different than what is found in the *Summa Theologiae*. The enumeration of individual differences between his earliest and his mature teaching would be lengthy. To point to some of the more obvious differences: in the *Scriptum*, grace is simply habitual. Aquinas worked out his ideas about *auxilium* in fits and starts over the intervening years, and only in the *Summa* do we have a detailed accounting of that grace.[26] In the *Scriptum*, moreover, Aquinas says little about perseverance; once grace is obtained, it does not seem all that difficult in the early writing for a person to keep on the way to God, simply by using that grace wisely. Further, the teaching about merit is relatively monochromatic. As in the later *Summa*, one can merit eternal life provided one has grace; and one can merit more habitual grace. But in detailing merit's contribution to the journey, Aquinas does not bother, as he does later in the *Summa*, with emphasizing what falls beyond the scope of merit.[27]

More illuminating than the simple articulation of differences, however, are the basic convictions at play in the development of the teaching of the *Scriptum* that give rise to these specific differences. The *Scriptum* and the *Summa* offer wildly divergent accounts of the respective roles of God and the human person in the person's salvation. If we were to ask what God does to accomplish salvation, the Aquinas of the *Summa* would say: God predestines some in love to eternal life; provides the grace needed to reach eternal life, through conversion and perseverance; motivates and empowers the person in the state of grace to merit rewards from God; and renders these rewards to the elect. As for the human person, that person is moved to convert and then to persevere, and is simply moved; at times (e.g., in the choice of means), that person is so moved that the person can will and do the meritorious good. In the *Scriptum*, on the other hand, the role of the human person is greatly expanded, reflecting the greater optimism about human capabilities that is characteristic of the early Aquinas. The human in this early version of salvation must do—and can do—a great deal to attain the desired end. In this scenario, God correspondingly takes on a lesser role. Considerations of predestination are much less explicit in the *Scriptum*'s version of salvation, and hardly integral to the depiction of grace. Rather, God makes a general offer of grace to all; it is up to each person to accept or reject this offer. God also constitutes Godself to be a respectful provider to humans. God freely promises to respect what people do. When people act correctly (as in opening themselves to the offer of grace), God will respond accordingly, giving them that grace. And when they then do good with the help of that grace, God has freely committed God to render to these acts the reward of eternal life. In comparison with the *Summa,* the initiative and principal responsibility for the person's salvation lies squarely with that person, although the structure of salvation is dependent on God's prior commitments to take human activity with full seriousness. God wants all to be saved, and provides the wherewithal to all to be saved. That any given person is saved is due to the good sense and good activity of that person.

The shift between the *Scriptum* and the *Summa* can perhaps best be seen in Aquinas' use in these works, in his account of conversion from non-grace to grace, of the saying *"facienti quod in se est, Deus non denegat gratiam"* (to one who does what is in him/herself, God gives grace). By Aquinas' time, the saying had a broad currency. In its obvious sense, it ascribes the initiative in the salvific process to the person; and this is how Aquinas takes it in the *Scriptum.*[28] When the person who lacks grace does something good, that person starts on the way to God. And God will respond to that good first step, giving that person grace, which ennobles the person and points the person to God as end. When the person in grace then does more good, God will give more grace, and eventually the good of eternal life, as that person's just reward. Why does God do all this? Considered on its own terms, as the act of a creature, the actions of the person are worth relatively little; God could justly ignore them. But God has promised to respond to good actions: to the good action of the non-graced, God promises grace and so gives grace when that person does good; to the good action of the graced, God promises more grace and then heaven, and so heaven is the reward of meritorious action. Without these promises, without God's self-commitment, what the person does would not matter. Given the promise, the actions of the person are accorded tremendous significance. They determine that the person will reach the state of grace and then heaven.

Aquinas retains the *facienti* in the *Summa* but offers a radical reinterpretation, making use in the process of his two kinds of grace and invoking God's predestining will. The key articles are *ST* I-II.112.2–4. In the first (a.2), Aquinas asks whether any preparation is required for grace in the first place. If one means *auxilium,* then no preparation is needed: it is simply given by God. If one is asking about habitual grace, then yes, a preparation is needed. As is the case with every formal perfection, first the matter must be prepared before the form can be produced or infused. In the case of the formal perfection that is habitual grace, the matter of the person must be prepared through a good act of the will. Yet, as Aquinas adds to complete the picture, the preparation of the person is itself worked by God's *auxilium:* God moves the will toward God, and habitual grace is then infused. A person takes the first step to God only as moved by God.

In the next article (*ST* I-II.112.3), Aquinas asks whether God must give habitual grace to one who is so prepared. There are two angles from which the preparation can be viewed. As worked in a creature, habitual grace need not be given; the creature in value falls far short of God and so cannot necessitate any act of God. But as worked in the creature by God—by God's *auxilium*—habitual grace will inevitably follow. For, God does nothing idly. When God works the preparation through *auxilium* for habitual grace, this is because God wants that person to receive habitual grace. Hence, once God works the preparation by *auxilium,* habitual grace will be infused. Here, God's intending will supplies the link between the two parts of the saying, rather than, as in the *Scriptum,* some promise of God to take the creaturely act with such seriousness.

Finally, in *ST* I-II.112.4, Aquinas explains that habitual grace will be greater in one than in another. Greater possession of habitual grace (that is, a more intense rooting of that grace in the person) will be due to a greater preparation for habitual grace. Thus, in those for whom God intends more habitual grace, God works a greater preparation, through the *auxilium* that readies a person, in accordance with God's will, for habitual grace.

What accounts for the rather different analysis of grace and human salvation by the time of the *Summa*? Scholars such as Lonergan have stressed that speculative developments are important, as Aquinas pondered in different writings the ways in which God and humans interact. Thus, as Lonergan insists in his study of the changes over the years in Aquinas' teaching about operative grace (including the invention by the time of the *Summa* of the grace of *auxilium* itself),[29] modifications in Aquinas' thinking about the human will and about human willing promoted, correspondingly, advances in his evaluation of grace. But Aquinas' historical researches should also receive their due; they too played an important role in the shift away from the human-centered teaching on salvation of the *Scriptum.* In his classic study of conversion according to Aquinas,[30] Henri Bouillard had observed that certain very late writings of St. Augustine had achieved a certain prominence in the late writings of Aquinas, shaping the way that Aquinas came to write about the move from non-grace to the state of grace. These later writings of Augustine, written against the Massilians as well as certain monks of North Africa, had fallen out of general theological circulation by the end of the Carolingian period. In these writings, Augustine is concerned to counter what might be termed an incipient version of the *facienti quod in se est* in its obvious sense, a view, namely, that accords the initiative in conversion to the human person. In the teaching of Augustine's opponents, once one moves to God, God will respond with the gift of grace. In his own writings, Augustine denies that conversion is the act of the human person. Rather, God works conversion in the person, doing so in accordance with God's predestining will. Bouillard postulated that in mid-career, Aquinas had rediscovered these later Augustinian writings and had recognized in the view attacked by Augustine a teaching rather close to what he himself had offered in the *Scriptum*. Hence, in order to bring his own account of conversion into accord with that of his great predecessor, Aquinas had thoroughly revised, by the time of the *Summa contra Gentiles* (and then the *Summa*), the way that he would put conversion into the state of grace.

Bouillard's proposal is more inspired, however, than he himself realized. While the occasion of these late Augustinian writings is a distasteful account of conversion, Augustine constructs in them a teaching on the working out of human salvation that anticipates remarkably the account offered in the *Summa*. Augustine, in fact, had argued well before his final works that conversion is a gift, worked by God; he argued the same in the second decade of the fifth century against Pelagius. What is innovative in these final writings is the insistence that in the case of the saved, predestination is toward eternal life (and not just to conversion) and a second operative grace, that of perseverance, must be given for the converted to continue successfully on the path to God as end.[31] God has also ordained that the Lord's Prayer will be the occasion for the granting of the grace of perseverance to those ordered to eternal life. At the same time, Augustine allowed for the merit of the elect, although restricting merit-talk to the post-conversion state alone. These late writings of Augustine, in other words, would find a receptive reader in Aquinas, as he put his own teaching on human salvation into its definitive form.

The Grace of Christ

In the final part of this account of grace in Aquinas, I turn to the case of Jesus Christ. My interest is not principally in Christ as the medium of grace, although he *is* surely the principal source of grace according to Aquinas.[32] God, for

Aquinas, has taken decisive action for human salvation through the life, sufferings, death, and resurrection of the Son of God become human; through Christ, humans come to God as their end. Rather, I will concentrate on the grace that Christ himself had, addressing in the process two related issues. To what extent do the discussions of grace and predestination earlier in the *Summa* help to illumine aspects of the account of Christ in the *Tertia Pars*? And, to what extent does Christ conform to the model of grace and of the human journey articulated in the *Prima Secundae*?

For sundry reasons, posing these questions seems appropriate. In recent times, highly influential Christologies have made much of theological anthropology to interpret Christ; and in this connection, there has been a self-conscious distancing from the more classical, incarnational approach to Christ favored by theologians such as Aquinas. Thus, as in his *Foundations of Christian Faith*, Rahner situates his account of Jesus in the context of a general account of what it means to be human.[33] Human beings search for their perfection or completion, impelled by a desire that leaves them unsatisfied with their present state. Correspondingly, humans have a capacity for self-transcendence, for surpassing themselves and becoming ever more what they should and can be. In acting in accordance with this desire, humans are aided by God's grace, by God's calling them to their self-realization. On this view, Jesus marks the highest realization of what it means to be human, precisely because he consistently responded to God's gracious promptings throughout his life, culminating in his death on the cross. What can hold true of other humans has in fact been the case in Jesus. Aquinas' own Christological starting-point and guiding convictions are rather different, and it would be impossible for him to have Jesus conform in a simple and uncomplicated manner to the general rule for divine-human interaction. Aquinas, along with other advocates of an incarnational approach, has been severely criticized for making his Jesus too unlike other humans in their graced relations to God. Thus, it is appropriate to examine what exactly Aquinas is arguing when it comes to the grace that Jesus had.

Another reason for including this topic should be cited here, one that is specific to this volume. All of the contributors are united in their appreciation for the coherence and integrity of Aquinas' theology. He is capable of subjecting discrete topics in theology to searching, precise, and detailed analysis. Yet as he looks at a new topic, he brings to bear what he has written elsewhere on related themes, in light of his basic conviction about the overall coherence of the Christian faith.[34] Thus, in looking at Christ's grace in this chapter, I can offer anew the recommendation already made in terms of linking the treatise on grace of the *Prima Secundae* to the discussion of predestination in the *Prima Pars:* to appreciate the full force and extent of a teaching, we should read questions from one Part of the *Summa* in tandem with questions in other Parts. Only that will reveal the full extent of Aquinas' thought on the crucial topics of religion.

The theme of Christ's grace weaves its way through different questions in the *Tertia Pars*. I will draw on the following questions: q.7, first and foremost, which looks specifically at Christ's grace and contemplates at length on how Christ in his grace is both similar to and differs from other graced humans; qq.18–19, on the unity of Christ's wills and operations; and briefly, q.24, on Christ's predestination. As is evident, these questions are scattered throughout the opening questions of the *Summa*'s treatise on Christ. Q.7 comes at the beginning of Aquinas' treatment of what is co-assumed by the Word in taking up human nature. In his questions on the "co-assumed," Aquinas looks at both the perfections and the defects that are co-assumed, shaping his analysis according to his sense of what is, and what is not, appropriate to the Christ who saves others. The other questions, 18–19 and 24, come in the course of his consideration of "what follows on the incarnation." As the questions included in this section (qq.16–26) indicate, "what follows on the incarnation" covers much: Christ in himself, in his unity of being, will, and operation (qq.16–19); Christ in relation to the Father (qq.20–24); and finally, Christ in relation to other humans, especially as the mediator between God and humans (qq.25–26).

However, before reaching those perfections that are co-assumed, including grace, Aquinas offers in the initial questions of the treatise a brisk overview of the center of the teaching: the account of hypostatic union as this is tailored to the making possible of human salvation. A more complete account of this teaching must await the next chapter of this volume. For my present purposes, it suffices to note what is pertinent in that teaching to Aquinas' engagement of the issue of the grace that Christ possessed.

Two points made repeatedly in the opening questions of the treatise on Christ are especially important for our topic. First, Christology and soteriology are intimately connected. In God's plan, Jesus Christ is geared toward human salvation; correct talk about the reality of Jesus secures the possibility of salvation for others. Aquinas nicely makes the point by the very ordering of the treatise on Christ. Before turning to the details of hypostatic union (in qq.2 ff.), he first ponders the "fittingness of the incarnation," showing in the very first question of the treatise the salvific dimensions of incarnation. The incarnation of God is fitting given the transcendent end to which God has called people.[35] As human, God shows people this end and the way to that end. As human, God reinforces the great love that God has for humans, becoming one of them to provide the way to God. As human, God can stimulate faith, hope, and charity, as well as provide a model for moral emulation. And by becoming human, God reveals definitively the dignity of the human person: humans should not sell themselves short, by becoming enslaved to the devil; they should act in accordance with their great standing before God. When they do so, in fellowship with the Jesus who provides their grace, they will attain eternal life.

Second, Aquinas plays nicely with two related senses of "incarnation." Incarnation can be viewed as an act: the second person of God does something, becomes human. Here, the focus is on the agent or subject of the act. In this sense, incarnation is one of many episodes or stages in the account of Jesus, along with his life in the world, his passion and then death, and finally his resurrection. But "incarnation" involves the description of the reality that is the result of that act. In the act, the Word of God becomes human. What is true of the Word of God prior to that act remains true of the Word at the term of that act. Thus, the incarnate Word of God remains the second Person of God, who from eternity is a distinct Person in the Godhead while being one and the same God as the Father and the Holy Spirit. But, by virtue of the act, something new comes to be true of the fully divine Word: the Word becomes flesh. That is, in the act of incarnation, the second Person without loss to itself takes up human nature and comes to be a true human being. Thus, the subject in the case of Jesus is the fully divine Word: it is the Word who lives, suffers, dies, and is raised. But, the Word does this as fully and truly human: it is the Word incarnate who lives, suffers, dies, and is raised.

On the basis of this teaching about hypostatic union[36]—that is, the union in the person or hypostasis of the Word of the two natures, the divine and the human—it is permissible to enumerate three sorts of statements that might be made of the Word. Some will be made of the Word as Word, that is, as a distinct Person in the Godhead. Such statements will be made only of the Word; other statements, peculiar to them, will be made of the Father and of the Spirit, respectively. Other statements will be made of the Word as God; and the same statements will be made of the Father and the Spirit, who are one and the same God as the Word. And finally, by virtue of the incarnation, a third set of statements will be made of the Word as incarnate. Such statements will have to do with the incarnate Word in its genuine humanity.

By virtue of incarnation, there is a surpassing intimacy in Jesus of the divine and the human. Here, the contrast with other humans is illuminating. For another human, there is a twofold difference between that human and God: God and the human differ in nature; the human also differs from God in person. In Jesus, there are two natures, and neither is to be reduced to or confused with the other.[37] But the Word is the person of Jesus, and the person of Jesus is one: the

Word of God perfectly expresses divinity, and does so from eternity; as incarnate, the Word perfectly expresses humanity, instantiating human nature in the case of Jesus. Aquinas can make his point by referring to the humanity of Jesus as the "conjoined instrument" of the divinity.[38] By talking about "instrument" he can reinforce the insight that the human nature is not the divine nature—it differs from that. He can likewise make the point that Jesus' human nature is in the service of the divine: it is the medium through which the divine Word works out the salvation of other humans. But, by speaking of an instrument that is "conjoined," Aquinas (here following the model of the Greek fathers, who also spoke in such terms)[39] can underscore the intimacy of the contact between the divine and the human in Christ. The human nature is not a separated instrument, in the way that an axe, say, would be separate from the woodsman who wields it. Rather, the human nature belongs to the Word as incarnate; indeed, in the case of Jesus it finds its subject in the Word become flesh. The incarnate Word has a body and soul (the chief constituents of human nature); the Word as incarnate employs its body and soul to bring about the salvation of others. The difference from other humans—and in particular, from other righteous humans— will be apparent. The righteous, those who stand in correct relationship to God, can be said to be God's instruments, inasmuch as through them God achieves God's will to proclaim the goodness of God outside of God. But the righteous are not themselves God. They are separate, ontologically, from the God who employs them; in the language of instrumentality, they are not conjoined instruments of the divinity. That is reserved to Jesus alone.

A considerable block of questions in the *Tertia Pars* is given over to the exploration of the humanity of the Word incarnate (qq.4–15). The first three are devoted to the human nature that is assumed, looking at the constituent parts of that nature as assumed by the Word. To be human means to have a human body and a human soul. By means of the soul, a human has the capacity to do human sorts of things: to will and to think discursively. Thus, as the consequence of the assumption of human nature, the incarnate Word has in fact two wills[40] and two intellects,[41] as is appropriate to one who has two natures in their integrity. A number of additional questions pursue the issue of Christ's humanity by looking at what is or is not co-assumed in the incarnation (qq.7–15). When he reviews the "co-assumed," Aquinas is looking at attributes that are not part of human nature, that is, they do not fall under the definition of being human. Yet a human is more than just his/her body and soul. Each human life is marked by various perfections and defects, in varying combinations. In the questions on the co-assumed, Aquinas asks about such perfections as grace (qq.7–8), knowledge (qq.9–12), and power (q.13), and about such defects (in qq.14–15) as sin and various consequences of sin (death, ignorance, concupiscence, difficulty in doing good), as well as such defects of body as hunger and thirst. Which of these defects and perfections mark the human nature as taken up and expressed by the Word? For Aquinas, as he attempts to summarize and thematize the scriptural account of Jesus in these terms, it is a matter of fittingness. What is fitting to the human nature that exists in such close proximity to the Word? What is fitting to the Word as incarnate, who is the principal means of the salvation of all?[42] Basically, Aquinas ascribes those perfections and those defects to Christ that will further his salvific work, confirm his genuine humanity, and allow him to serve as the moral exemplar of other humans who aspire to God as end. And he denies to Christ those defects that would put his salvific work in jeopardy. Thus, Christ was without the defect of sin, and did not have the consequence of sin that is concupiscence.[43] He did, on the other hand, take up such defects as dying (although as sinless he need not die) and hunger and thirst, for these defects would intensify his suffering and thus make his work of satisfaction on behalf of sinners all the more poignant.[44] And in terms of perfection, the Word in becoming human took up the fullness of knowledge, including the beatific vision while in this world, for these perfections would help to ensure that he would engage, and successfully, in his saving work on behalf of others.[45]

What about grace, the first of the perfections that Aquinas addresses in pondering the "co-assumed"? The issues addressed in *ST* III.7 are familiar from the treatise on grace in the *Prima Secundae* and the follow-up discussions of the virtues and the gifts of the Holy Spirit (in the *Secunda Secundae*). Does Christ have grace? How much? Does Christ have the virtues, including the theological virtues of faith, hope, and charity? And does Christ have the gifts that make the use of the virtues more prompt? As in the treatise on grace, Aquinas will make use of his standard analytical tool of the "journey" to discuss Christ, while also placing the case of Christ under God's predestining will. But though the terms of the discussion are familiar enough on the basis of our earlier discussion of grace, and though Aquinas will be conscious of those ways in which the case of Christ does conform to the general rule, Aquinas will also take care in q.7 to explain how Christ differs from other humans, taking his cue throughout from the scriptural account of Jesus.

What, then, is Aquinas' teaching about the grace of Christ? First, Christ did indeed have grace, and grace in his case performed the two functions described in the treatise on grace.[46] Christ's humanity is not his divinity, and for the humanity to attain to God as end requires a grace that elevates the human nature to the supernatural level. Thus, as with all other elect, by habitual grace the human nature of Jesus is ennobled and raised up to God's own level. Aquinas can also speak of the other function of grace, to justify and to make a human pleasing to God. In this regard, Aquinas attests to the perfect harmony both within Christ and of the incarnate Word in its humanity before God, as rendered possible by the granting of habitual grace.[47]

With regard to both of these functions, however, there is a difference between Jesus and other humans. In Jesus' case there is no story of lack of grace, including sin, followed by repentance and conversion, with the infusion of habitual grace as the term of conversion. Rather, throughout his entire life Jesus was without sin; and the grace that justified him was given from the moment of his conception. Consequently, Jesus was preserved from sin and so from the need for healing in that sense.[48] Rather, by that justifying grace, Jesus was rendered fully effective as a moral agent, perfectly attuned to the will of God; this is why he can serve as the moral exemplar of the elect.

With regard to the elevating function of grace, Jesus is also different. In others, grace provides an orientation to the end which is God. It raises one up to God's level and inclines one to the acts that will bring one to God as end. For others, however, there is a difference between the grace that characterizes life in this world and glory; when one reaches God in the next life, grace gives way to glory, and is not that glory itself. In Jesus, however, grace has been given so fully that it not only raises the humanity of the Word to God's level but provides the union, in this life, that for others comes only in the next. Because of the fullness of grace, Jesus is not a simple wayfarer; during his life, as gifted with the beatific vision, he was in fact a *comprehensor*.[49]

Actually, Aquinas eventually nuances the point, to make clear in what respects Jesus was and was not a *comprehensor*. As he argues elsewhere, the completion of the journey by entry into the presence of God involves the entire person, both soul and body.[50] In coming face-to-face with God, the person is perfected in the person's intellectual and voluntary capacities. And the glory that comes to the soul is passed on, as it were, overflowing to body and granting it a transformation. In sharing in the vision, the body is itself glorified, as befits what had been the needed instrument of the soul in this world. For Aquinas, Christ during his life was perfected in his soul, receiving the fullness of grace and the perfections of knowledge, including the beatific vision. But, "economically," glory was not extended to the body while the incarnate Word was in the world.[51] Rather, to promote Christ's salvific work, the body of Jesus in this world remained subject to suffering and change. Thus, it is better to say of Jesus that he was both wayfarer (with regard to his body) and *comprehensor* while in the world. Only when he passed to the next life did his body come to share in beatitude; only then was he, in his psychosomatic unity, fully *comprehensor*.

In discussing Christ's merit for himself, Aquinas repeats the performance of the question on merit in the treatise on grace. Aquinas is as intent on outlining what falls outside the scope of merit as on detailing what Christ could merit for himself. Most notably, Aquinas denies two signal possible rewards to Christ's merits: union with the Godhead; and the first grace. It is not as if there is a human actor—Jesus—who acts in a way that impresses God, who might then draw him into a close association with God. Rather, in Aquinas' incarnational approach, the divine identity of Jesus is settled from the outset of the story of Jesus. The Son of God is the bearer of the humanity; the Son has become human and lives and acts and suffers as truly human. Hence, it would be impossible for Jesus to merit becoming the Son of God; he is from the outset the Son of God because of the Son's act of incarnation.[52] Likewise, Jesus does not merit grace for himself in the first place; and here Jesus conforms perfectly to the rule sketched elsewhere. There is no room for the *facienti quod in se est* in its obvious interpretation. One is not first good and then the recipient of God's grace. Rather, the sequence for all humans, including Jesus, is that those who stand in God's special favor receive the grace that provides for their holiness. Jesus too is among the elect, and so is the beneficiary of God's love by receiving the grace that in his case provides for perfect holiness, while also constituting him as the source of the grace of all others who stand in God's predestining favor.[53]

The teaching that Jesus was *comprehensor* as to his soul, but wayfarer as to his body, helps to shape the rest of the account of Jesus' merit. With regard to the end of glory, Jesus will differ from other humans: while the elect through their graced good acts merit the glory that perfects both soul and body, Jesus as *comprehensor* will not merit through his graced good actions the glory of soul. He has that, as gift, throughout his entire earthly existence. However, since he was a wayfarer with regard to his body, he did merit for himself, through his graced good acts, the perfection of his body. Only in the next life does the glory of the soul pass over to his body, on the basis of his many good acts done in grace.[54]

The same teaching about Jesus' enjoyment of the beatific vision throughout his life also informs Aquinas' account of the theological virtues. In Aquinas' general account of the theological virtues, there is a pronounced eschatological dimension. These virtues, which flow out of habitual grace and perfect (at least inchoately) the powers of the soul, not only orient the justified to God as end but also provide a foretaste of the enjoyment of God that will come for others in the next life. One walks by faith now; in the next life, one will have the direct vision of God. One hopes now for union with God; in the next life, the beatified partake of that union. And one loves now, aspiring to the fullness of charity's expression that will come in the immediate presence of God, the ultimate good.

In comparison with what is to come, the theological virtues are imperfect; in the beatific vision each will have passed away, replaced by direct and immediate and personal knowing, loving, and adherence.

Since Jesus throughout his earthly existence enjoyed the beatific vision and so was perfected (not simply inchoately) as to soul, Aquinas concludes that he did not have the first two of the theological virtues (faith and hope) and that he had the third in its perfect form.[55] One does not believe certain things to be true when one knows them directly, in their Source; one does not hope for what one already has. And one does not love with the love of the wayfarer when one is linked directly to the One who is the most appropriate object of love.

That Aquinas' Jesus was without faith has elicited considerable negative comment from more recent theologians.[56] Is this not to deny to Jesus what is— or, at least, should be—most characteristic of the human's relation to God? By faith one shows one's openness to God; one accepts, before God, who one is and yields oneself to God's gracious promptings, thus fulfilling God's will for humans. If Jesus lacks faith and lacks such openness, he therefore stands as too distinct from those who, Aquinas thinks, should follow his example. He would fail to disclose how all humans should stand in relation to God.

The criticism, however, seems misplaced. Simply in terms of faith, it seems legitimate to ascribe to Jesus—as Aquinas does—certain privileges in keeping with his saving work. The savior, the one sent by God to effect human salvation, need not be—indeed, should not be—identical in every circumstance with those who are to be saved. But, in terms of revealing the correct relationship of humans to God, Aquinas' Jesus would seem to offer a most appropriate model. This may be an instance where too much has been made of a single word, and insufficient attention has been given to the main thrust of Aquinas' analysis. "Faith" in fact seems to be used equivocally by Aquinas and by more recent theologians. For Aquinas, faith is a virtue perfective of the intellect; by it one believes certain things, not susceptible to demonstration, to be true. In more recent theologians, on the other hand, "faith" is used as the equivalent of "faithfulness," perhaps even of "obedience." Hence, one expresses one's faith by obedience to God's calling. While Aquinas' Jesus differs in some respects from others in his standing before God (precisely as the fullest beneficiary of God's grace, as befits the Savior), in the main points of Aquinas' teaching about grace, predestination, and human salvation, his Jesus in fact sets the tone. As in his general account of God-human relations, in depicting Jesus Aquinas stresses divine prevenience and sovereignty in the salvific process; the need for a grace that is truly effective to attain God; and the importance of submitting one's own will to God's and of acknowledging all that God has done, and is doing, in one's life. In rendering Jesus in a way consistent with the fundamental teachings on grace, Aquinas is thus able to reinforce his main lessons about people in their relation to and dependence on God. Indeed, the lessons are advanced in a superlative way, for in Jesus one learns definitively about human possibilities as these are established and promoted by God through grace in accordance with God's saving will.

Notes

1. For the matter treated in this chapter, the following may be consulted: H. Bouillard, *Conversion et grâce chez S. Thomas d'Aquin* (Paris: Aubier, 1944); Prudentius de Letter, *De ratione meriti secundum Sanctum Thomam* (Rome: Gregorian University, 1939); J.-M. Laporte, *Les structures dynamiques de la grâce: Grâce médicinale et grâce élevante selon Thomas d'Aquin* (Montreal: Bellarmin, 1973); Bernard Lonergan, *Grace and Freedom: Operative Grace in the Thought of St. Thomas Aquinas*, ed. J. Patout Burns (London: Longman and Todd, 1971); B. McGinn, "The Development of the Thought of Thomas Aquinas on the Reconciliation of Divine Providence and Contingent Action," *The Thomist* 39 (1975): 741–52; Otto H. Pesch, *Die Theologie der Rechtfertigung bei Martin Luther und Thomas von Aquin* (Mainz: Matthias-Grünewald-Verlag, 1967); Joseph Wawrykow, *God's Grace and Human Action: 'Merit' in the Theology of Thomas Aquinas* (Notre Dame, Ind.: University of Notre Dame Press, 1995). See as well, on a topic of adjacent interest, U. Horst, *Die Gaben des Heiligen Geistes nach Thomas von Aquinas* (Berlin: Akademie Verlag, 2001).

2. See the prefatory paragraph to *ST* I.2, in which Aquinas sketches the main parts of the *Summa*: "Because the chief aim of sacred doctrine is to teach the knowledge of God, not only as He is in Himself, but also as He is the beginning of things and their last end, and especially of rational creatures . . . therefore, in our endeavor to expound this science, we shall treat: Of God; Of the rational creature's advance towards God; Of Christ, Who as man, is our way to God." For a recent discussion of the questions on grace in connection with others in the *Prima Secundae*, see Theo Kobusch, "Grace (Ia IIae, qq.109–114)," trans. G. Kaplan and F. G. Lawrence, in *The Ethics of Aquinas*, ed. S. Pope (Washington, D.C.: Georgetown University Press, 2002). Kobusch concludes this fine essay by expressing some doubts about the advisability of Aquinas' use, in the doctrine of grace, of categories (such as "motion") taken over from Aristotle's *Physics*. Are such categories really suited to matters that touch at the core of human freedom and expression? In my opinion, however, such "physical" categories are thoroughly contextualized and thus transformed by Aquinas, placed in the service of an account that does justice to the special relations between God and the people called into fellowship with God.

3. See, for example, the Blackfriars bilingual edition of *ST* I-II.106–114, entitled "The Gospel of Grace," *St. Thomas Aquinas, Summa theologiae*, vol. 30, trans. C. Ernst (London: Eyre & Spottiswoode, 1972).

4. For general accounts of medieval teachings on grace, see J. Auer, *Die Entwicklung der Gnadenlehre in der Hochscholastik*, 2 vols. (Freiburg: Herder, 1942–51); W. Dettloff, *Die Entwicklung der Akzeptations- und Verdienstlehre von Duns Scotus bis Luther* (Münster: Aschendorff, 1963); B. Hamm, *Promissio, Pactum, Ordinatio* (Tübingen: Mohr, 1977); A. E. McGrath, *Iustitia Dei: A History of the Christian Doctrine of Justification*, vol. 1 (Cambridge: Cambridge University Press, 1986).

5. The comments in the text about organization are based on the preface to *ST* I-II.109.

6. In these questions, Aquinas is principally concerned with *gratia gratum faciens*, sanctifying grace. Such grace has to do with the justifying and making holy of a person, and is oriented to that person's salvation. Aquinas also discusses in the treatise another grace, *gratia gratis data*. See *ST* I-II.111.1 and 4–5. By a *gratia gratis data*, a human can contribute to the justification of another. Aquinas has in mind such benefits as are enumerated by the Apostle Paul in 1 Corinthians 12:8 ff.

7. *ST* I-II.110.3–4.

8. See *ST* I-II.109.1c. From that discussion, it would appear that not all *auxilia* should be termed "grace"; even the acts of those outside of grace require a reduction to act by something already in act. The example given in that corpus is of knowing. Knowing things of this world on the basis of evidence provided by the senses requires a form—the intellect—and a moving of that form to act, by *auxilium*. In the rest of *ST* I-II.109, however, as in the rest of the questions on grace, Aquinas' focus remains resolutely on the grace of *auxilium*. In terms of the discussion later in the chapter, the grace of *auxilium* falls under predestination; the other *auxilium* falls under providence.

9. For the discussion of the partially healed person, see *ST* I-II.109.8c.

10. One might invoke here a saying that Aquinas on occasion uses: as at *ST* I.1.8 ad 2, "grace does not destroy nature, but perfects it." As employed by Aquinas, the saying makes two fundamental points. First, God as end transcends the natural capacities of the human person; hence the need for grace to raise up and perfect the person. Second, while the end is transcendent, it is not utterly incompatible with the human's native capacities, that is, the capacities for thinking and willing. One might draw a contrast in this respect with, say, a stone. The stone lacks the capacity for any thinking or willing. If the stone were to be brought to the presence of God as end, for the stone to enter into God's own life would require not a mere elevating but a radical reconstruction of the stone. The stone would have to be totally and essentially remade to become an entity capable of thinking and willing. There is, on the other hand, a continuity between the human's natural capacities and the transcendent end rendered possible through grace.

11. See *ST* I-II.109.9–10; 114.9.

12. See *ST* I-II.8–17.

13. See the prefatory paragraph to *ST* I.22: "having considered all that relates to the will absolutely, we must now proceed to those things which have relation to both the intellect and the will, namely providence, in respect to all created things; predestination and reprobation and all that is connected with these acts in respect especially of man as regards his eternal salvation."

14. *ST* I.20.2c.

15. *ST* I.20.4.

16. *ST* I.22.1 ad 2.

17. Aquinas refers to the predestination to salvation of *some* humans in *ST* I.23.2c and 4c; see too *ST* I.23.7, where he says the number of the predestined is certain both formally and materially.

18. *ST* I.23.4c. In this article, Aquinas repeats the contrast between human and divine loving (only the latter is causal) raised in *ST* I.20.

19. *ST* I.23.2 ad 4; 4 ad 1; 5c.

20. *ST* I.23.3 ad 2.

21. *ST* I.23.3 ad 1: "God loves all men and all creatures, inasmuch as He wishes them all some good; but He does not wish every good to them all. So far, therefore, as He does not wish this particular good—namely, eternal life—He is said to hate or reprobate them."

22. *ST* I.22.4 ad 1; 23.6c.

23. *ST* I-II.109.9c; 10 sed contra.

24. *ST* I-II.114.1 ad 2; see too *ST* I.23.5 ad 3.

25. The point has been made already in the treatise on grace in *ST* I-II.109.5c.

26. For a reliable account of the development of Aquinas' teaching on *auxilium* and his talk, by the *ST,* of grace as both *auxilium* (in a specialized sense) and habitual, see Lonergan, *Grace and Freedom*. While in the *ST auxilium* came to denote a specific kind of grace, Aquinas could also use it in a more general sense, even in the *ST,* simply as God's aid. At times, the word in this undifferentiated sense can even cover what elsewhere is called "habitual grace." God's help to the *viator* comes not just through *auxilium,* in the specialized sense, but through habitual grace. In the *ST,* nonetheless, there are the two kinds of grace specified in the text; it is just that sometimes the word (*auxilium*) for one of these graces also is used in a more general way, here reflecting the usage of Aquinas' predecessors. In an earlier work, the *ScG,* the terminological use is rather intriguing. There, Aquinas seems to have little interest in distinguishing the two kinds of grace or of specifying, as in the *ST,* what each does. Rather, he tends to refer to grace as *auxilium,* as God's engagement in the life of the person helping that person to God as end. Actually, in comparison with the *ST* and the much earlier *Scriptum,* in the *ScG* Aquinas displays relatively little interest in the peculiar characteristics of habitual grace (that is, as form that perfects). The stress seems rather on God's dynamic involvement in the life and action of the *viator*—that is, the bias would seem to be toward *auxilium* in the more specialized sense. The account of grace in the *ST* thus is more balanced. While Aquinas certainly is concerned to do full justice to *auxilium* in its specialized sense, he is also intent on describing the real contribution of habitual grace to the successful journey to God as end. By God's favor, the justified do receive a form that heals and elevates, and renders good action possible.

27. The discussion of merit in the *Scriptum* comes at II *Sent.* d.27 q.1 arts.3–6. For a detailed accounting of the early teaching on merit, see Wawrykow, *God's Grace,* ch. 2.

28. See Wawrykow, *God's Grace,* 84 ff.; the pertinent texts are listed in nn.47 ff.

29. Lonergan, *Grace and Freedom*.

30. Bouillard, *Conversion et grâce*.

31. For an excellent introduction to the main developments in Augustine's teaching about grace, see J. Patout Burns, *The Development of Augustine's Doctrine of Operative Grace* (Paris: Études Augustiniennes, 1980).

32. Other essays in this volume have as their focus the ways in which, through Christ, God brings about human salvation. See, e.g., O'Meara on Aquinas' ecclesiology and Van Nieuwenhove on soteriology. There is, of course, an intimate connection between Christ as mediator and the extent of his personal grace (the topic of this section of the present chapter): it befits Christ as savior to have the fullness of grace. The connection between the two is underscored in the *Tertia Pars* by the inclusion of two questions on Christ's grace: q.7 looks at his personal grace and q.8 at his grace as head of the Church. Q.7 in this sense prepares for q.8, as well as for later questions in the *Tertia Pars* that are concerned with the mediation of grace through Christ.

33. Karl Rahner, *Foundations of Christian Faith,* trans. W. V. Dych (New York: Crossroad, 1997), ch. 6.

34. For a fine statement of the point, see the opening of the essay by Walsh later in this volume.

35. For what follows in the text, see especially *ST* III.1.2c.

36. See *ST* III.2.2–3.

37. See *ST* III.2.1, in which Aquinas counters a monophysite Christology.

38. For the description of his humanity as the instrument of Christ's divinity, see, e.g., *ST* III.7.1 ad 3 and 8.1 ad 1.

39. See T. Tschipke, *Die Menschheit Christi als Heilsorgan der Gottheit,* Freiburger Theologische Studien 55 (Freiburg im Breisgau: Herder, 1940).

40. *ST* III.18.1c.

41. *ST* III.9.1.

42. See, e.g., *ST* III.7.1c; 9c.

43. *ST* III.15.1–2.

44. *ST* III.14.1c and ad 4; 3c; 4c and ad 2.

45. Aquinas discusses Christ's knowledge in *ST* III.9–12. See, e.g., *ST* III.9.2c, for Christ as *comprehensor* during his earthly life.

46. For the claim that Christ had habitual grace, see *ST* III.7.1c; that text also refers to the elevating brought about by that grace. That Christ had the fullness of grace, suitable for all the options and effects of grace, is maintained in III.7.9c.

47. See *ST* III.19.1.

48. *ST* III.7.9 ad 2: "It pertains essentially to operating grace to justify; but that it makes the ungodly to be just is accidental to it on the part of the subject, in which sin is found. Therefore the soul of Christ was justified by operating grace, inasmuch as it was rendered just and holy by it from the beginning of His conception; not that it was until then sinful, or even not just."

49. See, e.g., *ST* III.9.2; 34.1; and, in III.7.3 and 4, why therefore Christ did not have the virtues of faith and hope, which in other righteous people follow on the presence of habitual grace.

50. *ST* I-II.4.6.

51. *ST* III.14.4 ad 2: "The fullness of all grace and knowledge was due to Christ's soul of itself, from the fact of its being assumed by the Word of God; and hence Christ assumed all the fullness of knowledge and wisdom absolutely. But He assumed our defects economically [*dispensative*], in order to satisfy for our sin, and not that they belonged to Him of Himself. Hence it was not necessary for Him to assume them all, but only such as sufficed to satisfy for the sin of the whole nature."

52. See, e.g., *ST* III.2.11; 7.13; 24.2c.

53. See, e.g., *ST* III.19.3c.

54. Ibid.

55. See *ST* III.7.2–4; 9 ad 1.

56. Jon Sobrino, *Jesus the Liberator: A Historical-Theological View,* trans. P. Burns and F. McDonagh (New York: Orbis Books, 1993), 154 ff. Sobrino (155) notes that Aquinas' definition of "faith" differs from that that he pursues, characterizing it as "scholastic and non-biblical." He does not, however, recognize that what is covered biblically by "faith" is present in Aquinas, and in particular in Aquinas' presentation of Christ in his earthly existence.

Ten

Hypostatic Union

JOSEPH WAWRYKOW

Aquinas offers sustained meditations on Jesus Christ in many of his writings.[1] In terms of content, there is a remarkable consistency to Aquinas' teaching about Christ over the course of his theological career. He returns repeatedly to the same fundamental claims about Jesus: Jesus' centrality in the salvific process; the divine identity of Jesus from the outset of his story; and Jesus' genuine and full humanity, not simply divinity, on account of hypostatic union. Equally remarkable, however, is the diversity in presentation in Aquinas' various writings about Jesus. While he remains true to his central insights about Jesus, Aquinas taught Christ differently in his different writings. He can include diverse topics to promote the analysis of Jesus; alter the order of presentation; and pursue different tasks in proclaiming Christ in these various works. One will learn much about Aquinas' skill as a writer and teacher, as well as his intentions as a theologian, by paying close attention to the shape of the Christology in the major writings.

In this essay, I will focus on Aquinas' discussions of a key aspect of any incarnational Christology, hypostatic union, as found in three of his more important writings: the early *Scriptum* on the *Sentences* of Peter Lombard; the *Summa contra Gentiles* (also known as the *Liber de veritate catholicae fidei contra errores infidelium*); and, the *Summa Theologiae*. In each of these works, spanning his whole theological career, Aquinas insists that the two natures, the divine and the human, have been united precisely in the second Person of God. From eternity, the second Person is fully God, one and the same God as the Father and the Holy Spirit; the second Person is also a distinct Person in the Godhead, different from the other two Persons. Without loss to itself as Word, the second divine Person has taken up a second nature, and come to express human nature as well. The divine Word, because of incarnation, is also fully and truly human. Thus, in retelling the story of Jesus, one must attend to the divine and to the human dimensions. And yet the Christology of each of these writings has its proper feel. Aquinas proceeds differently in the *contra Gentiles* than he does in either the earlier *Scriptum* or the later *Summa:* while there is some overlap in theological tasks and ambition, in these writings he tries to do different things in subjecting Christ to close analysis. In developing his theology, Aquinas typically draws on a range of resources.[2] In these writings on Christ, he can deploy these resources in varying ways, in accordance with his ambitions in a given work. In this essay, I will highlight these formal features of Aquinas' Christological writings, as a way of displaying crucial aspects of his work as a theologian.

Especially important for this essay are what I will call "alternative Christologies." In teaching Christ, Aquinas does more than simply present his main claims. He relates his own position, worked out in conscious conformity to the tradition, that is, to other teachings about Christ, in order to show the advantages of what he takes to be orthodox proclamation about Jesus. These alternative Christologies can take two main forms: the Christologies advanced by historical figures, both orthodox and heterodox; and more speculative Christologies, which posit scenarios that differ from the revealed order. Aquinas plays off of these alternative Christologies in stating in his own writings his version of orthodox truth about Christ and in exploring its ramifications. The value of attending to the rhetoric of his Christology, including such use of authoritative texts, is significant.[3] It allows me to suggest the extent of Aquinas' debt to earlier traditions about Christ while making patent how at times he goes beyond them in his own constructive reflections about Jesus.

I begin with the *Summa contra Gentiles,* then turn to the *Summa Theologiae,* and finally to the *Scriptum* on the *Sentences.* As is apparent, I am proceeding out of chronological order, beginning with the middle work and ending up with what chronologically is the earliest of Aquinas' theological writings.[4] There is a twofold warrant for this order. First, the teaching of the *contra Gentiles* in my opinion is the most accessible of Aquinas' writings on Christ for a modern audience, which may be less versed in the intricacies of hypostatic union. Second, by leaving the *Scriptum* for last, it will be easier to make clear how Aquinas' grasp of the previous Christological traditions was enhanced over the course of his theological career to include, by mid-career, the Greek patristic heritage.

Summa contra Gentiles Bk. IV chs. 27–49

Aquinas devotes a number of chapters in the fourth book of the *contra Gentiles* to Christ. Earlier chapters (chs. 2–14) are given over to the trinitarian background of incarnational Christology, exploring the scriptural roots of the proclamation of the triune God as well as the relations between Father and Word. Chapters much later in the book (chs. 50–55) look in some detail at the saving effects of Christ's work, playing up, although not exclusively, how Christ in his death has overcome sin. The great bulk of the discussion (chs. 27–49), however, is given over to incarnation itself, considered as both act and as result of the act (recall my chapter on grace): the Word becomes human; Jesus, the result of this act of incarnation, is both fully human and fully divine.

Chapters 27–49 fall into two main parts. In chapters 27–39, Aquinas offers an orientation to the basics of hypostatic union. I do not think it an exaggeration to say that Aquinas is here much concerned to assert his continuity with the patristic tradition on Christ and that in fact he is following patristic precedent in the presentation of his own ideas about Christ. There is a threefold principle of organization in chapters 27–39. The first is the history of Christological heresy as the counterpart to the articulation of orthodox teaching about hypostatic union. Early Christian heresies by far predominate, although in a few of the later chapters Aquinas glances at some twelfth-century teachings (these, however, are assimilated to early Christian heresies). Thus, Aquinas looks in turn at the teaching of Photinus (who offers a more polished version of the Ebionite teaching) (ch. 28); then at the Manichaeans (ch. 29), Valentinus (ch. 30), Apollinaris (chs. 31–33), Arius (ch. 32), Theodore of Mopsuestia and Nestorius (ch. 34), Eutyches (ch. 35), Macarius of Antioch (ch. 36), and a few twelfth-century positions (chs. 37–38) as reported in what became the textbook of Scholastic theology, the *Sentences* of Peter Lombard.[5]

The second principle of organization is scriptural. Each of these positions is explained in terms of the reading of scripture. Each points to this or that scripture as the basis of its teaching; Aquinas' ambition in each case is to show how that reading of scripture is faulty, both in terms of the texts favored by his heretics and in terms of the scriptural witness as a whole. In the process, while showing how each heresy offers a partial and skewed reading, he demonstrates how the orthodox tradition on Christ best summarizes and restates what is essential to the scriptural message.[6]

While the ordering of heresies is roughly chronological (from earliest to latest), there is also a topical ordering, as a third principle of organization. Photinus, following Ebion, denies an incarnation, instead positing the "ascent" of a very good man into privileged status before God. The next group of heresies deny one or another of the constituents of human nature. The Manichaeans and Valentinus, dualists who deny the value of the material, deny that Jesus had a body: such would be inappropriate of the emissary of the good God. Apollinaris and Arius err with regard to soul, either denying a soul completely to Christ or part of the soul (after all, why would Christ need a human, rational soul, when the Word is Mind itself and so can supply for the rational soul in the case of Christ?). With Nestorius and Eutyches, the problem arises in their attempt to explain how the divine and the human in fact come together in Christ. As he considers in turn these heresies, Aquinas is at the same time able to show the fidelity of the dogmatic formula to scripture. Jesus has a complete human nature, both body and soul, as well as complete divine nature. The two natures are in fact united, but without confusion, in the person of the Word, who is the person of Jesus. The Word is fully divine and a distinct Person from eternity; without loss to itself, the Word has taken to itself a second nature, human nature, and come to express that as well. By the end of these chapters, Aquinas has made a compelling case for "hypostatic union" as the fullest and most accurate reading of the scriptural proclamation about Christ. And, by showing the link between dogmatic formulation and scripture, he has also offered a recommendation of the formulation for further reading of scripture. The formula provides a hermeneutical guide, which will prevent one from misreading any given scripture in the manner of the various heresies while also making more likely a fruitful encounter with the biblical text.

Certain scriptural passages enjoy a great prominence in this treatment of hypostatic union: John 1:1–18 and the Christ-hymn in Philippians 2 (vv. 6–11). Aquinas reads and deploys these passages with the full benefit of patristic debates over their correct interpretation. "The Word was made flesh" (John 1:14) testifies nicely to incarnation as act: the subject of this act is the Word, to whom something happens. The Word enters into history and becomes human. But, the choice of wording here is tricky. "The Word was made *flesh*." Does "flesh" here mean that the Word became or took on only a body?[7] If so, then those readers of John who deny to Jesus a human soul (e.g., Arius and Apollinaris) would seem to have important support for their analysis of Jesus in his ontological reality. But, to the contrary, "flesh" here should be taken as referring to the entire humanity of Jesus, to both body and soul. By referring to "flesh," to being human in its corporeality, this passage is a nice, scriptural refutation of dualist tendencies, which would insist that the physical is inappropriate to the Savior.[8] But this is not to say that the Word in entering history took up only the body. Here, the lower is used as representative of the entire human reality; the Word became truly and fully human, taking up and expressing both body and soul.[9]

The verb in this phrase also elicits considerable comment. For one thing, it bespeaks a certain intimacy. The Word does not "come to" flesh. If that were the claim, then the case of Jesus would be similar to that of the prophets, to whom God came and revealed. In their case, they exist as humans and God interacts with them. But, by stating that the Word "was made" flesh, the scriptural author is precluding such an interaction. By being made, the Word is—flesh. There is only flesh by virtue of the act of incarnation; and the bearer of the flesh is the Word.[10]

Even here there is the possibility of misunderstanding. A process is undoubtedly described in the statement that "the Word *was made* flesh." But is the process akin to what happens to the seed that gives way to the plant? If so, then the Word will cease to be the Word in becoming human. The Word will have been transformed, will have become something other than what it was.[11] With the orthodox tradition, however, Aquinas denies a "becoming" in this sense in the act of incarnation. Rather, what is true at the beginning of the statement continues to be true at the end of the statement; at the end of the statement, however, something else comes to be true (the Word is also, because of the act of incarnation, human). What is true of the Word from eternity is presented in the opening verse of John's Gospel. "In the beginning was the Word, and the Word was with God and the Word was God." In agreement with his orthodox predecessors, Aquinas will insist that in that verse, "God" supposits in two different ways. In the first use of the word, we meet an affirmation of difference in the Godhead. The Word is "with God" means that the Word is with "the Father," a distinct person in God with whom the Word is in relation. In the second use of the word "God" in this verse, we meet an essential claim. The Word is God, that is, everything true of being God is verified in the case of the second Person, just as it is for the Father (and the Holy Spirit) as well.

Thus, to offer a fuller reading of verse 14 in light of verse 1: the Word, who from eternity is a distinct Person in the Godhead and one and the same God as the Father and the Holy Spirit, without loss to itself as fully divine Word, takes up and comes to express what belongs to being human, that is, the human body and soul. In the one Person of the Word, two natures are joined and expressed. From eternity, the Word has fully expressed the divine nature. In incarnation, the Word continues to express that nature, but now also instantiates and expresses human nature. Because of incarnation, the Word is both fully divine and fully human.[12]

With the second main grouping of chapters in this discussion of hypostatic union, the analysis takes on a different cast. Chapters 40–49 are less insistently scriptural; they assume that the earlier chapters have succeeded in showing "one person, two natures" as the only adequate summary of the scriptural witness to Jesus. Nor are they as obviously patristic; other principles of organization inform this grouping of chapters. These chapters begin (ch. 40) with a series of objections designed to cast doubt on the plausibility or possibility of the scriptural, orthodox teaching. These objections take different forms. There is a worry, for example, that the teaching about incarnation will inevitably involve God in a change that is unacceptable on Aquinas' own grounds (e.g., ScG IV.40.2–3); or, will make Jesus utterly, and unacceptably, unusual, by saying of his person that it subsists in two natures (when in fact a person has but one substance or nature) (IV.40.5). The objections find their direct answer in the final of these chapters (ch. 49). But, from chapter 41 on, Aquinas has been preparing for their rebuttal, implying through a closer examination of various facets of the assertion of incarnation where the objections of chapter 40 have gone wrong. These intervening chapters are each devoted to a discrete topic: depicting an analogy from our more direct experience that can shed light on the union of the divine and human in Christ (ch. 41); pointing out the special suitability of the Word for becoming incarnate (ch. 42); and so forth. Together, however, they shed considerable additional light on the incarnation and so make Aquinas' task in chapter 49 all the easier.

For Aquinas, the incarnation is an article of faith. Throughout the Thomistic corpus, Aquinas is consistent in defining the articles of faith in contrast with what can be termed the "preambles of faith," and in specifying what reasoning can and cannot do in relation to each. Both the preambles and the articles are revealed by God and have to do with human salvation: God reveals God as the end of human beings; God reveals the way to that end for the rational creatures called to it. While revealed, the "preambles"—such truths as the existence and oneness of God—can also be known by reason; such have in fact been demonstrated by philosophers working without the benefit of Christian revelation. The articles of faith, on the other hand, are also revealed by God. But, they are above reason and so cannot be demonstrated by reason. They are not, however, contrary to reason; and so when arguments against them are constructed, those can be rebutted by reason working in service to the faith. And, although they are above reason, they are revealed by a God who acts for good purpose and in accordance with God's wisdom. Thus, they can be rationally explored. Their truth, to repeat, cannot be grasped or demonstrated by reasoning. But, in thinking about them in light of what is known of God's character and purpose in acting outside of God, their wisdom and plausibility can be shown by a reason working in the service of faith.[13]

The present chapters nicely conform to this understanding of the articles and what reason can and cannot do with them. Aquinas shows a keen awareness in these chapters of the incarnation as, precisely, mystery. That Jesus is both God and human is a matter of faith, as is the insistence that in the second person of God the two natures, the divine and the human, have been united. No human argument can demonstrate the full divinity as well as full humanity of Jesus; one must accept God's word, in faith. And yet, there are those who would doubt incarnation on rational grounds, as impossible or incoherent (ch. 40). As a theologian, Aquinas is under obligation to answer such arguments, in the process making clearer what is and what is not involved in the affirmation of Christ (ch. 49). The theologian can also pursue a better understanding of what God has revealed. Hence, as in chapter 41, Aquinas will suggest a suitable analogy, adverting to what is more accessible to us, to clarify incarnation. But the suggestion will be offered in due modesty, in full awareness that the incarnation is *sui generis* and that therefore even the aptest analogy will fail, finally, to grasp the mystery. The discussion will begin with faith. There will be growth in understanding of what God has revealed. But at the end of the discussion one will still be left in faith.[14]

While the "patristic" is less insistent and obvious in these chapters than in the preceding, Aquinas continues in these chapters to be in dialogue with the orthodox position, while countering those who put themselves in opposition to it. At least some of the objections in chapter 40 can be linked to heresies treated in the earlier grouping of chapters, attempting to show the reasonableness of another approach to Christ. In particular, some of these objections would seem to proceed from a perspective that can be fairly termed "Nestorian." Nestorius might fail as a reader of scripture, but his Christology does have much to recommend it, at least at first glance. For one thing, by insisting on a second person in Christ—a human person that expresses human nature, just as there is the divine Person who expresses the divine nature—Jesus is displayed to be in complete conformity with other humans. To be human means not simply having a human nature; it is to "have" a human person. But, in the position articulated by Aquinas, Jesus does not "have" a human person, at least not in the usual sense. Rather, the second Person of God has come to express this second nature. Is this not to make of Jesus a deficient human, lacking what is of greatest dignity for the human? Would it not be preferable to posit a second person and hypostasis, that is, a fully human person, to whom the divine person has come and with whom the divine person has formed a partnership for human salvation?[15] Indeed, if we allow God's perfection from eternity—and Christians insist on this—then it would seem that the union would have to be as Nestorius envisions it, that is, involving a forming of a team of two persons to work out human salvation. The one person (the divine), perfect and complete from eternity, would come to the other, itself independent in its existence; together they would as Christ save the world.[16]

Such objections are not peculiar to the *Summa contra Gentiles;* they will reappear in the *ST.*[17] Aquinas is aware of their emotive and intellectual appeal. He nonetheless remains firm in his adherence to the orthodox position. There is, it is true, no "human person" in the usual sense in the case of Christ as rendered by the orthodox. But there is a human person all the same. The second Person of God, without loss to itself as second divine Person, has taken up human nature and instantiated it; and as the bearer of the humanity, the divine Person is thus fully human. In this light, Aquinas can reject the worry about the supposed defectiveness of the Word made flesh. To say that the person of Jesus is the Word is not to detract from Jesus but in fact is to proclaim his proper and distinctive greatness. It is the fully divine Word that subsists in the human nature of Jesus; the human nature has been united to what is worthier, and thus Jesus' humanity is of greater worthiness.[18] And, by insisting on the divine person as the subject of the humanity, Aquinas can much more convincingly proclaim God's great love for humans. On the cross, it is not the merely human who dies, with the approval and sympathy of the divine partner in the partnership (as would seem to be the case in a Nestorian scenario, with a merely accidental union); it is God Godself, the second Person of God made human, who having entered the world to bring about human salvation, suffers and dies in the flesh for sinners. The human God dies on the cross, for us.

Chapter 41, in which Aquinas raises an analogy from human experience, also reveals Aquinas' continuity with and debt to patristic treatments. Indeed, the debt is profound and thorough. The chapter may be divided into three parts. In the first (IV.41.1–7), after an introductory defining of the key terms in putting forth the concept of hypostatic union ("nature," "person"), Aquinas offers a thumbnail history of attempts by theologians to bring the divine and the human together in Christ. Here, we meet anew the figures to whom chapters 28–38 are devoted. In the next part of the chapter (IV.41.8–9), Aquinas identifies the most appropriate analogy for describing hypostatic union: the union of body and soul. Finally, he concludes the chapter (IV.41.10–13) by specifying the ways in which that union both is and is not a suitable analogy for the union of the divine and the human in Christ. There are two ways of taking the union of body and soul: in terms of form (soul) informing matter, with the result that a human comes to be; and in terms of soul using body as its instrument. The latter, not the former, illuminates the union of divine and human in Christ. God is not a form and so does not, in incarnation, become the form of the human. Rather, the Son of God, in taking up all that pertains to human nature, takes up the human as its own and employs the human as the instrument of the divinity. There are, of course, different sorts of instruments. The axe is the instrument of the lumberman, for example. This is not how the human in Christ serves as the instrument of the divinity. The axe is a separated instrument and, moreover, is inanimate. But the humanity is conjoined to the divinity: the Word has taken up and come to express, and so persists in and is the subject of, the humanity of Jesus. The human nature of Christ, as instantiated by the Word made flesh, is intimately related to the divine nature while remaining in its integrity.

In the second part of the chapter, the special debt of Aquinas to the patristic tradition becomes apparent. The choice of body-soul to illumine the union of the natures in the person of the Word is not due solely to Aquinas' good theological sense (although that surely is involved as well). Rather, Aquinas here explicitly notes (IV.41.9) that the parallel with body-soul has already been observed, in the Athanasian Creed. Thus, in using this model to clarify hypostatic union, Aquinas is here too working in concert with the preceding tradition.

There are numerous similarities between chapters 27–49 and the earlier chapters in Book IV (chs. 2–14) on the person of the Word depicted in relation to the Father. Those chapters are divided into two main parts. In chapters 2–9, Aquinas again (as in chs. 27–39) follows a threefold principle of organization: patristic, scriptural, and topical. In chapters 2–9, the heretics that come to the fore are Photinus (chs. 4, 9), Sabellius (chs. 5, 9), and Arius (chs. 6–8), each of whom has erred when it comes to the distinction between Father and second person. Again, the fault of these heretics is to be ascribed to a misreading of scripture; and the principal achievement of the chapters is to show that the orthodox formulation of teaching on the Trinity alone safeguards the full scriptural teaching about God.[19] As with chapters 40–49, chapters 10–14 display a shift in tone in the analysis. Granted that the orthodox teaching about distinctions in the Godhead that are, however, not constitutive of different beings (one of whom would be God, another, lesser than God) is the accurate summary of scripture on God, are there not nonetheless serious difficulties with so describing God (ch. 10)? The final chapter (14) will address these objections, but only after the intervening chapters (11–13) have prepared the way, including the discussion of an apt analogy for figuring relations in the Godhead (11). In chapter 11, which thus parallels chapter 41, Aquinas points to intellection—to be precise, one's thinking oneself—as the best way for gaining a greater purchase on the plausibility and meaning of trinitarian relations. As in chapter 41, there is no claim here to fully grasp or explode the mystery. The exercise is carried out in due modesty and in recognition that even the best example will fall short of the reality of God. And in fact, when it comes to God thinking God, Aquinas is insistent on the ways in which that thinking will by necessity have to differ from a human thinking himself, precisely because of divine transcendence.[20] But perhaps the most striking parallel between this chapter and chapter 41 is that Aquinas is clear on the provenance of this particular image for illuminating the mystery of God. Again he claims no innovation or great originality. He has learned of the image as the most appropriate for putting God in scripture itself—in John 1:1, in which "Word" is used to name the second person—as this is mediated to him through Augustine, a great figure of the past who had already recognized, and so recommended, the image for talking appositely about God.[21] From this entire discussion of Christ in the *ScG* (Bk. IV, chs. 2–14 and 27–49), it seems safe to describe Aquinas' endeavor as a tradition-based inquiry, rendered possible by the work and insights of those who have come before, of all who have been concerned with the faithful transmission of God's saving word.[22]

Aquinas opens the *contra Gentiles* with a quote from Proverbs (8:7): "My mouth shall meditate truth, and my lips shall hate impiety." This nicely indicates his basic agenda for the entire work, including the chapters on Christ. On the one hand, he wants to teach the truth. He does not make up the truth, but receives it: from scripture; from the mediating tradition. And in interpreting the truth, he will bring whatever resources are to hand, including philosophical concepts that will help to maintain the truth. But the truth is not without its detractors; and thus, on the other hand, there is need to meet objections to the faith (the second part of the saying from Proverbs). Both the proclamation and the defense are evident in chapters 27–39. But both are evident as well in the chapters (40–49) that conclude this section of the fourth book. In these chapters, Aquinas has moved from arguing over the interpretation of scripture to plumbing more methodically the plausibility and wisdom of what God has done in Christ. Aquinas in fact is engaging in his own version of the Anselmian "faith seeking understanding." To those who say that hypostatic union still does not make sense, despite its success in rendering scripture (ch. 40), Aquinas not only provides arguments that show the flaws in the reasoning of the opponents (ch. 49) but also offers observations that show how the union of the divine and human in Christ might become more intelligible (by likening it to the union of body and soul, a figure which is more accessible to us; ch. 41), as well as show that the incarnation of, precisely, the Word makes eminent sense (ch. 42). The context of this inquiry is faith; and at the end of the inquiry one still has faith. The difference is that under Aquinas' tutelage, one will understand better what one believes.[23]

The Christology of the *Summa Theologiae:* Overview

In several ways the presentation of Christ in the *Summa Theologiae* differs from that in the *contra Gentiles*. For one thing, the discussion in the *Summa* is much more extensive, indeed exhaustive. Whereas the *contra Gentiles* hits only the main teachings—the high notes as it were—the *Summa* looks at those but many other topics as well. Second, Aquinas in the *Summa* follows a different pattern of organization, while pursuing many of the same theological tasks as the *contra Gentiles*. The fifty-nine questions on Christ in the *Tertia Pars* of the *Summa* fall into two main parts. Qq.1–26 look at "the mystery of the Incarnation itself." Qq.27–59 look at "those things which were done and suffered by the Savior, God incarnate."[24] Each of these main parts is further divided into groups of questions. There are three groupings of questions in the first main part. Q.1 stands by itself, looking at the fitness of the incarnation; here, Aquinas puts soteriological considerations at the forefront. This is his way of indicating the importance of negotiating properly what is to come: human salvation, the end of the incarnation, is dependent on Christ correctly understood. The next grouping of questions in the first main part runs from q.2 to q.15 and has to do with "the mode of union of the Word Incarnate." Aquinas begins (q.2) with the mode of union itself, here limning the basic contours of the teaching about hypostatic union by which the two natures are united in Christ. He then devotes the third question to the Person who assumes human nature and unites it to the divine; included in the eight articles of this question is a recommendation of the special suitability of the Word as the Person involved in incarnation (a.8), here paralleling the observations in *contra Gentiles* IV.42.

Qq.4 through 15 have to do with the nature assumed. Qq.4 through 6 look at the human nature itself, recalling the constituent parts of the nature and how the whole nature is assumed and so expressed by the Word. Qq.7 through 15 look at what Aquinas calls things that were "co-assumed." In these questions, Aquinas offers a methodical examination of such things that are associated with life in the world without being by definition part of human nature. This treatment is divided into two sets: those things that have to do with perfections (including grace, knowledge, and power; qq.7–13); and those things that have to do with defect, whether of body (q.14) or of soul (q.15). The analysis is intricate, but the basic rule of thumb is that if a perfection or defect is conducive to the success of Christ's saving work, then that perfection or defect was co-assumed by the Word in becoming human. If a defect would be counterproductive, then that defect would be denied to Christ. Christ needed to have the full use of his rational capacities to do his work and fulfill the will of the Father; he could not, therefore, have been mentally defective, one possible defect that can be attached to being human. In the previous essay in this volume, we have seen how this plays out in terms of Christ's own grace.

The remaining questions (qq.16–26) of the first main part of the *Summa*'s treatise on Christ have to do with "those things that follow on this union," and are divided according to whether such things belong to Christ in himself (qq.16–19); belong to Christ in relation to God the Father (qq.20–24; q.21, for example, is on his prayer); or belong to Christ in relation to us (qq.25–26), including as the mediator of God and humans (q.26).[25]

The second main part of the treatise on Christ (qq.27–59) is itself divided into four sections:[26] it covers in turn "those things that pertain to him coming into the world" (qq.27–39); "those things that relate to the course of his life in the world" (qq.40–45), including questions on his manner of life, temptations, and doctrine; "on his departure from this world" (qq.46–52), including an account of the passion and a more detailed analysis of Christ's saving work;[27] and "those things that pertain to his exaltation after this life (qq.53–59), with a number of these questions given over to his resurrection, also of importance for an account of Christ's salvific importance. The first main part of the treatise on Christ has to do with technical issues in Christology; it spells out, as it were, the grammar of Christ as approached incarnationally. The second main part of the treatise returns in detail to the gospel accounts of Christ, retelling the story of Jesus as informed by an awareness of his full identity as treated in the first main part. In comparison with the *contra Gentiles*, the second main part is innovative:[28] in the *contra Gentiles*, after showing how the account of hypostatic union is rooted in scripture, Aquinas does not go on to retelling the story of Jesus. In the *Summa*, on the other hand, he does return to the synoptics — the Gospel of Matthew is especially favored in the second main part — suggesting in practice how a better grasp of hypostatic union (as provided in the first main part) facilitates a richer reading of the gospel accounts.[29]

The *Summa* on Hypostatic Union

The differences between the two works extends to the presentation of hypostatic union (in qq.2 ff.), to the way in which Aquinas clarifies what is involved in this way of viewing Christ. The *Summa*, for one thing, reverses the order of procedure. In the *contra Gentiles* IV.27–39, after asserting the basic truth of incarnation (against Photinus and the Ebionites), Aquinas looks at the constituents of human nature (body, soul) and then ways in which theologians have tried to bring the divine and human together in Christ, showing in the process the preferability of the orthodox account. In the *Summa,* on the other hand, Aquinas begins with a basic account of hypostatic union (q.2), then turns to the Person in whom the union occurs (q.3), and then examines the human nature that is assumed in the act of incarnation (qq.4–6), in general (q.4) and then in terms of its constituent parts (q.5) and the order in which these parts are assumed (q.6). In these questions, Aquinas, moreover, is much less concerned to show how hypostatic union is the fairest, most comprehensive account of the scriptural witness to Christ. The intent to root dogmatic formulation in scripture is not entirely missing from these questions. But one has to wait until q.5, on the constituents of the human nature assumed by the Word, to find anything approximating *ScG* IV.27–39. For the most part, however, Aquinas simply assumes the connection between scripture and dogma as shown in the earlier writing.

Correspondingly, patristic discussions of Christ do not, as in the *contra Gentiles,* provide the structure of the account of hypostatic union in the *Summa.* Aquinas here follows a more purely topical, rather than historical, order in presenting the basic aspects of the union of the two natures in the Person of the Word.

The patristic voice in these questions nonetheless remains pronounced, and Aquinas adroitly employs historical Christologies in advancing his own. Indeed, the patristic contribution, and Aquinas' intention of presenting Christ as had the great figures of the orthodox past, can be quite striking. In the opening articles (aa.1–6) of the second question, Aquinas lays out the basics of Christ hypostatically construed. He opens by considering whether the union occurs in the nature (a.1), and then asks whether the union occurs in a person (a.2) and in a hypostasis or suppoit (a.3); he continues by asking whether by virtue of the union one can speak of a "composite person" (a.4) and of a union of body to soul in the taking up of human nature by the Word (a.5); and he concludes by asking whether the union of divine and human in Christ can be said to be "accidental" (a.6). The gains of the question are considerable. Aquinas is able to introduce and define at the beginning of the discussion the crucial terms (especially "nature," "person") needed to portray hypostatic union accurately. He is also able to show the preferability of the orthodox teaching of hypostatic union, while depicting the disadvantages of other teachings. Is there a "natural" union? Not in the monophysite sense: the union is not in the nature, whether involving the absorption of one nature by the other or a fusion of the two. Yet talk of "natural" union is permissible, in the sense that two natures, the divine and the human, have been united, without confusion, in the Person of the Word (a.1). Is there a "personal" union? Not in the sense that Nestorius would have it, as if one person were linked to a second union to form a team or partnership. Incarnation involves the taking up by the Word of a second nature, and coming to express that nature as well. But, in this vein, talk of "personal" union is thus acceptable, for, again, the natures are united precisely in the Person of the Word (a.2).

At first glance, however, at least one of the opening articles may seem redundant. Once one has spoken of "personal" union in the orthodox sense (a.2), need one ask (a.3) whether the union occurs in the "hypostasis" or the "suppositum"? After all, for Aquinas, "person," "hypostasis," and "suppositum" are in fact synonymous, and so to affirm the one is to affirm the others. Warrant, however, for including the third article—and indeed, also aa.4 and 5—is provided by the corpus of the sixth article, in which Aquinas explains why the union of the divine and human in Christ cannot be "accidental," since it is "personal" in the Person of the Word, who instantiates both natures. In aa.3-5, Aquinas is addressing in turn three Christological positions that had been described by Peter Lombard in *Sentences* Bk. III, distinction 6. There, in considering how the divine and human come together in Christ, the Lombard reports what he calls three Christological "opinions" that had found favor among his (twelfth-century) contemporaries.[30] In the literature, the three opinions have come to be designated the *homo assumptus* or two-supposit theory; the subsistent person or composite person theory; and the *habitus* theory. In the first, a *homo* is assumed into union with the second divine Person, presumably at the moment of conception. By talk of a "*homo,*" the idea seems to be that the human nature is concretized by a human subject or supposit, which then is united in assumption to a divine supposit, the second divine Person. Thus there are two natures and two supposits. However, there will be only one person. Normally, a supposit of a rational nature finds its perfection in coming to person, achieving its own personhood. But in the case of Christ this has not occurred for the human supposit. Rather, in his case the *homo* that is assumed receives its person from the divine Person, who is both supposit and Person. Hence, in this opinion, the full Christological formula would read: one person, two supposits, and two natures. The third opinion, the *habitus* theory, is very much concerned to deny a human person in the case of Christ. In its view, when body and soul come together, a human person is formed. Hence, in the taking up of human nature by the Word, the Word takes up each—body and soul—but does so separately; the two are kept apart, other than their respective union to the Word, and so there is not a distinctive person (a human) alongside the Person of the Word. The Word, in this view, puts on human nature the way one would put on clothing; hence, the union of the human and the divine in the case of Christ would be merely accidental, not "personal." As for the middle opinion, the subsistence theory, it affirms that the Word, who from eternity is a distinct person in the Godhead and fully God, takes up human nature and without loss to itself as fully divine second Person comes to express this second nature. As a result of the act of incarnation, the Person can be said to be "composite," for it subsists in two natures. In reporting these opinions, the Lombard refrained from asserting any of them as his own, although his disciples reported his own preference for the *habitus* theory.

In this light, the insertion of articles 3 through 5 makes eminent sense; in these articles, Aquinas is considering in turn the three opinions reported by the Lombard. But as q.2 a.6c makes clear, Aquinas cannot be satisfied with the Lombard's report, and in particular with the designation of the three as "opinions." Is the union of the natures an "accidental" one? What Aquinas offers in the corpus of this article is a pointed recapitulation of the history of attempts to account for the union of the divine and the human in Christ, running from the monophysites and the Nestorians through these more recent attempts. In this telling of the story, two of the three positions are not "opinions" but rather new expressions of a position condemned long ago by the Church meeting in council. Aquinas assimilates the first and the third positions to the Nestorian heresy. In Nestorius, there can be but an accidental union of the divine and the human in Christ, for one person is joined to another (there is not one person for the two natures). In *homo assumptus,* despite the refusal to speak of two *persons,* we find the same teaching, for there is an (accidental) union of two supposits. So too in the *habitus* theory, there is similarly a merely accidental union, for the Person has put on what pertains to the other nature the way one would put on one's clothing (and no matter how important clothing is to a person, the person is not that clothing). And likewise, the second opinion of the Lombard is not an "opinion" but orthodox truth, defined as such long ago by the Church meeting in council. As presented by Aquinas, the assimilation of the two opinions to Nestorius is offered as a historical judgment. Aquinas can offer the judgment because he is familiar with early conciliar documents. On that basis, he has an acute understanding of what the Church has in fact officially proclaimed and why, and what it has officially condemned and why, and so is able to recognize in these two twelfth-century opinions lapses into heresy. In making his case, Aquinas makes great use of that conciliar material, providing warrant for his judgment about these opinions and his championing of the second opinion by explicit quotation of the early conciliar documents.[31]

In designating those two opinions as "heresy," Aquinas adds that holders of these opinions "unwittingly" lapsed into such heresy.[32] Between the patristic period and the Middle Ages, there would seem to have been a serious disruption in the transmission of the Greek patristic heritage—both official ecclesial material and the discussions of theologians that had been attached to that official documentation. As a consequence, when western theologians in the twelfth century turned to the question of how the divine and the human come together in Christ, they did so without the benefit of a firsthand acquaintance with the earlier discussions. To the extent that they knew about the earlier discussions, it was principally through such intermediaries as Boethius. Thus, some of these theologians, in Aquinas' judgment, fell unwittingly into heresy, with their talk of *habitus* or of the assuming of a *homo* into union with the Word in Christ. For his part, however, Aquinas had by mid-career (that is, the early 1260s) rediscovered this Greek patristic material, in Latin translation, and had accordingly sharpened the presentation of his own Christology. In the *Summa Theologiae*, the results are remarkable. He offers extensive and repeated quotes of material emanating from the Third through Sixth ecumenical councils; in offering his own teaching on Christ, he self-consciously associates himself with such great figures of the Christian tradition as Cyril of Alexandria, the great opponent of Nestorius. The Christology of Nestorius is, indeed, a recurring theme in the *Tertia Pars*. Aquinas knows its surface attractiveness; throughout, taking up the torch from Cyril, he insists on why it will not work.[33]

Selected Questions in *ST* III.16, 3, and 17

Aquinas' engagement with the patristics—his effort to counter heresy while restating the essentials of the orthodox position as this had been worked out in the early Church—is evident throughout the first main part of the treatise on Christ in the *Tertia Pars*. *ST* III.16 offers another fine example of how this can play out. In the twelve articles of III.16, Aquinas considers in turn statements drawn from Christian literature. In most of these articles, he treats of individual statements, taken from the foundational documents and from important post-scriptural authors.[34] In two articles (aa.4, 5), he treats of important classes of statements. Hence, for example, in a.1 he asks about the statement "God is *homo*," and in a.2 its counterpart, "*homo* is God." In a.6 he investigates the statement "God was made *homo*," following that with what might seem its counterpart, "*homo* was made God." To handle each statement, Aquinas needs a good grasp of grammar, of how language works. But especially needed is a good grasp of the grammar of Christ, of what orthodox Christians mean when they speak of the full reality of Jesus. Thus, placement is significant. Aquinas will turn to difficult statements in the tradition only after he has worked the reader through the details of hypostatic union (in qq.2–15). Q.16 is appositely placed in the group of questions (running through q.26) on "what follows on the union."

The historical dimensions of the question are considerable. In asking whether a given statement is permissible and explaining how it should be taken, Aquinas draws on a healthy complement of historical Christologies. The fullest treatment comes in a.1, where Aquinas uses a full range of historical Christologies, as found in *ScG* IV.27–39, in reflecting on the statement "God is *homo.*" In other articles, Aquinas is content to use but one or two historical Christologies as a counterpoint to an orthodox reading. As should be expected, Nestorius is prominent in the question. The orthodox can say that "God is *homo*" and that "*homo* is God." For the subject of each nature is the one and the same Word, who, without loss to itself as fully divine Word, takes up and expresses human nature. Thus, for the orthodox, the *homo* of both statements (in aa.1–2) is the fully divine Word, as incarnate, as the one who instantiates in the case of Christ the human nature. So too the orthodox would say that "God was made *homo*" (a.6) but would not say that "*homo* was made God" (a.7). The problem, for the orthodox, with the last statement is that it would seem to presuppose an independent subject of the humanity, which would exist concretely prior to "divinizing." The two natures would each have their own subject, independent in existence from each other; and one who is human, in the usual sense, does not, cannot, become God. In Aquinas' telling, Nestorius, on the other hand, would not be able to make the statements considered in aa.1, 2, 6. Since in that Christology there would be an independent, human person (in the usual sense), God would not be *homo; homo* would not be God; and God would not be made human. Rather, there would occur in incarnation the forming of a team, a team of independently existing persons, one divine, the other human. But Nestorius *would* be able to make the statement analysed in a.7, for a human would "become God" in his version of incarnation, inasmuch as a *homo* would be joined to one who is God and come to share in that one's dignity.

In some articles Aquinas is concerned with another significant heresy, that of the Arians. Thus, for example, in a.8 he analyses the statement "Christ is a creature." Strictly in terms of the orthodox understanding of incarnation, the statement is allowable. For the nature taken up by the Word is creaturely; and so in its human nature, the incarnate Word is a creature. But, Aquinas notes in a.8c, the statement has a heritage that makes its use inadvisable. The Arians had made this claim of Christ, referring, however, to the other "side" of Christ, to what becomes incarnate. Even in terms of the subject of incarnation, for them Christ is a creature. Given that use, then, it is better to leave the statement to the side. Aquinas returns to cognate statements in later articles. Can one say that "Christ as human [*secundum quod homo*] is a creature" (a.10c)? Here, grammar is important. A term used in reduplication ("*secundum quod* x")—even a concrete term (as is *homo*)—supposits formally, or stands for the nature. Thus, the orthodox can make this statement, for the reduplication makes clear that the creatureliness has to do with human nature (not, as the Arians would want it, with the divine). But, Aquinas continues, if an insertion is made to the statement such that the reduplicated term supposits concretely, then the statement cannot be allowed. Can one say that "Christ as *this homo* is a creature"? Concretely, *homo* in the case of Christ refers to the second Person of God who has taken up and instantiated human nature; and the second Person of God does not cease being God in becoming incarnate. To make that statement would be to lapse into the Arian heresy.

While it is only in the first article that Aquinas subjects a statement to the full range of historical interpretations, preferring in other articles to concentrate on one or another heresy as a counterpart of the orthodox reading, it may be that he expects his readers to do on their own—for all of the statements—what he has provided the model for in a.1c. How would Photinus, the Manichaeans, and others, take the statements of aa.2–12? By engaging on their own in that more expansive exercise, Aquinas' readers would beyond doubt gain a better sense of these non-orthodox Christologies, as well as of the fuller adequacy of orthodox teaching. At any rate, by virtue of III.16, one is well prepared for a more fruitful reading of the texts from which these statements have been drawn.

In teaching Christ in the *Summa*, Aquinas is not, however, dependent solely on historical Christologies. His repertoire in this work includes more speculative Christologies, that is, Christological scenarios that differ from the revealed order.[35] In employing such speculative Christologies to advance his own, Aquinas is not innovative; he is following the lead of some of his Dominican predecessors, who had employed them in their own reflections on Christ.[36] In Aquinas, the use of speculative Christologies is much more modest and circumspect than that of historical Christologies: speculative Christologies appear only in a few questions, most notably III.3.[37] In III.3.6, Aquinas asks whether two or all three divine Persons might become incarnate; in the following article, he asks whether more than one human nature might have been taken up in the incarnation. In both cases, he answers positively: there could have been, due to incarnation, a multi-personed human (a.6); one Person could have assumed more than one human nature and come to express those without loss to itself (a.7). Aquinas in these articles is not particularly concerned with pursuing the details of such Christologies—for example, what changes to the foundational documents such Christologies would have required—but he does explain how in each scenario Christ would be correctly called "one *homo*." In the actual, revealed order (that is, where one divine Person has taken up one human nature and come to express that), there are two reasons for saying that Christ is "one *homo*": because the person is one, and because the human nature is one. In the scenario envisioned by a.6, there would be but one reason for saying that Christ is one *homo:* one human nature would be assumed.[38] So too, in the scenario envisioned by a.7, there would be one reason for saying the savior is one *homo:* the person would be one.[39]

On first reading, the impression made by these articles may not be entirely positive. Some may read them as confirmation of their worst suspicions about Scholastic theology, that it is engaged in pointless questioning and raising issues for no good reason. While challenging, these articles do, however, serve a purpose. In short, they set up nicely the final article of the question (a.8), in which Aquinas shows why the second person of God is especially suited to incarnation, trading here, among other things, on the close relation of humans and indeed all created reality to the Word on whom all things are patterned in their creation.[40]

Central to all eight articles of III.3 is the distinction between principle and term. By "principle," Aquinas means the power by which incarnation as act can occur. By term, Aquinas means the person in whom the assumption of human nature is terminated.[41] In terms of the actual, revealed order, the principle of incarnation is the divine power. Since the divine power pertains to all three divine Persons, Aquinas can thus affirm the common activity of the Trinity in the taking up of human nature. The term of the assumption, in the revealed order, is of course the second person of God: human nature is taken up, by the divine power, and united to the divine nature in the Person of the Word. It is the Word who is the term of the assumption of human nature.

As the question proceeds, Aquinas becomes more adventurous in the application of the distinction. Granted that it is the Word in whom the assumption of human nature finds its term, does that mean that the assumption of human nature had to terminate in the Word? Rather, as Aquinas makes clear in a.5, it was possible—that is, it lies within the divine power—for one of the other divine persons to have been the term of the assumption. By the divine power, human nature could have been assumed to the Father, or to the Spirit, as term. With the next article, we come to the first of the speculative Christologies that most concerns us. In asking about the possibility of multiple persons, Aquinas is not asking about the principle of assumption. That all three Persons are involved as principle is a point made very early in the question.[42] Rather, he is asking about the term of the assumption. It would not exhaust the divine power to assume human nature to a single Person; thus, it would be possible for God to assume human nature to all three Persons as term (6c). Likewise, divine power is not restricted to the assumption to God of a single human nature; it thus would be possible for God to assume more than one human nature (7c). In terms of the flow of q.3, however, this is not where Aquinas leaves things. The question culminates with the eighth article. In actuality, God has assumed one human nature to one divine Person, the Word; and as the eighth article shows in detail, the Word is eminently suited to be the term of the assumption. But, by virtue of the preceeding articles, one will not confuse suitability and fittingness with necessity. Yes, it makes great sense for God to have acted as God has. But matters could have been otherwise; God could have assumed more than one human nature (a.7) or assumed human nature to more than one divine Person (a.6) as term. The discussion of speculative Christologies, then, is not self-enclosed or for their own sake; Aquinas discusses them to shed additional light on the actual, revealed order.

In the discussion of Christ in the *Tertia Pars,* Aquinas pursues a number of tasks. He defines the key terms ("nature," "person," "union," "assumption," "principle," "term") and shows in various contexts how they may be correctly employed. He examines statements from scripture and the tradition, and on the basis of his facility with language and his knowledge of the orthodox teaching, is able to show how they may be correctly interpreted, and so facilitate a profitable return to the originating literature. In all of this writing on Christ, Aquinas shows himself to be the beneficiary of a deep encounter with the patristics; and his own work can be said to continue what has been initiated by such theologians as Cyril of Alexandria. However, it would seem clear enough that Aquinas is not simply repeating what he has found in his great predecessors. While in continuity with them, he also goes beyond them, and not simply in terms of the precision and clarity with which he can state his teaching about Christ. Aquinas' retrieval of the tradition includes making some Christological observations of his own, which help illumine the basic teaching about Jesus. In the course of the treatise on Christ, he can also advance claims that are distinctively his own. An outstanding example is found in the second article of q.17, in which Aquinas asserts that there is but one substantial *esse* (act of being) in Christ.[43]

Aquinas is well known for his use of the essence-*esse* distinction, between the "what" and the "that" of a being. Although in God the two must be said to be identical, in creatures the distinction is real: there is a difference between what a thing is (its essence) and that it is (its act of being); to define something is not to determine that it actually exists. For Aquinas, to be a creature means to receive one's entire reality from God: God grants to the creature its essence and act of being. Both are patterned on the divine essence and *esse,* while each falls far short of the divine essence and *esse*. And yet, each creaturely essence does "look like" God's essence, in the way established by God in God's wisdom. Hence, for example, human nature proclaims God by its will and rationality; again, human nature (and rationality and willing) is not divine nature (and rationality and willing). *Esse,* in turn, is proportioned to the essence; thus the act of being that realizes the potential constituted by the essence is a creaturely *esse*.

In the second article of q.17, Aquinas is trading on his metaphysics of being, in which the doctrine of creation is central, in order to show Jesus' distinctiveness. How many substantial *esse* does Jesus have? If *esse* follows on the nature, then there would be two substantial *esse,* for Christ has two natures. But *esse* has to do with the subject, the agent; and since there is one person in Christ, there is one substantial *esse*.

Much more interesting than this straightforward claim, however, is the observation that Aquinas makes in the response to the second objection in that article; it is here that Aquinas marks an advance over the previous tradition. The response reads: "The eternal *esse* of the Son of God, which is the Divine Nature, becomes the *esse* of man, inasmuch as the human nature is assumed by the Son of God to unity of Person." Much of this comment is familiar to us on the basis of our study of incarnational Christology. Thus, by the final words of the response ("the human nature is assumed by the Son of God to unity of Person") Aquinas is reaffirming hypostatic union, the union of the second nature to the first in the person of the Son. But what is striking in this response is the stuff at the beginning; this is new to the Christology, building nicely on Aquinas' metaphysics of being and the analysis by which he can distinguish God (in whom essence and *esse* are identical) from the world, on the basis of the essence-*esse* pairing. What we learn here is that an additional way of putting "assumption" is to speak of the communication of the divine *esse* to the human nature of Christ. Jesus then is a creature, inasmuch as the human nature which is received from God is creaturely. But in lieu of the human *esse* that is proportioned to the nature, the Word in taking up human nature shares with it, actualizes it through the giving of the divine *esse* that is the Word's as God. By virtue of this insight, we get a keener sense of what is involved in the act of incarnation. This is surely not to assert anything that would be unacceptable to, say, Cyril of Alexandria, who would appreciate the union of the two natures in the person of the Word. But in making the point about one substantial *esse* through the granting of the divine *esse* to the human nature taken up by the Word in becoming incarnate, Aquinas has gone beyond what is explicitly stated in the Christological tradition of which he is the beneficiary.

Christ in the *Scriptum* on the *Sentences,* Bk. III

While anticipating the *Summa* in some respects, the presentation of Christ in the earliest of the major writings, the *Scriptum* on the *Sentences* of Peter Lombard, differs from that in the later work in significant ways.[44] The differences can be obvious as well as more subtle. Perhaps the most palpable difference has to do with the topics included in the *Scriptum's* presentation of Christ. In the *ST,* a second part—on the life, death, and resurrection—follows on the first, which limns the grammar of Christ construed hypostatically. Some of the material of that second main part does find its way into the *Scriptum:* comments, for example, on the Virgin Mary, in terms of the conception of Christ,[45] and on the saving significance of Christ's death on the cross.[46] But the *Scriptum* does not set aside a separate part of the treatise that would be dedicated to the life, death, and resurrection as depicted in the scriptural accounts of Jesus and as read in light of the tradition's meditations on the incarnation. Rather, the distinctions on Christ in the *Scriptum* on the whole correspond simply to what is found in the first main section of the treatise on Christ in the *ST.*

The relationship between the *Scriptum* and the Lombard's *Sentences* is complex. Aquinas follows the order of topics found in the Lombard and discusses the topics treated by the Lombard. But the *Scriptum* is not a simple "commentary" on the Lombard's text, as if Aquinas were only concerned with highlighting and exploring claims advanced by Peter. Rather, Aquinas enjoys considerable freedom before the Lombard, inserting additional topics needed for a more adequate discussion of Christ. In including these additional topics, Aquinas displays his own theological sensibilities, as well as an awareness of Christological discussions subsequent to the compilation of the *Sentences.*

The relation between Aquinas' and the Lombard's texts can be shown in its complexity by reflecting on two of the distinctions especially concerned with the "mechanics" of the incarnation: d.1 and d.6 of Book III. In his d.1, Peter affirms the suitability of the second Person becoming incarnate for human salvation, although allowing that one of the other divine Persons could have taken up human flesh. Peter advances his teaching in a few pages and in straightforward, declarative sentences. Aquinas' own distinction 1, as is typical of all of his distinctions in this writing, is divided into three parts of unequal length. In the first, the *divisio textus,* Aquinas considers matters of organization—the internal organization of the Lombard's distinction and its place in the treatise on Christ as a whole. In the third part, Aquinas offers an *expositio* of the text, addressing difficult or intriguing phrases in the Lombard's text. The bulk of the distinction, however, is given over to the middle part, in which Aquinas investigates questions which he feels are occasioned by Peter's teaching. In his d.1, there are in fact two questions, each of which is comprised of a series of articles: four articles for q.1, five for q.2. In q.1 Aquinas follows the Lombard's lead in linking incarnation and salvation: the incarnation is geared to the saving of human beings. In q.2 Aquinas investigates the suitability of the second Person, rather than one of the others, becoming incarnate. In this question, Aquinas goes well beyond the Lombard, introducing speculative Christologies not considered by Peter: the possibility of two or three divine Persons becoming incarnate; the possibility of more than one human nature being taken up by the second divine Person. As is apparent, these two questions of Aquinas' d.1 correspond to the first and third in the *Summa's* treatise on Christ. By inserting in the later writing a new question (III.2) between these two—on the mode of union, in which he defines his terms carefully and provides a sound orientation to hypostatic union—Aquinas in effect is offering a comment on the adequacy not only of the Lombard's organization but of his own in the *Scriptum*. A general account (III.2) should precede the discussion of the Person who assumes (III.3).

The Lombard's distinction 6 is concerned with the three twelfth-century opinions which we have already met in *ScG* and *ST*. These opinions—*homo assumptus*, subsistence-theory, and *habitus*-theory—all speculate on how, exactly, the divine and human come together in Christ. This distinction is much longer than the first, reflecting, probably, the vivid interest in, and disagreement about, the topic among the Lombard's contemporaries. After stating each opinion, the Lombard provides a series of authorities—sayings by credible Christian authors—deployed by advocates in favor of that position. The authorities are almost all western; and Augustine in fact holds pride of place in each. The only eastern exception comes in the authorities for the second opinion; here, John Damascene, newly available in partial Latin translation, enjoys a certain prominence.[47] The early ecumenical councils, however, are not quoted in this distinction.

In the middle part of his own distinction 6, Aquinas raises three questions, each of which are again comprised of a series of articles, occasioned by the Lombard's account of the three opinions. He asks in turn about matters raised by the first opinion (q.1), the second opinion (q.2), and the third opinion (q.3). Hence, in q.1 he ponders the meaning of important terms (in the four quaestiunculae of art.1, he reflects on "hypostasis," "supposit," "individual," and "*res naturae*," showing the overlap among them); he asks whether the Son of God assumed a *homo* (art.2), and whether *homo* here means something composed of only two substances (art.3). In the three articles of q.2, on what pertains to the second opinion, he asks whether Christ is two in the neuter (art.1) and about the number of *esse* in Christ (art.2); and whether the person of the Word after the incarnation is "composite" (art.3). Finally, in q.3, on what pertains to the third opinion, he asks whether in Christ soul and body come directly together (art.1), and whether his human nature is united only accidentally to the Word (art.2). Even from this brief survey, it is apparent that in the later *ST,* Aquinas redistributes some of this material. Thus, what is found in d.6 q.1 art.2 is in the *ST* at III.4.3; d.6 q.2 arts.1–2 are set off as *ST* III.17 (aa.1–2); and d.6 q.2 art.3 is found at *ST* III.2.4. In none of these questions is Aquinas deliberating solely about the opinion that has occasioned that group of articles. He treats all three opinions in each question, explaining as needs be how each would handle the topic of the article. And, throughout all three questions, he makes absolutely clear his strong preference for the second opinion. It alone works, in bringing the divine and human together in Christ and in allowing for a single subject of the two natures.

As in the *ST,* in the *Scriptum* Aquinas again employs speculative and historical alternative Christologies in presenting his own. In terms of the former, their use would seem to be that found later in the *ST,* with one slight, yet meaningful, exception. In *ST* III.3, the speculative Christologies are placed in the midst of the analysis of the Person who assumes, and the final article of that question (a.8) is given over to the actual, the revealed order. It makes eminent sense for the second Person to have assumed human nature, although on the basis of aa.6–7 (in which the speculative Christologies are examined) one will not therefore conclude that only one divine Person could have become incarnate, or that only one human nature could have been assumed. In d.1 q.2 of the *Scriptum,* on the other hand, the point about the special suitability of the Word as Wisdom becoming incarnate comes earlier in the question (in art.2), and the question itself concludes with these speculative Christologies (arts.4–5). This placement may give the impression, at first glance, that Aquinas has incorporated discussion of these speculative Christologies for their own sake, not for the light that they may shed on the actual, revealed order.[48] In reorganizing the question in *ST* III.3, Aquinas will thus make more patent the point of including such speculative Christologies in the presentation of his own.

The distance between the *Summa* and the *Scriptum* is much greater when it comes to historical Christologies. In the early work, what holds for the Lombard's *Sentences* holds for the *Scriptum:* the authorities are (with the exception of the Damascene) western and the early councils are left out of account. The discovery by Aquinas of early Greek material was still to come, with important ramifications for the presentation of Christ. What this means is that the three opinions figure differently in the *Scriptum* than they do in the *Summa.* For one thing, he assesses them differently. The third opinion, it is true, is even here called a "heresy." But in the *Scriptum* this is because of a late twelfth-century conciliar judgment, not because of the affinity that could later (in the *ST*) be shown between this opinion and Nestorius.[49] As for the second opinion, it is preferred by Aquinas in the early writing; but he has not yet recognized that it is in fact a fortunate reinvention of what the Church had in fact declared in the early centuries to be orthodox truth. And so too, the first opinion is in the *Scriptum* a genuine "opinion." Remarkably enough, Aquinas in the *Scriptum* expressly asks whether the first opinion is a "heresy"; to be precise, he asks whether it falls under the heresy of Nestorius.[50] Dependent at this stage of his Christology for his knowledge of Nestorius not directly on the pertinent fifth-century writings and deliberations, but merely on reports of such intermediaries as Boethius and Cassian, Aquinas concludes in the *Scriptum* that the differentiation in this opinion between "person" and "suppositum" is enough to safeguard it from the charge of Nestorian heresy. By the time of the *Summa*, on the other hand, equipped with a more detailed and firsthand knowledge of what is involved in Nestorian teaching, he is more severe in his judgment. It not only does not work as a theological position (a point made as well in the *Scriptum*); it lapses into an error which the Church long ago had judged to fall outside the pale and to be contrary to what is central and binding to orthodox Christians, namely, the affirmation of the union of the two natures in the one and the same person of the Word.

Correspondingly, the three opinions assume in the *Scriptum* an importance that is denied them in the later writings. The three opinions do appear in the later writings. But there, they are read in the light of Aquinas' historical discoveries. They are thoroughly subordinated to the great Greek patristic disputes and decisions. In arguing against the first and the third opinions and deeming them heretical, Aquinas in the later writings is simply extending the argument already made in those writings against what he takes to be a more serious threat to the faith, the teaching about Christ of Nestorius, a teaching that would destroy Christ's unity and so put human salvation in jeopardy. And, his praise in the later writings of the second opinion is not for its own sake, but in recognition that it alone does justice to what the Church had long ago determined to be orthodox truth. In the *Scriptum*, on the other hand, the three opinions become his chief historical foil. Western patristic authorities come into account as deployed by these opinions; Aquinas situates his own position as a championing of the second opinion, in distinction from other positions held by twelfth-century theologians. The historical discoveries of the 1260s will be momentous for Aquinas, giving his subsequent analyses a finer texture as he argues, now self-consciously, in continuity with the great (Greek) patristic authors in proclaiming Christ.

Notes

1. On the Christology of Aquinas, see the following: I. Biffi, *I misteri di Cristo in Tommaso D'Aquino* (Milan: Jaca, 1994); B. Mondin, *La cristologia di San Tommaso d'Aquino* (Rome; Urbaniana University Press, 1997); F. Ruello, *La christologie de Thomas d'Aquin* (Paris: Beauchesne, 1987); H. Schoot, *Christ the 'Name' of God: Thomas Aquinas on Naming Christ* (Leuven: Peeters, 1993); J.-P. Torrell, *Le Christ en ses mystères: La vie et l'oeuvre de Jésus selon saint Thomas d'Aquin*, 2 vols. (Paris: Desclée, 1999); E.-H. Wéber, *Le Christ selon Saint Thomas d'Aquin* (Paris; Desclée, 1988); M. V. Leroy, "L'Union selon l'hypostase d'après saint Thomas d'Aquin," *Revue Thomiste* 74 (1974): 205–43; and M. Corbin, "La Parole Devenue Chair: Lecture de la Première Question de la Tertia Pars de la *Somme théologique*," *Revue des sciences philosophiques et théologiques* 62 (1978): 5–40. I am grateful to the Association of Theological Schools for a Lilly Faculty Research Fellowship in 1998–99 that allowed me a semester's leave to read more deeply in the Christology of Aquinas.

2. *ST* I.1.8 ad 2 nicely reflects Aquinas' basic convictions about the sources of theological work, and can for my purposes be taken as typical of his teaching. In this passage, we meet what might be termed a "hierarchy of authorities" in sacred doctrine and thus in the theology that pertains to sacred doctrine. Aquinas enumerates three such in this passage: God with the human authors of scripture; the church doctors; and philosophical writings. The authority of the first two are proper and internal to sacred doctrine. They have to do explicitly and directly with the passing on of the truth needed for salvation (for the need for a sacred doctrine, to promote human salvation, see *ST* I.1.1c). The authority of God and the human authors of scripture is also certain. God does not make mistakes; and God passes on saving truth to the human authors of scripture in such a way that they cannot be mistaken. As Aquinas states later in the *ST* (in the discussion of faith in the *Secunda Secundae*; see the later articles of *ST* II-II.1, in particular, II-II.1.9 ad 1), these main truths have been summarized by the church meeting in council, in the creed. The authority of the church doctors, while also internal to sacred doctrine, is, however, only probable. For God does not make a revelation to them. Rather, they have authority because they have been successful in interpreting scripture and have been deemed to be credible by the believing community. This process of discerning their authority would be a matter of time; and so by "church doctors" Aquinas is referring to such as Augustine and Cyril of Alexandria, whose interpretations of scripture have been shown much more often than not to be reliable and fruitful. The other authority mentioned in this passage, philosophy, has only probable and extrinsic authority. It is extrinsic because the philosophers were not concerned with saving truth, with sacred doctrine. Yet they have at times written about matters of interest to Christians, and have introduced concepts and terms that could be put to Christian use. And so Christians can bring their reflections to bear on Christian matters and can bring them into the project of sacred doctrine of passing on the truths needed for salvation. The determination of what from the "outside" should be brought in, and how, will be made from the perspective of Christian truth—that is, what is revealed as needed for salvation by God, as received in faith. In terms of the writing of theology, then, greater weight is given to scripture, when dealing with these saving truths, and to the creed, as summarizing the articles of faith. Lesser credence is given to the writings of the church fathers, yet more than that that would be given to those of the philosophers.

3. For some helpful general reflections on the value of attending to the pedagogy of the text and to Aquinas' compositional strategies, see the essay by my former colleague Mark Jordan,

"The Competition of Authoritative Languages and Aquinas's Theological Rhetoric," *Medieval Philosophy and Theology* 4 (1994): 71–90.

4. For the chronology of the works that make up the Thomistic corpus, see the studies by Torrell, Weisheipl, and Tugwell mentioned in the "Note on the Literature" appended to this volume. Aquinas lectured on the *Sentences* in 1252–56, preparing the lectures for copying shortly thereafter. He worked on the *Summa contra Gentiles* from 1259 through the mid-1260s and began the *Summa Theologiae* in 1266, working on it until he ceased writing in late 1273.

5. I discuss these twelfth-century Christological opinions in detail in the section of this chapter devoted to the *Summa Theologiae*, as well as in the treatment of the *Scriptum* on the *Sentences* with which the chapter concludes.

6. The point is nicely made at *ScG* IV.39.1: "From what has been set down above [chs. 28–38] it is clear that according to the tradition of the Catholic faith we must say that in Christ there is a perfect divine nature and a perfect human nature, constituted by a rational soul and human flesh; and that these two natures are united in Christ not by indwelling only, nor in an accidental mode, as a man is united to his garments, nor in a personal relation and property only, but in one hypostasis and one supposit. Only in this way can we save what the Scriptures hand on about the Incarnation. Since, then, sacred Scripture without distinction attributes the things of God to that man, and the things of that man to God (as is plain from the foregoing), He of whom each class is said must be one and the same."

7. At *ScG* IV.32.1, Aquinas calls this the reading of Arius, who was followed on this point by Apollinaris.

8. See, e.g., *ScG* IV.29.2, against the Manichaeans.

9. *ScG* IV.32.6 is worth quoting in full: "Manifestly, therefore, from the aforesaid there was in Christ a human body and a true human soul. Thus, therefore, John's saying (1:14), 'The Word was made flesh,' is not thus to be understood, as though the Word has been converted into flesh; or as though the Word has assumed the flesh only; or with a sensitive soul without a mind; but after Scripture's usual manner the part is put for the whole, so that one says: 'The Word was made man.' 'Soul' is sometimes used in place of man in Scripture; Exodus (1:5) says: 'And all the souls that came out of Jacob's thigh were seventy'; in the same way, also, 'flesh' is used for the whole man; Isaias (40:5) says: 'All flesh together shall see that the mouth of the Lord hath spoken.' Thus, then, 'flesh' is here used for the whole man, also, to express the weakness of the human nature which the Word of God assumed."

10. See, e.g., *ScG* IV.34.4.

11. See, e.g., *ScG*. IV.31.1, where Aquinas addresses the first of Apollinaris' Christological errors.

12. In these chapters, Aquinas also makes nice use of the Christ-hymn in Philippians (2:6–11). Some modern scholars have denied that the hymn is to be read incarnationally, preferring to read it in terms of a "second Adam" motif. Thus, a human did not aspire to equality with God, but instead lived in full obedience to God, in the process undoing the disobedience of the first Adam. In taking Philippians incarnationally, as had his great predecessors, Aquinas does not imagine that there is a "kenosis" that would entail the Word ceasing to be the Word (*that* reading is much later, indeed is early modern). Rather, there is an "emptying," in the sense that the eternally-divine Word condescends to become human and to live in the world as an authentic human, without loss to itself as Word. As is the case with John, some, according to Aquinas, have gone wrong in their encounter with Philippians, misinterpreting its exact presentation of incarnation. Such is the case, for example, with one of the Christological opinions reported by

the Lombard, the so-called *habitus* theory. See, e.g., *ScG* IV.37.11. In making such prominent use of John 1 and Philippians 2, Aquinas' text is somewhat reminiscent of the third of Athanasius' *Orations against the Arians*, a text that was highly influential on the development of Christological dogma in subsequent centuries (the *Orations* themselves, however, remained untranslated in the Latin Middle Ages and so unknown to Aquinas). The *contra Gentiles*, however, lack the venom of the Athanasian text, while continuing the struggle over the correct interpretation of scripture with other readers.

13. For the points made in the text, see the discussion at *ScG* I.3–8, which is meant to set the tone for the entire work. The division of the truth of sacred doctrine into two categories reappears in the first article of the *Summa Theologiae*, I.1.1c. A good but too-often neglected study of the preambles and their function in the teaching of Thomas Aquinas is Guy de Broglie, "La vraie notion thomiste des 'praeambula fidei,'" *Gregorianum* 34 (1953): 341–89.

14. For nice statements of the limits of inquiry and how the incarnation remains mystery, see, e.g., *ScG* IV.41.8 and 13.

15. *ScG* IV.40.9.

16. See the discussion of the union between two subjects as "accidental" at *ScG* IV.40.14.

17. See, e.g., *ST* III.2.2 objs.2–3. I will return to the importance of Nestorius for the presentation of Christ in the *ST* in the next major part of this essay.

18. *ScG* IV.49.9; see too *ST* III.2.2 ad 2.

19. See *ScG* IV.2–3. Aquinas makes his point especially well at IV.7.23: "Taught, therefore, by those mentioned and very similar testimonies of sacred Scripture, the Catholic Church maintains that Christ is the true and natural Son of God, eternal, equal to the Father, true God, identical in essence and nature with the Father, begotten, not created, and not made."

20. See, e.g., *ScG* IV.11.5 (at the end of the paragraph); 7; 9; 11; 13.

21. *ScG* IV.11.9–10.

22. As with chapters 11 and 41, chapters 12 and 42 stand in parallel. Both trade on a Wisdom Christology in which the continuity between creating and redeeming is especially important, as are God's purpose and concern for humankind.

23. The most reliable introduction to the *ScG* remains R.-A. Gauthier, *Somme contre les Gentils: Introduction* (Paris: Éditions Universitaires, 1993). The *ScG* is a highly controversial work; scholars disagree about the motive, ambitions, and intended audience of this writing. For representative, contrasting interpretations of the *ScG*, see T. Hibbs, *Dialectic and Narrative in Aquinas: An Interpretation of the Summa contra Gentiles* (Notre Dame, Ind.: University of Notre Dame Press, 1995), and N. Kretzmann, *The Metaphysics of Theism: Aquinas's Natural Theology in Summa contra Gentiles I* (Oxford: Clarendon Press, 1997). Both are reviewed, among others, in my "New Directions in Thomas-Research," *Religious Studies Review* 27 (2001): 34–41.

24. Aquinas explains the basic organization of the final Part of the *Summa*, including the two main sections of the treatise on Christ, in the prologue to the *Tertia Pars*. For a discussion of the organization, see J. Boyle, "The Twofold Division of St. Thomas's Christology in the *Tertia Pars*," *The Thomist* 60 (1996): 439–47.

25. The comments in the text are based on the following introductory paragraphs: those to *ST* III.1; 2; 4; and 16.

26. What follows in the text is based on the introductory paragraph to *ST* III.27.

27. On Christ's saving work, see the essay by Van Nieuwenhove in this volume.

28. In fact, the inclusion of the second main part of the treatise on Christ, concentrating on the scriptural narrative of the life and doings and sufferings of Christ, is an innovation in

terms of Scholastic theology as a whole. Aquinas was the first to include such a separate, extended treatment in a Scholastic treatise on Christ. See L. Scheffczyk, "Die Stellung des Thomas von Aquin in der Entwicklung der Lehre von den Mysteria Vitae Christi," in *Renovatio et Reformatio: Wider das Bild vom 'finsteren' Mittelalter*, ed. M. Gerwing and G. Ruppert (Münster: Aschendorff, 1985), 44–70.

29. For a good orientation to the use of scripture in the *Tertia Pars*, see W. G. B. M. Valkenberg, *Did Not Our Heart Burn? Place and Function of Holy Scripture in the Theology of Saint Thomas Aquinas* (Utrecht: Publications of the Thomas Instituut, 1990).

30. For a useful orientation to these opinions and to twelfth-century Christology, see L. O. Nielsen, *Theology and Philosophy in the Twelfth Century*, trans. R. Christophersen (Leiden: Brill, 1982).

31. On Aquinas' subsequent enhanced use of Greek patristic sources, see, e.g., I. Backes, *Die Christologie des hl. Thomas v. Aquin und die griechischen Kirchenväter* (Paderborn: Schöningh, 1931); G. Geenen, "En marge de Concile de Chalcédoine: Les Textes du Quatrième Concile dans les oeuvres de Saint Thomas," *Angelicum* 29 (1952): 43–59; M. Morard, "Une source de saint Thomas d'Aquin: Le deuxième concile de Constantinople (553)," *Revue des sciences philosophiques et théologiques* 81 (1997): 21–56.

32. *ST* III.2.6c: "Quidam autem posteriores magistri putantes se has haereses declinare, in eas per ignorantiam inciderunt. . . . Utraque autem harum opinionum incidit in haeresim Nestorii."

33. In "Thomas Aquinas and Christology after 1277," in *Nach der Verurteilung von 1277*, ed. J. Aertsen et al. (Berlin: Walter de Gruyter, 2001), 299–319, I have considered the reception of Aquinas' Christology in the final quarter of the thirteenth century, focusing on specific, controversial issues. It would appear that readers of Aquinas, whether disciple or foe, were stunningly inattentive to the new Greek documentation that Aquinas had attempted to introduce into Christological discourse, preferring to cite the usual Latin authorities, as transmitted principally through the Lombard's *Sentences*. This makes for a rather impoverished reception of Aquinas' Christology.

34. As a rule, in *ST* III.16 Aquinas has indicated in the *sed contra* of each article the source of the statement in question.

35. Speculative Christologies do not appear in the *ScG*, which is more streamlined in its choice of topics. They do figure, however, in the *Scriptum* on the *Sentences*. I will treat them briefly in the final main section of this essay.

36. These speculative Christologies involve the dialectic of the two powers of God. Scholarly work on the dialectic has tended to focus on its use in discussions of grace and the working out of human salvation, with especial attention to the heavy use made by Franciscan theologians. However, thirteenth-century Dominicans prior to Aquinas had employed the dialectic in Christology. There is need for a study of the use made by thirteenth-century theologians of speculative Christologies in presenting their own.

37. See as well *ST* III.4.4–5. *ST* III.4.5, which asks whether the Son of God ought to have assumed human nature in all individuals, may be seen as complementing *ST* III.3.7, in a sense taking the scenario envisioned in that article to the extreme (i.e., from more than one human nature to all human natures).

38. *ST* III.3.6 ad 1.

39. *ST* III.3.7 ad 2.

40. For a close reading of *ST* III.3.8, see my "Wisdom in the Christology of Thomas Aquinas," in *Christ among the Medieval Dominicans*, ed. K. Emery, Jr., and J. Wawrykow (Notre Dame, Ind.: University of Notre Dame Press, 1998), 175–96.

41. See *ST* III.3.1c.

42. In a.2.

43. Aquinas addresses the issue of Christ's substantial *esse* in a number of his writings, including the two other writings treated in this chapter. In all but one of these discussions, he argues, as described in the text, for a single *esse*. The exception is the *Quaestio disputata De unione Verbi incarnati*, a.4, which is roughly contemporary with *ST* III.17.2; there, he is—or seems to be—arguing for two personal *esse* in Christ. Scholars disagree sharply: has Aquinas there actually rejected what he argues for consistently in the *Scriptum*, *ScG*, and the *ST*? Or is it a merely terminological departure? For a good discussion of the issue, with literature, see S. Brown, "Thomas Aquinas and His Contemporaries on the Unique Existence in Christ," in Emery and Wawrykow, *Christ among the Medieval Dominicans*, 220–37. E. Hocedez has gathered major thirteenth-century discussions of Christ's *esse* in his *Quaestio de unico esse in Christo: A doctoribus saeculi XIII disputata* (Rome: Gregorian University, 1933). For a more jaundiced assessment of Aquinas' rendering of hypostatic union, including on the issue of Christ's *esse*, see R. Cross, *The Metaphysics of the Incarnation* (Oxford: Oxford University Press, 2002), ch. 2. In Cross's reading (e.g., at 58, n.28), Aquinas was from beginning to end of his career a monophysite, and was merely confirmed in his basic monophysite tendencies by the recovered Greek material, in which Cyril figured so prominently, and which I have highlighted in this chapter.

44. Lecturing on the *Sentences* played an important role in the training of the Scholastic theologian, and was the last major step in qualifying for employment at the university. Through the *Sentences*, one was exposed to major theological topics, as well as pertinent authorities on those topics.

45. For the discussion of Mary in relation to Christ, see III *Sent.* d.5 (itself composed of five questions); cf. *ST* III.27–30.

46. Cf. III *Sent.* dd.19–22 with *ST* III.46–48.

47. The discussion of Christ in the Damascene's *De fide orthodoxa* covers all of Bk. III and the opening chapters of Bk. IV. At the time of the composition of the *Sentences*, only the first eight chapters of Bk. III had been translated; the Lombard makes nice use of these. The translation of the rest of *De fide orthodoxa* occurred only later in the twelfth century.

48. See my "Wisdom in the Christology of Thomas Aquinas," 181–82, for more extensive comments along this line.

49. See III *Sent.* d.6 q.3 art.1 sol. and art.2 sed contra. Aquinas cites the twelfth-century declaration in the *ST* at III.2.6 sed contra and alleges earlier, patristic determinations in the corpus. For a critical assessment of Aquinas' understanding of the *habitus*-position, see W. Principe, "St. Thomas on the Habitus-Theory of the Incarnation," in *St. Thomas Aquinas 1274–1974: Commemorative Studies*, vol. 1 (Toronto: Pontifical Institute of Mediaeval Studies, 1974), 381–418.

50. See III *Sent.* d.6 q.1 art.2 sol.

Eleven

The Humanity of Christ,
the Incarnate Word

PAUL GONDREAU

"The good theologian," St. Thomas writes in his commentary on John's Gospel, "professes the true faith in both the humanity of Christ and the divinity of Christ."[1] In this statement Aquinas affirms the Chalcedonian definition of Christ as true God and true man, the divine Person of the Word substantially united to a human nature and a divine nature.

Many scholars, even Thomist ones, have often failed to appreciate the fact that a resolute anti-docetism is interwoven with Aquinas' adherence to the Chalcedonian conception of Christ.[2] St. Thomas has a genuine and, I would insist, unparalleled esteem for the full humanity of Christ. For the Master from Aquino, the doctrine of the Incarnation means that God has become man in the most fully human way possible. This understanding shines forth vibrantly in all of Aquinas' writings but especially in the Christological section of the *Summa Theologiae* (the *Tertia Pars*). The Christological treasures contained in this part of the *Summa* disclose a thinker who could not better qualify as the "good theologian" Aquinas himself describes in the *Super Ioannem*.

Not all share this view of Aquinas, however. Many contend that when it comes to the humanity of Christ, St. Thomas is hardly the model of a "good theologian." They insist that his "high Christology," a Christology that gives preference to Christ as the divine Person of the Word, cheapens if not eclipses Christ's full humanity. Some have even dismissed Aquinas, when he writes on Christ, as nothing more than a "glorified Hilary of Poitiers" (in his defense of Christ's divinity against Arianism, Hilary left little room for a human Jesus who, following Hebrews 2:17, "had to be made like his brethren in every respect").[3] Admittedly, Aquinas' deference to the mystery of the Incarnation causes him at times to hesitate in probing the human nature assumed by the Word as deeply as he probes other areas of inquiry. Nonetheless, Aquinas' opponents fail to render justice to what amounts to a lifelong defense of Christ's full and integral humanity. Aquinas' incessant endeavor to counter the glorified Christology of the same Hilary of Poitiers is one example of this. In many respects, this defense remains unsurpassed to this day. A profound anti-docetism at all times informs St. Thomas's Christology.

Aquinas' "High Christology" and the Integrity of Christ's Humanity

In reality, it is Aquinas' adherence to the divine Personhood of Christ—his high Christology—that accounts for his defense of the realism of the humanity assumed by the Word. With Aquinas we are far removed from the logic inherent in the "low Christologies" that dominate today's theological climate. These Christologies often assume that affirming Christ's full humanity is incommensurate, if not outright incompatible, with affirming his divinity or divine Personhood. For Aquinas, however, only the "bad" theologian considers a confession of Christ's divinity as a threat to an avowal of his full humanity. This is so because of the demands of the "true faith" concerning Christ. And the "true faith" always marks the point of departure, as well as the point of arrival, of any proper method of theological inquiry.

The good theologian knows that his discipline is a divinely orchestrated one, for which reason he works at all times within the framework of this "true faith." This framework, demarcated by the datum of divine revelation, is founded first and foremost on the incontrovertible source of revelation: sacred Scripture.[4] Aquinas' scriptural commentaries alone are proof that his reading of the "sacred page," as the medievals called the Bible, led him to confess a Christ who is both fully human and fully divine (his gloss on John's prologue in the *Super Ioannem* testifies to this especially).

Aquinas' reading of Scripture is also informed by the witness of the early church councils. Since it is the same God who authors Scripture and who guides the decisions of the ecumenical councils, the formulated doctrine of these councils offers the normative interpretation of the sacred page. Chalcedon, with its definition of the hypostatic union in 451, emerges as the most influential of the early councils in the formation of Aquinas' Christology. No less important is the celebrated defense of Christ's divinity at Nicaea in 325. The decrees affirming the integrity of Christ's humanity issued by the First, Second, and Third Councils of Constantinople in 381, 553, and 680–81 respectively, all of which Aquinas cites in his Christological writings, also have a significant impact on his thought.[5] These conciliar decrees, coupled with the revealed witness of the sacred page, made quite clear to Aquinas what the "true faith" holds concerning Christ: he is true man, i.e., fully man, and true God.

Closely related to the early conciliar decrees and thus to the proper bedrock and method of theology is the patristic witness. Here Aquinas' Christology draws from a rich and formidable patristic heritage, headed by Augustine (d. 430) and John Damascene (d. 749), on the issue of Christ's humanity.[6] This heritage bequeathed to Aquinas, through the works of Leo the Great (d. 461) and John Damascene, a Christological axiom that was formulated to repudiate the monophysitic denial of the integrity of the humanity assumed by the Word: "Each form accomplishes in concert with the other what is appropriate to it, the Word performing what belongs to the Word, and the flesh [or the human nature] carrying out what belongs to the flesh."[7] Delicately and finely balanced in its formulation, this axiom, which is at the forefront of Aquinas' mind whenever he drafts his remarks on Christ's humanity, affirms Jesus' divine Personhood without surrendering the integrity of his full humanity.

For Aquinas, then, the authoritative witness of Scripture, defined Church teaching, and the patristic writings combine to make up the lifeblood of any genuine Christological speculation. If philosophical principles and categories are employed in the theological enterprise, as they often are by Aquinas, their purpose is merely to clarify the givens of divine revelation.[8] Should one's Christology not be animated at all times by this lifeblood, one's conception of Christ risks turning into pure fancy.

And herein lies the problem for low Christologies. The bane of these Christologies is their faulty theological method. This method usually does not consist in attempting first to behold the divine logic and then to give coherence to this logic. Rather, it begins with a human conception of things, with human logic. Such a method will always struggle to see Jesus as something more than a common and morally frail man. And it will suppose, narrowly, that an avowal of Christ's divinity compromises a satisfactory theological account of his full humanity.

In reality, the integrity of Christ's humanity is safeguarded only by giving assent to the "true faith's" insistence that Christ's human nature is hypostasized not by a human person (Nestorianism) but by the divine Person of the Word.

As Aquinas insists in the *Summa Theologiae*, "our faith is in *both* the divinity and the humanity of Christ, such that belief in one *is not sufficient* without belief in the other."[9]

Hence Arianism (and Nestorianism) are as much an affront to Christ's humanity as to his divinity. Likewise, docetism (as well as monophysitism, Apollinarianism, and monothelitism) mark an assault as much on Christ's divinity as on his humanity. For in denying the part (i.e., part of the mystery of Christ), these heresies deny the whole (the whole Christ). One may call it a "high Christology," but Aquinas' Chalcedonian conception of Christ is the only one capable of maintaining the humanity of the incarnate Word: it alone retains the whole Christ, the *totus Christus*. And this *totus Christus* is the one divine Person of the Word united to two natures, human and divine. Ghislain Lafont notes that it "is truly unique to St. Thomas" to always look upon Christ's human nature as subsisting in a divine Person.[10]

Aquinas' Christology, then, does not *lose* the humanity of Christ; it *gains* it, since without his divinity there *is* no humanity of Christ. Only the bad theologian considers Christ's humanity in isolation from his divine Personhood. Though *verus homo*, Christ is not *purus homo*, to quote Jacques Maritain.[11]

In Aquinas' writings, the evidence that his high Christology champions the cause of Christ's full humanity is overwhelming. Though space does not permit an exhaustive presentation of this evidence, two points of inquiry will offer a sufficient sampling. The first is the role that Christ's humanity plays in the overall structural design, or *ordo disciplinae*, of Aquinas' Christology. In this essay I concentrate on the *Tertia Pars* of the *Summa Theologiae*, though I mention other works. The way that Aquinas integrates the humanity of the Word incarnate into his overall Christological vision tells us much of his regard for Christ's full humanity. The second point is the way in which Aquinas upholds Christ's consubstantiality with our humanity, whereby Christ's integral humanity is understood to own everything essential pertaining to human nature. This discloses for us Aquinas' genuine esteem for the full realism of the Incarnation.

The Place of Christ's Humanity in the *ordo disciplinae* of Aquinas' Christology

The clearest examples of the structured approach, or *ordo disciplinae*, that Aquinas adopts in his study of Christ appear when he drafts his comprehensive Christology. The first example occurs in Book III of his commentary on the Lombard's *Sentences*, composed at the beginning of his writing career. The second appears in the *Tertia Pars* of the *Summa Theologiae*, penned at the twilight of his career. (Though the *Compendium theologiae* contains an extensive Christological section, it is not comprehensive, since it gives only cursory consideration to the divinity of Christ.) Whereas in the *Sentences* commentary Aquinas simply follows the format established by Peter Lombard, in the *Summa* Aquinas lays out his own distinct and definitive vision of a comprehensive Christology. As M.-D. Chenu observes, only the *Summa* gives Aquinas the freedom to forge a theological synthesis of his own creation.[12]

The design of the Christological section of the *Summa*, the *Tertia Pars*, offers a glimpse into Aquinas' conception of the proper way one should understand the mystery of the incarnate Word. The structural design, the *ordo disciplinae*, of the *Summa* plays as much a didactic role in the theological vision of this work as the specific arguments themselves. Aquinas is a thinker who teaches both through his written words and through his arrangement of overriding themes and notions. How the humanity of Christ figures into the *ordo disciplinae* of the *Tertia Pars* is therefore most illuminating.

In his prologue to the *Tertia Pars*, Aquinas identifies two major lines of inquiry in examining the mystery of Christ: the first concerns the Incarnation itself, or the doctrine of "God made man" (*Deus factus est homo*), while the second concerns the historical events of Jesus' life, or what he "did and suffered" (*acta et passa*) in the flesh. The first line of inquiry, which covers qq.1–26, takes a more abstract and speculative approach. Here a distinctly deductive reasoning process, aided by the light of philosophical wisdom, predominates. The second line, which spans qq.27–59 and which some have termed the "mysteries" of Christ's life, follows a more descriptive method; it relies heavily on the witness of Scripture and the fathers of the Church.[13]

In examining *Deus factus est homo* (qq.1–26), Aquinas proposes that one best grasps this mystery by considering three principal notions. The first centers on the idea of *conveniens*, or "fittingness," more specifically, the fittingness of God clothing himself in a human nature (qq.1–3). Second, one examines the *assumpta*, or the Word's assumption of the essential elements of human nature (qq.4–6), such as a body and a soul. Yet a proper understanding of the *assumpta* remains incomplete without a consideration of the *coassumpta*, or the various nonessential features that enhance the existential condition of Christ's humanity (qq.7–15), such as his perfection in grace or the weaknesses of his body and soul (e.g., mortality, passibility).[14] Third and last, one explores the notion of the *consequentia unionis*, or the logical and necessary consequences of the Word's assumption of a true and integral human nature (qq.16–26). Such consequences include the possession of a human will and a divine will, the possession of a sensitive appetite, the possibility of atonement, and the like. As for understanding the incarnate Word's *acta et passa* (qq.27–59), Aquinas, in a move reminiscent of the *exitus-reditus* structure of the entire *Summa*, proposes consideration of Christ's entrance into the world (*ingressus*) (qq.27–39), his course of life (*progressus*) (qq.40–45), his passion and death (*exitus*) (qq.46–52), and his resurrection and exaltation (*exaltatio*) (qq.53–59).

As should appear obvious, the central place that Christ's humanity occupies in Aquinas' Christology is indicated by the sheer number and importance of the questions devoted to the matter. In fact, since the opening prologue to the *Summa* states that a comprehensive treatment of God must examine "Christ, who *as man*, is our way to God," one could even say the humanity of Christ plays a commanding role not only in Aquinas' overview of the study of Christ but in his entire overview (*summa*) of theology as well.[15] The *ordo disciplinae* of the *Summa* sends the clear message that a Christological synthesis worthy of its name is radically incomplete without an adequate grasp of the realism and integrity of Jesus' humanity.

In light of this division of the *Tertia Pars*, one can say that Aquinas' grasp of Christ's humanity is implied by his recognition of the following points: First, the human nature assumed by the Word represents a "fitting" way for God to reveal himself. Second, Christ's humanity lacks nothing essential pertaining to human nature (including a body made of "flesh and bones" and a rational soul). Third, Christ's humanity takes on not only singular perfections befitting the Savior of the human race (such as the fullness of grace and knowledge), but also defects and weaknesses befitting a man banded in solidarity with a human race suffering the consequences of sin (such as hunger, sickness, affliction, and mortality). Fourth, certain elements necessarily (or logically) follow upon the Word's possession of an integral human nature (including an intellect, a will, a sensitive appetite, and a particular sex). And, fifth, the human nature assumed by the Word was born of authentic human stock; it lived, breathed, ate, and slept among the humans it generously befriended at a particular time in a particular place, before meeting its end in an ignominious yet redemptive fashion, and attaining everlasting glory immediately thereafter.

Restated in the more general terms by which Aquinas divides the *Tertia Pars* in two equal sections, a proper understanding of the Son of God's real humanity means that a speculative beholding of the mystery of the Incarnation (qq.1–26) must be complemented by an analysis of Jesus' historical experiences (qq.27–59). Christological reflection cannot simply operate along the lines of purely abstract queries, such as whether the unity of Christ's being takes place in the Person of the Word, or whether what belongs to Christ's human nature can be predicated of God. Further, Aquinas' extensive treatise on Christ's historical *acta et passa* exemplifies how one moves beyond such queries. J.-P. Torrell, in fact, points to the singular achievement of Aquinas' treatise on Christ's *acta et passa* (it has no rival in either patristic or Scholastic literature) as evidence of Aquinas' "concrete or existential" Christology, namely, a Christology that strives at all points to show "that the Word was made man in the most human way."[16]

To emphasize the fact that the Word was made man in a fully human way, Aquinas typically employs the following terminology to affirm the human dimension of Christ. He avers the "truth of the human nature" (*veritas humanae naturae*) in Christ, or the "truth of the Incarnation" (*veritas incarnationis*). He stresses the "perfection of the human nature" (*perfectionis humanae naturae*) in Christ, or "the integrity of our nature" (*nostram naturam integram*) assumed by Christ. Aquinas insists that Christ possesses a real body (*verum corpus*), not an illusory (*phantasticum*) or heavenly (*caeleste*) one, and that this body is materially (*materialiter*) composed of earthly (*terrenum*) elements, such as "flesh and bones and blood" (*caro et ossa et sanguis*). He affirms that the Word incarnate is a "true man" (*verus homo*). And, echoing John 1:14, Aquinas makes constant references to the flesh (*caro*) of Christ, that is, to the material "stuff" of Jesus' humanity.[17] No doubt Aquinas intended such terms, which recur throughout his entire *opera*, to prevent his reader from slipping into a semi-docetic indifference toward the ontological realism of Christ's humanity. Little wonder that Gilbert Narcisse speaks of an "omnipresent theme of the realism of the Incarnation" in Aquinas' writings.[18]

The notion of *conveniens* (fittingness), mentioned earlier, merits brief comment. Aquinas relates the idea of *conveniens* to the fact of the Incarnation itself (*ST* III.1–3), whereby he considers it fitting for God to assume a human nature. He relates this concept as well to the existential features of Christ's humanity, inasmuch as the Word fittingly takes on a condition of mortality, including affective susceptibility, as well as moral perfection. In this sense, the notion of *conveniens* acts as a kind of wellspring of Aquinas' entire Christology, nourishing much of his reflection on the mystery of God made man.[19]

In itself, the idea of *conveniens* explores the coherence and beauty of the divine wisdom as manifested in the joining of an integral and ontologically frail human nature to the Son of God. Aquinas knows that God remains absolutely free in choosing the means by which to redeem the human race. The means chosen—becoming a true man—must therefore represent the most "fitting" or "suitable" way of achieving the end of human salvation. In view of God's economic plan of salvation, it was most fitting for the Word to substantially unite himself to a human nature. Aquinas has little difficulty in affirming the full manhood of God because he recognizes the eminent coherence of this assumed manhood. In Aquinas' vocabulary, *conveniens* signifies not only fittingness but also coherence, or even, in a more extended sense, ordered beauty.

The logic inherent in the notion of *conveniens* thus clears the way for giving full assent to Christ's genuine humanity. In fact, by making it the opening object of inquiry in his definitive Christological study, Aquinas suggests that the notion of *conveniens* opens the door to making proper sense of what otherwise remains a shocking and scandalous doctrine: the fact that the eternal transcendent God enters into substantial union with his limited, corruptible, and feeble material creation.[20] The notion of *conveniens* is no less the key to understanding the existential aspects of this substantial union between a divine Person and a human nature, such as Christ's bodily defects and weaknesses, his affectivity, his perfection in grace, his birth and circumcision, his prayer and spiritual priesthood, his poverty, his temptations, and his suffering and death.[21] Aquinas' evident admiration for the sublime beauty (*conveniens*) of the divine logic disclosed in the Incarnation offers a glimpse of how profoundly the humanity of Christ must have marked the heart of this Dominican friar's spiritual life: "Nothing more marvelous could be accomplished than that God should become man."[22]

The notion of *conveniens* fits hand in glove with another theme that figures prominently in the *ordo disciplinae* of Aquinas' Christology: credibility in the Incarnation. Aquinas understands that if the primary purpose of the Incarnation is to free the human race from sin (which, quoting Matthew 1:21, he affirms in the opening lines of the prologue to the *Tertia Pars*), then the Word must assume a human nature that accurately reflects the truth of human nature. Faith in a God incarnate, necessary for human salvation, can be achieved only to the extent that the human family views Christ's humanity as fully *believable*. As a result, Aquinas sees credibility as another manifestation of the coherence (*conveniens*) of the divine logic at work in the Incarnation. If God fittingly assumes a human nature, all the more fittingly does he assume a fully credible human nature.

This need for credibility determines the Word's assumption of various defects or weaknesses, such as mortality, hunger, and passibility: "it was fitting for the Son of God to assume flesh subject to human weaknesses," Aquinas explains, "in order to affirm belief in the Incarnation, since human nature is known only as it is subject to such defects."[23] If Jesus experienced no hunger, fatigue, fear, or the like, we would doubt the authenticity of his human nature. That is, a docetic interpretation of Christ's humanity could easily ensue if Jesus appeared as *too perfect* a human individual, for example, if he were immortal or immune to pain, fatigue, or affective suffering.

On the other hand, we would also doubt Christ's identity as Savior of the human race if he possessed defects incommensurate with his mission of salvation, such as lack of grace, or personal guilt due to sin. Therefore, no defect that undermines Christ's role as redeemer of the human race can have any place in the human nature assumed by the Word; nor, of course, is there room for any perfection that appears to abbreviate his humanity.

From this we can see that the need for credibility in the Incarnation involves two sides of the same coin: weaknesses that confirm Jesus' genuine humanness complemented by singular perfections that both verify his status as divine Savior and assist him in his role as Savior. Among the singular perfections called for by Christ's rank as Savior, Aquinas enumerates absolute sinlessness (and with it consummate grace, virtue, and enjoyment of the gifts of the Holy Spirit), as well as the fullness of knowledge and power. These perfections and defects that Christ takes on as a result of the need for credibility in the Incarnation form the proper subject matter of the treatise on the *coassumpta* in the *Tertia Pars* (qq.7–13 for the perfections, qq.14–15 for the defects). More importantly, these coassumed perfections and defects play an invaluable role in the human image of Jesus forged by Aquinas.

Christ's possession of a fully believable human nature adorned with singular moral perfections accommodates another theme that informs much of Aquinas' doctrine on the Word's assumed humanity: Christ as exemplar to emulate (*imitatio Christi*). Inspired by Scripture (1 Peter 2:21: "Christ suffered for you, leaving you an example, that you should follow in his steps") and rooted in a rich patristic tradition, this notion of *imitatio Christi* resounds throughout Aquinas' works, as evidenced by his penchant for the expression "Christ's action is our instruction."[24]

At its core, the theme of *imitatio Christi* emphasizes the fact that the human family yearns for a sure and concrete model to imitate in its drive for moral excellence and spiritual perfection. Obviously, no more "sure and concrete" model can be obtained than in God himself becoming man. Hence, the more credible or authentic, not to mention morally blameless, the human nature he assumes, the more this need is satisfied. To fully understand the human flesh taken on by the Son of God, and to understand why God clothes himself in this flesh in the first place, we must see how it meets the fundamental human need for exemplarity. And Christ satisfies this need in two unique ways. First, his sinless actions allow for the imitation of his outward comportment. It is in this "outward" sense that Aquinas speaks of Christ as moral exemplar. Second, Christ's actions become the source of the redeeming grace that transforms our lives. In this latter sense, Christ acts as ontological exemplar, or as an exemplar that helps shape our actions from within through the grace he bestows on us.

This theme of *imitatio Christi* discloses Aquinas' appreciation of the soteriological significance of the human nature assumed by the Word, or how Christ's humanity is useful for our salvation. Undoubtedly, such an appreciation stems from Aquinas' own personal devotion to the human example of Christ. In his work on Aquinas as spiritual master, J.-P. Torrell confirms that "Christ's exemplarity is always in the forefront of Master Thomas's mind."[25] This master theologian appreciates what it means, at bottom, to say God has taken on the same bodily apparatus as we possess, if only to allow us to see him with our eyes and hear him speak in a language we speak, making it all the easier to model our lives after God's own visibly cast ideal of human excellence and holiness. For Aquinas, the spiritual life is wholly "Christic," that is, Christ-centered, or conforming to Christ.[26]

This returns us to the issue of Christ's moral perfection and of Aquinas' "high Christology." For Aquinas, it is inconceivable to consider Christ's humanity apart from his sinlessness and his enjoyment of consummate grace and virtue. One reason centers on our need for a model to imitate: a sinless Jesus is a Jesus we can emulate, without hesitation or restriction, in all ways. The same reasoning carries over to the indispensable role that divine Personhood plays in Christ's exemplarity. Only a divine Jesus can stand as a model for the entire human race as such. Unless Christ is the divine Person of the Word, he cannot be the true exemplar for all humans, and he cannot fully disclose the truth of human nature. As Aquinas explains, "[T]he example of a mere human being would not be an adequate model for the entire human race to imitate. . . . And so we were given the example of the Son of God, which cannot err and which meets the needs of all human beings."[27]

Sinlessness coupled with divine Personhood equips Christ to serve as "the supreme model of perfection" (*summum exemplar perfectionis*), according to the *Super Ioannem* (commenting on John 12:6). Yet such exemplarity hinges no less on Christ's integral humanity as on his sinlessness and divine Personhood. For if his humanity is compromised in any way, his exemplarity dissolves with it. In Aquinas' vision, ultimate exemplarity follows upon the fusion of genuine humanness, absolute sinlessness, and true divine Personhood. We have here, then, further evidence of the fact that Aquinas' high Christology enhances and safeguards the full humanity of Christ.

Low Christologies, which view sin as natural to human life, of course tend to see sinlessness as a threat to Christ's full human consubstantiality.[28] Aquinas knows better, however. Following John Damascene, he goes to great lengths to point out that, metaphysically speaking, sin in no way belongs to the essence of human nature. Though one *can* speak of sin as a "natural" feature of human life if one considers the existential or historical condition of human nature (i.e., human nature since the original fall), sin remains an alien and intrusive accretion to God's created order.

It follows that a sinless Christ misses out on nothing "natural" and remains fully consubstantial to the human condition. As Aquinas argues, "Christ ought not to have assumed the defect of sin, since the truth of human nature is not proved by sin, as sin does not belong to human nature, a nature that has God for its cause."[29] Sinlessness does not turn Christ into any less of a true and full man. On the contrary, sinlessness allows Christ to illumine the true meaning of human existence. The Jesus of consummate moral integrity represents the supreme realization of all that it means to be human.

Aquinas on Christ's Consubstantiality with Our Humanity

"Nothing implanted in our nature by God," Aquinas writes in the *Summa*, "was lacking in the human nature assumed by the Word of God."[30] With this statement, to which other examples could be added, Aquinas confirms in the most explicit terms possible the fact that Christ's human nature is fully consubstantial with our own.[31] The Son of God assumes a fully integral human nature endowed with everything that belongs to the essence of this nature.

To delineate precisely what God has "planted" in human nature, and what, therefore, accrues to the Word's assumed humanity, Aquinas turns to an Aristotelian-inspired metaphysics of human nature. Here he makes one of his unique and lasting contributions to Christology. For Aquinas, only a sound Aristotelian (i.e., philosophical) conception of human nature can allow for a sufficiently penetrating grasp of Christ's consubstantiality with our humanity. "Metaphysics first" (i.e., metaphysics as the first tool used to clarify the givens of divine revelation) aptly encapsulates the method by which Aquinas examines Christ's humanity. Equipped with his Aristotelian anthropology, St. Thomas affirms that the humanity assumed by Christ is composed, most especially, of a body and a soul (hylemorphically united), as well as of such singular parts as a human mind, a will, a sensitive appetite, and a sex, to mention only a few.[32]

1. Christ's Assumption of a Genuine Human Body

In addressing the issue of Christ's body, Aquinas makes the most anti-docetically charged statements found in his entire *opera*. In the two articles from the *Tertia Pars* devoted to the matter (q.5, aa.1–2), Aquinas affirms Christ's possession of a real body no fewer than nine times. To emphasize this he follows Augustine's lead and repudiates (a total of fourteen times) the view that Christ's body was purely imaginary, illusory, or even heavenly.[33] Heeding the testimony of Luke 24:39 ("a spirit has not flesh and bones as you see that I have"), Aquinas insists that Christ's body is "carnal and earthly" (*corpus carneum et terrenum*), that is, composed of "flesh and bones and blood."

In these same two articles, Aquinas discloses the most fundamental reason for his anti-docetic adherence to the reality of Christ's humanity, to the point of singling out the "flesh and bones" of his body: it is because this flesh and these bones were beaten and broken for our salvation. The mystery of Christian redemption hinges on the reality of the tortuous crucifixion and death of Christ's body. As Aquinas explains, "[I]f Christ's body was not real but illusory, he underwent no real death . . . from which it follows that the true salvation of the human race has not been accomplished."[34]

Aquinas nowhere more explicitly confesses his appreciation of the soteriological significance of the incarnate Word's assumed humanity than when he asserts in the *Super Ioannem,* in words that echo the opening prologue to the *Summa,* that "the *humanity of Christ* is the way that leads us to God."[35] Without the humanity of Christ, without the true incarnate flesh of the second Person of the Trinity, there is no way to God and no reconciliation with God. The reality of Christian salvation succeeds or fails with the realism of Christ's humanity, of which his body forms an integral part.

Complementing this doctrine is Aquinas' appropriation of the soteriological principle that "what was not assumed by the Word was not healed by him," much celebrated for its widespread patristic usage.[36] Aquinas invokes this principle when establishing the essential parts of Christ's human nature, such as an intellectual soul, a sensitive appetite subject to movements of passion, and the like. Without the Word's assumption of such elements, the soteriological purpose of the Incarnation serves no intelligible end.

To strengthen his defense of the role Christ's humanity plays in the work of salvation, Aquinas, following John Damascene, turns to the Aristotelian notion of instrumental causality. This notion allows him to affirm that Christ, as a man, "causes" human salvation. Salvation, of course, can be achieved only by God himself, or, in Jesus' case, by the divine Person of the Word. However, the Person of the Word is substantially united to a human nature. For this reason the Word is able to produce effects proper to him as God *through* the mediation— through the active or free-willed mediation—of his human nature. When this happens, the Word acts as the "principal" cause (the one principally responsible for procuring salvation, the one proportioned to the effect as such), while the human nature acts as the "instrumental" cause (the one that is not proportioned to the effect as such but without whose proper mediated action the effect is not produced). Moved by the divine Person of the Word (like a brush moved by a painter), Christ's humanity truly produces or causes human salvation. Among his Scholastic contemporaries, only Aquinas avers that Christ's humanity acts as the conjoined "instrument" (*organum*) of his divinity, and he does so only later in his career (the *De veritate* marks the decisive turning point).[37]

This notion of Christ's human instrumental causality stands as a testament to Aquinas' commitment to probe deeply the human dimension of the Incarnation. And it offers another example of how Aquinas' "high Christology" pays sufficient honor and respect to Christ's humanity. For only inasmuch as it subsists in a divine Person can Christ's humanity enjoy the noble privilege of acting as the instrumental cause of salvation. Take away Christ's divine Personhood— or his humanity—and one eliminates human redemption. Both the principal cause (the divine Person of the Word) and the instrumental cause (Christ's humanity) together produce the effect of human salvation, just as a Caravaggio and his hand must work jointly to produce the chiaroscuro style of painting. The Son of God acts as savior of the human race *through* his assumed human nature, not apart, around, or in abstraction from it.

In addition to his soteriological concerns, Aquinas' affirmation of the reality of Christ's "carnal and earthly" body follows from another deeply held conviction: that of the fundamental goodness of material reality. Issuing from the creative hand of God, material reality *must*, Aquinas insists, be considered good (cf. 1 Timothy 4:4). No substance that has its source in God can be evil as such. In this sense, St. Thomas, whom G. K. Chesterton rightly dubs "St. Thomas of the Creator," counters an ever-present human tendency to demean the physical.[38] Aquinas' metaphysical instincts keep him close to all modes of being, even a corruptible and inferior one.

That the second Person of the holy Trinity has substantially united himself to genuine living, breathing, feeling human flesh confirms, definitively, the goodness of material creation. The dogma of the Incarnation stands as a pointed rebuttal to those who either refuse to take material reality seriously or who cannot bring themselves to recognize the nobility of that which God finds worthy enough to clothe himself in: "it pertains to the greatest glory of God to have raised a weak earthly body to such loftiness."[39]

This esteem for God's material creation as it relates to Christ's body stands out most clearly in Aquinas' passing remarks on the male sex Christ assumes. In a little known yet highly revealing passage in his commentary on the *Sentences*, Aquinas takes the occasion of a discussion, initiated by Augustine, on the fittingness of Christ's male sex to examine whether Christ had to assume any particular sex at all (*utrum Christus debuerit sexum aliquem accipere*).[40] Here Aquinas makes clear his refusal to allow the doctrine of the Incarnation to remain purely abstract (as it remains for many believers). Possessing both the objective clarity and the regard for material creation necessary to properly address an issue of such sensitivity, Aquinas has little difficulty affirming such far-reaching consequences of Christ's assumed humanity as his male sex. Genuine human consubstantiality *must* mean the Word's assumption of a particular sex: "Christ had to be like his brethren in all things natural, as Hebrews 2:17 says. *Yet sex is natural to man.* Therefore, he had to assume a sex. . . . Christ assumed a sex not in order to use it but *for the perfection of nature.*"[41]

"Sex is natural to man." With this short locution, so rarely found in patristic or medieval scholarship, Aquinas invites his reader to look upon sexuality (or the distinction between male and female) as part and parcel of God's creation.[42] Cognizant of the biblical witness (as in Genesis 1:27: "male and female God created them"), Aquinas appreciates the fact that to be human is to be a man *or* a woman. Put another way, to possess an *individuated* human nature is to own a bodily sexed nature. The "being man" and "being woman" of this man or that woman cannot be separated from their "being human." Though this might offend modern sensibilities, to deny it only snubs the dignity of God and his created order. And to deny it in Christ slanders the dignity of the human nature assumed by God.

Worse yet, to deny the historical and concrete elements of Christ's individuated humanity, including his sex, is tantamount to abandoning the truth of the Incarnation. The realism of this dogma does not allow for the assumption of an abstract or universalized, and unsexed or bodiless, "humanness." As Aquinas points out, quoting John Damascene: "human nature as it is separated or abstract from individuals 'is nothing but a pure idea, since it does not exist in itself.'"[43]

To preserve the notion of a credible incarnated humanity, then, Aquinas does not hesitate to claim that Christ takes on a particular sex "for the perfection of nature." That is, Christ assumes a sex for the integral completion of his individuated bodily nature. Little wonder that Aquinas interprets Jesus' circumcision, a deceptive event devoid of meaning if Christ is not endowed with a male sex, as proof of "the reality of his human nature."[44] Aquinas' anti-docetic esteem for the full existential and consubstantial realism of the humanity of Christ runs deep. More importantly, the fact that he speaks so candidly on a matter that causes no small uneasiness—even for contemporary theologians who embrace "low Christologies"—should lay to rest any lingering misgivings that Aquinas amounts to nothing more than a "glorified Hilary of Poitiers" when he writes on Christ.

2. Christ's Assumption of a Genuine Human Soul

If Christ's human consubstantiality involves the assumption of a (sexed) body, then no less does it require the possession of a soul, the animating principle of a human being. As Aquinas states, "the soul is the principle of the life of the body, as its form."⁴⁵

We should keep in mind, however, that for Aquinas body and soul unite as matter and form not in a merely loose Cartesian fashion (an excessive spiritualist anthropology), but in a wholly substantial or hylemorphic way. The human being is an integrated whole, a unified composite of body and soul. Commenting on this aspect of Aquinas' anthropology, G. K. Chesterton puts the matter succinctly: "a man is not a man without his body, just as he is not a man without his soul."⁴⁶

This holds to an unparalleled degree for Christ. Jesus' sinlessness gave him a share in the same harmony between body and soul that prelapsarian man enjoyed before the introduction of sin into the world, that is, before the disruptive impact of sin on human nature. For this reason, Aquinas speaks often of a dynamic hylemorphic exchange between Jesus' body and his soul, such that the experiences of one (like the bodily pain he endured in his torturous crucifixion) always affected (or "redounded into") the other. As Aquinas states early in his career: "Christ possessed perfect hylemorphic union, so that what he underwent on account of the greatness of his soul corresponded in equal measure to his body united to it."⁴⁷

Aquinas insists that the soul Jesus possessed was not just any soul but, contrary to the Apollinarian claim, a fully rational or intellectual (i.e., human) soul. As he observes, citing John Damascene: "[T]he Word of God assumed a body and an intellectual and rational soul,' since the body . . . is not truly human flesh if it is not perfected by a human, i.e., rational, soul. . . . For man is what he is on account of his reason."⁴⁸ This means that Christ owned both a human mind or intellect and an intellectual appetite or will. With his will he befriended and loved his human brethren in a genuinely human manner, including some more than others (cf. John 11:5; 21:7; Mark 10:21), as is natural for any human being. Also by his will he freely accepted to undergo his passion and death (cf. John 10:18; Matthew 26:39) and thus freely chose to redeem the human race. Aquinas knows full well that the reality of human salvation hinges strictly upon Jesus' possession of a human will: "by his free will Christ wished the salvation of the human race."⁴⁹ This explains the lack of tolerance Aquinas shows for monothelitism, the heresy denying a human will in Christ, which the Third Council of Constantinople, with the help of Maximus the Confessor, condemned.

Aquinas further develops the soteriological significance of Christ's human will, as well as of his humanity as a whole, in his theology of Christ's priesthood. In his remarks on Christ's priestly self-sacrifice, he explains that "by his humanity" (*per humanitatem Christi*) Jesus acts as priest. That is, as a man endowed with a human will, Jesus offers up his life "of his own free will" (*seipsum voluntarie*) for the expiation of human sin.⁵⁰

On the issue of Christ's human mind or intellect, the matter is more complicated, at least regarding the use of that intellect. Aquinas holds that Christ's degree of knowledge was required to match his unsurpassed dignity as God incarnate. For this reason he posits both beatific and infused knowledge in Christ. Beatific knowledge, of course, is the knowledge obtained when seeing the very essence of God in himself. In relation to Christ, it refers to the knowledge of the direct *visio Dei* that Jesus enjoyed, so Aquinas argues, from his very conception. However, such knowledge, commensurate with the essence of God, cannot be conceptualized as such. For Aquinas, what allowed Christ's human mind to conceptualize that which he gained from the light of beatific glory was infused knowledge. Yet infused knowledge is of an angelic sort; it is how angels know.

This means that if Jesus conceptualizes things in no way other than by an infused light, the use of his human mind *as human* is rendered superfluous. The human mind functions not by having intelligible concepts imprinted on it directly by God (infused knowledge) but by formulating concepts culled from sense data (which Aquinas terms "acquired" or "experimental" knowledge). If Jesus knows all things by a higher infused light, he gains nothing from sense experience. He gains nothing from the natural use of his mind. This, in fact, is the position of all early-thirteenth-century authors, including the young Aquinas.[51]

Pushed by his respect for the integrity of both God's creation and Christ's full humanity—"if in other things God and nature make nothing in vain, still less was there anything created in vain in Christ's soul"—Aquinas eventually acknowledged genuine acquired knowledge in Christ, "the kind of knowledge that is natural to the human soul."[52] Christ must not only possess a human intellect, he must also use it in an authentically human way.

Aquinas came to this position only at the end of his career. Although objections to his theory of Christ's knowledge might still be raised, however, it is significant that no other theologian of his day affirmed Christ's growth in acquired knowledge. We have here, then, further evidence of Aquinas' anti-docetic determination to preserve everything genuinely human in Christ, even if this should require a considerable rethinking of his theology.

Aquinas' appreciation of the human consubstantiality of Christ's soul leads to an extensive analysis of the "animal" side of Jesus' actions. Drawing upon his Aristotelian-inspired anthropology, Aquinas holds that Jesus' human soul, as with all human souls, subsumed the lower operational capacities commensurate with a sensitive (or animal) soul (i.e., sense knowledge and desire) and a vegetative soul (i.e., growth, nourishment through the assimilation of nutrients, and generation).[53] Since the sensitive soul acts as the principle of animal life, Aquinas has little difficulty ascribing a full animal nature to Christ (man, after all, *is* a rational animal): "the Son of God assumed together with the human nature that which belongs to the perfection of animal nature."[54]

Such language is unique to Aquinas. He alone emphasizes the integrity of Christ's "animal nature." In modern parlance, of course, the term "animal nature" carries a pejorative sense (a holdover from seventeenth-century rationalism). Yet Aquinas' objective metaphysical regard for human nature knows of no such pejorative understanding. He looks upon "animal nature" as nothing other than an expression of the goodness of God's creative will—which helps invigorate his endeavor to champion the cause of the realism of the Incarnation.

Aquinas points to Christ's possession of a sensitive appetite as the most evident manifestation of the "perfection of animal nature" in the Incarnation. This appetite pertains to the inclination of his animal (sensitive) soul to objects perceived by the senses as good and desirable, from which arise the passions or emotions. Aquinas adapts Leo's aforementioned axiom to argue for the full operation of Christ's sensitive appetite—"Christ allowed all the powers of his soul to do and undergo what was proper to them"—and thereby lays the theological groundwork for full-blown passions in the God-man: "He took on a true human nature with all its natural affections."[55]

On the issue of Jesus' passions or emotions, Aquinas knows no rival. He gives the matter more attention than any other thinker, patristic or medieval, and he drives the discussion deeper than all others. And considering how Christological reflection in the modern era has almost entirely neglected, if not purposely avoided, the subject of Christ's passions, Aquinas' analysis of Jesus' human affectivity remains unsurpassed to this day.

This modern neglect is rather amazing, particularly since it comes at a time when low Christologies purport to place in relief the side of Christ (his humanity) that classical theology has supposedly short-changed. For Aquinas, one simply fails to come to terms with Christ's full humanity until one examines what the Gospels make quite plain: Jesus is a man subject to movements of passion, even intense ones, such as sorrow, fear, compassion, joy, and, most reported by the Evangelists, anger.

What allows Aquinas to pioneer this field, besides his anti-docetic adherence to the realism of Christ's humanity, is his lucid metaphysics of human nature. He understands that to be human is to own a sensitive appetite and to experience the subsequent movements of this appetite. The passions enter into the essential makeup of the human being and the normal function of human appetite. To be human *is* to feel sad, angry, joyful, and hopeful at times. Jesus, a true man, undergoes the same: "the Lord [exhibited passions]," Aquinas writes in the *Super Ioannem*, "to prove the truth of his human nature, *since the passions certainly pertain to every human being*."[56]

This point of view squarely opposes Stoic philosophy. For the Stoics, the passions count as nothing more than "sicknesses of the soul." As such, they merit nothing but contempt and complete suppression. For Aquinas, who wages a relentless lifelong polemic against the Stoic view, the passions are in themselves morally neutral because they belong to man's animal nature. They can even assist in the work of virtue. Aquinas nowhere makes this clearer than when he inserts, at the beginning of the moral part of the *Summa* (the *Secunda Pars*), an extensive treatise on the passions (I-II.22–48), the longest treatise of the entire *Summa*. Such a tactical maneuver, entirely without precedent, sends the message that the passions play an indispensable role in the pursuit of moral excellence and holiness. This perspective grants Aquinas the objectivity needed to give an honest reading of the New Testament's account of Jesus' human affectivity.

Still, Aquinas remains clear on the singular moral quality of Christ's experience of passion. Jesus' sinlessness exempted him from the crippling effects of original sin on human affectivity, effects that otherwise touch every human being. The moral quality of Christ's passions is a vast topic explored throughout Aquinas' entire *opera*. At every turn those passions are affirmed as being wholly devoid of disordered movements: "the passions were in Christ otherwise than in us" is Aquinas' preferred expression.[57] Nonetheless, the disproportion between the moral quality of Jesus' passions and our own allows Christ, a real man subject to real movements of passion, to act as "the supreme model of perfection" (*summum exemplar perfectionis*) after whom we can mold our affective lives.

Aquinas encounters considerable difficulty reconciling the experience of disagreeable passions (sorrow and fear, principally) with the glory of soul that resulted from Jesus' enjoyment of the *visio Dei* (the condition of *simul viator et comprehensor*). Nevertheless, Aquinas' theology of Christ's human affectivity remains a remarkable Christological achievement. And it testifies, yet again, to the crucial role that Christ's full humanity enjoys in his theology.

Conclusion

Christian tradition knows of no greater defender of Christ's full humanity than St. Thomas Aquinas. Aquinas keenly perceives that what is essential to Christian faith, what sets Christianity apart, is its adherence to the tenet of God become man. As he writes in the *Super Ioannem:* "in our faith there are two things above all that must be believed: the mystery of the Trinity and the mystery of the Incarnation."[58] The Incarnation is the central historical event, and the realization of this marks the heart of this Dominican Master's theology.

Aquinas' labor to give intelligibility to the full human reality of the mystery of the Incarnation unfolds within the perspective of a "high Christology." That is, it unfolds within an awareness that Christ's incarnated human nature subsists in the divine Person of the Word. If anything, this awareness accounts for all the speculative powers that Aquinas brings to bear on ascribing full dignity to Christ's humanity. Aquinas knows that without the integrity of this humanity, everything that the Gospels recount for us and that the Church professes regarding the soteriological significance of the Word's accomplishments "in the flesh" is rendered meaningless. "After all," St. Thomas explains in his commentary on Matthew's Gospel, "it is *by his humanity* that Christ entered into the world, that he lived in it, and that he left it."[59]

Notes

1. *In Ioh.* 20:28, no.2562. This statement comes in Aquinas' gloss on the confession of faith of the Apostle Thomas in John 20:28, "My Lord and my God": "statim factus est Thomas bonus theologus, veram fidem confitendo: quia humanitatis Christi, cum dicit: 'Dominus meus.' Sic enim vocabant eum ante passionem.... Item divinitatis: quia 'Deus meus.'"

2. J.-P. Torrell deserves special recognition for his appreciation of Aquinas' anti-docetism. See his *Le Christ en ses mystères: La vie et l'oeuvre de Jésus selon saint Thomas d'Aquin*, 2 vols. (Paris: Desclée, 1999). For a more extensive treatment of Aquinas' esteem for the fullness of Christ's humanity within the context of his theology of Christ's human affectivity, cf. my *The Passions of Christ's Soul in the Theology of St. Thomas Aquinas*, Beiträge zur Geschichte der Philosophie und Theologie des Mittelalters 61 (Münster: Aschendorff, 2002).

3. The identification of Aquinas' Christology with that of Hilary of Poitiers is made by J. T. A. Robinson, *The Human Face of God* (Philadelphia: Westminster, 1973), 40, n.14. Another example of a low Christology is found in J. Moingt, *L'homme qui venait de Dieu* (Paris: Éditions du Cerf, 1993). For an example of Hilary of Poitiers' problematic Christology, cf. his *De trinitate*, Bk. X, chs. 23–27 and 47 (CCSL 62A, 477–501), where Hilary denies any kind of interior psychical suffering in Christ during the crucifixion.

4. *ST* I.1.1–2 and 8 ad 2. Also, in *ST* I.36.2 ad 1, Aquinas asserts: "we should not say anything about God that is not found in sacred Scripture, either explicitly or implicitly." É. Gilson, *Les tribulations de Sophie* (Paris: J. Vrin, 1967), 47, thus puts the matter well, and quite accurately, when he writes: "the entire theology of St. Thomas is a commentary on the Bible; he advances no conclusion without basing it somehow on the word of sacred Scripture, which is the Word of God." Within the context of a discussion on "low Christology," the remarks of J.-P. Torrell, *Le Christ en ses mystères*, 1:123, are pertinent: "the speculative part of Aquinas' Christology constantly refers to the Gospels, and thus to the starting point of every Christology 'from below.'"

5. It is well known that his stay at the papal court in Orvieto from 1261 to 1265 gave Aquinas privileged access to the conciliar decrees of the early Church. As a result, his firsthand knowledge of these documents was unparalleled for his day. For enlightening studies on this, cf.

C. G. Geenen, "The Council of Chalcedon in the Theology of St. Thomas," in *From an Abundant Spring: The Walter Farrell Memorial Volume of 'The Thomist'*, ed. staff of *The Thomist* (New York: P. J. Kenedy, 1952), 172–217, and M. Morard, "Une source de saint Thomas d'Aquin: Le Deuxième Concile de Constantinople (553)," *Revue des sciences philosophiques et théologiques* 81 (1977): 21–56. As for the councils themselves, Constantinople I (DS 150) professes, contra Apollinarianism, that the Word "became man" (ἐνανθρωπέω); Constantinople II (DS 424), also against Apollinarianism, affirms that the Word took on "human flesh animated by a rational and intellectual soul" (ψυχῇ λογικῇ καὶ νοερᾷ), and Constantinople III (DS 557) holds, contra monothelitism, that Christ owns a "human principle of operation" (ἀνθρωπίνην ἐνέργειαν), i.e., a genuine human will. Also, Chalcedon (DS 301) declares, contra monophysitism, that Christ is "consubstantial (ὁμοούσιον) with us as regards his humanity," and that he is "like us in all things but sin" (cf. Hebrews 2:17; 4:15).

6. For more on the impact of Augustine and John Damascene on Aquinas' regard for Christ's full humanity, cf. my *The Passions of Christ's Soul*, 51–66. For the patristic voice in Aquinas' theology, cf. C. G. Geenen, "The Place of Tradition in the Theology of St. Thomas," *The Thomist* 15 (1952): 110–35; idem, "Saint Thomas et les Pères," in "Thomas d'Aquin (saint)," *Dictionnaire de théologie catholique* 15, 1 (1946), cols. 738–62; and I. Backes, *Die Christologie des hl. Thomas von Aquin und die griechischen Kirchenväter* (Paderborn: Ferdinand Schöningh Verlag, 1931).

7. Leo the Great, *Tomus ad Flavianum* (DS 294): "Agit enim utraque forma cum alterius communione quod proprium est. Verbo scilicet operante quod Verbi est et carne exsequente quod carnis est." John Damascene, who was clearly influenced by Leo's work, reproduces the equivalent of this axiom throughout his *De fide orthodoxa*, Bk. III, chs. 19–20 (ed. E. M. Buytaert [St. Bonaventure, N.Y.: Franciscan Institute, 1955], 256–60). Though Aquinas does cite Leo's axiom (cf. *ST* III.19.1c), he prefers Damascene's use of it: cf., e.g., *ST* III.14.2c; 46.6c; III *Sent.* d.15 q.2 art.2 sol.2 ad 2. For the influence of Leo's work on Aquinas' Christology, cf. C. G. Geenen, "The Council of Chalcedon," 185.

8. *ST* I.1.5 ad 2.

9. *ST* III.53.2c, emphasis mine: "Est autem fides nostra et de divinitate et de humanitate Christi: non enim sufficit alterum sine altero credere." Cf. as well *ST* III.2.10 ad 1; 46.12; and *Comp. Theol.* ch. 209.

10. G. Lafont, *Structures et méthode dans la Somme théologique de saint Thomas d'Aquin* (Paris: Éditions du Cerf, 1996), 355–59. For more on Aquinas' conception of the hypostatic union, cf. J.-H. Nicolas, *Synthèse dogmatique: De la Trinité à la Trinité* (Fribourg: Éditions Universitaires, 1985), 301–58.

11. J. Maritain, *On the Grace and Humanity of Jesus*, trans. J. W. Evans (New York: Herder & Herder, 1969), 70.

12. M.-D. Chenu, *Toward Understanding Saint Thomas*, trans. A.-M. Landry and D. Hughes (Chicago: Henry Regnery Co., 1964), 298–310.

13. J.-P. Torrell's recent study on this section of the *Tertia Pars* in his *Le Christ en ses mystères* fills a great void in the history of Thomist research. Other scholars who have treated this section of the *Summa* include G. Lohaus, *Die Geheimnisse des Lebens Jesu in der Summa Theologiae des hl. Thomas von Aquin* (Freiburg im Breisgau: Herder, 1985); and L. Scheffczyk, "Die Stellung des Thomas von Aquin in der Entwicklung der Lehre von den Mysteria Vitae Christi," in *Renovatio et Reformatio: Wider das Bild vom 'finisteren' Mittelalter. Festschrift für Ludwig Hödl zum 60. Geburtstag*, ed. M. Gerwing and G. Ruppert (Münster: Aschendorff, 1986), 44–70.

14. Inspired by John Damascene (*De fide orthodoxa*, Bk. III, ch. 25 [ed. Buytaert, 269–70]), this distinction between *assumpta* and *coassumpta* was used by all the great thirteenth-century Scholastics, beginning with Alexander of Hales, *Summa Halensis* Bk. III, inq.1, tr.1, q.4, d.3 (Quaracchi Edition 4: 5866); cf. Albert the Great, *De incarnatione*, ed. I. Backes, tr. 4–6 (Cologne Edition, vol. 26 [1958], 204–35); Bonaventure, III *Sent.* d.15, a.1, q.2 ad 1 (Quaracchi Edition, vol. 3, 333). For more on this, cf. G. Lafont, *Structures et méthode*, 348–86. As for the *coassumpta*, L. Walsh (Introduction to *Summa theologiae*, vol. 49, *The Grace of Christ* [London: Blackfriars, Eyre & Spottiswoode, 1974], xviii) explains: "[t]he Word could have taken on human nature without them; no binding logic requires them."

15. *ST* I.2, prol., emphasis mine: "de Christo, qui secundum quod homo via est nobis in tendendi in Deum." Likewise, the *Comp. Theol.*, with its Christological section (chs. 185–246) focusing almost exclusively on Christ's humanity, also places the Word's real assumption of a human nature on center stage.

16. J.-P. Torrell, *Saint Thomas Aquinas: The Person and His Work*, trans. R. Royal (Washington, D.C.: Catholic University Press of America, 1996), 263–64: "This theologian [Thomas], who is believed to be abstract, knows the weight of the historical insertion of the Incarnate Word, and it is this that he labors to take into account."

17. For all the foregoing expressions, cf. *ST* III.1.6; 4.2 ad 2; 5.1–4; 9.1; 15.1 and 7 ad 2; 18.1 and 3 obj.1; 31.4; 33.1 ad 4; 35.1 obj.1; 54.3 ad 3; 55.6 ad 2; *De unione verbi incarnati*, a.1; Sermon *Attendite*, pt. 2; *In Ioh.* 1:14, no.169; 2:4, no.349; 3:6, no.448; 3:13, no.467; 3:32, no.533; 4:6, no.563; 6:63, no.990; 11:7, no.1535; 12:27, no.1652; 13:21, no.1798; 16:28, no.2162; 19:34, no.2458; *Comp. Theol.*, chs. 207 and 209; *ScG* IV.29, 34, 36, 39, and 55; *De Ver.* q.26 a.10; III *Sent.* d.2 q.2 art.1 sol.3 ad 3; d.3 q.5 art.2 ad 1 and ad 2; d.12 q.3 art.1 sol.1 ad 2; d.14 art.1 qc.2 sed contra 1; art.3 sol.2 ad 1; d.17 art.1 qc.3 arg.1 and sol.1–2; art.3 sol.1; d.21 q.2 art.4 qc.4 arg.3, and sed contra 2 and sol.4. *Caro* occurs in reference to Christ 228 times in the *Tertia Pars* alone (a prime example is *ST* III.16.2 sed contra: "Christ is man according to the flesh" [Christus secundum carnem est homo]). The closest Aquinas' predecessors come to something similar is in affirming the "truth of the human nature" assumed by Christ: cf. Damascene, *De fide orthodoxa*, Bk. III, ch.25 (ed. Buytaert, 270); Peter Lombard, *Sent.* Bk. III, d.15, ch. 1 (Quaracchi Edition, vol. 2, 95); Alexander of Hales, III *Sent.* d.15, n.25, Bibliotheca Franciscana Scholastica Medii Aevi, vol. 14 (Quaracchi: Edited by the Fathers of the College of St. Bonaventure [1954], 159); Albert the Great, III *Sent.* d.15, a.6 (Borgnet, vol. 28, 276 ff.); and Bonaventure, III *Sent.* d.15, a.1, qq.1–2, and dub.2 (Quaracchi Edition, vol. 3, 331–41).

18. G. Narcisse, "Les enjeux épistémologiques de l'argument de convenance selon saint Thomas d'Aquin," in *Ordo sapientiae et amoris: Image et message de saint Thomas d'Aquin à travers les récentes études historiques, herméneutiques et doctrinales*, ed. C.-J. Pinto de Oliveira (Fribourg: Éditions Universitaires, 1993), 149.

19. Narcisse, "Les enjeux," 146–47, affirms that a "torrent of suitabilities" runs throughout Aquinas' Christology, with the *Tertia Pars* alone offering 108 uses of *conveniens* in reference to Christ's ontology and psychology. Cf. as well *ScG* IV.54–55. The notion of the fittingness of the Incarnation is also appealed to by Peter Lombard, Alexander of Hales, Albert the Great, and Bonaventure. For more on the notion of *conveniens* in Aquinas' Christology, cf. J.-P. Torrell, *Le Christ en ses mystères*, 1:34–38; my *The Passions of Christ's Soul*, 181–88; O.H. Pesch, *Thomas von Aquin: Grenze und Grösse mittelalterlicher Theologie. Eine Einführung*, 2nd ed. (Mainz: Matthias-Grünewald-Verlag, 1989), 318–22; and M.-D. Chenu, *La théologie comme science au XIIIe siècle* (Paris: J. Vrin, 1969), 92–99.

20. If the doctrine of the Incarnation is shocking and scandalous to philosophical sensibilities, it is because of the inestimable gulf that separates material creation (including human nature) from God. For this reason, Aquinas on one occasion (*In Ioh.* 10:33, no.1456) holds that the mystery of the Incarnation "surpasses all understanding" (*opus incarnationis excedens omnem mentem*), since it seems too incredulous to hold that a man—though he is no common man—can bridge this gulf.

21. Cf. *ST* III.7.1; 21.1 and 3; 22.1; 35.8; 37.1 ad 1; 39.1–3; 40.2; 41.1–2; 46.1–4 and 9–11; 47.4; 50.1; *In Ioh.* 1:14, no.169; 5:27, no.789; *Contra errores Graecorum*, VII, 23–25; *Comp. Theol.*, chs. 226–28; *ScG* IV.54–55; and III *Sent.* d.15 q.2 art.2 sol.1.

22. *In Ioh.* 2:19, no.398: "Nihil enim mirabilius fieri potuit quam quod Deus factus est homo." For the same wording, cf. *In Ioh.* 6:35, no.914, and *ScG* IV.27.1.

23. *ST* III.14.1c. In ad 4 Aquinas adds: "although Christ's weaknesses concealed his divinity, they made known his humanity." Cf. as well *ST* III.15.7 ad 2; *In Ioh.* 7:1, no.1012, and 7:10, no.1027. Aquinas here follows in the tradition of Peter Lombard (*Sent.* III d.15, ch. 1 [Quaracchi Edition, vol. 2, 94]) and Bonaventure (III *Sent.* d.15, a.1, q.1 [Quaracchi Edition, vol. 3, 331]), who for their part stress the need for credibility in the Incarnation.

24. *ST* III.40.1 ad 3: "Christi actio fuit nostra instructio." For more on this expression, which occurs seventeen times in Aquinas' works, cf. R. Schenk, "Omnis Christi actio nostra est instructio: The Deeds and Sayings of Jesus as Revelation in the View of Thomas Aquinas," in *La doctrine de la révélation divine de saint Thomas d'Aquin*, ed. L. Elders (Vatican City: Libreria Editrice Vaticana, 1990), 103–31. For other texts affirming Christ's exemplarity, cf., e.g., *ST* III.14.1c; 40.2 ad 1; 41.1c; 46.1–4 and 9–11; 47.4; 50.1c; 51.1c; *In Ioh.* 11:33, no.1535; 12:27, no.1652; 13:1, no.1727; 13:15, no.1781; 13:21, no.1798; 15:10, no.2003; 15:13, no.2010; *In Matt.* ch. 4, lect.2; *Contra errores Graecorum*, VII, 23–25; *In I Cor.* 11:1, no.583; *Comp. Theol.*, chs. 227–28; and *ScG* IV.55. Cf. as well I. Biffi, *I Misteri di Cristo in Tommaso d'Aquino*, vol. 1 (Milan: Jaca Books, 1994), 391–93; and J.-P. Torrell, "Imiter Dieu comme des enfants bien-aimés: La conformité à Dieu et au Christ dans l'oeuvre de saint Thomas," in J.-P. Torrell, *Recherches thomasiennes: Études revues et augmentées* (Paris: J. Vrin, 2000), 325–35.

25. J.-P. Torrell, *Saint Thomas d'Aquin, maître spirituel* (Fribourg: Éditions Universitaires, 1996), 156–57.

26. This point is stressed by T. F. O'Meara, "Jean-Pierre Torrell's Research on Thomas Aquinas," *Theological Studies* 62 (2001): 798.

27. *In Ioh.* 13:15, no.1781: "exemplum quidem puri hominis humano generi non erat sufficiens ad imitandum. . . . Et ideo datur nobis exemplum Filii Dei, quod est infallibile, et ad omnia sufficiens." Here Aquinas points toward the position that Vatican Council II took in its Pastoral Constitution on the Church in the Modern World, *Gaudium et spes*, §22: "It is only in the mystery of the Incarnate Word that the mystery of man truly becomes clear. . . . Christ, the new Adam, fully discloses man to himself."

28. Robinson, *The Human Face of God*, 89–93, claims that Jesus' "real and total identification" with fallen humanity must preclude sinlessness, a doctrine that, he contends, is in any case purely "theological" rather than "historical."

29. *ST* III.15.1c. Cf. Damascene, *De fide orthodoxa*, Bk. III, ch. 20 (ed. Buytaert, 259). The principal anthropological text for Aquinas occurs in *ST* I.98.2c: "what is natural to man was neither acquired nor forfeited by sin." The distinction between the metaphysical and existential or historical senses of human nature comes from M.-M. Labourdette, "Aux origines du péché de l'homme d'après saint Thomas d'Aquin," *Revue thomiste* 85 (1985): 366–70.

30. *ST* III.9.4c.

31. Cf. e.g., *ST* III.18.2c: "The Son of God assumed human nature together with everything that pertains to the perfection of human nature"; III *Sent.* d.14 art.3 qc.3 sed contra 1: "Christ assumed everything natural that follows upon human nature" (*Christus assumpsit omnia naturalia que consequuntur humanam naturam*); and III *Sent.* d.17 art.1 sol.2: "Christ possessed all the perfections of human nature" (*in Christo fuerunt omnia quae sunt de perfectione humanae naturae*).

32. On Christ's possession of a body and a soul, cf. *ST* III.2.5c: "Christ is called a man univocally with other men, as being of the same species. . . . Now it belongs to the essence of the human species for the soul to be united to the body. . . . Hence, one must say that in Christ a soul was united to his body."

33. Cf. Augustine, *De diversis Quaestionibus 83*, q.14 (CCSL 44A, p. 20), quoted in *ST* III.5.1 sed contra. In the ensuing corpus Aquinas also cites Gennadius of Marseilles (d. c. 500), *De ecclesiasticis dogmatibus*, ch. 2 (PL 58, 981).

34. *ST* III.5.1c. Cf. as well *ScG* IV.29; and *In Ioh.* 5:28, no.791: "through the mysteries Christ accomplished in his flesh we are restored not only to an incorruptible life in our bodies, but also to a spiritual life in our souls." Already Ignatius of Antioch (d. c. 107) understood this quite well, since he criticizes severely those who allege that Jesus only "seemed" to have suffered and died; cf. *Ad Trall.*, chs. 9–10, and *Ad Smyrn.*, ch. 2.

35. *In Ioh.* 7:33, no.1074, emphasis mine: "Christi humanitas sit nobis via tendendi in Deum."

36. Though Aquinas prefers to cite Damascene's use of this principle (cf. *De fide orthodoxa*, Bk. III, ch. 6 [ed. Buytaert, 188]), it originates with Origen and is possibly rooted in Irenaeus' theory of recapitulation. Other fathers who employ the principle include Athanasius, Basil, Cyril of Jerusalem, Gregory of Nazianzus, Gregory of Nyssa, Ambrose, Augustine, and Cyril of Alexandria. For passages in Aquinas, cf., e.g., *ST* III.5.4c; *In Ioh.* 1:14, no.168; *ScG* IV.81.15; and III *Sent.* d.2 q.1 art.2, arg.1.

37. For Aquinas' definitive position on this matter, cf. *ST* III.19.1c and ad 2; and *In Ioh.* 6:52, no.959; the definition of instrumental causality comes in *ST* I.45.5c; for Damascene's remarks, cf. *De fide orthodoxa*, Bk. III, chs. 15 and 19 (ed. Buytaert, 239 and 258). Other scholars who have treated this issue, including the development of Aquinas' thought and the reasons thereof, include J.-P. Torrell, "La causalité salvifique de la résurrection du Christ selon saint Thomas," in *Recherches thomasiennes*, 214–41 (originally published in *Revue Thomiste* 96 [1996]: 179–208); É.-H. Wéber, *Le Christ selon saint Thomas d'Aquin* (Paris: Desclée, 1988), 179–87; and T. Tschipke, *Die Menschheit Christi als Heilsorgan der Gottheit unter besonderer Berücksichtigung der Lehre des hl. Thomas von Aquin* (Freiburg im Breisgau: Herder, 1940), 116–45. For the position of Aquinas' contemporaries on the matter (note that all were familiar with Damascene), cf. Albert the Great, *De resurrectione*, ed. W. Kübel, tr.2, q.1, sol. (Cologne Edition, vol. 26 [1958], 259); and Bonaventure, IV *Sent.* d.43, a.1, q.6, corpus and ad 4 (Quaracchi Edition, vol. 4, 895). Torrell, "La causalité salvifique," 220, n.3, observes that Bonaventure "sees [in Christ's humanity] no proper causality" with respect to the accomplishments proper to his divinity.

38. G. K. Chesterton, *Saint Thomas Aquinas* (Garden City: Image Books, 1956), 119. Among those who have insightfully discussed this aspect of Aquinas' thought, J. Pieper, *Guide to Thomas Aquinas* (San Francisco: Ignatius Press, 1991), 120–33, merits special mention.

39. *ST* III.5.2 ad 3.

40. III *Sent.* d.12 q.3 art.1 qc.1. In *De diversis Quaestionibus 83*, q.11 (CCSL 44A, 18), Augustine states that God became a man (male) because this represents the "more honorable sex" (*sexus honorabilior*), a view that Aquinas endorses in *ST* III.31.4 ad 1. Peter Lombard takes this

issue up for discussion in *Sent.* III d.12, ch. 4 (Quaracchi Edition, vol. 2, 83), from which it passes to the thirteenth-century *Sentence* commentaries. Yet only Aquinas adds the query on whether Christ had to assume any sex at all. For more on this whole matter, cf. my *The Passions of Christ's Soul,* 145–50.

41. III *Sent.* d.12 q.3 art.1 sed contra, and sol.1 ad 2, emphasis mine: "Christus 'debuit fratribus assimilari' quantum ad naturalia, ut dicitur He. II. Sed sexus est de naturalibus hominis. Ergo debuit sexum assumere. . . . [N]on assumpsit sexum ad usum sed ad perfectionem naturae." In the corpus of sol.1, Aquinas invokes the soteriological principle to argue the same.

42. For texts in which Aquinas affirms the integral role of sexuality in God's creation of man, cf. *ST* I.98.2c (where Aquinas takes to task the views of Gregory of Nyssa in *De hominis opificio* 17 [PG 44, 189], and John Chrysostom in *In Genesim*, homily 16 [PG 53, 126]); *ScG* III.126; *De ente*, ch. 5; and II *Sent.* d.20 q.1 art.2. We should note that Aquinas in some ways inherits this regard for sexuality from Albert the Great.

43. *ST* III.4.4 sed contra; cf. Damascene, *De fide orthodoxa*, Bk. III, ch. 11 (ed. Buytaert, 203). Also, in *ST* III.17.1c Aquinas states: "the [incarnated] human nature cannot be predicated of Christ in the abstract, but only in the concrete."

44. Cf. *ST* III.37.1c. It should be noted that Aquinas does acknowledge that, hypothetically, God could have assumed the female sex had he wished; cf. III *Sent.* d.12 q.3 art.1 sol.2.

45. *ST* III.5.3 ad 2.

46. Chesterton, *Saint Thomas Aquinas*, 37.

47. III *Sent.* d.15 q.2 art.3 qc.3 sed contra 2: "Christus fuit optime complexionatus, quod patet ex hoc quod habuit nobilissimam animam, cui respondet equalitas complexionis in corpore." Cf. as well *ST* III.19.2c. For the redounding effects of Christ's body into his soul, or vice versa, cf., e.g., *ST* III.14.1 ad 2; 15.6c; *Comp. Theol.*, ch. 231; *De Ver.* q.26 a.10; III *Sent.* d.15 q.2 art.1 sol.3 ad 3 and art.2 sol.1.

48. *ST* III.5.4c; cf. Damascene, *De fide orthodoxa*, Bk. III, ch. 6 (ed. Buytaert, 188).

49. *ST* III.18.6c. Cf. as well 18.1 and 4–5; 21.1 and 4; *In Matt.*, ch. 26, lect.5; *In Ioh.* 5:30, no.796; *De Ver.* q.26 a.9 ad 7; and III *Sent.* d.15 q.2 art.3 sol.2. For Jesus' free-willed love for his human brethren, cf. *Comp. Theol.*, ch. 232.

50. *ST* III.22.2c and ad 1.

51. Cf. Aquinas, III *Sent.* d.14 art.3 sol.5 corpus and ad 3; and d.18 art.3 ad 5; Alexander of Hales, III *Sent.* d.13, n.10 (Quaracchi Edition, vol. 14, 131); Albert the Great, III *Sent.* d.13, a.10 (Borgnet, vol. 28, 248–50); and Bonaventure, III *Sent.* d.14, a.1, qq.1–2 (Quaracchi Edition, vol. 3, 318–23).

52. *ST* III.9.4c; in this article Aquinas admits his change of opinion. Aquinas' theology of Christ's knowledge (qq.9–12) remains one of the more contested elements of his Christology today, particularly on the issue of Christ's direct possession of the *visio Dei*. For an overview of this debate, including a detailed analysis of Aquinas' change of opinion as well as an alternative view, cf. J.-P. Torrell, "S. Thomas d'Aquin et la science du Christ: Une relecture des Questions 9–12 de la Tertia Pars de la 'Somme de théologie,'" in *Recherches thomasiennes*, 198–213. Cf. as well D. Ols, "Plénitude de grâce et vision béatifique: Une voie peu fréquentée pour établir la Vision béatifique du Christ durant Sa vie terrestre," *Studi tomistici* 40 (1991): 315–29; and J.-H. Nicolas, *Synthèse dogmatique*, 408–9.

53. Cf. *ST* III.19.2c; and, for the human soul in general, I.78.1; cf. as well Aristotle, *De anima*, Bk. II, chs. 3–4 (414a28–415b28); and for those authors who appropriate this aspect of the Stagirite's thought and who have an influence on Aquinas, cf. Nemesius of Emesa, *De natura*

hominis, ed. G. Verbeke and J. R. Moncho, Corpus Latinum commentariorum in Aristotelem Graecorum, Suppl. 1 (Leiden: E. J. Brill, 1975), ch. 14 (pp. 91–92); Damascene, *De fide orthodoxa,* Bk. II, ch. 12 (ed. Buytaert, 118–19); and Albert the Great, *De homine,* ed. H. Anzulewicz and I. Söder, q.67, a.2 (Cologne Edition, vol. 27, 2 [2002]).

54. *ST* III.18.2. Cf. as well *In Ioh.* 6:4.

55. *ST* III.18.5c: "permittebat omnibus viribus animae agere et pati quae sunt ei propria" (this statement follows upon a citation of Damascene's phrasing of Leo's axiom); and III.21.2c: "veram naturam humanam suscepisse cum omnibus naturalibus affectibus." On Christ's possession of a sensitive appetite, cf. *ST* III.18.2; and III *Sent.* d.17 art.1 sol.2. For Aquinas' treatise on Christ's passions, cf. *ST* III.15.1–10; *Comp. Theol.,* chs. 226–28 and 230–33; *De Ver.* q.26 aa.8–10; and III *Sent.* d.15 q.2 art.1 qc.3 and art.2 qc.1–3; for an exhaustive study of this element of Aquinas' Christology, cf. my *The Passions of Christ's Soul.* For understanding the passions as "animal" movements of the soul, cf. S. Loughlin, "Similarities and Differences between Human and Animal Emotion in Aquinas's Thought," *The Thomist* 65 (2001): 45–65.

56. *In Ioh.* 12:27, no.1652, emphasis mine: "Dominus turbari voluit . . . veritatem humanae naturae approbaret: et ideo iam ad passionem appropinquans omnia humanitus agit."

57. *ST* III.15.4c. For the same wording, cf. *In Ioh.* 12:27, no.1651; *Comp. Theol.,* ch. 232; *De Ver.* q.26 a.8; and III *Sent.* d.15 q.2 art.2 sol.1.

58. *In Ioh.* 6:69, no.1004: "in fide enim nostra duo principaliter credenda sunt, scilicet mysterium trinitatis et incarnationis."

59. *In Matt.* 1:1, no.11, emphasis mine: "Per humanitatem autem Christus in mundum introivit, progressus est, et exivit."

"Bearing the Marks of Christ's Passion"

Aquinas' Soteriology

RIK VAN NIEUWENHOVE

An engagement with Aquinas' soteriology may appear unattractive, given modern concerns.[1] Modern soteriology puts less emphasis on salvation from sin than is the case in more traditional soteriologies. For Jürgen Moltmann, for instance, the perspective has shifted from sin to suffering, and in his work *The Crucified God* he develops a challenging soteriology, written in the shadow of Auschwitz. Even when sin remains in focus, the emphasis is now more on the social aspect of sin (social injustice), as in Liberation theology, rather than in terms of a broken relationship between God and the human person. Whereas Protestant theologians such as Moltmann and Jungel developed an interesting *theologia crucis* (and in doing so drew a close link between soteriology and theodicy), major Catholic theologians such as Schillebeeckx and Rahner fail—or refuse—to attribute any intrinsic salvific significance to the cross of Christ. Indeed, the cross has become somewhat problematic in modern Catholic theology. There appear to be a number of reasons for this.

First, focusing on the cross as the primary redeeming event appears to be one-sided and goes at the expense of Jesus' broader message of the Kingdom of God. More importantly, attributing redeeming value to the suffering of the Son seems to entail a rather problematic concept of God (evoking the specter of a cruel God whose divine anger had to be appeased by the sacrifice of his Son). This transactional view (a "sadistic and bloody myth," as Schillebeeckx occasionally puts it)[2] should be rejected, not only because of this problematic concept of God, but also because it might be misused as a glorification of innocent suffering. According to Schillebeeckx and others, Jesus' death is the side effect of his faithful adherence to his cause and is devoid of any redeeming value as such. Undoubtedly, the immense suffering of the twentieth century has alerted us to the obscenity of attributing redeeming value to the suffering of innocent people. In the face of such suffering, it is argued, we should keep silent and refrain from constructing theories, whether philosophical or theological: the problem of evil and suffering cannot be solved intellectually but only through praxis. These views may appear attractive at first, and they certainly meet some of our modern sensitivities. However, emptying the death of Jesus of all salvific power contradicts the New Testament witness (including, in all likelihood, the way Jesus himself viewed his passion) and the ensuing tradition of Christian reflection on the cross.

In my view, Aquinas' soteriology still proves useful because it can accommodate these modern concerns while remaining more faithful than some of the recent soteriologies to the way the New Testament views the central role of the cross. Also, although Aquinas sees Christ's salvific work primarily in terms of deliverance from sin, he is not inattentive to the social aspects of sin, or its link with suffering—in relation to the latter issue, this link is probably even closer in Aquinas' work than in modern understandings. Finally, although Aquinas clearly attributes salvific significance to the cross of Christ, this is not the sole focus of his soteriology; nor does it mean that he espouses a judicial or "transactional" theory of salvation. I hope to clarify these issues throughout this essay. I will pay particular attention to the problem of suffering and evil, not only because of the close link between soteriology and theodicy in modern theology, but also because sharing in the suffering of Christ is a major theme in Aquinas' soteriology. Although this essay is written with some of these modern concerns in mind, my primary goal is to expound Aquinas' doctrine as such, allowing his voice to be heard by referring to his own writings throughout the text.

In the first of the following six sections, my perspective is rather broad and somewhat preliminary: I consider the relation between divine and human causality—a topic that has bearings on the understanding of the "contingency" and "necessity" of the cross. Similarly, in the second section I examine in a fairly general vein the relation between divine providence and evil, and in the third, I discuss how Aquinas describes the nature of sin. The topic of the relation between sin and providence leads to a discussion of "punishment" in the fourth section, and of the meaning of "satisfaction" and its relation to punishment in the fifth. My treatment of satisfaction is intended to illustrate that Aquinas rejects a "judicial" or "transactional" theory of salvation. This point is further corroborated in the sixth section, on the notions of sacrifice and sacrament. There I deal in greater depth with our participation in the salvific role of Christ's cross and resurrection.

Divine Causality and Human Freedom: Some General Observations

The relation between divine causality and human freedom is dealt with in the contribution to this volume by Harm Goris. It has, however, immediate repercussions for one of the issues we set out to discuss, namely, how to attribute redeeming value to the cross of Christ without glorifying innocent suffering or espousing a transactional view of redemption. Aquinas avoids this dilemma by viewing the cross as both the result of all too human, sinful, and free (contingent) machinations and as part of the divine plan. In order to explain this, some general observations are in order.

First, divine foreknowledge (it would perhaps be better to speak of omniscience) does not imply for Aquinas that the "future" is predetermined. As Goris and others have shown, Aquinas is a proponent of what McTaggart called the "A-series" view of time: future events are genuinely contingent.[3] However, since God is beyond temporal distinctions, there is no present, past, or future for God. Similarly, divine causality does not abolish creaturely (including human) freedom: "divine providence works infallibly in all things, and nevertheless the effects of contingent causes come about contingently, inasmuch as God moves all things proportionately, each thing according to its mode."[4] Thus, the divine plan does not impose any necessity on genuinely contingent, historical events, and this also applies to the life and death of Christ.[5]

Once contingent events have taken place, however, they acquire a necessary character in an almost trivial sense: the past cannot be undone and is therefore necessary. This is subsequent necessity, not antecedent or intrinsic necessity. However, given the fact that God is eternal and omnipresent, talk of "subsequent" and "antecedent necessity" and "contingency" becomes strangely inapplicable to the way God relates to the world. Insofar as God relates to all events— past, present, and future—from an eternal "now," all events, including genuinely "contingent" ones, are equally "necessary" in the trivial sense of the word mentioned earlier. It then becomes the task of the theologian (whose perspective is theocentric, unlike that of the philosopher) to make sense of what has happened, and to see how it ties in (*convenientissimum*) with divine providence. Thus, divine providence—which is concerned with the bestowal of being on things and the direction of things to their end—should not be construed in terms of a plan which is being executed according to a preordained blueprint. Such a view is problematic for two reasons: first, because it seems to deny the genuine contingency of this world (it seems to imply a static, or, in McTaggart's terminology, a "B-series" view of time); second, because it sees divine and creaturely causality in terms of competition and therefore implies the abnegation of human freedom. Therefore, the metaphor of a jigsaw puzzle seems better suited to illustrate how the theologian understands events in the light of divine providence. If we were to have insight into the divine plan, we would be able to make sense of events which seem at first puzzling or incomprehensible (e.g., a destructive earthquake); we would see how each event "fits in" without meaning to suggest that every event is somehow predetermined.[6] Similarly, the theologian should attempt to make sense of the life and death of Christ and try to fathom how it fits in (*conveniens*) with the divine plan—which is exactly what Aquinas does in *ST* III.46.3–4. In short, Christ's death on the cross is a genuinely contingent historical event, yet it is "necessary" from a theocentric perspective, in the sense that it has as a matter of fact happened, in accordance with the divine plan, in order to redeem humanity. Once these two perspectives are grasped, it becomes clear how Aquinas can consider the death of Christ "a most grievous sin" (*ST* I.47.4) and yet attribute redeeming value to it.

Providence, Evil Done, and Evil Suffered

In the previous section I suggested that divine providence, causality, and omniscience do not exclude the genuine contingency of events, including the passion of Christ. However, whereas the issue of the relation between divine causality and creaturely freedom might occupy the minds of philosophers of religion, it is unlikely to stir the minds of "ordinary" Christians—at least not to the extent that the problem of evil and suffering does. Bad things happen to good people, and vice versa, with an arbitrariness that seems to suggest that God does indeed throw dice. Aquinas was well aware of this problem, and he states it clearly in the prologue to his *Commentary on Job:* "that just men should be afflicted without cause seems to undermine totally the foundation of providence."[7] So how can we square evil with divine providence?

Aquinas does not primarily understand providence in terms of efficient causality on a par with creaturely causality, but rather in terms of formal or constitutive causality (it creates the conditions of possibility for creaturely causality by conferring existence upon things) and final causality. Providence refers to the fact that all things are moved toward the divine goodness as their end.[8] This understanding of providence allows us to see how the existence of evil and suffering is not incompatible with providence—on the contrary. In willing himself God also wills created things, and he wills them to participate in his goodness by way of likeness.[9] God does not "impose" an order on his creatures—especially not on creatures endowed with free will—but he allows them to share in his freedom and causality; this, however, involves the possibility of evil: "it would be contrary to the rational character of the divine regime to refuse permission for created things to act according to the mode of their nature. Now, as a result of this fact, that creatures do act in this way, corruption and evil result in things. . . . Therefore, it does not pertain to divine providence to exclude evil entirely from the things that are governed."[10] Given the fact that evil is privation of goodness, Aquinas argues against those who take evil as an indication of the nonexistence of God ("If God exists, whence evil?") that the very existence of evil is a pointer toward God: there would be no evil if the order of good (which finds its origin in God) were taken away, since its privation is evil; thus: "If evil exists, God exists."[11] In short, the existence of evil does not mean for Aquinas that God's providence is somehow deficient. If evil were completely eliminated from things, they would not be governed by providence in accord with their nature; and this would be a greater defect than the particular defects eradicated. This applies especially to human beings. We can only attain the divine likeness through the exercise of free will, thereby mirroring God's own freedom.[12] This freedom, however, implies the possibility of turning away from God.[13] Thus, divine providence does not safeguard all things from evil, but rather sees to it that the evil that arises is ordained to some good.[14]

Can God, then, be said to want evil? In this context Aquinas distinguishes between *malum poenae* and *malum culpae*—a distinction I discuss in much greater detail in the next section.[15] The first, best translated as "evil suffered" or "affliction" rather than as "the evil of pain" or "punishment," refers to the afflictions that befall us against our will. The second, the evil of fault or "evil done," refers to the act of human sin or moral evil. When Aquinas states that God is the author of "evil suffered" but not of "evil done" (which is solely due to the exercise of our free will), he does not mean to suggest that God directly causes all our misfortunes (not even for the punishment of sins). What Aquinas says about *malum poenae* needs to be seen in the light of what he says on God as the cause of evil in *ST* I.49 and I.22.2.[16] Given the nature of evil (*privatio boni*), God can only be said to cause evil in things incidentally (*per accidens*). My failing eyesight is not caused by God: "the effect of a deficient secondary cause is derived from a non-deficient first cause with respect to what is real and complete there, not to what is defective."[17] Thus, God creates a world in which corruption of things occurs, but he does not directly cause the corruption.[18] However, these are merely philosophical arguments—a created world necessarily implies finitude and imperfection—and in the light of evil and suffering our theorizing has only a limited value. When Aquinas is developing these arguments, he is merely pointing out that evil and suffering are not incompatible with divine providence. They are obviously not to be seen as a justification of suffering and evil, nor do they reveal anything of their theological meaning.

Indeed, according to Aquinas, afflictions are not merely "bad luck" or simply part and parcel of a created world: even if they have not been directly caused by God, they are nevertheless theologically relevant in the light of human sin and can only be properly dealt with in the light of Christ's redeeming work. To explain this important point, I will first examine the nature of "evil done" (sin), how it affects the human person, and how it relates to God's providence. I then discuss in greater detail the relation between evil, sin, and suffering. This leads to a discussion of satisfaction, which allows us to treat of Christ's salvific work in the remaining sections of this essay.

The Disease of Sin and Theological Psychology

Before describing how we have been saved in Christ—the ultimate aim of this essay—it is useful to consider Aquinas' view of sin.[19] I will argue throughout that Aquinas develops a sophisticated theological psychology, which is essential for a proper understanding of the way he describes the remedial activity of Christ, the nature of justification and satisfaction, and so forth. Sin is described in "personalist" terms, i.e., as something that deeply affects the self of the human person and the way she relates to herself, other people, and above all, God. An indication of this "personalist" approach is the use of medicinal metaphors. Indeed, Aquinas describes (mortal) sin in terms of a disease of the soul that affects the whole human person. In his *Exposition on the Psalms* 6, 2, Aquinas draws a parallel between physical illness, which (according to Aristotle) results from a lack of order within the bodily fluids, and sin as a spiritual illness, which results from a lack of order within the personality.[20] It is no coincidence that the sin against the Spirit (i.e., choosing evil out of sheer malice) is described as "an incurable disease" because it causes us to refuse that which could cure us from it.[21] Through (mortal) sin we turn away from our goal—God—to whom we were previously directed in faith, hope, and charity.

In a beautiful passage in his *Commentary on John*, Aquinas allegorically interprets the different illnesses from which the people at the Pool of Beth-za'tha were suffering (John 5:1–9) as symbols of the effects of sin. Sinners are called "ill" because they are weakened by being subjugated to vices (such as concupiscence and envy). Some are suffering from "blindness" (sin darkens our capacity to judge reasonably), others from "crippledness" (the sinner, being unstable, lacks a proper focus in his life) and "paralysis" (the sinner, as Aquinas perceptively states, is "unable to love").[22] Similarly, in *ST* I-II.88.1 Aquinas writes: "since sin is a sort of sickness of the soul [*infirmitas animae*], a particular sin is classified as mortal by likening it to a mortal illness, one that brings on an incurable condition by destroying a vital principle. The principle of the soul's life, which is a life of virtue, is its relationship to the true ultimate end [*ordo ad ultimum finem*]. Once this principle has been destroyed, it cannot be restored by any resource within the soul itself, but . . . by the power of God alone."

Essentially, (mortal) sin is a turning away from God. God has directed all things toward him, but human beings have the freedom to turn away from their goal. Seeing that God inclines all things toward himself, sin is a departure from the order which is to God as the end: "Sin is by definition a withdrawal from the order of things which has God as its purpose. For his part, God inclines all things and draws them to himself, according to Dionysius."[23] If sin is essentially a turning away from God and at odds with our most fundamental orientation, salvation will have to be seen as a restoration of the divine order in which the human will is once again turned toward its ultimate end, i.e., a loving relationship between humanity and God will have to be restored. If this is a correct presentation of Aquinas' thought, we should resist interpreting the notion of "restoration of the divine order" in merely judicial terms.

Another way of approaching the same idea (namely, that by sinning we lose our fundamental orientation toward, and participation in, God) is by focusing on the role of the theological virtues in this life. The total human person is affected by the disorder which is sin: through the loss of God's grace, as the result of sin, the human being loses her central focus and sense of direction.[24] (Mortal) sin damages the order of our will to God at its root, i.e., the unity with our ultimate goal set up by the love of charity.[25] Although imperfect happiness can be attained through virtuous behavior, perfect happiness consists in the vision of the divine essence.[26] Obviously, since this vision surpasses our natural capacity and cannot be perfectly attained in this life, we need theological virtues (analogous to the intellectual and moral virtues), which direct us toward God and which are infused by God, namely, faith, hope, and charity. Faith relates to the intellect, and hope and charity relate to the will: hope makes us tend toward God, while charity refers to a kind of spiritual union of the human will and God.[27] Charity refers not only to love of God but also to a certain friendship with him, which implies reciprocity and communion.[28] This communion or fellowship with God is begun in this life by grace and will be perfected in the future life by glory. Indeed, through faith and charity we inchoatively participate in the trinitarian processions of intellect and will.[29] Charity is the first of all virtues;[30] it unites us immediately with our supernatural goal and is therefore the root and form of all virtues.[31] Through our incorporation in Christ we will be able to share in his charity, which allows us to reestablish fellowship with God in whom our perfect happiness is to be found.[32] Aquinas goes as far as drawing a parallel between our union with God through faith and charity and the hypostatic union of the divine and human natures in Christ.[33] In short, through (mortal) sin we lose the gift of charity which is the principle of our friendship with God. Through our participation in Christ's redemptive work, this friendship with God will be restored.

All human beings are directed toward God, but through sinning we lose this sense of direction; we still pursue what we consider to be good, but we are mistaken in assessing what constitutes this goodness. We take creaturely goods as our ultimate goal. It is not that love for creatures and love for God are incompatible; on the contrary, love for God results in love for creatures. However, a love for creatures which is not also a love for God is a form of idolatry. This leads to the question of how sin relates to God's providential ordering: if sin is a turning away from God, then it might seem that it falls outside the scope of God's providence which directs all things toward him. However, Aquinas argues, perhaps somewhat unconvincingly, that this is not the case: "Because it is the universal cause of all things, God's will cannot but achieve its effect. So whatever seems to depart from his will from one point of view returns to it from another. Thus a man who in so far as he can abandons the divine will by sinning nevertheless re-enters its plan when by divine justice he is punished."[34] In other words, although the sinner acts against God's antecedent or absolute will, his acts do not fall outside the scope of God's providence. In this sense, evil suffered becomes theologically relevant. It is important to develop this argument in more detail. In the passage just quoted, Aquinas seems to link sin and punishment. It is bad enough to suffer; however, if the theologian explains suffering in terms of a punishment for sin, he seems to even further victimize the sufferer. Does Aquinas really teach that sufferings are a punishment for sin?

Punishment, Sin, and Suffering

Throughout his works Aquinas suggests that there is a connection between our afflictions and bodily defects (including illness and death), on the one hand, and (original) sin, on the other.[35] Many texts appear to suggest that he regards it as part of the teaching of the Catholic Church that what we call "natural evil" is a punishment from God. This view seems problematic for a number of reasons. First, the claim that "evil suffered" is a punishment for (original) sin seems to entail a traditional understanding of original sin and its transmission—a view in need of some reinterpretation, to put it mildly. Second, as suggested earlier, calling afflictions "punishments" seems to victimize the victims even further. Third, it seems to make the problem of theodicy totally unsolvable: does not God subject his mercy to his justice? Also, is the immensity of suffering not such that the "punishments" are totally out of proportion and suggest a God who is cruel rather than kind?

I hope to demonstrate that, despite appearances to the contrary, Aquinas does not teach that all afflictions are penal. Having said that, it cannot be denied that for Aquinas there is a close connection between sin and affliction, between evil and punishment. Ironically, while nowadays people are more inclined to accept misfortunes (such as an earthquake, or AIDS) in a matter-of-fact way— since attributing them to God seems at odds with God's goodness in his dealings with people—Aquinas uses this very same argument to defend the view that they are not merely "bad luck" but part of God's providential plan: given the goodness of God and the dignity of humanity it is impossible, Aquinas reasons, that bad things "just happen": all fall within the scope of God's providence.[36] If the link between sin and punishment were absent, and given the fact that all events are part of God's providence, God could indeed be rightly accused of cruelty.[37]

Also, the fact that sins are punished—here or in the afterlife—does not imply that God's mercy is subject to an external law of justice. The opposite is the case: the order according to which sin is punished and goodness is rewarded is a manifestation of God's goodness and justice.[38] It simply means that the hope that evil will not have the last word is not futile—a perspective that has acquired a new significance in the light of suffering witnessed in the last century. Moreover, Aquinas could make the argument that human society punishes its transgressors, too. This line of reasoning carries some weight, not because God is behaving in the same manner as humans do, but because human justice is part of God's providence: it is correct to say that human punishment can function as the way God punishes the sinner.[39]

Finally, it is important to examine how Aquinas views the nature and the purpose of punishment. With regard to the nature of punishment, Aquinas considers that the gravest punishment—namely, an evil contrary to the human will— is to be cut off from beatitude or divine enjoyment; next in order of severity is the deprivation of virtue; then disorder of the natural powers of the soul; next, bodily injury; and finally, the loss of exterior goods.[40] Aquinas is well aware that most sinners would reverse this order—which just goes to show that they, being sinners, do not get their priorities right! Given this hierarchy, the loss of exterior goods may actually be a blessing in disguise in the case of a good person (for instance, when she is becoming too consumerist), even though it retains its penal character insofar as it goes against her will, while the enjoyment of wealth by an evil person obviously does not mean that he is being favored by God.[41] All of this goes some way in qualifying—and making somewhat more plausible, if not more tolerable—Aquinas' seemingly harsh statements concerning the relation between evil and suffering.

With regard to the purpose of punishment, Aquinas distinguishes between two closely related aspects. First, punishment for sin can be remedial: punishment is a means of healing the disorder that is sin. Thus, punishment of sin can have a medicinal character (which, given the description of sin in terms of disease, should not surprise us),[42] although not necessarily: afflictions and loss of temporal goods might have the opposite effect, by enticing the sinner to move even further away from God. Second, punishment restores the right order violated by sin. It safeguards God's justice in the world: evil will not have the last word.[43] Whereas Anselm emphasized the second aspect,[44] Aquinas puts the emphasis firmly on the first aspect, and he understands the second aspect in terms of the first, as is clear from the following passage:

> Punishment is inflicted as a medicine that is corrective of the sin and also to restore right order violated by the sin. Punishment functions as a medicine inasmuch as fear of punishment deters a man from sinning; that is, a person refrains from performing an inordinate action, which would be pleasing to his will, lest he have to suffer what is opposed to his will. Punishment also restores the right order. By sinning, a man exceeds the limits of the natural order, indulging his will more than is right. Hence a return to the order of justice is effected by punishment, whereby some good is withdrawn from the sinner's will.[45]

The order of justice is restored when the will is redirected to God: clearly, the medicinal aspect shapes the restorative aspect. This is in line with Aquinas' understanding of sin as a sickness of the soul and with the theological psychology outlined earlier. Once more, it alerts us to refrain from interpreting Aquinas' soteriology in judicial terms.

These arguments go some way toward clarifying the close link in Aquinas between sin and punishment, and between affliction and evil. Nevertheless, afflictions often befall good people. Aquinas is aware that there is not necessarily a link between suffering and sin. He explicitly teaches that temporal misfortunes, such as the loss of external goods or even bodily goods, are not necessarily punishments for personal sin.[46] This is the main theme of his *Commentary on Job*. Here Aquinas argues that the view that all afflictions in the present life are caused by past sins is deeply mistaken. If the connection between sin and punishment and between virtuous behavior and reward were as close as some of the previous passages might suggest, our relationship with God would be in danger of becoming a mercenary affair.[47]

When our sufferings function as a way in which the divine glory is revealed in us, they lose their penal character—a view which can only be properly understood in the light of our participation in Christ's sufferings and which goes to the heart of what Aquinas has to say on our redemption in Christ. This explains why God, when allowing afflictions to occur to good people, does so only insofar as they contribute to the persons' ultimate good.[48] In commenting on the man who was born blind (John 9:23), Aquinas argues that misfortunes such as bodily infirmities do not necessarily befall us because of our sins. Aquinas refers to the passage in the *praefatio* V, 12 from *Moralia in Job*, where Gregory the Great had written that God sends afflictions for several reasons, such as the beginning of our punishment for sins; as correction; as prevention from future sins; and as a means for allowing the divine mercy and power to show itself in the one afflicted. Such was the case, Aquinas claims, with Job and the man born blind in John's Gospel.[49] Clearly, not all afflictions are punishments for sin in the proper sense. This important conclusion is further supported by a discussion of the concept of satisfaction.[50]

Satisfaction

The notion of satisfaction occupied a major role in Anselm's treatise *Cur Deus homo*, although it actually has patristic roots.[51] In the twentieth century Anselm's theory has been severely criticized, usually for the wrong reasons. It has been alleged that it entails a transactional, legalistic view of God; that it evokes the specter of a vindictive Father who demands the sacrifice of his Son; that Anselm's God would be guilty of subjecting his mercy to his justice; and so forth.[52] I will deal with some of this criticism, albeit in a rather summary fashion, because Aquinas adopts the notion of satisfaction and seems to develop an argument similar to that of Anselm, as the following passage suggests:

> The tradition of the Church, moreover, teaches us that the whole human race was infected by sin. But the order of divine justice—as is clear from the foregoing [*ScG* III.158]—requires that God should not remit sin without

satisfaction. But to satisfy for the sin of the whole human race was beyond the power of any pure man, because any pure man is something less than the whole of the human race in its entirety. Therefore, in order to free the human race from its common sin, someone had to satisfy who was both man and so proportioned to the satisfaction, and something above man that the merit might be enough to satisfy for the sin of the whole human race. . . . Therefore, it was necessary for man's achievement of beatitude that God should become man to take away the sin of the human race.[53]

Since popular misrepresentations of Anselm's thought are bound to affect one's appreciation of Aquinas' soteriology, a few words on *Cur Deus homo* are not out of place.

The popular critique that the justice of Anselm's God overrides his mercy shows a disturbing lack of firsthand knowledge of Anselm's text. Anselm explicitly states that one of the main purposes of his work is to show how divine justice and mercy are harmonized in the cross of Christ.[54] Justice requires that evil will not prevail and will be penalized; however, the "satisfaction" Christ effects through his obedience and love, as displayed in his passion, renders "punishment" unnecessary. Whereas "satisfaction" is popularly misunderstood in terms of meeting the demands of vindictive justice (Christ is being punished on our behalf), for Anselm satisfaction rules out punishment: *aut poena aut satisfactio*. In short, Anselm's view on the relation between satisfaction and punishment implies a critique of the popular misinterpretations of his theory.

This is not to say that Anselm's theory is devoid of weaknesses, or even inconsistencies,[55] and Aquinas will make some significant qualifications when adopting the notion of satisfaction. For instance, he develops the link between Christ's redemptive activity and our participation in it in much greater depth by espousing the Pauline notion of the Body of Christ. Aquinas also takes the edge off the Anselmic "necessity" of the incarnation, and, finally, he links his understanding of Christ's soteriological activity to the theological psychology expounded earlier.[56] As we have seen, sin affects the whole human person; it creates a disorder in the soul as the human will turns away from God toward creaturely things. In *ScG* III.158 Aquinas, relying on this theological psychology, explains how, having received grace, we are freed from sin by an opposite movement of the will:

because man is chiefly directed toward the ultimate end, and also turned away from it, through his will, it is not only necessary for man to abandon sin in the external act, but also to renounce it in his will, for the purpose of rising again from sin. Now, man renounces sin in his will provided he repents his past sin and forms the intention of avoiding it in the future. . . . the movement whereby one moves away from something is contrary to the movement whereby one approaches it; thus whitening is contrary to blackening. Consequently, the will must abandon sin by moving in a contrary direction from those movements whereby it was inclined toward sin. Now, it was inclined toward sin by appetition and enjoyment in regard to lower things. Therefore, it must move away from sin by means of certain penances whereby it suffers some injury because of the sin that it has committed. For, just as the will was drawn toward consent to the sin by means of pleasure, so it is strengthened in the detestation of sin by means of penances.[57]

The will must be turned away from seeking its ultimate enjoyment in lower things (such as money, honor, food) and toward God as its ultimate goal. Note, however, that this does not entitle us to grace or forgiveness. The opposite is the case: having received grace in Christ, we are in a position to make satisfaction or to be purified.[58]

Clearly, Aquinas, like Anselm, understands satisfaction in terms of purification and penance, and he shares Anselm's view that satisfaction excludes punishment. The main difference with respect to punishment is that the person who makes satisfaction to God freely submits herself to penance so as to renounce sin in her will.[59] Therefore, whether afflictions are actually "punishments" depends on the attitude of the person who is subject to it—another indication that the connection between "evil suffered" and "punishment" is not as strict as some of Aquinas' texts might at first lead us to believe. If we accept afflictions about which we ourselves cannot do anything,[60] they lose their penal character and acquire instead a "satisfactory" character.[61] The purpose of both punishment and penance is purifying the sinner and restoring the "right order," which means that God (and not any creaturely idols) should be our ultimate concern, or our enjoyment or fruition, as Aquinas puts it in Augustinian fashion.[62] Hence, Aquinas states that punishment and penance can be dispensed with if we have sufficient love for God, for it is through charity that we are oriented toward God. This illustrates, once more, that "punishments" are not inflicted by God for their own sake, "as if God delighted in them," but for something else, namely, redirecting creatures toward their true goal. It is this that Aquinas has in mind when he talks of the right order of the universe.[63] God is not subject to an external law; he only wants his own goodness and the fulfillment of his creatures in him.

There is a second difference between satisfaction and punishment. Whereas punishments are always personal (if Tom sins, Tom is the one to be punished), somebody else can "satisfy" for another if the two are united in love. Quoting Aristotle that "things we can accomplish through the efforts of our friends we seem to do ourselves," Aquinas states that, just as a person can make satisfaction to God by himself, he can also do it through another person: "the love of charity in the person who suffers for a friend makes his satisfaction more acceptable to God than if he suffered for himself, for in the one case it is prompted by charity; in the other, by necessity. It may be taken from this that one person can make satisfaction for another provided both abide in charity."[64] This teaching could be easily misconstrued in terms of penal substitution—a widespread practice throughout the Middle Ages (and a very profitable one for the Catholic Church).[65] However, Aquinas' point is clearly Christocentric in inspiration.

The merit of Christ's satisfaction is derived from his love and obedience.[66] Through identification with Christ's redemptive work and by sharing in his charity, we become utterly transformed and become part of him, and vice versa. This idea of incorporation in Christ—becoming part of the Body of Christ— is crucial to preclude a misunderstanding of Aquinas' soteriology in transactional or even substitutional terms. I therefore strongly disagree with Gerald O'Collins' statement that Aquinas contributed to "a monstrous version of redemption: Christ as the penal substitute propitiating the divine anger."[67] Participation in the strong sense, as Aquinas advocates here, excludes substitution: because Christ and his Church form as it were one single mystical person (*quasi una persona mystica*), Christ's satisfaction extends to all the faithful as to his members.[68] Aquinas develops this idea of participation in a number of ways: we can share in Christ's roles of priest, king, and prophet by sharing in his sacrifice, by freedom from the bondage of sin, and by receiving the Holy Spirit, respectively.[69] I have suggested that Aquinas grounds this soteriology in a "psychological" manner, describing in medicinal terms the effects of sin and the remedy offered in Christ.[70]

Through our incorporation in Christ through faith and charity, we begin to share in the trinitarian life—the processions of the Word and Love. In *ScG* IV.54.4 Aquinas explains that in faith (which relates to our intellect and knowledge) we obtain a certain foretaste of the vision of God. Christ revealed this knowledge, which is not a body of propositions but an inchoative participation in the divine life.[71] Similarly, in *ScG* IV.54.5 Aquinas explains that the human will had to be disposed toward a desire for the enjoyment of the divinity. God's movement of love toward us in Christ elicits a corresponding response from us to love him in return: "nothing, of course, so induces us to love one as the experience of his love for us."[72] God demonstrated his love for us (and thereby elicited ours) by wanting to be united to humanity in person, for it is typical of love to unite the lover with the beloved as far as possible.[73] Thus, through Christ we begin to share in the trinitarian processions of intellect and will.

Aquinas describes the death of Christ as a universal cause of salvation, parallel to the sin of the first man, the universal cause of damnation. Nevertheless, this remedy still needs to be applied individually: "the effect of the death of Christ comes to each one in a spiritual regeneration in which the man is somehow conjoined with Christ and incorporated into him."[74]

Through our incorporation in Christ our sufferings may acquire a "satisfactory" value. Indeed, when dealing with the objection that it appears odd to claim that Christ saved us, if death and the other penalties for sin are still with us,[75] Aquinas makes some points of considerable significance for a proper understanding of his soteriology. He points out that it is fitting that the afflictions (*poenalitates*) remain even when the fault is taken away because, among other reasons, the misfortunes and sufferings allow us to achieve conformity to Christ as members to the head: "hence, just as Christ bore many sufferings, and thus arrived at the glory of immortality, it was also becoming to his faithful to undergo sufferings and so to arrive at immortality, bearing in themselves, so to say, the marks of the passion of Christ [*quasi portantes in seipsis insignia passionis Christi*], in order to achieve a likeness to his glory."[76] It is not surprising that Aquinas refers in this context to Romans 8:17. Indeed, this teaching is thoroughly Pauline, even according to its most recent interpretations: Paul's view is that Christ did not die in the place of others that they escape death; rather, Christ's sharing their death makes it possible for them to participate in Christ's life and death.[77] Ultimately, Aquinas shares this view.[78]

In summary, satisfaction does not refer to a legalistic transaction. Christ's death, which functions as a sign of his utter humility and obedience,[79] atones (*satisfacit*) because of the charity in which he bore it. This "satisfaction" changes us (and our relationship with God), not God as such.[80] Seeing that sin is a turning away from God, through our incorporation in Christ we begin to share in the divine life through faith and charity. In this sense Christ can be said to take away the sins of the world. Although God could have forgiven sins without "satisfaction," this would have been less fitting, for in satisfying we are allowed to put matters right with God. Through Christ, humanity regains the confidence to approach God.[81] In other words, although salvation is from God alone, through Christ's satisfaction we begin to participate in God's redeeming work: satisfaction is an inchoative participation in our abiding with God.

This interpretation of Aquinas' soteriology gains further support from his analysis of the death of Christ as sacrifice. This notion of sacrifice receives an emphasis and attention in *ST* it did not enjoy in the *ScG*. Perhaps Aquinas' growing personalist perspective explains why "satisfaction" (which was still the most important category governing Aquinas' exposition of the salvific activity of Christ in the *ScG*) becomes in the *ST* merely one among several categories, such as "sacrifice," "reconciliation," and "redemption,"[82] aimed at denoting Christ's salvific work and our participation in it. Or perhaps this emphasis on sacrifice needs to be seen in the light of Aquinas' more profound engagement with scripture during the later years of his life: unlike "satisfaction," "sacrifice" is a truly scriptural notion.

Sacrifice and Sacrament

In *Comp. Theol.* 228 Aquinas raises the question why Christ willed to suffer death on the cross. He enumerates three reasons. First, Christ's death was a salutary means of satisfaction—a topic we discussed at length in the previous part. Second, Christ's death on the cross acted as a sacrament of salvation—in dying, Christ made clear that we, too, ought to die to our carnal life and be transferred to a spiritual life. Third, Christ's death was an example of perfect virtue. In this section I will deal with the second of these aspects: Christ's death as sacrament and sacrifice. As will become clear, the two notions are closely linked.

Drawing on Book X of Augustine's *De civitate Dei*, Aquinas makes the point that what matters most is not the external sacrifice, but rather the internal spiritual sacrifice of the soul: always referring in this context to Psalm 50:19, Aquinas states that the external sacrifice represents the interior spiritual sacrifice, whereby the soul offers itself to God.[83] Thus, "every work performed for the purpose of being united to God in holy fellowship" can be considered a sacrifice. This is a highly attractive view, for it suggests that all the activities of the Christian (and not just the ones performed in a liturgical setting) assume a character of a sacrifice if they are being done in order that we may cling to God in holy fellowship.[84] Similarly, it suggests a close link between Christ's self-gift on the cross[85] and the gift of self of every Christian. In short, Christ's sacrifice functions as the source and model of the spiritual sacrifice of the Christian. Interestingly, Aquinas deploys a "hierarchy" of signification: the sacrifices of the Old Law refer to (and draw their salvific efficacy from) Christ's sacrifice on the cross, which, in turn, is nothing but a visible sign of the invisible sacrifice of his obedience and love; and it is in this sacrifice that the Church can share.[86]

When commenting on Romans 12:1–2, Aquinas describes in detail how believers can share in Christ's sacrifice. Using a threefold division derived from Aristotle's *Nicomachean Ethics* (1098b12), Aquinas argues that our soul, body, and external goods should become an offering to God. The sacrifice of our external goods refers to giving alms. We offer our bodies when we expose them to suffering and death for God's sake, and by engaging in acts of justice and worship. Finally, we offer our souls to God when we refrain from conforming to the ways of the world and are radically focused on God.[87] This perspective on the sacrifice of Christ and our participation therein corroborates our interpretation of satisfaction in the previous sections; it is also in deep harmony with the more personalist soteriological views Aquinas increasingly developed throughout his career.

I suggested earlier that there is a close link between sacrifice and sacrament. This link is evident in the sacrament of the Eucharist,[88] but, given the fairly general nature of the notions of "sacrifice" and "sacrament," it also has a more general application. In *ST* III.48.3 ad 2 Aquinas argues that Christ's passion, although signified by other figurative sacrifices (under the Old Law), is itself a proper sign (or sacrament) of some reality which we ought to observe (*signum alicujus rei observandae a nobis*). This reality refers to our willingness to suffer with Christ and to be intent upon God.[89] Therefore, Christ's passion is the sacrament of our salvation. However, it is not just Christ's passion that functions in a sacramental manner. A sacrament is a sign of a sacred reality (*sacrae rei signum*) inasmuch as it has the property of sanctifying men.[90] In this general sense, the whole life, death, and resurrection of Christ acquire sacramental status: they signify our salvation in him. Conversely, the sacraments in the strict sense are signs of the salvific efficacy of Christ's redeeming work. (This point is developed in Liam Walsh's contribution to this volume.) To explain the first point, namely, how the life, death, and resurrection of Christ act as a sacrament of our salvation, we must examine Aquinas' description of the manner in which God effects our salvation through Christ's humanity, which is described as the instrument of the divinity.

Aquinas' claim that the humanity of Christ is the instrument of the divinity may at first suggest that he does not give the human nature of Christ its due weight, but he explicitly denies this:[91] "the human nature has its proper operation, distinct from the divine, and vice versa. Yet at the same time the divine nature employs the operation of the human nature as the operation of an instrument; and in the same way the human nature participates in the operation of the divine nature, as an instrument shares in the operation of its user."[92] God was acting in Christ (and therefore all the activities of Jesus of Nazareth draw their salvific efficacy from God acting in him) without, however, abolishing the specific human character of Christ's activity in the world. On the contrary, insofar as Christ's humanity is an instrument of the divinity, it actualizes Christ's human potential to share in the life of the Trinity.[93] In short, in Christ the human and divine natures and operations retain their distinct character, although they concur inasmuch as one nature acts in union with the other. Aquinas gives the example of a leper who is being touched (a human act) and healed (a divine act) by Christ.[94] Given this relation between the divine and human natures and their operations, how then does Christ's humanity (and his passion in particular) bring about our salvation? Since Christ's humanity is the instrument of his divinity, all of Christ's acts and sufferings work instrumentally in virtue of his divinity in bringing about our salvation. Thus, in the humanity of Christ we encounter God.[95] This explains the salvific efficacy of Christ's body, both historically (for example, in his healings) and in the Eucharist—a connection Aquinas explicitly draws in *In Ioh.* 6:52.[96] It also explains how Christ's resurrection can function both as the cause of our spiritual resurrection (justification) and our bodily resurrection.

Indeed, through our incorporation in Christ in faith and love, Christ's death functions as the sign (sacrament) of our death to sin (which especially takes place in baptism), while his resurrection functions as a sacrament of our life in God.[97] Through Christ's death we die to sin and through his resurrection we attain life in God. As Aquinas puts it when commenting on Romans 4:25:

> as the humanity of Christ was so to speak the instrument of his divinity, as John Damascene says, all the sufferings and works of the humanity of Christ have salvific value for us, as they are derived from his divine power. But because the effect resembles the cause, the Apostle says that the death of Christ, by which his mortal life has been extinguished, is the cause of the extinction of our sins; and similarly, the resurrection by which Christ came to new life, is the cause of our justification, by which we come to a renewal of justice.[98]

This text and the parallel text in *ST* III.56.1 and 2 are remarkable, since they attribute an exemplary and instrumental causality to Christ's resurrection. It is therefore untenable to claim that Aquinas does not have a theology of the resurrection.[99] Thus, just as the passion of Christ in an exemplary manner causes the remission of our faults (for we die to sin), the resurrection causes our justification.[100]

The resurrection is not merely the exemplary cause but also the efficient cause of our resurrection: "just as all the other things which Christ in his humanity accomplished or suffered for us are saving acts through the power of his divinity, so too the resurrection is the efficient cause of ours through the same divine power whose proper effect it is to raise the dead."[101] Christ's resurrection operates as efficient cause through the power of God that extends to all places and times. Since Christ's humanity is the instrument of the divinity, his flesh is "vivifying" both in the Eucharist and in the resurrection.[102] Of course, Aquinas' claim that the resurrection acts as the efficient cause of ours through the divine power should not be understood in crude physical terms. As Torrell points out, "it is not a case of 'corporeal' but of 'spiritual' contact, through the efficacy of the *virtus divinitatis.*"[103]

In summary, whereas in the *ScG* Aquinas focused on the notion of satisfaction to explain Christ's salvific activity, in the *ST* he places an equal emphasis on a number of other categories, such as merit, redemption, and sacrifice. The notion of sacrifice, understood in an Augustinian sense as sign (or sacrament) of an inner sacrifice, allows Aquinas to further develop the idea of our participation in Christ's salvific work—an emphasis already present in earlier works. I have indicated the different ways Aquinas describes this incorporation in Christ's sacrifice. The central notion of our incorporation in Christ makes clear how Christ's death and resurrection can function as a "sacrament" of our death to sin and of our spiritual rebirth (justification), respectively. Aquinas strengthens this notion of the sacramental value of Christ's life, death, and resurrection by adopting John Damascene's notion that Christ's humanity is the instrument of his divinity. This, in turn, allows him to develop a highly original theology of the resurrection.

Conclusion

Major theologians of the thirteenth century, such as Bonaventure and Aquinas, managed to uphold a synthesis between theological insights and spirituality (or mystical theology, as they would have preferred to call it)—a synthesis that soon withered away, to the impoverishment of both disciplines.[104] This general background should alert us to the fact that Aquinas' soteriology is more than a "theory" of salvation. Given the centrality of the idea of our incorporation into the Mystical Body of Christ,[105] we should refrain from reducing his soteriology to a "theory" of salvation; and we certainly should not construe it in transactional or legalistic terms. Christ's satisfaction on the cross is not aimed at appeasing the paternal wrath of a vindictive God (a "blood-myth," in the words of Schillebeeckx); its salvific value is derived from his charity and obedience, in which we are called to share. Thus, Christ's satisfaction and sacrifice should not be understood in isolation from our participation in them, and vice versa: our sacrifices and penances only acquire their meaning in the light of those of Christ—which suggests that the tidy scholarly distinction between "objective" and "subjective" theories of salvation is totally inapplicable to Aquinas' soteriology. In short, interpreting Aquinas' central soteriological categories in terms of meeting the demands of a vindictive justice or even in terms of substitutional penance is misplaced: as I argued, satisfaction excludes punishment, and the emphasis upon participation in Christ excludes substitution. Aquinas describes sin in terms of a sickness of the soul whereby the sinner loses her proper focus in life; our incorporation in Christ through faith and charity radically transforms us, heals the soul, and allows us to begin to share in the trinitarian life.

Although my primary aim was to expound Aquinas' teaching, a secondary aim was to show that, given our modern concerns, an engagement with Aquinas' soteriology remains a meaningful enterprise. Aquinas argues that because Christ's humanity is the instrument of his divinity, every aspect of Christ's life, death, and resurrection acquires salvific value for us, and every aspect of Christ's humanity has sacramental meaning. He also shows us that we can attribute salvific significance to the death of Christ without espousing a problematic concept of God or glorifying innocent suffering. Christ's death, itself a most horrible crime, becomes a means of salvation in accordance with God's providential plan. Insofar as we share in it and allow ourselves to be changed, it takes away the sins of the world. Given the close connection between sin and suffering in Aquinas' thought, it is not surprising that Christ's death also suggests to us a way to deal with suffering, namely, by treating our suffering as an instrument to become more Christlike. This is not to deny the crushing reality of afflictions, nor to explain them,[106] and even less to justify them. It is merely a pointer as to how to deal with them in Christ. Simone Weil wrote near the end of her brief life: "The extreme greatness of Christianity lies in the fact that it does not seek a supernatural remedy for suffering but a supernatural use for it."[107] Aquinas would agree.

Notes

1. Perhaps this is the reason why relatively little is being published on Aquinas' soteriology. In English, see R. Cessario's study *The Godly Image: Christ and Salvation in Catholic Thought from Anselm to Aquinas* (Petersham, Mass.: St. Bede's Publications, 1990). A helpful recent article is Matthew Levering's "Israel and the Shape of Thomas Aquinas's Soteriology," *The Thomist* 63 (1999): 65–82. In French, see the beautiful work (with extensive bibliography) by J.-P. Torrell, *Le Christ en ses Mystères: La vie et l'oeuvre de Jésus selon saint Thomas d'Aquin*, vol. 2 (Paris: Desclée, 1999). Other works that deal with Aquinas' Christology in general are E. H. Wéber, *Le Christ selon saint Thomas d'Aquin* (Paris: Desclée, 1988); F. Ruello, *La Christologie de Thomas d'Aquin* (Paris: Beauchesne, 1987); and B. Catao, *Salut et Rédemption chez S. Thomas*

d'Aquin (Paris: Desclée, 1965). There are a number of useful articles in recent issues of the *Revue Thomiste* (here, *RT*), such as J.-P. Torrell, "Le sacerdoce du Christ dans la *Somme de théologie*," *RT* 99 (1999): 75–100; G. Remy, "Sacerdoce et médiation chez saint Thomas," *RT* 99 (1999): 101–18; G. Berceville, "Le sacerdoce du Christ dans le Commentaire de l'épître aux Hébreux de saint Thomas d'Aquin," *RT* 99 (1999): 143–58; D. Chardonnens, "Éternité du sacerdoce du Christ et effet eschatologique de l'eucharistie," *RT* 99 (1999): 159–80; G. Emery, "Le sacerdoce spirituel des fidèles chez saint Thomas d'Aquin," *RT* 99 (1999): 211–43; T. D. Humbrecht, "L'eucharistie, 'représentation' du sacrifice du Christ, selon saint Thomas," *RT* 98 (1998): 355–86; J.-P. Torrell, "La causalité salvifique de la resurrection du Christ selon saint Thomas," *RT* 96 (1996): 179–208; J. H. Nicolas, "Le Christ est mort pour nos péchés selon les Écritures," *RT* 96 (1996): 209–34; G. Remy, "Le Christ médiateur dans l'oeuvre de saint Thomas d'Aquin," *RT* 93 (1993): 183–233.

2. E. Schillebeeckx, *Church: The Human Story of God* (London: SCM, 1990), 120. At 125 we find: "Many existing theories of our redemption through Jesus Christ deprive Jesus, his message and career of their subversive power, and even worse, sacralize violence to be a reality within God. God is said to call for a bloody sacrifice which stills or calms his sense of justice."

3. See H. Goris, *Free Creatures of an Eternal God: Thomas Aquinas on God's Infallible Foreknowledge and Irresistible Will* (Leuven: Peeters, 1996). The distinction between A-series and B-series of time is indebted to McTaggart's paper, first published in 1908. The A-series refers to a dynamic or "tensed" view; the B-series refers to the static or "tenseless" view on time.

4. *De Malo* q.6 a.un. ad 3; *ST* I.22.4.

5. See J.-P. Torrell, *Le Christ en ses Mystères*, 310–22.

6. In *De Ver.* q.5 a.5 ad 6, Aquinas gives the example of a man entering a carpenter shop who is puzzled by the "useless" multiplication of tools: only he who knows the trade will see that all these tools exist for a very good reason.

7. For a translation, see *Thomas Aquinas, The Literal Exposition On Job: A Scriptural Exposition concerning Providence*, trans. A. Damico, introduction by M. Yaffe (Atlanta: Scholars Press, 1989), 68.

8. *ScG* III.1; 64; 74; 115.3. Compare *ST* I.22.1c: "ratio ordinis rerum in finem, providentia in Deo nominatur."

9. *ScG* I.75.

10. *ScG* III.71.4; I have used the translation by Vernon Bourke from Saint Thomas Aquinas, *Summa Contra Gentiles, Book Three: Providence*, Part I (Notre Dame, Ind.: University of Notre Dame Press, 1975), 238–39. Moreover, as Aquinas states in *ScG* III.71.6, without evil much good could not materialize. Also, the good of the whole takes precedence over the good of a part (*ScG* III.71.7).

11. *ScG* III.71.10.

12. *ScG* III.73.4.

13. *ScG* III.71.4.

14. *Comp. Theol.* I, 142. Given that redemption is ultimately a restoration of friendship with God (see *ScG* III.95.5; *ST* I.20.2 ad 3), the freedom to respond to, or turn away from, God's call is a necessary precondition of this restoration. Aquinas' notion of satisfaction should be interpreted from this perspective, as I argue throughout this essay.

15. *ST* I.48.5.

16. In *ST* I.22.2 ad 2 we learn that God creates things that are subject to corruption. This is for the sake of the good of the universe: the order of the universe requires that there should be some things that can, and sometimes do, fail.

17. *ST* I.49.2 ad 2.

18. Similarly, "God wills no good more than his own goodness, though with regard to particular goods he wills one more than another. Hence moral evil, which upsets the ordering of things to divine good, he in no way wills. Physical evil or suffering, however, he does will by willing the good to which it is attached. For instance in willing justice he wills penalty, and in willing to maintain the balance of nature he wills that some things should follow their constitutional course and die away" (*ST* I.19.9). God neither wills evils to be nor wills evils not to be; he wills to allow them to happen (*ST* I.19.9 ad 3).

19. Aquinas follows the same order: his description of sin and its effects always precedes that of salvation.

20. In his *In Ioh.* 11:1 and 11:34 (nos.1472 and 1536 in the Marietti edition), Aquinas sees Lazarus as the symbol of the sinner who is resuscitated from the death of sin by the saving power of Christ.

21. The sin against the Spirit is unforgivable, not on God's account but because we contemptuously reject the things that would assist us in withdrawing from sin (*ST* II-II.14.3).

22. *In Ioh.* 5:3, no.706.

23. *ST* I-II.79.1. See also *ScG* III.162.2 and III.143.2.

24. More specifically, the sinner turns from that in which her last end really consists, but she does not turn away from the intention of the last end, which intention she mistakenly seeks in other things (*ST* I-II.1.7 ad 1).

25. *ST* I-II.87.3.

26. *ST* I-II.5.5. Only the universal good can satisfy our longing for happiness: see *ST* I-II.2.8.

27. *ST* I-II.62.1 and 3.

28. *ST* I-II.65.5; *ST* II-II.23.1.

29. *ST* I.38.1; 93.6–8.

30. *ST* I-II.62.4.

31. *ST* II-II.23.8.

32. *ST* I-II.65.5.

33. *In Ioh.* 6:58, no.977.

34. *ST* I.19.6.

35. See *De Malo* q.1 a.4 and q.5 a.4; *ScG* III.141.7; IV.52; *ST* I-II.85.5; *ST* II-II.164.1.

36. *ScG* IV.52.4.

37. *ST* I-II.87.3 ad 3.

38. *ScG* III.158.4.

39. *ST* I.22.3 ad 4: human providence is included under the providence of God. See also *ST* I-II.87.8 ad 2. In *ScG* III.146.2 Aquinas explicitly makes the point I am arguing here.

40. *ScG* III.141.

41. See *ScG* III.141. Absolutely speaking, punishment is not an evil but a good: "the evil of punishment is indeed an evil insofar as it is the privation of some particular good, yet absolutely speaking it is a good, insofar as it is ordained to the last end" (*ST* II-II.19.1).

42. Aquinas defends this idea by referring to Aristotle's *Nicomachean Ethics*. See *Ethics* II, 3 in *ST* I-II.87.6 obj.3.

43. See *ScG* III.140.

44. *Cur Deus homo*, I, 13; II, 4. For a new translation, see Anselm of Canterbury, *The Major Works*, trans. B. Davies and G. R. Evans (Oxford: Oxford University Press, 1998), 260–356.

45. *Comp. Theol.* I, 121. Translation from Thomas Aquinas, *Light of Faith: The Compendium of Theology* (Manchester, N.H.: Sophia Institute Press, 1998), 131–32. Compare *ST* II-II.108.3 ad 2 and 108.4; *ST* I-II.87.6 ad 3 and 87.7; *ScG* III.144.10 and 158.6; *In Ioh.* 9:3, nos.1301–2. The "medicinal" character of sin seems in opposition to the eternal punishment in hell. Aquinas is aware of the difficulty and argues (in *ScG* III.144) that eternal punishments are for the correction of the behavior, not of the sinner himself, but of others.

46. See also *ST* II-II.108.4.

47. *In Iob* 1:10: "it is manifest that the good things which we do are not referred to earthly prosperity as a reward; otherwise it would not be a perverse intention if someone were to serve God because of temporal prosperity. But in the like manner of speaking, temporal adversity is not the proper punishment for sins, and the discussion in the book will generally concern this point." Aquinas also argues that temporal goods are not only extremely precarious but are useless without good souls, while good persons can, even when they temporally suffer, still enjoy some participation in divine wisdom, which is far more valuable (*In Iob* 27:8 ff.; see also *ST* I-II.87.7 ad 2). However, ultimately the problem of suffering cannot be intellectually "determined," as Yaffe argues in his introduction to the English translation, 61–63.

48. *Ad Rom.* 8:28 and 11:11, nos.695–98 and 879; *In Ioh.* 9:3, no.1301; *ST* II-II.108.4.

49. *In Ioh.* 9:3, nos.1301–2.

50. For a thorough examination of the role of "satisfaction" in Aquinas' soteriology, see Cessario, *The Godly Image,* and Nicolas, "Le Christ est mort."

51. *Cur Deus homo* can be translated as "Why did God become Man?" or even "Why the God-Man?" Tertullian used the notion of satisfaction in *De poenitentia,* ch. 5, CCSL 1.328. The title of Tertullian's treatise is significant: "satisfaction" was a crucial aspect of the penitential system of the Catholic Church, which was developing just at that time. See J. Pelikan, *The Christian Tradition: A History of the Development of Doctrine,* vol. 3, *The Growth of Medieval Theology (600–1300)* (Chicago: University of Chicago Press, 1978), 143–45: "'Satisfaction', then, was another term for 'sacrifice.' And Christ's sacrificial act of penance made even human acts of satisfaction worthy, since of themselves they were not." See in this context Boso's second reply in *Cur Deus homo* I, 20.

52. Von Harnack first attacked Anselm's theory and is to this day quoted with approval by modern theologians. See, for instance, H. Kung, *On Being a Christian,* trans. E. Quinn (New York: Image Books, 1984), 423: "this theory of redemption is in fact more or less dominated by a legalistic logic." This sort of critique reveals more about modern commentators than about Anselm's treatise. For a good discussion of Anselm's theory, see D. Bentley Hart, "A Gift Exceeding Every Debt: An Eastern Orthodox Appreciation of Anselm's *Cur Deus Homo,*" in *Pro Ecclesia* 7 (1998): 333–49.

53. *ScG* IV.54.9; translation by Charles O'Neil from Saint Thomas Aquinas, *Summa Contra Gentiles, Book Four: Salvation* (Notre Dame, Ind.: University of Notre Dame Press, 1975), 232.

54. See *Cur Deus homo* II, 20 (summary of the book); I, 6, 12, 25.

55. One of the major weaknesses of *Cur Deus homo* is that Anselm fails to clarify the connection between Christ's satisfactory activity and our participation in it, a feature which has given fuel to misunderstanding his teaching in transactional terms. Moreover, whereas in Book I, 9 and 10, Anselm seems to adhere to a Augustinian understanding of sacrifice—the soteriological significance of Christ's suffering is derived from his obedience and love rather than from his actual suffering—he seems to develop a more problematic reasoning in Book II, 14: here the value of Christ's sacrifice seems to be derived from the value of his Person.

56. It must be said that Anselm's emphasis upon the "necessity" of the incarnation on account of God's goodness (II, 5) is not all that different from Aquinas' argument of fittingness or "convenience."

57. *ScG* III.158.1; translation by Bourke, 257; see also *ST* I-II.87.6.

58. *ScG* III.157.

59. *ScG* III.158.

60. An important qualification: otherwise we might be in danger of tempting God. See *ST* II-II.97.1 ad 3.

61. *ST* I-II.87.6 and 7; *ScG* III.158.5.

62. *ScG* III.145.3: "the man who puts his end among created things does not use them as he should, namely by relating them to his ultimate end."

63. *ScG* III.144.10.

64. *ScG* III.158.7, translation by Bourke, 259; see also *ST* I-II.87.8.

65. See R.W. Southern, *Western Society and the Church in the Middle Ages* (Harmondsworth: Penguin Books, 1990), 225–28.

66. *ScG* IV.55.25–26, translation by O'Neil, 246.

67. See G. O'Collins, *Christology: A Biblical, Historical, and Systematic Study of Jesus* (Oxford: Oxford University Press, 1995), 207. Matthew Levering has made the very same point in "Israel and the Shape of Aquinas's Soteriology," albeit for different reasons. His main argument is that Aquinas' soteriology is unified by his insight into how Christ's passion fulfills the Old Law. I do not deny that this is an important theme, especially in the *ST* and even more so in *In Ioh*. However, Aquinas is perfectly capable of expounding his soteriology without any reference to the Old Law (e.g., in *Comp. Theol.*), and in *ScG* this theme does not receive any major attention either—which suggests that the claims made by Levering, although not incorrect, need to be nuanced. The link Levering sees between the different aspects of the ceremonial precepts and Christ's passion (see 71) is somewhat tenuous. Moreover, for Aquinas the sacrifice of Christ has priority over the sacrifices of the Old Law, which are mere prefigurations; in other words, we need to understand the Old Law in the light of the Christ-event, and not the other way around, as Levering seems to suggest.

68. *ST* III.48.2 ad 1.

69. See Emery, "Le sacerdoce spirituel," especially 218 ff., and the quotation from IV *Sent.* d.13 q.1 art.1 qc.1 ad 1: "Every good person can be called 'priest' in a mystical manner when he offers to God a mystical sacrifice by giving himself to God, that is, 'as a living offering to God.' (Romans 12:1)."

70. Given the fact that moral fault is found primarily in the act of the will (see Aquinas' analysis of moral action in *ScG* III.10), participation in Christ's satisfaction through our own penances results in the reordering of the will toward God. See *ScG* IV.72 for a similar approach to the sacrament of penance, described in terms of "spiritual healing," while Christ is described as the "physician of our souls."

71. *ScG* IV.54.2 and 55.2.

72. See also *ST* III.46.3.

73. *ScG* IV.54.5. Aquinas refers to the Pseudo-Dionysius, *The Divine Names*, IV.

74. *ScG* IV.55.29.

75. *ScG* IV.53.26.

76. *ScG* IV.55.28, translation by Charles O'Neil, 245; compare *ST* I-II.85.5 ad 2: "It is right that we should first of all be conformed to God's sufferings, before attaining to the immortality

and impassibility of glory, which was begun in him, and by him acquired for us. Hence it behooves that our bodies should remain, for a time, subject to suffering, in order that we may merit the impassibility of glory, in conformity with Christ." The other reasons are as follows: if we immediately attained immortality, many would approach Christ for these bodily benefits, rather than for spiritual goods; finally, if those who come to Christ were immediately rendered incapable of suffering and death, this would somehow compel man to accept faith in Christ. See also *ST* III.56.1 ad 1.

77. See J. D. G. Dunn, *The Theology of Paul the Apostle* (Edinburgh: T&T Clark, 1998), 223.

78. For another striking example of a text that illustrates how we should suffer with Christ, see *Ad Rom.* 8:17, no.651, and *ST* III.56.1 ad 1.

79. *ScG* IV.54.20.

80. This is a commonplace in medieval theology, given the idea of the immutability of God. See *ST* III.1.1 ad 1 and *ST* III.49.4 ad 2.

81. *ScG* IV.54.8.

82. *ST* III.48.6 ad 3.

83. See *ST* II-II.85.2. The theological psychology mentioned earlier has bearings on the relation between external and internal sacrifice. Given the fact that human beings rely on the senses to receive knowledge, it is appropriate that we should employ sensible signs in order to signify our devotion and subjection to God (*ST* II-II.85.1; *ScG* III.119). This general principle has obvious Christological implications: Christ's suffering—which is an external representation of his inward spiritual sacrifice—affects our sensible nature (see *ScG* IV.55.7). This idea also provides a rationale for the popular medieval piety of the cross.

84. *ST* II-II.85.3 ad 1.

85. *ST* III.48.3.

86. See Emery, "Le sacerdoce spirituel," especially 229. Other articles in the same volume of *Revue Thomiste* by Chardonnens, Berceville, Remy, and Torrell on the priestly role of Christ are equally helpful (see note 1 above).

87. *Ad Rom.* 12:1–2, nos.957–67. Aquinas develops this idea in several other places. For a more in-depth discussion, see Emery, "Le sacerdoce spirituel," 230–34.

88. See, in the same volume of *Revue Thomiste,* Humbrecht, "L'eucharistie."

89. *ST* III.48.3 ad 2, quoting 1 Peter 4:1 ff. The link between sacrifice and sacrament is inspired by a quotation from Augustine's *De civitate Dei,* X, 5: "sacrificium visibile, invisibilis sacrificii sacramentum, id est, sacrum signum est."

90. *ST* III.60.2.

91. In another passage Aquinas points out that Christ's humanity is not a "passive" instrument but is animated by a rational soul (*ST* III.7.1 ad 3). For a captivating discussion of this notion and its relevance for Aquinas' theology of the resurrection, see Torrell, "La causalité salvifique."

92. *ST* III.19.1 (my translation).

93. Compare *ST* I.93.4 with I.35.2 ad 3 and I.93.3 ad 2.

94. *ST* III.19.1 ad 5.

95. See also *In Ioh.* 6:44, no.936.

96. *In Ioh.* 6:52, no.959.

97. See *Ad Rom.* 6:11, no.491.

98. *Ad Rom.* 4:25, no.380. See also *Comp. Theol.* 239: "Christ's death is the cause of the remission of our sins: the efficient cause instrumentally, the exemplary cause sacramentally, and

the meritorious cause. In like manner Christ's resurrection was also the cause of our resurrection: the efficient cause instrumentally and the exemplary cause sacramentally."

99. See O. Pesch, *Thomas von Aquin: Grenze und Größe mittelalterlicher Theologie* (Mainz: Matthias-Grünewald-Verlag, 1988), 330: "es geriete zu einem etwas krampfhaften Unternehmen, eine 'Theologie der Auferstehung bei Thomas' zu erarbeiten."

100. *ST* III.56.2.

101. *ST* III.56.1 ad 3.

102. *In Ioh.* 6:52, no.959. The parallel is not complete: whereas unbelievers do not receive the benefits of the Eucharist, they do benefit from the resurrection of Christ as the efficient cause of their own. See Torrell, "La causalité salvifique," 198.

103. Torrell, "La causalité salvifique," 201: "il n'y a pas ici de contact 'corporel', mais il y a bien contact 'spirituel', 'virtuel', c'est-à-dire, par l'efficacité de la virtus divinitatis."

104. See the classic study by D. Turner, *The Darkness of God: Negativity in Christian Mysticism* (Cambridge: Cambridge University Press, 1995). See also Mark A. McIntosh, *Mystical Theology: The Integrity of Spirituality and Theology* (Oxford: Blackwell Publishers, 1998).

105. This idea governs Aquinas' soteriology as a whole (especially in his later works), and this should be taken into account when interpreting his key notions, such as "satisfaction" and "sacrifice." See *ST* III.48.1; III.48.2 ad 1; III.49.1; III.49.3 ad 3; *Ad Rom.* 12:4–5, nos.972–75; *In Psalmos* 21:2 ("Christ transforms himself [*transformat se*] in the Church and the Church in Christ").

106. Although, as we have seen, Aquinas links suffering and punishment for sin, this link is—thankfully—not unmitigated, and in this life there remains a surplus of suffering we cannot account for.

107. S. Weil, *Gravity and Grace* (London: Routledge, 1992), 73.

Thirteen

Theology of Church

THOMAS F. O'MEARA, O.P.

Until the twentieth century the theme of the church in the thought of Thomas Aquinas was not much discussed. Then, in the century just ended, the ecclesiologies of medieval theologians began to be studied. The theology of the church—which was related to such topics as ecumenism, episcopal collegiality, an emphasis upon the local church, and the expansion of ministry—became prominent, and the twentieth century was called by some the time of the church. Scholars of a historical and creative bent researched the theology of Aquinas as it touched on the church. Curiously, while in the first half of the twentieth century a neo-scholastic revival and a papal centrism flourished, neither of them in fact drew much from medieval theologies of the church. It was the creative theologians whose thought was preparing for Vatican II who unfolded the ecclesiology of Aquinas, men who were at times personally and intellectually at odds with the exaggerated Pian claims to power for the church, that is, for the papacy.

Aquinas did not compose an ecclesiology: that is, there is no section of the *Summa Theologiae* on church forms. Why? Some answer that society in the thirteenth century saw the church to be mainly the universal church rather than parish or diocese. Others argue that in Aquinas' view the central topics of theology were the great themes of Christian revelation, and ecclesiastical structures are hardly on the same level with the Trinity or Incarnation. Perhaps Aquinas presumed that faith and theology, life and liturgy, are lived against the backdrop of the church,

within a context of the church. Like the great cathedrals, the church was important but secondary: it offered the physical place, the structures of laws and ad-
ministrators, the architecture and art, the array of human forms realizing grace
and voicing its special presence.[1] M.-D. Chenu noted: "It is significant that this
theology (of the church) is not formed into a separate treatise . . . , but develops
totally—both as institution and sacrament—within a theology of Christ and
the Incarnation. The church is the very body of Christ animated by the Spirit
whose organic realities come from its apostolic foundation now under the guidance of the pope. The church is at the same time a body (a corporation in the
sociological sense of the word) and a mystery of Christ living on mystically and
sacramentally."[2] Chenu and a few others found in Aquinas not a treatise but
brief treatments of ecclesial motifs, insights seminal for a theology of the church.
These the following essay pursues.

But first, can we find echoes or traces of a personal ecclesiology in Thomas
Aquinas' life and career? As a young man he left the institutions of the feudal
past: the monastery under the Benedictine rule with its monastic school and patristic and Neoplatonic meditative theology of symbols. Early on he avoided possible ecclesiastical positions like abbot or bishop and resolutely embraced the new
movements of university and friar. He lived amid the medieval city and world
and became the advocate of emerging new forms of ministry in the church seeking to restore the work of Jesus, and his theology clearly stated that some legal
and political forms of the church have human origins and are not of the institution of the twelve apostles. He had intimations that history and biblical origins
modify church offices. Aquinas, however, is not so clear about the identity and
limits of what comes from medieval society and ancient philosophy and what
came from the age of Jesus; a number of ecclesiological aspects are colored by his
medieval focus upon the priesthood of the Eucharist as central and special and
by his regard for Pseudo-Dionysius. Regardless, he chose to live his life amid institutions being born or in flux, and, as we will see, his theology of the church
is one of Spirit rather than of feudal form.

Discovering an Ecclesiology

When he was thirty-five, in 1939, Yves Congar published a remarkable article
on the place of Thomas Aquinas in medieval ecclesiology and in the history of
explicit ecclesiologies composed during the following centuries. "It is true that
on the church St. Thomas wrote no separate treatise, characterized by a study
of the distinctive marks of the church, of its organization in the form of a king-

dom, or of the authority which rules it. But it seems quite clear that St. Thomas has in his works answers to these questions, answers which are compact though scattered."[3] Following upon essays by German historians such as Martin Grabmann and J. R. Geiselmann,[4] Congar pointed out some basic ecclesiological aspects in Aquinas. First, he analyzed Aquinas' use of terms for the church. It is a congregation of the faithful, a people, a social body. Next he noticed the central place of Christ as the head of humanity and the head of the church: from him grace flows to human beings through the sacraments celebrating creation and humanity.[5] Christ not only teaches but bears in himself ontically the economy of saving life moving toward God. Finally, he saw how the psychology of grace in the entire Second Part of the *Summa Theologiae* relates Christians to an active society, to a church. Explicit ecclesiological topics also occur in the treatments of the virtue of faith and the religious states of life and offices within society. Congar found a deeper ecclesiology in Aquinas, one not of laws and offices but of the life of the entire church, of a collective person enjoying the vitality of the Holy Spirit. The Holy Spirit is the soul of the Body of Christ, and the virtues, gifts, charisms, and ministries are its living powers and voices. For Aquinas, "Someone is said to be of Christ not only because that person has faith in Christ but because they move under the influence of the Spirit of Christ to virtuous works."[6] Aquinas commented: "As in a human being there is one soul and body, yet a diversity of members, so the Catholic Church is one body and has different members. The soul vivifying this body is the Holy Spirit. . . . The one who says church says congregation, and the one who says holy church says congregation of believers, and Christian person means member of that church."[7] Members of the church as empowered by the love of God not only believe and hope together but care for each other; the redemption of Christ gives a spiritual anointing of grace to individuals, to all peoples called to be the church.

As the decades passed, other writings by Congar located the church within the economy of salvation.[8] "The church is the ensemble or supernatural unity of spirits, men and women vivified by the grace of Christ, a 'work' or 'effect' of 'grace.'"[9] Aquinas' theology joins a supernatural dynamism to a psychological realism to explain a particular (and universal) corporate identity of men and women. Congar expresses in modern language this theology where the church is ultimately an "absolute of theologal communion."[10]

Jesus Christ, church, and liturgy step forth from a similar pattern, the pattern of divine grace active in human lives. In fact, the church is the background to sacrament, word, grace, and life where the Incarnation continues in history after the Ascension of the risen Christ. The church, for Aquinas, has an inner vitality as well as a public concreteness: "The beauty of the church consists chiefly in an inner life, in inner acts [of grace]. But external activities also belong to this beauty insofar as they proceed from the interior [reality] and carefully preserve its inner beauty."[11] Even while being a visible society with failings and sins, the church furthers the sign and power of God's grace in the world. While Congar found ecclesiological ideas in a few questions of the *Summa Theologiae* devoted to the graced individual, there were also sacramental and social dimensions to the church; it is a kind of city or community with its customs and forms of life. Aquinas described the church as a river of graces in people, an overflow of the fountain that is Christ.[12] The influence of Jesus from birth to resurrection upon the fallen human race gives the church its presence and its service. Because of the presence of God and the dignity of men and women, the church cannot be simply a tribe or a theocracy but is a people of persons and charisms. Congar continues: "The church is both anthropological or moral, and pneumatological or theocentric. The substance of the church is composed of the new life which people receive by the three virtues of faith, hope, and love. This life is driven Godwards, for it has God for its end and the divine life as its determining principles. The church is the whole economy of the return towards God. . . . Its movement and return finds in the Holy Spirit its power and agent, the principle of the divine life which is influencing the dynamic movement towards the objects of the life of God; the soul of the church."[13] The sacramental liturgy exists not to appease an angry deity but to celebrate the power of grace, ecclesial grace in Christians as the Body of Christ.

Sixty years after Congar's essay, Jean-Pierre Torrell's magisterial overview of the medieval Dominican's thought also approaches Aquinas' ecclesiology through the missions of the Trinity ending in the graced gifts of the Christian life. "If the church is not treated in a special way [in the *Summa Theologiae*], it is in reality often present in the movement of the human return to God."[14] There are a few elements of medieval political theory in the *Summa Theologiae*, although the influential lines of thought on the church are biblical and theological motifs rather than juridical principles. Aquinas' commentaries on the Gospel according to Matthew and on the Letter to the Ephesians speak of the church of the Holy Spirit as a college of believers whose head and rector is God, "Our Father." Baptism bears one into the church, where the food is Eucharist and the life is charismatic. Torrell has written an essay on the pastoral theology of Aquinas as it is found in the commentary on the creed; there one finds the church related to the Holy Spirit and not to moral exhortation or apologetics for church leaders.[15] He concludes that seeds from Aquinas' theology bore ecclesiological fruit at Vatican II and notes that the interplay of nature and grace in the Christian is rich in principles and applications for the life of the Christian in the church and in society.[16]

In the thirteenth century canon law was attracting a growing body of interpreters. Some canonists and dutiful bureaucrats of a system of clerical offices wanted to give the church indiscriminate political power and to turn the body of Christ into a machinery of rules. Aquinas refused that direction by making the church the Body of Christ and a people vivified by the Spirit. He occasionally mentioned canonical questions in his systems of theology, but his ecclesiological approach is biblical and theological: the church is a society mainly of grace rather than of law.

Toward Defining *Ecclesia*

Communities large and small are not necessary evils but realize the convivial nature of humanity. The church, like the family, the clan, the city, and the parish, expresses the social nature of men and women who enjoy creating social bonds. Just as human forms of life for men and women lead to societies, the forms of grace too should unfold a community, a kind of city or community with its customs and forms of life. Aquinas began not with buildings or laws or with Jesus' founding words but with the human need for church.

Several metaphors and theological terms, some biblical and some political, describe the church. Aquinas compared states and groups in secular society with "that people called a church,"[17] a people coming from all nations and from all levels of society. He discussed metaphors for the church—ship, ark, spouse of Christ—but he offered his theology in terms like "people," "the congregation of believers," or "the mystical body of Christ."[18] Did this seem unusual to his contemporaries leaving an age of political feudalism and philosophical descending emanation? Congar notes: "The church is basically and first a future community with God in heaven; here on earth a community with God through grace and faith."[19]

The church is unusual: it is not a regional kingdom, not a sacral fortress or a merely human organization. The church is a social reality, a body with, like every living thing, a soul: "a soul is said to be the existence of the activity of an organic body, that is, a body constituted through different organs."[20] In this case the soul, pondered through the lens of the exciting new Aristotelian psychology, is the Holy Spirit. Congar observed: "Because, relative to Christ as its standard, leader and principle, this 'work of grace' merits the name of 'body of Christ,' Thomas conceived the mystical body first simply as a 'society of saints' without including at this level the note of visibility or of hierarchical structure. Finally, in terms of human beings, one can say that the church, at the most basic level, encompasses totally the return to God, *reditus ad Deum*, i.e., the entire Second Part of the *Summa theologiae*."[21] The called gathering (*ecclesia*) is a society, a community where grace lives explicitly and visibly in people. According to M.-D. Chenu, "The church is at the same time a body (a corporation in the sociological sense of the word) and a mystery of Christ living on mystically and sacramentally."[22] If the church is a visible society with institutions, offices, and laws, its forms serve the reign of God on earth in a state of pilgrimage and embattlement. A heavenly community, living already in the eschaton, draws the pilgrim church on earth forward.[23] Now, however, the terrestrial church mixes the good with the bad; it is struggling to be the Spirit's new creation, but its members can pursue misdirected goals and prefer selfish power to holy service. Aquinas observed: "Someone moves away from the unity of the Spirit by seeking to transform the church's good into their own. Just as in the terrestrial state peace is removed by the fact that individual citizens seek their own benefit."[24] As both institution and community, the church strives to be the body of Christ amid human society passing through history.

The church is universal, open to all, made up of many, and diverse in its activities. Aquinas wrote: "The aggregation of believers—they are the church and the house of God—is drawn from diverse kinds of men and women, for instance, from Jews and Greeks, from slaves and free."[25] This congregation drawing from the human race in each culture around the globe is also universal in time: it endures from Abel to the end of the world.[26] It includes potentially all men and women: all who actually respond to grace and revelation, and all remaining in degrees of potentiality to Christ but who will choose evil.[27] Did Aquinas think the visible church and the kingdom of the saved were coterminous? Did he find only sin outside of baptized public membership in the church? Was there no salvation outside the church? No. Five times Aquinas' writings refer in passing to the axiom "*extra ecclesiam nulla salus*," but none of these instances refers to huge populations in which baptism or faith in Christ are absent. Three passages in the *Summa Theologiae* apply that phrase and principle to the Eucharist: "the reality of this sacrament is the unity of the mystical body without which there can be no salvation."[28] A fourth mentions faith, and a fifth censures acts which prompt excommunication. Aquinas interpreted the axiom not as an arbitrary decree about members of other religions (they are never mentioned) but as an ecclesiastical issue touching upon faith and the sacraments. Aquinas' usage of this ancient formula was intra-ecclesial: it censored church members who had separated or were considering separation from unity, and in no citation is any application made to groups outside of Christendom.[29] For those who did not know Christ and would not have received baptism, his theology held the saving portals of implicit faith and baptism by intention. Christ had been known in many centuries and many cultures outside of the preaching of his revelation, known in different ways.[30]

The church is not simply a religious version of a state (Aquinas' employment of "*Christianitas*" is rare).[31] It is not a natural society with a veneer of rituals nor an intimate, active cell of enthusiasts. Thomas had no interest in a solely interior Christianity or in a small sect where the elect congratulate each other. "Congregation" brings notions of breadth and universality, while the phrase "Body of Christ" implies activity and diversity. Drawn from the Pauline letters, the metaphor of body expresses the variety of activities in the members of the church,[32] for actions and ministries compose and display the church's institutional and social organism.

The thirteenth century was partly molded by a Neoplatonic theology of ecclesial authority, namely, hierarchy. In that society the pattern of descending levels of beings or offices molded mysticism, aesthetics, and politics. One philosophical source for the ecclesiology of the Middle Ages was the quasi-mythical Dionysius the Areopagite. For the educated citizens of Paris, the Dionysius converted by Paul on the Areopagus in Athens (Acts 13:33 ff.) found his way to Gallo-Roman Paris, evangelized its citizens, and before he died wrote mystical, philosophical treatises such as *The Divine Names, The Celestial Hierarchy,* and *The Ecclesiastical Hierarchy,* works in fact composed by a Neoplatonist Syrian monk from the sixth century. Because of his Pauline conversion and Parisian ministry, Pseudo-Dionysius' synthesis of Christian and Platonist motifs held a singularly high position in the cultural world of Paris: in the abbey of St. Denis dedicated to him, the royal family was buried and Gothic art began. Congar argues that the Western churches resisted such a dominance of abstract hierarchy until the twelfth century, but that "in the second half of the thirteenth century the texts of Denis [Pseudo-Dionysius] imposed themselves as an authority."[33] The Dionysian thought-form of hierarchy can be seen in the façade of Gothic churches, although these churches' art presented cosmological theories more than political ones, art in which the seasons, zodiac, and nature intimated heavenly hierarchies.[34] Through layers of statues a vertical line ascends, representing in images an elevation from the material to the spiritual. Ministerial and magisterial aspects of the church were constrained by a vertical hierarchy. That hierarchy was also a ladder of descending illuminations where, reflecting an unfortunate metaphysical principle, a higher office and order contains the lower.[35] The higher illumines the lower because such is the pattern coming from the Trinity and the angels. With the angels as analogue and with a Neoplatonic metaphysics of light as model, Aquinas too described the ecclesial hierarchy as a descending illumination: the lower is perfected, illumined, and directed by actions moving downward but not by influences moving upward. When this form and dynamic are applied to the church, office speaks and acts only downward. The community is absent. What could the lower contribute to higher ranks? Service has become authority, authority without constraint from others. A higher office and order contains the lower eminently. What could a lower order contribute to a higher one which possesses all beneath it? Movement upward in illumination or sacred action is impossible because it is redundant. We see here a pyramid of hierarchy replacing a circle of different graced agents.

Life in the Church

For Aquinas life in the church unfolds through the sacraments, through teaching and preaching, through service and governance. Grace is the faithful sharing in the life of the Trinity "by a kind of participation of likeness,"[36] and so Christians are clearly not to be subjected to a theocratic and hierocratic regime like that of the Jewish people of the Bible. Chenu explained why life and organism were prominent in the mid-thirteenth century:

> The Gothic age was involved more and more audaciously in a spirituality of *Incarnation* rather than in one of *the sacred* (so characteristic of Carolingian and Romanesque times). There is a progressive affirmation of the human being, and that affirmation of the human affirms the world. From an idealist universe one passes to a world where the vitality of realistic novels, nature, science, history, and activity finds further forms in the birth of secular art. The encyclopedia, *Mirror of the World*, composed by Thomas' confrère Vincent of Beauvais, adviser and librarian to Louis IX, gives to this vision in its great panels of nature, thought, tradition, and history a significant expression.[37]

Thus life in the Spirit is active incarnationally in liturgy and ministry.

1. Sacramental Liturgy

Through his incarnation Jesus of Nazareth became the cause and the exemplary path of human lives leading toward the eschaton. The effects of Jesus' life continue after his departure from earth, as he offers the Spirit's life through the biblical word and the sacraments to nourish the lives of his followers. There is a line of incarnation reaching from the historical and risen Christ to the community. George Sabra rightly sees the ministers and receivers of the sacraments as living between Christ and the Spirit in the church, for Aquinas speaks of "visible human beings having spiritual power."[38]

Where created material reality meets grace there is incarnation and sacrament. Liturgy is a primary activity of the Christian community, for sacraments deepen, celebrate, and vitalize the graced life of the members. In the thirteenth century sacramental signs and personal ministry were centered in the Eucharist, although other sacraments and liturgical sacramentals shared transitorily in the real presence of Christ's salvation. Aquinas evaluated the signs and activities of a liturgy in a monastery or parish not according to the standards of asceticism or miraculous power but by how well they brought people together with God. Visible and effective sacraments do serve the unseen, for externals express that inner dialogue of Spirit and personality. Liturgy is the source and expression of love, and both liturgy and ministry exist for people whose lives unfold in time. The sacraments are stages of the journey of life toward the fulfilling eschaton. "The sacraments are set up for certain important effects which are necessary in the Christian life."[39] On life's journey we move to the divine future not with steps but by means of our personal actions and lives. There are a number of sacraments, in Aquinas' view, to mark the key moments of life on earth: they fashion a kind of life-cycle of sacraments. "The sacraments of the church have for their purpose to serve a human being's need in the spiritual life. Now the spiritual life runs parallel to that of the body, since bodily things are shadows of spiritual realities."[40]

A society has laws but aims at community, social friendship. The theme of friendship appears at key moments in the *Summa Theologiae*. Christian life is a life not of waiting and misery but of conversation with the Spirit. How rarely it occurs to Christians to link community with friendship. The church, however, is a place where God's Spirit welcomes and meets friends. "Because there is a sharing of God with people according to a communication of God's own happiness to us, a kind of friendship can be grounded in that sharing."[41] God's love for men and women and their response in love bring God and people together because human beings in grace share God's own life. Friendship also gives the deepest reason for the sacrament of real presence, since at the Eucharistic real presence friends meet at a meal. "What is most characteristic of friendship is for friends to be together, and because of this [Christ] has promised us his bodily presence as a [future] reward [Matthew 24:28]. But meanwhile he has not wanted to leave us fully deprived of his corporeal presence during our journey of pilgrimage. So he joins us to himself in this sacrament through the truth of his body and blood. . . . This sacrament is the sign of the greatest love, a support of our hope because of the friendly presence of Christ with us."[42] The church is not primarily a center of control and judgment but a milieu for the many ways in which creatures enact an instrumental causality through liturgy and art. The church's liturgy is not a theater of religious cult but the ordinary worship of the Trinity active in believers. God gives knowing and living, revelation and grace. Although only God is the proper cause of grace—creatures cannot be the controllers (but only the instruments) of grace—the ministers and people of the church are true sacramental causes. "The spiritual physician Christ works in two ways: interiorly through himself as he prepares the human will to will good and hate evil; in another way through ministers externally offering sacraments."[43] Aquinas ponders the mysterious phrase "the foundation of every law lies in the sacraments."[44] So grace from God in people is the source, the active form, and the goal of all that human beings create in religion.

2. Preaching

The community hears the gospel proclaimed and knows the words of everlasting life. A member of the preaching friars, Aquinas labored to reestablish content and vigor in sermons. For the Dominicans preaching and teaching went together, and neither is conceivable without study. Preaching involves theology, since preaching is the communication of the faith through a theological interpretation. The preached words lead to the Word incarnate in Jesus Christ. Word and sacrament support each other. The sacrament of orders deputes some to give the community information about faith. Bishops and preachers are to explain thoroughly and practically the gospel and not to offer only a few phrases from catechisms, creeds, or dogmas. Everyone who preaches should know enough scripture and theology to deal with the issues brought up in daily life, while bishops and theologians ought to be able to present and resolve more difficult topics and problems.[45]

3. Governance

The community has a social order, but, as we have seen, it is an order of an organic body with many activities serving their goals. The bishop's office—which for Aquinas is not clearly an order distinct from the priesthood but is definitely an important office[46]—exists to instruct and to govern the church. Preaching and teaching find a climax in the ministry of the bishop. Explaining and interpreting the gospel, the bishop instructs at a high level, and his teaching office cannot be delegated to others.[47] The highest in the hierarchy of ecclesiastical offices is the bishop; at that ordination (Pseudo-Dionysius had observed) the scriptures are placed over the head of this high priest to show that he receives the fullness of light and that he illumines all. "He who preaches should have what he preaches permanently and integrally."[48] The bishop illumines the people in his local church. Aquinas, however, contrasted the episcopal teaching of the truths of Christianity with rare papal and conciliar texts. Bishops as teachers in the church have a "pastoral teaching office" (*magisterium*), interpreting in an ordinary, pastoral way the gospel in terms of pressing issues. Theologians too have a teaching office, not one of pastoral care and of the preaching of revealed doctrines, but a teaching role given by the academic professorship, a *cathedra magistralis* destined for the explanation of revelation. In the area of important church teaching, the bishops present the basics of Christian faith, although this does not replace theological interpretations needed for new times and new problems. "Some [theological] disputation belongs to the university and has as its goal not to remove errors but to instruct people and to lead them toward an understanding of the truth. It is right for this to use investigative reasons to reach the heart of the truth . . . and not to determine questions by authority alone."[49]

While Aquinas saw bishops receiving areas of their jurisdiction from the bishop of Rome, he did not think that their sacramental power and ministerial identity are derived from the papacy.[50] The bishop's fullness of power in the church seems to include a relationship to the bishop of Rome and to bishops outside his diocese, a kind of collegiality.[51] Ultimately the goal of the episcopal *officium* is to serve the good of the community. "A prelate exists for the church, and not vice-versa."[52] Despite the role of the papacy in the creation and sustenance of the friars, Aquinas did not much develop in his writings a theology of the See of Peter. Apart from two articles, the papacy is not treated formally in the *Summa Theologiae,* and later centuries' questions, precise and difficult, about this ministry are left unmentioned. In the opening question on faith the *Summa Theologiae* discusses how express statements of Christian faith find their public form. The verbal elements, the "articles" of faith, are gathered together to be more easily preached, and this collection is called a *symbolum* or creed. When in time errors arise, there needs to be a new "edition" of the creed, and since the pope is the only permanent entity who has the care of the entire church, it belongs to him to call an ecumenical council or "to determine those things which are of faith."[53] "Just as a later council has the power both of interpreting the creed formulated by an earlier one and of adding certain things, so also the Roman

Pontiff can do this by his authority."[54] The theological context for the discussion of authority here is not the church but the virtue of faith. The papal "determination" (a technical term, meaning to give a high level of ecclesial formulation and advocacy) has a special and universal nature but is not solitary or charismatically miraculous. Determination also involves approval and reception within the church and its councils.[55] The bishop of Rome has an impressive role, but the term "infallible" is not used by Aquinas. In the precise meaning of the word for Aquinas, only God could be *infallibilis:* revelation and the church's teaching about revelation can have a participatory lack of error.[56] Aquinas saw degrees and levels of authorities, sources, and media of revelation. He had a nuanced approach to the interpretation of sacred teaching by witnesses living and dead, for the source of any charism or role in teaching was the Holy Spirit, the inspirer of all truth. The goal of each was to serve one faith among the faithful.[57] Individuals did not act apart from the body, from the church. Ultimately "the universal church cannot err."[58]

Aquinas has severe things to say about Christians seeking church office as a reward for ambition. Ambition drives people who think they have abilities they do not have and who presume they can do something they cannot. Unrealistic ambition is a vice, one opposed to the virtue of magnanimity where personal generosity acts for the reign of God.[59] Ambition desires honor and power apart from the reference of all things to God and pursues ecclesiastical office for personal benefits and not for the common good. "Adults in the faith adhere to God alone . . . ; if they adhere to their prelates it is only because those prelates adhere to Christ."[60] If authoritarian control and ecclesiastical dictatorship were unacceptable to Aquinas, he was also aware that the hierarchy of sanctity and union with Christ does not necessarily correspond to the hierarchy of sacred ministries. Aquinas' theology was not, as in Congar's phrase, "a hierarchology"[61] but a social pneumatology. "In the body of the church the peace among diverse members is sustained by the power of the Holy Spirit who vivifies the body of the church."[62] An equality in grace—the highest power and dignity—comes first. Love is the source and the soul of the church, and love is the community's goal, not display or control. "When someone joins the army of a king, he wears his insignia; the insignia of Christ are the insignia of love."[63]

The Church in Ministry

Do the scattered insights of Aquinas make a contribution to the church's self-understanding today? Unlike the thirteenth century, the century just ended has been an age of ecclesiology, replete with insightful ecclesiologists and varied theologies of the church.

A particularly prominent area today is the expansion of ministry. As Congar saw decades ago—one presumes that his exploration of Aquinas led to his studies on the laity and on tradition—the church is a political organ where Christians are active. Ministry in that body animated by the Spirit is fundamental; the church is active and functional, diverse and universal, even as it is directed by authority amid various enterprises and for particular goals. Aquinas' teaching and writing had once served the expansion of ministry. As Congar observed, "The mendicants were men of a world that was changing."[64] What was ecclesially new in the thirteenth century was not today's restoration of some of the ministries of the first century of the Christian era or the granting of public roles beyond monastic ones to women (there were attempts in the decades before Francis and Dominic, all suppressed, to give women evangelizing ministries of preaching),[65] but rather new forms of a life imitating Jesus and the apostles. Should orders like the Franciscans and Dominicans exist? Do regional groups of men imitating Jesus the preacher have the right to restore forms of poor service, to fashion new forms of ministry in the church? In the Middle Ages, and subsequently in the Baroque church and in the decades before Vatican II, diversity in ministry appeared in the diversity of religious orders and confraternities. Aquinas' theology, however, does contain openings toward the broader interpretation of ministry occuring after 1965. First, his thought on ecclesial states, sacramental orders, and the gifts of the Spirit underscores a diversity in the Body. Second, by noting that some of the treatment of church and ministry belongs to the human polity of canon law ("For the study of offices so far as it pertains to other acts is a matter for jurists; and so far as it pertains to the sacred ministry it is a matter of orders"),[66] he suggested a legitimate re-expression of ministry in diverse cultural forms.

The Pauline theology of the Body of Christ proclaims a diversity of activities and gifts. "Each human being," Aquinas wrote, "has a body and a soul and through them diverse members. So it is with the Catholic church: one body and yet different members; the soul vivifying this body is the Holy Spirit."[67] Life flows not into static being but into various capabilities for acting to a purpose: organs act for goals. As a body the church has a "multitude of people ordered to a goal according to distinct acts and offices."[68] The church is a collective organism owning an inner life with diverse functions. According to Congar, "Life is determined, like all movement, by its objects; for people to live the life of God means having the 'ends' and objects of the life of God."[69] The human image of God is knowing, loving, and being free, and the collective Body of Christ lives by service. Ministers receive a power, a power similar to Christ's power, a power in the realm of the spiritual, a power that is not personal and sacral for them, but functionally ministerial, a power to serve grace. As one would expect from a thinker deeply engaged with Aristotelian natural science, offices have activities and activities have goals. They are not states of honor or locations of divine favor. Neither a hieratic state nor a community of elite charismatics protecting people from history and society, the church exists to preach the Gospel's view of salvation history and to further love among human beings. Aquinas gave three reasons for a diversity of roles in the church.[70] In nature and in political groups diversity visibly assists life and order, and similarly, grace centered in Christ seeks a diversity in the members of the body of Christ. Second, the church needs to have a variety of services to help people. Third, the church displays a beauty through this diversity. Movements, religious orders, mystics, and charismatics are visible representatives of freedom and diversity in the Spirit. Each office, like every being, is teleological. If all ministries point to the Eucharist, it is equally true that every office has its own proper *telos* by which it makes grace accessible and stands at the service of the divine.[71] A charism, an office, a ministry, an ordination—these have their activities and goals in achieving something for the church.

Church and society by the thirteenth century had largely replaced the biblical term *diakonia* (ministry) with Roman legal terms like *officium, status,* and *ordo.* Services outside liturgy were entrusted to religious orders and lay confraternities. The variety of the church's ministries had been reduced; the diaconate had for some centuries existed only in a transitional, liturgical form. Ministry in a public way existed in the priesthood of priest and bishop. The theology of the Christian life at the end of the Second Part of the *Summa Theologiae* treats not ministries but extraordinary charisms, the active and contemplative lives, and a few church offices. Aquinas' psychological theology of the graced individual encourages, however, the ministerial and charismatic contribution of all the baptized and argues that, in terms of nature and grace, people should be selected for church ministries because of their qualifications, qualifications evident in their lives and activities. Authority should be concerned with the individual life of each Christian and with the efficacy of the church, for the true goal of the church is to serve the Christian life.[72] Endowed with virtues and gifts, men and women are baptized to extend the work of the Trinity.[73]

One effect of the sacraments of baptism and confirmation is a spiritual form deputing a man or a woman to Christian worship, called a "character," that is, a lasting capability not only to be but to act. Those sacraments, bestowing a certain participation in the priestly office of Jesus Christ, the redeemer of the world, qualify the person to enter fully and maturely into the liturgy of the church. Ordination to special ministries in the church, for instance, the temporary ceremonial deacon or the priest, builds on this initial baptismal priesthood. Offices cannot be solely positions of ecclesiastical governance or honors because they are to continue the work of Jesus and his Spirit. Everything in the church-as-institution, namely, laws, rites, and even rubrics, is "dispositive to the grace of the Holy Spirit."[74] The new law, the ultimate reality of the Gospel, is the inner divinizing presence of the Spirit, and, as important as they are, created forms, even scripture and Eucharist, serve this primary reality.

Aquinas situated church offices in a dialectic of form and tradition. He can distinguish what is central to God's plan from contingent, historical moments (the plan itself is not necessary but is one *ratio* from a number of ways to relate to humanity).[75] Some ensemble of different ministries has always existed, but church offices, ecclesiastical teachings, and church laws are partly forms structured by human beings. Some arrangements of the structures of the church come not from revelation but from church law; some are of divine tradition, but not a few change with the times and are the results of church law.[76] In the age of the apostles the basic ministries were present, but their names and descriptions were not the same then as those appearing in later ecclesial organization. Aquinas, however, tended to collapse the varied names in the New Testament for ministries into one office, and to find variety in ecclesiastical distinctions between officeholders with canonical rights.[77] But then why did one sacrament of orders have different forms and ordinations (albeit largely extinct outside of monastery and cathedral), like those of subdeacon or acolyte? There is one sacrament of orders, Aquinas responded, but it has seven ordained stages or modes. Orders compose a unity with diversity, a unity that is a particular kind of totality, a "potestative whole."[78] Ordained ministry is a vital totality, an organism from whose life various powers could emerge, which leaves open the issue of whether in theory and practice ministries beyond those of leadership might be different in kind and number from age to age, culture to culture. The rediscovery of deeper meanings and realizations for baptism, ministry, and liturgy was furthered by Congar, Edward Schillebeeckx, J.-M. Tillard, and other scholars who used Thomist principles to explain the recent expansion of church life.

What did Aquinas think of women active in the church? His theology could hardly have transcended the long tradition before him or the medieval social forms in which he lived. But why are women not ordained? He gives no argument from a papal document or a New Testament passage.[79] The fact that the church has not ordained women comes not merely from canon law but from some more serious factor.[80] On the topics of women preaching or being ordained to lead the local church, he did not argue from biblical examples or from maleness in Jesus and his disciples. In the young Dominican's treatise on orders—part of a youthful commentary on the Lombard's *Sentences,* which is reproduced in the supplement of the *Summa Theologiae*—the reason given for excluding women from priesthood and episcopacy is that state of subjection found in the Jewish scriptures: a passage from Genesis argued that after the Fall, women are subject to men.[81] A personal (or religious) subjection given by the Fall apparently brings a social diminishment, for Aquinas also gives an argument from medieval sociology. Mention is made of a lack of "a grade of eminence" necessary for the symbolic aspect of leadership in the ordained.[82] What does this idea that women do not have the signification of being a public figure mean? Aquinas, as a medieval theologian, might have meant that an abbess or a duchess did not appear to her society as a public leader, or he might have been thinking of a theological subjection as in Genesis 3:16.[83] When the question of women preaching arose, Aquinas argued that women can preach to small groups.[84] Although he replied to questions about women as priests and preachers in terms of sociological symbolism or the theological origin of the woman and the cursed subjection, Aquinas also cited Paul in Colossians to support without discussion women baptizing and being sponsors at confirmation as "ministers of Christ."[85] Of course charisms from the grace, the milieu, and the gift of the supernatural order, such as prophecy or mystical experience, are no less accessible to women than to men. So we have a sparse theology on this topic, making few claims on Christian revelation and tradition and located explicitly in a social context.

Conclusion

In the last analysis, Aquinas composed no systematic ecclesiology. Still, some of his theological insights are richer than much of the textbook ecclesiology of the nineteenth and twentieth centuries; he is more dynamic and more person-centered than many Neo-Thomist epigones. Nonetheless, we should not ignore the absence of the ecclesial and the social in the thirteenth century. Aquinas' church is a universal body reaching in all directions in space and time. It is not a parish, an entity to which he devoted little thought and left as a subepiscopal unit.[86] Aquinas lived in a Europe enjoying a new universality. The particularity of individual churches and the differences of regions and rites were not what the cultural moment held up as significant. Dioceses were administrative segments of the one church. The new religious orders were supranational, not subject to local bishops but directed by each order's central administration in Rome. In the church, as in the world of nature, a universal *politique* joins a multitude of regional groups. Congar noted that the new contexts of friar and theology lead to an emphasis on the universal church over a previous monastic and national regionalization.[87] "The Middle Ages are dominated by the idea of unity and ponder issues in the framework of a universe obeying a divine plan. . . . Medieval political or ecclesio-canonical theories have as their context the universal or cosmic world . . . , and it is clear that in ecclesiology that procedure carries the danger of assimilating too quickly the structures of the church to those of nature and losing from sight what is specifically biblical or evangelical."[88] The great cathedrals are places for crowds of pilgrims, for assemblies passively attending sermon or Eucharist, and are not assembly points for ministry. Those were the priories of the friars.

As we have seen, in Aquinas' theology the motifs of Spirit and individuality were never fully captured by a hierarchical and feudal clericalism. Although he related episcopal ordination generally to ideas from Pseudo-Dionysius, Aquinas also defined hierarchy rather broadly as the leadership of one directing an ordered multitude.[89] Congar finds limitations in Aquinas' ecclesiology: the lack of attention to the parish, the meagre theology of the episcopacy, and the tying of ministry too closely to the Mass, that is, by defining the priest principally in terms of the power of Eucharistic consecration.[90] Ultimately, Aquinas' fundamental theology of Christianity, the ground of ecclesiology, was terrestrial, an economy of grace in people. Grace comes according to the receptivity and capability of the personality and according to God's plan for that individual. Commenting on the main portal of Notre Dame in Paris, Alain Erlande-Brandeburg observes: "The annunciation of the end of the world and of the return of Christ is no longer presented as an apocalyptic vision. Here the more humane depiction from the Gospel according to Matthew is basic. . . . Christ appears in the tympanum as redeemer, showing his wounds and surrounded by angels with the instruments of his Passion. The Virgin and John are prominent as intercessors for humanity . . . , and angels watch this dramatic event."[91] Christ is the head of the church, and according to their external roles and inner gifts, all members of the church can share in the communion of goods of the society given by the Spirit; there is a kind of Platonism of the flow of grace.[92] In fact the hierarchical architecture of the facades of church buildings actually held not princes and cardinals in arrangements of superiority, but men and women from the church whose public lives were exemplary. Not feudalism but the salvation history of Bible and grace provided the content of life. Men and women receiving grace give a more horizontal Aristotelian dynamic of the Christians living the ministries of the Body and serving the ecclesial gathering. Thus there was in Aquinas' thought a tension, a dialectic. In terms of an institutional model,

Aquinas retained something of the forms of a pyramidical hierarchy, with cleri-cal offices culminating in the pope, although that ecclesiology was inserted in a deeper theology where missions of Word and Spirit came to and formed a people. The hierarchical was modified by the universality of graced life offered in a col-lective person, and the life of virtues and charisms complemented the reduction of all real ecclesial ministry to the priest. Ultimately, the church was an organic so-ciety of all the baptized whose graced life flowed out into actions serving love.

What can we learn from Aquinas' ecclesiology? Little, if we are looking for a contemporary theology of diocesan offices, but quite a bit if we look beneath and find an ecclesial theology of intimations. Ecclesiology is pneumatology, or so-cial life for the transcendent Spirit loose in the world. When we say in the creed that we believe in the church, Aquinas wrote, this means not that the church is di-vine but that Christians believe in the divine Spirit animating the church.[93]

Notes

1. See G. Sabra, *Thomas Aquinas' Vision of the Church* (Mainz: Matthias-Grünewald-Verlag, 1987), ch. 1. Sabra's book is a rich and insightful overview.

2. M.-D. Chenu, *St. Thomas d'Aquin et la théologie* (Paris: Éditions du Seuil, 1959), 98.

3. Yves Congar, "The Idea of the Church in St. Thomas Aquinas," *The Thomist* 1 (1939): 332; reprinted with revisions in "The Idea of the Church in Thomas Aquinas," *The Mystery of the Church* (Baltimore: Helicon Press, 1960), 53–74. The French version appeared as "L'idée de l'Église chez saint Thomas d'Aquin," *Revue des sciences philosophiques et théologiques* 29 (1940): 31–58. Congar published a Latin version of his ideas in "Traditio thomistica in materia ecclesi-ologica," *Angelicum* 43 (1966): 405–28.

4. J.R. Geiselmann, "Christus und die Kirche nach Thomas von Aquin," *Theologische Quartalschrift* 107 (1926): 198–222; for Martin Grabmann, "The union of grace and humanity sug-gests the church be viewed as a kind of sacrament on 'the plane of grace and divine-theological life'" (*Die Lehre des heiligen Thomas von Aquin von der Kirche als Gotteswerk* [Regensburg: G.J. Manz, 1903], 89 f.). Mannes Dominikus Kloster began his pioneering work with Aquinas' the-ology, *Ekklesiologie im Werden* (Paderborn: Bonifacius-Druckerei, 1940). Reginald Garrigou-Lagrange, mentioning Ambroise Gardeil and Charles Journet, wrote that "throughout the *Summa* we find the lineaments of a treatise on the church." A later apologetic approach, he argued, led to "a disregard for the theological treatment of the inner constitution of the church," while in Aquinas we find the areas of the grace of headship, the mystical body, and faith, and a church of body and vitalizing soul (*Reality: A Synthesis of Thomistic Thought* [St. Louis: Herder, 1950], 267).

5. *ST* III.8.1 and 3; III.69.5.

6. *ST* II-II.124.5 ad 1.

7. *The Sermon-Conferences of St. Thomas Aquinas on the Apostles' Creed*, ed. Nicholas Ayo (Notre Dame, Ind.: University of Notre Dame Press, 1988), 125.

8. A number of Congar's essays on themes and terms in Aquinas' ecclesiology have been collected in *Thomas d'Aquin: Sa vision de théologie et de l'Église* (London: Variorum Reprints, 1984).

9. Yves Congar, *L'Église de saint Augustin à l'époque moderne* (Paris: Éditions du Cerf, 1970), 234.

10. Yves Congar, "Vision de l'Église chez Thomas d'Aquin," *Revue des sciences philosophiques et théologiques* 62 (1978): 525.

11. IV *Sent.* d.15 q.3 art.1 ad 1.

12. *In I Cor.* 12:4, no.721.

13. Congar, "The Idea of the Church in Thomas Aquinas," 339. Jean-Pierre Torrell, mentioning Congar's unfulfilled desire to write an ecclesiology according to Thomas, argues that the medieval Dominican's view of the church is original in its pneumatology and anthropology of grace but not in its Christology, and that through Congar's own work Aquinas' ecclesial directions were influential on the Catholic Church after 1950 ("Yves Congar et l'ecclésiologie de Saint Thomas d'Aquin," *Revue des sciences philosophiques et théologiques* 82 [1998]: 201–42).

14. J.-P. Torrell, *Saint Thomas d'Aquin, maître spirituel. Initiation 2* (Paris: Cerf, 1996), 386; see 392–96.

15. J.-P. Torrell, "La pratique pastorale," *Recherches Thomassiens* (Paris: J. Vrin, 2000), 282–314. Otto Pesch sketches Aquinas' discussion of church as a legal entity and as the realm of the age of grace in *Thomas von Aquin: Grenze und Grösse mittelalterlicher Theologie. Eine Einführung* (Mainz: Matthias-Grünewald-Verlag, 1989), 373–78, while Avery Dulles arranges texts from Aquinas' works into a modern outline of an ecclesiology in "The Church according to Thomas Aquinas," *A Church to Believe In* (New York: Crossroad, 1982), 149–92.

16. A. Bandera compares Aquinas' ecclesiological themes with the documents of Vatican II and with contemporary issues in *Eclesiología histórico-salvífica en la escuela de Tomás de Aquino* (Barcelona: Esin, 1996).

17. IV *Sent.* d.20 q.1 art.4. There are also passages where the social and ministerial structure of the church does resemble that of feudal society, where the bishop is a prince and other ministers derive their powers from him (e.g., IV *Sent.* d.7 q.2 art.1).

18. On Aquinas' terms, see Sabra, *Thomas Aquinas' Vision of the Church*, ch. 2. H. W. M. Rikhof warns against turning the medieval theologian's view of the Body of Christ into an anonymous corporation hierarchically presided over by Christ or a bishop ("Corpus Christi Mysticum: An Inquiry into Thomas Aquinas' Use of a Term," *Bijdragen. Tijdschrift voor Filosofie en Theologie* 37 [1976]: 149–71); see M. Morard, "'Corpus Mysticum' et 'Persona Mystica' dans l'oeuvre de Saint Thomas d'Aquin," *Revue Thomiste* 95 (1995): 653–64; W. Swierzawski, "Christ and the Church: Una persona mystica in the Pauline Commentaries of St. Thomas Aquinas," in *S. Tommaso Teologo: Ricerche in occasione dei due centenari accademici*, ed. Antonio Piolanti (Vatican City: Libreria Editrice Vaticana, 1995), 239–51; Achille Darquennes, *Hat sociaal corps van de kerk volgen Sint Thomas van Aquino* (Brugge-Brussel, 1945); *De juridische structuur van de kerk volgens Sint Thomas von Aquino* (Leuven: Universiteitsbibliotheek, 1949); "La Définition de l'Église d'après S. Thomas d'Aquin," *Études présentées à la commission internationale pour l'Histoire des Assemblées d'États* 7 (1943): 1–53.

19. Yves Congar, *Die Lehre von der Kirche: Ekklesiologie von Augustinus bis zum abendländischen Schism. Handbuch der Dogmengeschichte* III/3c (Freiburg: Herder, 1971), 151.

20. *In I Cor.* 12:12, no.732.

21. Congar, *L'Église de saint Augustin*, 234.

22. Chenu, *St. Thomas d'Aquin et la théologie*, 98.

23. *ST* III.61.4 ad 1; III.63.5 ad 3.

24. *ST* II-II.183.2 ad 3.

25. *In Heb.* 3:1, no.163.

26. See Congar, "Ecclesia ab Abel," in *Abhandlungen über Theologie und Kirche*, ed. M. Reding (Düsseldorf: Patmos-Verlag, 1952), 79 ff.

27. *ST* III.8.3c.

28. *ST* III.73.3c.

29. See III *Sent.* d.25 q.2 art.2; *Super Primam Decretalem*, #683 (this was the decretal *Firmiter* of the Fourth Lateran Council in 1215); *In Ioh.* 6:54, nos.968–69; *In Symbolum Apostolorum*, a.9; *ST* III.73.3c.

30. On Aquinas and grace outside of biblical salvation history, see M. Seckler, "Das Heil der Nichtevangelisierten in thomistischer Sicht," *Theologische Quartalschrift* 140 (1960): 39–51; Thomas O'Meara, "The Presence of Grace outside of Evangelization, Baptism, and Church in the Theology of Thomas Aquinas," in *That Others May Know and Love*, ed. M. Cusato (St. Bonaventure: Franciscan Institute, 1997), 91–132; Sabra, *Thomas Aquinas' Vision of the Church*, 158 ff. For Aquinas this topic of wider grace does not concern the Jews. They stand in the line of God's covenant of the supernatural order and are in an always distinguished way the source of the Christ and his gospel. "The passion of Christ had the effect of salvation among the Jews, and then through the preaching of Jews the effect of the passion of Christ passed on to the peoples" (*ST* III.47.4c). The Jews had—and still retain—covenantal beliefs and sacramental rites (*ST* I-II.101.4; 102.5; III.62.6), some of which anticipated prior to Pentecost the Messiah. Some of the theologically educated, the "*majores*," had an intimation of Trinity and Incarnation (*ST* II-II.2.7). Aquinas interpreted the Jewish rituals as valuable, even in his own time, to Christian as well as to Jew; they were sacraments (*ST* II-II.10.11; I-II.101.4). There are no circumstances which would permit the forced baptism of Jewish adults or children, because of their sovereignty as human beings (*ST* III.68.10). For literature on the Dominican opposition to any forced baptism of Jews, see U. Horst and B. Faes de Mottoni, "Die Zwangstaufe jüdischer Kinder im Urteil scholastischer Theologen," *Münchener theologische Zeitschrift* 40 (1989): 173 ff.; see also D. Berg, "'*Servitus Judaeorum*': Zum Verhaltnis des Thomas von Aquin und seines Ordens zu den Juden in Europa im 13. Jahrhundert," in *Thomas von Aquin: Werk und Wirkung im Licht neurer Forschungen*, ed. A. Zimmermann, Miscellanea mediaevalia 19 (Berlin: Walter de Gruyter, 1988), 439–58; W. Eckert, "Thomas von Aquino und seine Stellung zu den Juden und zum Judentum," *Freiburger Rundschau* 20 (1968): 30–52.

31. See A. Melloni, "Christianitas nelli scritti di Tommaso d'Aquino," *Christianesimo nella storia* 6 (1985): 45–69.

32. *ST* III.8.1; 48.2 ad 1.

33. Congar, *L'Église de Saint Augustin*, 224 ff.

34. See M.-D. Chenu, *Toward Understanding St. Thomas*, trans. A. M. Landry and D. Hughes (Chicago: H. Regnery Co., 1964), 172. The triadic form of a Neoplatonic schema had to be trimmed to the empirical phenomenon of the church, and so a double, not a triple, form was posited for the ecclesiastical hierarchy. Bishops, priests, and deacons worked on the passive triad of monks, laity, and the catechumens. The episcopal hierarchy was said to possess a triple spiritual power to purify, to illuminate, and to unify; see R. Roques, *L'univers dionysien* (Paris: Aubier, 1954); David E. Luscombe, "Thomas Aquinas and Conceptions of Hierarchy," in *Thomas von Aquin: Werk und Wirkung im Lichte neuerer Forschungen*, ed. Zimmermann, 261 ff.

35. IV *Sent.* d.24 q.2 art.1 ad 1. Aquinas, following Gratian and Lombard, admitted an influence from pagan sources upon the monarchical aspect of the church (IV *Sent.* d.24 q.3 art.2 qc.2 ad 2; see Congar, *L'Église de Saint Augustin*, 154).

36. *ST* I-II.112.1c.

37. Chenu, *St. Thomas d'Aquin et la théologie*, 130.

38. *ScG* IV.74.1.

39. *ST* III.62.2c.

40. *ST* III.73.1c.

41. *ST* II-II.23.1c.

42. *ST* III.75.1c.

43. *ST* III.68.4 ad 2.

44. IV *Sent.* d.7 q.1 art.1 ad 1.; see M. Useros Carretero, *"Statuta Ecclesiae" y "Sacramenta Ecclesiae" en la eclesiologia de Santo Tomás* (Rome: Libreria Editrice dell'Universita Gregoriana, 1962).

45. *ST* Supplement, 36.2.1c.

46. *ScG* IV.76; see Sabra, *Thomas Aquinas' Vision of the Church*, 107–43.

47. *ST* II-II.185.3c; III.67.2 ad 1.

48. *ST* III.41.3 ad 1; see too *ST* II-II.184.5; J. Lecuyer, "Les étapes de l'enseignement thomiste sur l'episcopat," *Revue Thomiste* 57 (1957): 29 ff.; and Walter Kasper, "Episcopal Office," in *Leadership in the Church* (New York: Crossroad, 2003), 76–113.

49. *Quodl.* 4, 18; see A. Dulles, "The Teaching Role of the Magisterium and of Theologians," *Proceedings of the Catholic Theological Society of America* 24 (1969): 239 ff.

50. Congar, *L'Église de saint Augustin*, 237.

51. Congar, *Die Lehre von der Kirche*, 154.

52. *In Col.* 4:1, no.193.

53. *ST* II-II.1.10c.

54. *De Pot.* q.10 a.4 ad 13. The creeds articulate what the Bible holds and the church believes (*ST* II-II.1.6 ad 1; II-II.1.9 ad 1; II-II.110.3 ad 1).

55. *ST* II-II.1.10 ad 2 and ad 3.

56. Ulrich Horst, "Kirche und Papst nach Thomas von Aquin," *Catholica* 31 (1977): 152; see Yves Congar, "Saint Thomas Aquinas and the Infallibility of the Papal Magisterium," *The Thomist* 38 (1974): 81–105.

57. *ST* II-II.1.1; II-II.1.10. "One speaks with the Holy Spirit moving and dwelling within that person. . . . Not only does that person confess verbally [the truth] but the heart reverences the Spirit as Lord and obeys the Spirit in works" (*In I Cor* 12:3, no.718).

58. *ST* II-II.1.9 sed contra.

59. *ST* II-II.131.1 and 2.

60. *ST* II-II.43.5c.

61. See Thomas O'Meara, "Beyond Hierarchology: Johann Adam Möhler and Yves Congar," in *The Legacy of the Tübingen School*, ed. Michael Himes and D. Dietrich (New York: Crossroad, 1997), 173–91.

62. *ST* II-II.183.2 ad 3.

63. *In Ioh.* 13:35, no.1839.

64. Yves Congar, "La Querelle entre mendiants et séculiers," *Archives d'histoire doctrinale et littéraire du Moyen Age* 29 (1962): 147.

65. See Herbert Grundmann, *Religious Movements in the Middle Ages*, trans. S. Rowan (Notre Dame, Ind.: University of Notre Dame Press, 1995).

66. *ST* II-II.184, prol.

67. *The Sermon-Conferences of St. Thomas Aquinas on the Apostles' Creed*, 125.

68. *ST* III.8.4c.

69. Congar, "The Idea of the Church in Thomas Aquinas," 336. At that time Congar saw the activity of the church in terms of virtues and ethics, and not yet, as he did after World War II, in terms of activities ministering to the church.

70. *ST* II-II.183.2c.

71. IV *Sent.* d.24 q.2 art.1 ad 3; d.24 q.1 art.3 qc.2 ad 1.

72. *ST* I-II.106.1 ad 1.

73. John Mahoney writes: "For Aquinas the Church is essentially 'the Church of the Holy Spirit,' and this underlies his teaching that those in authority in the Church be sensitive to the purpose of their decisions and decrees as providing a timely, and when necessary temporary, expression of the grace of the Spirit in the community of the faithful. And not only should all in the Church be open to the possibility of the unexpected from the Spirit, and to the Spirit's response through his Church to the needs of men in every generation. They should also respect the Christian dignity of all the faithful and realize that the New Law of the spirit is not . . . a burden . . . but a clearly visible expression of the love and freedom which the Spirit imparts" ("The Church of the Holy Spirit in Aquinas," in *Seeking the Spirit: Essays in Moral and Pastoral Theology* [London: Sheed and Ward, 1981], 115).

74. *ST* I-II.106.1 and 2. In contrast to Albert and Bonaventure, it is not faith that is the pinnacle of membership in the church but participation in the priesthood of Christ, the power to act in Christian worship (Congar, *Die Lehre von der Kirche*, 153).

75. Yves Congar, " 'Ecclesia,' et 'populus (fidelis)' dans l'ecclésiologie de S. Thomas," in *St. Thomas Aquinas, 1274–1974: Commemorative Studies* (Toronto: Pontifical Institute of Mediaeval Studies, 1974), 170.

76. *ST* I-II.97.1; *ST* II-II.184. In the age of the apostles the basic ministries were present, although their names and descriptions were not the same as those appearing in later ecclesial organization. "Since in one city there are not many bishops, this expression in the plural must include the presbyters. . . . In the beginning, although the orders were distinct, still the names of the orders were not" (*In Phil.* 1:1, no.6). "In the early church, because of the small number of faithful, all lower ministries were confided to deacons. . . . All those powers were contained in the single diaconal power. But with time, divine service was expanded and that which the church possessed in one order it has distributed in many" (IV *Sent.* d.24 q.2 art.1 ad 2). Aquinas spoke of the beginnings of the church and its progress as the subject of the apostles' letters in the New Testament (*Breve Principium Fratris Thomae de Commendatione Sacrae Scripturae, Opuscula theologica* 1 [Turin, 1954], 439).

77. *In I Cor.* 12:28, nos.755–58.

78. *ST* Supplement, 37.1 ad 2; IV *Sent.* d.24 q.2 art.1.

79. We do not find a formal treatment of this topic in the *Summa Theologiae* because that work was left incomplete before it treated of the sacrament of orders; the "Supplement" gives the teaching from Aquinas' earlier commentary on the *Sentences* (John Hilary Martin, "The Injustice of Not Ordaining Women: A Problem for Medieval Theologians," *Theological Studies* 48 [1987]: 303 ff.). Dennis Michael Ferrara argues convincingly that the phrase concerning the priest acting "in the person of Christ" meant for Aquinas the recitation of Jesus' consecratory words at the last supper and not that the priest as a male is a symbol of the incarnate Word ("Representation or Self-Effacement: The Axiom *In Persona Christi* in St. Thomas and the Magisterium," *Theological Studies* 55 [1994]: 195 ff.).

80. *ST* Supplement, 39.1.

81. *ST* I.92.1 ad 2.

82. *ST* Supplement, 39.1. This passage has been taken from the early IV *Sent.* d.25 q.2 art.1. It can be left to sociologists of the Middle Ages to research the meaning of this subjection coming from sin and from a lesser position in that society. Aquinas would not have accepted the theology that the Word of God became incarnate in a "male" rather than in a human being, for the Word directly assumed human nature in an individual human being (*ST* III.4.3).

83. To this Aquinas adds two arguments: one about women inciting to sensuality, and one about women being not well educated (*ST* II-II.177.2c). On the other hand, "Colossians says that 'in Christ Jesus there is neither male nor female' and therefore it makes no difference whether a man or a woman is a sponsor in confirmation" (*ST* III.72.10 ad 3).

84. *ST* II-II.177.2c.

85. *ST* III.67.4c; see too *ST* III.72.10 ad 3.

86. "In terms of an organisation, St. Thomas saw the *corpus ecclesiae,* the body that is the church, in the categories of his time.... This organisation is a little pyramidical in analogy with society at that time.... But one must add with Aquinas an important precision: even at the level of the parish, looking at each believer, the church is 'city', for the faithful exercise the most lofty activities in the city of God, those of the virtues of faith, hope, and love" (Congar, "Vision de l'Église chez Thomas d'Aquin," 528 f.).

87. Yves Congar, "Saint Thomas et les archidiacres," *Revue Thomiste* 57 (1957): 670.

88. Yves Congar, "La Querelle," 145.

89. *ST* I.108.2.

90. Congar, "Vision de l'Église chez Thomas d'Aquin," 536–38.

91. A. Erlande-Brandeburg, *Notre Dame in Paris, Geschichte, Architektur, Skulptur* (Freiburg: Herder, 1992), 108.

92. See Congar, "The Idea of the Church in Thomas Aquinas"; Janez Vodopivec, "La 'Gratia Capitis' in S. Tommaso in relazione all'Ecclesiologia di comunione," in *Prospettive teologische moderne* (Vatican City: Libreria Editrice Vaticana, 1981), 327–38.

93. *ST* II-II.1.9 ad 5.

Fourteen

Sacraments

LIAM G. WALSH, O.P.

There is, indeed, a theology of sacraments in Aquinas. It does not, however, come in the form of a "treatise on sacraments." Thomas Aquinas,
like other Scholastic masters, was not writing a theology of this or that.
The subject of his theology was God. When he dealt with this or that,
it was as it comes forth from God and returns to God. This means
that when these other things come explicitly into view, as the sacraments of the Church do at the end of the *Tertia Pars* of the *Summa
Theologiae,* what he says about them is not all he has to say about them.
Many theological things already said are assumed to be on the mind of
the reader, who is expected to read the new material in their light. Like
the other masters, Aquinas had to decide when and where the sacraments should come into view in his theology. Peter Lombard had put
sacraments in Book IV of his *Liber Sententiarum,* and in the prologue
to his *Scriptum super Libros Sententiarum* Aquinas explained how he understood that choice.[1] He will maintain the positioning of consideration of the sacraments that he found in the *Sentences,* and the eschatological perspective that it entails, in his *Summa contra Gentiles* and in
the *Summa Theologiae.*[2]

Sacraments in the *Summa*

The *Summa,* like the Bible, requires a continuous reading as well as the
piecemeal reading of it that is often imposed by a theological curricu-

lum or a research project.[3] The progression of Aquinas' theology, as it appears in its most refined state in the *Summa,* is not linear: he does not pass from one thing to another. He is looking at everything all of the time, but in a perspective that moves gradually from the more abstract and universal to the more particular. The subject is always God, and what comes forth from God and returns to God. In the *Prima Pars*[4] this subject is dealt with in its most general terms, in the great questions about God, creation, and divine government. The move toward the concrete has, however, already begun in the *Prima Pars.* Created reality has its center of interest in Man and Woman, introduced in terms of the account of their creation provided by Genesis. Their unique openness to God as creatures made in God's image and likeness, with the unique ability this gives them to act and interact within the world governed by God, is brought into focus in the end questions of the *Prima Pars.* The carried-over presence of these analyses of God and humans from the *Prima Pars* makes Aquinas' discussion on the sacraments both a genuine theology and a genuine theological anthropology.

The *Prima Secundae* analyzes the God-human relationship on the general level of human moral action in quest of blessedness and of God, the giver of blessedness, acting on humans through the community-forming power of law and grace. The consideration remains abstract, but there is a growth in concreteness with the introduction of certain temporal events: the original fall and its consequences for human solidarity in sin is introduced into the general consideration of moral fault; the giving of the law through Moses and the institutional establishment of God's people is integrated into the discussion on law; and the coming of the New Law in the grace of the Holy Spirit gives body to the discussion on grace. By recalling these analyses of the *Prima Secundae* one can look at sacraments in the *Tertia Pars* as rituals that are God-given and God-driven acts of human moral choice, made in community, in which humans seek out the blessedness of eternal life.

In the *Secunda Secundae* God is seen as acting in the more specifically biblical virtues and states of life by which humans return to God. Here is a growth in concreteness because this is the way of life that is lived in the Church. Although the *Secunda Secundae* introduces many features of life in the Church of the New Testament, the concept of Church is still sufficiently abstract to correspond to the *ecclesia ab Abel justo* and the different historical forms that it takes in gathering all humanity into salvation. This biblical and ecclesial analysis of God's presence in human life will be at work when Aquinas refers to the ecclesial reality of sacraments.

The *Tertia Pars* makes the God/human relationship that has been explored throughout the first two parts of the *Summa* historically concrete in the Person of the Word Incarnate. All that has previously been said about the divine and the human is being said again, but now about a historical event and Person. This account of Christ, carrying with it everything that has already been said about God and humans, is the master theological key to understanding what Aquinas says about sacraments at the end of the *Tertia Pars.* The sacraments of the Church are the ultimate concretizing of God's action, in Christ and the Spirit, on the universe God has created. They bring to fulfillment at the end of human history the human moral striving for blessedness, in which all that God has made is brought back to God. Thus the theology of the sacraments is the most concrete level of the theology that Aquinas has been building from the beginning of the *Prima Pars.* It is eschatology in the flesh. It examines what Aquinas called, in his prologue to the *Scriptum super Libros Sententiarum,* the preparation phase of the latter times: it is the way that Christians live the "already" of Christ in the "not yet" that waits the return of all things to God in the glory of the resurrection.

How the *Summa* Has Been Read on Sacraments

One cannot read Aquinas' theology of sacraments today without being aware of the way it has been received and transmitted in the ongoing work of theology. It held its own easily in the Middle Ages. Although other authors put forward variants of more or less significance, there were no major disagreements on the subject of sacraments among the Scholastic masters. Those who received and commented on their work, however, often concentrated on the more metaphysical subtleties of the teachings of the masters, and the technical discussions they introduced tended to distort the biblical and patristic shape that the masters had given their sacramental theology. Then Nominalism began to eat away the epistemological and metaphysical foundations of the medieval constructions, and the teaching on sacraments was undermined. What the Reformers came to know as the sacramental theology of Aquinas was unbiblical, rational, and clerical; they would have none of it.

The Council of Trent drew certain key elements of its teaching on the sacraments from Aquinas. But when one looks at its coolness toward the concept of "sign," one can hardly claim that Trent promoted a well-rounded understanding of Aquinas' teaching. Sixteenth-century and later commentators recovered a good deal of the strong points of Aquinas on the sacraments. But apologetical concerns to defend the teaching of Trent against Protestants gave an emphasis to causality in the theology of sacraments that was not always in keeping with the delicate balance Aquinas established between sign and cause. Among the neo-scholastics one begins to find traces of a more sensitive appreciation of the balance of Aquinas. But only when the historical method began to be applied to his text during the first half of the twentieth century did a more authentic reading become possible, as forgotten features emerged. The monumental work of Edward Schillebeeckx,[5] translated into more accessible terms in his *Christ the Sacrament of the Encounter with God*[6] and attractively expressed in Aimé Roguet's contribution to the *Revue des Jeunes* edition of the *Summa*,[7] allowed Aquinas' theology of sacraments to find a comfortable place in the liturgically enriched debate on sacraments that accompanied Vatican II.

Contemporary Readings and Issues

Schillebeeckx drew freely from contemporary personalist philosophy in his reading of Aquinas on the sacraments. Other twentieth-century philosophical currents, from phenomenology to various forms of linguistic analysis, seemed to be reasonably comfortable with Aquinas' way of thinking about sacraments, and were thought to be able to contribute to a contemporary elucidation of it.[8] However, one of the most important present-day theologians of the sacraments, Louis-Marie Chauvet, has challenged these comfortable alliances.[9] Basing his arguments on Heidegger's critique of metaphysics and adopting an alternative anthropological position grounded on the philosophy of language, he offered a radical critique of Aquinas' sacramental theology and claimed that it has led to serious misunderstandings. The principal criticism bears on Aquinas' employment of the category of causality, which, Chauvet claimed, leads to a "productionist" view of sacramental action, and on the "representational" sense that Aquinas gave to the concept of sign. Chauvet also voiced criticisms raised by others as well about the absence of pneumatology in Aquinas' theology of sacraments and the weakness of its liturgical and ecclesiological grounding.

1. Theology and Anthropology

The issues raised by Chauvet confirm that it is necessary to begin reading Aquinas' theology of the sacraments not in the *Tertia Pars* but in the *Prima Pars*. These issues are in fact general issues of theology that Aquinas discusses long before he brings the sacraments themselves into view. The positions he takes on them are assumed to be available and are put to work in the questions on sacraments without much further explanation. The first issue is surely the relationship between theology and the anthropological sciences. The profound influence of Odo Casel on the twentieth-century revival of liturgical theology requires that sacraments, as mystery, must be considered as acts of God. Theology, understood as a word about God, must have the principal say about them. Sacraments are also, of course, human actions. Anthropology is indispensable for understanding them. The question is, can one start studying sacraments from the standpoint of any kind of anthropology, and particularly of an anti-metaphysical anthropology, and be reasonably certain of being able to combine anthropological analysis with truthful theological statements about the divine reality of sacraments? Or must one secure the theological ground and verify the possibility of affirming divine action, before exploring the complex divine-human reality of sacraments? This is a version of the question of whether one should do theology from below or from above, or how one should combine the above and the below. Here is not the place to debate this matter, which entails serious issues of fundamental theology. What one can attempt to do, however, is to read Aquinas in terms of the option that he took, in order to see whether the way he handles the theological issues allows him to develop an anthropology of sacraments that escapes the impasses that Chauvet detects. One might even find that the approach of Aquinas brings out the best in contemporary anthropological reflection on the sacraments and saves it from some of the impasses that it creates for itself.[10]

2. The Appeal to Divine Causality

A particular feature of the relationship between God and humans that is important for sacramental theology is divine causality. When Aquinas analyzes the action of God in the *Prima Pars*, he proposes a remarkable integration of its final, formal, and efficient components. In crude terms, God never does anything without having an end in view and without generating a form for what is to reach that end. Where there is divine energy there is, inseparably, divine design and divine desire.[11] Much has been written in Scholastic theology about sacramental causality. The concentration has been on efficient causality in a way that often leaves aside the final and formal components of God's action. When Chauvet criticizes the reliance of a Scholastic theology of sacraments on the concept of causality, he seems to be envisaging causality as efficient, in isolation from final and formal causality. However, if one is to do justice to Aquinas' analysis of divine causality, one must recognize his position that when God acts he is simultaneously giving finality and form, as well as existence, to what he is doing. Divine goodness is present as desire in everything that is. Divine ideas are the exemplars that are present as form in everything that is, including events that occur contingently in time.[12] And when God is acting in humans, made in his own image and for the purpose of coming to know and love him, the action of humans is God-formed and God-directed, as well as being God-moved. Sacraments are human actions, having all the features of human symbolic activity and life choices. They take the form of signs that have been given by God; they represent the choice of an eternal life that has been offered by God; and God is acting in them to bring into existence the good that he has promised in the way he has promised it. Sacraments are acts of God occurring within wholesome and moral human actions.

3. Pneumatology in the Theology of Sacraments

Whereas the *Prima Pars* studies what humans think and believe about God and about themselves, the *Secunda Pars* studies how these thinking and believing humans act and tend toward God as their ultimate blessedness, and how God is present in their moral striving through law and grace. Here, Aquinas sets out his basic theology of grace, which he calls the grace of the Holy Spirit. Much of his pneumatology, of which the foundations are laid in the trinitarian questions of the *Prima Pars,* is developed in the *Secunda* rather than in the *Tertia Pars.*[13] It is to be found in the discussion on grace,[14] in the discussions on the gifts of the Holy Spirit, and in the discussion on the charisms. Aquinas does not often mention the Holy Spirit in his questions on the sacraments. One could say that he matches the pneumatological reticence of the Roman liturgy. But one must recognize that whenever he talks about grace in those questions on sacraments, he is talking about the grace of the Holy Spirit;[15] and when he is talking about the faith and charity and religion that come into play in sacraments, he understands these Spirit-formed virtues as accompanied by the corresponding gifts of the Holy Spirit; and when he is talking about the Church, it is the Church formed and animated by the Holy Spirit.[16]

4. The Grace of Christ in the Theology of Sacraments

The *Tertia Pars* deals with the way in which the return of all things to God is concretely and historically realized in the man Christ, in whom God is uniquely present through incarnation. Christ is the Savior sent by the Father because he is the Word through whom all things were formed and made, and in whose humanity all reach their end in returning to the Father. The grace of Christ, his human created grace, the grace of the Holy Spirit, is what makes it possible for him to unite all things and all people in himself and bring them with him to the

Father. Questions 7 and 8 of the *Tertia Pars* establish this recapitulative role of the grace of Christ and give it its ecclesial expression. All this is assumed in the often laconic statements that Aquinas makes about sacraments giving grace. Receiving grace in a sacrament is thought of not as an isolated and isolating production of sanctification but as a bonding of believers with Christ in the unity of his Mystical Body.

The Christological and ecclesiological setting of the sanctifying efficacy that will be attributed to sacraments is further enhanced by the way Aquinas combines the movements of sanctification and of worship in his analysis of sacraments. He appeals to this twofold movement at several key points in his questions on sacraments.[17] He has been criticized for placing an excessive emphasis on the sanctifying movement of sacraments, as God giving grace to humans, and not enough emphasis on their cultic movement, as worship given by humans to God. However, one must remember that the cult movement of all human action, its *ordo ad Deum,* has already been established in his theology of religion, and sacraments have been expressly identified as acts of religion.[18] What is new in the *Tertia Pars* is the presence in the sacraments of the divine action through Christ in the grace of the Holy Spirit. The movement of Aquinas' thought requires one to understand their grace-giving movement of sanctification as being for the fulfillment of the *ordo ad Deum,* which is realized in human worship. Sanctification is received in worship and flowers in worship.[19] This perspective enables Aquinas to regard his discussion on the sanctifying power of sacraments as the completion of the task he had set himself in his prologue to the *Summa,* and which he describes as *ea quae ad Christianam religionem pertinent . . . tradere.* Christianity is a "religion" because it brings about the return of all things to God in Christ. That is what the sacraments, like everything else, are for. What is novel about them, and so has to be analyzed explicitly, is how they do it, which is by making the sanctifying action of Christ present to his members in a unique way. That action is, as Aquinas will explain in his analysis of the sacramental characters, the action of Christ the Priest. It is worship, and it makes those who are sanctified by it exercise their worship of God in the form of participation in the priestly worship of Christ.

What Kind of Thing Is a Sacrament? (q.60)

The move from questions about Christ to questions about sacraments is made by Aquinas[20] in a way that shows there is no break in continuity, and that everything that has been said about Christ must be kept in mind when new topics are dealt with in the questions about sacraments—just as things previously said about God and humans must be kept in mind when reading the questions about Christ. The movement from Christ to sacraments is not deductive. It could be described as hermeneutical. A new subject is being brought into view—the seven rituals practiced in the Church that are called sacraments. These are to be examined within the horizon provided by what has been established about Christ. The related use of *mysterium* and *sacramentum* in the prologue invites one to bring the biblical, patristic, and liturgical studies of the past century about "mystery" to bear on one's reading of Aquinas.

The prologue announces five questions *de sacramentis in communi*, to be followed by questions on the individual sacraments. What is being offered is not a generic notion of sacrament that will then be specifically differentiated into seven sacraments. Aquinas is instead raising some general questions about the entire sacramental economy that comprises seven sacraments—as the medieval Latin Church had come to accept by the twelfth century—before going on to look at the individual sacraments. The first question he asks concerns the formal constituent of sacramentality: what kind of thing is a sacrament? (q.60). From the formal he goes on to the final: what makes sacraments necessary? (q.61) and what good do they do? (qq.62–63). Then comes the existential question: what agents actually bring them into being? (q.64). And finally Aquinas asks the more material question of how many of them there are (q.65).

1. A Sacrament Is a Kind of Sign

Aquinas' answer to the question of what formally constitutes a sacrament is careful. He does not quite say that sacraments are signs: he says they are *in genere signi*, that is, they are of the kind of things that are classed and spoken of as signs. He is not very categorical about this, as if nothing else could usefully be said about sacraments. He is making a methodological choice to follow Augustine, whom he quotes in the sed contra of q.60 a.1. Other options open to him are listed in the difficulties he deals with in this article. *Sacramentum* comes from *sacer*, which means holy, and comparison with other words ending in *-mentum* suggests one should think about sacraments as causes, that is, causes of holiness. Some medieval theologians thought this was the safest way to respect the originality that the tradition of faith attributed to the rituals of the New Testament: in Augustine's language, they contain and have the power to give grace. Or one could think about them, following the etymology provided by Isidore, as hidden or secret sacred realities—and that option, whether Aquinas knew it or not, can claim credence from the original meaning of the Greek *musterion*, which lay at the origin of the use of the Latin *sacramentum*. Or one could think of sacraments as being like oaths—and that would be holding on to an original meaning of the Latin *sacramentum*. Aquinas sees some merit in each of these postulates but in the end decides that the best way to get at the truth about sacraments is to think about them as one thinks about signs. He is locating sacraments, then, in an area of human experience that has its own logic and its own language. Whatever he says subsequently about sacraments has to be understood as the kind of thing one says about signs. They are signs of the sacred.

2. Sign of Christ Sanctifying Humans

Aquinas now has to consider why the Christian tradition, which sees signs of the sacred everywhere—and the difficulties put forward in a.2 are reminders of that—does not call all of them sacraments. Aquinas must add a qualification to "sign of the sacred" before it can serve as a statement of what a sacrament is. He does so by making what is again a firm methodological choice: from here on (*secundum quod nunc de sacramentis loquimur*), the specific kind of sign that he will use to understand sacraments is the sign of a sacred reality that is sanctifying humans. In making this choice Aquinas is working from the assumption that a sign is always a sign of something, and of something other than itself. He knows that in the language of Augustine, the something signified is called *res*, and that this something is other than and beyond the familiarity of the sign. In working out a way of thinking about sacraments, he is much more interested in this Augustinian correlation of *signum/res* that in another bit of Augustiniana of which he was also aware. Current in medieval circles was a definition of "sign" taken from the *De doctrina christiana:* a sign is that which, over and above the form which it impresses upon the senses, makes something else enter into our cognition.[21] This definition emphasizes the cognitive role of a sign. Aquinas quotes it when it suits him[22] but does not give it a major place in his theology of sacrament. Some of his commentators, notably John of St. Thomas, offer elaborate analyses of the cognitive notion of sign as a help to understanding what Aquinas means by saying sacraments are signs. Their work has been valuable for semiotics, but one wonders if it was necessary or useful for the theology of sacraments. Aquinas seems satisfied with a rather generic notion of sign, whose specific quality comes not from an inner differentiation of the notion of sign, but from the reality that is being signified (*res sacra . . . sanctificans homines*).

The point of Aquinas' choice becomes clear when he explains in a.3 that the reality signified in signs called sacraments is none other than Christ. He has already explained in his analysis of Christ's grace how Christ is the unique and universal principle of sanctification.[23] Now, in q.60 a.3, he explains the mysterious way in which the grace-filled Christ, head of the Church, is the sanctifying reality signified in sacraments. He is a reality that is at once of the past, of the present, and of the future. He became the one who sanctifies in his passion; he is now the one who sanctifies in giving the grace of the Holy Spirit; he is the one who will bring ultimate sanctification in eternal life.

What is interesting about this understanding of sacrament is that it brings together signification and causality. Respect for the findings of historians that the theology of sacraments has been marked by an alternating emphasis on sign and on cause has made some readers of Aquinas assume that his preference for sign requires him to put causality in a secondary place; they tend to raise the question of causality only when they discuss q.62, where Aquinas inquires about how grace is an effect of sacraments. But once Aquinas has chosen to think about sacraments as "signs of a sacred reality sanctifying humans," he is thereby thinking about them as causes: they are the reality of Christ, the one who sanctifies, in the form of sign. The sign allows an encounter to occur between Christ and believers in which Christ is the efficient cause of holiness (which he became in his passion); the formal cause of human holiness (which he is as the unique image and measure of human grace); and the final cause of holiness (which he is as the culmination of the return of all things to God). Christ's causality in the sacraments reflects the threefold pattern of God's causality to which I have drawn attention earlier: that it is efficient is more than adequately stated by the kind of language used about it; that it is also final and formal is an underlying postulate of Aquinas that is brought to light now and again, as it is here in his reply to the third difficulty of q.60 a.3.

3. Made up of Words and Elements

The decision to define sacraments as signs of a reality that is actively sanctifying entails putting an accent on the "downward," sanctifying movement of sacraments. I have already pointed out that this does not mean that Aquinas separates the "downward" from the "upward" movement of worship in his theology of sacrament. But it does mean that he wants to think of sacraments as acts of God from the very beginning. The whole weight of his theology of grace has to be brought to bear on his theology of sacrament. It is only in that light that the novelty of sacraments can be considered. Their novelty lies, of course, in the divinization of an anthropological exercise: they allow God to act humanly in signs made by humans. They are signs made by humans that allow God to act humanly. In q.60 aa.4–8 Aquinas does some anthropologico-theological marking of the signs that make sacraments. He asks how they are made and why.

The first thing to be said about the sign that is sacrament is that it is made up of things that touch the senses. In the sed contra of a.4 Aquinas quotes with approval a famous phrase of Augustine that expressed an important principle for Latin sacramental theology: "The word is added to the element and this becomes a sacrament."[24] Here Aquinas is looking at the *elementum,* the sense-touching item that will be twinned with words to make the sign. The element is more down to earth than the words, and it engages the senses more immediately than they do. The senses are the door to human knowing, and Aquinas wants to inject the sense-grounded realism of his epistemology into his theology of sacrament. If there is a bit of Aristotelian intellectualism peeping through what he says, there is also a hint of Platonism in the way he regards bodily-perceived images as giving access to the spiritual reality that is active in sacraments. His interest is in the images generated by sense impressions. That is clear from the very liturgical parallel that he draws between Scripture and sacrament: both operate by sense images, evoked by the reading of words in one case and by the touch of things in the other. The argument of the article is theological and the references are to scriptural texts and to patristic texts from Pseudo-Dionysius and Augustine, rather than to the philosophers.

4. Instituted by God

Anthropology, especially cultural anthropology, suggests that a variety of things could serve to signify what God is doing in sacraments. The difficulties put forward in q.60 a.5 evoke a problem that is with us even more acutely today, in a Church that talks encouragingly about inculturation of the liturgy. Aquinas needs to understand why, in spite of the arguments favoring choice in sacramental signs, the Church then, as now, seemed to be saying that it has no room for choice about the sign to be employed. He tries to offer something to both sides in the argument. He makes explicit for the first time his underlying assumption that there is a double movement in the making of sacraments: the worship of God (which one can imagine as going upward) and the sanctification of humans (coming downward). Here he reasons that the upward movement is somehow the business of humans in their relating to God; the downward is God's affair in his relating to humans. Aquinas claims that because sanctification is God's business it is God, not humans, who must determine the signs of sanctification. He draws no conclusions here about what humans might determine for themselves in the sacraments they make. Later he will say that what they determine about the rite is meant "to impart a certain solemnity to the sacraments so as to excite devotion and reverence in those receiving them."[25] But here he is satisfied with drawing a conclusion only about the movement of sanctification. He is carrying out the task he has set himself of refining the distinctive features of "sign" as it is used to understand sacraments: he does that here by explaining why the sign used in the Church must be the one instituted by God.

The issue of institution is introduced in aa.4–5 of q.60 as a theological issue, not as the apologetical issue it will become with the Reformation and the Council of Trent. Aquinas' knowledge of liturgical history is limited. He assumes with the Church of his day that the Scriptures and their tradition identify one sign for each of the seven sacraments. He makes the best sense he can of this. He turns once again to the bond between Scripture and sacrament, to say that the particular sacramental signs received by the Church are as much word of God as are the inspired words written in the Scriptures. God does humans a favor by determining sacramental signs, just as he does by speaking to them in the Scriptures. It is well to note that when Aquinas comes to study individual sacraments, he never sets out to "prove" from the Scriptures or the Tradition that Christ instituted each of the seven sacraments. Rather, he tries to find a place in the Word of God where the significance of what the Church of his day was doing is seen to have been determined by God. In a.5 he considers a third difficulty against the position he wants to adopt: it argues from the freedom of choice that was allowed in the Old Testament regarding signs of cult to the claim that the God of the New Testament should be even more broad-minded and less monocultural about the signs of worship. Aquinas does a neat side step in his reply by switching the issue from cult to sanctification, and by making the actual sanctifying presence of Christ the distinctive thing about New Testament worship: this stance requires that God determines the signs to be used. But Aquinas does recognize the cultural problem. He offers the palliative that at least for the two most necessary sacraments, baptism and Eucharist, the elements chosen by God are not discriminatory because they "are either in everyone's possession or can be had with little trouble." His world was smaller and flatter than ours. And yet his argument for the decisive, once-for-all institution by God of essential sacramental signs, linked as it is to the once-for-allness of Christ and confirmed by the once-for-allness of Scripture, cannot be written off in the debate about inculturation.

5. Sacramental Words

Article 6, which examines the need for words in sacraments, is full of the tradition of Scripture and the fathers, with Augustine as its principal spokesperson. In the first difficulty it recognizes, with Augustine, that the "bodily sacrament" is already a "visible word" before anything is said, and so asks why audible words need to be added. Aquinas is able to offer three arguments for vocalizing sacraments. The first looks at sacraments from God's side. It draws on what is almost a commonplace in patristic literature: as the Word was joined to palpable flesh in the Incarnation, so a word is added to a palpable element to make a sacrament. The second argument looks at things from the side of humans. The reasoning is drawn from the tradition of body/soul anthropology. Aquinas returns to the medicinal analogy for understanding sacraments that he had used so frequently in his commentary on the *Sentences,* arguing that sacramental healing matches the body/soul constitution of humans in that a visible thing touches the body and a word is believed in the soul. Here, under the prompting of Augustine, the language is careful: a clear distinction is made between the way the element works and the way the word works. The sacramental touch of water, oil, bread, and wine and the touch of human hands are felt as healing by the body just because they touch it. But words act differently. They, too, could be soothing and healing for the soul, and they are so used in all sorts of healing rituals. But in a sacrament the healing is sanctification and not merely soul-comforting consciousness. The words are neither an enlightenment, nor a mantra, nor a reassuring spell: they are a call to saving faith. They work, as Augustine says, "not because they are said but because they are believed." The sacramental word signifies, and therefore makes a sacrament, only as a word of faith. The third argument draws a reason for having words in sacraments from their formal constituent as signs. Words carry signification more precisely than things. The human mind can manage them in a way that lets it express its finest thoughts in them. The signification of things is largely given, and it is often polyvalent. Words pin down the signification of things.

6. Matter and Form

The argument for having words determine the signification of things in sacraments is surely a good one as far as it goes. But it carries the risk of equating signification with "making clear." There is a whole register of signification that is, indeed, opened up by sacramental words but that merges again into the opaqueness and ambivalence of the material component of the sign. Sacraments are mysteries. Their signification, embodied in matter, not only draws from the clarity of words but in its very materiality can breathe unexpected depths of meaning into the words that are spoken. It is surely this that Aquinas wants to express by insisting that sacramental words and elements must be taken together as forming a single sign. He makes this point, in his reply to the second difficulty, with the help of an analogy between the complementarity of word and element in sacramental signification and the complementarity of form and matter in material things. Aquinas is surely remembering that the forms of material things are drawn out of the potentiality of matter and have no existence apart from matter; the malleability of matter leaves the forms of material things fickle but also open to enhancement. What bread and wine, water and oil say to us is indeed held in check by the sacramental words that accompany them; but they, in their turn, can push the meaning of those words into overtones and undertones that take them well beyond their merely rational signification.

Unfortunately this analogy between the constitution of sacramental signs and the constitution of material substances often lost its status as an analogy in the theology of sacraments. Matter and form were turned into canonical categories that had the effect of separating words and elements instead of uniting them in the making of a single sign. The canonists were happy to have a way of classifying the different requirements they prescribed for elements and for words so that one could be sure of having a canonically valid sacrament. Requirements for the element were said to constitute the matter of the sacrament; those concerning the words constituted its form. Medieval theology allowed itself to be heavily influenced by canon law, and nowhere more than in its discussions on sacraments. The distinction between matter and form came to be seen as convenient for theological analysis. Aquinas uses it again in dealing with individual sacraments. But this use of what came to be called "sacramental hylomorphism" was too easily caught up in, and itself contributed to, a forgetfulness of signification as the key to understanding what sacraments are. It materialized the components of sacraments: it made a preoccupation with getting things and words right get in the way of making the words and elements come together to be a telling sign of the presence and action of God in Christ.

7. Words and Actions

More needs to be said about the words spoken in sacraments. In replying to difficulties in a.6 Aquinas drops two important hints. He notes at the end of his second reply that sacramental words accompany actions and not merely things: they speak and determine the meaning of what is being done with things. Later he explains that the sacramental sign of baptism is not provided by water but by a washing with water (or immersion in it), of which the sacramental words determine the signification.[26] This is an important qualification of the matter/form analogy. It might be canonically convenient to call water the matter of baptism. But water signifies in the sacrament only when something is being done with it.

The words "inform" by saying what the action means, rather than simply what the water means. And since both words and actions require a person to make them happen, matter and form can never mean impersonal objects waiting around for someone to pick them up. There is matter and form, and therefore a sacrament, only when persons are doing and saying something significant.[27]

The second hint about sacramental words comes when Aquinas notes (in his reply to the third difficulty) that under the Old Law the priests who ministered the sacraments and the children of Israel who received them spoke words, and observes that these were words of worship—a blessing and a profession of faith, in the examples he gives. This reference to worship is something that one might hope Aquinas would say at this point about the sacramental words of the New Law. It would help dissipate the criticism that his theory of sacramental form impedes an appreciation of the liturgical reality of sacraments. However, his assumption that sacraments are acts of worship as well as of sanctification entitles one to claim that what he is saying about sacramental words here does not preclude the possibility that they are also words of worship. He simply does not need to say it explicitly at this point, because his concern here is to establish that the core sacramental words are words of God, fixed like the words of Scripture. He puts the sacramental words in their worship setting when he talks about the liturgical rites of the individual sacraments.[28] And of course the fact that he presents the sacramental words as words of faith entails that they belong to the most fundamental of liturgical acts, which is the profession of faith.

There are other consequences to be drawn from the faith standing of sacramental words. Aquinas explains in his replies to the difficulties of a.7 that because the words work in sacraments as expressions of faith, not as vocal sounds (*non quia dicitur sed quia creditur*, as Augustine said), it is their meaning for faith that has to be maintained, not their oral accuracy. They can be in any language as long as the faith meaning is maintained. So, there is no question of giving preference to any "sacred languages" in sacraments. Nor does Aquinas think that the wording in sacraments should be exotic: they use the most common words available in the particular language. The words can be garbled, especially the endings of words, and yet hold their meaning.[29] The awareness of linguistic complexity shown in these replies to practical difficulties should prevent us from interpreting in a rigid manner Aquinas' use of the matter/form analogy in the body of a.7 to establish that the sacraments must employ set words. The texts he quotes in the sed contra indicate that he is basically trying to understand why the Church has always considered itself bound to use the set Gospel words given by Jesus for baptism and the Eucharist.

8. Doing What the Church Does

In the final article of q.60 Aquinas introduces what seems to be a casuistical discussion of how modifications of the sacramental words might affect the reality of a sacrament. He makes some interesting remarks here about the role of the Church in the making of sacraments. He recognizes that the sacramental elements and actions and words are put together by human ministers, and that human error and human willfulness affect their make-up. Anyone who is familiar with sacramental practice knows that errors can occur, and also that cavalier creativity can give rise to doubts about whether what is being done is really the sacrament of the Church. Some criteria are needed to deal with such difficulties. Aquinas introduces a few that were, or later became, classical. Like the matter/form terminology, they quite often turned into canonical rules of thumb rather than theological insights. Aquinas is talking theology here. He does not use the canonical terminology of validity to judge the effect of changes made to the sacramental words. Rather, he uses the theological terminology of truth: he speaks of *veritas sacramenti* and *perfectio sacramenti*. A sacrament must truly express what is supposed to be going on within it. Aquinas is no stickler for verbal exactitude. His basic criterion is one of meaning: once verbal variants leave intact the meaning of the established words, there is a true sacrament.

The "meaning" in question is, of course, the meaning that faith gives the words. The examples given in this article of changes that would destroy the truth of a sacrament are various forms of tampering with the expression of trinitarian and Christological faith. Verbal differences that do not imperil faith are no problem for the truth of sacraments. Aquinas notes in the sed contra that the Church itself employs two different forms of words for baptism: the Latin Church says "John/Mary, I baptize you in the name . . ." and the Greek Church says "Let Mary/John be baptized in the name. . . ."

In dealing with the difficulties that can arise with changes in wording, Aquinas is assuming that there are some established words that the changes are measured against, and that these words are known from what the Church does. Throughout his reflection on individual sacraments he constantly invokes this authority of what the Church does. It is important to note that, in these general questions on sacramentality, he does not say that the words to be maintained are determined by the Church; he says that they are received by the Church. In discussing deliberate changes to the established words, he states that there would not seem to be a sacrament if the changes were done with the intention of making a rite other than the one received in the Church (*alium ritum inducere, quae non sit ab ecclesia receptus*). To make a sacrament, one must want to do what the Church does (*id quod facit ecclesia*).

But Aquinas' formulation makes it clear that it is not the Church that decides what it should be doing. Sacramental words are from God: they are given to and received by the Church, not designed by it. In this they are like the words of Scripture, as he explains in his reply to the first difficulty of a.9. However, they are not as untouchable as the words of Scripture. To delimit what is untouchable in them, Aquinas uses a term that will have a great future in Catholic sacramental theology: he says one cannot change those things that are *de substantia formae sacramentalis*. It is clear from the way he uses the term that by *substantia* he understands the core meaning (*sensus*) of the words, not the words themselves, and that the meaning is on the level of faith. Later Catholic theology is often hard put to resist the canonical pressure to make *substantia sacramenti* mean a minimal set of things and words that the Church must impose for the validity of sacraments, and that the Church itself has no power to change. For Aquinas *substantia* does indeed designate what ensures the truth and reality of sacraments. But because sacraments are signs, their truth and reality must be in the domain of meaning, not in their fidelity to certain fixed sights and sounds.

Human Need for Sacraments (q.61)

What and whose purpose do these sacraments serve? Aquinas believes they meet a real human need. But, more importantly for him, they meet a divine need. They allow God to bring about his providential design for the return of all things to himself in a way that treats humans for what they are and for what they have become through their history. The first of the reasons for the necessity of sacraments given in q.61 a.1 concludes, "And so divine wisdom appropriately gave humans the aids needed for salvation in various bodily and sense-experienced signs, which is what sacraments are." The finality of sacraments is God's before it is of humans. God wants humans to receive divine gifts even more than humans do. The three considerations around which Aquinas weaves his explanation of the necessity of sacraments in article 1 are, then, formally anthropological: humans are led to spiritual and intelligible realities from bodily and sense experience; they are sinners who need healing at the point where their malady is located; they busy themselves above all else with bodily concerns.

The anthropological considerations to which Aquinas appeals as making sacraments necessary have been examined at length in the *Prima* and *Secunda*

Pars. Here he evokes them briefly on a general theoretical level in a.1; in the remaining articles he puts them in a historical framework that takes account of how they might operate in the successive phases of an economy of grace that reaches its fullness in the coming of Christ. Article 2 asks about humans in the grace of original justice and argues that the kind of spiritual relationship they had with God would have taken them beyond any need for sacraments. Some mystics, who seem to have outgrown the need for much sacramentality, might take comfort from his argument. Articles 3 and 4 are about historical and sinful humanity, burdened with original sin and its consequences, and redeemed from sin by Christ. Sinful humanity is characterized by busyness with material and bodily things, which in the domain of the religious can, as Aquinas pointed out in the third anthropological reason for sacraments in a.1, turn into superstition and various forms of the cult of demons. Sacraments are needed because Christ is needed. They were needed both before and after his coming. They had to be different after his coming because they signified him as already present rather than as one yet to come. The signification is, as always for Aquinas, in the domain of faith. As he says in a.4 in a finely Protestant phrase, "sacraments are various signs protesting (*protestantia*) the faith by which humans are justified."

What Sacraments Do (qq.62–63)

Sacraments meet the needs of God and of humans by doing something: they have effects, which bring things forward to eternal fulfillment. This is what Aquinas now goes on to study. Given the place at which he introduces sacraments in the *Summa* and his explanation of what they are and what they are for in qq.60–61, what they do can only be what Christ does. They are his continuing active presence in the world, transforming it through time until the consummation of all things at his coming again in glory.[30] Christ is the *res sacra sanctificans homines* of which sacraments are the signs. What Christ does must be the giving of the grace of the Holy Spirit. Aquinas announced this when speaking about the New Law in the *Prima Secundae.*[31] He examined that grace in general terms in the final questions of the *Prima Secundae.* He dealt with it there as the action of God and as the moral reaction of humans, including their possibility of refusing grace. In his scheme of things that was not yet the place to deal with the historical, existential giving of grace. This comes in III.7–8, where the man Christ is seen as the concrete, historical embodiment of the fullness of grace and as the head of a Church that is his mystical body, gathering humans together in grace in view of the recapitulation of all things.

How Christ's own grace, acting and made visible in his life, death, and resurrection, made him the active, historically present cause of grace for the members of his body is examined in the series of questions on the *acta et passa* of Christ (qq.27–59). The giving of this grace of the Holy Spirit to the members of his body, gathered as believers in the Church and celebrating its sacraments, is examined in qq.62–63. Because there is a double movement in sacraments and a giving and receiving in grace, two separate questions must be asked about the effect of sacraments. The first is how and why the grace of Christ is actually given in sacraments (q.62). The second is about how and why a bond with Christ and his Church, which allows people to cooperate sacramentally in the giving and the receiving of grace, is an effect of some sacraments, an effect that can occur even when the grace of that sacrament is not actually received. The Latin tradition of faith, consolidated by Augustine, had come to recognize that certain sacraments are not repeated because they have a Christ-conforming effect that occurs even when those who receive the sacrament do not then and there open their hearts to the grace of the Holy Spirit. The bond can become active later, when obstacles to grace are removed and the sacrament can have its full effect. This discussion had led medieval theology to a wider consideration of what this sacramentally-given bond with Christ is and how it operates in any receiving or giving of grace. This issue is dealt with in the question devoted to the character effected by sacraments (q.63).

1. Sacraments Give Grace (q.62)

There can be no doubt that when a sacrament is celebrated in the Church, grace is given. The *res sacra* signified by a sacrament is present and at work, and the Church gives thanks in and for the sacrament. Aquinas argues for the grace-effectiveness of sacraments succinctly and profoundly in a.1 of question 62: "By the sacraments of the New Law a person is incorporated into Christ, as the apostle says about baptism in Galatians 3:27, 'those who are baptized into Christ have put on Christ.' But one is not made a member of Christ except by grace." What is open to question, however, is whether the sacramental sign itself—the ritual of words and actions performed in the Church—has a causal role in this giving of grace; or is it merely a sign that God is doing something in Christ?

The kind of instrumental prepositions that Paul uses when talking about the role of baptism in justification suggests some real form of causality for the ritual. Similar things are said in the Scriptures about the Eucharist. The patristic tradition that gravitates around "mystery" and "sacrament" suggests that the rite itself somehow possesses a divine power. Augustine talked about the *virtus sacramenti* and about how sacraments "contained grace." The theological problem is to find a realistic rather than a merely metaphorical explanation of how a humanly-made rite could have a causal role in divine grace.

In a.1 Aquinas looks first at an unsatisfactory proposal that attributes to sacraments a kind of moral causality. He thinks this would leave sacraments as no more than signs of grace. He proposes instead to think of sacraments as acting, under the primary causality of God, as instrumental causes of grace. He has used this concept of instrumental causality already to explain how the humanity of Christ could serve his divinity as a real cause of grace.[32] He cites John Damascene as his authority and so puts himself in line with the Greek fathers, who described the humanity of Christ as the *organon* of his divinity. In Christology the concept has the advantage of not compromising the divine origin of grace (only God is its principal cause), while at the same time giving real value to the human mediation exercised by Christ (raised beyond itself under the movement of God and yet contributing a distinctive human modality to the divine action); it also respects the personal unity of Christ. It has an analogous value in the theology of sacraments and provides another useful junction between it and Christology. The human make-up of a sacrament, the putting together of elements and words in an act of human ritual, is taken hold of by the power of God—a power that has already been given decisive human form in the humanity of Christ— and used to cause in those to whom the sacrament is directed the kind of grace that it signifies.

But can one have it both ways? Can sacraments be at once signs and causes? The theologians of Aquinas' epoch tended to think they had to choose one or the other. Later on, Reformation theologians, both Protestant and Catholic, also tended to take sides. And some contemporary theologians seem to think that if one is to do justice to the symbolic value of sacraments, one must renounce using the language of causality about them. Aquinas deals with the difficulty in his reply to the first objection. He has no intention of letting go of his thesis that sacraments are signs. The difficulty raised was that signs must be effects rather than causes: they show what is at work rather than make something work. He turns the argument around and sets out to establish that a cause can be a sign. He allows that a principal cause cannot be a sign of its own effect. But an instrumental cause can, provided it has some visibility. An instrumental cause is already an effect of the principal cause that is acting upon it and through it. In its visibility as instrument, as something seen to be acting under the movement of a principal cause, it can be a sign of its principal cause and of the proper effect of its action. This, says Aquinas, is the meaning of the adage widely used in his day about sacraments: *efficunt quod figurant*—they do what they signify. Sacraments are only causes when they are signifying the God who is working through them. Aquinas coins an aphorism of his own for it in the *De veritate: sacramenta significando causant.*[33]

His resolution of the sign/cause dilemma may appear somewhat tortuous. A less metaphysical explanation of the causality exercised by sacraments would have made it easier to maintain their status as signs. His theory of instrumental causality met with opposition or attempts at dilution. Strong Thomists, like Cajetan, defended it stoutly. Some of the refinements they proposed in order to overcome difficulties raised against it, however, pushed it in dubious directions. One of the things often sacrificed in a concern to maintain the realism of Aquinas' conception was the connection between instrumentality and signification. Perhaps this happened because a metaphysical analysis of instrumentality focused attention almost exclusively on efficient divine causality. But if one keeps in mind that God's action in sacraments occurs simultaneously along the three great axes of causality, one recognizes that any instruments God uses are formed according to the divine ideas and similitudes and are chosen to achieve God's purposes. Aquinas states in the body of a.1 that the sacraments of the New Law are causes of grace because they are used *ex divina ordinatione ad gratiam in eis causandam.* The form they take and the purpose they serve, as well as the grace-energy they transmit, are works of God. Their instrumentality is like that of Christ himself, in that they reveal what is being done through them. They serve to manifest God and God's intentions as well as to convey his power. From God's standpoint they are both signs and causes.

That Aquinas is thinking of sacramental causality as formal and final, and not only as efficient, is made clear in a.2, where he asks why one can speak of graces as sacramental. The article is also an important indication of the fact that all the moral teaching of the *Secunda Pars* is meant to be present in his theology of sacraments. It recalls that the grace that sanctifies humans radiates into their powers of action in the form of virtues and gifts of the Holy Spirit. But, Aquinas now adds, Christian life has a history and goal as well as a form. It has a beginning and an end, and a number of critical turning points in between. Sacraments make grace enter human lives at these critical moments in a form that makes these lives be lived successfully, in terms of the goal to which the sacrament itself gives form. Aquinas notes in his reply to the second difficulty that sin is a feature of the existential reality of Christian life. Sacraments are particularly directed toward overcoming the baneful effect of sin in human existence. They are necessarily remedial. So Aquinas concludes that in the Christian dispensation the grace, virtues, and the gifts of the Spirit that sanctify humans and make their moral action reach out to eternal life are marked inherently by the sacramental moments through which they come to be and are developed. That marking entitles one to talk of graces as sacramental and to name them from the sacrament in which they are signified and given. It also requires one to say that in the Christian dispensation all grace is sacramental.

2. Grace and the Mystery of Christian Worship

In the remaining articles of q.62 Aquinas uses the notion of instrumental causality that he has fashioned for understanding how sacraments act in God's giving of grace, to clarify some traditional language and to ground his theology firmly on the Bible and the patristic tradition. Medieval theology, inspired by its reading of Augustine, held that sacraments "contain grace" and that there is a *virtus* in them to give grace. These were risky claims because they could make grace seem like a product to be stored and doled out. Aquinas goes to some metaphysical lengths in a.3 and a.4 to show that his concept of instrumental causality allows one to maintain a true understanding of grace as divine gift, while using this kind of metaphorical language about sacraments. In a.5 and a.6 he clinches his theory of instrumental causality both Christologically and biblically. He argues that the instrumentality of sacraments is a prolongation of the instrumentality of Christ's humanity. The grace of the Holy Spirit is given by God through Christ, the Word made flesh. His humanity, joined to his divinity in hypostatic union, is an attached (*coniunctum*) instrument of the divine; his sacraments are detached (*separatum*) instruments by which the divine causality of grace, active in his humanity, reaches humans in place and time.

The argument connecting the instrumentality of Christ's humanity and the instrumentality of the sacraments supposes a real connection between the human action of Christ and the human making of sacraments. In q.62 a.5 Aquinas finds the connection not in any appeal to the institution of the sacraments by Christ, but in the mysterious reality of his passion. In a passage that seems almost an anticipation of the *Kultmysterium* thinking of Odo Casel, he argues from Scripture (quoting Ephesians 5:2, "He offered himself as oblation and victim to God") that by his passion Christ inaugurated Christian worship (*per suam passionem initiavit ritum Christianae religionis*). The reference to the resurrection in Aquinas' reply to the third difficulty indicates that by "passion" he must mean what the term "Paschal Mystery" has come to mean in contemporary theology. Sacraments give access to this mystery of worship. To explain how they do so, Aquinas returns once again to the double movement of sacraments. The downward movement of sacraments does two things: it takes away sin, and it "perfects the soul in those things that belong to the worship of God according to the religion of Christian life." The downward movement does not exist without the upward movement. Sanctification occurs in human worship. This is an application of Aquinas' general theology of grace and its reception in human freedom. He analyzes further how this occurs in sacraments when he turns to the sacramental "character" and its participation in Christ's priesthood.

Aquinas grounds the relationship between sanctification and worship in sacraments on the mystery of Christ. He explains that sacraments give grace because they are acts of worship that join those who make them to the passion of Christ. The passion was the act by which Christ took away sin, meritoriously and by way of satisfaction, and simultaneously was the act by which he set up the only worship that is now acceptable to the Father. To be sanctified by Christ is not only to receive the remission of sin; it is to be joined to him in worship. It is to be made able to give oneself to the Father in him. Aquinas gives full Pauline realism to this joining with Christ: "The sacraments of the Church take their power especially from the passion of Christ, whose power is somehow joined [the Latin has the grossly realistic *copulatur*, which must be reminiscent of Paul's sexual language about membership of Christ in 1 Corinthians 6] to us by the reception of sacraments." He drives home the point by recalling the water and blood that flowed from the side of Christ and that evoke baptism and the Eucharist, which are the principal sacraments.

Through the sacraments the sanctifying power of Christ's Paschal Mystery reaches his members in their body as well as in their spirit. Because it comes from the human Christ it affects them as exemplar as well as efficient cause, as Aquinas notes in q.62 a.5 ad 1.[34] In them it takes the form of justifying faith.[35] The sanctifying power of sacraments is inconceivable for Aquinas apart from justifying faith. Sacraments, however, are more than a stimulus to faith. They have a depth of mystery that no other call to faith has. Aquinas explains this by raising in a.6 the classical question of the difference between the sacraments of the Old and the New Law. He recognizes that the sacraments of the Old Law were signs that called the ancient fathers to faith in the saving passion of Christ. By this faith they were justified by Christ who was to come. But the sacraments of the Old Law had no power within themselves to cause justifying faith in the cross of Christ. They carried the minds of believers to Christ, but did not themselves make Christ present to those believers in body as well as in spirit. They could not, because Christ did not yet exist in his physical, historical reality: he had not yet died and risen from the dead. Only when this Paschal Mystery had been actually accomplished could the glorious Christ take hold of human rituals, celebrated in space and time, and empower them to be his presence in body and spirit, sanctifying those who believe in him. The real mystery of the rituals celebrated in the Church—that which makes them sacraments—is the active presence of the mystery of Christ's death and resurrection within them.

3. The Sacramental Character (q.63)

The idea that some sacraments give a "character" to those who receive them, and that this character is something other than grace, was too solidly established in Latin theology for Aquinas to ignore it.[36] The postulate of a character had, to a large extent, grown out of the reception of Augustine's anti-Donatist reflections on the non-repetition of baptism. The medieval theology on this topic also owes much to certain passages of *The Ecclesiastical Hierarchy* of Pseudo-Dionysius. When it became a subject of independent analysis in the Middle Ages, it succumbed to the risk of becoming little more than a kind of "feather in the cap" of sacramental efficacy—decorative but not particularly useful. The Reformers disposed of it as a Scholastic superfluity. But if they knew something of Aquinas' theological thinking about it, they may have found deeper reasons for refusing it. In Aquinas the character becomes an integral element in his understanding of the nature of sacraments and their role as unique, active presences of the mystery of Christ. It is a key element of his understanding of the Church as the Body of Christ. The reason he gives in q.63 a.1 for the existence of sacramental characters, and the refinements he adds in subsequent articles, extend far beyond explaining why baptism is not repeated.

Underlying Aquinas' argument for the existence of character is the double movement that is inherent in sacrament. How the movements that he had earlier called sanctification and worship actually occur in sacraments is now spelled out in terms of grace and character. He takes up again an analysis he had introduced when discussing the grace of sacraments in q.62 a.5. The downward movement from God does the two things that sacraments are designed to do: it takes away sin, and it "perfect[s] the soul in all that concerns the worship of God according to the rite of Christian life." Now he adds that while sin is taken away by the gift of grace, qualification for worship is provided by the giving of character. Aquinas argues that those who are empowered to do something are normally marked out for their task: Christians are marked out for divine worship, and this marking is called character. The downward movement of sanctification thus has two component gifts: holiness of life and consecration for holy actions.[37] The upward movement of the sacrament is the grace-filled worship of persons so sanctified, exercising their role as consecrated people in virtue of their character, and having holiness of life to offer to God in virtue of grace. When one brings Aquinas' theology of grace and the virtues to bear on this double movement of sacraments, one can understand how sanctification and worship are not successive but simultaneous and interactive movements: grace is at work in the fact that it is received; the character is at work in the receiving of grace as well as in the flowering of grace as worship.

In the remaining articles of q.63 Aquinas' discussion of character becomes quite technical. Some of the technicalities have to do with defining its ontological status in terms of Aristotelian physics and psychology. If one believes the character is a reality, one must be able to give it a place in the categories by which one analyzes reality. Aquinas explains that it can be conceived as a spiritual power, instrumental, inhering in the cognitive faculties of the soul, and indelible. But what is far more interesting is the way his exploration of the notion of character evokes serious ecclesiological, Christological, and even trinitarian thinking.

4. Character and Ecclesiology

Aquinas notes as early as his reply to the first difficulty of a.1 that the character is a designation for acts that belong to the Pilgrim Church (*praesenti Ecclesiae*); in this it differs from the designation to life in the Glorious Church which is given by predestination and grace. Contemporary Thomists like Schillebeeckx are right to say that Aquinas' theology of character is an important contribution to what theology now calls the ecclesial dimension of sacraments. In his reply to the final difficulty of a.6, which evokes the classical Scholastic trilogy of *sacramentum tantum, res et sacramentum,* and *res tantum,*[38] Aquinas recognizes that the character belongs to the level of *res et sacramentum,* which is identified by contemporary theologians as the ecclesial level of sacramental analysis. The character empowers one to do ecclesial actions. It thus provides a satisfactory explanation of how one remains a member of the Church even when one refuses the full grace of membership. It explains how actions of those marked by the character can be recognized as acts of the Church, and therefore how sacraments given and received even by sinners can be true sacraments.

To understand the relationship between character and membership in the Church, it is helpful to look at the way Aquinas explains, in his reply to the second difficulty of q.63 a.1, how the character can be both inner spiritual reality and sign (*res et sacramentum* in Scholastic language). It is sign through its relationship with the visible sacramental rite in which it is given and whose giving is remembered in the Church (records are kept of baptisms, confirmations, ordinations, and other ecclesial actions that depend on these sacraments). The rituals of external membership signify the reality of belonging to Christ on the spiritual level of the character, and they also give that belonging its visibility. The Church is thus made, and seen to be made, the sacrament of Christ by the characters.

5. Character and Christology

Being in the Church means being related to Christ its head. Aquinas' ecclesiology of the character is grounded on Christology. In a.3 he sets out to establish that the sacramental character gives a relationship to Christ. As the difficulties put forward in the article suggest, the tradition could also suggest that the character, as a seal, is a relationship to the Holy Spirit or to the whole Trinity. One can find in the sed contra the reason Aquinas opted for the Christological understanding of character. He takes a current definition of character and explains it in the light of Hebrews 1:3. Reading from the Latin, with an evocation of the Greek, he interprets Hebrews as saying that Christ is "the character of the Father's substance." From this he argues that the eternal character, from which by definition the sacramental character is derived, is Christ, and that therefore the character has to be of Christ. Combining this with his position that the character is a designation for worship, Aquinas now reasons that the character must be a participation in Christ's priesthood. The reason he gives is that all Christian worship, the giving and receiving of the gifts of God that believers[39] do in the Church, is derived from the priesthood of Christ. He had already made this same point in q.62 a.5, putting it in terms of the cultic value of the passion. Here he draws the conclusion that the sacramental character, as designation for worship, is the character of Christ and is specifically a direct participation in the priesthood of Christ. As an instrumental capacity it allows Christ to use the believer to sacramentalize his worship in the Church. Aquinas will spell out this thought more fully in a.5. The rich thinking of that article is at the service of what might seem a peripheral curiosity—that sacramental characters are indelible. But this "curiosity" was an important issue in the explanation of the Church's refusal to reiterate certain sacraments. The indelibility of the character must not, however, be taken to invalidate Aquinas' persuasion that the character is given for acts appropriate to the Pilgrim Church.[40]

6. Character and the Trinity

The analysis of the character brings a Christological depth to the sacramental theology of Aquinas and through that to his ecclesiology. Even more noteworthy is the emergence of trinitarian theology in his thinking about the character. Before identifying the sacramental character as the character of Christ, he wants to do justice to the tradition that understood the sealing of the Christian as the work of the Holy Spirit. In a.3 he explains that the believer is signed (sealed) in view of two goals. The first is the enjoyment of the life of glory, and the signing for this is the grace of the Holy Spirit. The second goal is the ability to give and to receive the things that make up the worship of God. Aquinas sees the signing for this as configuration to Christ, because the worship of believers is the work of Christ, being what he brought into existence on the cross. In this worship and from it comes the grace of the Holy Spirit. One can suggest that Aquinas' distribution of sacramental effects between the Son and the Spirit is not merely appropriation but is real economic trinitarianism. Sacraments are made by those whom Christ the Savior has made his own by marking them with his character. That they bring the fullness of his justifying grace is the gift of the Holy Spirit. Grace is given by the Father through Christ in the sending of the Spirit. It is the gift that flowers in glory but is already at work in the time of waiting, in the Pilgrim Church. Its presence is manifested in the life of virtue and the gifts of the Spirit, and also in the charisms. Its divine provenance is authenticated in the worshipful giving and receiving that goes on in the sacraments. In these, the work of Christ is given ecclesial visibility in his members who, through their characters, participate in his priesthood. This allows the Spirit of holiness to be received and the Father to be glorified through Christ in the Spirit.

When Aquinas was discussing Christ's headship over the Church in q.8 of the *Tertia Pars*, he alluded briefly to this trinitarian reality of grace. In replying to the third difficulty, which involved an argument from a superiority of the heart over the head in the body, he wrote: "The head has an observable supremacy over the external members, whereas the heart has an influence that is hidden. And so the Holy Spirit is likened to the heart, since it is he who invisibly gives life and unity to the Church. But Christ is likened to the head by reason of his visible nature, in which he stands out as a man among men." Aquinas' analysis of the headship of Christ throughout q.8 is primarily in terms of grace and the way it is appropriated in faith and charity. But headship requires visibility, and it is in Christ's humanity that the divine is visible. Likewise it is in Christ's humanity that grace was gained and is actively given. Because Christ is the visible and economic cause of the grace that animates his Mystical Body, grace is said to be his, even though it is formally the grace of the Holy Spirit. The level of analysis in q.8 is Christological and the theme is the grace of Christ; the Church is being viewed for what it says about Christ. In q.63 the subject is the Church itself, in the sacraments that it makes and by which it is made. Similarly, in q.63 grace that is given in its eschatological fullness in the Church is attributed to the Holy Spirit, while the visible ecclesial giving and receiving of grace, which is orchestrated by the sacramental characters, is attributed to Christ. The priestly worship of his Paschal Mystery is given visibility through space and time in the Church that is his Body, and in that worship the grace of the Holy Spirit is given to and received by the faithful who await their resurrection at the Coming of Christ in glory.

7. Character and the Sacramentality of the Church

The final article on character can be read in a way that further clarifies Aquinas' understanding that sacramentality, in its sevenfold realization, constructs the Church. He deals with the organic unity of the sacramental system in q.65 a.1, arguing that it is articulated in seven sacraments to meet the various crucial needs of the life of grace. The explanation given in q.63 a.6 is more ecclesial, amounting to a demonstration that the deepest reality of the Church is expressed in the organic unity of its sacraments. This is worked out in an argument that ostensibly explains what by his time had become standard teaching in the Latin Church, namely, that three of the sacraments and only three—baptism, confirmation, and ordination—give characters. But one can read a lot more than this in the argument.

The starting point of the demonstration is once again the double movement, of sanctification and cult, inherent in sacramentality. A differentiation between sacraments can be discovered in the cult movement. Aquinas states that Christian worship is an action, and an action entails an agent and a recipient.[41] As cult actions of the Church, the different sacraments can be ranged according to this pattern. The cult action takes place uniquely in the Eucharist, which is the sacrifice of the Church. This sacrament does not give a character to anyone, because it is not a designation for worship but is worship itself in its fullness. It is the sacrament of Christ himself, the unique Priest, giving himself to the Father in his Paschal Mystery. But since it is as a sacramental action that Christ's sacrifice is being offered in the Church, there have to be agents and receivers: the Eucharist has to be made by people who can sacramentalize Christ's priesthood by their being designated for his worship as it is carried out in the Church. A sacrament has givers and receivers. What is done in it is a gift of God, and the gift aspect is sacramentally represented and brought home to the celebrating Church by the ministry of those who exercise a giving role; the receiving role, acted out sacramentally as receiving in relation to a minister who gives, makes what is done in the sacrament be experienced as a grateful and grace-filled response to God.

Here Aquinas is not distinguishing roles that are passive against roles that are active, but is distinguishing the roles of agent and of recipient.[42] In Christian worship receiving is every bit as active as giving, because it is the taking hold of grace. It is, indeed, the action that lasts forever. The roles are sacramental. One has to be careful of the word *potestas* that Aquinas sometimes uses to speak of them. It has often been misrepresented, especially in relation to the "power" that is attributed to the ordained. What the characters give are sacramental roles. These roles are ordered to actions of signifying, in its giving and receiving modalities. They join with the signification of elements and words in the making of a sacrament. And they must both be present for the making of a sacrament. There is no such thing as a sacrament celebrated for no one.

Aquinas uses the agent/recipient schema to explain how ordination and baptism (with confirmation) build up the sacramental worship of the Church and thus build up the Church as a eucharistic communion. The tradition would have suggested that baptism should be mentioned before ordination, but the schema required that the agent be put before the recipient, which is what Aquinas does. A clerical view of the Church will be comfortable with his priority, but should not read more into it here than schematic neatness.[43] Aquinas in fact recognizes the primacy of baptism by quoting the adage that baptism is "the door to all the sacraments." There would be no point in having ordained ministers if there were not a community of baptized persons desiring, by the very urge of their baptism, to celebrate the Eucharist. The only other sacrament that Aquinas mentions explicitly is penance. In the course of saying that it does not give a character, he suggests that its sacramental role is to restore people to the state they were in after their baptism and make them ready once again for full participation in eucharistic worship. He might attribute the same restorative role to the anointing of the sick, in line with what he will say about that sacrament in q.65 a.1. What he says about marriage there could also prompt thinking about it here in terms of ecclesial worship. In his reply to the third difficulty he suggests that what corresponds to the character in the non-character sacraments is their *res et sacramentum,* that is, the level of ecclesial qualification on which they operate. But these ecclesial qualifications will always suppose the presence of the original ecclesial belonging that is given in the character sacraments.

What makes Aquinas' understanding of the sacramental characters amount to a statement about the Church is the attention given to persons. For Aquinas both the characters and the *res et sacramenta* of the non-character sacraments make persons significant, capable of doing significant things. The Church is a community of persons. They are persons who believe and celebrate sacraments.[44] In celebrating sacraments they act as significant people capable, because they are marked out for it, of doing things that sacramentalize the priestly action of Christ. Christ culminates this sacramentalizing of worship by being himself present sacramentally as person, person of flesh and blood, in the Eucharist.[45] This community of sacramentalizing persons, both the head and the members, is the Church. Aquinas could have no difficulty about calling the Church a sacrament, because it is the sum total of sacramentality, and never more so than when it is celebrating the Eucharist. The Eucharist, like all the Church's character-grounded worship, is for sanctification. Aquinas shows very little interest in celebrations of sacraments where the characters work but grace is not given. His theology of character can, indeed, provide an explanation of how a sacrament can be truly a sacrament even when its grace is being refused. But it is much more designed to explain how the fullness of holiness, as grace and worship, is realized when believers open themselves to the full richness of the sacramental economy. And it is the Church of believers, built out of the priesthood of Christ and the grace of the Holy Spirit that flows from it, that reaches the visible summit of its being in the Eucharist.

Who Makes Sacraments? (q.64)

The crucial test of any theology of sacraments is the understanding it offers of how sacraments are actions of God. The whole tradition carried by the words *musterion* and *sacramentum* requires that the obvious anthropological structure of the rites be so explained that the divine event of salvation that occurs in them is affirmed in its full theological reality. In questions 60 – 63, Aquinas has been using anthropological categories to explain what sacraments are (their form), and how they operate to achieve their finality. At the same time he has been establishing that their form comes ultimately from God, and that their finality is the divine finality of the return of all things to God in Christ and the Spirit. However, it is in q.64 that he offers the decisive affirmation of the divine reality of sacraments.

The question is devoted to the agents that bring sacraments into existence. Because of what sacraments are and do, because of what the whole tradition of faith says about them, their originating cause can only be God: they must be understood as acts of God. This is so obvious that Aquinas hardly seems to think it necessary to establish it. His main concern in q.64 is to explain how, given their divine reality, sacraments can also owe their reality to created agents: they can be simultaneously divine and human realities. He makes the crucial distinction between how God acts and how creatures act in introducing the question: the causes of sacraments will be either originating or ministerial (*causa . . . sive per auctoritatem, sive per ministerium*). His answer throughout all the articles is dominated by the concept of instrumentality, which he now translates into the language of ministry (a.1: *eadem ratio est ministri et instrumenti*). His first article establishes the possibility of ministerial action in the making of sacraments. While it is true that only God can touch the spirit from within, created agents can touch it from outside, in the kind of sign-making address to the senses, imagination, and desire that sacraments entail. God can use this anthropological impact of the sacrament instrumentally to cause the interior effects of grace and character.

1. Institution of Sacraments by God

For human activity to serve God instrumentally, it must be done in the way God wants it to be done. This is the point made by the introduction of the question of the institution of sacraments by God in a.2. The issue is not whether God instituted this or that sacrament, but that nothing can be a sacrament unless instituted as such by God. The argument is that ritual actions made by humans do divine things because the power of God is in them. Only God can confer divine power on things that are not themselves divine. That is what God does by instituting certain rituals as sacraments. In fact, the only way one can know if a sacrament is an act of God is if it is an action that can claim divine institution.

The principle of divine institution of sacraments is clear, and Aquinas will hold firmly to it for the best of theological reasons throughout the remaining articles. But he does not spell out very clearly what it is and how it is done. It is something peculiar to the sacraments of the New Law. It seems to consist in giving power to rituals rather than in creating rituals. The presence of the power depends on certain necessary features being maintained in the ritual. These features have been determined by Christ, whose human actions were actions of God. They were determined more by what he did than what he said. Thus Aquinas says in q.66 a.2 that Christ instituted baptism by being baptized himself, rather than by his command to baptize in the name of the Father, Son, and Holy Spirit; and in q.73 a.5 Aquinas is content to say that Christ instituted the Eucharist at the Last Supper, without drawing special attention to what are sometimes called "the words of institution." What Christ did about sacraments is known to us from the Scriptures but also from what Aquinas (quoting 1 Corinthians 11:34, "about the other things I will give directions when I come") calls the "household tradition of the Apostles." Aquinas thinks that Christ gave to his followers all that is essential for sacraments. Later generations were able to add ritual niceties, but these are not of the essence of the sacrament. The business of the Church is to receive what has been handed on to it from Christ. Aquinas puts the apostles and their successors firmly in their place with a stirring piece of ecclesiology in his reply to the third difficulty of a.2: "The Apostles and their successors are the vicars of God in regard to the government of the Church, a Church that is instituted by faith and the sacraments of faith. And so, just as they cannot constitute a different Church, so they cannot hand on another faith or institute other sacraments; rather, the Church of Christ is built up by the sacraments that flowed from the side of Christ hanging on the cross."

2. Christ, Maker of Sacraments

The role of Christ in making sacraments obviously goes beyond the designation of the essential features of their ritual form. Aquinas devotes article 3 to exploring this role. It is a powerful reprise of his Christology, put at the service of understanding sacraments. Christ acts to make sacraments as God and as man. As God he acts as their originating cause. As man he acts as an instrument of divinity. His instrumental role is unique. It is that of the one who, in his Paschal Mystery, merited all the grace that is given to humans in sacraments, and was established in power as the sender of the Spirit, and hence as the one who actually gives grace. In virtue of that power, which Aquinas calls *potestas excellentiae,* Christ can act in sacraments, can have them celebrated in his name for the sanctification of those who believe in him, can institute them as he wills, and can bypass them when necessary, giving their proper effects of grace outside their actual celebration.

In calling the power that the human Christ has in the making of sacraments a *potestas excellentiae,* Aquinas wanted to separate it from any power that other humans might have in sacraments. However, it remains a human power, and in a.4 Aquinas is willing to entertain the possibility that Christ could have communicated it, in some subsidiary form, to other humans. It is an interesting speculation, which might have some relevance for contemporary discussion about the power authorities of the Church have to change certain features of the sacramental economy. The discussion might also take note of Aquinas' reasons for saying that Christ did not, in fact, communicate this power to other humans: it could tempt the faithful to rely on people other than Christ; it could give them the impression that the Church had other heads than he, and so could lead to divisions in the Church.

3. Ministers of Sacraments in the Church

Sacraments, which are acts of God, of Christ, and of the Church, find their most obvious actor in the minister who brings them to the believers coming to be sanctified. The minister is the last in the chain of instrumentality that brings the saving power of God actively to bear on God's people in sacraments. Believers exercise their sacramental role of reception, which is also instrumental in virtue of the "character," in contraposition to the one who ministers the sacrament. The tradition, firm in the Latin Church since Augustine's solution of the issue raised by Donatism, required Aquinas to say a few important things about the minister. He had to explain why the sinfulness of human ministers does not take away the reality of sacraments they provide. The concept of instrumentality provides an explanation of how Christ uses the sacramental action of a human minister: it is an explanation that allows one to understand how this ministerial action can serve Christ even when it is provided by a sinner who is refusing the grace of God in his own life. Of course, Aquinas recognizes that these ministers are meant to be themselves holy, and that it is incongruous and sinful for them not be so when they celebrate the sacraments of Christ and his Church. Nor is there any justification for sacramental automatism in his explanation of the ministerial role. What the minister does must be a truly human action: it must be done deliberately, with the intention of doing what the Church does when it celebrates such a sacrament.

Aquinas' appeal to the intention of doing what the Church does is ecclesiologically founded. The Church, in its faith and intention, carries responsibility for the action of those it authorizes to be ministers of its sacraments. This paring down of the minister's contribution to its ultimate essentials may have contributed historically to the development of a minimizing casuistry that did little to encourage ministerial excellence in the Church. On the other hand, it is worth noting that there is no trace in the *Summa* of the *ex opere operato* formula that Aquinas dabbled with in his commentary on the *Sentences*[46] and that continued to find favor in other Scholastic authors. Because *ex opere operato* became a prime target of the Reformers, and because the denial of it served as an expression of their rejection of general Catholic sacramental doctrine, the formula found its way into the condemnations of the Council of Trent and thence into Counter-Reformation theology. For Aquinas, however, a sacrament sanctifies not because it is a rite that is done, but because it is a sign of Christ and an instrument of his saving power.

Sacraments and the Life of Grace (q.65)

For methodological reasons question 64 concentrated attention on the agents of sacraments and left the recipients somewhat out of the picture. Question 65 puts the recipients back at the center, where they belong in the overall structure of

Aquinas' theology of sacraments. The question is about the numerical multiplication of sacraments. Technically, one might describe the topic as having to do
with material causality: how and why is the sacramental economy, which has been
analyzed as an organic unity up to now, made up of seven numerically distinct
sacraments? Historically, this question had taken a long time to be formulated and
an even longer time to be answered in the Church. In the eight difficulties regis-
tered in the first article, there are traces of the variant answers that Latin theology,
nourished on Augustine's lavish use of the term "sacrament," had considered until
the number seven became commonly accepted in the twelfth century. It is this
theological tradition, which would be canonized by the Latin Church at the
Council of Lyon in 1274, that Aquinas works on and tries to understand.

What is most interesting theologically about his approach is not its neat
schematizing, but the way it takes the life of grace, lived in the complexity and
historicity of human existence, as the ground for understanding the sacramental
system. This is the life that Aquinas has been analyzing progressively throughout
the *Summa,* in its constitution in the anthropological questions of the *Prima
Pars,* in its moral and grace-driven structure throughout the *Prima Secundae,* in
its virtuous activity and social interactions in the *Secunda Secundae,* and as it is
lived and redeemed in Christ in the *Tertia Pars.* Aquinas is now at the point of
seeing how that life is perfected. He knows that its ultimate perfection is in the
resurrection. But he believes that perfection is eschatologically realized, as an
"already" within a "not yet," in the sacraments, in which the Christian religion
comes fully alive. One can hear him saying this in the opening words of a.1: "The
sacraments of the Church are ordered to two things: to making humans perfect
in all that pertains to the worship of God according to the religion of Christian
life; and also to being a remedy against the damage done by sin."

The seven sacraments provide, in Aquinas' view, what humans need in order
to be eschatologically perfect. He describes this perfection as being achieved in
the worship of God as practiced in the Christian life. He has somehow transcended the double movement of grace and worship, the up and down schema
with the often heavy accent on the downward movement of sanctification. Sanctification is for worship, because God graces us so that we will turn to God and
give ourselves in worship. Christian life is a journey of return to God. Ultimate
holiness is achieved in the heavenly liturgy. This prioritizing of worship ensures
that the reception of sacraments, for all the passive language that is used about it,
is eminently active, being that most intense of all activities which is worship. In
the time of waiting, sacraments correspond to the sorrows as well as to the joys
of human life and manifest the pain as well as the glory of Christ's redeeming
passion, as Aquinas has analyzed these realities in the *Secunda* and *Tertia Pars.*

Sacramental grace keeps its remedial role: it purifies from sin and repairs the damage it does. This role is prominent in the sacraments of penance and anointing. But they too are acts of worship and passages toward the Eucharist.

1. The Eucharist and the Other Sacraments

The final article of Aquinas' six questions on the sacraments gives some specifications on how the different sacraments are necessary for salvation. But the real climax of his discussion comes in the third article, where he explains why the Eucharist is the most important among the sacraments. He takes his lead from Pseudo-Dionysius in the sed contra with a text that relates the Eucharist to "hierarchical perfection." The sense of ultimacy and perfection pervades the three reasons given for the greatness of the Eucharist. The first is that in the Eucharist, Christ himself is contained *substantialiter*. This is an interesting anticipation of the key role that *substantia* will have in Aquinas' teaching about the Eucharist. There is more to this reason than an evocation of what will come to be called the real presence. The Platonic-style contrast between *per essentiam* and *per participationem* that Aquinas uses is a contrast between full and transient reality. From the point of view of the one who receives it, the Eucharist gives a bonding with Christ himself, in the full reality of his being, whereas the other sacraments give a transient, functional contact with Christ. The Christ received in the Eucharist is Christ in the fullness of his priesthood and the fullness of his glory. He is received as the head of the Church. Aquinas re-echoes the *substantialiter* of the article in his reply to the first difficulty, where he says that "the common good of the whole Church is contained substantially [*substantialiter*] in the sacrament of the Eucharist."[47]

The Eucharist, then, is the sacrament in which the eschatological fullness proper to the sacramental economy is most fully realized and manifested.[48] There is nothing further to be done when one has received the Eucharist, whereas there always is another step to be taken after the reception of other sacraments. Aquinas offers as a second reason for the primacy of the Eucharist the fact that all the other sacraments are ordered to it as to their end. And his third reason, attributed again to Pseudo-Dionysius, appeals to liturgical practice to confirm that all sacraments are "consummated" in the Eucharist.

Aquinas is careful not to let the primacy of the Eucharist be taken as an excuse for belittling any of the other sacraments. He gives them each a significant place, and in the body of the article and in his replies to the difficulties he calls attention to particular ways in which each of them has some preeminence of its own. To grasp his thinking about sacraments, then, one should go on to study what he has to say about particular sacraments. It is disappointing that he left the task unfinished in the *Summa,* and also that he was not able to say his final word, promised in the prologue to the *Tertia Pars,* about how the gifts of the Savior to humanity, that we take hold of during life on earth in his sacraments, are brought to their fullness in immortal life through his final gift of resurrection. But at least he was able to give his full theology of the Eucharist. It wonderfully completes his theology of sacrament. At the same time, his theology of the Eucharist can only be fully understood in the light of his general theology of the sacramental economy.

Notes

1. I *Sent.,* prol. In this comparatively lengthy prologue to the commentary (pages 1–5 in the Mandonnet edition, vol. 1), Aquinas views the *Sentences* as being about the wisdom of God: in his wisdom God reveals himself, and this revelation of God is the matter dealt with in Book I; in God's wisdom creatures are produced, and that is the matter of Book II; in wisdom God restores, through the mystery of Christ, what has gone wrong in the created world, and this is the matter of Book III; finally, in his wisdom God brings things to perfection, in the attainment of their end, and that perfection is dealt with in Book IV. Aquinas explains that sacraments belong to this phase of perfection, as the immediate preparation provided by Christ for the entry into glory, in which the end is reached. It is the phase of the Church—the Church which Aquinas goes on to present as the paradisal garden, watered by the sacraments, in preparation for the glory of the resurrection, in which blessedness is reached.

2. Even in the *De articulis fidei et sacramentis,* which contains the only other substantial consideration of the sacraments in Aquinas' writings, the great creedal themes of God the Father, Son, and Spirit, of Creation, Incarnation, and Redemption, are developed before the sacraments are introduced. The final paragraph of this work (no.629 in the Marietti edition, 1954) confirms the connection Aquinas sees between sacraments and eschatology: it begins, "By the power of these sacraments humans are brought to future glory," and continues with a brief presentation of the seven *dotes* of soul and body, in which glory consists. On the *dotes* or "dowries," see the essay by Leget in this volume.

3. English translations of texts from the *Summa* in this essay are from the version published by Benzinger Bros. in 1947 (*St. Thomas Aquinas: Summa Theologica,* trans. Fathers of the English Dominican Province), and from the Blackfriars Latin/English edition published 1966–1975; the translations have occasionally been modified by the author.

4. The points being made here are borne out by the successive prologues to the Parts of the *Summa.*

5. E. Schillebeeckx, *De Sacramentale Heilseconomie: Theologische bezinning op S. Thomas' sacramentenleer in het licht van de traditie en van de hedendaagse sacramentsproblematiek* (Antwerp: 't Groeit Antwerpen, 1952).

6. E. Schillebeeckx, *Christ the Sacrament of the Encounter with God,* trans. P. Barrett and N. D. Smith (London: Sheed & Ward, 1963).

7. *Somme théologique: Les Sacrements,* trans. A.-M. Roguet, Éditions de la Revue des jeunes (Paris: Desclée, 1951).

8. Cf. K. Rahner, "Introductory Observations on Thomas Aquinas's Theology of the Sacraments in General," *Theological Investigations* 14 (New York: Crossroads, 1982), 149–85; H. McCabe, *The New Creation* (London: Sheed & Ward, 1960).

9. L.-M. Chauvet, *Symbole et Sacrement: Une relecture sacramentelle de l'existence chrétienne* (Paris: Cerf, 1987).

10. I have dealt with this question in more detail in "The Divine and the Human in St. Thomas's Theology of Sacraments," in *Ordo Sapientiae et Amoris: Hommage au Professeur Jean-Pierre Torrell,* ed. Carlos-Josaphat Pinto de Oliveira, O.P. (Fribourg: Éditions Universitaires, 1993), 321–52.

11. Texts that illustrate the presence of the threefold pattern of causality in the early questions of the *Summa* include the conclusion to the *quarta via* in *ST* I.2.3c: "Therefore there must also be something which is to all beings the cause of their being [efficient], goodness [final], and every other perfection [formal]; and this we call God." In Aquinas' answer to the question "Whether all things are good by the divine goodness" (*ST* I.6.4), he concludes: "Everything is therefore called good from the divine goodness, as from the first exemplary, effective and final principle of all goodness. Nevertheless, everything is called good by reason of the similitude of the divine goodness belonging to it, which is formally its own goodness, whereby it is denominated good. And so of all things there is one goodness, and yet many goodnesses." An even more comprehensive statement of the pattern comes in *ST* I.5.4c: "Since goodness is that which all things desire, and since this has the aspect of an end, it is clear that goodness implies the aspect of an end. Nevertheless, the idea of goodness presupposes the idea of an efficient cause, and also of a formal cause. For we see that what is first in causing, is last in the thing caused. Fire, e.g., heats first of all before it reproduces the form of fire; though the heat in the fire follows from its substantial form. Now in causing, goodness and the end come first, both of which move the agent to act; secondly, the action of the agent moving to the form; thirdly, comes the form. Hence in that which is caused the converse ought to take place, so that there should be first, the form whereby it is a being; secondly, we consider in it its effective power, whereby it is perfect in being, for a thing is perfect when it can reproduce its like, as the Philosopher says (*Meteorologica* iv); thirdly, there follows the formality of goodness which is the basic principle of its perfection."

12. *ST* I.15.3c: "So far as the [divine] idea is the principle of the making of things, it may be called an exemplar, and belongs to practical knowledge. But so far as it is a principle of knowledge, it is properly called a type, and may belong to speculative knowledge also. As an exemplar, therefore, it has respect to everything made by God in any period of time; whereas as a principle of knowledge it has respect to all things known by God, even though they never come to be in time...." God makes things according to their divine exemplars by an act of his will. I have noted in "The Divine and the Human" (339–40) that Aquinas introduces the notion of *signum* to speak of various modalities in which divine willing is expressed, and that one might make a useful connection between this use of the word and its use for the understanding of sacraments.

13. On the general issue of pneumatology in Thomas, cf. J.-P. Torrell, *Saint Thomas d'Aquin, maître spirituel, Initiation 2* (Fribourg: Éditions Universitaires, 1996), ch. 7, "Parler du Saint Esprit," 203–31.

14. Cf. the key statement in *ST* I-II.106.1.

15. In contrasting the "sealing" of grace with the "sealing" that is the sacramental character à propos Romans 5:5, Aquinas writes (*ST* III.63.3 ad 1): "The Apostle speaks there of that sealing by which a man is assigned to future glory, and which is effected by grace. Now grace is attributed to the Holy Spirit, inasmuch as it is through love that God gives us something *gratis*, which is the very nature of grace: while the Holy Spirit is love. . . ."

16. *ST* III.8.1 ad 3.

17. *ST* III.60.5; 62.5; 63.1; 63.6; 65.1.

18. *ST* II-II.89, prol.

19. On the relationship between *sanctitas* and *religio* and on the worship component of sanctification, cf. *ST* II-II.81.8 and ad 1.

20. This move is made in the prologue to *ST* III.60: "Now that we have completed our consideration of the mysteries of the Incarnate Word, our next field of investigation is the sacraments of the Church, seeing that it is from this same Incarnate Word that these derive their efficacy."

21. Augustine, *De doctrina christiana* II, 1 (PL 34, 35).

22. In *ST* III.60.4 ad 1.

23. *ST* III.7.9–13.

24. Augustine, *Tractatus super Joannis* 80.

25. *ST* III.64.2; 66.10. On *solemnitas* cf. *ST* 72.4.

26. *ST* III.66.1.

27. This is true of the Eucharist: the sacrament is made when people and priest take bread and wine, pray over them in a prayer that includes the core sacramental words, and receive them in the act of eating and drinking. There are good reasons for reserving the sacrament after the Mass has ended, but it is always intended that its sacramentality will be completed in its being eventually consumed.

28. *ST* III.83.4—concerning the Eucharist.

29. One hopes that Aquinas was not indulging in a bit of linguistic vanity in pointing out here that he knew the garbling could be more serious in Greek than in Latin because Greek inflected words at their beginning as well as at the end!

30. Cf. *ST* III, prol.

31. *ST* I-II.106.

32. *ST* III.8.1 ad 1.

33. *De Ver.* q.27 a.4 ad 13; q.28 a.2 ad 12.

34. Cf. *ST* III.56.1 ad 3 on the efficient and exemplar causality of Christ's resurrection.

35. *ST* III.62.5 ad 2: "virtus Christi copulatur nobis per fidem."

36. E. Schillebeeckx, *Christ the Sacrament of the Encounter with God*, ch. 6; J. Galot, *La nature du caractère sacramentel: Étude de théologie médiévale* (Paris: Desclée de Brouwer, 1958); B. Leeming, *Principles of Sacramental Theology* (London: Longmans, 1956), 129–279.

37. On the character as sanctification/consecration cf. *ST* III.63.5; 63.6 ad 2.

38. The medieval analysis of sacrament recognized three levels in it: the *sacramentum tantum* is the external ritual; the *res tantum* is the divine grace that is given to those for whom the sacrament is celebrated; the *res et sacramentum* is an intermediate level on which the persons taking part in the sacraments are spiritually qualified by the sacraments they are receiving, or have already received, to make sacred actions that signify the receiving or giving of the grace of Christ. The need to recognize the intermediate level emerged in the course of reflection on how people could make real sacraments even when they were not living in the grace of the Holy Spirit. It

was, from the beginning, a way of recognizing that Christ could always be counted on to act when his members performed a true sacrament.

39. Aquinas regularly designates the character actors as "believers" in these articles (e.g., in 63.3 ad 3); this corresponds to his locating the character in the "cognitive power of the soul" in which faith resides (63.4 ad 3).

40. In *ST* III.63.5 ad 3 he allows that the character remains in heaven, but as something to be shown off rather than to be used.

41. In *De Ver.* q.23 a.2 Aquinas introduces a discussion on God's action with the words: "in qualibet actione est aliquid considerandum ex parte agentis et aliquid ex parte recipientis."

42. The character of baptism is sometimes described as "passive" in comparison with the active character of orders. In *ST* III.63.6, however, Aquinas' contrast is not between *agens* and *patiens*, but between *agens* and *recipiens;* he also speaks about the *potestas recipiendi.*

43. The suggestion of Galot (*La nature*, 181) that in working out the theology of character, Aquinas moved from taking baptism as the primary model of understanding to giving that place to ordination, does not seem at all well founded.

44. Cf. *ST* III.64.2 ad 3: "Ecclesia instituta per fidem et fidei sacramenta."

45. Aquinas explains the presence of Christ in the Eucharist in terms of instrumentality and of *res et sacramentum* in *ST* III.73.1 ad 1 and ad 2.

46. In order to affirm that a sacrament has a power to give grace that is not dependent on the holiness, or lack of it, of the one who administers the sacrament, Scholastic theologians said that sacraments gave grace not *ex opere operantis* (literally, "not because of the work of the worker"), but *ex opere operato* (literally, "because of the work worked"). It was a smart way of expressing the objective value of a properly celebrated sacrament, over against the value of any other exercise of piety in the Church (such as prayers offered for people) that depends on the subjective goodness, or lack of goodness, of the one who performs it. It was never meant to suggest that subjective dispositions were of no account in sacraments, either in the minister or, more particularly, on the part of the one who receives the sacrament. It was taken as obvious that, without exercising faith and charity, the recipient could gain no saving grace from a sacrament, for all its objective reality. The limitation of the expression *ex opere operato* is that it says nothing about the reason why sacraments have their objective reality. And it carries the risk of suggesting that the rite has some inherent power that works independently of all personal factors. By taking the trouble to explain that sacraments work as they do because they are signs and instruments of the active presence of Christ, by pointing out that the minister acts in them as an instrument of Christ, and by leaving no doubt that they only cause grace in those who participate in them with faith and love, Aquinas obviates the need for the *ex opere operato* formula or at least guards against its risks. On this see Schillebeeckx, *Christ the Sacrament*, 100–109.

47. It is interesting that a reflection on the sacrament of marriage provoked this strong ecclesiological statement from Aquinas. He also recognizes the ecclesiological connection between marriage and Eucharist in the body of the article, when he says: "Marriage touches [Eucharist] at least in its signification, insofar as it signifies the joining of Christ and the Church, in a unity that is represented by the sacrament of the Eucharist."

48. This is how Aquinas will explain the name *viaticum* given to the Eucharist in *ST* III.73.4c: "[This sacrament] has a third signification with regard to the future. It prefigures that enjoyment of God which will be ours in heaven. That is why it is called *viaticum*, because it keeps us on the way to heaven."

Eschatology

CARLO LEGET

Is there a life after death? What may we hope for? What should we think of heaven and hell? Questions like these are traditionally subsumed and treated under the heading of "eschatology," the doctrine of the Last Things. Contemporary theology has great difficulty answering them. Although the twentieth century has known an enormous revival in the study of eschatology, both in theology and in pastoral care there seems to be a crisis: the old images do not function any longer, and nothing new has emerged to replace them. Has Thomas Aquinas anything to say in this mysterious area of Christian faith? Can the medieval author still be a source of inspiration, a guiding light, despite his outdated cosmology and anthropology? Before these last questions can be addressed, a clear idea must be developed about what exactly Aquinas teaches on the topic.

A first glance through Aquinas' *Summa Theologiae* is disappointing. Aquinas never finished the last part that was planned to deal with eschatology. Due to an overwhelming experience during Mass on the feast of St. Nicholas, he stopped writing halfway through the treatment of the sacrament of penance. In some editions of the *Summa* the remainder of the treatise on the sacraments and on eschatology is supplied by a so-called *supplementum*. As a matter of fact, however, this supplement was composed by Aquinas' personal secretary, Reginald of Piperno, from material taken from Aquinas' commentary on the *Sentences* that had been written twenty years earlier.[1]

Those who know Latin—the commentary on the *Sentences* is still not available in any of the modern languages—and turn to the source of this cut-and-paste work are likely to meet a strange world of medieval fantasy and future-telling. Will the resurrected have hair and nails? (Yes.) Will all be of the masculine sex after resurrection? (No.) Will all resurrect in the same age, as young people? (Yes.) Can a glorified body be in the same place as a non-glorified body simultaneously because of its subtlety? (No.)[2]

How do we relate to this way of thinking? How can we begin to appreciate the faith that animated the intellectual labor to which these texts testify? And what is the relevance for theology today? Various routes are possible here. I start with Aquinas' treatment of death, which leads to his reflections on the concept of "life." His discussion of "life" gives us a key to Aquinas' eschatology, enabling us to grasp its place in his systematic theology, its connection with the doctrine of God, and its "logic." From this perspective I offer an interpretation of the peculiar questions with which Aquinas deals. Finally, I address the question as to what contribution Aquinas' reflections can make to contemporary eschatology.

Death

Human beings are corporeal beings. They are part of the material world. This means that they are subject to processes of development, growth, and decay. But they also participate in the spiritual world. By their intellectual capacity they share in the immaterial world, a realm of being outside the coordinates of materiality and time. What, according to Aquinas, is a human being, which participate in two worlds, and what happens when a human being dies?

A human being, in Aquinas' view, is a unity of body and soul. Men and women are not intellects that are accidentally wrapped up in a bunch of muscles and bones. Corporeality is a necessary element for speaking of a human being. Contrary to common sense experience—according to which the soul seems to be a function of the body—Aquinas follows Aristotle in stating that metaphysically the soul contains the body rather than the reverse.[3] The body is held together by the soul. The soul is regarded as the form (*forma*), motor, and goal of the body (*matter*). Thus, metaphysically the soul is the stronger of the two.[4]

From a theological perspective, human beings hold a unique central position in creation. They are the bridge between the material and the spiritual world. This central position is a privileged one. Consequently, Aquinas calls a human being "a little world" (*minor mundus*) and considers humanity to be more perfect—in the sense of containing all dimensions of creation—than, for example, angels, who intellectually are far more gifted than the most brilliant human minds.[5]

The central position of human beings—a position showing an "overlap"—is reflected in their soul. Following Aristotle, Aquinas speaks of three parts of the soul: a vegetative, sensory, and intellectual part.[6] These parts can be distinguished without challenging the unity of human nature. They interact and need one another so as to live as a corporeal creature that is aimed at a spiritual goal: full participation in God's abundant life.

Theologically speaking, again, Aquinas assigns a hierarchy to the different levels of being that flow together in human nature. Since humans are created for knowing and loving God—in which consists their happiness—and since God can only be known by the intellect (although not without God's help), all human faculties are ordered to the working of the intellect. According to Aquinas' theological cosmology, the world is at the service of the corporeal dimension of man; the corporeal dimension is at the service of the spiritual one; and the spiritual dimension is at the service of the union with God. Sometimes Aquinas takes the three steps as one, saying that the universe is created for the sake of the beatitude of the saints.[7]

If one looks in Aquinas' extensive *oeuvre* for a clarification of the nature of death, one discovers that he does not devote any questions or articles to this topic.[8] For example, for what concerns the moment of dying, Aquinas takes a very sober approach. We can recognize the process of dying, being a process of a living creature and pertaining to the realm of being. We can recognize a corpse: a body bereft of its natural form. The transition between the two of them, however, is not open to our knowledge. Nowhere does Aquinas speculate about it, in contrast with twentieth-century discussions by theologians who regard the moment of dying as one of decisive importance.[9] Nevertheless, two definitions appear throughout his works: separation of the soul from the body (*separatio animae a corpore*)[10] and privation of life (*privatio vitae*).[11] Both of them frame Aquinas' reflection on our fate after death.

The expression "separation of the soul from the body" seems to suggest that both elements have a certain subsistent existence of their own, so that they can be separated. We know what happens to the body in this case: separated from the soul, it dissolves.[12] But what happens to the soul? Aquinas speaks of a separated soul (*anima separata*) that continues to exist after death.[13] What then is this separated soul like? Does it reveal anything about the situation, or even "life," after death?

Aquinas indeed speaks of the human soul after death. But the separated soul is no longer a human being. By the separation of form (*forma*) and matter (*materia*), human nature is destroyed. Thus, neither the separated soul nor the remaining corpse can be called a "human being," and neither can be called a "person" in the Boethian sense.[14]

Although the separated soul is not a human being, Aquinas states that it subsists after death. What, then, is the status of this immortal substance, and why does he reflect on it? Aquinas regards the separated soul as a damaged substance, neither a person nor belonging to human nature. Stripped of the functions of the vegetative and sensitive parts, which are intrinsically connected with the bodily human nature, all that remains is the rational part, which cannot be corrupted because of its immateriality.[15] This situation of a form, existing apart from the matter it was meant to inform, is against human nature.[16] It has a different, non-natural mode of being and, consequently, a similar mode of knowing, according to which it is not able to use the images (*phantasmata*) that are so important for and characteristic of the human mode of knowing.

In the condition of the separated soul a tension comes to the fore that—according to a metaphysics inspired by Aristotle—cannot remain forever. Aquinas uses this philosophical insight as an argument that it is not unreasonable to believe in a resurrection of the body.[17] And it is within this theological context that Aquinas' view on the separated soul gains its full meaning and coherence.

Two more considerations bring us to the realm of theology. To begin with, Aquinas is well aware of the fact that the dead are cut off from communicating with the living by divine ordination.[18] In speculating about these topics one touches upon boundaries that were set by God. Nevertheless, questions emerge, not least because of stories in Holy Scripture like that of Lazarus and the poor man (Luke 16:19–31). Thus exegesis is the motor of Aquinas' philosophical analysis. And second, because Aquinas focuses strictly on the separated soul, one easily forgets that in Aquinas' view the separated soul is always in purgatory, in heaven, or in hell. In other words, its mode of being is totally determined by its relationship with God.

So far, we must conclude that Aquinas does not enlighten us regarding our situation after life. He has a very sober and "negative" appreciation of death. It can only be known as a departing from the life of which it is a privation. This leads us to the second definition mentioned above. By defining death as privation of life, it is presented as a defect, an evil. Aquinas agrees with Aristotle that death is the greatest corporeal evil of this earthly life, naturally filling man with horror.[19]

Because death is seen as an evil, it has no ontological status of its own. It cannot be known immediately. Since things can only be known insofar as they exist—insofar as they "have being"—death can only be known by the mediated knowledge of the being of which it is a privation. Following this negative definition, we may hope to gain some insight by studying the concept of "life." This is not such a bad idea, since the Christian tradition (the Creed) speaks of "eternal life" as the promise for those who are united to Christ, a promise that transcends the boundaries of earthly existence. This brings us to the heart of Aquinas' theology.

Life

In contrast to his reserve with regard to the concept or moment of death, Aquinas devotes considerable attention to the subject of "life." For instance, at the beginning of his *Summa Theologiae* he investigates the question whether "life" can be a name of God.[20] His answer is both revealing and of importance to eschatology, for one cannot understand Aquinas' eschatology without understanding his doctrine on God.

"Life" appears to be a keyword in Aquinas' theology. It can be used as a name both of God and of creatures; it refers to the human mode of being, the destination of our existence ("eternal life"), conversation with God, and so forth. Given this wide application of "life," it is clear that Aquinas places human existence in a larger framework. Theologically, the challenge he meets is a very precise determination of the various ways in which the word "life" is used in these divergent contexts. Because the concept "eternal life" is among the ones involved, eschatology is involved as well.

In Aquinas' systematic reflection on the various contexts and meanings of "life," two directions of thinking are developed simultaneously. On the one hand, there is continuity between God and his creatures, based on the idea that the Creator is known by and interested in the work from his hands. On the other hand, Aquinas tries to do justice to the fundamental discontinuity between creature and Creator, which marks our knowledge of God. God is not an "oversized creature," and the distinction between Creator and creature is principally different from any distinction by which creatures differ from one another.[21] God differs "differently."

According to the line of continuity of living things, properties like movement and autonomy become more advanced and complex in higher forms of life. In the scale of living creatures, ranging from plants, animals, and human beings to angels, God can thus appropriately be called "living" since he cannot be considered to have any of the limitations that are characteristic of created forms of life. In Scripture and tradition God has made himself known as free and pure activity (no mere unmoved mover). On the other hand, we must conclude that our created concepts continuously fall short when we try to think the concept of life in its most perfect form. This, however, is not so strange, because already in the third question of his vast *Summa Theologiae* Aquinas concludes: "Of God we do not know how he is. Rather how he is not."[22] God is a mystery, a divine mystery that should be approached as such, even when studied by theologians or philosophers.

Theologically speaking, Aquinas' approach leads to an important reversal of perspective as regards life. As a consequence of his line of reasoning, we must say that although by knowing various created forms of life we have some notion of what life is, the ultimate criterion according to which the concept of life is defined remains beyond our grasp. We can point in a certain direction, that of the Creator and spring of life. The object of our pointing, however, which—or rather who—is most appropriately called "living" or even "Life itself," is not known directly and in a way that corresponds to his infinite perfection.

This epistemological reversal is accompanied by an ontological perspective. By considering the natural life of human beings within the larger framework of the life of God, Aquinas is able to work out the idea that human beings have participation in divine life as their destination. The life and work of Christ opened a new horizon to humankind: a horizon of glorified human nature, fully participating in divine glory. Eschatology is precisely that part of theology that reflects on the perfection of creation, the glorification and sharing in God's life. In Aquinas' theology, "eternal life" is a name for both the destination of human-kind and for God.

When we reflect on the nature of eschatology, knowing how Aquinas speaks of life, some salient features come to the fore. In the first place, eschatology is profoundly theocentric in character. It has nothing to do with future-telling, with making extrapolations or having a privileged access to the future as Christians. It deals with God's perfecting activity, not ours. This God-centered character is expressed in a further feature: Aquinas deals with eschatology from the perspective of God, as we shall see later. Even the question of whether I will have nails in heaven is answered by reasoning from the role these might have in perfect communion with God. And finally, because our knowledge of God's life is limited in earthly life, our knowledge of the perfect participation in eternal life is subject to the apophatic quality of God-talk.

The Eschatological Dimension of Theology

Considering the nature of eschatology, one might say that it is the part of theology that deals with God's glorifying work.[23] As such, within Aquinas' theology it is not a separate discipline but a dimension inherent in the consideration of every theme that is questioned with respect to God (*sub ratione Dei*). When reading the *Summa Theologiae*, it is easy to show that the eschatological dimension is present in every treatise.[24]

Already in the very first question of the *Prima Pars*, the need for another (sacred) doctrine, distinct from philosophical studies, is based on the fact that God is the ultimate end of human life: this end should be known so that men can direct their intention and actions toward it.[25] Subsequently, this sacred doctrine is defined from the perspective of the perfect knowledge that God and the beatified have.[26] And in discussing the nature of our earthly knowledge of God, the beatific vision is regarded as the criterion by which all knowledge should be measured. The primacy of the perspective of eternal life emerges prominently when Aquinas examines the completion of the work of creation on the seventh day: the end (*finis*) of the entire universe is the perfect beatitude of the saints.[27] And in his anthropological passages, he makes clear that man as image of God is a dynamic concept. Human beings are images of God in three ways: by their natural abilities to both know and love God, insofar as they—with the help of God's grace—actually know and love God, and finally when they reach eternal life.[28]

The second part of the *Summa* opens with an investigation into the ultimate end of creation and the special character of the ultimate end of man.[29] The eschatological perspective remains a guiding one throughout the "moral" part of the *Summa* that deals with the various possible emotions, habits, virtues, and actions that contribute toward attaining this end. The distinction between mortal and venial sins is based on the possibility of missing the ultimate end (eternal death);[30] the theological virtues are directed at the blessed communion with God in heaven;[31] only theological virtues are called virtues in the proper sense, because they alone make the ultimate end attainable;[32] and within the context of the examination of the particular virtues, the question as to whether the virtue concerned will remain in eternal life has a regular place.[33]

In the third part of the *Summa*—dedicated to Christ, the sacraments, and eschatology—the latter constantly determines the perspective. The Word has become flesh so as to enable mankind to enjoy perfect communion with God. The life and work of Christ is the beginning of the divine work of glorification that is studied in eschatology. Christ is *viator* ("on the way," according to his human nature) and *comprehensor* ("having arrived," according to his divine nature). His resurrection is the first fruit of the perfection of creation and reveals to us something of the nature of God and what he wants us to become.[34] As regards the sacraments, Aquinas teaches that they not only refer to the cause of our sanctification and the life of grace that is effected in us by virtue of Christ's passion; they also refer to the eternal life that is the ultimate end of our earthly existence.[35]

Although Aquinas never reached the treatise on eschatology in his *Summa Theologiae,* these examples tied to crucial parts of his theological structure are convincing enough to see that eschatology is perfectly integrated in his theological approach. In fact it is a structuring principle of his theological approach.[36] With this in mind, our attention can be focused on the treatise itself.

From the Last Supper to the Last Things

In the prologue to the *Tertia Pars*, Aquinas formulates the intention to close the *Summa Theologiae* by considering "the end which is immortal life."[37] By placing this tract at the end of his work, he is in line with Peter Lombard's *Sentences* and the order of the creeds.[38] From the perspective of the history of salvation, the location seems to be natural since it concerns the end of time.

When the place of this tract is examined more closely, one discovers that Aquinas attaches the perspective of immortal life to the life, death, and resurrection of Christ.[39] Christ is "the Way, Truth and Life" (John 14:6): it is through him that we enter the Life of God.[40] Thus eschatology must be seen in the light of the redemptive work of Christ. The life of glory is the perfection of the life of grace that is bestowed on human beings through the sacraments, by which the restorative work of Christ is mediated.

According to Aquinas, Christ came for the restoration of our relationship with God. His life, death, and resurrection, however, are the beginning of a process that needs to be applied to every individual human being. In Christ the spiritual restoration is completed by his corporeal resurrection. Thus, as head of the Church, he reveals the destination of humankind: life with God involving all dimensions of man, both spiritual and corporeal. In the community of Christ's followers, spiritual restoration is obtained by the sacraments; the corporeal side is delayed until the end of time.[41]

The life, death, and resurrection of Christ thus have a double eschatological character. First, in terms of causality: with Christ the process of restoration of life with God begins. From that moment on, the Holy Spirit is rooted in the history of humankind as the Spirit of Christ, communicated through the sacraments. With this new beginning, the process of sanctification of creation has begun— a process which will be consummated by the glorification at the end of time. Second, in terms of revelation: with the resurrection of Christ the plenitude and abundance of the restored (or rather, glorified) life with God is revealed to humankind. Thus, the resurrection of Christ has an important hermeneutical function for Aquinas when he interprets the eschatological passages in Holy Scripture.

The fundamental importance of Christ with regard to our relationship with God is based on the union of human and divine natures in his Person. Christ embodies the perfect relationship between God and man: his human life is entirely God-centered, and the glorification of his human nature is the consummation of this God-centered life. In examining Aquinas' eschatology, one recognizes this

God-centered perspective as the guiding principle of his reflection. Everything is considered under the idea of perfecting the relationship with God, on the model of Christ's resurrection, and with the help of biblical stories. The decisive framework, then, is that of a corporeal resurrection by which human nature is restored and the relationship with God is enjoyed and expressed in the integrity of body and soul. According to this ultimate perfection, there can only be two states: that of total union with God (heaven) and that of total rejection of him (hell).

This corporeal resurrection, however, will not take place until the end of time, when the entire creation is purified, judged, and reorganized in the light of our relationship with God.[42] This entails that the souls of those who die before the end of time "wait" for reunion with their body, in order to enjoy the life of the beatified in accordance with the two dimensions of human nature. Aquinas also considers this situation of waiting from the perspective of the relationship with God. Since the will is fixed at the moment of death, the relationship with God—measured in terms of charity—does not alter. Therefore, one could say that the quality of this relationship is decided upon at the moment an individual human being dies. In this particular judgment (*iudicium singulare*) it has already been decided whether or not there is a relationship of God in grace that can be consummated in glorification. Thus, in Aquinas' view, immediately after dying the separated soul endowed with charity is united with God in the beatific vision; and the soul without charity is separated from God. In Aquinas' day, however, the conviction had grown that a third option was possible: the situation of the soul endowed with grace, which, nevertheless, is in need of purification because of venial sin. The name for this state is purgatory.[43]

Keeping in mind this God-centered perspective, it becomes clear that for Aquinas the notion of the incorruptibility of the soul occupies only a subordinate position within the larger theological framework. For the theologian—who considers everything with respect to God—and for the believer—who considers everything from the God-centered perspective of charity—the question is not "what happens to me after death?" but "what happens to my relationship with God, after death?"[44] Aquinas' conviction that the soul is incorruptible because of its immateriality allows him to conceive the continuity between earthly human life and life after death, but has no value apart from the relationship with God. To put it bluntly: because the relationship with God continues to exist after death—since God's life (the life of grace) surpasses the boundaries of natural life—there has to be a created entity to which this love is addressed. This, and nothing more or less, is the separated soul.[45]

The subordinate position of the separated soul is also evident when looked at from another perspective: as part of the damaged human nature, it is entirely directed at fully human participation in eternal life. Only after the resurrection of the bodies can one speak of the glorification of human beings. Thus the resurrection of the body is not a bit of "extra dessert" after the immortality of the soul; it is part of the "main meal" and, more precisely, the part by which the glorification of human life takes place in accordance with the coordinates of (glorified) materiality and time, characteristic of the human condition.

The Theological Nature of Eschatology

Eschatology is not the same as futurology. The reason why Christian theology deals with the future from a theological perspective is because Holy Scripture contains passages that speak of God bringing to completion what he has begun when creating the world. With the resurrection of Christ, moreover, for the first time in history God revealed the glorification of a human being. If eschatology is the part of theology that deals with creation in the mode of perfection, doesn't it lift the veil all the same? Isn't it a pious way of future-telling despite the various reservations that were expressed above? And isn't this especially true in relation to Aquinas' detailed questioning about what has been called "the furniture of heaven and the temperature of hell"?

Although a superficial reading of selected passages from Aquinas' eschatological treatises might suggest this, a thorough examination of the consequences of what has been said makes clear that his picture of heaven is anything but a travel guide for the hereafter. The main reason is that life after death lacks the dynamism toward a goal that is characteristic of life on earth. The hierarchy of elements that structure Aquinas' anthropology—world, body, soul, God—are present, but in a different way. The union with God glorifies the soul; the glorified soul expresses itself in a glorified body; the glorified body is endowed with a glorified creation. In this scheme, the same elements appear in a reversed order, this time organized radically from the central point at which the elements in earthly life are directed.

This reversed order is characteristic of the peculiar nature of God's glorifying work: the structure, according to which everything is connected, no longer has a character of finality (in the sense of showing a correlation of ends and means). Its character is rather one of overflowing, copious expression. This is hardly thinkable from the perspective of a world in which everything is moving toward the ultimate end. But if one takes the ultimate end seriously, it cannot be conceived except in terms of total arrival: all striving comes to total rest. In fact, here we come close to the very same incomprehensible non-motion of

God's own life. Indeed, it is "eternal life" of which we are talking. Nevertheless, the distance between Creator and creatures remains. What, then, does heaven look like?

Heaven

1. The Glorified Soul

The human intellect is organized so as to obtain knowledge by abstraction of information provided by the senses. God, however, is not an object in the sensible world. He cannot be distinguished with the help of the same procedure by which created objects are distinguished, namely, by looking for differences. As stated earlier, God differs "differently." He is outside any genus or species, and none of our concepts or words is used univocally when naming the divine essence. Nevertheless, in Holy Scripture the promise is made that God "will be seen face to face and known as I am known" (1 Corinthians 13:12). How can God ever be known directly when the human intellect and the divine perfection seem to be so incompatible?

Proceeding from the created intellect as faculty, Aquinas teaches that it should be strengthened and made available in order to be able to receive God. This is accomplished to the extent that the will is assimilated to God by charity. The result of this in the intellect is a similitude, a God-likeness (*deiformitas*) of the faculty of seeing, which Aquinas calls "light of glory,"[46] according to the verse: "In you is the source of life, by your light we see the light" (Psalm 36:9). This light is a created light, since it is a created participation in God's intellectual power.[47] Apart from strengthening the intellectual power, God also provides the intelligible species, because of the fact that the glorified intellect is immediately united to God himself. In earthly life the agent intellect forms an intelligible species by which the object known is presented to the intellect. Because God is outside any genus, no intelligible species can contain him. The only way of knowing him directly is the manner in which God knows himself: by being at one and the same time knower, object known, medium by which the object is known, and act of knowing—thus discerning what, according to divine simplicity, cannot be separated. Therefore, in the beatific vision God is not only object of knowing, but also medium by which the object is known.[48] Here we reach the borders of what is comprehensible. The object, as well as the medium by which we know, is God's incomprehensible being. This is true participation in God's knowing, which is his very being. The abundance of this sharing in God's perfection is expressed in the fact that the borders of the potency of the glorified soul—the soul strengthened by light of glory—are transcended.

Eternal life is God's life in God's mode: it is knowing God with the double help of God. It is a life of perfection according to which all striving and desiring have come to rest. The ultimate end is attained and there is no further end or further future.[49] For this reason eternal life has a character of overflowing expression. The nature of this structure is the same as that of creation. God did not need to create for any goal. For the blessed the same is true: there is no further end apart from sharing in God's beatitude. Both motives flow together in the notion of eternal life: in giving eternal life, the triune God gives himself, and giving oneself is a sign of great love (John 15:13). In eternal life we are assimilated to God's overflowing goodness (or love), sharing the same copious beatitude that is at the origin of creation.[50] In the state of glory everything is there as an expression of this beatitude, including, in the first place, that which is by nature closest to the glorified soul: the body.

2. The Glorified Body

As we saw above, Aquinas rejects any dualistic anthropology according to which the soul can only be blessed when it is separated from the body. In his view the ultimate perfection of the soul cannot exclude its natural perfection, according to which it should be united to the body. In his account of the role of the body, however, he tries to keep a balance between two demands. On the one hand, the perfect disposition of the body is necessary for a beatitude that is perfect in every respect. On the other hand, this perfect disposition of the body does not contribute to the essence of beatitude: its role is preceding and subsequent.

The perfection of the body precedes perfect beatitude to the degree that it causes no hindrance for the operation of the intellect; it is subsequent to perfect beatitude by the fact that it shares in the perfection of the intellect by overflowing (*redundantia*).[51] The body is thus indispensable for perfect beatitude, but nevertheless does not contribute to its essence. The relation between body and soul in the state of consummated life with God is one of overflowing expression. In eternal life, human life is still material, corporeal, but now radically "redefined" in the light of our completed relationship with God. In this "redefinition" everything is consistently based upon the relationship with God.[52] The human capacity for God is located in the soul, not in the body. The body that has helped us to grow unto eternal beatitude is not able to reach it directly. It can only receive it from the soul by overflowing.[53] In this God-centered eschatology the corporeal dimension of human existence is not denied, but radically subjected to its core: life with God.[54]

In the glorified soul, the faculties are in perfect harmony. Since the soul is the form of the body (*forma corporis*), the perfection of its faculties results in a perfect operation of those powers that are connected with the body.[55]

The passage of Scripture which is most influential in the appreciation of the resurrected body is 1 Corinthians 15:42–44. Here the re-creation of man, proceeding from his relationship with God, is qualified as the resurrection of a spiritual body instead of an animal-like one. The animal-like body—perfected by the soul—is the one that is inherited from the first man, Adam. The spiritual body is the one that is entirely directed at the spiritual dimension of human life. Moreover, the word "spiritual" simultaneously refers to the life of grace. Here Christ is the ancestor, giving access to the life-giving Spirit.[56]

In medieval theology, the perfection of the glorified body is discussed under the notion of "dowries" of the body (*dotes corporis*). Aquinas distinguishes four dowries that God gives to the glorified so that the body shares in the glory of the soul: subtlety (*subtilitas*), lightsomeness (*claritas*), the incapacity of suffering (*impassibilitas*), and agility (*agilitas*).[57] The dowries are not descriptions of the glorified materiality of the body. The four concepts express the relation between soul and body: corporeal dowries are the dispositions in the glorified body by which the body is made perfectly subjected to the soul.[58] The glory of the soul as form of the body is revealed in the first three dowries, and the function of the soul as motor is perfected in the fourth. Subtlety is not a property that enables the resurrected to walk—like the resurrected Lord—through closed doors; it is a term that denotes the perfect accommodation of the body to the "spiritual man."[59] Lightsomeness does not refer to a luminous skin, but indicates that the clarity of the soul is materially expressed in the beauty of the body.[60] The incapacity of suffering corresponds to the perfect operation of the soul with regard to the preservation of the body.[61] Agility, finally, concerns the perfect control of the soul over the body with regard to corporeal movements.[62]

The dowries materially express the spiritual perfection of the glorified human being. Nevertheless, although body and soul are in greater harmony than in earthly life, the operations of the glorified can hardly be imagined. During life on earth, corporeal activities are directed at the continuation of the individual and the species. Human beings need food in order to survive and procreation in order to ensure their existence. In eternal life these two central activities are no longer necessary. The body is so completely informed by and filled with the glorified soul that it no longer has the function of ensuring the basis of natural life.[63]

3. The Glorified World

Above we saw that in Aquinas' view, man holds a central place in creation. All creatures contribute to the perfection of man, and in this perfection the entire creation arrives at its consummation. For this reason, the eternal life of man has its impact on the entire universe: all creatures take advantage of the restoration of man.[64] This radical anthropocentric perspective can be found in all places where Aquinas examines the renewal of the world at the end of time.[65] All corporeal creatures are adjusted to a state that is in harmony with that of the glorified man. For the heavenly bodies, endowed with an incorruptible nature, this entails that they will cease moving, not only because this is in conformity with the timelessness of eternal life—time is measured by the motion of the heavenly bodies—but also for a more specific, related reason. According to what Aquinas has learned from Aristotle, generation and corruption in the world are caused by the motion of the heavenly bodies. In the state of the world after the Final Judgment, all corruption is banned and man is given an incorruptible body.[66]

The cessation of generation and corruption has no drastic impact on those creatures that are—partly or entirely—incorruptible by nature. For those that are entirely corruptible—like plants, animals, and bodies consisting of two or more elements—this cessation is more far-reaching: Aquinas sees no reason for further existence. They do not directly participate with man in the beatific vision, as angels do, for they lack the rational nature that is a precondition to being endowed with charity.[67] Neither do they occupy a subservient place in the eternal life of man. Their function of supporting the corporeal life of man has ended. Nutrition, shelter, help, and whatever other services they provide are no longer needed, since the glorified human body is entirely and perfectly kept in existence by the glorified soul.[68] All functions that are related to the pursuit of further ends are incompatible with the superabundant nature of eternal life. Having attained one's ultimate end (*finis ultimus*), there is no further finality.

Aquinas considers that the lack of animals, plants, and minerals in the glorified universe is in agreement with Saint Paul's promise in 1 Corinthians 7:31 that the world, as we know it, will pass away.[69] The new form of the world will be entirely in congruity with glorified man, and for this reason the remaining bodies are endowed with glory;[70] whereas in the world in which we live, all corporeal creatures do contribute to the knowledge of God, in the glorified universe this function is no longer thinkable. The most complete knowledge of God is directly obtained by beatific vision. The glorification of corporeal creation pertains to the superabundant nature of eternal life. As comfort for our corporeal eyes, which cannot attain the vision of God, they are enabled to see the divinity in his corporeal effects: from the clarity of the resurrected body of Christ to the bodies of the glorified souls and the heavenly bodies.[71]

In the glorified universe everything expresses the situation of consummated relationship with God. Even the location of the body within the glorified creation expresses this. The more noble the soul, the higher and closer to God the body is. Thus the fitting place for the glorified soul is high in heaven, like Christ, "who went up above all heavens to fill all things" (Ephesians 4:10).[72] Similarly, the location of those who turn away from God is expressed by distance from heaven.[73] This brings us to eternal death, the opposite of glorification.

Hell

God's glorifying work concerns the perfection of what is begun by the life of grace. The will, which is averted from God by mortal sin, is fixed. The aversion from God inevitably has the character of eternal privation of the life of grace and glory. The privation of life is called death, so the name of this eternal privation is "eternal death."[74]

Like eternal life, eternal death is characterized by a lack of development. In this mode of existing there can be no more change or correction. Again, in conformity with eternal life, eternal death has a "post-final" character of overflowing expression: there is no development toward any further end. What then does this "overflowing," or superabundant, eternal death look like?

Aquinas' account of hell is in every respect the reverse of heaven. At the core of it is the greatest privation of all: eternal exclusion from communion with God and the saints.[75] As punishment this evil is greater than sensitive inflictions for which hell is known in popular images.[76] This primacy of the relationship with God brings back to mind the hierarchy of elements (soul, body, world) discussed above. There is also a similitude with the punishments for original sin. There, the core was the broken relationship with God, resulting in a disorder in soul, body, and world. The punishment of eternal death has the same structure: the eternal privation of life with God is expressed in a disorder according to which soul, body, and creation are turned against the punished.

The happiness of eternal life is composed of the vision of God and the fruition of his goodness. In hell the will is not directed at God but averted from him. Whereas the center of the beatified, who is endowed with charity, has shifted toward God, and everything—even one's own degree of beatitude—is desired in accordance with God's will, in hell everything is sought in accordance with one's own profit. Averted from God, the will is fixed at a temporal good which can never fully satisfy all human desire. Thus the longing in hell has the character of pursuing an impossible objective. Running against the order of creation, one necessarily frustrates oneself. This frustration is brought about by an act of the free will and—as a result of the fixation of the will after death—is unchangeable. Because God does not bestow his grace against the free will of his creatures, it is the fixed will of the mortal sinner by which the gate of hell is closed: hell is locked from the inside.[77]

Aquinas sees a mechanism according to which this self-centeredness of hell—in contrast with the God-centeredness of heaven—results in an increase in suffering. Those who are in hell wish damnation for all people (which is the opposite of friendship that makes one wish the best for one's neighbor), although this only increases their suffering.[78] Closely related to this is the idea that the demons are charged with tormenting the inhabitants in hell, a role that contributes to their own suffering.[79]

In eternal life, the glorified soul is endowed with four dowries that concern the perfect control of the soul over the body. In hell, the material dimension of man leads to torment instead of expression of glorification. The misery of the soul is expressed in the body of the damned. Thus the bodies of the damned show qualities that are the reverse of the four dowries that are bestowed on the beatified. Instead of the subjection to the spiritual, which is denoted by subtlety, the body is carnally oriented. Instead of agility, the disobedience to God is reflected in a disobedience of the body in respect of the soul: thus the body becomes ponderous, burdensome, and in a sense unbearable to the soul. The torment of the soul, being entirely frustrated in its natural desire for beatitude, is reflected in a capacity to suffer with regard to sensible affliction. The fact that the soul is excluded from the light of divine cognition is reflected in an opaque and dark body, lacking the clarity of the beatified.[80] Thus the material dimension of man—originally intended to lead toward God in accordance with the human condition—becomes a source of suffering, leading further away from God, because man used it contrary to what it was meant for.

Conclusion

Is there a life after death? What may we hope for? What should we think of heaven and hell? As we have seen, Thomas Aquinas is very clear in answering these questions. Moreover, in his sermons on the Creed, Aquinas lists four reasons why faith in, and hope for, corporeal resurrection is useful. First, it tempers the sadness we experience from the loss of our beloved ones. In the second place, it takes away the fear of death. Because we believe in another, better life after death, no one ought to fear death or commit evil out of fear of death. Without this perspective death would be seriously feared and people would do whatever possible to escape from death. Third, the perspective of receiving "eternal goods" after resurrection incites us to perform good actions. If earthly life were everything, people would not be motivated to act well. In the fourth place, it withdraws one from evil: just as the hope for reward attracts one to good actions, the fear of punishment withdraws one from evil.[81]

Many things have changed in culture, theology, and philosophy since Aquinas wrote his works more than seven hundred years ago. So the question of whether he has anything to say to contemporary theology becomes inevitable. I think some lessons can be drawn from Aquinas' eschatology, lessons that are contrary to the first impression any superficial reading of these texts may give.

Aquinas teaches that eschatology is not a highly speculative appendix to any systematic theology, but a dimension characteristic of and inherent in all God-talk. Eschatology is the theological reflection on God's glorifying work, the perfection of creation. This eschatological dimension of theology functions as the horizon of our reflection and is the theological expression of the object of our hope.

Because eschatology deals with God's action, its hallmark is the same apophatic nature that characterizes all God-talk. Eschatology is not futurology, and it cannot provide us with a travel guide to the hereafter. The "picture" of heaven, painted by Aquinas, is in fact a collection of different sketches that may help us to understand the various images that are presented in Holy Scripture. These sketches give access to Scripture by showing their appropriateness, instead of proposing a doctrinal whole that replaces the Bible. This access is given by presenting the framework that constitutes the inner "logic" of heaven: a new creation, this time organized as proceeding from the consummated relationship with God. Despite the apophatic and overflowing character of heaven, it may function as a magnifying mirror showing more clearly what is hard to see in earthly life. The relationship with God, which pertains to the most hidden core of a human being, is exposed in its full glory. Every element of eternal life points to this core, being the expression of it, either spiritually or materially.[82]

By functioning as a magnifying mirror, the perspective of eternal life brings back all attention to the here and now. For eternal life is nothing else but the completion and glorification of the relationship with God that was given to us in the sacrament of baptism. This is why Aquinas speaks of faith as the "beginning of eternal life."[83] In the theology of Aquinas, living with God on earth and the eschatological realities are two sides of the same coin. Both are modes of living with God. The more one is involved in this relationship with God, the less one worries about the hereafter. For the theological virtue of hope gives us confidence that God will help us reach our destination, no matter how unattainable it seems.

Notes

1. Aquinas stopped writing after *ST* III.90. Following his experience while celebrating Mass on December 6, 1273, he could not write any further, for, as he said: "all that I have written seems like straw to me." Three months later he died (cf. Jean-Pierre Torrell, *Saint Thomas Aquinas,* vol. 1: *The Person and His Work,* trans. R. Royal [Washington, D.C.: Catholic University of America Press, 1996], 289 – 95). Because of the indirect authorship, the *Supplementum* is left out of consideration in this chapter. My main sources are IV *Sent.* dd.43 – 50; *ScG* IV.79 – 97; *Comp. Theol.* I, 149 – 84; *ST* I.12; *ST* I-II.1 – 5; and selected fragments of other works. The edition of the *Scriptum* edited by Mandonnet and Moos (see the list of abbreviations at the head of this volume) terminates at Bk. IV, d.22. References in this chapter to Bk. IV, distinctions 23 ff., are to the Parma edition, as reprinted in the Musurgia Publishers edition introduced by Vernon J. Bourke: *Sancti Thomae Aquinatis Doctoris Angelici Ordinis Praedicatorum Opera Omnia* secundum impressionem Petri Fiaccadori Parmae 1852 – 1873 Photolithographice Reimpressa (New York: Musurgia Publishers, 1948), vol. 7. The content of this chapter is worked out more extensively in Carlo Leget, *Living with God: Thomas Aquinas on the Relation between Life on Earth and 'Life' after Death* (Leuven: Peeters, 1997).

2. See IV *Sent.* d.44 q.1 art.2 qc.2; d.44 q.1 art.3 qc.3; d.44 q.1 art.3 qc.1; and d.44 q.2 art.2 qc.2.

3. *ST* I.76.3c; I *De An.* 14. Aristotle's text is in I *De anima* 14 (411b6 – 8); cf. also J. Lotz, "'Magis anima continet corpus . . . quam e converso' (*Sth* I,q.76.a.3): Zum Verhältnis von Seele und Leib nach Thomas von Aquin," *Zeitschrift für katholische Theologie* 110 (1988): 300 – 309.

4. *Quaestio disputata de anima* 8.

5. *ST* I.91.1c.

6. *ST* I.96.2c.

7. *ST* I.73.1c.

8. Aquinas' view on death has been studied most extensively by L. F. Mateo-Seco. His (Spanish) papers and those of other authors are listed in Leget, *Living with God,* 275 – 89.

9. In the twentieth century Aquinas' account of death has been a point of departure of a theological discussion about the moment of dying and the situation of the soul after death for scholars such as P. Glorieux, K. Rahner, L. Boros, and L. Scheffczyk. For an overview cf. Leget, *Living with God,* 269 – 71.

10. Cf. III *Sent.* d.21 q.1 art.3 sed contra 2; *Comp. Theol.* I, 229; *Quaestio disputata de anima* 8, obj. 4.

11. Cf. *Quaestio disputata de anima* 14, obj. 8; *ST* III.53.1 ad 1.

12. II *De An.* 1.

13. Cf. *ST* I.89; *Quaestio disputata de anima* 15–21.

14. Boethius' definition of a person as "individual substance of a rational nature" (*rationalis naturae individua substantia*) is found in his *De duabus naturis*, ch. 3 [PL 64, 1343]. Cf. also *In I Cor.* 15:2. Cf. W. Kluxen, "Seele und Unsterblichkeit bei Thomas von Aquin," in K. Kremer, *Seele: Ihre Wirklichkeit, ihr Verhältnis zum Leib und zur menschlichen Person* (Leyden: Brill, 1984), 66–83.

15. Cf. R. Heinzmann, "Anima unica forma corporis: Thomas von Aquin als Überwinder des platonisch-neuplatonischen Dualismus," in *Philosophisches Jahrbuch der Görres-Gesellschaft* 93 (1986): 256.

16. In *ST* I.89.1c Aquinas speaks of *praeter naturam,* and in *ScG* IV.79.10 of *contra naturam,* meaning the same thing. Cf. A. Pegis, "Between Immortality and Death: Some Further Reflections on the *Summa contra Gentiles,*" *The Monist* 58 (1974): 12–13.

17. Cf. *ScG* IV.79.10.

18. *ST* I.89.8c. This, however, does not mean that the living and the dead are not concerned about each other. Cf. ad 1.

19. *ScG* III.48.6.

20. *ST* I.18. For a detailed interpretation of this quaestio, cf. Leget, *Living with God,* 25–45.

21. R. Sokolowski, *The God of Faith and Reason: Foundations of Christian Theology* (Washington, D.C.: Catholic University of America Press, 1995).

22. *ST* I.3, prol.

23. Cf. *In Psalmos,* prol.

24. There is a very long debate on the structure of the *Summa.* In an interesting overview article B. Johnstone makes a case for the resurrection as the important element. Cf. his "The Debate on the Structure of the *Summa Theologiae* of St. Thomas Aquinas, from Chenu (1939) to Metz (1998)," in *Aquinas as Authority: A Collection of Studies Presented at the Second Conference of the Thomas Instituut te Utrecht, December 14–16, 2000,* ed. Paul van Geest, Harm Goris, and Carlo Leget (Leuven: Peeters, 2002), 187–200.

25. *ST* I.1.1c.

26. *ST* I.1.2c.

27. *ST* I.73.1c.

28. *ST* I.93.4c.

29. *ST* I-II.1–5.

30. *ST* I-II.88.1.

31. *ST* I-II.62.

32. *ST* I-II.65.2c.

33. *ST* I-II.67; and in *ST* II-II in several places when discussing each virtue separately.

34. Cf. Johnstone, "The Debate on the Structure."

35. *ST* III.60.3c. Each sacrament is called a *signum rememorativum, demonstrativum,* and *prognosticon.*

36. Cf. P. Künzle, "Die Eschatologie im Gesamtaufbau der wissenschaftlichen Theologie," in *Anima* 20 (1965): 231–38.

37. *ST* III, prol.

38. On the history of the place of the eschatological tract before Aquinas, see the classical study of N. Wicki, *Die Lehre von der himmlischen Seligkeit in der mittelalterlichen Scholastik von Petrus Lombardus bis Thomas von Aquin* (Freiburg, Switzerland: Universitätsverlag, 1954), 7–56.

39. See also the way in which Aquinas opens his examination of eternal life in *ScG* IV.79: "Quod per Christum resurrectio corporum sit futura."

40. *ST* III, prol.: "Quia salvator noster Dominus Iesus Christus . . . viam veritatis nobis in seipso demonstravit, per quam ad beatitudinem immortalis vitae resurgendo pervenire possimus, necesse est ut, ad consummationem totius theologici negotii . . . de ipso omnium Salvatore ac beneficiis eius humano generi praestitis nostra consideratio subsequatur." Notice how John 14:6 is implicitly quoted, in order to connect Christology and eschatology.

41. Cf. *Comp. Theol.* I, 174.

42. Cf. IV *Sent.* dd.43, 47, and 48.

43. Cf. J. Le Goff, *The Birth of Purgatory*, trans. Arthur Goldhammer (Chicago: University of Chicago Press, 1984). On the different locations after death, which are organized from the perspective of the relationship with God, cf. IV *Sent.* d.45 q.1 art.3c.

44. Cf. G. Mansini, "Similitudo, Communicatio, and the Friendship of Charity in Aquinas," in *Thomistica,* ed. E. Manning (Leuven: Peeters 1995), 1–26.

45. In recent decades various studies have shown that one cannot play off Aquinas' account of the incorruptibility of the soul against a so-called more biblical idea of corporal resurrection. See for example L. Scheffczyk, *'Unsterblichkeit' bei Thomas von Aquin auf dem Hintergrund der neueren Diskussion* (Munich: Beck, 1989). I want to stress the importance of appreciating what J. Ratzinger calls the "dialogical character of immortality," which, in Aquinas' case, is entirely organized proceeding from the relationship with God. Cf. J. Ratzinger, *Eschatology: Death and Eternal Life,* Dogmatic Theology 9 (Washington, D.C.: Catholic University of America Press, 1988).

46. *Lumen gloriae;* cf. *ScG* III.53 and *ST* I.12.5.

47. Cf. Aquinas' indication of the light of glory: *ST* I.12.2c; I.12.2 ad 1; I.12.6c; I.12.7c.

48. *ScG* III.51.2.

49. *ST* II-II.18.2 ad 2; cf. also *De Spe* 4, ad 3.

50. Although the infinite distance between the divine and the human nature remains in heaven: cf. *ST* II-II.19.11 ad 3.

51. *ST* I-II.4.6c; IV *Sent.* d.49 q.1 art.4. Aquinas sketches a steadily increasing line: earthly life, where union with the body is a hindrance for the perfect operation of the soul; after death, when the separated soul is liberated from the hindrance of the body; and after corporal resurrection, when the operation of the soul is intensively increased by union with the body. In *ST* I-II.4.6 the role of the body in the third state is limited to a contribution to the beauty or perfection of beatitude (ad 1: "aliquem beatitudinis decorem vel perfectionem"), consisting in non-hindrance (ad 2: "requiritur perfectio corporis, ut non impediat elevationem mentis") and total subjection (ad 3: "non autem [requiritur abstractio] a corpore spirituali, quod erit totaliter spiritui subiectum").

52. *In I Cor.* 15, lect.5.

53. *ST* II-II.25.5 ad 2.

54. Cf. also the strong expressions in *ST* II-II.18.2 obj.4; *ST* III.7.4 ad 2. Cf. also *ST* III.15.10c and ad 2.

55. *In I Cor.* 15, lect.6.

56. *In I Cor.* 15, lect.6; further, *In I Cor.* 15, lect.7. Cf. also *In Ioh.* 5, lect.5, where the resurrection of body and soul is connected with conformity to the Word.

57. Cf. IV *Sent.* d.49 q.4 art.5 qc.1–3; *ScG* IV.86; *Comp. Theol.* I, 168. For the developments which have led to this exegesis, cf. Wicki, *Die Lehre,* 202–37. Apart from the four dowries of the body, Aquinas also distinguishes three dowries of the soul (*dotes animae*): vision (*visio*), enjoyment (*fruitio*), and love (*dilectio*). Cf. IV *Sent.* d.49 q.4 art.5; *ST* I.12.7 ad 1; *De articulis fidei et ecclesiae sacramentis* 2 (Leonine edition, vol. 42).

58. IV *Sent.* d.49 q.4 art.5 2c.

59. IV *Sent.* d.44 q.2 art.2 1c. Cf. also IV *Sent.* d.44 q.2 art.2 qc.2–5.

60. *ScG* IV.86.1. Cf. IV *Sent* d.44 q.2 art.4 qc.1–3.

61. *ScG* I.86.4. Cf. IV *Sent* d.44 q.2 art.1 qc.1–4.

62. *ScG* IV.86.3. Cf. IV *Sent* d.44 q.2 art.3 qc.1–3.

63. IV *Sent* d.44 q.1 art.4 qc.4; *ScG* IV.83; *Comp. Theol.* I, 156.

64. Cf. IV *Sent.* d.48 q.1 art.1c.

65. Cf. IV *Sent.* d.48 q.2 art.1–5; *ScG* IV.97; *De Pot.* q.5 a.9; *Comp. Theol.* I, 169–71.

66. *ScG* IV.97.2.

67. Participation in eternal life is determined by the amount of charity. Plants and animals are excluded from charity, since they have no rational nature; cf. *ST* II-II.25.3.

68. Cf. *De Pot.* q.5 a.9c. Cf. also *ScG* IV.97 and IV *Sent* d.48 q.2 art.5.

69. *ScG* IV.97.5.

70. *ScG* IV.97.7. This is connected with Revelation 21:1 and Isaiah 65:17–18.

71. IV *Sent.* d.48 q.2 art.1. Cf. also *Quodl.* 8, 9, 2.

72. Quoted in *ScG* IV.87.1.

73. *ScG* IV.89. This is connected with Psalm 54:16 and Revelation 20:9–10.

74. *Mors aeterna: ST* II-II.10.12 obj.2; *ST* II-II.24.12 sed contra; *ST* III.68.11 obj.3.

75. *Comp. Theol.* I, 174.

76. *Collationes in Symbolum Apostolorum* XII (*vitam aeternam*). (Marietti edition.)

77. Cf. J. Pieper, *Über den Begriff der Sünde* (Munich: Kösel Verlag, 1977), 115 (Josef Pieper, *The Concept of Sin* [South Bend, Ind.: St. Augustine's Press, 1997]).

78. IV *Sent.* d.50 q.2 art.1 4c.

79. IV *Sent.* d.47 q.1 art.2 4c.

80. *ScG* IV.89.2. Cf. also IV *Sent* d.44 q.3 art.1 qc.1–3, and *Comp. Theol.* I, 176.

81. *Collationes in Symbolum Apostolorum* XI (*carnis resurrectionem*).

82. *Collationes in Symbolum Apostolorum* XII (*vitam aeternam*).

83. Cf. *ST* II-II.4.1c; *De Ver.* q.14 a.2c; *Collationes in Symbolum Apostolorum* prol.; *In Hebr.* 11:1.

Sixteen

Thomas Aquinas as Interpreter of Scripture

THOMAS PRÜGL

The medievals seem not to have recognized a distinction between systematic and historical theology, or between dogmatics and exegesis. A medieval professor of theology typically was expected to teach all aspects of the faith and to be conversant with all sources of theological knowledge. "Sacred doctrine," therefore, was not restricted to any one of the theological specializations familiar to us today. Rather, it was seen more broadly, as the process of transmission of saving knowledge having its origin in God and reaching humankind through church doctrine, Scripture, and theology. The work of interpreting Scripture by a professor thus took place within a full and rich context of explanation, instruction, and transmission, and presupposed his grounding and training in the extensive range of the faith and its appropriation. Through the efforts of preachers, themselves increasingly in the High Middle Ages the beneficiaries of university instruction, "sacred doctrine" and the interpretation of God's word in Scripture were in turn passed on to the faithful. This is why medieval theology could understand itself as, especially, "exercise on Holy Scripture."[1]

We must be mindful of the unified character of medieval theology in approaching Aquinas' interpretation of Scripture, shaped as we are by a rather different, modern, and more specialist understanding of exegesis and biblical theology. Nevertheless, Aquinas did interpret several books of the Bible in the classroom, and most of these interpretations saw publication. Lecturing on Scripture was in fact his main task as a university professor—the technical designation of the theology professor was, indeed, "master of the sacred page"—and so it is legitimate to single out this part of his work for special consideration in this essay. In the following, therefore, I shall deal with a specific segment of his literary production—namely, his scriptural commentaries—while also examining the methods he employed in his interpretation of Scripture. Last, but equally important, I will locate Aquinas' exegesis, in terms of its function and intent, within the whole breadth of his theological thought. I begin this presentation with (1) a review of Aquinas' exegetical writings, followed by (2) an examination of the hermeneutics and the methodology of his exegesis, highlighting at the same time (3) general tenets, particularly the theological characteristics of Thomistic exegesis and its relevance for theology.

The Exegetical Writings of Aquinas

Of all the works of Aquinas, the commentaries on the Scriptures have traditionally challenged scholars the most. Although lecturing on a specific book of Holy Scripture was central to the academic life of a medieval professor, the history of the texts and the chronology of many of Aquinas' commentaries have remained uncertain. Many medieval theologians did not themselves prepare their most important lectures for publication. In fact, as a rule, these lectures were handed down only in the form of notes, so-called *reportationes*, made by students. Aquinas appears to have revised for publication only a handful of his commentaries. Such are the commentary on the Book of Job and parts of the commentary on St. Paul's Letter to the Romans; we also have the autograph of his lecture on Isaiah. Only these works, prepared by Aquinas himself for copying, are termed *expositio;* the taking of notes is referred to as *lectura.* In the following, I provide an overview of when and where, according to scholarly consensus, Aquinas commented on various individual books of the Bible:[2]

prior to 1252	Cologne	*Expositio super Isaiam ad litteram; Super Ieremiam et Threnos*
spring 1256	Paris	*Principium Rigans montes de superioribus; Hic est liber mandatorum Dei*
1261–65	Orvieto	*Expositio super Iob ad litteram*
1263/64	Orvieto	*Glossa continua super Evangelia (Catena aurea)— in Matthaeum*

1265–68	Rome	*Catena aurea—in Marcum, Lucam et Iohannem; Lectura super epistulas b. Pauli apostoli*
1269/70	Paris	*Lectura super Matthaeum*
1270/72	Paris	*Lectura super Iohannem*
1272/73	Naples	*Expositio super epistulam b. Pauli apostoli ad Romanos* (cc. 1–8); *Postilla super Psalmos*

Thus far there are critical editions only of the expositions of Job and of Isaiah.[3] According to Weisheipl, Aquinas is supposed to have interpreted the Prophets Isaiah, Jeremiah, and the Book of Lamentations under Albertus Magnus in Cologne, when Aquinas was *Baccalaureus biblicus*. The particular task of the *Baccalaureus biblicus*, or *Cursor biblicus*, was a "cursory" interpretation of Holy Scripture, that is to say, a brisk and basic understanding of the text's literal sense. This characterization fits, however, only part of the commentary on Isaiah. Not only are chapters 1–11 commented in greater depth; they do not dispense with the *quaestiones*, which are typical of a "magisterial" interpretation.[4] A peculiar feature of the commentary on Isaiah is the so-called *Collationes*, which Aquinas himself designed in the margins of the manuscript. These constitute lists of keywords indicating various ways in which the literal meaning of the scriptural text could be appropriated for the purpose of spiritual talks (*collationes*). It appears that Aquinas followed up his lectures by sharing these reflections with his confrères.[5]

The commentary on Jeremiah has been handed down in incomplete form. It too is accompanied by *Collationes*. As for the brief commentary on Lamentations ascribed to Aquinas, its authenticity has not been established. Although the oldest catalogues list it among his writings, the only extant manuscript is attributed to the Augustinian hermit Augustinus of Ancona. Both the manner in which the scriptural text is interpreted and the general lack of theological insight render its authenticity doubtful.[6]

On the occasion of his appointment as professor, Aquinas delivered in spring 1256 two lectures in which he addressed the interpretation of Scripture and the theological plan of the biblical canon, in the process expressing basic convictions that would inform his subsequent theological career. In the first lecture, the so-called *principium*, Aquinas explains the dignity and task of professors, who share a particular responsibility for the mediation of "sacred doctrine." His second lecture, the so-called *resumptio*, emphasizes the "truth of Holy Scripture" (*commendatio sacrae scripturae*) and presents a classification of the biblical canon (*partitio sacrae scripturae*).[7] As a professor, Aquinas was now primarily responsible for delivering lectures on Holy Scripture. It is therefore regrettable that modern scholarship has yet to identify the book on which Aquinas commented during his first teaching assignment in Paris.

More certain, however, is his subsequent work as biblical commentator. During the next stage of his career as a teacher in the Dominican convent at Orvieto, Aquinas wrote a commentary on Job. This *expositio* is considered one of his masterpieces, although it was published only posthumously. Here, for the first time in the Middle Ages, Job was explained exclusively in its literal sense; Aquinas thus abandoned, although he did not condemn, the kind of allegorical interpretation of the book sketched out previously by Gregory the Great in the *Moralia in Iob.*[8]

At the same time (1263–64), Aquinas at the request of Pope Urban IV began the work which became known as the *Catena aurea,* which was to be his most widely read exegetical work during the Middle Ages.[9] Its actual title, *Glossa continua super Evangelia,* delineates the nature of the work more clearly. Aquinas collected a number of patristic interpretations of the Gospels and arranged them in the form of a continuous commentary. He also had translations made of Greek patristic catenae that had hitherto been unknown to Western Christianity, which he employed from the second Gospel on. In arranging the interpretations by the fathers, he was concerned more with the meaning of these texts than with accurate translations; this afforded him a certain license in rendering their contents more succinctly or in accentuating certain passages.[10] Far from being a mere string of patristic quotations, this work comprises two levels of interpretation. The first probes the degree of insight present in the patristic commentaries, the second adapts them to a given passage in Scripture. In preparing the *Catena,* Aquinas gained great familiarity with patristic writings, which in turn were to exercise an influence on his Christology as expressed in the *Tertia Pars* of the *Summa Theologiae.*

His later interpretations of Matthew and John, on which he lectured during his second teaching assignment in Paris (in 1270–72), also reveal a frequent use of the *Catena aurea.* The commentary on Matthew has been handed down in the form of a *reportatio,* although the printed editions lack the section on the Sermon on the Mount. The first publisher of Aquinas' works, Bartholomeo Spina, O.P., supplemented the missing sections using the commentary on Matthew by Petrus de Scala.[11] Fifty years ago, however, a manuscript was discovered in Basel containing the complete text, parts of which have already been edited.[12] The dating of the commentary on Matthew to the years 1269–70 is supported by passages paralleling the opuscule *De perfectione spiritualis vitae,* penned by Aquinas during the renewed mendicant controversy. In particular, the commentaries on

Matthew 10 and 19 contain his highly controversial views on apostolic poverty and the imitation of Christ.[13]

The *Lectura in Iohannem* is based on the outstanding note-taking of Reginald of Piperno, Aquinas' closest collaborator and secretary, which Reginald supplied at the request of Adenulf of Avagni, the provost at St. Omer. The quality of these notes was so remarkable that they were accepted by the University of Paris as an exemplar, that is, an official copy serving as an authentic text for further copying.[14] Contrary to the views of several biographers, Aquinas appears not to have edited these notes himself, a fact that Reginald would certainly have mentioned.

Of all of Aquinas' commentaries, those on the letters of St. Paul raise the most difficulties. Although there are many indications that Aquinas lectured twice on the Pauline corpus, the complicated manuscript tradition reveals only one coherent block of commentaries, from 1 Corinthians 11 to Hebrews inclusively, in the *reportatio* of Reginald of Piperno.[15] On the other hand, medieval catalogues already list the first part of the commentary, from Romans 1 to 1 Corinthians 10 (or 11), as a separate work that had been personally edited by Aquinas. In fact, "la partie où sa main est assez directement perceptible comprehend les huit premiers chapitres des Romains."[16] No commentary on 1 Corinthians 7–10 has been preserved; it was replaced in the printed editions by the corresponding section from the commentary by Petrus de Tarentasia.[17] These findings allow us to conclude that Aquinas interpreted the letters of St. Paul twice, stopping at 1 Corinthians 7 (or perhaps only at Romans 8) during his second attempt. After his death, secretaries filled in the missing parts, borrowing passages from the first interpretation. These editorial efforts may also be responsible for the well-known interruptions and lacunae. At any rate, as the preface to the commentary on Romans suggests, Aquinas viewed the letters of St. Paul as a single coherent work, which was to be interpreted as a whole.

When did Aquinas comment on the Pauline letters? The problems concerning the textual transmission of the work complicate establishing a convincing chronology. Proceeding from the perfectly developed teachings on grace in the commentary on Romans, modern scholarship assumes that the second interpretation was delivered during the last two years of Aquinas' life and that mental exhaustion and ultimately his death put an untimely end to this undertaking. Regarding the first cycle of preserved commentaries on the letters of St. Paul, which begins with 1 Corinthians 10, most scholars, without offering any convincing proof, accept as given that he delivered it in the years 1265–68 when he was commissioned by his order to develop a school at Santa Sabina in Rome. J.-P. Torrell adopts this date with the caveat, however, that St. Thomas had not made the *Summa Theologiae* the subject of his lectures during his stay in Rome.[18] Michèle Mulchahey, on the other hand, following Leonard Boyle, makes precisely such an assumption. In this view, Aquinas would have lectured on the *Summa* in the morning, while in the afternoon lecturing on Pseudo-Dionysius' *De divinis nominibus*.[19] If this assumption is correct, then Aquinas did not comment on any book of the Bible while in Rome, having only recently completed the *Catena aurea*. This leads me to suggest that Aquinas' first commentary on St. Paul may be dated to his first teaching assignment in Paris.[20]

Because Aquinas' interpretation of the Psalms remained unfinished, it is assigned by Mandonnet to the final year of his life. Certainly, the commentary hardly seems a work of Aquinas' maturity. For this reason, Tugwell, following a suggestion by Bataillon, prefers to place this commentary at the beginning of Aquinas' teaching career.[21] The old catalogues list the commentary on the Psalms under the heading *Lectura super tres nocturnos psalterii*. In fact, until the end of the last century, the commentary was known only up to Psalm 51. Uccelli discovered an additional section that furnished the interpretation up to Psalm 54. Unfortunately, this manuscript was destroyed during air raids on Naples during the Second World War; fortunately, Uccelli had published the text. Aquinas largely follows a traditional interpretation: he felt obliged to interpret this book not only literally, but also *mystice* in accordance with official Church tradition.[22]

Finally, all of the early catalogues of the writings of Thomas Aquinas mention an interpretation of the Song of Songs. According to his biographer, William of Tocco, Aquinas dictated this commentary while already on his deathbed in Fossanova.[23] However, no manuscript of such a commentary has ever been discovered. The two interpretations of the Song of Songs which were included in the first edition of Aquinas' complete works are without doubt inauthentic.

The Method and Hermeneutics of Aquinas' Exegesis

Aquinas never wrote a separate treatise on hermeneutics comparable to Augustine's *De doctrina christiana* or Hugh of St. Victor's *De scripturis et scriptoribus*. However, he was familiar with these texts and internalized them to an extent that must not be underestimated.[24] The extensive exegetical tradition of the fathers must be kept in mind when turning to Aquinas' principles of scriptural interpretation. Especially in his discussions of "theology," with which he introduces such systematic works as his commentary on the *Sentences* and the *Summa Theologiae*, Aquinas devotes himself to the question of the four senses in the Scriptures. However, any attempt to reduce his exegesis to a wrestling between the spiritual and literal sense would represent a gross misunderstanding of his concerns. The discussion of different senses in Scripture illustrates merely one aspect of his exegesis; the characteristics of his exegesis must be gleaned largely from the commentaries themselves, that is to say, from his actual exegetical practice.

1. The Four Senses

The first question in the *Summa Theologiae* examines "sacred doctrine," with a special concern for its "scientific" character. Articles 2 through 7 ask about sacred doctrine's scientific character according to the criteria of "science" outlined in Aristotle's *Posterior Analytics;* the eighth article investigates the use of reason in sacred doctrine, asking what argument can and cannot accomplish with regard to sacred truth. In the final two articles Aquinas turns to matters connected to exegesis. The ninth article asks whether it is appropriate for "sacred scripture" to use metaphors; the tenth, about levels of meaning in Scripture. At first glance, these two articles might appear out of keeping with the earlier articles, and their inclusion might seem surprising.[25] However, already in the earlier articles, the close connection between "sacred doctrine" and "sacred scripture" had become clear; at times, Aquinas comes close to using the two terms synonymously. This has been noted by several scholars and bespeaks the extensiveness of the concept of "sacred doctrine." There are two basic aspects of "sacred doctrine": what is taught; and the process of teaching what is taught. In the latter, the focus shifts to teaching as act. As act, sacred doctrine is an extensive process, beginning with Revelation, understood as teaching from and by God, and ending with preaching, understood as teaching the basics of faith.[26] Aquinas views Scripture as a part—indeed, a central part—of this encompassing project of transmitting divine knowledge, which starts in God's wisdom, continues in the revelation of the incarnate Logos, arrives at the apostles as main witnesses of Christ's deeds and words, and is eventually transmitted from the biblical authors to the interpreters of Scripture. The aim of this process is the "manifestation of truth."[27] Just as the revelation of God's truth is the purpose of Scripture, so theological reflection must concern itself with the very same *manifestatio veritatis.*

In this perspective, the final two articles of *ST* I.1 gain both purpose and meaning. While stating in article 8 that "sacred doctrine" relies on argumentation (*utrum sacra doctrina sit argumentativa*), that is to say, it is based on scientific evidence in the Aristotelian sense, Aquinas wants to make clear in the final two articles that the transparent procedure of reasoning is not obfuscated by either the "dark" poetic style of Scripture or by what might be taken as an arbitrary method of interpretation. Thus, securing the ability of the theological technique to be conclusive depends on determining the proper methods for interpreting Scripture. Not only the pictorial language of the books of the Bible (a.9), but also the multiple senses of Scripture, including the spiritual, appear to argue against this procedure (a.10). How are we to deal with interpretations that extrapolate seemingly arbitrary results from the sacred texts?[28]

Aquinas counters these fears not only by asserting Scripture as a source and legitimate component of "sacred doctrine," but also by defending a centuries-old practice of interpretation despite the fact that it might appear to be in tension with the ideal of his own scholarly method. However, Aquinas defends the spiritual senses of Scripture not simply because of the venerable age of this doctrine and the honorable people who sought these spiritual senses in their meditation on the Bible. He affirms the spiritual senses primarily because Scripture itself, which is incapable of error in matters necessary for salvation, employs this very procedure. Thus the hermeneutic interest displayed by Aquinas at the end of the first question of the *Summa Theologiae* arises from his concern for scriptural clarity and for the inclusion of Scripture in the theological project of "transmission" that aims for the *manifestatio veritatis*.

1.1. *Sensus spiritualis* and *sensus litteralis*

Scripture assumes an extraordinary position in this process of transmission because God (respectively, the Holy Spirit) is its originator. Whereas prophets and evangelists participate in the authorship of Scripture only in an instrumental capacity, God is the *auctor principalis*. However, God's "language" has at its disposal more possibilities than are available to human beings. While the language of humans depends on words with which to designate things, God is able to transcend words by turning things, events, indeed even the entire course of history, into possible ways of expressing Himself. He is able to appropriate things and events to which Holy Scripture "refers using words," that is, "significations," for different things and events.[29] These two levels of signification are the reason for a second level of scriptural meaning of the Bible. The first important level of signification on which the divine truth is expressed by words corresponds to the *sensus litteralis*, while the designated reality of the literal meaning itself becomes a reference to something different, and then the text is understood in its *sensus spiritualis*. Of course, human authors are also wont to employ symbols and comparisons and to resort to imagery. Aquinas would argue, however, that human authors are not able to use the reality they describe as another means of expression operating beside the written text. Their use of symbols or comparisons notwithstanding, these operate only on the first level of signification. The spiritual sense, on the other hand, probing as it does the "language" of God in the story of salvation, is able to use historical reality as a further noetic system inherently present in Holy Scripture and testifying both to the dignity of Holy Scripture and to the authority of its progenitor. No book other than this, authored by the Holy Spirit, possesses such deeper level of signification.

The distinction between spiritual and literal sense derives from the distinction between a divine and a human author. The spiritual sense is further divided according to its contents. Its three variations are informed by the three epochs of salvation history. Allegorically speaking, the facts of the Old Testament are interpreted as *figurae* for the events in the New Testament. Morally speaking, the acts of Christ in the New Testament signify the conduct required of Christians; while the anagogic meaning reveals the life of the Church, especially that of the early Church, as foreshadowing future glory. Thus, all three spiritual meanings interpret the objects of a certain *status* in salvation history as a sign of a subsequent status, revealing in fact a uniform direction of salvific activity.[30]

While the objects of the spiritual sense reveal the impressive panorama of a divine plan, Aquinas continues to insist on the fundamental significance of the literal sense. In addition to stating that every spiritual interpretation needs to be built on the literal sense, the literal sense is seen itself to contain all that is necessary for the salvation of mankind. Moreover, the contents of the spiritual senses do not extend beyond the literal sense. Aquinas emphasizes that every insight one can derive from the spiritual sense of one passage in Scripture may also be discovered in the literal sense of a different passage in Scripture. Therefore, based on this view, the spiritual sense is not necessary for salvation; and, it may even be ignored by theology.[31] Whereas the spiritual sense will never be unequivocal because it is always based on a linguistic comparison, that is, on association, it will be impossible to be mistaken about the literal sense.[32] Regarding the scientific method in theology that searches for the reasons behind its objects, Aquinas emphasizes the priority of the literal sense, since allegorical meaning is unfit for use in an argument: *ex sensu spirituali non potest trahi argumentum.*[33] Only the literal sense avoids the confusion that would be fatal to theological argument. Images, metaphors, and poetic and rhetorical stylistic devices must be interpreted literally in order that their underlying purpose may be comprehended. Due especially to the apologetic function of theology, Aquinas values the unequivocal authority of the Scriptures so highly because "sacred doctrine" is also supposed to assume the complementary function of the *manifestatio veritatis*, that is, the refutation of errors.[34] This is precisely why Aquinas insists so firmly on the importance of the literal sense and why he almost exclusively interprets Scripture literally.

1.2. *Sensus scripturae* and *veritas* — the Plurality of the Literal Sense

It will be helpful to follow this initial overview with an examination of what precisely Aquinas understands by *sensus* and how he thinks exegetes discover the meaning of a specific biblical passage.[35] One must first acknowledge that Aquinas understood under *sensus* both the level of interpretation and the concrete meaning of a text. On the level of the *sensus litteralis*, on which I will now focus exclusively, the interpreter discovers the sense or senses, that is, the meaning of a given text. A faith that is anchored in the *articuli fidei*, the official creed that summarizes the truths needed for salvation, serves as the criterion for recognizing the correct meaning of given scriptural passages. In a manner of speaking, the meaning of a given passage in the Bible emerges from the text during interpretation; it is derived synthetically by a careful reading based on a prior dogmatic understanding. Nevertheless, the meaning remains rooted in the text and must not be arbitrarily separated from it by the interpreter. The interpretation must reveal the intention of the author in such a way that, hermeneutically speaking, both biblical author and exegete can meet during the investigation. Not surprisingly, according to Aquinas there may be several meanings within the literal sense of certain passages. For every interpreter at any point in history applies his experiences, existential needs, and intellectual abilities to the revealed text. Thus the interpretation of Scripture will never come to an end.

One text in particular, which has been the source of serious controversy among scholars of Aquinas for several years, is pivotal for determining Aquinas' position on the plurality of literal senses.[36] In his discussion of the character of *materia prima* in the *Quaestiones disputatae de potentia*, Aquinas notes a discrepancy between the interpretations of St. Augustine and St. Basil of Genesis 1:2 ("the earth was void and formless"). Whereas St. Augustine contended that God had created the world in a single instant, Basil insisted on a successive creation in time and therefore in a successive state of *materia prima* and of individual objects formed from it. Whose interpretation was in error? In his response, Aquinas attempts to maintain the authority of both fathers of the Church by making interesting observations about the interpretation and the meaning of Scripture. Since the problem appears to deal less with theology than with philosophy of nature, he begins by distinguishing between truth and the interpretation of Scripture. Not everything that is true is *eo ipso* also revelational truth. Conversely, one must not insist on the truth of anything that contradicts the revealed faith, that is, Scripture. What this means for scriptural exegesis is that many questions typically possess a range of interpretations capable of doing justice to both.

Therefore, says Aquinas, the solution to what seems to be a contradiction between (immanent) truth and the (transcendent) authority of Scripture is found in the legitimate possibility of multiple literal interpretations of biblical passages. Scripture, whose ultimate author is the Holy Spirit and which cannot therefore be based on even a single error, must not be reduced to one specific interpretation. Instead, salvific truth, which in itself is invariable, is therefore comprehended differently, depending on the location, the time, and the intellectual faculties of the interpreter. The meaning of a biblical passage will then emerge from the agreement of what is recognized as the truth and the biblical text: "Every truth which, without violating the wording, is able to be fitted to divine Scripture is its sense."[37] According to Aquinas, the resulting multiplicity of interpretations can reach a point where circumstances may lead to a meaning not specifically intended by the biblical author, that is, the interpreter may reach beyond the *intentio auctoris* to the more comprehensive *intentio Spiritus sancti*. As a matter of fact, the interpretation of Scripture is never final because the Holy Spirit imbues the texts with a degree of vitality that continues to affect the Church in ever new ways and at all times.

1.3. The Language of Images and Metaphors

By favoring the literal sense Aquinas was able to devote himself more intensively to the rich language of images present in Scripture. He rarely misses an opportunity to refer to *locutiones figurativae* or *similitudines metaphoricae* and to explain them. Aquinas carefully distinguishes between pictorial words, comparisons, and parables; however, he does so not for reasons of literary criticism or rhetorical interest but because he is aiming for an appropriate theological interpretation of the text. Metaphors play a special role in this connection. By going beyond pictorial words, metaphors reach a deeper theological level of meaning without ever leaving the interpretive framework of the literal sense. This is illustrated by the interpretation of the blessing in St. Paul's Letter to the Ephesians: the Christological statement, "And he has put all things under his feet" (Ephesians 1:22), is supposed initially to represent a *locutio figurativa et similitudinaria*, that is, a figurative image, but one could understand it also in the sense of a *locutio metaphorica*. In the first case, the verse states figuratively that creation is entirely subjected to Christ. However, metaphorically speaking, it contains additional information. Taken as a metaphor, the same verse points to a much larger context of imagery since it leads further than the figurative expression. As the lowest part of the body, "feet" in Ephesians 1:22 also implies their counterpart, the head. Aquinas views both the head and the feet as metaphors for the two natures of Christ. Thus the metaphorical interpretation of Ephesians 1:22 leads to the conclusion that creation is subjected to the Son of God not only on account of his divine nature, but also because of Christ's human nature. For Aquinas, this metaphor amounts to an "image within an image" whose dual figurative transfer (*transsumptio*) leads to a deeper theological understanding.[38]

But, should one not raise the same objection against the use of images and metaphors that Aquinas raised against the spiritual sense, namely, that pictorial language is not suitable as a scientific language since it is not the language of choice in arguments? Aquinas would at one level concede the objection, since he rejects the use of images as arguments. Yet images, just like objects perceptible to the senses, are necessary to the act of cognition insofar as the human intellect derives its concepts from impressions made on the senses. Because pictorial statements about God and his works are more "connatural" to human cognition on account of its dependence on sensual perception, Aquinas not only defends the imagery present in Scripture, he even considers it highly appropriate to its revelational content.[39] However, images require interpretation once they have been consciously employed as stylistic devices. Behind the images stands the author who had intended to express concrete theological facts. Once again, Aquinas places the *intentio auctoris* at the center of his exegesis, insisting that the intention of the author can be recognized only in the literal sense which includes everything that can be gleaned accurately from the meaning of the words. And whether by figures, comparisons, metaphors, or whatever the kind of pictorial language, the intention of the author is always expressed by words.[40]

2. The Praxis of Aquinas' Interpretation of Scripture

We must now attempt to verify the hermeneutical reflections of Aquinas by considering his exegetical writings. To what extent and how has Aquinas translated his theoretical reflections into his exegetical praxis? Here, too, Aquinas was clearly a man of his time. He did not invent the methods of his Scholastic exegesis, but simply followed an established tradition and development. His importance for the history of biblical exegesis rests not on any revolutionary innovation, but rather on the masterful way in which he adopted and accentuated traditional elements.

2.1. Philological Aspects of Aquinas' Exegesis

Aquinas' philological interest in the text of the Bible seems modest. There are hardly any comments on grammar in his commentaries, not to mention observations of textual criticism. Moreover, quite a few of his interpretations appear almost to do violence to the original intention of the scriptural text. We ought, however, to refrain from applying modern standards of historical and critical exegesis in our efforts to appreciate Aquinas's sensitivity to the peculiarities of the biblical text. Granted, he is content with the largely defective text of the Vulgate in the version approved by the University of Paris. He hardly takes advantage of the efforts of the Dominicans at St. Jacques to obtain textual alternatives, although this would have greatly helped him with many difficult passages — especially while working on his interpretation of the Book of Job.⁴¹ Whenever he introduces philological information, he borrows from the prefaces in St. Jerome's Vulgate or the *Glossa ordinaria*. In contrast to Albertus Magnus or Roland of Cremona, Aquinas refrains from overburdening his commentaries with philosophical or scientific erudition. Instead, he concentrates entirely on their theological content, i.e., a precise illumination of their *sensus*. Only by first recognizing the absolute priority of the theological intent in Aquinas' interpretation of the Scriptures will we also realize that Aquinas possessed a keen sense for linguistic peculiarities in the Bible.

As pointed out in the reflections on the *sensus litteralis*, Aquinas assigns great importance to the *circumstantia litterae*, the concrete wording of a passage and precise meaning of words. He takes the Latin form of the text before him very seriously. However, he lacks ultimate interest in the philological characteristics of the biblical text. Usually Aquinas is conscious of the peculiarities of the various literary genres. For instance, at the beginning of the quarrels in Job 3, he points out that from the third chapter on the Book of Job reads like a poem. Nevertheless, his principal concern is to analyze the quarrels in terms of logically corresponding arguments. Usually Aquinas is cognizant that lyrical texts vary their subject by resorting to figures of speech and images. Nevertheless, he tries minutely to discover a substantial logical progression in the synonyms expressed by Hebrew parallelisms.⁴² Usually Aquinas is aware of the peculiarities of the original languages of the Bible, but he chooses not to use translators.⁴³ If we assess his efforts only from this narrow philological perspective, it seems that the language of the biblical text remains alien to Aquinas. On the other hand, on principle, i.e., for theological reasons, he refuses to be overly interested in biblical philology, insisting that one must not waste time on such things unless one can gain from the text "solid truth."⁴⁴

Instead, Aquinas prefers to direct his attention to the peculiarly biblical "way of speaking" (*modus loquendi*), which he sees realized particularly in the rich semitic imagery of the Old Testament. Elaborating on the scene in which God allows Satan to test Job's virtue, Aquinas states that by resorting to symbolic and enigmatic explanations he follows the practice of Scripture itself, which describes spiritual contexts in physical terms.⁴⁵ Whenever the Bible expresses spiritual matters through images, the task of the exegete is to uncover and draw attention to them. Aquinas thus never misses an opportunity to advert to the anthropomorphic images of God in Scripture. For instance, the "wrath of God" describes not a divine emotion, but the punishment that God occasionally metes out to human beings in the form of sufferings here on earth.[46] The "ways of the Lord" are God's commands and laws to which we are subjected throughout our lives.[47] And "God's eye" signifies the "foresight" of divine providence.[48] While Aquinas is careful to analyze the metaphors of God, he is nevertheless quite capable of masterfully explaining many an obscure passage by supplying his own imagery in the form of examples, comparisons from nature, and observations from daily life. The commentary on Job in particular is full of numerous such "plausible" explanations, into which Aquinas inserts in a rather refreshing manner not only his scientific knowledge but also his psychological insights.[49]

Aquinas engages sparingly in philological discussions. Whenever he does treat these matters, however, he subjects them entirely to the theological point he is trying to make about a passage in the text. This concentration on the main topic of the biblical book and its interpretation dominates all of his exegetical methods, the details of which cannot be introduced here.[50] Let it suffice to mention merely one aspect: Aquinas relies just as sparingly on *auctoritates*. In the commentaries, he quotes from patristic texts only if they truly contribute to the reasoning underlying his interpretation. Because of his preliminary work in the *Catena aurea*, this occurs more frequently in the later commentaries on Matthew and John than in his commentaries on the Old Testament. When his scriptural commentaries are compared not only to Albertus Magnus but also to his own *Summae*, Aquinas employs even quotations from Aristotle quite sparingly. Indeed, even quotations from other books of the Bible, which accompany each and every interpretation offered by medieval exegesis, tend to be deemphasized in favor of progressive reasoning. In fact, Aquinas' selection of quotations seems more judicious in comparison to the more profligate practice of his contemporaries.

2.2. The Prologues

Medieval commentaries on Scripture follow in the tradition of the philological and philosophical commentaries of late antiquity.[51] A striking feature of this literary genre is the prologue, into which important information about the work and about the underlying principles of interpretation is woven. Moreover, Aquinas also alludes in his prologues to key concepts and articulates the theological framework that will be filled out by the actual commentary. The prologues continue the so-called *accessus ad auctorem*, which is characteristic of the rhetoric of late antiquity. During the twelfth century, a special version of the *accessus* took hold in all scientific disciplines, which, following the research of R. W. Hunt, is referred to as "type C."[52] This type, which appears in its purest form in Boethius' commentary on Porphyry, concentrates the classical introductory questions on the following aspects: *Titulus — nomen auctoris — intentio auctoris — modus agendi — ordo libri — utilitas — cui parti philosophiae supponitur*. We encounter these concepts in almost all of Aquinas' commentaries, although in abbreviated forms of this type.[53] The prologue to his Isaiah commentary unfolds with discussions of *auctor, modus*, and *materia* and also includes within the *modus* questions about the *ratio explanationis* and *utilitas*. He follows the pattern of *auctor — materia — modus — utilitas* in the prologues to the early commentaries on Jeremiah and the Lamentations. Whereas the commentary on the Book of Job departs from this pattern, Aquinas emphasizes especially *materia* and *modus* in the prologue to the interpretation of the Psalms. As late as the interpretation of the Letter to the Romans, he relies on the pattern *auctor — materia — modus — utilitas*, despite the fact that this prologue was likely edited and enlarged because of the second period of lecturing on the letters of St. Paul.

When dealing with the question of authorship in the commentary on the Book of Isaiah, Aquinas concludes that the actual author must be the Holy Spirit while the prophet Isaiah served merely as a minister, a person who wrote and spoke as *organum spiritus sancti*. The Apostle Paul is extensively credited as the *auctor* in the prologue to the Letter to the Romans (which was intended as a prologue to the whole *Corpus Paulinum*). Paul is the "chosen vessel" (*vas electionis*) through which the teachings of the apostles are passed on within the Church.[54] Regarding the *materia* of St. Paul's letters, Aquinas proclaims that they contain the complete teachings of Christ. From this point of view, the letters of St. Paul parellel the Psalms because both books contain "nearly the whole doctrine of theology." This corresponds to the formulation of the prologue of the Psalms commentary, where we read that the psalms contain the "basic material of all theology" (*generalem materium totius theologiae*). The *materia* of the psalms, he says, is so rich that they ought to be viewed more like gospels than prophesies.[55] Their *materia*, he claims, is "Christ and his members." On the other hand, he views the *materia* of the letters of St. Paul more specifically: "Their whole doctrine is about the grace of Christ." According to Aquinas, the *materia* of Isaiah encompasses the threefold manifestation of the Son of God (in the flesh, in the faith, and on Judgment Day), which accounts also for the fact that the Church reads this book during Advent.

Whereas the *materia* circumscribes the doctrinal contents or the undergirding theological argument, the *modus* deals with the literary style of the book.[56] As mentioned above, the latter is equally important to interpretation because the epistemological character of the Scriptures is connected also to its literary form. High Scholasticism discussed the *modi* of Scripture not only in the prologues to the commentaries on the Scriptures but also in the prologues to commentaries on the *Sentences*. By contemplating the *modi*, Alexander of Hales was led to the fundamental distinction between the narrative aspects of the biblical text and the argumentative and systematic book of the *Sentences*. Whereas Peter Lombard is said to prefer a *modus artificialis* that, assisted by the *artes* (that is, by employing scientific methods), tries to convince reason, the *modus* of Holy Scripture is presumably directed at the religious disposition of human beings, i.e., the *affectus pietatis*. However, this *modus* of Holy Scripture is further divided, extending from a *modus praeceptivus* in the Pentateuch and the Gospels, a *modus exemplativus* in the historical books of the Old Testament, and a *modus exhortativus* in the wisdom literature and the epistolary literature in the New Testament, to a *modus revelativus* in the Prophets and a *modus orativus* in the Psalms.[57] Aquinas borrows these classifications, varying them slightly except for one rather essential aspect. While Alexander of Hales and the Franciscan school after him separate the Bible from the *Sentences* depending on their literary and thus also scientific objectives, Aquinas insists that the *modus argumentativus* is also represented in the Bible, thus preserving the uniformity of the "sacred doctrine" in its most important document.[58] Aquinas resumes the listing of the *modi* in his prologue to the commentary on the Psalms in the manner in which he had introduced them in the commentary on the *Sentences*, now also providing examples for the "scientific" *modus*, namely, the Book of Job and the letters of the Apostle Paul.[59]

2.3. Divisio Textus

The most typical characteristic of textual exegesis at medieval universities[60] is the particular manner in which the text was thoroughly subdivided, from the first rough subdivision of the entire book down to the very last half of the last verse. Unlike modern form criticism, this method does not search for smaller literary units that comprise the entire book. It covers rather the entire book with a logical net of coordinates within which all parts can be brought into relationship with one another.[61] In doing so, the exegete seeks to highlight the presumed logical progression of the thought of the biblical author in an effort to make the intentions of his words transparent. This is accomplished at the beginning of each chapter by progressing from summing up larger textual units, indicating their beginning and end and their respective content, to ever smaller textual units and more detailed descriptions of their contents. This approach corresponds precisely to the method of the *modus argumentativus*, which was also referred to as *modus divisivus et collectivus*. In order to capture a line of reasoning one must break it down into its components. Once the text is reduced to its smallest segment, the procedure is reversed by gathering all individual insights into a single systematic summary.[62]

In addition to this systematization, the division also serves a didactic purpose which is particularly characteristic of Aquinas' commentaries. Aquinas sums up the core statement of each preceding section and combines it with the following section: "Above the apostle explained how charity should be applied to those who need it, now he explains how it should be applied also to enemies."[63] Through these brief summaries, Aquinas tries to get especially close to the *intentio auctoris*, or the *propositum*, as he frequently calls it. The *propositum* is the principal idea from which the interpretation takes its cue and at which it is directed. The *propositum* is justified, illustrated by examples, defended against objections, extended by following parallel themes, and so on.[64] Naturally, the excessive application of these motives to the act of interpretation leads occasionally to forced and frequently arbitrary divisions, and therefore at times to divisions that are hardly of any help. As a rule, however, Aquinas is surprisingly accurate when fleshing out the tensions and original intention of a biblical text.

2.4. Doctrinal Interpretation

Aquinas considered every biblical book to be an organic unit that was composed with a certain doctrinal plan in mind.[65] Whatever is expressed in concentrated form by the articles of faith is presented in Scripture in a larger, more expansive way, although at times also in a more obscure fashion.[66] It is therefore the task of the theologian to try always to uncover the "doctrinal order" in Scripture, especially when commenting on Scripture. Included in this task is the duty to point out the systematic order of all the Scriptures. Aquinas meets this task by remaining faithful to the plan sketched in his inauguration lecture *Hic est liber mandatorum Dei*, in which he undertakes a division of the canon.[67] Holy Scripture provides all human beings with stepping stones for attaining eternal life. Therefore, Aquinas assigns to each book of the canon particular kinds of aid, having distinguished previously between commandments in the Old Testament and grace in the New Testament. Within the Old Testament, one has to distinguish the obligatory laws of the Pentateuch from the mere admonitions contained in the remaining Old Testament writings. In the New Testament, Aquinas differentiates grace with respect to its origin (in the Gospels), its effective powers (in the letters of St. Paul), and the implementation of this effectiveness (in the remaining New Testament Scriptures). He thus goes into ever greater detail until each individual book is systematically "networked." Moreover, this "order of Scripture" assigns to every book a specific topic (*materia*) as well as a specific function (*modus*). At the same time, Aquinas carefully outlines themes that are overarching and highly central to the teaching of the faith, to avoid both restricting interpretation or basing the teaching of the faith on too narrow a textual platform. His division of the canon is not a matter of mere theological acrobatics, as is shown by the preface to his interpretation of the letters of St. Paul, which itself follows the "doctrinal plan" of St. Paul's letters. Again, the great theme of grace is central to the interpretation:[68] The Letter to the Hebrews deals with grace in Christ, the head of the mystical body, while the remaining letters of St. Paul deal with grace within the mystical body itself. Within the latter group, the Letter to the Romans deals with grace as such (*secundum se*), while 1–2 Corinthians and Galatians are devoted to sacramental grace, and, beginning with Ephesians, the topics are both love and unity in the Church.

The concrete interpretation that proceeds verse by verse, while still observing the initially established *divisio textus*, tends to return consistently to the "theme" of each respective book. This serves as a key to interpretation, permitting the understanding of entire passages and thus providing a point of view on the basis of which individual verses can be explained and through which the interpretation itself gains both factual direction and precision. Proceeding from the scriptural text, the *quaestiones* and the detailed discussion, with which Aquinas injects a certain degree of recurring "rhythm" into his interpretation, are also devoted to a particular aspect of the main theological theme. Thus they do not detract from the ongoing interpretation, but serve on the contrary the very theological context that exegesis must provide.

Regarding Aquinas' Theological Interpretation

The purpose of Aquinas' exegesis is not the establishment of dogmatic proof based on Scripture. It aims rather at an agreement or a correspondence between Scripture and the doctrine of faith; or, as he himself put it, the continuation of *manifestatio veritatis* by interpreting the fixed form of this manifestation. Thomist theology and its theological exegesis are not fixed on dogmatics or individual dogmas; they breathe rather the vastness of Revelation in its entirety. The difference between a "systematic" *Summa* and an "exegetic" commentary is therefore modest. Both aim at the "manifestation of truth," and both deal with the rational understanding, order, and permeation of the revealed word. The "advantage" of the *Summa* lies in the fact that its endeavors are not tied to the continuous text of a biblical book; its topics are instead "freely" arranged according to the requirements of the theological discipline (*secundum ordinem doctrinae*, *non secundum quod requirebat librorum expositio*).⁶⁹ On the other hand, the commentary possesses the advantage of being able to uncover within the biblical text "more" than is necessary for the systematic description of a theological subject. What this means is that, depending on opportunity, Aquinas' interpretation of the Scriptures occasionally puts more effort into a theological subject in an attempt to do justice to the spiritual or affective dimension of Scripture than is the case with the exclusively argumentative method of the *quaestiones disputatae* or the *Summae*.⁷⁰ The commentary on Job aims specifically at the argumentative character of the Book of Job, which Aquinas views as a great disputation, and contains a plethora of such "spiritual" texts. Without them, the commentary would lack its present liveliness and freshness.⁷¹ Moreover, in commenting on Scripture, Aquinas was perhaps particularly aware of the needs and expectations of his fellow Dominican brethren and students who were preparing for their own preaching office.

Furthermore, the commentary on the Book of Job provides an opportunity to clarify the theological character of Aquinas' exegesis. Aquinas considered the Book of Job a treatise about God's providence. In the prologue to his commentary, he explains that God's providence is misunderstood by many, among them philosophers of nature, leading to an obscuring of the truth about God (*manifestatio veritatis*). The sufferings of the just constitute one of the most serious objections to divine providence. For this reason Aquinas argues especially against these objections in order to make more evident God's concern for the world and humanity. The intentions of this commentary agree with the program followed by the contemporary *Summa contra Gentiles*, to affirm the truths of faith in rational terms and to disarm objections against them. As is the case of the *Expositio super Iob* the entire third book of the *Summa contra Gentiles* also deals with the final destiny of the world and God's providence. This thematic correspondence not only testifies to the fact that both works were written contemporaneously, but also illustrates that Aquinas assigned a central place to *providentia divina* within the whole horizon of his theology. In fact, in the *Summa Theologiae* he even went as far as to proclaim that the existence of God and of divine providence are the two most important and fundamental truths of faith to which the whole Revelation and all theology can be reduced.⁷² In this regard, the commentary on Job can be likened to Aquinas' theological testament, since he elaborates on the basis of a difficult biblical text those aspects of faith in divine providence that appear to be of the highest importance to him.⁷³

Another illustration of how systematic theology and the interpretation of Holy Scripture overlap in the works of Thomas Aquinas may be found in his interpretation of the letters of St. Paul. As pointed out already in the discussion of the prologue to his commentary, Aquinas treats the letters of St. Paul as grandly designed teachings about grace. One aspect of grace is its active presence in the mystical body, that is, the Church. All of Aquinas' collective interpretations of Ephesians, Colossians, and the First Letter to Timothy in fact amount to an astoundingly original, biblically-founded ecclesiology which he deduces consistently from the contemplation of the mystical body.[74] There is not a hint in this fundamental, grace-based ecclesiology of the later controversies and the juridical reduction of ecclesiology to the *potestas ecclesiastica.* For instance, many of the interpretations of the First Letter to Timothy may be read like a handbook for bishops,[75] touting bishops as teachers, preachers, and examples in faith. This ecclesiological section within the interpretation of the letters of St. Paul serves as further illustration of the way in which the exegetical writings of Aquinas complement the teachings of his *Summae.* The interpretation of 1 Timothy is even more remarkable because Aquinas does not construct an explicit *Tractatus de Ecclesia* in his systematic writings.[76]

St. Thomas's exegesis—especially the *divisio textus* method and his primary interest in the doctrine of each individual book of the Bible—may be criticized by today's historico-critical exegesis as nonliterary and unhistorical. However, does that mean that his interpretation of the Scriptures is meaningless, or even "false"? If we ask at the end of this essay about the ideas that a modern theology may derive from Aquinas' interpretation of the Scriptures, there is certainly no desire to recommend the simple imitation of the method of Aquinas or to declare it as supra-temporally normative. However, since all understanding is transmitted by history, it seems sensible to come face-to-face with the ideas and results of earlier theological models, especially if they were designed by theologians who exercised a tremendous impact.

Regarding the way he both posed and answered his questions step by step, Aquinas developed his entire theology on the basis of a close and direct reference to Scripture. This observation is all the more significant because, on account of his use of Aristotelian terminology, he has been accused of neglecting the biblical foundation and biblical spirit of theology. Nevertheless, it is a matter of fact that Scripture was both the source and the measure of Aquinas' theology.[77] In the process, Aquinas takes a surprising amount of liberty with Scripture, a freedom that is rooted in his principal understanding of theology. Despite its normative character, Scripture is neither the (only) foundation nor the (exclusive) objective of theological thinking. That is God alone, the "divine truth." Scripture is already a part of a theological process that originates in God's self-communication. This self-communication extends from the incarnation of the Logos to the witness of the Apostles, prophets, and evangelists to any kind of *manifestatio veritatis,* which must be reclaimed each time anew by academic as well as pastoral interpretations of Scripture. Aquinas permits a plurality of interpretations as long as they do justice to the goal of uncovering the truth of the works of God. He vehemently rejected claiming an exclusive and exhaustive interpretation of any biblical text. No interpretation, including his own, is able to grasp fully the richness of God's word.[78]

The "liberty" apparent in Aquinas' interpretation of the Bible is further illustrated by the creativity and stimulation he received from the Latin text of the Vulgate version of the sacred texts. Whenever Aquinas establishes relationships between different books of the Bible based on word associations, he rarely engages in mere linguistic playfulness (for which there existed concordances and other aids). They are rather an expression of the systematic and creative powers with which he was able to disclose and unfold from any point of the revealed text the whole panorama of "sacred doctrine." Although a modern reader may become irritated when reading these medieval interpretations of the biblical text, such irritation or alienation may lead in turn to a broadening of the theological horizon, capable of enriching a preliminary knowledge of the scriptural text. Anyone who devotes himself or herself to the theology of St. Thomas will soon discover how this great thinker was always preoccupied with the most important task of theology: encountering the ultimate and greatest mystery of faith, God and the ways in which He reveals Himself to humanity for our salvation.[79]

Notes

1. Petrus Cantor, *Verbum abbreviatum,* ch. 1, PL 205, 25: "In tribus igitur consistit exercitium sacrae scripturae, circa lectionem, disputationem et praedicationem." Thomas de Aquino, *Principium Rigans montes,* ed. R. A. Verardo (*S. Thomae Aquinatis Opuscula Theologica,* vol. 1 [Turino-Rome: Marietti 1954]), 442 (no.1213): "Et de his tribus officiis, scilicet praedicandi, legendi et disputandi, dicitur Tit 1 (9): Ut sit potens exhortari, quantum ad praedicationem; in doctrina sana, quantum ad lectionem; et contradicentes revincere, quantum ad disputationem."

2. The research done by Eschmann and Weisheipl, and incorporated by J.-P. Torrell, *Initiation à saint Thomas d'Aquin: Sa personne et son œuvre* (Fribourg: Éditions Universitaires, 1993), 493–98, is fundamental to the establishment of these historical dates. See E. T. Eschmann, "A Catalogue of Saint Thomas's Works," in É. Gilson, *The Christian Philosophy of St. Thomas Aquinas* (New York, 1956), 393–99; J. A. Weisheipl, *Friar Thomas d'Aquino* (Washington, D.C.: Catholic University of America Press, 1983), 368–74. L. J. Bataillon offers interesting observations concerning the dissemination of the scriptural commentaries in "La diffusione manoscritta dei commenti biblici di San Tommaso d'Aquino," *Angelicum* 71 (1994): 579–90. Thus, older research, such as that of P. Mandonnet, "Chronologie des écrits scripturaires de saint

Thomas d'Aquin," *Revue Thomiste* 33 (1928) and 34 (1929), and of P. Glorieux, "Essai sur les Commentaires scripturaires de saint Thomas et leur chronologie," RTAM 17 (1950): 237–66, has to be corrected.

3. *Expositio super Isaiam ad litteram*, Leonine Edition, vol. 28 (Rome, 1974); *Expositio super Iob ad litteram*, Leonine Edition, vol. 26 (Rome, 1965).

4. On the difference between "cursory" and "magisterial" interpretation, see G. Dahan, *L'exégèse chrétienne de la Bible en Occident médiéval, XIIe–XIVe siècle* (Paris: Cerf, 1999), 110 f.

5. P.-M. Gils, "Les 'Collationes' marginales dans l'autographe du commentaire de S. Thomas sur Isaie," *Revue des sciences philosophiques et théologiques* 42 (1958): 254–64; J.-P. Torrell and D. Bouthillier, "Quand saint Thomas méditait sur le prophète Isaie?" *Revue Thomiste* 90 (1990): 5–47; D. Bouthillier, "Le Christ en son mystère dans les 'collationes' du 'super Isaiam' de saint Thomas d'Aquin," in *Ordo sapientiae et amoris: Hommage à J.-P. Torrell à l'occasion de son 65e anniversaire*, ed. C.-J. Pinto de Oliveira, Studia Friburgensia, n.s. 78 (Fribourg: Éditions Universitaires, 1993), 37–64; Torrell, *Initiation*, 40–52.

6. Bataillon, "La diffusione manoscritta," 585.

7. Regarding the ceremonies accompanying the inauguration, see Torrell, *Initiation*, 73–78. The text of the two lectures are edited in *S. Thomae de Aquino Opuscula theologica*, vol. 1, 435–43. For an English translation, see R. McInerny, ed. and trans., *Thomas Aquinas: Selected Writings* (London: Penguin Books, 1998), 5–17.

8. L. Elders, "El comentario de Santo Tomás de Aquino sobre el libro de Job," in *Miscellanea Bruno Gherardini*, Studi Tomistici 61 (Vatican: Libreria Editrice Vaticana, 1996), 37–64; P. Zerafa, "Il commento di san Tommaso al libro di Giobbe tra esegesi antica e esegesi contemporanea," *Angelicum* 71 (1964): 481–507; for additional literature, see below, note 73.

9. Since Pope Urban IV was already dead by October 2, 1264, Aquinas was able to present him only with the *Catena in Matthaeum*. The remaining three gospel glosses, which Aquinas completed while in Rome during the course of the next four years, are dedicated to his former student, Cardinal Annibaldo degli Annibaldi. See Bataillon, "La diffusione manoscritta," 582–83; Bataillon, "Saint Thomas et les Pères: De la Catena à la Tertia Pars," in *Ordo sapientiae et amoris*, 15–36; C. G. Conticello, "San Tommaso ed i Padri: La Catena aurea super Ioannem," in AHDLMA 65 (= vol. 57) (1990): 31–92; Torrell, *Initiation*, 200–206.

10. In his letter of dedication to the pope, Aquinas gave an account of his exegetical methods as well as his intentions: "In assumendis autem Sanctorum testimoniis, plerumque oportuit aliqua rescindi de medio ad prolixitatem vitandam, nec non ad manifestationem sensum vel, secundum congruentiam expositionis, litterae ordinem commutari; interdum etiam sensum posui, verba dimisi, praecipue in Homiliario Chrysostomi, propter hoc quod est translatio vitiosa. Fuit autem mea intentio in hoc opere non solum sensum prosequi litteralem, sed etiam mysticum ponere; interdum etiam errores destruere, necnon confirmare catholicam veritatem." *Catena in Matthaeum*, Epistola dedicatoria, ed. A. Guarienti (Turin-Rome: Marietti, 1953), 4.

11. The passages in question are Matthew 5:11–6:8 and Matthew 6:14–19. This corresponds to paragraphs 444–582 and 603–10 in the Marietti edition.

12. H.-V. Shooner, "La Lectura in Matthaeum de S. Thomas (Deux fragments inédits et la Reportatio de Pierre de Andria)," *Angelicum* 33 (1956): 121–42; J.-P. Renard, "La Lectura super Matthaeum V, 20–48 de Thomas d'Aquin," RTAM 50 (1983): 145–90.

13. E. Panella, "La 'Lex nova' tra Storia ed Ermeneutica: Le occasioni dell'esegesi di s. Tommaso d'Aquino," *Memorie domenicane*, n.s. 6 (1975): 11–106, esp. 40–59; U. Horst, *Evangelische Armut und Kirche: Thomas von Aquin und die Armutskontroversen des 13. und beginnenden 14.*

Jahrhunderts, Quellen und Forschungen zur Geschichte des Dominikanerordens, N. F. 1 (Berlin: Akademie, 1992), 77–81; B. Smalley, *The Gospel in the Schools c. 1100–c. 1280* (London: Hambledon Press, 1985), 257–71. Based on these clear indications, the thesis presented by M. Arges in "New Evidence Concerning the Date of Thomas Aquinas' 'Lectura' on Matthew," *Mediaeval Studies* 49 (1987): 517–23, dating the *Lectura* to the year 1263, must be refuted.

14. Bataillon, "La diffusione manoscritta," 589; J. A. Weisheipl, "An Introduction to the Commentary on the Gospel of Saint John," in *St. Thomas Aquinas: Commentary on the Gospel of St. John,* Part I (Albany, N.Y.: Magi Books, 1980), 3–19; Pierre-Yves Maillard, *La vision de Dieu chez Thomas d'Aquin: Une lecture de l' 'In Ioannem' à la lumière de ses sources augustiniennes,* Bibliothèque Thomiste 53 (Paris: Vrin, 2001); G. Ferraro, *Lo Spirito e l' 'ora' di Christo: L'esegesi di san Tommaso d'Aqino sul quarto vangelo* (Città del Vaticano: Libreria Editrice Vaticana, 1996); L. Jansen, "Was hat der inkarnierte Logos mit Aristoteles zu tun? Thomas von Aquins Gebrauch der Philosophie in der Auslegung des Johannesprologs und eine holistische Interpretation seiner Schrifthermeneutik," *Theologie und Philosophie* 75 (2000): 89–99; S. Cipriani, "Riflessioni esegetiche su 'Super Ionannis Evangelium lectura' di S. Tommaso," in *Tommaso d'Aquino nel suo settimo Centenario,* vol. 4 (Naples: Edizioni Domenicane Italiane, 1976), 41–59.

15. The Letter to the Hebrews was also handed down separately in several manuscripts. The textual difficulties are augmented by the existence of an *altera reportatio* spanning the first seven chapters of Hebrews, because parts of this variant tradition were incorporated into the printed editions. Bataillon, "La diffusione manoscritta," 586–87; M. Grabmann, *Die Werke des hl. Thomas von Aquin: Eine literarhistorische Untersuchung und Einführung* (BGPTMA 22/1.2), 3rd ed. (Münster: Aschendorff, 1949; reprinted in 1967), 266–72.

16. Torrell, *Initiation,* 496; see in general, 365–76; H. Bouillard, *Conversion et grâce chez s. Thomas d'Aquin: Études historiques,* Théologie 1 (Paris: Aubier, 1944), 225–41 (Appendice: Date du commentaire de Saint Thomas sur l'épitre aux Romains); T. Domanyi, *Der Römerbriefkommentar des Thomas von Aquin: Ein Beitrag zur Untersuchung seiner Auslegungsmethoden,* Basler und Berner Studien zur historischen und systematischen Theologie 39 (Bern-Frankfurt-Las Vegas: Lang, 1979); D. O'Connor, "St. Thomas' Commentary on Romans," *The Irish Theological Quarterly* 34 (1967): 329–43.

17. Paragraphs 336–581 in the Marietti edition.

18. Torrell, *Initiation,* 367.

19. M. Mulchahey, *'First the Bow Is Bent in Study . . .' Dominican Education before 1350,* Studies and Texts 132 (Toronto: Pontifical Institute of Mediaeval Studies, 1998), 278–306.

20. It is possible that the impending publication of the critical edition of the commentary on St. Paul's Letter to the Romans by P. Grandpré will shed more light on these questions. I give further arguments for my hypothesis below in note 68.

21. *Albert and Thomas: Selected Writings,* trans., ed., and introduced by S. Tugwell (New York: Paulist Press, 1988), 248 and n. 474; cf. Torrell, *Initiation,* 377.

22. Torrell, *Initiation,* 376–81; Bataillon, "La diffusione manoscritta," 589 f.; see also the French translation: *Thomas d'Aquin, Commentaire sur les Psaumes,* introduction, traduction, notes et tables par J.-E. Stroobant de Saint Eloy; préface par M. D. Jordan (Paris: Cerf, 1996). For a critical evaluation, see M. Morard, "À propos du Commentaire des Psaumes de saint Thomas d'Aquin," *Revue Thomiste* 96 (1996): 653–70; C. Pandolfi, *San Tommaso filosofo nel Commento ai Salmi: Interpretazione dell'essere nel modo 'esenziale' dell'invocazione* (Rome: Edizioni Studio Domenicano, 1993); most recently, Thomas F. Ryan, *Thomas Aquinas as Reader of the Psalms,* Studies in Spirituality and Theology 6 (Notre Dame, Ind.: University of Notre Dame Press, 2000).

23. C. Le Brun-Gouanvic, *Ystoria sancti Thome de Aquino de Guillaume de Tocco (1323)*, édition critique, introduction et notes, Studies and Texts 127 (Toronto: Pontifical Institute of Mediaeval Studies, 1996), 196 (c. 57).

24. J. Wawrykow, "Reflections on the Place of the '*De doctrina christiana*' in High Scholastic Discussions of Theology," in *Reading and Wisdom: The 'De doctrina christiana' of Augustine in the Middle Ages*, ed. E. D. English (Notre Dame, Ind.: University of Notre Dame Press, 1995), 99–125.

25. *ST* I.1.9 and 10. These two articles were introduced in *Quodl.* VII, q.6, where Aquinas elaborated on the matter more broadly. *Quodl.* VII was already debated in April 1256, that is, shortly after the *venia legendi* was bestowed on Aquinas. See the preface by R. A. Gauthier in the Leonine Edition, vol. 25 (Rome, 1996), IX* and 58*–60*; for the text see 27–32. Within ten years, Aquinas had resumed the discussion of these ideas, in the *ST*.

26. J. A. Weisheipl, "The Meaning of 'Sacra Doctrina' in 'Summa Theologiae' I, q. 1," *The Thomist* 38 (1974): 49–80; J.-P. Torrell, "Le savoir théologique chez saint Thomas," *Revue Thomiste* 96 (1996): 355–96 (reprinted in Torrell, *Recherches Thomasiennes*, Études revues et augmentées, Bibliothèque Thomiste 52 [Paris: J. Vrin, 2000]); A. Patfoort, "Théorie de la théologie ou réflexion sur le corpus des Écritures?" *Angelicum* 54 (1977): 459–88 (reprinted in A. Patfoort, *Thomas d'Aquin: Les clefs d'une théologique* [Paris: FAC, 1983], 13–47); Y. Congar, "Tradition et 'Sacra doctrina' chez saint Thomas d'Aquin," in *Église et Tradition*, ed. J. Betz and H. Fries (Le Puy-Lyon: Éditions Xavier Mappus, 1963), 157–94 (reprinted in Y. Congar, *Thomas d'Aquin: Sa vision de théologie et de l'Église*, Collected Studies 190 [London: Variorum Reprints, 1984]); T. C. O'Brien, "'Sacra Doctrina' Revisited: The Context of Medieval Education," in *The Thomist* 41 (1977): 475–509; M. F. Johnson, "God's Knowledge in Our Frail Mind: The Thomistic Model of Theology," *Angelicum* 76 (1999): 25–45; B. J. Shanley, "'Sacra doctrina' and the Theology of Disclosure," *The Thomist* 61 (1997): 163–87; L. Donohoo, "The Nature and Grace of 'Sacra Doctrina' in St. Thomas's 'Super Boetium de Trinitate,'" in *The Thomist* 63 (1999): 343–401.

27. "Sacra scriptura ad hoc divinitus tradita est ut per eam nobis veritas manifestetur necessaria ad salutem," *Quodl.* VII, 6, 1 (Leonine Edition, vol. 25, 28, lin.52–54). Regarding the theology of Revelation in Aquinas, see C. Berchtold, *Manifestatio Veritatis: Zum Offenbarungsbegriff bei Thomas von Aquin*, Dogma und Geschichte 1 (Münster: Lit, 2000); L. J. Elders, "Aquinas on Holy Scripture as the Medium of Divine Revelation," in *La doctrine de la révélation divine de saint Thomas d'Aquin*, Studi Tomistici 37 (Città del Vaticano: Libreria Editrice Vaticana, 1990), 132–52; E. Menard, *La Tradition, Révélation, Écriture et Église selon saint Thomas d'Aquin*, Studia 18 (Bruges: Desclée, 1964); B. Decker, "Schriftprinzip und Ergänzungstradition in der Theologie des hl. Thomas von Aquin," in *Schrift und Tradition*, ed. Deutsche Arbeitsgemeinschaft für Mariologie, Mariologische Studien 1 (Essen, 1962), 191–221.

28. In one of the objections in this article (*ST* I.1.10 arg.1), Aquinas describes this danger as follows: "Multiplicitas enim sensuum in una scriptura parit confusionem et deceptionem"; furthermore, in *Quodl.* VII, 6, he speaks of "*deceptio*," "*occasio erroris*," "*multiplicitas sensuum obnubilat intellectum.*"

29. *Quodl.* VII, 6, 1 (Leonine Edition, vol. 25, 28, lin.59–63): "Spiritus sanctus non solum est auctor verborum sed etiam est auctor rerum, unde non solum verba potest accommodare ad aliquod significandum, sed etiam res potest disponere in figuram alterius." Aquinas borrowed this idea from Hugh of St. Victor, thus endorsing a patristic tradition that began with Augustine and continued through Gregory the Great. Cf. M. Aillet, *Lire la Bible avec s. Thomas: Le passage de la 'littera' à la 'res' dans la Somme théologique*, Studia Friburgensia, n.s. 80 (Fribourg: Éditions Universitaires, 1993), 69–76.

30. *Quodl.* VII, 6, 2; *ST* I.1.10. Cf. Aillet, *Lire la Bible avec s. Thomas,* 151–70. The theological benefits of the spiritual meaning are emphasized by H. de Lubac, *Der geistige Sinn der Schrift,* mit einem Geleitwort von H. U. v. Balthasar (Einsiedeln: Johannes, 1952). The standard work concerning the allegorical interpretation of Scripture during the Middle Ages remains H. de Lubac, *Exégèse médiévale: Les quatre sens de l'Écriture,* 4 vols. (Paris: Aubier, 1959–64; reprinted, Paris, 1993); about Aquinas, see vol. 4, 272–302; see also H. J. Spitz, *Die Metaphorik des geistlichen Schriftsinnes: Ein Beitrag zur allegorischen Bibelauslegung des ersten christlichen Jahrtausends* (Munich: W. Fink, 1972); H. Brinkmann, *Mittelalterliche Hermeneutik* (Tübingen: Niemeyer, 1980); L. Valente, "Une sémantique particulière: La pluralité des sens dans les Saintes Écriture (XIIᵉ siècle)," in *Sprachtheorien in Spätantike und Mittelalter,* ed. S. Ebbesen (Tübingen: G. Narr, 1995), 12–32 (with extensive bibliography).

31. *Quodl.* VII, 6, 1, ad 3 (Leonine Edition, vol. 25, 29); *ST* I.1.10 ad 1: "nihil sub spirituali sensu continetur fidei necessarium, quod Scriptura per litteralem sensum alicubi manifeste non tradat."

32. *ST* I.1.10 ad 3: "Sensui litterali sacrae scripturae numquam potest subesse falsum."

33. *Quodl.* VII, 6, 1, ad 4 (Leonine Edition, vol. 25, 29). A sentence from Pseudo-Dionysius runs like a thread through Aquinas' hermeneutical deliberations: "simbolica theologia, id est que ex similitudinibus procedit, non est argumentativa," *Quodl.* VII, 6, 1, arg.4 (Leonine Edition, vol. 25, 28; parallel passages are found in the apparatus of sources in Bataillon's edition). As for the meaning of the literal sense in Aquinas, see R. G. Kennedy, "Thomas Aquinas and the Literal Sense of Sacred Scripture," Ph.D. dissertation (University of Notre Dame, 1985), especially 98–149; M. Arias Reyero, *Thomas von Aquin als Exeget: Die Prinzipien seiner Schriftdeutung und seine Lehre von den Schriftsinnen* (Einsiedeln: Johannes Verlag, 1971), 153–68. The fundamental priority of the literal sense over allegorical interpretation was never in doubt. The greater attention paid to it was propagated by Hugh of St. Victor, who thus decisively influenced the development of Scholastic exegesis. B. Smalley, *The Study of the Bible in the Middle Ages,* 3rd ed. (Oxford: Blackwell, 1983), especially 93–106, 214–41; C. Spicq, *Esquisse d'une histoire de l'exégèse latin au moyen âge,* Bibliothèque Thomiste 26 (Paris: J. Vrin, 1944), 267–88; Dahan, *L'exégèse chrétienne,* 239–97; G. R. Evans, *The Language and Logic of the Bible: The Early Middle Ages* (Cambridge: Cambridge University Press, 1984), 67–71.

34. *In II Tim.* 3:16, no.127: "Effectus huius scripturae est duplex, sc. quia docet cognoscere veritatem et suadet operari iustitiam. . . . Est enim ratio speculativa et est etiam ratio practica. Et in utroque sunt duo necessaria, sc. quod veritatem cognoscat et errorem refellat. Hoc enim est opus sapientis. . . . Sic ergo quadruplex est effectus sacrae scripturae, sc. docere veritatem, arguere falsitatem, quantum ad speculativam; eripere a malo et inducere ad bonum quantum ad practicam." Concerning the apologetic task of scriptural interpretation, see S. Baldner, "The Use of Scripture for the Refutation of Error according to St. Thomas Aquinas," in *Hamartia: The Concept of Error in the Western Tradition, Essays in Honor of J. M. Crosset,* ed. D. V. Stump et al., Text and Studies in Religion 16 (New York: Edwin Mellen Press, 1983), 149–69.

35. Hugh of St. Victor proposed the three-step procedure of *littera-sensus-sententia* as a method of interpreting the Bible (*Didascalion* III, 9; PL 176, 771D) by means of which he penetrated ever more deeply into the text, from the (superficial) meaning of the words and their "sense" to a deeper understanding. Aquinas did not adopt this three-step procedure. To be sure, he occasionally talked about the *superficies litterae* at which one must not stop and by which one must not be deceived; as a rule, he turned immediately to *sensus* as the primary goal of exegesis.

36. The issue has finally been put to rest by M. F. Johnson, "Another Look at the Plurality of Literal Sense," *Medieval Philosophy and Theology* 2 (1992): 117–41, where the entire controversy

is documented. Johnson introduces a new, decisive argument based on a passage from the *alia lectura*, that is, the revised commentary on the *Sentences* on which Aquinas lectured during his stay in Rome prior to his decision to write the *ST.* There Aquinas states (134): "Item aliud proprium est quia in ista (sc. scriptura) sunt plures sensus litterales et quilibet est verum."

37. *De Pot.* q.4 a.1: "Unde omnis veritas, quae salva litterae circumstantia potest divinae Scripturae aptari, est ejus sensus."

38. *In Eph.* 1:22, nos.65 ff. See G. Dahan, "Saint Thomas d'Aquin et la métaphore: Rhétorique et herméneutique," *Medioevo* 18 (1992): 85–117; Dahan, *L'exégèse chrétienne,* 426–35. Occasionally, when Aquinas speaks of a *sensus parabolicus seu metaphoricus* he makes an attempt to create a new level between the literal and the spiritual sense; he prefers to contribute to the clarification of concepts because it is up to the literal sense to interpret imagery: "sub sensu litterali includitur parabolicus seu metaphoricus." See also Arias Reyero, *Thomas von Aquin als Exeget,* 169–206; Kennedy, "Literal Sense," 201–12. The fact that Aquinas still locates the metaphor between the literal sense and allegory is illustrated by his interpretation of Isaiah 30:25 (Leonine Edition, vol. 28, 139, lin.188–96): "Iudei dicunt haec *ad litteram* complenda in fine mundi. . . . Vel potest esse *metaphorica locutio,* ut per aquam significetur consolatio quam post reditum de captivitate et Babilonis destructionem habuerunt. Vel *mistice* de doctrina Christi . . ." (emphasis mine).

39. *ST* I.1.9: "Utrum sacra scriptura debeat uti metaphoribus." *Expositio super Isaiam,* prol. (Leonine Edition, vol. 28, 3, lin.40–47): "Ponit enim pulcras et curiales similitudines, que quidem sunt necessarie nobis propter connaturalitatem sensus ad rationem: est enim naturale rationi nostrae accipere a sensibilibus, unde perspicacius capit ea quorum similia ad sensum videt; unde Dionysius in Epistula ad Titum secunda demonstrat hoc, scilicet quod necessarie sunt sensibiles figurae in Scripturis."

40. *Quodl.* VII, 6, 2 (Leonine Edition, vol. 25, 30, lin.57–61; *In Is.* (Leonine Edition, vol. 28, 47, lin.38–43): "Ad aliquid enim significandum spiritualiter inducuntur sensibiles figurae spiritualium in sacra scriptura, sicut dicit Dionysius, et ille erit litteralis sensus, sicut etiam in locutionibus metaphoricis non illud quod significatur per verba, sed quod loquens per verba vult significare."—"Sacra scriptura non proponit nobis divina sub figuris sensibilibus, ut ibi intellectus remaneat, sed ut ab his ad immaterialia ascendat. Unde etiam per vilium rerum figuras divina tradit, ut minor praebetur occasio in talibus remanendi, ut dicit Dionysius in II c. Celestis ierarchiae." *De Trin.* q.6 art.2 ad 1 (Leonine Edition, vol. 50, 165, lin.144–50). The *intentio auctoris* was also at the center of Aquinas' thoughts in the prologue to the opuscule *Contra errores Graecorum.* In addition, the exegetical principles contained in this text apply to Aquinas' interpretation of Holy Scripture and are emphasized by M.D. Jordan, "Theological Exegesis and Aquinas's Treatise against the Greeks," *Church History* 56 (1987): 445–56.

41. A. Dondaine, in his preface to the *Expositio super Iob* (Leonine Edition, vol. 26, 24*–25*. Regarding textural criticism during the thirteenth century and the so-called *correctories* of Dominicans and Franciscans, see Dahan, *L'exégèse chrétienne,* 175–90; specifically regarding Aquinas, see C. Spicq, "Saint Thomas d'Aquin exégète," in *Dictionnaire de Théologie Catholique* 15/1 (1946), 694–738, esp. 708–11.

42. *In Iob,* ch. 3 (Leonine Edition, vol. 26, 21, lin.129–40): "Sicut Hieronymus dicit in Prologo . . . , hexametri versus sunt, dactylo spondeoque currentes'; et sic patet quod liber iste ex hinc per modum poematis conscriptus est, unde per totum hunc librum figuris et coloribus utitur quibus poetae, ut vehementius moveant, ad eandem sententiam diversa inducere."

43. This is typically illustrated by the following observation: "Matthaeus enim Evangelium Hebraeis conscripsit, et ideo in scribendo modum Iudeorum servavit. Consuetum est autem apud Hebraeos sic loqui. . . ." *In Matt.* 1:2, no.12.

44. *In Tit.* 3:9, no.100: "Et doctor ad duo intendere debet, sc. ad utilitatem et ad veritatem. . . . Non est ergo intromittendum se de inutilibus, et quae non habent solidam veritatem. Scire enim singularia, ut sunt genealogiae, non est ad perfectionem intellectus nec ad instructionem morum, nec fidei. Et sunt vanae, quia non habent solidam veritatem."

45. *In Iob*, ch. 1 (Leonine Edition, vol. 26, 7, lin.223–34. For an example of the frequently mentioned *modus loquendi sacrae scripturae* in the commentary of the Book of Job, see for instance ch. 2 (ed. cit., 16, lin.50–57, where the text speaks of God "*figuraliter more humano*"); ch. 7 (ed. cit., 51, lin.461–63); ch. 13 (ed. cit., 86, lin.158–60); ch. 26 (ed. cit., 145, lin.98–99) ("loquitur enim secundum aestimationem vulgarium hominum pro ut est moris in sacra Scriptura").

46. *In Iob*, ch. 3 (ed. cit., 26, lin.551).

47. *In Iob*, ch. 21 (ed. cit., 124, lin.133).

48. *In Iob*, ch. 34 (ed. cit., 182, lin. 241). In the *Expositio super Iob* alone I discovered more than sixty similar references to anthropomorphic attributes of God. In the *Expositio super Isaiam*, ch. 2 (Leonine Edition, vol. 28, 24, lin.365), we encounter the expression "loquitur de Deo ad similitudinem hominis per figuram antropostratos," which Aquinas uses only a total of five times (twice each in the Isaiah commentary and in the Jeremiah commentary and once in the interpretation of the Psalms).

49. "Assez souvent saint Thomas prépare son auditeur à l'explication qui va suivre par une considération d'ordre général, simple et évidente; le commentaire en sera l'application à un cas particulier." Dondaine, in his preface to the Leonine Edition, vol. 26, 29*.

50. For a good overview, see Spicq, "Saint Thomas d'Aquin exégète"; cf. the very thorough discussion in Domanyi, *Römerbriefkommentar*, 77–158. Dahan in his *L'exégèse chrétienne*, 121–59 and 239–71, offers a comprehensive compilation of the philological aspects of the interpretation of the Scriptures during the Middle Ages.

51. A. J. Minnis and A. B. Scott, eds., *Medieval Literary Theory and Criticism, c. 1100–c. 1375: The Commentary Tradition* (Oxford: Clarendon Press, 1988), especially 1–11 (general introduction); *Les prologues médiévaux*, ed. J. Hamesse, Textes et Études du Moyen Âge 15 (Paris-Turnhout: Brepols, 2000); F. del Punta, "The Genre of Commentaries in the Middle Ages and Its Relation to the Nature and Originality of Medieval Thought," in *Miscellanea Mediaevalia* 26 (Berlin: W. de Gruyter, 1998), 138–51; Nicolaus Häring, "Commentary and Hermeneutics," in *Renaissance and Renewal in the Twelfth Century*, ed. R. L. Benson and G. Constable (Cambridge, Mass.: Harvard University Press, 1982), 173–200.

52. R. W. Hunt, "The Introductions to the 'artes' in the Twelfth Century," in *Studia mediaevalia in honorem R. J. Martin* (Bruges: Apud Societatem Editricem 'De Tempel', 1948), 85–112; A. J. Minnis, *Medieval Theory of Authorship: Scholastic Literary Attitudes in the Later Middle Ages* (London: Scolar Press, 1984); D. Kelly, "*Accessus ad auctores*," in *Historisches Wörterbuch der Rhetorik*, vol. 1 (Tübingen: M. Niemeyer, 1992), 27–36.

53. Quite surprisingly, Aquinas did not employ the so-called Aristotelian prologue in his commentaries on the Scriptures, i.e., the type of prologue that discusses the introductory literary questions on the basis of the four *causae* (*materialis, formalis, efficiens, finalis*). Regarding this type of prologue, which occurs for the first time in Hugh of St. Cher (ca. 1230) and which was already used exclusively by Bonaventure, see Minnis, *Medieval Theory of Authorship*, 28–30; Kelly, "*Accessus ad auctorem*," 33; B. Faes de Mottoni, "I prologhi dei commenti al Vangelo di Luca di Giovanni della Rochelle e di Bonaventura," in *Les Prologues médiévaux*, 471–513. See also the introduction to *Thomas von Aquin: Prologe zu den Aristoteleskommentaren*, ed., trans., and with an introduction by F. Cheneval and R. Imbach (Frankfurt am Main: V. Klostermann, 1993), lvii–lxx.

54. O. H. Pesch, "Paul as a Professor of Theology: The Image of the Apostle in St. Thomas' Theology," *The Thomist* 38 (1974): 584–605.

55. "... ut fere videatur evangelium, et non prophetia." Aquinas may have been reminded of St. Jerome's preface to the Vulgate translation of the prophet Isaiah: "... non tam propheta dicendus sit quam evangelista." *Biblia Sacra: Iuxta vulgatam versionem*, 4th ed., ed. R. Weber and R. Gryson (Stuttgart: Deutsche Bibelgesellschaft, 1994), 1096.

56. Minnis, *Medieval Theory of Authorship*, 118–59.

57. *Summa Halensis*, Tractatus introductorius, q.1, ch. 4, art.1, ad 2.

58. Aquinas, I *Sent.*, prol., q.1 art.5. Regarding the question of the scientific status of theology as discussed by the introductory questions of the commentaries on the *Sentences*, see M.-D. Chenu, *La théologie comme science au XIIIᵉ siècle*, Bibliothèque Thomiste 33, 3rd ed. (Paris: J. Vrin, 1969), especially 38–53; U. Köpf, *Die Anfänge der theologischen Wissenschaftstheorie im 13. Jahrhundert*, Beiträge zur historischen Theologie 49 (Tübingen: Mohr, 1947), especially 156–76; C. Trottmann, *Théologie et noétique au XIIIᵉ siècle: À la recherche d'un statut*, Études de Philosophie Médiévale 78 (Paris: Vrin, 1999). The consequences of these distinctions for biblical exegesis are mentioned in Dahan, *L'exégèse chrétienne*, 416–22.

59. For instance, Aquinas detects an "argumentative" process in 1 Corinithians 15:12, where St. Paul concludes from Christ's resurrection to the general resurrection of all mankind (*ST* I.1.8; I *Sent.*, prol., art.5 ad 4). Terms such as *modus divisivus, collectivus, disputativus, diffinitivus, probativus* were all considered to be variations of the *modus argumentativus*, according to Köpf, *Anfänge*, 159, n.22. All these *modi* aim at rational argumentation. Whereas the Franciscan school refused to acknowledge this "rational" *modus* in Holy Scripture, Albertus Magnus finally got himself to accept the Thomist idea in his old age. He still repeated Alexander of Hales' dual viewpoint in his commentary on the *Sentences;* however in his second *Summa Theologiae* he also accepted the existence of the *modus disputativus* in Holy Scripture, namely, in the Book of Job. Albertus Magnus, *Summa*, Tract. I, q.5, ch. 4, arg.13 (Cologne Edition 34/1; Münster, 1978), 21.

60. Dahan, *L'exégèse chrétienne*, 74–120, divides medieval exegesis into the three epochs of "exégèse monastique" (until the twelfth century), "exégèse de l'école" (twelfth century), and "exégèse universitaire" (from the thirteenth century on).

61. For a descriptive overview of such a division of an entire commentary, see the "Index synopticus-generalis" of the *In Matt.* (*Lectura in Evangelium S. Matthaei*, ed. R. Cai), 397–429.

62. In this context, M. M. Rossi, "La 'divisio textus' nei commenti scritturistici di s. Tommaso d'Aquino: Un procedimento solo esegetico?" *Angelicum* 71 (1994): 537–48, speaks appropriately (541) of a centrifugal and centripetal movement of this method; see also M. M. Rossi, "La 'divisio textus': Indizio di un genere letterario?" in *Studi 1995*, ed. D. Lorenz and S. Serafini, Studia Pontificiae Universitatis a S. Thoma Aq. in Urbe, Istituto San Tommaso, n.s. 2 (Rome, 1995), 183–203.

63. *Ad Rom.* 12, lect.3, no.996.

64. *Ad Rom.* 2:6–12, nos.189–90: "Postquam apostolus *proposuit* veritatem divini iudicii exclusa *contraria opinione*, hic *manifestat* divini iudicii veritatem; et primo *proponit quod intendit*, secundo *manifestat propositum*.... *Proponit* autem primo veritatem divini iudicii quantum ad duo ..." (emphasis mine).

65. Spicq, "Saint Thomas d'Aquin exégète," 715; M. D. Chenu, *Toward Understanding St. Thomas*, trans. A.-M. Landry and D. Hughes (Chicago: H. Regnery Co., 1964), 249–53.

66. *ST* II-II.1.9 ad 1: "Veritas fidei in Sacra Scriptura diffuse continetur et variis modis, et in quibusdam obscure, ita quod ad eliciendum fidei veritatem ex Sacra Scriptura requiritur

longum studium et exercitium. . . . Et ideo fuit necessarium ut ex sentenciis Sacrae Scripturae aliquid manifestum summarie colligeretur quod proponeretur omnibus ad credendum."

67. Regarding the two *principia*, see n.7 above. It was a common practice during these "inaugural lectures" to include a so-called *Commendatio S. Scripturae*. Dahan, *L'exégèse chrétienne*, 402–9, points out the importance of these texts, quoting the Cornell University Ph.D. dissertation of N. Spatz, "Principia: A Study and Edition of Inception Speeches Delivered before the Faculty of Theology at the University of Paris, ca. 1180–1286" (Ithaca, N.Y.: 1992).

68. Surprisingly, the mentioned *principium* lacks—at least in the manuscript on which the text of the Marietti edition is based—the classification of the letters of St. Paul (see 439 in the Marietti edition, including relevant observations by the editor). Is this an indication that Aquinas may have begun his teaching career in Paris in 1256 with the interpretation of the letters of St. Paul? Because he had intended to interpret this book anyway during the days following the *principium*, he could have refrained (perhaps because of time pressures) from classifying St. Paul's letters, simply referring to the lecture that was to follow.

69. *ST* I, prol.

70. Certainly, this view merely intends to point out one tendency in Aquinas' writings. Aquinas was, of course, masterfully able to combine "argumentative theology" with spiritual warmth. The most telling example of this is found in the hymn *Adoro te devote*. See R. Wielockx, "Poetry and Theology in the 'Adoro te devote': Thomas Aquinas on the Eucharist and Christ's Uniqueness," in *Christ among the Medieval Dominicans: Representations of Christ in the Texts and Images of the Order of Preachers*, ed. K. Emery and J. Wawrykow, Notre Dame Conferences in Medieval Studies 7 (Notre Dame, Ind.: University of Notre Dame Press, 1998), 157–74. Regarding the spiritual dimension of Aquinas' theology, see especially J.-P. Torrell, *Saint Thomas d'Aquin, maître spirituel, Initiation 2*, Vestigia 19 (Fribourg: Éditions Universitaires, 1996).

71. A few references may suffice: God's concern for man which is taken as proof (!) for life after death (*In Iob*, ch. 7 [Leonine Edition, vol. 26, 50 f., lin.395–419]); the praise of friendship (ch. 2; ed. cit., 18 f., lin.220–52); the location of wisdom (ch. 28; ed. cit., 152 f., lin.145–85); the award for the just in this life (ch. 27; ed. cit., 148 f., lin.84–157); the proximity of God (ch. 17; ed. cit., 106 f., lin.49–71); moderate sadness (ch. 3; ed. cit., 20, lin.16–44). Concerning sadness, see T. Prügl, "Tristitia: Zur Theologie der 'passiones animae' bei Thomas Aquin," in *Einheit der Person: Beiträge zur Anthropologie des Mittelalters, Festschrift für R. Heinzmann zum 65. Geburtstag*, ed. M. Thurner (Stuttgart: Verlag W. Kohlhammer, 1998), 141–57.

72. *ST* II-II.1.7c: "Omnes articuli implicite continentur in aliquibus primis credibilibus, sc. ut credatur Deus esse et providentiam habere circa hominum salutem. In fide autem providentiae includuntur omnia quae temporaliter a Deo dispensantur ad hominum salutem, quae sunt via in beatitudinem."

73. Concerning the theology in the commentary on the Book of Job, see D. Chardonnens, *L'homme sous le regard de la providence: Providence de Dieu et condition humaine selon l'"Exposition littérale sur le Livre de Job' de Thomas d'Aquin*, Bibliothèque Thomiste 50 (Paris: J. Vrin, 1997); A. Wohlman, *Thomas d'Aquin et Maimonide: Un dialogue exemplaire* (Paris: Cerf, 1988), 207–66; A. Wohlman, *Maimonide et Thomas d'Aquin: Un dialogue impossible*, Dokimion 16 (Fribourg: Éditions Universitaires, 1995), 69–99; T. P. Jackson, "Must Job Live Forever? A Reply to Aquinas on Providence," *The Thomist* 62 (1998): 1–39; F. Coggi, "Dolore, Providenza, Rissurrezione nel libro di Giobbe: Validità di un'intuizione esegetica di S. Tommaso," *Sacra Doctrina* 27 (1982): 215–310; S. Ausin, "La providencia divina en el libro de Job: Estudio sobre la 'Expositio in Job' de Santo Tomás de Aquino," *Scripta Theologica* 8 (1976): 477–550; L. Hödl, "Die Disputation Hiobs mit

seinen Freunden als Zeugnis der theologischen Toleranz nach des Thomas von Aquin Iob-Kommentar," *Universalität und Toleranz: Der Anspruch des christlichen Glaubens, Festschrift für G. B. Langemeyer,* ed. by N. Klimek (Essen: Ludgerus-Verlag, 1989), 69–84; E. Stump, "Aquinas on the Sufferings of Job," in *Reasoned Faith: Essays in Philosophical Theology in Honor of Norman Kretzmann,* ed. E. Stump (Ithaca, N.Y.: Cornell University Press, 1993), 328–57.

74. The interpretation of the Letter to the Ephesians offers a particularly dense ecclesiology, especially in ch. 4, lectio 5 (pp. 54–56). W. Swierzawski, "Christ and the Church: 'Una Persona Mystica' in the Pauline Commentaries of St. Thomas Aquinas," in *San Tommaso Teologo,* a cura di A. Piolanti, Studi Tommistici 59 (Città del Vaticano: Libreria Editrice Vaticana, 1995), 239–50. I did not have the opportunity to examine the study by C. T. Baglow, *"Modus et forma": A New Approach to the Exegesis of Saint Thomas Aquinas with an Application to the Lectura super epistolam ad Ephesios,* Analecta biblica 149 (Rome: Pontificio Istituto biblico, 2002).

75. *In I Tim.* 1:3, no.7: "Et est haec epistula quasi pastoralis regula."

76. The combination of exegesis and systematic theology is relevant not only to the commentaries on the Scriptures. One merely needs to remember the three large "exegetical blocks" within the *Summa Theologiae,* namely, the interpretation of the six days of Creation (*ST* I.67–74), the portrayal of Old Testament law (*ST* I-II.98–105), and the mysteries of the life of Jesus (*ST* III.27–59). Chenu, *Toward Understanding St. Thomas,* 259–60; B. Smalley, "William of Auvergne, John of La Rochelle and St. Thomas Aquinas on the Old Law," in *St. Thomas Aquinas 1274–1974: Commemorative Studies,* vol. 2 (Toronto: Pontifical Institute of Mediaeval Studies, 1974), 11–71 (reprinted in her *Studies in Medieval Thought and Learning from Abelard to Wyclif* [London: Hambledon Press, 1981], 121–81); O. H. Pesch, *Das Gesetz: Kommentar zu Summa Theologiae I-II, 90–105,* Die deutsche Thomas-Ausgabe, vol. 13 (Heidelberg-Graz: F. H. Kerle and Verlag Styrie, 1974), especially Exkurs 4: ". . . Exegese des Alten Testaments bei Thomas," 682–716; A. Paretzky, "The Influence of Thomas the Exegete on Thomas the Theologian: The Tract on Law (Ia-IIae, qq. 90–108) as a Test Case," *Angelicum* 71 (1994): 549–78; J.-P. Torrell, *Le Christ en ses mystères: La vie et l'œuvre de Jésus selon saint Thomas d'Aquin,* vol. 1 (Paris: Desclée, 1999); I. Biffi, *I misteri di Cristo in Tommaso d'Aquino* (Milan: Jaca, 1994).

77. W. G. B. M. Valkenberg, in *Words of the Living God: Place and Function of Holy Scripture in the Theology of St. Thomas Aquinas,* Publications of the Thomas Instituut te Utrecht, n.s. 6 (Louvain; Peeters, 2000), 48–53, writes about "primary and secondary functions of scripture" in Aquinas, claiming that Aquinas treated scriptural texts as theological arguments but also that, in turn, Holy Scripture determined his theological queries. This dependence on Scripture is felt more strongly in the *Summa Theologiae* than in the commentary on the *Sentences* (ibid., 188 f.).

78. *De Pot.* q.4 a.1.

79. Cf. the pertinent reflections in Valkenberg, *Words of the Living God,* 214–27; also the stimulating ideas in M. M. Rossi, "(L')Attenzione a Tommaso d'Aquino esegeta," *Angelicum* 76 (1999): 73–104.

Seventeen

Philosophical Theology and Analytical Philosophy in Aquinas

PAUL O'GRADY

> "[There are] some who in their complete ignorance want to
> oppose the use of philosophy. This is especially true among
> the Dominicans, where no one stands up to contradict them.
> Like brute animals they blaspheme against things they do
> not understand."
>
> —*Albertus Magnus*[1]

What is the relationship of philosophy to theology in the thought of
Thomas Aquinas? A fruitful initial procedure is to examine in general
the possible relations (or lack of relation) which could exist between
them. First, one general view is that there is no relationship between
philosophy and theology. This "no-relationship" view can be divided
into three positions: either philosophy subsumes theology, leaving it
no independent status, or theology subsumes philosophy in the same
manner, or they coexist totally independently of each other with no
connection. It is clear that Aquinas rejects the first and third position.
The first has been historically defended by Averroës[2] and Hegel[3] and is
probably the attitude of a great number of contemporary professional

philosophers. There is no rational space for a revealed religion; at best it constitutes a primitive and underdeveloped attempt to articulate what is better expressed in philosophy. Aquinas nowhere accepts this. The third position holds that philosophy and theology are totally different enterprises, which do not clash. One could, perhaps, think of this in terms of Kuhnian incommensurability or think of them as postmodern discourses without any overarching framework connecting them. For Aquinas such a view would not make sense. Both philosophy and theology address the fundamental nature of reality and in doing so address the same thing. That means that the relationship between these disciplines needs to be clarified; they cannot exist totally independently of each other (assuming, against the first position, that theology exists in its own right). However, the second position, that theology subsumes philosophy within itself, has been recently defended as a correct interpretation of Aquinas. He speaks on occasion of the miraculous transformation of the water of philosophy into the wine of theology.[4] Therefore the question of the relationship of philosophy to theology in Aquinas, while apparently natural, is misleading since philosophy no longer exists as a distinct enterprise. I shall reject this reading of Aquinas (and in so doing reject the entire "no-relationship" view).

If both disciplines exist, are not reducible to each other, and cannot ignore each other, what are the possible relations that might hold between them? Such relations can be examined in terms of their respective objects, methodologies, and epistemic status. The object of philosophy and of theology, as of all sciences, is reality. Under what aspect? Philosophy attempts a most general investigation of the most fundamental features of reality. Theology also claims to do this, insofar as God is regarded as the source and origin of all creation. However, the methods of theology differ from those of philosophy. Philosophy uses rationality, subjecting its principles and arguments to the tribunal of rational adjudication. Theology, while using rationality, also uses further material which does not derive from such a purely rationalistic approach. It accepts certain beliefs on the basis of revelation, from an authoritative teaching tradition claiming direct transmission from God. Many philosophers have doubts about such a move. Theologians, however, hold that such material is essential for a correct understanding of reality and because of its source is in fact epistemologically superior to anything deriving from unaided human reason. Furthermore, the claim is that these truths are not available to mere philosophical inquiry—and so theology allows access to a greater range of truths than philosophy. Nontheistic philosophers challenge this epistemic status, querying the reality of the purported extra truths, and so a kind of standoff occurs. In the face of this challenge, some theologians adopt a fideistic stance. Recent developments in philosophy have aided this. Certain internal movements in philosophy have challenged the very notion of rationality. Under the general label of "anti-foundationalism" it is held that reason cannot perform the foundational task the Enlightenment project set up for it. Therefore philosophy is in no position to challenge theology's use of revealed principles, since philosophy itself relies on a dogmatic faith in reason.[5]

Whatever the validity of such an approach, it seems clear that it is not that of Aquinas. He accepts that there is reasoning which is universally valid and which does not use premises derived from revelation (a good rebuttal of the curiously common view that the Enlightenment somehow generated such an idea). This reasoning is philosophy and is the *lingua franca* of all educated people. There is also reasoning which essentially uses revealed principles. This is theology and is restricted to those with faith. Philosophy and theology may come to the same conclusions, but they use different methods. For example, one may assert the existence of God or the separated intelligences (the angels) on the basis of metaphysical reasoning or on the basis of scriptural authority. Fewer people may pursue the former approach than the latter, for various reasons. As Aquinas says, commenting on Aristotle, "even though all men desire knowledge, still not all devote themselves to the pursuit of it because they are held back by other things, either by pleasures or the needs of the present life; or they may even avoid the effort that learning demands because they are lazy."[6] Nevertheless, both approaches are possible and legitimate ways to reach the same conclusion. In the theological approach, which uses revelation, philosophical reasoning may be used to clarify, analyze, supplement, and articulate the beliefs held on the basis of faith. This is the sense in which philosophy can be called the *ancilla theologiae*, an aid to theological reflection. However, this does not imply that philosophy cannot also be used outside theology, as an independent means of acquiring truth where it is not merely ancillary.

The aim of this chapter, then, is to argue that Aquinas advocates a relation between philosophy and theology, such that they use different methods of inquiry and philosophy is a methodologically independent means of acquiring knowledge of reality. Philosophy is available both as a nonrevealed means of reaching some truths about God (what Kretzmann[7] calls "natural theology") and also as a means of regimenting revealed truths (what Kretzmann calls "philosophical theology"). Such a view was common in neo-scholastic interpretations of Aquinas. Such neo-scholasticism had many problems, including a lack of historical sensitivity, a ghetto defensiveness, and a failure to engage genuinely with other positions, and has been rightly abandoned. Nevertheless, some recent reactions to it have thrown out the philosophical baby with the neo-scholastic bathwater. My means of presenting Aquinas' view on the relation of philosophy to theology will be through a critique of these recent interpretations. Having established a robust philosophical presence in Aquinas, I shall furthermore argue that his method is quite close to that of contemporary analytical philosophy and that this interpretation poses a challenge to certain features of contemporary theology.

Objections to Aquinas as a Philosopher

In recent interpretations of Aquinas, various challenges have been leveled at any reading which sees Aquinas as a philosopher, let alone a philosopher close to the analytical tradition. The fundamental point made in such challenges is that Aquinas is a theologian, a member of a specific faith-community, and to interpret him in any way that downplays his theological commitments is to falsify his work. As noted, this is mostly a reaction to Catholic neo-scholastic readings that posit a two-tier system in Aquinas, with a separable philosophical component that can stand alone, followed by a theological component that builds on the philosophical. This critique comes in two forms. The "mild" critique primarily concerns the interpretation of Aquinas as a correction to anachronistic readings of his work, situating him in his proper theological setting. It makes no substantive claims about the possibility of philosophy independent of theology; rather, it seeks to emphasize the theological goals and methods evident in Aquinas' works. The "radical" critique, however, attacks the pretensions of philosophy and denies that one can find a philosophy independent of theology in Aquinas' works. The radical critique will be my chief target here.

Étienne Gilson and Jacques Maritain were the two most famous exponents of Thomistic philosophy in the twentieth century.[8] They presented Aquinas' views in a way that made those views relevant to contemporary philosophical debate, treating his work as articulating truths which should engage with their contemporary philosophical scene. That scene has changed significantly, and some of their work bears the mark of time unfavorably. Recent interpreters of Aquinas have focused more on a faithful historical presentation of his views, including the notion that his thought went through periods and changed, rather than existing as a kind of static Platonic reality which took Aquinas about twenty years to transcribe between the mid-1250s to his death.[9] While this historically sensitive process sharpens our understanding of Aquinas, it has also had the effect of removing him further from the intellectual mainstream, insofar as the effort to relate his work to contemporary philosophical and scientific concerns has receded.

Two main strategies are evident in this. The first is the historicizing move itself. This treats historical accuracy as the main goal of research and assumes that it is academically improper to inquire into the truth of first-order issues in an unhistorically relativized way. Many scholars in the Catholic tradition have taken this route. That is, one treats a particular thinker in a purely internal fashion, making coherent the views, tracing the developments, bringing out subtle nuances, but without inquiring in a larger manner into the truth or value of that work. Whatever the merits of this approach, clearly it is not that of Aquinas himself. He did not inquire into Aristotle or Augustine merely to get clear on what they said; he sought the truth and readily disagreed with his historical interlocutors in the process of finding it. This strategy fits readily with the mild critique, as an attempt to get a historically accurate picture of Aquinas. Insofar as it goes it is good, but it is not enough. Truth is the goal of inquiry; clarifying meaning is a means of reaching that goal.

The second strategy is the relativizing move—using postmodern criticisms of rationality to advocate a multiplicity of "rationalities," alternative paradigms where one does not have to answer to the universal constraints of reason. Theology is relieved of the burden of making itself intelligible to outsiders, since it is its own "framework," "paradigm," or "conceptual scheme." Evident in this strategy is an eschewal of universal claims and an embarrassment about talk of truth, or at least of philosophical universal claims or philosophical truth. Curiously, often coupled with this rejection of the universal claims of secular rationality is the claim that theology has dominion over all other inquiries, since it inquires into the deepest, most profound aspects of reality. The demise of secular reason makes space for the hegemony of faith. Attempts are made to recruit Aquinas to this project, and this is the radical critique.[10] So what case can be made for finding the radical project in Aquinas? I shall select four arguments which have been recently used in this manner. The first is the historical argument, which claims that a correct reading of Aquinas' historical context makes clear that he does not operate as a philosopher, but is a theologian who denies the independence of philosophy; various texts of his are cited in support of this. The second is the subsumption argument, which denies the independence of philosophy from theology. Third is the coherentist argument, which claims on epistemological grounds to show that there cannot be two different disciplines holding truths about God. Finally, the "Simple Being" argument holds that God cannot be known by faith and reason simultaneously, leaving no room for reason.

1. The Historical Argument

According to the historical argument, Aquinas was primarily a theologian. He did not accept modern distinctions such as that between philosophy and theology. "To ask how his philosophy is related to his theology supposes that he would admit to having two separate doctrines and that he would agree that a doctrine was his in any important sense. Aquinas was by vocation, training and self-understanding an ordained teacher of an inherited theology."[11] His major writings are theological. When he did explicitly philosophical work, such as the commentaries on Aristotle, he did so to make sense of Aristotle, not to present his own "philosophy." Texts which are fully philosophical, such as the *De ente et essentia* and the *De unitate intellectus,* are either minor (the former) or polemical (the latter). He uses the term *philosophus* in a pejorative sense, as it often had in the thirteenth century, contrasting it with "Christian."[12] Hence it is a mistake to view Aquinas as articulating a distinctive philosophical position or indeed as a philosophical innovator.

Now it is clear that Aquinas was indeed a theologian by profession. This fact, however, is compatible with being an important philosopher as well. While articulating a distinctive philosophy may not have been his primary aim and self-understanding, he nevertheless succeeded in doing so. His appropriation of Aristotle is not mere exposition, but a careful critical analysis of Aristotle's own views and, moreover, a synthesis of these with Neoplatonism. The distinctive position articulated in *De ente et essentia* recurs in greater detail in subsequent works, continuing into his second period at Paris, when the *Commentrary on Aristotle's Metaphysics* and the other great Aristotelian commentaries appear. Sections of the *Summa contra Gentiles* and the *Summa Theologiae* can be read as straight philosophy, not relying on revealed premises. These passages may be seen differently and given nuanced meanings in the overall context of the work that contains them, but the essential arguments remain valid—and are characterized by a lack of reliance on revealed premises. The fact that an author does not produce individual volumes clearly labeled "philosophy" is not sufficient reason to impugn his or her status as a philosopher.

Yet the argument is sometimes advanced that philosophy is changed when used in the theological context—it no longer remains a separate, methodologically distinct enterprise. Aquinas himself says that "those who use the works of the philosophers in sacred doctrine, by bringing them into the service of faith, do not mix water with wine, but rather change water into wine."[13] Philosophy (as water) is changed into theology (wine) when used in the service of faith. However, the context of this passage is instructive. It occurs in a question in his *Expositio super librum Boethii de Trinitate* entitled "Is it permissible to use philosophical reasonings and authorities in the science of faith, whose object is God?" The fifth objection to the use of philosophy in theology states:

Secular wisdom is often represented in Scripture by water, divine wisdom by wine. But in Isaiah 1:22 innkeepers are blamed for mixing water with wine.

Consequently those teachers should be condemned who mingle philosophical doctrines with sacred teaching.

Aquinas' answer is clearly affirmative about the use of philosophy. In certain contexts it is assimilated into theology—thus defusing the scriptural objection. However, the assimilation of water into wine in some contexts in no way impugns the existence of water or its appropriate use in other contexts. Because philosophy is assimilated to theology in some contexts (i.e., philosophical theology) does not mean it is assimilated in all contexts—so this text does not support the claim that philosophy is totally assimilated (that there cannot be natural theology). Also, what would such an assimilation be? Does it mean there are special theological modes of reason, for example, theological logic as distinct from Aristotelian logic, or theological truth as distinct from philosophical? Aquinas holds that the principles and premises of theology differ from those of secular reasoning—but theology, insofar as it uses reason, does not offer "alternative modes of reason" in the manner sometimes associated with postmodern rhetoric. Aquinas is quite traditionalist in this respect, following the account of Aristotle's *Posterior Analytics* about the correct deductive structure of knowledge.

Aquinas does indeed point out some of the problems associated with philosophy. He draws attention to the weakness and fallibility of human reason.[14] He notes the pride and self-love which can accompany philosophy.[15] He accepts that if a conflict occurs between philosophy and revealed truth, the latter always triumphs.[16] None of these points, however, deny the methodological independence of philosophical reasoning and assert a theological hegemony. Many philosophers have drawn attention to the limits of reason while still pursuing philosophy.[17] Many point to the hubris which can accompany philosophical inquiry. Many accept some external curb on philosophical theorizing—for example, common sense or scientific knowledge or political realities.[18] All of these admissions of limit are compatible with being a philosopher. Also, Aquinas seems to think that many of these problems arise from the *bad use* of philosophy, but that philosophy is intrinsically good in itself. Just as nature may be flawed, it is essentially good insofar as it exists. As he puts it: "Secular wisdom is said to be opposed to God in regard to its abuse, as when heretics misuse it, but not in regard to its truth."[19] But what about passages where Aquinas seems to explicitly impugn philosophers? He uses the terminology of "them" and "us," contrasting the way of faith with that of reason.[20] In response to this, one can say that it is historically clear that for Aquinas, Christian revelation is of primary importance. He regards it as infallible and epistemically superior to all else. Accepting that human reason is fallible and that human motives are often mixed, it follows that there is no contest between faith and reason. Reason cannot impugn faith. However, Aquinas does seem to regard reason as indispensable in explicating matters of faith. Compare the way he does theology with that of earlier writers, such as St. Bernard, where allegorical and symbolic readings of scripture predominate. In Aquinas the stamp of university teaching, of dialectical reasoning, and of logical sophistication is all-pervasive. Furthermore, philosophical investigations not explicitly linked to theological themes are also important for Aquinas. While accepting that they cannot contradict revelation, he accepts that it is appropriate and important to pursue truth, using reason alone. The role of revelation in these contexts is, to use Kretzmann's helpful image, "a navigational aid"—it helps show when things go wrong, but has no methodological role.[21] Aristotle is the paradigmatic instance of such use of reason, and while writing the *Summa Theologiae*, Aquinas simultaneously produced a series of commentaries on Aristotle's work. What is historically significant about this is that producing an Aristotelian commentary would be the appropriate work of a scholar working in the lower, arts faculty of the university. Yet Aquinas, having served his time as a scholar and having reached the pinnacle of university life—a regent master in theology— returned to the task of clarifying Aristotle. This is not the activity of one who regarded philosophy as dispensable. For example, questions 75–88 of the *Prima Pars* of the *Summa Theologiae* are an example of an extended philosophical treatise on human nature, where the majority of the discussion is prosecuted purely in relation to Aristotle. The historical argument correctly emphasizes the theological context and goals of Aquinas' work. However, it does not succeed in showing that Aquinas lacks a distinctive philosophical position which is integral to his work.

2. The Argument that Theology Subsumes Philosophy

Eugene Rogers[22] has recently advanced an ingenious and detailed argument which denies that one can find a separable philosophical component in Aquinas' work and concludes that his position ultimately comes close to that of Karl Barth. The argument has many facets. Rogers examines the historical context, defending the view that Aquinas changed his mind on this issue. He presents a close reading of *Summa Theologiae* I.1 and the *Commentary on Romans* and makes an argument based on the Aristotelian notion of science. All of these serve to show that Aquinas lacks a separable philosophical component. I cannot do justice to all these elements within this chapter, but I shall focus on what I take to be Rogers' central systematic argument and maintain that it is both invalid and untrue to Aquinas.

Rogers' chief claims are twofold. The first, historical claim is that Aquinas changed his mind on the relation of philosophy to theology. In the *Summa contra Gentiles* and earlier work (particularly the *Expositio super librum Boethii de Trinitate*), he defended a view that allowed the methodological independence of secular reasoning, but in the *Summa Theologiae* there is no genuine space for such reasoning—everything is subsumed within theology, understood as *sacra doctrina*. The second, substantive claim is that this sublation of metaphysics into *sacra doctrina* is correct. The first claim rests heavily on the work of Michel Corbin.[23] I will not mount a detailed critique of this historical view, because my main focus will be the substantive incorrectness of the position. However, I will indicate below why I think it unlikely Aquinas held it (other than its being false).

Rogers' argument involves three stages. He presents a reading of the Aristotelian understanding of science which emphasizes the realism inherent in that view. He then specifies certain respects in which *sacra doctrina* differs from that Aristotelian view. Putting these two elements together, he argues that there is no genuine space for methodologically distinct metaphysical reasoning under the correct Aristotelian understanding of *sacra doctrina*. I will examine these steps in some detail.

The Aristotelian notion of a science essentially involves the notion that a discipline proceeds from first principles. These principles are sources of explanation for other elements derived from them. The logical and explanatory connections between *explanans* and *explanandum* constitute the scientific nature of the discipline. Distinct disciplines have distinct principles—disciplinary boundaries are set up by differing principles. There may be interconnections between sciences, where a more derived discipline draws on the principles of a higher discipline to allow explanation. For example, musicians may appeal to mathematical principles to explain the laws of harmony. In this case the derived discipline (harmony) is called a subalternated science, as distinct from the initial self-contained science (arithmetic). Now one way of thinking about such principles is to regard them as mental representations, as being on the mental side of a mind-world dichotomy. On this view, science is primarily a reflective mental activity, logically structured and articulated in a deductive fashion. Rogers holds that this would be an incorrect way of reading Aristotle, who preceded the characteristically modern mind-world dichotomy. Principles exist both in the mind and in the world itself as forms. Intelligibility is built into reality, as it were. The very same form which exists in the world—in birds, for example—is that which is considered by ornithologists in their scientific endeavors. The objects of science already exist, waiting to be discovered in reality, rather than being derivative linguistic representations of that reality. So first principles can be thought of as existing both in thought as the ultimate explanations of certain phenomena and in reality as those self-same explanations. Science has two inseparably linked aspects. Modern conceptions of science tend to emphasize one aspect (the mental) over the other (the real). Aquinas clearly endorses the realism of the Aristotelian position—the principles of a science are really existent in reality.

Theology, understood as *sacra doctrina*, has a curious status as a science. The principles of this science are derived from elsewhere—so in that respect it is a subalternated science, like harmony. However, the principles of this science are not genuinely grasped by human reasoning, unlike a regular subalternated science (it is possible that arithmetic could be grasped by musicians). Rather, *sacra doctrina* receives its principles through revelation. These are fully understood by God, but not by humans to whom they are passed. Aquinas therefore describes theology as a quasi-subalternated science. However, the epistemic status of such a science is powerful indeed. Insofar as the principles derive from God, who has complete knowledge, and are reliably transmitted to humans through revelation, they have a certitude no other principles could have.

The notion of revelation is surely alien to the Aristotelian outlook, and Rogers notes how Aquinas alters that framework. The first principles of reality lie outside the world in the mind of God in a manner inaccessible to us on the basis of reason. They are understood only in the context of revelation. The science known to God is complete; he knows all things in their exemplary ideas. *Sacra doctrina* is a sharing in this knowledge, albeit in a lesser way for us now, compared to after death. *Sacra doctrina* leaves out nothing; all things are necessarily governed by it. Hence all things can be viewed in two ways. They can be viewed as *intelligibilia* (things grasped by our minds using reason alone) or as *revelabilia* (things revealed by God from his divine knowledge). Rogers distinguishes *revelata* (the actual deliverances of revelation—passages of scripture) from *revelabilia* (the way of looking at things from the perspective of *sacra doctrina*). The latter clearly has a far greater extension than the former, applying to all things. *Sacra doctrina* is therefore the most complete science and based on the most secure knowledge.

Rogers notes that a key maxim for Aquinas is that the same thing cannot both be an object of knowledge and an object of faith for a believer at the same time. Thus there is an exclusivity between things in the world viewed as *intelligibilia* or as *revelabilia*. They cannot be viewed as both together. Metaphysics views the world as comprising *intelligibilia*, *sacra doctrina* as *revelabilia*. Metaphysics aspires to talk about God, as a *scientia divina*, reaching conclusions about God based on secular premises. However, once one has come to the understanding of things in the world as *revelabilia*, there is no conceptual space for an independent understanding of them as *intelligibilia*. Everything is subsumed within *sacra doctrina.* Lower disciplines are termed "manuductions" which are "led by the hand" into theology, the supreme science of the way reality is as understood by God. Therefore theology replaces metaphysics. One can regiment this argument into the following succinct form.

1. The Aristotelian model of science is realist in having both a discursive and an ontological aspect.
2. Aristotelian secular reasoning understands things as *intelligibilia.*
3. *Sacra doctrina* is fundamentally God's own knowledge of reality.
4. God shares this knowledge in revelation, presenting things as *revelabilia.*
5. The knower cannot treat the same objects of inquiry as both *intelligibilia* and *revelabilia*—they are incompatible ways of knowing reality. Therefore,
6. *Sacra doctrina* excludes metaphysical knowledge of God, and so,
7. Theology renders philosophy redundant as an independent inquiry into ultimate things.

This conclusion is to be taken as a first-order truth claim and as a historically accurate attribution to Aquinas.

A first objection to this argument is that it seems to blatantly fly in the face of much of what Aquinas himself has said, in holding that two distinct approaches to knowledge of God are possible. To cite some relevant texts in chronological order:

> We are said to know God as unknown at the highest point of our knowledge because we find that the mind has made the greatest advance in knowledge when it knows that his essence transcends everything it can apprehend in the present life. Thus, although what he is [*quid est*] remains unknown, that he is [*quia est*] is nonetheless known.[24] [ca. 1258]

> We can use philosophy in sacred doctrine . . . in order to demonstrate the preambles of faith, which we must necessarily know in the act of faith. Such are the truths about God that are proved by natural reason, for example that God exists, that he is one, and other truths of this sort about God or creatures proved in philosophy and presupposed by faith.[25] [ca. 1258]

> There is a twofold mode of truth in what we profess about God. Some truths about God exceed all the ability of the human reason. Such is the truth that God is triune. But there are some truths which the natural reason also is able to reach. Such are that God exists, that he is one and the like. In fact

such truths about God have been proved demonstratively by the philosophers, guided by the light of the natural reason.[26] [ca. 1260]

The existence of God and other like truths about God, which can be known by natural reason, are not articles of faith, but are preambles to the articles; for faith presupposes natural knowledge, even as grace presupposes nature, and perfection supposes something that can be perfected. Nevertheless there is nothing to prevent a man, who cannot grasp a proof, accepting as a matter of faith something which in itself is capable of being scientifically known and demonstrated.[27] [ca. 1268]

Aquinas holds that some truths about God can be demonstrated using philosophical reasoning. Those incapable of that reasoning can accept these truths in faith. Various other truths are not amenable to philosophical reasoning. However, just as grace does not obliterate nature, neither does theology obliterate philosophy. So Rogers' reading faces massive textual problems. To sidestep these he has to claim that Aquinas changed his mind (another unsignaled "*kehre*," perhaps?), and that by the time he wrote the *Summa Theologiae* Aquinas had come to the view articulated by Rogers. However, the last passage cited above, from that work, is pretty forthright. So too is the following passage from the *Sententia super Metaphysicam,* dating from this later period, characterizing the kind of inquiry pursued by Aristotle:

It is called divine science or theology inasmuch as it considers the aforementioned substances [God and the intellectual substances]. It is called metaphysics inasmuch as it considers being and the attributes which naturally accompany being. . . . And it is called first philosophy inasmuch as it considers the first causes of things.[28] [ca. 1271]

While it is clear that this kind of inquiry is not itself *sacra doctrina* and that any results conflicting with *sacra doctrina* should be rejected, there is no hint that this is a methodologically inappropriate enterprise for one already conversant with *sacra doctrina*. So there is a lot of textual evidence against this reading. However, the argumentative case is even stronger.

Rogers makes two questionable assumptions. The first is that the principles about reality pertaining to God are totally beyond human cognition:

For Thomas, unlike Aristotle, the structural first principles of the world—its set-up—lie radically outside the world, in the mind of an unreachable God.

And for Thomas the intellectual first principles of the understanding—that which the human creature demands and desires—lie radically beyond our capacity.[29]

Sacra doctrina has to be totally inaccessible to unaided human reason. Aquinas does not hold this. We have some knowledge of God on the basis of natural reason. Metaphysics, as a science, investigates the principles of being, God, and the intelligible substances. Indeed what is actually meant by "God" is partially governed by the meaning of being. That God is understood as pure actuality and necessary existence is by no means a complete grasp of God's essence—but it sets boundaries as to how God is to be understood. For example, it allows an explanation as to how goodness is not an arbitrary whim of God's will, but yet it is not some external standard which compromises divine omnipotence. Such metaphysical understanding can allow for a correct interpretation of scriptural information about God and hence play a part in *sacra doctrina*. A clear strength of Aquinas' position is that such cooperation of faith and reason occurs.

The second dubious assumption is Rogers' way of interpreting the mutual exclusiveness of faith and reason. Faith and reason are two different attitudes to a specific content. The same target cannot be the object of both faith and reason at the same time in the same respect for the same person. However, Aquinas holds that some things are capable of being known by reason or by faith at different times by different people. Other things can only be known by faith at any time by anyone. Of the former, it is possible for many truths about God to be known by those capable of having such knowledge, while other truths are known by faith. The total exclusion required by Rogers' argument is not part of Aquinas' conceptual framework.

Apart from resting on questionable assumptions, the argument also brings unhappy results in its train. No discipline (let alone metaphysics) has autonomy apart from *sacra doctrina*—physics, biology, and so forth, are also manuducted into *sacra doctrina*. It is clear that Aquinas thinks all things are absolutely dependent on God at an ontological level—they would not exist without him. However, this does not mean that at an epistemological level there cannot be independence (that physicists are made redundant by theologians, for example, or that nontheistic physicists are not possible). In fact, Aquinas specifically rejects the view that human reason is incapable of knowing without a special illumination from God. He says, rejecting a special illumination account, that "the human mind is divinely illumined by a natural light."[30] This quotation nicely captures the idea that God is operational at one level (the ontological), but this does not count as a special intervention at another level (the epistemological). Hence,

Aquinas says, "the intellectual light that is connatural to the mind also suffices to know some truth."[31] Rogers' position, which makes our knowledge of God totally dependent on a special revelation, ironically has the effect of turning Aquinas into Augustine, whose views on cognition he explicitly rejected for the more secular Aristotelian model.

3. The Coherentist Argument

Bruce Marshall[32] presents other arguments to claim that there is no room for metaphysical knowledge of God in Aquinas' system. He initially characterizes Aquinas' thought as coherentist in character—epistemic justification comes from coherence with a stable set of beliefs. This coherentist perspective does not allow for separate methodologies for theology and philosophy—instead there is a single integrated system. Just as nature is transformed by grace, philosophy is transformed by theology. Marshall then highlights some texts in which Aquinas uses an argument from the metaphysical notion of simplicity to discredit non-Christian attempts to know God.

Marshall asks "under what conditions for Aquinas can one assert a proposition which is true, that is which conforms the mind to reality."[33] The response is that for matters of Christian belief, the proposition must cohere with the verbal expressions of revelation and creed. Aquinas distinguishes between the material and formal objects of faith. The material object is the content of the actual proposition believed. The formal object is the means of demonstration appropriate to that content. For example, in arithmetical truth, the material object could be 2 + 2 = 4 and the formal object would be the demonstration appropriate to justifying such a truth. In the case of faith, the formal object is what Aquinas calls "the first truth," namely, God. Marshall interprets the content of this formal object of faith as the Christian creeds, understood as a summary of scripture. He states, "My proposal then is that for Thomas, Christianity is a complex and variegated network or web of belief, in which the truth of any one aspect is measured by its coherence with the others."[34]

But there is an obvious counterexample to this claim, which Marshall discusses. Some beliefs seem to be justified on independent grounds, such as the existence of God, which is justified on deductive grounds from metaphysical premises. This would seem to go against the coherentist understanding of faith, since believers also hold to the existence of God, which should be justified as part of the web of belief. Unbelievers seem to have independent justification for the same beliefs. To defuse this objection, Marshall maintains that unbelievers cannot genuinely hold that God exists, citing Aquinas in support:[35]

Unbelievers, even those with demonstrative arguments, do not in fact believe that God exists, or hold any other beliefs about God which Christians
hold.... [This] is a remark about epistemic justification. Unbelievers do not
really [*vere*] believe that God exists, or whatever else they may say about
God, precisely because "they do not believe that God exists under those conditions which faith determines."[36]

The unbelievers' propositions about God lack the necessary coherence with other
beliefs to make them epistemically justified in coherentist fashion. Hence they are
unjustified in their utterances, and this argument does not compromise the coherentist account of faith.

    There are three objections to Marshall's argument. The first is that it seems
to be question-begging. Marshall defends proposition P (Aquinas holds a coherentist view of justification) against objection Q (some beliefs shared by Christians and non-Christians are justified for non-Christians in a non-coherentist
manner) by denying that non-Christians can hold these beliefs. However his
case for this latter is merely a reassertion of P, namely, that Christian beliefs are
held in a coherentist fashion, without an independent argument. However, even
if question-begging, doesn't the quotation show that Aquinas did hold just such
a view? No, because the second objection is that Marshall seems to misinterpret
a crucial passage in making this argument. He cites Aquinas at *ST* II-II.2.2 ad
3: "dicendum quod credere Deum non convenit infidelibus sub ea ratione qua
ponitur actus fidei" (Unbelievers cannot be said to believe in a God as we understand it in relation to the act of faith. For they do not believe that God exists
under the conditions that faith determines). In my view, this sentence should
be interpreted as follows. Unbelievers (such as Aristotle) do not believe in God
under the conditions that faith determines; they believe under different conditions, those of rational demonstration. To say that they do not believe under the
conditions of faith is not to deny *simpliciter* that they cannot believe in God at
all. That part of Aquinas' text is of no help in defusing the objection to the coherentist reading. The third objection is that Aquinas explicitly dismisses coherentism as an account of epistemic justification in his *Sententia super Posteriora
Analytica*. There he endorses the Aristotelian argument that coherentism is vi-
ciously circular and ends up begging the question.[37] It would be odd if the supreme science, from his point of view, operated with such flawed epistemology.
The principles of faith are articulated in the creed—but their epistemic status
is foundationalist. That God guarantees them serves to remove the need for any
other justification. So it seems that the coherentist case for dismissing philosophy has little going for it.

4. The "Simple Being" Argument

But there is a further argument used by Marshall that, prima facie, has a lot more going for it. This relies on the remaining part of the text of *ST* II-II.2.2 ad 3, where Aquinas states, "hence they do not truly believe in a God, since, as the philosopher observes, to know simple things defectively is not to know them at all." This argument is repeated in the *Lectura super Iohannem*.[38] Since God is simple, with regard to God a defect of knowledge can only be a total lack of knowledge. Metaphysics only allows defective knowledge if at all, and so it allows no knowledge. Marshall takes this to imply that "in the absence of Christian faith there is, with regard to God, no *adequatio mentis ad rem*, and so no knowledge."[39]

Divine simplicity is a notoriously difficult topic to clarify.[40] Many of the positions it entails seem quite counterintuitive—that there are no distinctions within God and so the divine attributes do not genuinely differ; hence, for example, God's knowledge is not distinct from his will. The central element seems to be to deny that God has a nature, in the sense that creatures have a nature. God's nature or essence is to exist, and God is unique in this respect. Now, for Aquinas, does anyone—believer or unbeliever—have full knowledge of God's nature? The answer is clearly no; even with revelation one can have only a partial grasp of the divine reality. So the contrast alluded to cannot be that Christians have full knowledge and non-Christians have none, since Christians do not have full knowledge. But following the logic of the quotation, as Marshall uses it, anyone without full knowledge cannot have any knowledge, hence Christians cannot have any knowledge, either. This would be an odd conclusion for Aquinas to draw. Thus, the quotation must be understood in some other way.

Aquinas distinguishes two kinds of demonstration.[41] The first is the detailed explanation from first principles to conclusion, which explains exactly why things are the way they are. It follows the order of being, that is, it explains reality abstracted from considerations about how we might know it. The second argues from effect to cause and follows the order of knowledge. Some things in reality are epistemologically accessible to us but require further explanation, and we reason back to their cause. We cannot give a definition of the thing whose existence we are seeking to show, since a definition presupposes the existence of the thing. So this second kind of demonstration is carried out in ignorance of the essence of the thing under discussion. Precisely this second kind of demonstration is used to show God's existence. Since it does not claim to articulate the essence of God, this kind of demonstration is consistent with the charge that it is ignorant, in a certain sense. The further details of the nature of God (insofar as it can be known) are subsequent to the initial demonstration of the existence of something which needs further clarification. This subsequent clarification is informed by revelation. However, this doesn't mean that a demonstration of the existence of an initial mysterious reality requiring further clarification is impossible—and both believers and nonbelievers can argue for that existence. So the Simple Being argument fails.

Aquinas as an Analytical Philosopher

The upshot of the above is that Aquinas is rightly viewed as a philosopher as well as a theologian. The burden of this section is to claim, furthermore, that he should be viewed as an analytical philosopher. Why so, and what is the significance of such a claim? Theologians have long been suspicious of analytical philosophy, amounting in many cases to genuine antipathy. A certain kind of neo-scholastic philosophy manual tended to label philosophical schools by their errors and list catechetical-style responses to the views so described, thus rendering further exploration of original texts redundant.[42] While most theologians today would never produce that kind of work, the prejudices underlying it unfortunately remain. This is reflected in a study Fergus Kerr cites,[43] when he notes that of the four thousand items in a database of research projects in theology in the United Kingdom and Ireland between 1994 and 1998, few had any acquaintance with analytical philosophy. This is fairly representative of the wider theological field—analytical philosophy is generally to be avoided. Other kinds of philosophy are indeed well represented—phenomenology, hermeneutics, critical theory, process thought, and postmodernism, to mention the more obvious ones. Philosophy per se is not being shunned by theologians. Yet the results of a recent influential survey of American and British philosophy departments,[44] which provides relative rankings of graduate schools, gives pause for thought. The top fifty American and top fifteen United Kingdom departments are overwhelmingly analytical in character. In academic philosophy, the analytical is a very powerful (if not dominant) tradition, while academic theology largely chooses to ignore it (even in the English-speaking world). What are the reasons for this apparent anomaly?

The exact details of what constitutes the analytical tradition are disputed, but there is broad agreement on certain points.[45] It began toward the end of the nineteenth century and early twentieth century with the work of Frege, Russell, Moore, and Wittgenstein. It proliferated through the work of the Logical Positivists and the twentieth-century American Pragmatists, and flourished in the linguistic heyday of Oxford ordinary language philosophy. Post-positivistic analytical philosophy diversified into many schools, with names such as W. V. Quine, P. F. Strawson, Donald Davidson, Hilary Putnam, and Michael Dummett among the luminaries. The style of reasoning used by these philosophers tends to be focused, argumentative, explicit, dealing with narrowly circumscribed issues, privileging clarity and conceptual exactitude. So why do theologians avoid it?

One possible reason is that many analytical philosophers appear to share beliefs that are inimical to religion and transcendence in general. These include an admiration for the advances of physical science and an endorsement of Enlightenment views about the ability of human reason to unravel the mysteries of the universe — hence, analytical philosophers are held to have an impious hubris about reason. Another explanation is the infamous period of verificationism, where analytic philosophers waged war on metaphysics, especially religiously-oriented thought. Analytic philosophers sought to banish theology from academia. Again, the very exactitude of studies in the tradition has led to charges of excessive narrowness, lack of depth, and a failure to come to terms with the reality and importance of mystery. Given this charge sheet, it comes as no surprise that even ecumenically-minded theologians wrinkle their brows on coming across such a shallow and godless crew.

Yet this is an imperfect description of the analytical tradition. There is indeed some truth in it, but the truth has been distorted into a caricature; as if an account of Aquinas' Church consisting only of inquisitions, crusades, and clerical scandals gave a true picture of it. Closer inspection yields a richer and more diverse picture. Contemporary analytical philosophy has a rich vein of metaphysics running through it. Studies on substance, essence, causation, necessity, and other traditional topics appear regularly in cutting-edge journals. The focus on language evident in the tradition is carried on for its own sake, illuminating semantical and syntactical puzzles, but is also used to resolve problems in epistemology, ethics, and metaphysics. Critics sometimes accuse the tradition of adhering to a kind of naive realism, but a strong thread of anti-realist thought is also evident — for example, in the works of Dummett and Putnam.[46] Other critics point to the scientism in the tradition — uncritical adulation of the physical sciences. Clearly there is a great deal of reflection on science in the tradition — but by no means uncritical reflection. Strawson defends ethical beliefs against the dominance of science,[47] Nelson Goodman defends the parity of aesthetic with scientific thought,[48] Thomas Kuhn famously supplied a historical means of evaluating scientific progress.[49] The reason for such an engagement is that the physical sciences are intellectually and culturally a dominant force in the contemporary world, and that any work in epistemology and metaphysics needs to take them into account. For example, discussions of human nature must be aware of and take into account developments in genetics, psychology, and cognitive science. Those who believe that their accounts of human nature, for example, need not address these nitty-gritty issues, perhaps because their account is "metaphysical," merely leave the field of genuine intellectual endeavor. If one thinks that something is lacking in the scientific results, one can only make this claim from a position of knowledge of these results, not by avoiding engagement with them. One of the strengths of analytical philosophy as a tradition is its willingness to make such an engagement.

But what of the claim that the tradition is still generally opposed to religious belief, with famous combatants such as Bertrand Russell, Anthony Flew, John Mackie, and J. J. C. Smart undermining religious belief? Many schools of contemporary philosophy can boast luminaries who reject religious belief, for example, in hermeneutics (Heidegger), phenomenology (Sartre), and critical theory (Habermas)—schools of philosophy often now favored by theologians. There is nothing intrinsic to analytical philosophy that pushes it more one way than another on the theism question. Indeed, outstanding philosophers who are Christian, such as Richard Swinburne, Alvin Plantinga, William P. Alston, Nicholas Wolterstorff, Peter Geach, G. E. M. Anscombe, and Peter Van Inwagen, are firmly in the analytic camp. Furthermore, many of the objections to religious belief deriving from continental philosophy, from Nietzsche, Marx, Freud, and subsequent hermeneuticians of suspicion, deal with unwanted results or dubious causes of religious belief, but fail to tackle head-on issues about the truth of the beliefs and whether such beliefs are rational. These latter are the issues of interest to the analytical school and allow for robust defenses of theistic belief—which many of the above-mentioned philosophers have produced. In fact, a recent group of writers have appropriated the title "analytical Thomism" to characterize their style of philosophy, reading Aquinas in the light of contemporary analytical concerns.[50] What connections are there between Aquinas' approach and that of the analytical tradition?

First, in terms of writing style, he clearly endorsed the need for explicit argumentation. His texts are difficult for the nonprofessional to read, because they presuppose a body of knowledge and a skill acquired in tertiary education. They show a lack of interest in literary matters and a desire for argumentative rigor. One of the sloganistic objections to analytical philosophy is that it is too "scholastic," meaning that it revels in making subtle distinctions and displaying dialectical skill and is not easy to comprehend without effort, an objection often directed at Aquinas. So the works of both Aquinas and analytical philosophers are not literary or easily accessible.

Another contemporary objection to analytical thought is that it is limited in its scope. It deals with narrow technical questions, far removed from the existentially important topics of interest to most people. Granted, it is narrow in the sense that it attempts to reach conclusions and not leave loose ends dangling. The main literary genre is the paper in a journal, which is focused and to the point. A useful comparison can be made with Aquinas' use of the *quaestio* technique throughout his work. This derives from thirteenth-century university disputations, where a thesis was debated, objections advanced, the thesis defended, and the objections defused. This pedagogical method is reflected in Aquinas' use of the article as his main unit of writing, which defends a specific claim. It is narrow in scope, in that the argument is focused on a specific end and prosecuted in a limited amount of space. It relies on doctrines established earlier and refers to them when necessary. Aquinas defends a bewildering variety of theses in this manner, from the grand-scale discussion of the existence of God[51] to more specific issues, for instance, whether concepts allow direct intellectual contact with reality or only mediate contact.[52] Likewise, in analytical philosophy one finds papers discussing large issues, such as the existence of God, or more technical points such as whether direct or representative realism is correct. The core issue in common is that a claim is made and defended, and knowledge is advanced by evaluating the effectiveness of the dialectical defense of the claim and the defusal of objections. Isn't this the case with all philosophy? Not necessarily. Some styles are more ruminative, others aphoristic, others again more literary. In particular, some are more verbose, returning to points again and again and layering reflection on reflection without a clear argumentative pattern emerging, relying on the larger shape of the discussion rather than specific details. Such methods are avoided by Aquinas and analytical philosophers in general.

Aquinas and analytical thinkers also share a similar attitude toward history. In dealing with history of philosophy, the emphasis is firmly on the philosophy rather than on the history. While both groups engage with the heritage of the past, the chief concern is the present, and positions are examined, not to clarify the past or for the sake of disinterested scholarship, but to address a first-order current concern. So while historical acuity may be valued (e.g., Aquinas notes the Proclean provenance of the pseudo-Aristotelian *Liber de causis* on textual grounds),[53] historicism is avoided.

If the style and method of analytical philosophy parallels that of Aquinas, so also does the intellectual environment from which it arises. Aquinas wrote in a professional educational context. He was a university master. By the mid-thirteenth century, the university of Paris had developed from earlier schools and guilds of teachers, with its own regulations, ceremonies, and form of life. The methods of teaching were prescribed as a certain style of lecturing and of disputation, the details of which were clearly outlined. Graduate students were trained in a specified way, dealing with topics which were well worked over by the intellectual community. It was an international community, with clear criteria for success or failure, centrally involving knowledge of the Aristotelian corpus and manifesting competence in dialectical reasoning. Just as this kind of intellectual enterprise is not to many modern theologians' taste, it also attracted criticism in Aquinas' time. Suspicions of secularism, over-subtlety, and excessive technicality followed his own career. The famous condemnation of Étienne Tempier in 1277, along with those of John Peckham and Robert Kilwardby, show the resistance to this kind of work by a certain kind of conservative intellectual.[54] But in later philosophy too there was a reaction to the Scholastic method; many of the great modern philosophers were not university teachers, and derided the cooperative venture of a movement such as Scholasticism. One thinks of Bacon, Descartes, Hume, Spinoza, Schopenhauer, and Nietzsche, to mention a few. Yet the development of analytical philosophy, from its foundation with Frege, Russell, Moore, and Wittgenstein, returned in a more marked form than any other philosophical school to the pedagogical model of Scholasticism. Central topics are regarded as worthy objects of study, and canonical texts are regarded as central to the tradition. The modern analogues of the disputation, the tutorial and seminar, are central to the process of imparting dialectical skills to students. An international community with fairly clear criteria for success is evident. The corpus is not Aristotelian, but shares with Aristotle a desire to be aware of and attuned to the best research in natural science, while dialectical skill is a sine qua non. While acknowledging these similarities in style, method, and intellectual context, there are also more substantive agreements on important philosophical theses. I briefly address three of them; first, attitudes toward epistemology, second, attitudes toward contemporary science, and third, attitudes toward language.

Modern philosophy has been dominated by the Cartesian conceptual framework, and many of the distinctive movements of twentieth-century philosophy can be characterized as ways of trying to dismantle that framework, for example, phenomenology, pragmatism, and analytical philosophy. One striking feature of the Cartesian paradigm is the need to respond to skepticism as a genuine worry. This means taking the skeptical challenge at face value and attempting to answer it by appeal to kinds of knowledge that are purportedly skeptic-proof. Post-Cartesian philosophy attempts to undermine the skeptical challenge by highlighting unacceptable assumptions of skepticism itself, that is, by refusing to let it get off the ground. Hence epistemology is no longer dominated by the theme of rejecting skepticism, and the shape of contemporary epistemological theories is not thereby skewed. One important kind of response to this situation has been the development of naturalized epistemology, with its associated developments such as reliabilism and virtue epistemology. This is an attempt to show how questions about knowledge and justification can be addressed starting with the resources of empirical science, how normativity can emerge from descriptive material, and how an epistemological "ought" can arise from a psychological "is." This is Aristotle's approach and also that of Aquinas. Their discussion of sensory knowledge, involving an account of the alteration of the physical organs leading to the formation of concepts and subsequent accounts of judgment and reasoning, is a developmental account housed in a comprehensive natural philosophy yielding normative epistemology. The discussion is not driven by skeptical worries.

Aquinas was acquainted with the best scientific knowledge of his era. His training at Naples and with Albert in Cologne had immersed him in Aristotelian natural philosophy. His first teacher, Peter of Ireland, was known for his commentary on Aristotle's scientific work,[55] and Albert was renowned as a polymath, particularly in relation to technological applications of scientific knowledge. Many of the examples Aquinas uses throughout his work derive from natural philosophy—discussions of natural place, of the process of heating, details about changes in organs of perception on perceiving, and discussion of the heavenly movers. Even though these accounts are now archaic, they played an important part in Aquinas' method. His metaphysical claims were rooted in and built on a grasp of the natural realm. Analytic metaphysics follows suit in that respect.

Aquinas did not engage in the kind of logical speculation that characterized later thirteenth-century and early-fourteenth-century philosophy—presenting elaborate theories of signification, supposition, consequences, and *insolubilia*.[56] Nevertheless, attention to language is important to him as a source of metaphysical insight. The categorial distinctions between terms in language reflect deeper metaphysical distinctions in the realm of being. One place where this is evident is his discussion of existence. He rejects the view that existence is some accidental modification of an essence, that it is some attribute, even an essential one.[57] Rather, existence is something that cannot be captured in a concept. It is expressed in a judgment, where concepts are conjoined. Existence has the character of an activity, an actualization, and so it is linguistically expressed as a verb, "*esse*," rather than reified as a noun. Such a distinction can be found reflected in Frege's view of existence as a second-order predicate. It is not a regular predicate, the extension of something captured by a concept. Rather it operates at a meta-level, indicating that certain specific concepts are instantiated.[58]

In not having his account of knowledge dominated by skeptical worries, in being attentive to the results of natural science, and in using language as a tool for metaphysics, Aquinas is thus in accord with the broad approach of the analytical tradition. He differs from those who regard descriptive scientific material as philosophically irrelevant, who pursue introspective psychological rather than linguistic inquiry, and whose interest in language is not for cognitive purposes.

Two points emerge as crucial in contrasting Aquinas' theology with much of contemporary theology. Aquinas had a deep engagement with the best scientific knowledge of his age. He believed that intellectual inquiry is a unified pursuit and cannot be prosecuted in isolation within the academy. Second, his treatment of predecessors, while respectful, was directed toward the first-order goal of the resolution of a specific problem, rather than merely clarifying the actual meaning of the predecessor.

Conclusion

What is so attractive about Aquinas as a thinker is the way he connects issues in faith and reason, allowing philosophy and theology distinct and complementary roles. The problem with recent revisionist readings is that they tend to make Aquinas look like a fideist and so diminish his actual achievements. What were those achievements?

He took on board the best philosophical and scientific results of his age and used them to further his religious outlook. He held that faith and reason are not contrary to each other; he did not endorse a "two truth" approach, and he tried to show that reason can lead one to many of the beliefs that faith also holds. He did not attempt to sidestep troublesome issues by claiming that he was operating in an alternative paradigm, or that philosophical conceptions of truth, justification, or demonstration had to be watered down to make space for religious analogues of them. Specifically, he took on the burden of explaining some of the more troublesome aspects of religious belief in a way that was rationally compelling to any disinterested observer. For example, the notion of an afterlife is central to Christian belief. The favored account of this in the early thirteenth century was a Neoplatonic substance dualism, which let the soul exist as a substance separate from the body. Aquinas took Aristotle's account of the soul (so unattractive to the conservative Augustinian element in Paris) and developed a hylomorphic argument for the existence of soul as an immaterial entity after death. What is distinctive about his treatment of this issue is the marked lack of any reliance on revealed authority. It is hard-nosed philosophy.

Compare that with today's situation. The analogue of Aristotelianism is cognitive science—the most advanced account of the mental we have. Is there a worked-out theological response to this? Apart from the somewhat odd move of thinking that Aquinas' thirteenth-century account is sufficient, it seems that a lot of theological energy is devoted to showing how such an enterprise is not needed. For example, retreat to special pleading about the Enlightenment is a standard move—the Enlightenment made an idol of reason, the postmodern situation allows us to be relaxed about that, and so there is no need to exert ourselves in this way. Science has its paradigm, theology has its own. One can talk about the afterlife in a theological context ("we live on in a very special way") without having to connect it to any of the realities in the rest of the academy. Aquinas is not an Enlightenment thinker, but it is clear what his judgment on such an evasion would be.

The basic advantage of reading Aquinas with his philosophical side intact and furthermore situating that philosophical side in the analytical camp is that it serves as a constant reproach to certain evasionist tendencies in current theological practice.

Notes

I thank Rik Van Nieuwenhove for his perceptive comments, Martin Cogan, O.P., for his support, and the Dominican Community at Tallaght, Dublin, for access to their library and for first having introduced me to the thought of Thomas Aquinas.

1. Albert the Great, *Super Dionysii Mysticam Theologiam et Epistulas*, ed. Paulus Simon (Cologne Edition, 37/2, 1978), 504, lin.27–32. Such was the situation Albert found before the mid-thirteenth century—it ceased to be generally true of the Dominicans by mid-thirteenth century. See Paul Hinnebusch, *A History of the Dominican Order*, vol. 2 (New York: Alba House, 1973), and Frederick J. Roensch, *Early Thomistic School* (Dubuque, Iowa: Priory Press, 1964). Neither is it true of most of the current resisters of philosophy, who display knowledge and ingenuity in their resistance. However, the quote shows that the impulse to sideline philosophy is not new and was pressing in Aquinas' formative years.

2. See Averroës, *Tahafut Al-Tahafut* (*The Incoherence of the Incoherence*), trans. S. van den Bergh (Oxford: Oxford University Press, 1954).

3. See Hegel, *Phenomenology of Spirit*, sections 748–87: "The Revealed Religion."

4. *De Trin.* q.2 a.3 ad 5.

5. I am unsympathetic to such an approach in philosophy in general and specifically as used by theologians. See my "Anti-Foundationalism and Radical Orthodoxy," *New Blackfriars* 81

(2000): 160–76; my review of *Radical Orthodoxy*, ed. John Milbank et al., *Religious Studies* 36 (2000): 227–31; and my *Relativism* (Montreal: McGill-Queen's University Press, 2002), ch. 5.

    6. *Meta.* IV.

    7. N. Kretzmann, *The Metaphysics of Theism* (Oxford: Clarendon Press, 1997), 23–25.

    8. See especially É. Gilson, *The Christian Philosophy of St. Thomas Aquinas*, trans. L. K. Shook (London: Victor Gollancz, 1957), and Jacques Maritain, *The Degrees of Knowledge*, trans. M. R. Adamson (London: Centenary Press, 1937).

    9. The work of M.-D. Chenu pioneered the historically sensitive reading of Aquinas, especially *Introduction à l'étude de S. Thomas d'Aquin* (Paris: Vrin, 1950). The recent splendid work of Jean-Pierre Torrell also focuses on historical accuracy, for example, his *Initiation à Saint Thomas d'Aquin: Sa personne et son oeuvre* (Paris: Éditions du Cerf, 1993).

    10. I will treat Mark Jordan, Bruce Marshall, and Eugene Rogers, Jr., as proponents of the radical critique.

    11. Mark D. Jordan, "Theology and Philosophy," in *The Cambridge Companion to Aquinas*, ed. N. Kretzmann and E. Stump (Cambridge: Cambridge University Press, 1993), 232.

    12. M.-D. Chenu, "Les 'Philosophes' dans la philosophie chrétienne medievale," *Revue des sciences philosophiques et théologiques* 26 (1937): 27–40.

    13. *De Trin.* q.2 a.3 ad 5.

    14. For example, *De Trin.* q.3 a.1; *ScG* I.4–5; *ST* I.1.1.

    15. For example, III *Sent* d.35 q.1 art.1.

    16. For example, *De Trin.* q.3 a.2.

    17. Hume and Wittgenstein are two obvious examples.

    18. Think of G. E. Moore on common sense, W. V. Quine on science, and the Frankfurt School on politics.

    19. *De Trin.* q.2 a.3 ad 2.

    20. For example, *ST* II-II.19.7.

    21. Kretzmann, *The Metaphysics of Theism*, 7.

    22. Eugene F. Rogers, Jr., *Thomas Aquinas and Karl Barth: Sacred Doctrine and the Natural Knowledge of God* (Notre Dame, Ind.: University of Notre Dame Press, 1995).

    23. M. Corbin, *Le Chemin de la théologie chez Thomas d'Aquin*, Bibliothèque des archives de philosophie, n.s. 16 (Paris: Éditions Beauchesne, 1974).

    24. *De Trin.* q.1 a.2 ad 1.

    25. *De Trin.* q.2 a.3 resp.

    26. *ScG* I.3.

    27. *ST* I.2.3 ad 1.

    28. *Meta*, prol.

    29. Rogers, *Thomas Aquinas and Karl Barth*, 32.

    30. *De Trin.* q.1 a.1 sed contra.

    31. Ibid.

    32. Bruce D. Marshall, "Aquinas as Postliberal Theologian," *The Thomist* 53 (1989): 353–402, hereafter APL, and "Thomas, Thomisms and Truth," *The Thomist* 55 (1991): 499–524, hereafter TTT.

    33. APL, 370.

    34. APL, 377.

    35. APL, 381.

    36. *ST* II-II.2.2 ad 3.

37. *Post Anal.* 1, 7–8.

38. *In Ioh.* 17:25, no.2265.

39. TTT, 506.

40. See, for example, C. Hughes, *On a Complex Theory of a Simple God* (Ithaca, N.Y.: Cornell University Press, 1989), who delivers a negative verdict on the coherence of Aquinas' account of divine simplicity.

41. *ST* I.2.2 resp.

42. For example, Iosephus Gredt, *Elementa Philosophiae Aristotelico-Thomisticae* (Freiburg: Herder, 1926).

43. Fergus Kerr, "Theological Research Initiative," *New Blackfriars* 79 (1998): 66–67.

44. See http://www.philosophicalgourmet.com, accessed December 3, 2003.

45. See, for example, M. Dummett, *Origins of Analytical Philosophy* (London: Duckworth, 1993); P. Hylton, *Russell, Idealism and the Emergence of Analytical Philosophy* (Oxford: Clarendon Press, 1990); A. Coffa, *The Semantic Tradition from Kant to Carnap* (Cambridge: Cambridge University Press, 1991).

46. See, for example, M. Dummett, *Truth and Other Enigmas* (London: Duckworth, 1978), and H. Putnam, *Reason, Truth and History* (Cambridge: Cambridge University Press, 1981).

47. Peter Strawson, *Skepticism and Naturalism: Some Varieties* (New York: Columbia University Press, 1985).

48. Nelson Goodman, *Ways of Worldmaking* (Indianapolis: Hackett, 1978).

49. T. S. Kuhn, *The Structure of Scientific Revolutions* (Chicago: Chicago University Press, 1962).

50. See, for example, special issues of the following journals: *The Monist* 80 (1997); *New Blackfriars* 80 (1999).

51. *ST* I.2.3.

52. *ST* I.85.2.

53. See Torrell, *Initiation*, 324.

54. See J. Wippell, "The Condemnations of 1270 and 1277 at Paris," *Journal of Medieval and Renaissance Studies* 7 (1977): 169–201.

55. Magistri Petri de Hybernia, *Expositio et Quaestiones in Aristotelis Librum de Longitudine et Brevitate Vitae*, ed. M. Dunne (Louvain: Editions Peeters, 1993).

56. See N. Kretzmann, A. Kenny, and J. Pinborg, eds., *Cambridge History of Later Medieval Philosophy* (Cambridge: Cambridge University Press, 1982), sections IV and V.

57. *De Ente*, ch. 4.

58. G. Frege, "On Concept and Object," in *Translations from the Philosophical Writings of Gottlob Frege*, ed. P. Geach and M. Black (Oxford: Basil Blackwell, 1952).

Eighteen

Faith and Reason Follow Glory

EUGENE F. ROGERS, JR.

Protestant skepticism about the theology of Thomas Aquinas focuses on his doctrine of grace. Protestants worry that Aquinas has too high a view of human nature, that grace for Aquinas is so reliable as to impugn divine freedom, and thus that humans could exact grace from God. Proof of the Pelagian defect is supposed to be Aquinas' reliance on Aristotle, the natural philosopher *par excellence.* To this critique I will reply that Aquinas has so arranged things that the more Aristotelian he is, the greater is the power of grace.

Chief among Aquinas' Protestant detractors are Martin Luther and Karl Barth. Luther's polemic against Aquinas is well known.[1] Less well known are ways in which Luther might have turned Aquinas to his own purposes, had he known Aquinas better. For example, as Otto Pesch has pointed out, "In explaining Romans 4:5, Thomas . . . does exactly that which offended Catholic exegetes so much in the case of Luther: without hesitation [Thomas] joins the '*sola*' to the '*fides*,' the 'alone' to the 'faith,' and interprets the verse to mean: the sinner receives . . . justification 'by faith alone without works.'"[2]

In the *locus classicus,* Barth blames Aquinas for the dependence of Catholic theology on an "analogy of being" characterized by Barth in 1940 as "*the* invention of the Antichrist."[3] As Barth explains, "Natural theology was able, . . . after the rediscovery of Aristotle, to get the upper hand over medieval theology, which at last and finally became apparent in the formulas of the First Vatican Council (in the canonization of

Thomas Aquinas as its supreme achievement)."[4] But after Hans Urs von Baltha-sar's *Karl Barth* appeared in 1951, Barth went out of his way to praise von Balthasar's understanding, seemed to accept the account of the *analogia entis* offered there, and had, by 1953, dropped his polemic against Aquinas.[5] By 1956 Barth could write:

> the world which has always been around [the Gentiles], has always been God's work and as such God's witness to himself. Objectively the Gentiles have always had the opportunity of knowing God, his invisible being, his invisible power and godhead. And again, objectively speaking, they have always known him. In all that they have known otherwise, God as the Creator of all things has always been objectively speaking the proper and real object of their knowledge, exactly in the same sense as undoubtedly the Jews in their law were objectively dealing with God's revelation. . . . How can the Gospel be God's almighty power (1:6), if the Gentiles could exculpate themselves by saying that God is a stranger to them, that they are living in some forgotten corner of the world, where God is not God or cannot be known as God . . . ?[6]

The denial of God-forsakenness for the Gentiles amounts in effect to a doctrine of nature. By the end of his life, in 1968, Barth could claim, "On the contrary, I would gladly concede that *nature* does objectively offer a proof of God, although the human being overlooks or misunderstands it."[7]

And yet, if that were all, Aquinas' Protestant detractors could still regard the argument that Barth accepted the validity of a doctrine of nature as mere proof-texting. Fully aware of Barth's movement and of the texts cited above, a prominent Barthian (George Hunsinger) could still assert that Barth disagrees with Aquinas

> that in justification (and thus in salvation) grace actualizes a possibility inherent in human nature. Barth considers justification to be a miracle in the very sense that Aquinas rules out. Indeed, Barth must do so, precisely because he disallows a key premise articulated by Aquinas in this text, namely that "the soul is by nature capable of or open to grace."[8]

Hunsinger's complaint, too, can be disposed of. It depends on the misunderstanding of a technical term. When Aquinas uses "nature" without the possessive article, he means integral nature, which is elevated by grace.[9] Otherwise, and quite rarely, he uses "*natura sua*," one's own proper nature, abstracted from the way it really is, suspended in grace. The soul is by nature (nature-elevated-by-grace) capable of or open to grace, or by grace is open to grace; the fact that nature is open to grace is a contingent grace that God did not need to grant yet did, just as God created Adam and Eve in grace, though he need not have done so.[10] The openness of nature to grace and the grace "itself" are not two graces, one of which is domesticated, but rather one integral grace: God carrying out his will for creatures over time and among contingencies, a grace rendered dynamic and courteous to creatures.

Yet Aquinas' doctrine of grace still needs to be explained, not case by case in response to specific charges, but so that such claims stand in a context less likely to offend Protestant ears. The issue is a large one: Does God continually intervene in justification, or does God delegate power to human beings such that we could boast of our power? Protestant detractors such as Hunsinger, who have come a long way in acknowledging that justification in Aquinas is always by grace, nevertheless fear that the language of habit makes grace our own possession. Treating the *kontroverstheologische* issues either seriatim, or in the context at most of grace and nature, faith and reason has sometimes failed to persuade. The issues turn finally upon a trinitarian question about how Son and Spirit relate—a question, happily, on which Protestant and Catholic agreement is growing, in dialogue with Eastern Orthodoxy.

In what follows, I address the traditional issues in the larger context of Aquinas' trinitarian theology, especially his Christology and pneumatology. Does Aquinas leave the Holy Spirit free to blow where it wills? Does he allow human habit to constrain the Spirit? Or does he falsify this alternative? Of central importance are the ways in which grace initiates the human creature into the trinitarian life, and by which Aquinas preserves the trinitarian pattern that (in a formula of the ecumenical dialogues) the Spirit rests upon the Son. I occasionally refer to John Paul II's encyclical *Fides et ratio* in developing this approach, suggesting a relevance to the most recent deliverances of the Catholic magisterium. However, I leave this to others to elaborate.[11]

Trinity

Protestants and Catholics alike often sum up the end of the human being with God in a word, "salvation," that arises from the starting point of a movement. Conceptually, "salvation" is tied to what we are saved *from*. It often leads Christians to foreclose the end of their movement toward God prematurely, as if "redemption from sin" or "reception of grace" were the end of the story. Christians may divide human beings into two groups, unsaved and saved; or they may consider two states, nature and grace; two habits of mind, reason and faith; or two varieties of good works, splendid vices and infused virtues. Catholics may accuse Protestants of ignoring the continuity, and Protestants may accuse Catholics of ignoring the break. But for both, the second member of the pair tends to become the unitary goal: salvation, faith, grace, even good works. Grace, in a word, is it.

Yet grace too is *for* something, Protestants and Catholics alike admit, if pressed, that grace is for glory. Thomas Aquinas preserves, indeed insists upon, a threefold movement: nature, grace, and glory. The first two make sense only in light of the third. Difficulties about continuity and discontinuity, nature and spirit, or habit and intervention become insuperable only in isolation from the triune God, who naturalizes and inspires, habituates and intervenes with us, and who kills and makes alive. Faith and reason, the good works of the justified and the splendid vices of the pagan, all make sense as proleptic human participations in the life of the triune God, as anticipations of that "participation in the divine nature" promised us in 2 Peter 1:4. It is only by God that we know God, and only by God that we do good, just as it is only by God that we participate in God. As in the early Christological controversies, so it is here: only God saves; only God divinizes; only God reveals God. And God's revealing is just the beginning of God's divinizing. In faith and reason and every good deed, God is revealing—as Karl Barth and Vatican II agree—Himself. In faith and reason, grace and nature, God is beginning to bring us to God's own self, into God's very life. In faith and reason, grace and nature, God anticipates glory. Although that way of putting the matter may sound Eastern Orthodox, it might just as well be Calvinist; in the first question of the *Westminster Catechism*, it is "the chief end of man" to "glorify God and enjoy Him forever," just as it is for Thomas Aquinas.

The great merit of *Fides et ratio* is that it, too, makes hints in this direction and admits of interpretation in this light. There are two ways of reading the encyclical. One takes the exposition of Romans 1 to indicate a charter of reason, of human independence from God. This is to read the encyclical against the grain. Rather, according to a second, more charitable and more accurate reading, reason descends from faith, faith from glory, and glory from the Spirit of Truth. On that reading, we start from the Spirit of Truth and the invitation to join in the Spirit's glorification of the love between the Father and the Son. Everything depends on sharing in this fellowship, which is a way of participating in the divine nature. From friendship in and with God comes fellowship with Jesus and other people. Reason develops in an Aristotelian fashion from living in community with others, and counts therefore as a gracious, merciful leftover from and anticipation of the great communion which is life with God. Reason and faith both derive, at a greater and lesser remove, from the trinitarian fellowship, the friendship of and with Jesus, and the community that celebrates his thanksgiving. Martyrdom is the form that friendship and thanksgiving take in the face of evil. On this reading, Romans 1 is a story of the culpable failure of reason because the Gentiles had detained the truth in unrighteousness and ingratitude. Although "we *could* say that this important Pauline text affirms the human capacity for metaphysical inquiry," John Paul II implies that we should not. Rather, we should say that "reason became more and more a prisoner to itself" (para. 22). On this reading, even when the pope speaks of philosophy as inquiry and science, his references to a set of traditions and a perennial conversation mean what is implicit in transcultural convictions, in habits and ways of life. Thus he is not doing epistemology; he is doing moral psychology. It would be impossible to do epistemology, since "natural knowledge had lapsed into idolatry" (para. 36). Thus the important part about paragraph 27 cannot be certitude, but must be *desire.* In paragraph 31, truths cannot be reached *alone,* but must be reformed in community. In paragraph 33, the search for truth becomes at last a search for "a person to whom they might trust themselves." Moral psychology returns such notions to their proper place in community and among friendships, chief among them the community that makes up the triune life. By the time one reads that "certain basic concepts retain their universal epistemological value and thus retain the truth of the propositions in which they are expressed," (para. 96), the word "universal" has been glossed by the diversity of Acts 2 (para. 71), and the word "epistemological" has been interpreted by the life of Christ, so that nineteenth-century pretensions are rejected even if their language may survive.

In Aquinas, faith and reason are characteristically human modes of adherence to the First Truth and, in the truth, to its creatures. Human creatures may adhere to the First Truth, however, only by attraction. "No one comes to the Father except one whom the Father shall draw" (John 6:44). Human creatures participate in that truth when the Holy Spirit draws them into its own characteristic activity of bearing witness to—of glorifying—the love between the Father and the Son.[12] This state of being drawn into the Spirit's own proper activity is already here on earth; it is an anticipation of the dancing day to which Christ invites human beings at the wedding of the Lamb, a dance which will be the human participation in the trinitarian perichoresis; it is a being drawn to the Father already in this life by taking on the name of the Son in the community gathered by the Spirit. It is the eternal mission of the Son (compare Barth on the Son's eternal election) to be the temporal author of a human holiness that elevates our reason.[13] It is the eternal mission of the Spirit to be the material index of human holiness that enlarges the heart.[14] Because God graciously gives himself, the entire Trinity,[15] to dwell in the human being as in a temple,[16] God can be the

One known in the knower and the One loved in the lover; for this reason, God can engage the human being's own characteristic powers of knowing and loving without ceasing to be their entire activity.[17] As in Barth (and Athanasius and Augustine), so in Aquinas: the human being does not know and love God, except by God. God's own knowledge and love of God might exclude us, since God is complete without us and possesses all riches in himself; God has no need of us. Nevertheless, by grace God creates us—and, grace on grace, includes us. God's own knowledge and love, by the incarnation of the Son and the work of the Spirit, come to flow, circulate, or dance through us. When this happens, God's participation of us in God's own knowledge and love of God does not cease to have its trinitarian form. How could it, since it is God's own? In God's knowing and loving God, as it occurs graciously through the finite and sinful medium of human beings, God allows us to participate in God's own trinitarian life. In God's knowing and loving God, as it occurs graciously through us, the Father, Son, and Holy Spirit preserve their character and characteristically enact themselves. Part of that pattern is reflected in the economy characteristic of relations in the Trinity. Just as the office of the Spirit within the trinitarian life is to witness, celebrate, and feast the love between the Father and the Son, similarly, the Spirit prepares the world to celebrate the Son, in the prophets, in John the Baptist, in the womb, in the desert, on mount Tabor, in the Last Supper: in all these activities, we appropriate to the Spirit the preparation for the wedding of the Lamb. And similarly, the Spirit also rests upon the Son in the world, in the words of the prophets, the baptism in the Jordan, the temptation in the desert, the transfiguration on Tabor, and in the Eucharist and the sacraments from first to last. In all these things the Spirit prepares and rests upon the Son below in a temporal activity that reflects the one celebration that leaves the trinitarian love not without a witness, not without a celebrant. It is no necessity or obligation, but rather a delight of character, that the Spirit can scarcely resist incorporating human beings into the testimony and celebration of the trinitarian love.[18] Thus Aquinas sees the pattern also in us, that the Spirit prepares for and rests upon the Son. The Son and the Spirit are sent for no other purpose than for the gift of grace making graced—for beginning human participation in the trinitarian dance.[19]

Knowledge of the Son

In Aquinas the knowledge of God has a downward movement in the incarnation of the Word and a dependent, returning upward movement in the life of grace, which is the law of the Spirit. In complicated medieval epicycles, four kinds of knowledge are attributed to Christ.[20] As God, Christ must enjoy the factitive omniscience of the Creator; with the Father and the Spirit, Christ is the only comprehensor. As human, Christ must enjoy all created perfections: so he is learner, prophet, and beator. These four kinds of knowledge are not in conflict, not least because in Christ, divine and human are not rivals, do not compete. They are in concert, rather, because they perfect four different powers, not the same one. As comprehensor, Christ exercises the power of the Almighty to create, heal, forgive, resurrect. He cannot do those things by learning. As learner, however, Christ follows a discursive structure of composing and dividing that begins in sense impressions received in the ordinary way. God the comprehensor of all does not "ordinarily" receive information by light on the eyes; it is no part of divinity to do so, but rather part of the divine humanity. As prophet Christ receives visions infused apart from sense impressions—visions of eschatalogical justice, we might add—in a human mind.

Here is the one of the four kinds of knowledge important for salvation (cf. *Fides et ratio,* para. 10, "Contemplating Jesus as revealer"). As perfect human being, Christ continually enjoys the beatific vision. He does not do this as comprehensor: it is something that he receives from God in his humanity. It is something for which he depends utterly on another. He does not receive it as learner. The human experiences of suffering and death do not lead to it. Indeed part of his suffering is that experience and death seem to lead so far away, that because as *beatus* he may not retreat, that because as *beatus* he is also *passus et sepultus.* Christ's enjoyment of God is not a rival to his obedience unto death. Christ's enjoyment of God is not only received but also *enacted* in his obedience unto death. "Blessed are those who. . . ." Beatitude below, as above, is a received *activation*—in Aristotle's terminology, an unimpeded activity fulfilling a purpose—that is, the activity of love, and in Christ's case therefore also the activity of suffering. Beatitude characterizes the whole life of Christ, because the whole life of Christ is enacted in obedience to his purpose. "For human beings are brought to the end of beatitude by the humanity of Christ."[21] This is the tropos of Christ's character, that what he undertakes is what he undergoes. As Athanasius might have put it, he knew as human, that we might know the divine.[22]

This tropos of the Son gives the lie to those who see here an intellectualistic distortion of Christianity. They worry that if the beatific vision is vision, *scientia,* and its beginning in us arises from Christ's own enjoyment of perfect *scientia,* then this is all too Aristotelian. The human being desires to understand, both in Aristotle and in Aquinas; and earth like heaven is rendered sterile in mere contemplation. But this is to divide what Aquinas unites. For the union of knowledge and love is guaranteed and enacted, not, to be sure, by human persons all too prone to separate and sterilize them, but by trinitarian persons for whom separation and sterility are impossible. Thus, early in the *Summa* in Aquinas' discussion of the mission of the Persons, we read that the Son instructs us *for a breaking out of love*. Why? Because the Son is not just any kind of Word, but a Word breathing love.[23]

Christ's suffering is not the whole story, as it would be if he were mere learner, temporary prophet, and comprehensor in a way permanently inaccessible to the human creature. Unlike the other kinds of knowledge, the beatific vision is the destiny of the human creature. Unlike prophecy, it is not temporary. Unlike learning, it is not swallowed up in suffering and death. Unlike divine comprehension, it is not the power of the Creator we may never share. The beatific vision is, by God's gift on gift, a *human* potential, the perfection of the human love of God which the Spirit works in our hearts while fulfilling, not violating, them. That Christ enjoys this gift, in technical Aristotelian language, reduces potency to act.[24] In enjoying the beatific vision, Christ begins in us what we could not begin in ourselves. Life itself, similarly, is a power *of* the creature only as a gift *to* the creature.

To mix physical and parental metaphors: The beatific vision is like a gift on a high shelf that the human child cannot reach. Because of its height it has a certain potential energy. Yet that potential energy cannot be actualized by the child below. It must be actualized by the parent above. Once the parent brings down the gift, however, it is "actual" to us. It can be shared. Actual to us here below, the light of glory becomes the light of faith.

The beatific vision, or life with God, is thus possible in two ways. It is theoretically possible—God can give it if he wants to, without exploding ("violating") the human creature. In Christ, however, the gift is actually, irrevocably given. A human creature enjoys full fellowship with God. This fellowship is now not just givable from above, but sharable among us. It is sharable among those who participate at a distance in the life of Christ, the whole form of which was enjoyment of God, even the suffering. We do this by taking on his character, sharing in the community gathered in his name, and partaking in the breaking of the bread by which the body of God breaks itself open for us. It is thus that the knowledge of Christ that is his human beatific vision reduces to act also for us. It is active in the gift of faith.

The Law of the Spirit

Another Protestant worry may arise here. Protestants may misread the previous section by supposing that if Christ only gets the process started, human beings can continue it by their own power. In that interpretation, Christ becomes mere precondition. But that objection would ignore the trinitarian role of the Spirit. When the Father sends the Son, he does not send the Son alone, but sends the Son with the Spirit. The same pattern obtains among those whom the Father will draw to himself in the Son. The Father does not abandon us, and the Son sends us a Comforter. Human beings are most decidedly never left alone when they are initiated into the trinitarian communion. To imagine that the Son begins something that the Spirit abandons is to deny the trinitarian pattern that the Spirit abides with, rests upon, and witnesses to the Son and those who belong to him. The sort of worry that plagues Protestant readings of Aquinas is not really one based on anthropology. It is at best one that misunderstands the depth of his trinitarian thinking—at worst, one that mistrusts the reliability of God's trinitarian acting.

So the trinitarian God does not leave us alone with the work of Christ, but initiates us into the trinitarian community, the love stronger than death. It is characteristic of the triune God not only to come down to us, but also to bring us up to himself. Aquinas describes this movement in terms of grace. But grace simply is the Holy Spirit dwelling in our hearts and writing a new law upon them. When we bless God, we are doing what the Spirit does in the life of the Trinity. When the Spirit writes a new law on our hearts, it comes out in human acts, and therefore in habits, which are as new and as reliable as the Spirit. The movement from the human creature up to God is no independent human movement, but belongs within the movement from God to God by which the Spirit adds a new song to the love between the Father and the Son.

Aquinas takes up a Pauline expression when he defines grace as "the law of the Spirit." Consider the glorious piling up of characterizations in Romans 8:1–2. We read first of "the law." As if to confute those who would divorce the spirit from the letter, it becomes "the law *of the Spirit.*" In case anyone would think that this is another spirit, or suppose that law had gotten the upper hand over liberty, Paul goes on to specify it as "the law of the Spirit *of life.*" And lest that be just any spirit of life, any biological vitality, with its Darwinian laws, Paul characterizes it finally as "the law of the Spirit of life in *Christ Jesus.*" In choosing this passage as rubric for his tractate on grace, Aquinas wants to affirm, I think, that grace is a *structure that liberates.* It is no *nomos,* which gives rise to an antinomian rebellion. Rather, it completes and consummates *the life in Christ Jesus.* As Anselm wrote so beautifully in *Cur Deus homo,* "God would complete what he began." As a structure that liberates, it is the consummation of Torah, of the law of the Psalms that is "a delight to walk in," of the songs of the Spirit, of what completes human beings not measurelessly but humanly, from measure to measure.[25]

As the giver not of legalisms but of newness of life, the Spirit appropriates two features of human nature that Protestants hate to see deified. They are reason and habit—the structure of knowing and the reliability of love. In appropriating these, the Spirit takes hold of the human being *in toto*, and redeems us in a bodily way. For both reason (composing and dividing) and habit (a settled disposition to act) depend upon sense impressions and temporal sequence, that is, upon bodies.

Protestants may say, Wait! Reason and habit are the very places where the human rebellion against God takes place. Reason, in Luther's famous phrase, is the devil's whore. Habit is where sin persists even in the justified. Is it not a perverse denial of what Reinhold Niebuhr called the only *empirical* feature of Christian doctrine—namely, sin—to speak of the work of the Spirit in reason and habit, of all places?

Aquinas' reply, I think, would be consistent with the famous line of Bernard in speaking of good works. "The entire work is *in the will*," Bernard wrote, "just because the entire work is *from grace*."[26] Will and grace, reason and faith, habit and spirit are not rival agents.[27] While Aquinas would not want to deny that human beings are agents, he would want to deny that they are agents of such a kind as to rival grace. Bernard's language of agent and *place* locates God's agency in a human field—under conditions of sin, in a human battlefield. Reason and habit *must* be the places where grace works, just because they are the places where sin reigns. This is a matter of what Aquinas would call *convenientia* or fittingness: the suitedness of the story to the case, and indeed evidence that God has a sense of dramatic irony. Catholics tend to express God's dramatic irony with the words of the vigil, "Felix culpa, quae tantum ac talem meruit Redemptorem: O happy fault, that merited such and so great a Redeemer." Protestants can express God's dramatic irony in the observation of Luther that God insists on working *sub contrario*. It suits God's sense of dramatic irony to take the worst that human beings can do (with their wills, their reason, their settled dispositions to sin, and finally their crucifixion of the Son), and use precisely *that* as the means of salvation. That the sacrifice of the cross, and the great thanksgiving, should come together in the Eucharist represents the Church's participation in and celebration of God's work, that God makes the worst that we can do the occasion of our benefit. As it is in salvation history, so it is in the cure of souls. The Father elects reason and habit—the very places where we rebel—to be the places where the Spirit redeems. How indeed could it be otherwise?

1. The Spirit in Reason

As is well known, everything in Aquinas' tractate on grace happens by grace except one. It is not possible to repent of sin but by grace, to receive grace but by grace, to merit further grace but by further grace, to persevere in grace but by grace, and so on. But it is possible to know truth without grace.

It is a misunderstanding to regard this exception in Aquinas, as in the encyclical *Fides et ratio,* as a human claim upon God. Rather, it is a concession by God to the sinful creature. It is a concession—a mercy—a grace! Reason is that gift which remains because, like salvation history, it works over time. God has left the gift which is appropriate to the reception of his further gifts. Otto Pesch has put it best: Reason is the *Vorauswirkung* of the creator's will for the grace that saves.[28] Reason is not a demand that turns a gift into a given, by which we extort something from God on the basis of an exalted creaturely status; reason is a part of the human destiny to glorify God, which God gives us in advance. The pope cites Aquinas to this effect, greatly against the grain of much handbook Thomism, when he quotes the line "Whatever its source, truth is of the Holy Spirit" (*Fides et ratio,* para. 44, *ST* I-II.109.1 ad 1).

Again the clue is the reason of Christ, the principle of his human learning.[29] Christ learns, to glorify God. Christ learns language, to sing Psalms in a humanly appropriate way. Christ learns to preach and to give thanks. Christ learns to argue with the religious authorities by composing and dividing, and he learns to teach in parables. He learns to lay hands on the sick, to wash his disciples' feet, to quote scripture to the devil, and to expound it to his disciples. In this his reason serves his faith as his faith enacts his vision. In learning he does a divine thing—glorifying God—humanly. In learning he does a human thing—composing and dividing, preaching and ministering—divinely, or with divinizing results.

In this light, various flaws of the encyclical may appear in the best light. Political gestures—like the sly modal of "we *could* say" that Paul praises metaphysical inquiry—are overwhelmed by the great Thomistic descent of glory to faith to reason, the Spirit of Truth returning us by the Way to the participation in the First Truth. If human reason receives too philosophical a narrowing (end of para. 61), or if Spirit and Law are contrasted in a supersessionist way (para. 68), or if "eclecticism" or "pragmatism" are defined in unimaginative ways, these flaws are minor compared with the assertion that "The very heart of theological enquiry will thus be the contemplation of the mystery of the Triune God" (para. 93).

2. The Spirit in Habit

Protestants worry that habits give too much continuity to the creature. Before turning to a defense of that continuity, I point out two ways in which Aquinas' habits are just as eventful as human action in Barth. In Aquinas, virtuous habits depend upon God's constant intervention for both their origin and their very working out. Good habits are nothing other than the gently condescending courtesy of grace, or the robust, insistent humanity of God.

Luther famously imagined that virtuous habits, informed by theological virtues, are disciplines that Thomists falsely believed could be built up by our own natural powers. This is a supposition that the language of *infused* virtues in Aquinas is supposed to block. If all human action, to be human, is habitual, then it is habitual in two ways. First, all human acting *arises* out of structures or pathways previously laid down; second, all human action *builds* or *blazes* such structures or pathways. An infused virtue is a grace not previously worked out by a human being, from which real human acting arises. If a human being does a good deed, therefore, the habit from which it arises must be a divinely laid down one. The infusion of virtues insists upon and protects the absolute prevenience of grace in the transformation of the human agent. Any human building up of true virtue must have a divine intervention behind it. Infused virtues are settled dispositions to act, not because we have so disposed ourselves, but because God has so disposed us. In Irenaean fashion, God respects our time- and body-boundedness by working within them, habitually. Indeed, every divine intervention, if it leaves any trace at all in the human being, must leave a trace in the form of an incipient habit. If God transforms the human agent without violating the creature, then God dramatically or gently changes human habits. For Aquinas this statement is not controversial. It follows logically. If God redeems us, God habituates us.

Is God's work, then, just the first intervention, leaving us to work out our salvation on our own? By no means. God's intervention is constant, unceasing, and eventful. Aquinas signals this fact with a much controverted word, *auxilium.* Non-latinist Protestants see this word translated as God's "help" and imagine that *auxilium* is a matter of God and the human being engaged in Pelagian or semi-Pelagian collaboration, God and the human being pulling on the same rope. Catholics see the same word and think of sixteenth-century controversies about the mechanics, physical or otherwise, of God's intervention. Neither the Protestant reduction nor the sixteenth-century inventions are helpful.

I believe that Aquinas does use *auxilium* as a technical term, but not one hitched to a theory about how it works. *Auxilium* is a technical term, in the pragmatic sense that it always does the same work.[30] Like "infusion," it always marks the spot where God intervenes—powerfully, sovereignly, redemptively—in human acting. But also, like "infusion," it is an *x* that marks the spot where God intervenes, much like the Barthian word "event." A theory would only obfuscate the simplicity of the claim, Here God acts. This claim is a mystery in the strict sense, an act of God that surpasses human understanding not because it is absurd, like evil, but because it is dazzlingly *good.* God's *auxilium* is a mystery, as if it were "too good to be true": namely, that God acts in us in such a way

that we act. It is part of God's mercy and justice, that God gives us to participate in good works—all God's work—so that we are not left out of our salvation, but are involved in it. In *auxilium,* God bears, carries, moves, engages our
wills. The correct translation is not "help," a word that truthfully expresses God's
courtesy and nonviolence toward us but that remains far too weak. A better translation is "engagement." There is no good human act without God's ongoing,
eventful engagement of it. God's act is causative of such acts. If human agency
is also causative, that is only by God's gracious granting of an analogy between
our goodness and his, a participation which is already a share in God's own life
and agency, since only God is intrinsically good, and we are good only in leaning
upon God. The gracious and unexacted event of God's grant of such an analogy
or share is God's *auxilium* or engagement of us in God's act.

Final Reflections

What does the preceding account suggest for the further working out of a theology of faith and reason, nature and grace, of help to Protestants, Catholics, and
Orthodox alike?

First, faith and reason are both effects of the triune God's destining human
beings for fellowship with Father, Son, and Spirit. (Reason might have been an
effect of the triune God's destining us for an Edenic life without that fellowship,
but that is a different story from the actual one.) Therefore, our work ought to
focus on our destiny to share God's life, whether we name that sharing in Protestant, Catholic, or Orthodox terms as calling, beatific vision, or *theosis.*

Second, faith and reason are ways in which the triune God can engage and
involve human beings in that activity of self-revelation, self-communication, and
self-interpretation by which Father, Son, and Spirit know one another in ex-
changes of gift and thanksgiving. In knowing God we come to trace the path of
the trinitarian dance, a virtuous circle, in which God the Father is revealed by
God the Son to God the Spirit, so that we come to be related to the Father by
the Son as the Spirit prays in us in sighs too deep for words. Therefore our work
ought to focus on ways in which faith and reason derive from the relations
among the persons of the triune God.

Third, the light of faith and the light of reason are derivative, secondary
lights that anticipate and participate in advance in and exist for the sake of the
light of Glory. The light of Glory is the light by which the Holy Spirit manifests the love of the Father and the Son. In it we come to participate in the Holy
Spirit's own proper work of witnessing, already in the triune communion, to

the love of the Father and the Son. Therefore our work ought to focus on the work of the Holy Spirit in catching us up, already here below, into its witness to their love. That means focusing first of all on pneumatology and second on sacramentology, since baptism, Eucharist, ordination, and marriage are all ways in which the Spirit catches us up into witness of the love between the Father and the Son.

To conclude: topics of our study should include *theosis,* Spirit, and Trinity, as ways in which the Church articulates the marvel that the triune God desires us to join in the work of the Spirit in celebrating the love of the Father and the Son, with faith and reason as nearer and remoter ways by which the Spirit may catch us up into the dance.

Notes

Much of this essay was worked out in response to an invitation from Robert Jenson and Wallace Alston of the Center of Theological Inquiry in Princeton to join a workgroup on faith and reason. Although I was not able to participate in the workgroup because of family commitments, I wish to record here my thanks to them for posing a series of provocative questions.

1. See Denis Janz, *Luther on Thomas Aquinas: The Angelic Doctor in the Thought of the Reformer* (Stuttgart: F. Steiner, 1989).

2. Otto Hermann Pesch, "Paul as Professor of Theology: The Image of the Apostle in St. Thomas's Theology," *The Thomist* 38 (1978): 594–95. The passage from the Commentary on Romans offers two complementary expositions. The first concerns eternal rewards and adds the "*sola*" to the "*fides.*" The second addresses the event rather than the consequence of justification; Aquinas characterizes the second exposition as literal. See *Ad Rom.* 4:5, nos.330–31:

> Deinde, cum dicit "Ei vero," etc., ostendit qualiter se habeat merces aeterna ad fidem, dicens "ei vero qui non operatur," scilicet exteriora opera. . . . "Deus qui iustificat, reputabitur fides eius," *scilicet sola sine operibus exterioribus,* "ad iustitiam," id est, ut per eam iustus dicatur, et iustitiae praemium accipiat, sicut si opera iustitiae praemium accipiat, sicut si opera iustitiae fecisset, secundum illud infra, x.10 "Corde creditur ad iustitiam," et hoc secundum propositum gratiae Dei, id est, secundum quod Deus proponit ex gratia sua homines salvare.

The alternative is perhaps even more fiducial and Lutheran-sounding than that one:

> Alia expositio est ut hoc referatur ad hominis iustificationem. . . . "Ei vero, qui non operatur," ut scilicet per sua opera iustificetur, "credenti autem in eum qui iustificat impium," computabitur haec eius "fides ad iustitiam secundum propositum gratiae Dei," non quidem ita quod per fidem iustitiam mereatur, sed quia ipsum credere est primus actus iustitiae quam Deus in eo operatur. Ex eo enim quod credit in Deum iustificantem, iustificationi eius subiicit se, et sic recipit eius effectum.

Et haec expositio est litteralis, et secundum intentionem Apostoli, qui facit vim in hoc quod in Gen. XV, 6 dictum est "Reputatum est illi ad iustitiam," quod consuevit dici quando id, quod minus est ex parte alicuius, reputatur ei gratis, ac si totum fecisset.

Et ideo Apostolus dicit quod haec reputatio locum non habaret, si iustitia esset ex operibus, sed solum habet locum secundum quod est ex fide.

For more on Aquinas and Luther, see the magisterial work by Otto H. Pesch, *Die Theologie der Rechtfertigung bei Thomas von Aquin und Martin Luther: Versuch eines systematisch-theologischen Dialogs,* 2nd ed. (Mainz: Matthias-Grünewald, 1985). The index to citations from Luther and Aquinas is extraordinarily useful. In English, the claims without the evidence appear in Pesch, "Existential and Sapiential Theology," in *Catholic Scholars Dialogue with Luther,* ed. Jared Wicks (Chicago: Loyola University Press, 1970). See also S. Pfürtner, *Luther and Aquinas on Salvation,* trans. E. Quinn (New York: Sheed and Ward, 1965), and Denis Janz, *Luther on Thomas Aquinas.*

3. Karl Barth, *Die Kirchliche Dogmatik,* 4 vols. in 12 (Zürich: Zollikon, 1932-); in English, *Church Dogmatics,* ed. and trans. G. W. Bromiley and T. F. Torrance (Edinburgh: T. & T. Clark, 1936-); here, *CD* II/1, 82.

4. *CD* II/1, 127, translation modified.

5. Hans Urs von Balthasar, *Karl Barth: Darstellung und Deutung seiner Theologie* (Köln: Jakob Hegner, 1951); in English, *The Theology of Karl Barth,* trans. Edward T. Oakes (San Francisco: Ignatius Press, 1992). See esp. Part III, ch. 2: "The Concept of Nature in Catholic Theology," 267-325. See Barth's comment at *CD* IV/1, 768 (written in 1953).

6. Karl Barth, *Kurze Erklärung des Römerbriefes* (Munich: Christian Kaiser, 1956); in English, *A Shorter Commentary on Romans* (Richmond, Va.: John Knox Press, 1959), 28-29.

7. Karl Barth, letter to Carl Zuckmayer of 7 May 1968, in *Gesammtausgabe: Briefe,* V, 286; in English, *A Late Friendship: The Letters of Karl Barth and Carl Zuckmayer,* trans. Geoffrey Bromiley (Grand Rapids, Mich.: Eerdmans, 1982), 42. Barth adds, "I would not venture to say the same of natural science, whether ancient or modern." But it is easy to show that Aquinas' arguments then belong on the side of "nature," that is, theological nature, rather than on the side of natural science (ancient or modern).

8. George Hunsinger, *How to Read Karl Barth* (Oxford: Oxford University Press, 1991), 146. Hunsinger quotes *ST* I-II.113.10c.

9. For a terminological distinction between integral (graced) and defective nature, see *In Ioh.* 6:44, nos.934-38.

10. *ST* I-II.19.1 and 85.1 with I.95.1c and I.100.1c and ad 2. Briefly, grace is a gift *to* nature in such a way that it becomes a good *of* nature, as life is a gift to a body which it cannot give or restore to itself. For discussion with additional citations, see Pesch, *Theologie der Rechtfertigung,* 489.

11. Neither this essay nor my book *Thomas Aquinas and Karl Barth* (Notre Dame, Ind.: University of Notre Dame Press, 1995), it should go without saying, explicitly addresses faith and reason as construed by Anglo-American analytic philosophy. Rather, they address mainline Catholic and Protestant intramural theologies, especially as advanced by French and German scholars (Corbin and Pesch) innocent of analytic philosophy. Thus I am flattered by the attention in this volume from Paul O'Grady, and grateful for his kindness in allowing me to see his essay as it stood in July 2001. Let me state the following points of full or qualified agreement:

1) I too see a family resemblance between Aquinas' methods and those of analytic philosophy. Indeed, I dedicated *Thomas Aquinas and Karl Barth* to a Thomist trained (at Princeton and

Oxford) in analytic philosophy—my teacher Victor Preller. To those interested in how my theological approach can be pursued with p's, q's, entailment signs, entity realism, and so on, I frequently cited, and heartily commend, his book *Divine Science and the Science of God* (Princeton:
Princeton University Press, 1967), a reformulation of Aquinas in the light of Wittgenstein and
Wilfred Sellars.

2) I agree that a Christian may do philosophy without doing theology, and that a non-
Christian philosopher may read the *Summa* with understanding. Indeed Aquinas insists as much
at *ST* I.1.6 ad 3, where he says that what is needed for teaching sacred doctrine is not the wisdom that comes from the Holy Spirit but the wisdom that comes from study! My concern in
Thomas and Barth was to articulate the way in which the *Summa* requires sacred doctrine to stick
to its last, not to deprive analytic philosophers of their vocation. Did I not think so, I could
hardly write an essay for *Grammar and Grace: Aquinas and Wittgenstein,* ed. Robert McSwain
and Jeffrey Stout (London: SCM, forthcoming), a volume in memory of Victor Preller.

3) I agree with O'Grady that my argument "*seems* to blatantly fly in the face of much of
what Aquinas himself has said," as evidenced by a catena of texts interpreted synchronically. But
I regard that seeming as the seeming of all Thomistic objections, in which what seems to be the
case is not. After centuries of synchronic interpretation, one does not hear the stages of Aquinas'
development without lining up the texts in parallel columns, as one has learned to hear the differing voices of the synoptic Gospels. Granted that the diachronic interpretation must bear the burden of proof, I hold that the burden has been discharged with regard to just these texts by some
eight hundred pages of Michel Corbin's *Chemin de la théologie chez Thomas d'Aquin* (Paris: Beauchesne, 1974), which O'Grady cites, but explicitly does not engage. See esp. 535–44, 652–66,
700–709, 727–43. Aquinas did not write one work, the *Opera Omnia,* and he did not exempt
himself from the observation that human inquiry takes place *per longum tempus.*

4) I agree with O'Grady's theses 5–7 with qualifications:

5) Knowing, for Aquinas, is a perfection of a power (which is not the same as a nineteenth-
century faculty). Aquinas does not use a Latin word for "knower" as a synonym for the human
being. Christ can know the same things in four different ways, as perfections of the powers of
beatification, of learning, of prophecy, and of divine comprehension. By analogy with the case
of Christ, the student of Aquinas therefore might solve the apparent problem this way: Philosophy perfects the power of learning; sacred doctrine, if done with faith and love, may participate
in the perfection of the power of beatification, incomplete until the next life.

But in fact Aquinas solves this difficulty in a simpler way. Of *intelligibilia* human beings
can have *scientia.* Of *revelabilia* in this life they can have only *cognitio,* indeed, the sort of *cognitio* better known as *fides.* As Preller (*Divine Science and the Science of God,* 32) observed in 1967,
"The ordinary word for 'know' in Aquinas is *scire,* which is never used in connection with cog-
nitions of God through natural reason. *Cognitio* and *cognoscere* are the broadest possible generic
terms, referring to any state of mind connected with the apprehension of reality." Aquinas expressly denies that human beings can have *scientia in divinis* in this life at *ST* II-II.9; we only
know what to believe, and believing is the substance of things not seen, II-II.4.1. Aquinas at
least twice asserts that we have *scientia* that in this life "we are joined to God as to One *un*known
(*ignoto*)," at *ST* I.12.13 ad 1 and *Ad Rom.* 1:19, no.114.

So Aquinas would agree with the modified statement, "The human being cannot have *scientia* of the same objects of inquiry as both *intelligibilia* and *revelabilia* at the same time and *in
the same way,*" and indeed cannot in this life possess *scientia* of *revelabilia* at all. The beatific vision is indeed like philosophy, in that it is vision, or *scientia;* it is like faith in that it adheres to

the truth by the power of another, God, or by love. Sacred doctrine is the peculiar case of a *discipline* that counts as *scientia* on account of its principled character, but has in this life no "scientists," or Aristotelian knowers—except Christ, who enjoys beatitude to start us on its path. See my *Thomas Aquinas and Karl Barth*, 36.

6) Sacred doctrine *includes* metaphysical knowledge of God. This is not "no relation," but a relation of participation in the medieval sense, or (more Christologically) of assumption. Sacred doctrine *must* include metaphysical knowledge of God, because by the ancient dogma what is not assumed is not redeemed.

7) The *scientia* of the blessed in heaven renders both theology and philosophy redundant. Here below, no human inquiry is redundant, because all human inquiry proceeds "by a few, over a long time, and with an admixture of many errors" (prologue to *ST*). For my account of how followers of Aquinas might deal with conflict between theological and scientific inquiry where one seems to be in error, see the chapter "Nature and Justice when Science and Scripture Conflict" in my *Sexuality and the Christian Body: Their Way Into the Triune God* (Oxford: Blackwell, 1999), 127–39, also available in an earlier version in "Aquinas on Natural Law and the Virtues in Biblical Context: Homosexuality as a Test Case," *Journal of Religious Ethics* 27 (1999): 29–56. Integrity in this life belongs not to the human being in his or her power(s) of knowing, but to the completed discipline of sacred doctrine, described in the *Posterior Analytics*. But of course the discipline will not be completed in this life, either—or perhaps I should say, in this world. The integrity—and the scientific character—of sacred doctrine makes an eschatological claim.

12. The formulation is meant to be neutral as to the Filioque. The Spirit bears witness as an independent trinitarian Person: not a mere bond of love, but a witness or celebrant of it, whose characteristic activity makes it new.

13. *ST* I.43.7c and ad 4.

14. *ST* I.43.7c: "Filius visibiliter missus est tanquam sanctificationis Auctor: sed Spiritus Sanctus tanquam sanctificationis indicium."

15. *ST* I.43.5c: "Per gratiam gratum facientem tota Trinitas inhabitat mentem, secundum illud Ioan. 14, [23]: 'Ad eum veniemus, et mansionem apud eum faciemus.'"

16. *ST* I.43.3c.

17. Ibid. For more on Aquinas' trinitarianism, see A. Malet, *Personne et amour dans la théologie trinitaire de saint Thomas d'Aquin* (Paris: Vrin, 1956).

18. On the pattern of Rom. 8:11.

19. *ST* I.43.3c and ad 1, 2.

20. *ST* III.9.

21. *ST* III.9.2c.

22. I owe this way of stating the matter to Troy Dahlke, "The Christologically Effected Knowledge of Faith," unpublished typescript, 1.

23. *ST* I.43.5 ad 2: "Filius autem est Verbum, non qualecumque, sed spirans Amorem: unde Augustinus dicit, in IX libro de Trin. [ch. 10]: 'Verbum quod insinuare intendimus, cum amore notitia est.' Non igitur secundum quamlibet perfectionem intellectus mittitur Filius: sed secundum talem instructionem intellectus, qua prorumpat in affectum amoris . . . in Psalmo [38:4]: 'In meditatione mea exardescet ignis.'"

24. *ST* III.9.2c.

25. I owe the last phrase to Sergei Bulgakov (Serge Boulgakof), *Le Paraclet*, trans. Constantin Andronikof (Paris: Aubier, 1944).

26. Bernard of Clairvaux, *De gratia et libero arbitrio*, in finem, as translated in Hans Küng, *Justification: The Doctrine of Karl Barth and a Catholic Reflection*, 2nd ed. (Philadelphia: Westminster, 1981), 266, italics modified.

27. For the best treatment of the noncompetitive relation between nature and grace, see Kathryn Tanner, *God and Creation: Tyranny or Empowerment?* (Oxford: Basil Blackwell, 1988), esp. 48.

28. Pesch, *Theologie der Rechtfertigung*, 526.

29. Cf. *Fides et ratio*, para. 11: "God's revelation is therefore immersed in time and history. Jesus Christ took flesh 'in the fullness of time' (Gal. 4:4)."

30. I have been confirmed in this impression by a word-study by Michael Lockaby.

A Note on the Literature

For an insightful introduction to the life and career of Aquinas, see J.-P. Torrell, *Saint Thomas Aquinas*, vol. 1, *The Person and His Work*, trans. R. Royal (Washington, D.C.: Catholic University of America Press, 1996). The value of the volume is further enhanced by the inclusion (330–61) of a "Brief Catalogue of the Works of Saint Thomas Aquinas," prepared by Gilles Emery, indicating the availability of editions and of translations in the major modern languages. Other serviceable introductions to Aquinas' career are M.-D. Chenu, *Toward Understanding Thomas Aquinas*, trans. A. M. Landry and D. Hughes (Chicago: H. Regnery Co., 1964); James A. Weisheipl, *Friar Thomas d'Aquino: His Life, Thought and Works*, rev. ed. (Washington, D.C.: Catholic University of America Press, 1983); and Simon Tugwell, ed. and trans., *Albert and Thomas: Selected Writings* (New York: Paulist Press, 1988), "Thomas Aquinas: Introduction," 201–67 and 291–344.

Handy one-volume surveys of the scholarship are found in Vernon J. Bourke, *Thomistic Bibliography, 1920–1940* (St. Louis: The Modern Schoolman, 1945); Terry L. Miethe and Vernon J. Bourke, *Thomistic Bibliography, 1940–1978* (Westport, Conn.: Greenwood Press, 1980); and Richard Ingardia, *Thomas Aquinas: International Bibliography 1977–1990* (Bowling Green, Ohio: The Philosophy Documentation Center, 1993).

More comprehensive are the reviews of the scholarship that appeared on a yearly basis throughout much of the twentieth century: *Bulletin Thomiste* (Soisy-sur-Seine: Société thomiste), 1924–65; and *Rassegna di letteratura tomistica* (Naples: Edizioni domenicane Italiane), 1966–93.

With the end of publication of the *Rassegna*, students of Aquinas must look to other sources for information on the literature. The *Revue thomiste*, 1893–, published by the Dominicans of the Province of Toulouse, offers regular reviews of new publications.

The web can be an important resource. The Thomas-Instituut at Utrecht maintains a helpful site (www.ktu.ruu.nl/Thomas/); one of its more valuable features is regular interviews with leading scholars in the field. See also the "Grand Portal Thomas d'Aquin" (www.thomas-d-aquin.com/), which maintains many useful links.

Index